Coaching for the Inner Edge

Advanced Praise for Coaching for the Inner Edge by Robin S. Vealey

"Robin Vealey's book, Coaching for the Inner Edge, *is a comprehensive, practical, invaluable resource for coaches at all levels who want to assist athletes in their quest for competitive excellence. Written by an experienced and respected expert in sport psychology, this book is a 'must read' for anyone interested in facilitating optimal performance through mental skill training. Topics, activities, and implementation strategies are creatively and realistically packaged to offer practical suggestions for athletes committed to developing their Inner Edge. Techniques are brought vividly to life through inspiring stories of some of the world's finest athletes and coaches. Vealey's performance enhancement blueprint is wonderfully written, enjoyable to read, easy to understand, and important to apply."*

Dr. Colleen M. Hacker, mental training consultant for the U.S. Women's National Soccer Team that achieved the gold medal in the 1996 and 2004 Olympic Games, silver medal in the 2000 Olympic Games, and won the 1999 World Cup. Dr. Hacker also coached the Pacific Lutheran University women's soccer team to three NAIA national championships, and in her 15 years of coaching compiled a .780 winning percentage at PLU. She is currently Professor and Assistant Dean in the School of Physical Education at PLU.

"Vealey's text is special in several ways—her engaging writing style, integration of diverse and current literature relevant to coaching, use of anecdotes and stories, and many creative learning activities . . .

"Vealey's text is one that I will recommend to every sport psychology student, coach, and colleague I have. It is what I consider a dynamic active text that guides the reader through the reflective process of knowledge creation . . .

"Vealey's book is unique in that it integrates practice, theory, and application unlike any other textbook I've seen . . .

"This book was easy to read because the author's passion for the topic was clearly evident. Her willingness to share her own personal experiences (success stories as well as mistakes), and the tremendous use of quotes, anecdotes, and 'personal plug-ins' creates a sense of empathy and sharing. Never did I feel like the author presented herself as an 'expert' telling the reader how they should coach. I strongly believe that this style will allow students and coaches to make a strong personal connection with the material . . .

"Vealey accomplished her stated purpose of helping coaches learn how to create and implement sport psychology strategies through an experiential learning approach. I have yet to find another coaching or sport psychology text that captures the essence of the mental aspect of coaching in such a comprehensive and creative way."

Dr. Wade Gilbert, professor at Fresno State University, leading scholar in the study of coaches and coaching practice.

"Even though the chapters contain a great deal of information, they are organized very well to provide practical points that clarify concepts and are even inspirational and motivational . . .

"Specific sport examples used to illustrate concepts are very helpful."

"The book contains excellent exercises for helping coaches and athletes understand where they are in their mental development. These should be helpful to coaches to better understand their athletes . . .

". . . provides specific outlines for putting together a mental training program. The emphasis is on keeping it simple and starting off slowly. Great guidelines for coaches, educators, and sport psychologists . . .

"The book enables those working with athletes to find information quickly and get ideas for helping athletes to increase their mental skills . . .

"An outstanding book—very user friendly with outstanding tools to apply the material covered in each chapter."

Dr. Challace McMillin, professor, mental training consultant, and former head football coach at James Madison University

Coaching
for the Inner Edge

Robin S. Vealey, PhD
Miami University of Ohio

Fitness Information Technology
A Division of the International Center
for Performance Excellence
262 Coliseum, WVU-PE
PO Box 6116
Morgantown, WV 26506-6116

Library of Congress Card Catalog Number: 2004117281
ISBN: 1-885693-59-1   ISBN: 978-1-885693-59-4

Production Editor: Corey Madsen
Cover design: Jamie Merlavage
Proofreader/Indexer: Maria denBoer
Typesetter: Jamie Merlavage
Printed by Sheridan Books
Printed in the United States of America

10 9 8 7 6 5 4 3 2

Fitness Information Technology
A Division of the International Center for Performance Excellence
262 Coliseum, WVU-PE
PO Box 6116
Morgantown, WV 26506-6116
800.477.4348
304.293.6888 (phone)
304.293.6658 (fax)
Email: icpe@mail.wvu.edu
Website: www.fitinfotech.com

In Memory
A Dedication

To Mary Lou Vealey, who challenged and inspired everyone she taught, especially me. Thanks, Mom, for being the best coach I could ever have, in the biggest game of all. I'll always have the Inner Edge because of you.

Thank you
Acknowledgments

Thanks to Andy Ostrow at FIT for his patient support in waiting for me to finish this book, and to Corey Madsen at FIT for his editing expertise and guidance. The book was greatly improved by review comments I received from Wade Gilbert and Challace McMillan. As a leading researcher in the study of coaching, Wade led me through a much more thorough review of the scholarly and applied coaching literature. He also provided key insights as to how to challenge coaches to become more self-reflective when reading it. Challace's comments were insightful based on his unique dual role as former college football coach and sport psychology professor. His expertise helped me focus specifically on what coaches need and want. In addition, I have been very positively influenced and inspired by the applied sport psychology work of Terry Orlick, Ken Ravizza, Doug Newburg, Dan Gould, Damon Burton, and Yuri Hanin.

Thanks to all the athletes I had the pleasure of coaching. I learned more from them than I ever realized until I started writing this book. Likewise, thanks to all the athletes that I've learned so much from in my sport psychology consulting. I must also acknowledge the important contributions to the development of the book by the graduate students in my spring 2004 mental training class. They ran a hilarious contest to see who could identify the best name for the book, and proudly presented me with 50 tentative book titles - all on a bar napkin! So thanks to David DiMauro, George Pappas, Lindsay Ronayne, Katie Mellus, Nick Galli, and Josh Fenton.

Thanks to all my former coaches for providing me the opportunity to compete. Special thanks goes to Sue Gregg, my high school basketball and track coach, who in those pre-Title IX years did it because she loved coaching and loved us. I would not have had a college basketball career without her. I also would like to express appreciation to Jane McIlroy, former Athletic Director at Linfield College, who took a chance on me as a young coach and allowed me to grow myself as we grew the program.

Thanks to Rainer Martens, my doctoral advisor and demanding mentor, who challenged me to move beyond my comfort zone and sparked my life-long love affair with sport psychology.

Thanks to my father, Sherman Vealey, for all he has contributed to my success. His affirmations of "there's no free lunch," you do "whatever it takes," and "you've got to compete" shaped my strong drive to achieve. In addition, his rock-solid unconditional love and support have given me the confidence and perspective needed to pursue the challenging goals that have made my life so fulfilling.

Thanks to Jordan and Jackson, the children I thought I would never have, but whom I could never now imagine being without. The fathomless love that I feel for them has opened me up to greater reflection about the importance of relationships with others. I know now that's why we're on this earth, and it provided me with unique insights in writing the book.

Finally, thanks to Melissa Chase for believing in me over the several years that it took to polish off this book. Because she understands how much I've loved writing it, she sacrificed greatly to provide me with the space and time that I needed. But most of all, she's supported me with unflinching loyalty, unwavering support, and a goes-without-saying understanding of who I am and what I have to do to be me.

Contents

Detailed Contents

Part 2 Mental Training Tools

Part 3 Mental Skills for Athletes: The Big Three

Chapter 14 Self-Confidence

Part 4 Putting It All Together

Chapter 15 Implementing Mental Training: Selecting from the Menu

Chapter 16 Common Challenges Faced by Coaches: Special Recipes

Introduction

Coaches constantly search for ways to gain the "edge" on their opponents. They work tirelessly to get their athletes in top physical condition, to develop athletes' physical skills, and to implement successful tactics and strategies for their teams. This physical training is designed to provide athletes with the "outer edge," which is a sharpness or keenness of performance that creates an advantage over less physically skilled opponents. However, as most coaches realize, there is an "inner edge" that is also needed by athletes to perform successfully. This **Inner Edge** is *the advantage that athletes create for themselves by honing the sharpness or keenness of their mental skills.* The Inner Edge is gained when athletes learn to manage their energy in pressure situations, to focus effectively despite distractions and obstacles, and to maintain stable self-confidence despite performance setbacks.

How can you help your athletes get the Inner Edge that they need? Here are some of the typical questions I hear from coaches about the Inner Edge:

- how can I prepare athletes to keep them from folding under pressure, or "choking"?
- what is the best way to motivate my athletes?
- how can I use mental training techniques like visualization to help my athletes perform better?
- how can I create the right "chemistry" in my team to help us perform better?

These questions have been asked and answered by researchers in sport psychology, and this information is contained in scholarly journals. But the problem is that most scientific research is conducted and written in a technical style that is impractical and boring to most coaches.

The purpose of this book is to provide coaches with practical information about sport psychology so they can help their athletes get the Inner Edge they need to be successful. The information in the book is taken from the research literature, but I've attempted to "package" the information in useful and interesting ways for coaches. In attempting to create a book that appeals to coaches, I relied on my practical experiences as a college basketball player and coach, and my more recent work as a sport psychology researcher and consultant. Another important source for the material in this book is knowledge derived from master coaches that have been innovative sport psychologists their entire careers. Throughout the book, you'll read examples, quotes, and exemplary ideas from outstanding coaches about the ways in which they coach to gain the Inner Edge. In addition, you'll learn from elite athletes in stories and examples about how they have developed the Inner Edge. I learn about the Inner Edge every day from coaches and athletes, and you can learn from them as well by reading this book.

The book is targeted for current coaches as well as prospective coaches such as students in coaching courses. Athletes and other practitioners such as teachers, athletic trainers, and consultants may find the material in the book of interest as well. Material in the book may be applied to various levels of competition (i.e., youth, high school, college, elite). I want to make your learning about sport psychology as meaningful and experiential as I can. I want to spark your interest in and commitment to helping your athletes gain the Inner Edge. I want to help you move beyond the popular myths and clichés regarding such issues as motivation, mental toughness, and self-confidence.

Take time to work through the study questions at the end of each chapter, as well as the "personal plug-ins" located throughout the book, to internalize the information in deeper and more meaningful ways. Key words are printed in bold type throughout the book, and these words are included in the glossary at the end of each chapter to help you to review the meaning of typical terms used in sport psychology. A resource guide for coaches is provided at the end of the book, in case you want to pursue additional information about topics of interest to you. The resource guide includes books about the Inner Edge and other topics of interest to coaches, as well as videotapes, DVDs and web sites related to the Inner Edge.

It is my hope that the material presented in the book may "hook" you into developing a passion for sport psychology and the pursuit of the Inner Edge. I hope that you will incorporate some of the concepts from this book in your unique coaching situations. You'll be amazed at how your perspective about the world of sport is transformed through your new knowledge about sport psychology. I will have succeeded as an author if you begin to "see" the ideas in the book when you look at your world. I urge you to be innovative - to think about interesting and novel ways to apply the concepts presented in this book. Hey - go out on a limb! Why? Because that's where the fruit is. Good luck, and good coaching.

Part One

Establishing a Solid Foundation

Learning to coach for the Inner Edge begins with the basics. The first six chapters in Part 1 are designed to provide you with a solid foundational understanding of sport psychology. In the first chapter, the field of sport psychology is explained as it relates to coaching effectiveness. Then, we move on to the basic topics of coaching philosophy, motivation, communication, leadership, and team cohesion. As shown below in Figure 1.1, these basic topics form the building blocks needed for the Inner Edge. Your athletes gain the Inner Edge when they are part of a program in which

- there is a consistent and effective coaching philosophy,
- motivation is nurtured and enhanced in athletes,
- communication flows easily and honestly,
- innovative leadership is provided, and
- the whole is stronger than the parts through team cohesion.

Read with an open mind. Learn from the master coaches and elite athletes who are described throughout these chapters. Consider the ways in which you can use this knowledge in your program with your athletes. Be thoughtful, innovative, and willing to move beyond your comfort zone and familiar ways of thinking. Get the Inner Edge!

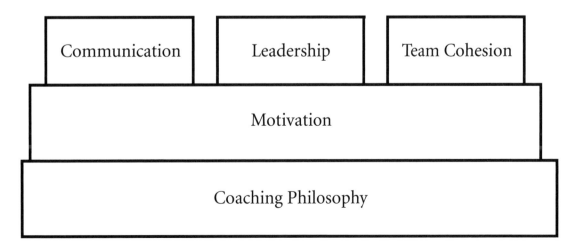

Figure 1.1 Building Blocks for the Inner Edge

Chapter

One

Understanding Sport Psychology

Chapter Preview

In this chapter, you'll learn:
- what sport psychology is about
- how sport psychology integrates with other sport sciences
- how the objectives of sport psychology may be thought of as a "triad"
- about research in sport psychology that supports the triad

Michael Johnson let the pressure wash over him as he stood on the track waiting for the start of the 200 meter race in the 1996 Atlanta Olympic Games. The entire world knew that he was attempting to become the first man to strike Olympic gold in both the 200 and 400 meter races. Amazingly, Johnson seemed eager to create more pressure for himself by confidently stating his intention to win both races and then appearing on the track in glistening gold shoes as a public declaration that anything less than gold medals in both races would be a failure. He won the 400 meter race in Olympic record time, and now faced his second challenge, which he wanted the most. Later, Johnson revealed what he was thinking at this moment: "There was pressure from the . . . people who expect you to win . . . But I crave [pressure]. I live for that very moment in the blocks" (Moore, 1996, p. 30). Johnson exploded from the blocks to win the race in a world record 19.32 seconds, a time that most track aficionados would not have predicted to occur until a few decades later.

Most all athletes have experienced the intoxication of peak performance in sport, although most of us will not achieve our peak performances in the Olympic Games as did Michael Johnson. Sport arouses passion and competitive intensity in us because we all have at least briefly experienced *being in the zone* or performing at a level commensurate with our physical and mental potential. What a feeling it is to experience this *zone* where performance seems so automatic and even effortless! However, it is far more typical for athletes to perform when they are *not* in this automatic, optimal performance zone. This requires athletes to be mentally skilled, to focus effectively and manage their thoughts, emotions, and actions during competition. The goal for any athlete is to perform optimally, whether that involves performing in the *zone* or being mentally skilled to perform well when things are not automatically clicking. The quest to understand, and help athletes achieve, optimal performance in sport has spawned the various sport sciences, or areas of systematic study and research, such as sport physiology, sport biomechanics, sport medicine, and sport psychology.

Consider how Michael Johnson used knowledge from the sport sciences in achieving his peak performance. Sport physiology was important in designing appropriate fitness training for the specific energy demands of the 200 and 400 meter sprint races. Sport biomechanics was important in helping Johnson develop and refine his individualized running technique, which allowed him maximum acceleration and minimum drag to enhance his speed. Sport medicine played an important role in providing the latest injury treatment and rehabilitation in his training for the Olympics. And finally, Johnson utilized principles from sport psychology to remain mentally tough throughout years of grueling workouts, to develop and maintain a competitive focus free of distraction, and to optimize his energy level at the point of competition to enable his mind to control his body to achieve its maximum performance.

Although sport psychology is the focus of this book, it should be noted that all of the sport sciences work in an integrated fashion to enhance sport performance. Michael Johnson had earned his ability to be confident based on his persistence in a sound physiological training program. His physical and mental energy levels were primed at their optimal point in relation to the physiological needs of this specific event. His competitive focus was developed in concert with his biomechanical technique training in which he learned how most efficiently to direct his attention to run using proper mechanical form. Effective sport performance is the culmination of knowledge gained from all the sport sciences, although our primary interest in this book is in sport psychology.

What is Sport Psychology?

Sport psychology is the study of how individuals think, act, and feel when participating in sport. Thus, sport psychologists are interested in *how the thoughts, behaviors, and emotions of athletes influence and are influenced by their sport participation.* Think about this relationship. What are examples of ways that athletes' thoughts, feelings, and behaviors are linked to the social context of sport? Why does an intelligent, easy-going ice hockey player drop his gloves and fight with an opponent on the ice? Why do athletes believe that it's harder to win on the road than at home (and often let this belief affect their performance)? Why would a talented high school basketball player, who is being wooed by every college coach in the country, suddenly lose her shooting touch in the championship playoffs?

These questions all capture the **psychosocial aspects of sport participation**—which is the focus of study in sport psychology. This simply refers to the ways in which psychological factors (e.g., personality of the athlete) interact with social factors in sport (e.g., competitive pressure, leadership style of coaches, crowd size) to influence athletes and their performance. The hockey player fights because hockey is marketed as an aggressive sport, and hockey players are encouraged and expected to fight to increase fan attendance. The home advantage has been documented in sport meaning that statistics show that teams win more at home than on the road. However, the home advantage has been talked about so much by coaches and the media that athletes often put themselves at a psychological disadvantage by believing it. This socially constructed belief affects athletes' competitive behavior in terms of effort and confidence, which subsequently hurts their performance on the road. The talented basket-

Personal Plug-In

What questions do you have about the psychosocial aspects of sport participation? Identify 3-4 questions about sport psychology that you think are the most interesting. Be creative—ask hard questions!

ball player in our example probably fell prey to competitive stress based on the increasing pressure of performing well to carry her team to a championship, earning a college scholarship, and gaining the approval of her parents and coach. In other words, the social pressures she faced influenced her thinking, and detracted from her ability to relax and focus on the process of playing.

Objectives of Sport Psychology: The Triad

From a practical standpoint, three objectives of sport psychology are presented in this chapter for athletes and coaches. These three objectives represent a *triad* that emphasizes that the field of sport psychology attempts to help athletes achieve (a) *optimal performance*, (b) *optimal development*, and (c) *optimal experiences* in sport.

Achieving Optimal Performance

Research has shown that sport psychology interventions, or mental training, can enhance athletes' performances in a variety of sports (e.g., Greenleaf, Gould, & Dieffenbach, 2001; Greenspan & Feltz, 1989; Patrick & Hrycaiko, 1998; Thelwell & Greenlees, 2001). Several of the techniques presented in this book, such as imagery, relaxation, and purposeful self-talk, have been shown to enhance athletes' performance. At the elite level, such as the Olympics and World Championships, a consistent finding is that successful athletes engage in systematic mental preparation more so than less successful athletes (Greenleaf et al., 2001; Gould, Eklund, & Jackson, 1992a, 1992b, 1993; Gould, Guinan, Greenleaf, Medbery, & Peterson, 1999). In a study of professional baseball players, mental skills were just as predictive of batting averages as were players' physical skills, and for pitchers, their mental skills were more important in predicting their success than their physical skills (Smith, Schutz, Smoll, & Ptacek, 1995). In addition, mental skills were predictive of players' survival in professional baseball two and three years later (Smith & Christensen, 1995).

Clearly, coaches understand that athletes who are mentally skilled in terms of confidence, coping ability, and concentration typically perform better than those athletes who are less mentally skilled. Research supports this observation, and in addition demonstrates that mental skills can be taught to athletes, which in turn enhances their performance. Thus, *helping athletes achieve optimal performance* certainly is an important objective of sport psychology. But does that mean that sport psychologists are only concerned with performance? Absolutely not. The two other important objectives of sport psychology are *helping athletes achieve optimal development* and *helping athletes achieve optimal experiences*. Because performance (and winning) is so important in our society, the objectives of optimal development and experiences for athletes are often overlooked.

Achieving Optimal Development

Earl Woods says, "If you treat your child with admiration, respect and love, a miracle will occur" (Reilly, 1995, p. 66). The miracle in this case is Earl's son—Tiger Woods—who at age 21 won the prestigious Masters golf tournament, and has since fulfilled predictions that he could be the greatest golfer of all time. In Tiger's first big tournament as a child, Earl took him to the first tee and said, "Son, I want you to know I love you no matter how you do. Enjoy yourself" (Reilly, 1995, p. 65). The rise of Tiger Woods to stardom has been chronicled not only due to his outstanding physical abilities as a golfer, but also due to the unique environment in which he developed his competitive skills. His father prepared him to handle the psychological rigors of competition, but he did it in a way that allowed Tiger to develop his physical and mental skills without the stress of disappointing or letting down his parents which has been shown to be a source of stress for many young athletes. And not once did his parents ever insist that he practice. Tiger Woods developed the internal motivation to learn and improve his game without constant needling from his parents or coaches.

Tiger Woods, a megastar on the professional golf tour, represents the second objective of sport psychology—*optimal development*. Not everyone can become a successful and famous professional athlete like Tiger Woods, but the field of sport psychology attempts to help all athletes experience the optimal development of their physical skills as well as the optimal development of important self-perceptions such as feelings of self-worth and competence.

A great deal of research in sport psychology supports the importance of optimal development as an important goal for sport psychology. This research indicates that by focusing on personal development, individuals can enhance the quality of their sport participation. Children join sport teams to develop skill, have fun, and be with their friends (Lee, Whitehead, & Balchin, 2000; Weiss & Petlichkoff, 1989). Sure, winning becomes an important objective for athletes at later ages, but it's clear that kids really just want to learn how to play. All developmental theories of motivation emphasize that children must develop a sense of autonomy or ability to master physical skills to feel personally competent before they can engage in intense social comparison such as competition. Children lose motivation to participate in sport when they set unrealistically high standards usually in comparison to other athletes or when they play only for external reasons (e.g., pleasing their parents, winning trophies). For example, researchers have shown that 8-12-year-old children who participated in a mastery-oriented sport climate that emphasized personal improvement developed higher skill levels and were more motivated to continue than children who participated in a competitive-oriented sport climate (Theeboom, De Knop, & Weiss, 1995). The secret to keeping kids motivated to participate in sport is to help them to develop skills and improve, so that later they can meet the challenges of competition.

Many people mistakenly believe that an emphasis on development is important for children, but that adults should have a more mature perspective and focus on outcomes. But this is not true! Research has shown that one of the characteristics of highly successful Olympic and World Champion athletes is that they clearly define personal performance goals for each day of training and that their competition focus plans emphasize a task performance focus, as compared to less successful athletes that tend to think more about possible outcomes and upcoming competitors (Gould, Eklund, & Jackson, 1992a; Orlick & Partington, 1988). In Chapter 8, you will learn how to design individualized goal maps so that you can chart the developmental progression of athletes in achieving their goals in sport.

Achieving Optimal Experiences

Consider the following quotes to better understand why optimal experience is an important objective in sport psychology.

"The most memorable match I ever had as a pure tennis player, playing for the love of the game and the competition, was a match I lost—the Wimbledon final of 1990 against Edberg. I was down two sets to love, I came back and had a 3-1 lead in the fifth. Eventually, I lost 6-4 in the fifth. It isn't important that I lost that match, because I was on top of my game, I sensed the beauty and joy of the game, I stuck with it through the ups and downs and I played like a champion. That's good enough for me." **Boris Becker**, winner of six Grand Slam events, including three Wimbledon titles *(Becker, 1998, p. 54)*

"As a white-water canoeist I discovered that the challenge of running a river is not a conflict between human and nature, it is a melding together of the two. You do not conquer a river, you experience it. The calculated risk, the momentary sense of meaning, and the intensity of the experience let you emerge exhilarated and somehow better. It is a quest for self-fulfillment rather than a quest for victory over others or over the river. Many sports can be viewed in the same way. Each experience or exploration can lead to enlightenment and discovery. There is no way to fail to experience the experience, and experiencing becomes the goal. The experience may lead to improved performance, self-discovery, personal satisfaction, and greater awareness, or it may simply be interesting in its own right." **Terry Orlick**, internationally-known sport psychology consultant *(Orlick, 1990, p. 5)*

"I had learned what it means to ride the Tour de France. It's not about the bike. It's a metaphor for life, not only the longest race in the world but also the most exalting and heartbreaking and potentially tragic. It poses every conceivable element to the rider . . . and above all a great, deep self-questioning. During our lives we're faced with so many different elements as well, we experience so many setbacks, and fight such a hand-to-hand battle with failure, head down in the rain, just trying to stay upright and to have a little hope. The Tour is not just a bike race, not at all. It is a test. It tests you physically, it tests you mentally, and it even tests you morally." **Lance Armstrong**, six-time winner of the Tour de France *(Armstrong, 2001, pp. 68-69)*

What do you notice about these quotes? It seems that Boris Becker, Terry Orlick, and Lance Armstrong were highly motivated to achieve optimal experiences as they faced the challenges of professional tennis, raging rivers, and the French Alps. Becker is a great tennis champion who won multiple Wimbledon titles, Orlick is a highly successful consultant and author, and Lance Armstrong is a six-time Tour de France champion. Yet they clearly indicate that for them, focusing only on the outcome misses the essence of what their sports mean to them. These examples emphasize the importance of the third objective of sport psychology, which is to help athletes understand how to achieve optimal experiences in their sport participation. Sport psychologists want to help athletes enjoy quality sport experiences, to have fun, to feel more competent and worthy, and to gain personal fulfillment and meaning through their sport participation. Athletes don't have to be world-class tennis players or Olympians to enjoy optimal experiences in sport. Thus, the material in this book is designed for coaches at all levels who want to apply some basic ideas from sport psychology to help athletes more fully enjoy their sport experiences.

Can you remember a time when you were engaged in an activity that was so absorbing that you completely lost track of time? If you can, then you are recalling your experience of *flow*. Flow, originally defined by Csikszentmihalyi (1990) as *an optimal mental state involving total absorption in a task*, is what most athletes refer to as being *in the zone*. Most everyone involved in sport has enjoyed this feeling of sheer absorption, or flow, and it is this feeling that typically leads individuals to fall in love with sport and seek out these feelings when playing sport.

Flow is not the same as peak performance, but in sport, flow often coincides with or results in peak performance, and the strategic use of mental skills during competition is associated with achieving flow (Jackson, Thomas, Marsh, & Smethurst, 2000). Interestingly, athletes indicate that getting into flow involves such factors as maintaining an appropriate task focus, keeping a positive mental attitude, and feeling physically ready to perform. Research with hundreds of elite athletes from various sports has supported several common characteristics of the peak performance state such as effortless perfor-

mance, sense of control, lack of conscious thinking about performance, extraordinary awareness of what other athletes are going to do, and feeling highly energized (Cohn, 1991; Jackson, 1992; Loehr, 1984; Ravizza, 1977). Consider the following description of an athlete's flow experience:

> I felt like I could do almost anything, as if I were in complete control. I really felt confident and positive . . . I felt physically very relaxed, but really energized and pumped up. I experienced virtually no anxiety or fear, and the whole experience was enjoyable. I experienced a very real sense of calmness and quiet inside, and everything just seemed to flow automatically . . . Even though I was really hustling, it was all very effortless (Garfield & Bennett, 1984, pp. 37, 95).

These characteristics of flow and peak performance seem to fuel athletes' passion for their sport participation. Flow experiences are described as *autotelic*, which means that *the experience of playing sport is a reward in itself without concern for the outcome*. Thus, sport psychology often focuses on ways to help athletes achieve optimal experiences to enhance the joy and personal meaning that sport participation can often provide.

In summary, sport psychology attempts to enhance the quality of athletes' participation in sport by helping them achieve

- optimal performance,
- optimal development, and
- optimal experience.

Personal Plug-In

Recall in as much detail as you can an event in which you experienced flow. This experience could be in sport or in other recreational or leisure activities. Some people get into flow while they work. Identify your flow experience and jot down as many specific characteristics of this experience as you can remember.

These three objectives form the sport psychology *triad*. The examples of Michael Johnson, Tiger Woods, Boris Becker, Terry Orlick, and Lance Armstrong used in this chapter illustrate the three factors that make up the sport psychology triad. The essence of sport participation involves the thrill of experiencing an *optimal performance*, the feeling of pride and accomplishment that we experience through the *optimal development* of competency, and the satisfaction and savoring of an *optimal experience* that has great meaning in one's life. Sport psychologists work as teachers, researchers, and consultants to develop and apply knowledge about the psychosocial aspects of sport participation that influence the triad. A common misconception about sport psychology is that it focuses only on performance enhancement. However, the triad emphasizes the importance the field of sport psychology places on not only optimizing the performance of athletes, but also optimizing their development and experiences.

A *Big Picture* of the Inner Edge

In summary, the objectives of sport psychology include the triad of optimal performance, development, and experience for athletes. In the remaining chapters of the book, the various topics in sport psychology that can help coaches and athletes gain the Inner Edge are introduced. In these chapters, you'll get specific tips about how you as a coach can use sport psychology to get the Inner Edge. Take a look at the *big picture* of the Inner Edge in Figure 1.2 for an illustration of the sport psychology topics that are in the upcoming chapters of this book.

A Balanced Triad for the Inner Edge

The pinnacle of the Inner Edge shown in Figure 1.2 is the triad representing optimal performance, optimal development, and optimal experience. Notice that the triad, shaped as a triangle, is perfectly balanced, meaning that the Inner Edge is achieved when the objectives of optimal performance, development, and experience are in balance. (This is discussed in more detail in the next chapter.) All the other parts of the *big picture* serve to keep the triad in balance so athletes can achieve the Inner Edge.

Building Blocks (Chapters 2-6)

The building blocks that form the foundation for the Inner Edge, shown at the bottom of Figure 1.2, are discussed in the rest of the chapters in Part 1 of the book. A practical and meaningful philosophy for coaches and athletes is the most basic building

Photo by Navy Sports, courtesy of USMC

block to provide a stable and consistent grounding for the Inner Edge. In Chapter 2, the importance of developing and living an effective coaching philosophy is discussed. Motivation (Chapter 3) is the next building block for the Inner Edge, because motivation is the energizer that turns your coaching philosophy into behavioral action in your athletes. The remaining three building blocks are communication, leadership, and team cohesion. The essential human skill of communication is discussed in Chapter 4 to emphasize how your interpersonal skills influence your effectiveness as a coach. In Chapter 5, leadership is discussed as another critical building block for coaches to help athletes achieve optimal performance, development, and experiences in sport. Chapter 6 focuses on team cohesion, so that you may better understand how the elusive *team chemistry* influences the Inner Edge.

Overall, the five building blocks discussed in Chapters 2-6 ensure that athletes

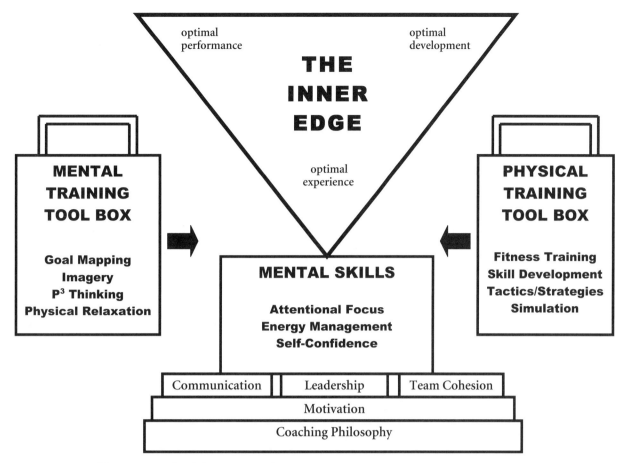

Figure 1.2 The "big picture" of the Inner Edge

- are advantaged by having a coach with a sound and practical coaching philosophy,
- have strong internal motivation to achieve and a coach who understands motivation,
- thrive in a climate characterized by skillful and effective communication,
- reap the benefits of effective decision-making and leadership, and
- belong to a cohesive team.

If any of these building blocks were removed, the foundation for the Inner Edge would be shaken, athletes' mental skills could be disrupted, and the triad might tip precariously and become unbalanced (see Figure 1.2). We don't want this to happen! Thus, Part 1 of the book is dedicated to helping coaches understand how to design and build a solid foundation for the Inner Edge.

Mental Training Tool Box (Chapters 7-11)

With these solid building blocks in place, coaches and athletes are now ready to move on to mental training. Part 2 of the book begins with Chapter 7, which introduces coaches to the basic premises behind mental training and attempts to dispel myths about sport psychology and the nature of mental training. The remaining four chapters in Part 2 introduce coaches to the mental training tool box (shown on the left side of Figure 1.2), or the four mental training tools that can be used by coaches to build mental and physical skills in athletes. In Chapter 8, the concept of goal mapping is presented as a tool to help athletes develop a sense of purpose, and to plan and actively pursue their goals in a purposeful manner. In Chapter 9, imagery is introduced as a mental training tool that helps athletes visualize their way to success in sport. In Chapter 10, P^3 Thinking is presented to help athletes engage in effective thinking to optimize their performance, development, and experiences. In Chapter 11, physical relaxation is explained as a tool to help athletes identify and reduce physical tension in their bodies. All of these tools are part of the mental training tool box that coaches and athletes carry with them, providing the needed tools for developing and maintaining the Inner Edge.

Although not the focus of this book, a physical training tool box is also shown in Figure 1.2 to emphasize that mental and physical training work hand in hand to help athletes achieve the Inner Edge. Sound fitness training, repetitive practice for skill development and execution, and the effective use of tactics and strategies all contribute to the Inner Edge for athletes. Simulation of competitive situations in training is an extremely important tool to get the Inner Edge in performing in different types of pressure situations. Examples of practicing mental skills through simulation in physical training sessions are provided throughout the book.

Mental Skills (Chapters 12-14) and Implementation Tips (Chapters 15-16)

Part 3 of the book presents the three mental skills of attentional focus, energy management, and self-confidence. The ability of athletes to achieve optimal performance, development, and experiences in sport is dependent on their ability to focus attention (Chapter 12), manage competitive energy (Chapter 13), and compete with confidence (Chapter 14). As shown in Figure 1.2, the mental training tools in the tool box are used to enhance the mental skills of athletes. The mental skills rest on the foundational building blocks so that athletes have a consistent and productive environment within which to enhance their focus, confidence, and energy management.

Part 4 of the book (Chapters 15-16) is dedicated to help you integrate your sport psychology knowledge into personalized mental plans that meet the specific needs of your athletes and your program. A cursory knowledge of isolated mental training concepts is not necessarily helpful to coaches and athletes, so Part 4 is designed to help you integrate your knowledge into useful mental training ideas. In Chapter 15, implementation ideas for how to select from the mental training *menu* are provided, and sample mental training plans are provided for different situations. In Chapter 16, *special recipes* are provided for common challenges faced by coaches, such as slumps, burnout, inconsistency, and rehabilitation and return from injury.

Wrapping Up

You now have the *big picture* of how to get the Inner Edge as presented in this book. The **Inner Edge** is *the advantage that athletes create for themselves by honing the sharpness or keenness of their mental skills*. You as the coach can help your athletes gain the Inner Edge in many ways, as shown in Figure 1.2. You can set the foundation by establishing a consistent and effective coaching philosophy, understanding motivation and team cohesion, and being a strong communicator and leader. You can use tools in your mental training and physical training tool boxes to help athletes develop and hone their mental skills to be more focused, energized, and confident. And you can help athletes balance the objectives of optimizing their performance, development, and experiences in sport. The remainder of the book is designed to help you do all these things.

Although the breadth of information may seem overwhelming, it is my intent to provide you with practical examples of how to get started in small ways to incorporate sport psychology into your coaching. Actually, you probably know more than you realize! Many coaches are masters of the Inner Edge. Hopefully, the ideas presented in the book can enable you to more consistently and effectively use sport psychology concepts in training your athletes.

Summary Points for Chapter 1

1. Sport psychology is the study of how the thoughts, behaviors, and emotions of athletes influence and are influenced by their sport participation.

2. Knowledge about sport psychology is most useful to sport practitioners when it is integrated with knowledge from the other sport sciences.

3. Sport psychology professionals engage in research, teaching, and consultation with athletes and coaches to develop and apply knowledge related to the psychosocial aspects of sport.

4. All sport psychology topics examine the ways in which the psychological characteristics of athletes interact with the social characteristics of sport and society.

5. The main objectives of sport psychology represent a triad that focuses on gaining the

Inner Edge by helping athletes achieve optimal performance, optimal development, and optimal experiences.

6. Research supports that mental skills and the systematic use of mental preparation enhances athletes' performances in a variety of sports.

7. Flow occurs as an optimal experience for athletes when they are totally absorbed in the activity to the point where playing sport is a reward in itself without concern about winning and losing.

8. Research has shown that athletes believe that personalized physical and mental preparation strategies enhance their ability to achieve flow and peak performance.

9. By focusing on personal development and improvement, athletes of all ages can enhance their motivation and feelings of personal competence and self-worth.

10. The *big picture* of the Inner Edge demonstrates how the building blocks, the mental and physical training tool boxes, and mental skills all interact to help athletes achieve optimal performance, development, and experiences.

11. Achieving the objectives of the sport psychology triad requires the effective implementation and mastery of the sport psychology knowledge in this book along with the optimization of physical skill and training.

Glossary

autotelic: the experience of playing sport is a reward in itself without concern for the outcome

flow: an optimal mental state characterized by total absorption in the task; typically called *in the zone*

Inner Edge: the advantage that athletes create for themselves by honing the sharpness or keenness of their mental skills

psychosocial aspects of sport: the ways in which psychological factors, such as the personality of the athlete, interact with social factors in sport, such as competitive pressure and crowd size, to influence athletes and their performance

sport psychology: the study of the how the thoughts, emotions, and behaviors of athletes influence and are influenced by their participation in sport

Study Questions

1. Define sport psychology.

2. What do we mean by the term *psychosocial?* Provide several examples of psychosocial phenomena in sport.

3. Explain the *triad* that represents the three objectives of sport psychology. For each objective, identify at least two questions that represent areas of interest or study for the field of sport psychology.

4. Define and explain *flow.* What are the characteristics of flow that have been identified by athletes?

5. Many people associate sport psychology with performance enhancement. Although this is one objective of the field, explain why the other objectives are just as important as performance enhancement for athletes of all ages. Cite some research to support your answer.

6. Why is it important to integrate knowledge from sport psychology with knowledge from other sport sciences in helping athletes achieve the highest quality sport participation?

7. Why are the building blocks shown in Figure 1.2 important in maintaining mental skill over time?

Reflective Learning Activities

1. The Zone

All athletes have experienced playing in flow, or the zone, where performance is effortless, their awareness is sharp, and they are focused on the quality and enjoyment of playing their sport, as opposed to the pressure to perform perfectly and win. Although flow is an elusive quality, many athletes believe that they can do things to increase their ability to get in the zone.

Consider the following questions about flow, and brainstorm to think of several answers for each.

a. What are some things athletes can do in (choose a specific sport here) to increase their chances of getting into flow?

b. What are some things that coaches can do in (specific sport) to help athletes get into flow?

c. What are typical things in this sport that disrupt flow for athletes?

d. How do coaches disrupt flow in athletes (often unknowingly)?

(10 minutes in groups of 3-4; participants divided into groups that represent specific sports and ages)

2. Megatrends

Emerging social forces are changing the nature of sport in our society. Identify several of these social forces that are influencing or will influence the nature of sport participation. Discuss how these emerging social forces may interact with psychological characteristics of athletes to affect the sport psychology triad (or the ability to achieve optimal performance, optimal development, and optimal experiences). (8 minutes in groups of 3 and then overall 10 minutes large group discussion).

Chapter

Two

Developing and Living a Practical Coaching Philosophy

Photo courtesy of UT Lady Vol Media Relations

Chapter Preview

In this chapter, you'll learn:

- why sport psychology is based on philosophy
- why it is important to develop and live an effective coaching philosophy
- about "balancing the triad" as a coaching philosophy
- how coaches can keep the "triad" from becoming unbalanced

"Some of the winningest coaches . . . were philosophers, people of learning and wisdom. For these coaches, philosophy and sport are not mutually exclusive. Indeed they are one and the same. To coach is to believe in something: the game, the athlete, the quest for excellence, the process of challenging one's self and striving to overcome. [They] could transform people and inspire them to dazzling heights of achievement. The athletes of these coaches were blessed with . . . a deeper perspective on life, on people, on themselves." **Gary M. Walton**, from his book *Beyond Winning: The Timeless Wisdom of the Great Philosopher Coaches*

W hen philosophers held court in ancient Greece, their ideas were respected and revered. Today, philosophy is viewed by most people as abstract, boring, and impractical. In this chapter, we're going to explore how a well thought out philosophy serves as a concrete, exciting, and practical foundation for coaches to effectively apply knowledge from sport psychology to help athletes achieve success in sport and fulfillment in life.

Socrates, one of the greatest philosophers in history, is famous for saying "The unexamined life is not worth living." Socrates didn't know a thing about sport psychology, but with these words he captured the most critical building block for the

Inner Edge. We have to examine our lives—to understand what is important to us and what we value. The key to developing an effective personal philosophy, as Socrates knew, is to know yourself. This is why the study of sport psychology must begin with an understanding of one's philosophy. This is particularly crucial for coaches, who need a deeply rooted guidance system that keeps them on course as they face difficult decisions and challenges. Not only is it important for coaches to develop a sound philosophy, but they must also live this philosophy every day. Effective coaching for the Inner Edge begins with you *walking the walk* along with *talking the talk*. Thus, a sound coaching philosophy is the most basic building block (see Figure 1.1 in Chapter 1) in helping your athletes develop the necessary mental and physical skills to be successful.

Who Needs Philosophy? We All Do!

A **philosophy** is simply the *basic beliefs that guide our behavior every day*. Our philosophy helps us to interpret the events in our lives, and it gives our lives meaning and direction. It helps to keep us consistent and directed by a sense of purpose when we face the daily stresses and obstacles of life. Consider the following philosophies and the ways in which these philosophies have influenced the behavior of the individuals:

> *"I try to think like nature to find the right questions. You don't invent the answers, you reveal the answers from nature. In nature, the answers already exist."* **Dr. Jonas Salk**, inventor of the Salk polio vaccine
>
> *"I am an educator. I have always felt my responsibility was broader than wins and losses."* **John Thompson**, former men's basketball coach at Georgetown University
>
> *"I'm no role model."* **Charles Barkley**, former professional basketball player known for his many off-the-court scuffles
>
> *"I'm not afraid of storms, for I have learned how to sail my ship."* **Louisa May Alcott**, famous author
>
> *"Genius is 10% inspiration and 90% perspiration."* **Thomas Edison**, famous inventor
>
> *"In the end, all business operations can be reduced to three words: people, product, and profits. People come first. Unless you get a good team, you can't do much with the other two."* **Lee Iacocca**,

> business executive who saved Chrysler from corporate disaster
>
> *"What I owe to my team is to make sure everybody plays and works hard and I have an opportunity to play them."* **Joe Paterno**, legendary Penn State football coach, after his team won the game but dropped in the national polls because he refused to leave his starters in to run up the score
>
> *"I am just a common man who is true to his beliefs."* **John Wooden**, winner of 10 national titles as UCLA basketball coach

Philosophies are more than words—they are personal *how to* manuals that guide our decisions and behavior. Clearly, the philosophies just presented have influenced the decisions and behavior of the individuals who held the philosophies, as well as others who were touched by the implementation of these philosophies. Lee Iacocca's philosophy influenced thousands of workers in his corporation, and John Thompson's, Joe Paterno's, and John Wooden's philosophies have enriched the lives of many college athletes. Consider your beliefs, values, and philosophy about sport participation and your role and responsibilities as a coach. Do you think that coaching philosophies should differ for coaches at the youth, high school, collegiate, and professional levels? Why or why not? Regardless of your answer, coaches at all levels should spend some time in self-reflection to understand their beliefs and values regarding their role as a coach, and their objectives and the ways in which they pursue these objectives when working with athletes.

Your coaching philosophy is based on your personal values and beliefs about your role as coach in relation to the lives of your athletes (Lyle, 2002). It is not simply a tactical philosophy, such as "pressure defense and push the ball" or "conservative, ball control." A coaching philosophy is much broader, and focuses on how your beliefs and values about your role as a coach impact your behavior toward your athletes and team every day. If coaches forego the important step of reflecting upon and developing their coaching philosophies, they lack a basis for all their decisions and coaching practices. Your coaching philosophy is like a well. Athletes come to you all the time for water (questions, problems, need for guidance and teaching), and if you don't have a deep, steady source of water from your coaching philosophy well, you will be unable to consistently hydrate your athletes when they need it.

You can learn from the coaching philosophies developed by others by reading popular books written by coaches or books on coaching effectiveness. Coach Mike Krzyzewski's (2000) *Leading with the Heart*, Tony DiCicco and Colleen Hacker's (2002) *Catch Them Being Good*, and Anson Dorrance's (2002) *The Vision of a Champion* are all good sources to learn about the philosophy and leadership styles of highly successful coaches. Coaching philosophies suggested in popular coaching effectiveness books include "Athletes first - winning second" (Martens, 1997) and the "double-goal" model (Thompson, 2003). The "athletes first - winning second" philosophy suggests that coaches keep the three objectives of fun, winning, and development of athletes in perspective by prioritizing the wellbeing of athletes ahead of the team outcome of winning. The "double-goal" model emphasizes the equal priority of the coaching objectives of striving to win and teaching life lessons to athletes. The key to all the philosophies presented in these books is how they help coaches keep their values and coaching objectives in perspective and in mind to guide them in the myriad of daily decisions they must make regarding their athletes, their teams, and their overall programs. That is, your coaching philosophy logically leads you to such specific behaviors as use of practice and training time, recruitment practices, communication with athletes, rewards and discipline, decision-making, leadership style, goal mapping, and even your personal motives for coaching (Lyle, 2002).

Balancing the Triad: A Basic Coaching Philosophy

In the previous section, you learned about the importance of philosophy as the foundation for all other sport psychology principles. Based on the example philosophies presented, it should be clear that developing a coaching philosophy is a deeply personal and individualistic experience. Nowhere is a sound philosophy more needed than in competitive sport. Sport in our culture is wildly popular, and athletes at young ages are receiving stunning social and economic rewards for achieving athletic excellence. It may be hard for parents, coaches, and young athletes to keep their lives in perspective when they

---

Personal Plug-In

On a blank sheet of paper, jot down some thoughts that represent your current philosophy about coaching. This might include what you see as your most important objectives as a coach, and the values and beliefs that will guide you in making everyday decisions about your athletes and your team. Consider your coaching philosophy a work in progress—don't worry if it's not well developed at this time.

---

believe that multi-million-dollar professional contracts, Olympic gold, and lucrative endorsements are readily available.

In this section, I offer a philosophy that serves as the foundation for this book, and it represents a philosophy that seems useful for coaches. It is my belief that to effectively understand and practice the basic tenets of sport psychology, the three objectives in the sport psychology triad introduced in Chapter 1 (optimal performance, optimal development, and optimal experience) must be kept in balance or perspective. As shown in Figure 2.1, *balancing the triad* means that the quality of sport participation is enhanced by focusing on the complete triad, as opposed to overemphasizing one side of the triad at the expense of the others. Keeping the triad in balance, or at least keeping all three objectives in perspective, is critical to successfully apply the principles of sport psychology presented in this book. Keeping the triad in balance or perspective, then, is critical in coaching for the Inner Edge.

Look at the triad pictured in Figure 2.1, and consider how an overemphasis on each objective can create an unbalanced perspective on competitive sport. Obviously, the balance between performance, development, and experience undergoes continuous shifts when you consider situational and developmental factors. At various times in an athlete's career, he or she may be more fixated on one corner of the triad than others. A coaching philosophy appropriate for young children should clearly emphasize the development of skills and enjoyable sport experiences over high-level performance expectations. An elite athlete undergoing rehabilitation from a serious injury should shift to more of a developmental focus and use a systematic goal mapping plan (presented in Chapter 8) to facilitate her return to top competitive

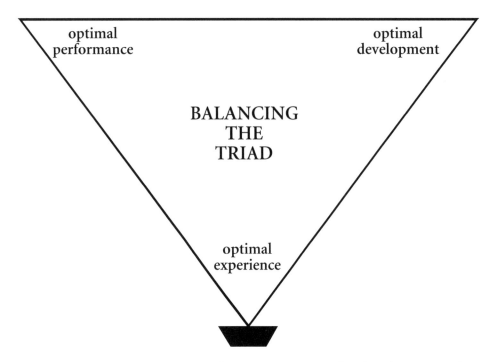

Figure 2.1 Balancing the triad provides perspective needed for the Inner Edge

form at a high-performance level. Due to the extreme social pressure to win and perform perfectly, a philosophy that embraces a balanced triad of performance, development, and experience is often ignored due to an overemphasis on performance. Research has shown that youth sport coaches typically state that their philosophies emphasize development and experience (fun), but that their behaviors often emphasize performance (winning) over the other two objectives (Gilbert, Trudel, & Haughian, 1999; McCallister, Blinde, & Weiss, 2000; Wilcox & Trudel, 1998). This problem is discussed in the next section.

A Tilted Triad: Is Winning Really "the Only Thing"?

Vince Lombardi was misquoted. Lombardi, the legendary coach of the Green Bay Packers, is popularly associated with the quote "Winning isn't everything, it's the only thing." In reality, what Lombardi really said was "Winning isn't everything—but making the effort to win is." Lombardi's foundational philosophy won him the respect of his players. His former quarterback Bart Starr said,

> "Lombardi felt that every fiber in your body should be used in an effort to seek excellence, and he sought this goal every day of his life with complete dedication . . . He never expected more from us than he was willing to give of himself" (Flynn, 1973, foreword).

Vince Lombardi's misquote has influenced the coaching philosophies of youth football coaches in America more than any coaching clinic or sport psychology textbook. A big problem in sport is the overemphasis on performance outcomes and the neglect of the essential objectives of development and enjoyment of the sport experience. Let's examine several examples of how philosophies that are based on a tilted triad with performance overriding the other two objectives can be destructive.

Christy Henrich, an elite American gymnast, paid the ultimate price when her compulsive and perfectionistic devotion to gymnastics ended with her death from the eating disorder anorexia nervosa. In a tragic attempt to make her body fit society's expectation of a petite spunky gymnast, Henrich starved herself to death.

A softball game in Cincinnati, Ohio, between two teams of eight-year-olds ended in a brawl among parents and multiple lawsuits when the game was postponed due to extreme heat. Never mind that the soaring heat and humidity had already forced three of the young players to be taken to the hospital for observation due to heat exhaustion. The parents of the players whose team was winning at the time of the postponement verbally and physically attacked the umpires and opposing parents, while the eight-year-old players from both teams sat and watched with confusion and embarrassment from under a nearby shade tree.

A soccer dad pleaded no contest to an assault charge after he punched a 14-year-old boy who had scuffled for the ball with the man's 14-year-old son, leading to both boys' ejections from the game. The punch split the victim's lip, and the father was sentenced to 10 days of community service and ordered to undergo counseling (Nack & Munson, 2000).

These true stories illustrate out of balance competitive philosophies where an over-emphasis on performance outcomes caused irrational and even tragic consequences. Many people fail to understand that optimal performance in sport is most likely to occur when athletes focus on developmental goals and the enjoyment of optimal experiences in their sport. Even if you disagree with the balanced triad philosophy because you believe that winning is everything, the point is that winning (or optimal performance) is most likely to occur when the triad is in balance! Consider the following example of two Olympic figure skaters.

Midori Ito and Kristi Yamaguchi arrived at the 1992 Albertville Olympic Games with very different mindsets. Ito arrived in Albertville with the hopes of an entire country on her shoulders—no Japanese woman had ever won a gold medal in the Winter Games. As the 1989 world champion and the first woman to perform a triple Axel jump in competition, the pressure on her to win the gold was tremendous. "I was the favorite," said Ito, "and I knew the Japanese people expected a gold medal" (Swift, 1992, p. 72). As the competition approached, the normally chatty Ito became aloof and withdrawn, and in her practices she began missing her jumps. When Ito fell during her long program, the gold medal was lost and the headlines back in Japan read "Midori Fails."

Kristi Yamaguchi had just the opposite experience from Midori Ito. Even though Yamaguchi was the reigning world champion, she and the press considered herself an underdog to Ito at the Olympics. Unburdened by high expectations and pressure, Ya-

©iStockphoto.com

maguchi concentrated on enjoying the experience of being a part of the Olympic Games. She marched in the opening ceremonies, stayed in the Olympic Village, and went dancing with other athletes. Yamaguchi admits that she was mentally prepared to live with the result if Ito won the gold medal over her. This acceptance and Yamaguchi's focus on the experience of the Olympics freed her from the pressure and expectations that Ito faced, and Yamaguchi went on to win the gold medal.

The philosophies of Kristi Yamaguchi and Midori Ito served as the basis for one athlete to relax and allow her body to perform optimally, and for the other athlete to lose focus on the rational perspective needed to calm her negative thoughts and feelings. The point is that it was easier for Yamaguchi to achieve optimal performance because she had the balance of savoring the optimal experience of the Olympics and accepting whatever outcome occurred as part of her development. Ito, in contrast, fell victim to the performance pressure that resulted from an overemphasis on winning the gold medal, which overshadowed her personal developmental goals and robbed her of her enthusiasm for the Olympic experience. It should be noted that even though Ito had failed in the eyes of many Japanese, she did win the silver medal and responded by saying, "I was never disappointed for myself, only that I had let down the people of Japan" (Swift, 1992, p. 73).

It is important to realize that an unbalanced triad or unrealistic coaching philosophy is often influenced by the cultural and competitive structures of society, such as nationalistic pride in the case of Midori Ito, the exploitation of college athletes by overzealous coaches who yearn for big contracts and fame, and society's shallow belief that winning is the essence of sport as opposed to the *pursuit* of winning and personal achievement. Consider the following reaction from Dan Jansen, who although he won an Olympic gold medal in 1994, wrote about his experiences in a chapter titled "There's More to Life than Skating Around in a Circle" (Jansen, 1999):

> "In 1984, my only goal was to make the Olympic team; to represent the United States at the Olympic Games. I hit that mark … [and] once I made the team, I hoped that with a great race, a top ten finish might be possible. I finished fourth, just 16/100ths of a second from winning a bronze medal, and was overjoyed. When I returned home… one of the most common reactions I received was, 'That's too bad, no medal.' That's when I realized the disparity in how various people define success" (p. 4).

Canadian figure skater Brian Orser won a silver medal in Calgary in 1988, and returned home to the following headline in the *Toronto Star*: "Orser Magnificent—But Still A Loser" (Perman, 2002). Nike ran an ad during the 1996 Atlanta Olympic Games with the slogan "You Don't Win the Silver, You Lose the Gold." So according to the popular press and an influential marketing firm, Midori Ito, second best in the *world*, Brian Orser, second best in the *world*, and Dan Jansen, fourth best in the *world*, were losers. Incredible.

These examples reinforce the constant interaction of the psychological characteristics of athletes with the social aspects of sport and society discussed in Chapter 1. Christy Henrich fell victim to our cultural expectation that gymnasts are petite and lean as well as society's overemphasis on physical attractiveness in females. Burnout in athletes typically occurs as the result of our culture's insatiable desire to push child athletes to specialize early at the expense of a balanced triad and an enjoyable childhood. Other problems in sport, such as aggression, violence, and a lack of sportsmanship, occur due to an imbalanced triad brought on by our cultural obsession with winning and irrational reasoning that violence against others is part of the game. It is essential that coaches and athletes recognize how society and the sport subculture create pressures to conform to behavioral codes that are unhealthy and destructive. This may be referred to as **hyperconformity,** which is defined as *a rigid code of behavior defined by the sport structure that athletes are expected to follow without question.*

Clipboard

Frosty Westering - Balancing the Triad

In over 20 years as head football coach at Pacific Lutheran University in Tacoma, Washington, Forrest "Frosty" Westering's teams never had a losing season while winning three national championships and playing for three others at the NAIA Division II level. Westering's coaching style was not to motivate by fear as many football coaches do, but rather to inspire his players to play for each other, which gave them a source of inner strength typically lacking in externally motivated athletes. Football practice under Westering (now retired) began at a three-day breakaway camp on an Oregon beach, where they played softball, built human pyramids, and competed in bizarre relays. The purpose of breakaway camp was to bond as a team, learn to trust each other, and enjoy the experience of being a PLU football player. Then, when the real practice and contact drills started, the players worked hard because they wanted to work hard. As a coach, Westering was a football workaholic, and everyone worked hard for him because Westering lived, breathed, and sweated every slogan that he spouted (e.g., "Doing your best is more important than being the best"). Westering's empowering coaching style instilled commitment and motivation in his players. During the season, PLU players always held hands when they entered and left the field. Once before an important game, Westering ordered his players to partner up and play an impromptu game of rock-paper-scissors before taking the field. After winning a national championship, Westering was most touched by a note from a stadium janitor who said in all his years he had never seen a team leave a locker room in such good condition as did PLU. Westering is a legend in the Pacific Northwest; he never yearned to leave PLU, which is evident in the book he wrote titled *Making The Big Time Where You Are.* If Westering sounds like an isolated eccentric, maybe we should reconsider what we accept as the norm that defines coaching practices. Perhaps we should start to consider Frosty Westering as the norm and begin to view with skepticism the controlling and dehumanizing coaching practices commonly seen in college football.

Let's take time out here for a quick gut check.

- Do you think that a coaching philosophy that includes an emphasis on optimal development and experience is unrealistic or naive in today's society?
- Is it possible to achieve a balanced perspective and philosophy when nineteen-year-old athletes sign professional contracts worth more than the gross national product of many small countries?
- Do you actually believe that the greatest athletes in the world care about optimal experiences and optimal development as much as the bottom line, which is based on performance?

My response to the gut check? No, it's not unrealistic or naive to focus on development and experiences along with performance. Yes, it's possible to achieve a balanced competitive philosophy in today's society. And, yes, I believe that the greatest athletes—the ones who raised the level of their sports along with their performance—such as Martina Navratilova, Mia Hamm, Michael Jordan, Wayne Gretzky—all possessed a sound and balanced philosophy that allowed them to perform their best when it meant the most.

In 1999, at age 42, Payne Stewart surprised the golfing world by winning the prestigious U.S. Open over many young golfers in their prime, such as Tiger Woods, David Duval, and Ernie Els. Stewart attributed his win to his philosophical maturity, which allowed him to retain his competitive fire yet keep his work as a professional athlete in perspective. Stewart worked with Richard Coop, a sport psychologist, who summed up Stewart's philosophical development:

Photo by Dale Sparks, All-Pro Photography

"An athlete is used to proving himself by what he does on the field, and Payne was no different. But that approach ultimately makes the result too important, and the resulting pressure gets in the way. It's better to prove yourself by what you are in life. Then the understanding that you remain a good person no matter the outcome on the playing field allows you to release the pressure and more easily have a good outcome" (Diaz, 1999a, p. G56).

The greatest athletes know how to keep competitive pressure in perspective because they focus on the joy of playing that drew them to sport in the first place. Legendary basketball center Bill Russell won two national collegiate championships, an Olympic gold medal, and 11 National Basketball Association World Championships in his illustrious career. Yet in his book titled *Second Wind: The Memoirs of an Opinionated Man* (Russell & Branch, 1979), he admits that championships were not his motivation for playing. Russell states that his greatest pleasure in basketball came during competition when both teams were playing at their peak, which in Russell's mind elevated the game to unprecedented levels of excellence. He admits that on some nights when the caliber of play escalated to this level, he found himself even rooting for the other team to keep up the challenge. Russell admits, "when the game ended at that special level, I literally did not care who had won" (Russell & Branch, 1979, p. 157). This powerful statement from one of the winningest athletes in basketball history is a personal testimony to the power of flow and peak experience in sport.

Therese Brisson, member of the Canadian Women's Ice Hockey team that won the gold medal at the 2002 Olympic Games, explains the importance of perspective and how it affected her team's performance:

> *"It's not all about the medal. In fact, athletes who seem to have the most success think the least about the outcome. The focus is on the process and on being the best you can be the day that it matters the most. My team was not able to do that in Nagano . . . After this disappointment . . . at the 2002 Winter Olympics in Salt Lake City, we won the gold . . . The difference was that we were able to focus on the journey so that we would be the best we could be on the night it mattered most"* (Starkes & Ericsson, 2003, p. x).

Even though optimal performance is an important objective, all athletes can enjoy sport simply for the pleasure and excitement that it provides. Tennis champion Pete Sampras has talked of the intense personal meaning that he felt when playing at Wimbledon, much like the intensity of meaning that professional golfers feel when playing a round at St. Andrews in Scotland, where the game of golf was born. Coaches should help athletes reflect on what sport means to them to develop a strongly rooted competitive philosophy, which may help them regain meaning when they face pressure and lose perspective and balance in their sport participation. Bob Rotella (1995), a successful sport psychology consultant, believes that athletes with healthy philosophies naturally and effortlessly think better than athletes with unhealthy philosophies. Rotella's point illustrates the direct link between how athletes think, feel, and act (sport psychology), and the values and beliefs upon which these thoughts, feelings, and actions are based (philosophy). As illustrated in the quote above by Therese Brisson, focusing on the experience frees ath-

Photo by Nick Manning, courtesy of © stock.xchng iv

letes up to perform their best, as opposed to focusing on the pressure of having to perform well to win. Keeping the triad in balance actually helps athletes to win, so help your athletes adopt a healthy perspective to serve as the foundation for their Inner Edge!

Wrapping Up

Don't let the P-word fool you! Remember that philosophy is not impractical and boring, but rather a practical guide to help you maintain a productive perspective when coaching for the Inner Edge in the challenging world of sport.

In this chapter, I've attempted to challenge you to develop and refine a strongly rooted coaching philosophy from which your operational plan as a coach can flow. Keep in mind that a coaching philosophy is a work in progress—something that is constantly developing and changing as you gain additional experiences and new perspectives. It is important that you consider not only the words that describe your coaching philosophy, but also that you identify key behaviors that represent your philosophy in action. Remember to walk the walk by modeling your commitment and belief in your philosophy every day. Living your philosophy makes it real and powerful to athletes, and allows them a firm grounding within your program from which they can face and overcome obstacles in their pursuit of excellence. This is the first essential step in moving beyond coaching a *team* to developing and maintaining a *program*. Plan, develop, and live a coaching philosophy that allows your program to flourish in the long-term as a fertile and challenging climate for athletes.

Also in this chapter, I've introduced a philosophy that serves as the basis for the rest of the book, and one that I believe is crucial for gaining the Inner Edge. All coaches should develop their own coaching philosophy based on their individual beliefs, values, and personality, yet I believe that keeping the sport psychology triad in perspective serves as a basic guide for any coaching philosophy. All of the psychosocial principles discussed in this book, such as goal mapping, self-confidence, and focusing attention, must start with a mentally healthy perspective about competition.

Summary Points for Chapter 2

1. Because a coaching philosophy requires self-reflection and an understanding of personal values and beliefs, it is the foundation for the Inner Edge.

2. Philosophies guide our behavior every day by helping us interpret events that happen to us, by serving as the foundation through which our lives develop meaning, and by keeping us consistent and goal-directed.

3. Because sport achievement in our society is so highly valued and publicized, it is essential for coaches to develop and maintain a sound philosophy to maintain a proper perspective when faced with difficult decisions.

4. The coaching philosophy espoused in this book is *balance* or *congruence* between the three sport psychology objectives of optimal performance, development, and experience.

5. Although developmental and situational factors may at times cause athletes to emphasize one part of the triad over others, an effective philosophy serves to keep the three objectives of sport psychology in perspective.

6. The most common source of imbalance in the sport psychology triad is an emphasis on performance outcomes, while ignoring the essential objectives of development and enjoyment of the sport experience.

7. Most great athletes understand that competitive pressure is kept in perspective by focusing on their enjoyment of and personal development through sport, even as they strive intensely to perform well and win.

Glossary

hyperconformity: a rigid, and typically harmful, code of behavior within the sport subculture that athletes are expected to follow without question

philosophy: the basic beliefs that guide our behavior every day

Study Questions

1. Why does philosophy serve as the foundation for the Inner Edge?

2. Explain why an athlete, a coach, and an athletic administrator could benefit from the development of and adherence to a sound philosophy of competition.

3. Explain the concept of the balanced sport psychology triad as the philosophy provided in this chapter. Generate several examples of how the triad becomes unbalanced in different ways.

4. Discuss how coaching philosophies are developed as psychosocial phenomena. That is, explain how society influences the types of philosophies that coaches adopt.

Reflective Learning Activities

1. Tilting The Triad

Brainstorm examples that you have experienced as an athlete or coach of an out-of-balance sport psychology triad and the consequences that occurred due to this imbalance. Also, can you think of personal examples where the triad was out of balance due to optimal experience and/or optimal development overshadowing optimal performance?

(25 minutes total; groups of three for 10 minutes to identify examples and 15 minutes for overall class discussion)

Example

1:_____

Describe triad imbalance:_____

_____

_____

Consequences:_____

_____

_____

Example

2:_____

Describe triad imbalance:_____

_____

_____

Consequences:

_____

_____

Example

3:_____

Describe triad imbalance:_____

_____

_____

Consequences:_____

_____

_____

2. Buck the System

The sport psychology triad is often tilted out of balance due to the unquestioning acceptance of sport norms by athletes and coaches. Norms are commonly accepted social rules that govern behavior in a society. An example of a sport norm is that females should not participate in high school wrestling because it is a male sport. Norms are very powerful because they become internalized values that are accepted without question or reflection, and lead to hyperconformity by athletes who follow these norms even to the point of personal physical harm and violence toward others. It is extremely important that coaches and athletes learn to be reflective about sport norms so that they may question the appropriateness of certain sport practices and develop an effective philosophy about sport participation to change negative and even destructive social norms.

  a. Identify several examples of unquestioned sport norms by athletes and coaches.
  b. For each norm, discuss why the norm exists and how it is sanctioned or controlled.
  c. Discuss the implications of these norms, and outline ways in which negative sport norms could be broken to enhance the quality of sport participation.

(24 minutes total; 12 minutes in groups of 4; then 12 minutes for large group discussion)

3. Developing Your Philosophy

The balanced sport psychology triad was presented in this chapter to set the philosophical foundation of the book. Do you agree that it is a useful and relevant philosophy or not? How might your coaching philosophy differ from the balanced triad?

Take some time to reflect upon your goals and beliefs, and then draw a model that represents your coaching philosophy. Your model could be a geometric figure like our triad or it could take a very different form. Be creative and honest in drawing out your philosophy.

(Overnight individual assignment and then spend 20 minutes in groups of four with each person presenting his/her model to the group followed by questions/discussion

Chapter

Three

Motivation

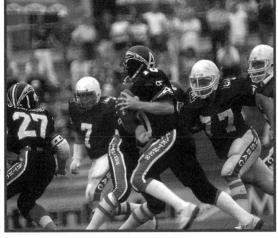

©Media Focus, LLC

Chapter Preview

In this chapter, you'll learn:
- truths and myths about motivation
- that motivation is related to human needs
- why self-determination is critical to motivation
- how motivation may be developed and enhanced

"The will to win is worthless if you do not have the will to prepare." **Thane Yost**

"I have failed over, and over, and over again. That is why I succeed." **Michael Jordan**

Nothing is more important than motivation. Nothing. There is no substitute—not even talent. Talented athletes who lack motivation will enjoy success only to a point, after which they will fail when they reach competitive levels that require intensity in training and persistence in overcoming challenging obstacles. Research in sport psychology has overwhelmingly supported motivation in the form of commitment and self-control as the biggest psychological predictor of elite status in sport (Orlick & Partington, 1988; Williams & Krane, 2001).

Cal Ripken, major league baseball's iron man, surpassed one of the most invincible records in sport on September 6, 1995, when he broke Lou Gehrig's record of playing in 2,130 consecutive games. Consider that over 3,600 players had gone on the disabled list during Ripken's streak. Also consider that the other major league teams used over 340 players at the shortstop position during the years that Ripken played the position every night for the Baltimore Orioles. Ripken's preparation routine for games bordered on obsessive. Prior to each game, he used an indoor batting cage to hit, run, and throw in total solitude before batting practice began on the field. After breaking the record, Ripken extended his streak to 2,632 consecutive games played, a record that most feel will never be broken.

Jackie Joyner-Kersee grew up in East St. Louis, one of the nation's most impoverished cities, and went on to become one of the world's greatest track and field athletes. She learned to long jump by leaping off the family's porch into a makeshift pit filled with sand that her sisters brought from a nearby park in potato chip bags.

Jerry Rice, proclaimed by many as the finest wide receiver in NFL history, adheres to a workout regimen that is legendary. He worked out so hard during one off-season that his starved body began burning his muscles for energy, at which point the team trainer ordered him to start eating ice cream.

Although these outstanding athletes possess exceptional physical skills, it is their motivation that has enabled them to extend their careers and achievements beyond others in their sports. Why is motivation so important? Simple—motivation is the fuel used to ignite behavior. Individuals that refine their burning motivation to achieve into committed behavior and take effective control of their lives, expend greater effort, and persist despite setbacks. Time and time again we read testimonials from successful athletes who earned their success the old-fashioned way—through focused, deliberate, repetitive practice of their skills even in the face of obstacles and setbacks.

Defining Motivation

How do we know that people are motivated? They act like it! **Motivation** is *a complex set of internal and external forces that induces one to behave in a certain way*. All human behavior is purposeful. Even though human behavior is not totally consistent or predictable, it is definitely not random, and thus it is controlled by motivation. Thus, sport psychologists are interested in studying motivation because it gives them insights into why people behave as they do.

The behaviors most typically associated with motivation are *choice*, *effort*, and *persistence*. Motivation is all about choices, such as choosing to join a sports team, choosing to go to practice, or choosing to run an extra set of wind sprints. Cal Ripken *chose* to play every day, and Jackie Joyner-Kersee *chose* to practice in less than desirable conditions. The word commitment is often used to describe the behavioral choices of highly motivated athletes. A successful Olympian canoeist describes it this way:

> "*Everything I do, whether it is weights, or running, or the normal training things, or the leisure activities I do, it is all geared toward how it's going to affect my paddling. Everything is opportunity/cost. If I go out to a movie instead of going hiking as my leisure activity, what is the cost of that? . . . Does that help or hurt my paddling? I've got to judge that. I've always thought this way . . . maybe that's different from other people*" (Orlick & Partington, 1988, p. 110).

Most people associate motivation with *effort* or the intensity with which people direct their energies toward a goal. People assume that Jerry Rice is motivated based on the intense effort he expends in keeping his body fit. Lance Armstrong, cancer survivor and six-time Tour de France champion, is renowned for training harder than anyone else in his sport. His teammates and competitors alike speak admiringly of his single-mindedness and commitment to training: "I am very passionate about cycling, but I cannot match Lance. Mentally, he is unique" (Dutch rider Erik Dekker as cited in Murphy, 2001, p. 39). Armstrong himself says, "What is a sacrifice? You suffer a little during a training ride, you suffer dur-

ing a race, and I like that. I would be really upset if I never had the opportunity to suffer" (Thomsen, 2000). Successful English Channel swimmers that were interviewed discussed how they practiced vomiting and swimming at the same time (they would drink the salt water or stick their finger down their throat to induce vomiting) to test their tolerance and recovery abilities in relation to their upcoming swim of the Channel (Hollander & Acevedo, 2000). This surely qualifies as intense effort or motivated behavior directed toward an important goal!

Quotable Quote

"Success is the ability to go from one failure to another with no loss of enthusiasm." **Winston Churchill**

Without question, *persistence* is the most important achievement behavior associated with motivation. An unflappable commitment to persist despite numerous obstacles is one of the strongest predictors of highly successful athletes and people. Henry Ford's first two car companies failed. Thomas Edison tried and failed more than 1,000 times in the process of inventing the light bulb. Consider the fate of a man who failed as a businessman, suffered the death of his two young sons, was defeated twice as a Congressional candidate and twice more as a Senate candidate, and was defeated as Vice Presidential candidate. His name is Abraham Lincoln, and he is considered one of the most successful Presidents in American history.

When *Newsweek* magazine polled a dozen athletes known as "dominators" in their respective sports (e.g., Martina Navratilova, Joe Montana, Michael Jordan, Wayne Gretzky, and others), they all agreed that persistent preparation and quality of practice were the defining characteristics of dominating performers in sport (Gordon, 2001). These dominators believe that the vast majority of athletes have a much lower tolerance for persistent preparation than those athletes who reach megastar status. Montana explains, "A lot of guys say, 'Yeah, I watched two hours of game film last night.' But they're not really studying what's going on. They may as well have been watching television" (Gordon, 2001, p. 45). Gretzky states, "No matter who you are, no matter how good an athlete you are, we're creatures of habit. The better your habits are, the better they'll be in pressure situations" (Gordon, 2001, p. 45). Navratilova says, "Every great shot you hit, you've already hit a bunch of times in practice" (Gordon, 2001, p. 45).

Clipboard

Persistence

Runner Aimee Mullins, the first disabled member of a Division I collegiate track team, was born without fibula bones in her shins and had both legs amputated below the knee. She has competed in athletics all her life, always against non-disabled athletes. She states,

> *"Perfection isn't winning every time. Perfection means doing as excellent a job as you could on that particular day. The people I admire most . . . are the people who keep coming back and doing it, time after time" (Compton, 1998, pp. 60-61).*

In summary, then, motivation is a set of internal and external forces that interact in complex ways to influence the choices we make and the amount of effort and persistence that we expend. Sport psychologists study motivation to try to understand its link to behavior. Research questions about the motivation-behavior link include these questions: Why do some athletes persist in the face of all obstacles, while other athletes give up easily? Why do some youth sport athletes enjoy participation and develop a lifelong commitment to physical activity, while other young athletes burn out or drop out of sport? Why do some athletes work harder than others? Is motivation hardwired in humans and set early in life, or can motivation be taught and developed? As you read through the chapter, you'll develop a deeper understanding about motivation, and in particular you will consider the various ways in which motivation may be developed and enhanced. But first . . . a test!

Test Your Motivation I.Q.

Everyone wants to know what successful athletes use to fuel their intense motivation. This question cannot be answered by providing a simple solution or a quick fix—motivation is far too complex. Due to the many myths and misunderstandings about motivation, I thought it would be helpful to challenge you to test your Motivation I.Q. Circle your answer to the following questions, and then after you've read the chapter, look back at your answers to see how your ideas about motivation may have changed.

1. Motivation in athletes is the responsibility of the coach.
    Yes   No   Sometimes

2. Trophies and other awards keep children motivated to stay in sport.
    Yes   No   Sometimes

3. The most important need for young athletes is to experience success in the form of winning, which keeps them motivated.
    Yes   No   Sometimes

4. Forcing athletes to take responsibility for themselves enhances their motivation.
    Yes   No   Sometimes

5. The home advantage in sports is an effective motivator for athletes.
    Yes   No   Sometimes

Motivation Myths

Too often, coaches and athletes looking for the Inner Edge fall prey to myths, or popular ideas that are largely untrue, about motivation and sport performance. In this section, three common motivation myths are identified, and then explanations are provided as to why these popular ideas represent flawed thinking.

Jug-and-Mug Myth

The most frequent question asked by coaches is "How do I motivate my athletes?" As you will see later in the chapter, this is really the wrong question to ask about motivation. The question itself has perpetuated the most common motivational myth believed in sport: *the jug-and-mug* myth.

This myth about motivation is termed jug-and-mug because it assumes that coaches and other external motivators, such as fans, possess motivation (contained in a *jug*), and that they dispense this motivation to athletes by pouring from the jug into each athlete's individual *mug*. A common example of the jug-and-mug approach to motivation is the pep talk, in which coaches engage in fiery or tearful orations to provide what they view as necessary pre-competitive "motivation" for athletes. Grant Teaff, former football coach at Baylor, chewed up a worm for some unknown reason in his attempt to motivate his players. Mississippi State football coach Jackie Sherrill arranged for a bull to be castrated in front of his team before a big game against the Texas Longhorns. Southwest Texas State football coach John O'Hara halted practice, asked the captains to step forward, and then pulled a pistol from his coaching shorts and fired a shot at each captain. Luckily, the pistol was loaded with blanks. To the horror of his athletes, a high school coach from Libertyville, Illinois, staged his own phony shooting, complete with fake blood, to "motivate" his team. One of the high school players captured the absurdity of the situation by saying, "Obviously, the shock of the idea we were going to die overshadowed any point he was trying to make."

Coaches also attempt to use gimmicks as part of the jug-and-mug approach, using fancy awards, catchy slogans, or posters. Another common example of the jug-and-mug motivational approach is the increasing emphasis of the *home advantage* as a means of motivating athletes. The home advantage is the consistent research finding that home teams in sport competition win over 50% of the time, assuming a balanced home and away schedule (Courneya & Carron, 1992). Coaches emphasize this territorial motivation by challenging athletes to defend *our house* against all opponents, and many athletes admit that they are extremely motivated by big home crowds. Some coaches buy canned motivational packages in the form of videos, workbooks, and/or consultants who call themselves motivational specialists. Again, all of these approaches assume that athletes have empty mugs when it comes to motivation, and that coaches, cheering crowds, and motivational specialists must bring their jugs of motivation to fill up athletes so they will want to excel in sport.

The jug-and-mug myth assumes that coaches must *make* athletes want to excel and that coaches have the magical ingredients for motivation that they can give to their athletes on cue. If only it were this easy! The jug-and-mug myth incorrectly assumes that athletes possess the same goal or drive that is in the coach's jug, and obviously the coach's jug cannot con-

©iStockphoto.com

tain the appropriate type of motivation for everyone. Some football players like the fiery and eccentric pre-game pep talks given by coaches, but many players admit that it's an act that gets old, and one that doesn't really affect their motivation to play the game. And what about the home advantage? Why shouldn't this be used as an important source of motivation? Well, common sense would argue that if athletes are more motivated to play at home, then they must be less motivated to play on the road. You can't have it both ways! Also, being motivated to perform only in front of big crowds is representative of a shallow motivation where athletes are too lazy to engage in the self-discipline and motivation necessary to consistently and successfully pursue excellence. Pep talks, home advantage, and motivational packages are superficial motivators or quick fixes—short-term approaches to what is really a long-term challenge.

Clipboard

Knute Rockne's Views on the Jug-and-Mug

Historical archives indicate that Notre Dame football coach Knute Rockne's famous "win one for the Gipper" pep talk was misunderstood. Coleman Griffith, a pioneering sport psychologist at the University of Illinois in the 1920s and 1930s, wrote to Rockne in 1924 to learn what the famous coach thought about motivating his players prior to games. Here was Coach Rockne's reply:

"Dear Mr. Griffith:

I feel very grateful to you for having written me, although I do not know a great deal about psychology. I do try to pick men who like the game of football and who get a lot of fun out of playing. I never try to make football hard work. I do think our team plays good football because they like to play and I do not make any effort to key them up, except on rare, exceptional occasions. I keyed them up for the Nebraska game this year, which was a mistake, as we had a reaction the following Saturday against Northwestern. I try to make our boys take the game less seriously than, I presume, some others do, and we try to make the spirit of the game one of exhilaration and we never allow hatred to enter into it, no matter whom we are playing.

Thank you for your kindness, I am

Yours cordially,

Knute Rockne

(From the Coleman Griffith Collection, University Archives, University of Illinois at Urbana-Champaign, as cited in Gill, 2000.)

You-Have-It-or-You-Don't Myth

A second popular motivational myth is the polar opposite of the jug-and-mug myth. Whereas the jug-and-mug approach incorrectly assumes that coaches control all the motivation available to athletes, the *you-have-it-or-you-don't* myth incorrectly assumes that motivation is totally innate and fixed, that individuals either possess motivation or they do not, and that motivation cannot be nurtured or enhanced. Based on this myth, coaches feel they must choose or select motivated individuals and exclude individuals that lack motivation. Pat Summitt, winner of six national collegiate basketball titles at the University of Tennessee, states, "I don't want average people. Average people cut corners. Winners know there are no shortcuts" (Sexton, 1998, p. 20). Summitt goes on to say that she is in the business of teaching life skills, yet her comments indicate that she selects a certain type of player who mirrors her motivational intensity.

The you-have-it-or-you-don't myth contains some truth, for as Pat Summit stated, there are inherent differences between individuals in their moti-

vation. Obviously, athletes differ in the choices they make, the effort they will give without prodding, and especially in their will to continue to achieve when running into obstacles, such as injuries or performance setbacks. However, the problem with the you-have-it-or-you-don't perspective on motivation is that it is oversimplified and often used as an excuse by coaches. Sure, some athletes are more motivated than others, and always will be, yet coaches should take some responsibility to develop and enhance motivation in athletes. Research has supported that the motivational climate established by teachers and coaches greatly influences the learning and performance of students and athletes (Theeboom, De Knop, & Weiss, 1995). Thus, although coaches should not assume that they carry the magic jug full of motivation, they should assume that their organizational and communication skills clearly bear on athletes' motivation. Also, the you-have-it-or-you-don't perspective on motivation is unrealistic for most coaches who may not have choices about their players. We all don't have the pick of the litter like Pat Summitt at Tennessee!

The Natural Talent Myth

You may remember the movie titled *The Natural*, which starred Robert Redford as a baseball player whose prodigious talent is seen as God-given or innate. Our society glorifies exceptional individuals, whose performance is vastly superior to the rest of the population. We commonly attribute these individuals' outstanding performances to special gifts, or natural talent. However, research indicates that although there are inheritable characteristics that influence sport performance (e.g., speed, body type, physical stature and limb length, eyesight), the characteristics believed to reflect innate talent are actually the result of intense practice over a number of years (Ericsson, 2003). Simply put, expert performance in sport is typically the result of deliberate practice, as opposed to natural inborn talent. Thus, the third motivational myth is that *natural* athletes don't require the motivation to engage in extensive practice, because high level performance is so easy for them to attain.

When Tiger Woods won the prestigious Masters golf tournament in 1997, most people assumed this achievement was the beginning of a successful career for an athlete who was considered a golf prodigy since the age of three. Of course, the focus was always on Woods's talent, as opposed to the fact that he began repetitive, specialized, deliberate practice in golf when he was still a toddler. However, after winning the Masters, his first major championship, he worked with his coach to totally restructure his golf swing, because he realized that his current level of technical performance was inadequate to withstand the varied demands of different course layouts. As stated in *Sports Illustrated*, "that Woods asked coach Butch Harmon to help him change his swing only weeks after the most commanding performance in a major championship this century—and knowing that it would take a year or more for his rebuilt swing to become natural—speaks volumes for his long-term commitment to peak performance" (Diaz, 1999b, p. 49). Tiger Woods may be popularly known for his enormous talent and his flair for dramatic shots and wins, yet his motivation to be the best as demonstrated by his commitment to disciplined practice is what truly makes him one of the best golfers in the world. In 1999, after patiently waiting for his new swing to jell, Woods became only the eleventh PGA Tour player to win eight tournaments in a season, a feat even more remarkable in the modern era of golf. In 2000, he won three of the four major championships of men's golf, and in 2001 won another major (to hold all four major championships at one time), and ended up as the leading money winner and number one ranked golfer in the world for the third straight year. Woods's dominance and drive to be the best in his sport is the result of not only his talent, but especially his disciplined commitment and persistent practice to harness and maximize his talent.

Exploding Motivational Myths

What does all this mean? Should coaches never use pep talks or motivational packages? If the jug-and-mug idea doesn't hold water, then why isn't it true that athletes either have-it-or-they-don't when it comes to motivation? And is motivation really more important than talent? Take a moment to revisit the definition of motivation given previously in the chapter, to remember that we're talking about a set of internal and external forces that interact in a complex way to influence our behavior. The key word is complex. The internal motivation of an athlete is constantly interacting with external motivators in the environment to influence how that athlete thinks, acts, and feels.

Personal Plug-In

There are many motivational myths. Can you think of some others? Identify common myths about motivation and consider why they are typically accepted as true.

Motivation is the direct personal responsibility of each individual, and athletes cannot abdicate their personal responsibility for their own motivation to the coach, home crowd, or some motivational specialist. However, coaches can help develop and enhance motivation in athletes indirectly by setting up the competitive environment so that athletes are optimally challenged to pursue their goals. Coaches play a large role in shaping the motivational climate for their athletes in such ways as providing appropriate feedback and reinforcement, establishing and adhering to a solid and consistent philosophy, being effective teachers and communicators, and meeting the specific needs of athletes depending on their age and level of participation.

The bottom line is that motivation is a complex, uniquely personal, and dynamic force that ebbs and flows throughout a sport season or an athletic career. There is no one size or type of motivation that fits everybody—rather motivation is very individualistic. Thus, it is much more important to gain a basic understanding of motivation, rather than worry about finding out the "secrets" about motivation. Once you understand the basic underlying foundations of human behavior, you can develop all kinds of innovative ideas to enhance motivation. So yes, gimmicks and packages and inspirational talks can *sometimes* be very motivational, but only if they are used as part of an overall philosophy built on a basic understanding of human motivation (see Clipboard). Also, it will always be apparent in sport that some athletes work less and still perform as well as other athletes. But don't assume that this means that an outstanding athlete performs well only because of innate talent. As stated at the beginning of the chapter, talented athletes that lack motivation will enjoy success only to a point, after which they will fail when they reach competitive levels that require disciplined training and persistence in overcoming obstacles. Tiger Woods understood this and demonstrated the motivation and commitment needed to extend his talent to a higher level.

You may be thinking, "This sounds complicated. I don't care about theories of motivation. Just give me some ideas about how to motivate—give me the secrets." If it were that easy, you would have heard about these secrets long ago. Face it—there are none! There are no absolutes about motivation. Many times coaches hear about motivational ploys used by famous coaches, and they attempt to try this ploy only to see it bomb miserably. To understand *how* to motivate, we must learn more about *why* people are motivated.

Clipboard

A Motivational Philosophy - Vince Lombardi

Jerry Kramer (1968) tells of an experience during his first year with the legendary Vince Lombardi as coach of the Green Bay Packers:

> *"He drove me unmercifully during the two-a-days. He called me an old cow one afternoon and said that I was the worst guard he'd ever seen. I'd been working hard, killing myself, and he took all the air out of me. I'd just lost seven or eight pounds that day, and when I got into the locker room, I was too drained to take my pads off. I just sat in front of my locker, my helmet off, my head down, wondering what I was doing playing football, being as bad as I was . . . Vince came in and walked over to me, put his hand on the back of my head, mussed my hair and said, 'Son, one of these days you're going to be the greatest guard in the league.' He is a beautiful psychologist. I was ready to go back out to practice for another four hours" (pp. 78-79).*

Vince Lombardi was able to successfully reverse the management principle of providing praise in public, and chewing out players in private—and his players understood that. Lombardi would push players hard early in the week, but as game day approached and the physical work was done, he emphasized pride and confidence in his players. He cared deeply for his players and would not tolerate any form of prejudice or special privilege. Lombardi's ability to motivate his players emanated from his foundational philosophy that won him the respect of his players. The Green Bay Packers under Vince Lombardi won five NFL championships and two Super Bowls (Walton, 1992).

Athletes' Needs and Motivation

Sport psychologists view motivation differently from athletes and coaches. Coaches view motivation very narrowly by asking *how* to motivate. Sport psychologists, on the other hand, believe that all behavior is motivated. Think about it. Human behavior is never random—we all seek rewards and satisfaction for what we do. If a student is not paying attention in a class, the instructor may infer that she is not motivated. But in reality, she missed breakfast, so she is extremely motivated by the most basic physiological need of increasing her blood sugar! From this perspective, motivation may be defined as *a response directed toward the reduction of a need*. The student is extremely motivated by hunger and seeks to reduce her need by eating.

Thus, an important motivational guideline is that *people are motivated to fulfill their needs* (Martens, 1990). If you remember this guideline, it will go a long way in helping you to understand why people act in ways that seem puzzling to you. Some coaches incorrectly assume that athletes are not motivated when they balk at doing everything the coach's way. But often athletes who balk at the directives of coaches are highly motivated to play sports—they're just not motivated to play according to the structure and methods dictated by the coach. This conflict between coach and athlete often emanates from coaches seeking to meet their own needs through the team rather than considering the athletes' needs.

Coaches often lament that they cannot meet all of their athletes' needs and that often certain athletes' needs are inappropriate within a team structure. For example, an athlete may state that he needs to be in the starting lineup, yet he fails to put out quality effort or demonstrate adequate ability in practice. Obviously, this need is inappropriate, and, as explained by Nakamura (1996), it's really more of a *want* than a *need*. Wants are usually frivolous and non-essential, while needs are important and essential for optimal development. For example, athletes may want prestige and attention, but they need recognition. Similarly, athletes may want approval and permissiveness, but they need acceptance and discipline. Athletes may want permissiveness and sympathy, but they need discipline and empathy. Do you see the difference? Motivation is enhanced when we meet the important basic needs of athletes, as opposed to caving in to their superficial and immature wants.

Overall, research has supported three prominent needs that athletes seek to fulfill by participating in sport (summarized by Martens, 1987):

- the need to experience stimulation and challenge
- the need to be accepted and belong to a group
- the need to gain and demonstrate competence to feel worthy

Need for Stimulation and Challenge

All humans possess the need for a certain amount of stimulation and challenge. Sport is a terrific environment to meet this need because most all athletes begin and continue sport participation because it is fun! The joy and stimulation we experience in sport often leads to flow or peak experiences. Flow, as described in Chapter 1, is the feeling of being totally absorbed in an activity that is usually enjoyable and fulfilling.

Coaches often lament that meeting athletes' needs for stimulation requires an over-emphasis on fun at the expense of accomplishment. But why do we automatically assume that fun and accomplishment are incompatible? After all, sport is inherently an achievement activity, and much of the fun that athletes experience is in achieving, such as improving their skills. Also, remember that challenge is part of this need for stimulation. Research with youth athletes has shown that children don't want to have fun in totally unstructured, disorganized, permissive practices, but rather that they want to have fun by developing competence in practices where they are op-

Photo courtesy of Robin Vealey

timally challenged (Horn & Harris, 1996). The issue is one of degree—the best coaches know how to use practice time effectively with a variety of activities to meet athletes' needs for stimulation and challenge while at the same time developing their skills. In any practice, some activities require more disciplined adherence and attention, while other activities are more fun and stimulating. Clearly, the difference between athletes' need for stimulation and their want of frivolous play should be differentiated. Overall, motivation is developed and enhanced when athletes' needs for optimal stimulation and challenge are met.

Strategies to enhance motivation through stimulation and challenge:

1. Time should be built into practices for some fun drills or activities to make the athletes laugh and build a sense of team. It works great to divert to a fun and stimulating activity for a few minutes to keep athletes fresh and motivated for more rigorous training.

2. The difficulty of the practice challenge should be appropriate for the developmental ability of the athlete. Athletes lose motivation when they see no progress toward their goals or when they constantly fail. Athletes need to experience some success, although it shouldn't be too easy.

3. Training and practices should not become too routine. Variety and novelty keep motivation fresh.

4. Time should be allotted in practices for athletes to just play the game without being constantly evaluated by the coach. This is difficult for perfectionist coaches, but it is important to allow athletes to experience the flow of the sport.

5. Motivation is enhanced by enthusiastic, exciting, and challenging leaders. Coaches should be motivational models and attempt to transform the sport environment into a stimulating, exciting, and challenging place where athletes *want* to be.

6. Goal mapping strategies (see Chapter 8) fuel motivation as they turn abstract dreams into finite objectives to be pursued.

7. Athletes must keep in mind what drew them to sport in the first place. Motivation is enhanced

when we focus on participating for enjoyment, which probably hooked us on sport in the beginning. Professional golfers often use off days to play a fun round with each other, making small wagers to keep it exciting and challenging.

8. Athletes should seek out stimulating and challenging practice situations where training partners, teammates, and/or coaches share their specific needs to experience optimal challenge. Research shows that athletes who perform in motivational climates that are congruent with their personal motivational goals are more satisfied, motivated, and productive.

Need for Acceptance and Belonging

The second motivational need of athletes in sport is the need for acceptance and belonging. Research has shown that adolescents drop out of school when they lack a sense of belonging or feel that they don't fit in with others. The need to fit in, belong to a group, or be accepted by others is a fundamental need that can be easily met through sport. Young athletes join sport teams to be with their friends or to be a part of something that is important to them. Coaches should understand this important need and attempt to make every team member feel that he or she is a valued and important contributor to the team. This is often difficult at higher levels of sport where ability is the primary factor in determining playing time. Yet coaches can help athletes define and accept their roles on the team, and create a team environment where all roles are valued and esteemed (see Clipboard).

Clipboard

MVP Season - A True Story of Gaining Acceptance

Leann was the most unskilled player on her small college basketball team. She rarely saw playing time, getting into games only in a mop-up role when her team held a huge lead. However, Leann understood and accepted her role, although of course she would have preferred to play more. Her goal was to be a part of a college team, and she was thrilled to make the team. She worked extremely hard in prac-

tice, first of all to improve her own skills, but also to push her teammates. Although Leann lagged behind her teammates in terms of physical skill, it became apparent that she was a student of the game and she demonstrated an advanced understanding of basketball tactics and strategies. As she sat at the end of the bench during games, Leann would keep notes regarding various strategies, and at half time or after games would confer with the coaches about her observations. The coaches and players grew to respect Leann's basketball knowledge, and she developed much credibility with her teammates due to her intense effort in practice and in particular her efforts in helping to make her teammates the best they could be. Leann's inspirational attitude was infectious, and her teammates took her lead and became less self-centered and more team-oriented. After winning the championship, the team elected Leann as their Most Valuable Player, and she cried as she received the award at the banquet in front of a large crowd. Today, Leann is a top high school basketball coach, winning multiple state championships and undoubtedly helping many young athletes understand and accept their roles within the team.

Strategies to enhance motivation through acceptance and belonging:

1. Team-building activities (see Chapter 4) may be used to build cohesion and make the group attractive and significant to the athletes.
2. Social activities where athletes can get to know each other beyond the competitive environment may enhance motivation to belong to the group.
3. A mentoring system could be established so that returning team members serve as mentors to new team members.
4. Coaches should demonstrate their sincere interest in each athlete on the team. Athletes should feel that parents and coaches unconditionally accept them irrespective of their performance and accomplishments. For athletes to develop self-esteem and acceptance of

themselves, they must have significant others who care for and accept them.

5. Coaches should work to understand their personal biases (which we all have) that affect their ability to accept athletes for who they are. Working to identify and understand our own biases help us to honestly accept and relate to other people. This takes time and self-reflection, but it is crucial to better understand the ways in which we may send subtle messages of acceptance or non-acceptance to athletes.

6. Besides helping athletes define and accept roles within the team, coaches should repeatedly and consistently demonstrate their beliefs in the value of these roles. When athletes successfully fulfill their respective roles on a team, this role fulfillment should be recognized and rewarded.

Quotable Quote

"The deepest urge in human nature is the desire to be important." **John Dewey**

Need to Feel Competent and Worthy

The inherent need of humans to feel competent and worthy represents the third and most important motivational need. Although there is no such thing as a born competitor, human beings are born with an innate need to be competent. All motivational theories are based on the premise that people strive to be competent at something which makes them feel worthy as human beings.

Think about the activities in which you are motivated to participate. Do you really like to do things at which you're not very good? Or do you prefer to spend time in activities at which you are skilled? Of course, we choose to do things that make us feel competent and worthy. This relates to the previous need for stimulation because we enjoy doing things that we are good at doing. This is called the *positive cycle of motivation*:

- If we enjoy something, we do it more.
- If we do it more, we get better at it.
- When we get better at it, we enjoy it more.

Can you then see how developing a negative cycle destroys motivation? Often motivation is snuffed out early when sport is made so unfun that children drop out. But motivation can also be destroyed by unrealistic performance expectations and pressure that makes athletes feel incompetent and unsuccessful so that sport becomes unenjoyable. So the need to feel competent and worthy often dovetails with the need for stimulation and challenge to affect our motivation.

A big problem in meeting athletes' need to feel competent and worthy is the intense public social comparison that is inherent in sport competition. Very young children base their perceived competence on feedback from significant adults, so early in life children typically can feel worthy and competent as they achieve personal competency milestones like riding a bike, swimming the length of a pool, or jumping over a hurdle. However, during the late elementary years, children begin to base their feelings of competence and self-worth on how they compare to their peers (Horn & Weiss, 1991). Do you see the problem here? Realistically, they will be unable to always ride the fastest, swim the farthest, or jump the highest.

Adding to the difficulty is the strong link that we all make from our perceived competence to our beliefs about our own personal worthiness. In our society, children quickly learn that their self-worth is often linked to their ability to achieve (Martens, 1990). However, our inherent worthiness as individuals is not conditional upon our achievement, especially in sport. As discussed earlier in this chapter, coaches should strive to demonstrate an unconditional acceptance and belief in each athlete's personal worthiness, *despite* that athlete's ability to perform in sport. However, this is easier said than done in our achievement-oriented, sports-crazed society! We all have experienced the enhanced self-esteem and social prestige that comes from hitting the game-winning shot, as well as feeling the self-derogation and embarrassment from choking at a crucial moment.

Although it is very difficult in competitive sport, athletes must learn to base their competence on their own performance standards and their ability to improve and develop skills *in relation to themselves*. One way to do this is for athletes to view competition as a place where they can go to get information about how their skills are developing. Of course we're going to compare ourselves to others—that's

© MediaFocus International, LLC

what sport is—but we can use that comparison process to gauge ourselves and test how well our skills are progressing. As humans, we all strive to be judged as competent and successful by others, but a mature and rational approach to motivation teaches us to be able to judge our own abilities in the absence of approval from others.

Other coaching books (e.g., Martens, 1987, 1990) have simplified motivational theory (Atkinson, 1974; Bandura, 1997; Weiner, 1986) to describe different types of motivation that are commonly seen in achievement situations like sport. In particular, these books and theories identify the behavioral consequences of different motivational orientations related to perceptions of competence and self-worth. Martens (1987, 1990) termed these different types of motivation as *success-oriented* and *failure-oriented*. Read on, and you will easily recognize the difference in success and failure-oriented athletes—I'm sure you've coached both types!

Success-oriented athletes. Success-oriented athletes perceive that they are competent and typically gauge their success and failure on their own personal standards. Their feelings of self-worth are quite stable because they have learned to view themselves as successful even if by normative social comparison standards they do not always win or place first. Suc-

cess-oriented athletes have learned to make productive **attributions**, which are the *reasons people accept as to why they succeed and fail*. When success-oriented athletes succeed, they attribute this success to their own hard work, effort, preparation, and ability. This attributional pattern of taking credit for success fuels their self-worth and motivates them to work harder. When success-oriented athletes fail, they often attribute the failure to factors that they believe they can control and change. For example, a success-oriented high school pole-vaulter fails to qualify for the state track meet, which was a major goal for him. Although he is extremely disappointed, he moves past the negative emotion to understand that he progressed far in one year, and that with increased practice and physical maturity, he can qualify for the state meet next year. Attributions are not excuses (although some people use them for that), rather they are important self-reasoning explanations that we use to either fuel or destroy our subsequent motivation. Our pole-vaulter remains motivated and confident because he knows he has the ability to train and improve. His feelings of self-worth remain high because he has learned that his parents, friends, teammates, and coaches all believe in him and accept him no matter how he performs.

Failure-oriented athletes. Failure-oriented athletes are constantly threatened by sport because they are typically unable to separate their performance from their feelings of self-worth. These athletes have learned to view themselves as unsuccessful athletes, and they lack confidence in their ability to perform. Failure-oriented athletes often make attributions that doom them to a negative motivational cycle. For example, failure-oriented athletes typically attribute their failures to the notion that they are no good—they reason that they lack the ability to succeed, so why try? The difference between this and success-oriented attributions is controllability. Failure-oriented athletes feel they have no personal control over the failures and obstacles that they have encountered. This lack of control also permeates their attributions for success, because they assume success occurs due to luck or the fact that it was an easy task. As you can see, these attributions do not provide the necessary fuel to enhance feelings of self-worth and motivation.

Often, failure-oriented athletes drop out of sport because it is too threatening for them. However, failure-oriented athletes do remain in sport, and you can sometimes recognize them from certain behaviors that they display. First of all, they typically will not try very hard, putting out a token effort, which is often mistaken by coaches as a lack of motivation (Martens, 1990). But remember, athletes are motivated to fulfill their needs, and these athletes are extremely motivated to protect their self-worth. They are apprehensive about trying hard, because then their lack of ability would be noticed even more. Not trying very hard gives them an easy excuse to fail.

Quotable Quote

"All of us do not have equal talents, but all of us should have an equal opportunity to develop our talents."

John F. Kennedy

Second, failure-oriented athletes fail to persist when obstacles appear. Again, this makes sense, because if you don't believe that you can control your performance and success, then why persist? And finally, failure-oriented athletes differ in the choices they make about achievement. Whereas success-oriented athletes seek out optimal challenges, failure-oriented athletes prefer very simple tasks or unreasonably difficult tasks. Can you explain why? Hint: the answer relates to the excuses they use to protect their self-worth.

Clipboard

Living up to a Legend

A great example of a success-oriented athlete is Michael Jordan, who returned to the NBA after retiring in 1993 and pursuing a limited career as a professional baseball player. To many people, Jordan had absolutely nothing to gain from his return to the NBA. He was a perennial league MVP, scoring leader, and defensive star, and his Chicago Bulls had won three NBA championships from 1990 to 1993, years in which he was MVP of the Finals all three times. His status as the greatest basketball player in NBA history was only heightened by his early retirement, and his decision to return to basketball in 1995 put him in the pressurized situation of having to compete with his own larger-than-life legend. No problem. Jordan's return to the game was based on the simplest motivators of all . . . enjoyment and challenge. "Eventually, I just decided that I loved the game too much to stay away," he stated. "All of this is about challenges," he said of his return to the Chicago Bulls. "Every time I go on the court, it's a challenge" (Taylor, 1995, p. 22). Because Michael Jordan is fueled by his strong success-oriented motivation, he refused to become a spectator to his reputation. His motivation to experience the stimulation and challenge of basketball far outweighed any pressure he felt to live up to his prior performances. And what a great choice it was. Upon his return to pro basketball, he and the Chicago Bulls won three more NBA Championships to rank them as the sport's dynasty of the 1990s. Jordan polished off his legacy by again winning the MVP of the Finals each year. Truly, he lived up to his own legend.

Strategies to enhance motivation through competence and self-worth:

1. When coaches are effective teachers, they enhance motivation in athletes by building competence and confidence. Athletes want to learn skills in sport and need appropriate technical instruction.

2. Coaches should maintain high expectancies for skill development from all of their athletes in relation to their own personal ability levels. In sport, talented athletes are often given more attention because they are viewed as more vital to the team's success. However, all athletes should be given opportunities to develop their skills by focusing on individual improvement and progress toward important goals.

3. The difference between learning and performing must be explained repeatedly to athletes (Martens, 1990). When learning skills, errors are a typical and natural part of the learning process. These errors should not be interpreted as failures, but rather as indicators that athletes are challenging themselves to get better at their

sport. Athletes tend to lose motivation when they focus on performing in practices, as opposed to working to get better so they can perform more effectively in competition. Research indicates that elite athletes spend more practice time working on the weakest parts of their game as compared to less successful athletes who tend to spend more time practicing well-learned skills.

4. Help athletes develop productive attributional patterns to feel personally responsible for their success achievements as well as optimistic and hopeful that they can overcome their failures and setbacks. Athletes should examine their personal attributions and work on making them more personally controllable to fuel their motivation. Research in psychology shows that successful people tend to have optimistic, hardy personality characteristics, which serve to inoculate them against stress, depression, and illness. Specifically, **hardiness** involves *being committed to and invested in life pursuits, feeling in personal control over life events, and seeing change and problems as opportunities for growth* (Kobasa, 1979). Chapters 7-17 of this book are designed to provide you with information about mental training that focuses on helping athletes attain mental skills such as hardiness and learned optimism.

5. Coaches should help athletes to always honor themselves in their pursuit of excellence. An important mental skill is the ability to affirm that you are a special and worthy person despite setbacks and failures. Likewise, another important mental skill is to avoid self-deprecating thoughts and comments (more on this in Chapter 10). Our self-image directly influences our motivation, which ultimately influences who we become.

Self-Determination: The Most Misunderstood Motivational Need

You've now learned that motivation is based on a person's needs. In the previous section, the motivational needs of stimulation/challenge, acceptance/belonging, and competence/worthiness were discussed. The take-home point was that athletes' motivation is best developed and enhanced by meeting these basic needs. However, there is still one big need to be discussed in relation to human motivation. That need is **self-determination**, and because it is so important, so encompasses sport psychology literature, and is so often misunderstood by coaches, this section of the chapter is devoted to it.

Personal Plug-In

Examine your own personal motivational orientation. What drives you—what are your most important needs that drive your motivation to achieve? How do these needs affect your behavior? Are your motivational needs consistent, or do they vary across different areas of your life?

One of our most basic human needs is for **autonomy**, which refers to *the ability and opportunity to govern one's self*. Self-determination is similar to autonomy in that humans are motivated when they *perceive that they possess control over themselves and their actions—when they feel that they determine their own course of behavior*. Thus, self-determination as a sense of self-empowerment leads to perceptions of autonomy. It makes sense, then, that athletes' motivation is boosted when they are allowed to be self-determining. Why, then, do we develop elaborate reward structures to artificially entice athletes to do their best? Why do many coaches believe that an autocratic, controlling coaching style that motivates through fear, punishment, and dehumanization is a better motivator than an autonomous coaching style that allows and even expects athletes to be responsible for their own motivation and subsequent behavior?

To answer these questions, let's revisit our definition of motivation. As defined earlier in the chapter, motivation is a complex set of internal and external forces that induces one to behave in a certain way. As stated in this definition, people can derive motivation from internal as well as external sources. External sources of motivation are easier to understand because they are more tangible, such as trophies, contracts, scholarships, and rewards and punishment doled out by coaches. Internal sources of motivation, such as pride, curiosity, and joy, are harder to understand because they aren't always necessarily visible. Thus, it is popularly assumed that the best motiva-

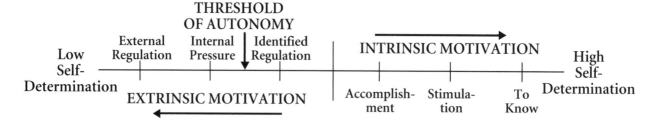

Figure 3.1 Continuum of self-determination

tors are external sources such as material gain or controlling coaches that can get the best out of their athletes. Is this true? Read on to decide for yourself!

Because motivation involves both internal and external forces, it is best conceptualized across a continuum of self-determination (see Figure 3.1). As shown in Figure 3.1, human behavior can be more intrinsically motivated or extrinsically motivated as we move along the continuum of self-determination (adapted from Pelletier, 1995). Thus, both intrinsic and extrinsic motivation represent two different sources of motivation available to athletes and coaches. These different forms of motivation are not dichotomous or distinct, as they often operate simultaneously and interact in complex ways. Notice the threshold of autonomy marked on the continuum, which represents the motivational point at which individuals feel they are independent and self-governing. As you will see, all types of motivation are useful, but it is critical to understand how and when the various types of motivation should be used.

Intrinsic motivation

Intrinsic motivation (IM) refers to *engaging in an activity purely for the pleasure and satisfaction derived from doing the activity* (Deci & Ryan, 1985). When people are intrinsically motivated, they will voluntarily engage in a behavior in the absence of material rewards or external constraints. IM stems from our innate need as humans to be competent, self-determining, and autonomous. This is why IM lies toward the right end of the continuum of self-determination (see Figure 3.1)—activities that allow individuals to experience feelings of competence and self-determination will be engaged in because of IM. Three types of IM have been supported in sport: IM to know, IM for stimulation, and IM for accomplishment (Pelletier et al., 1995).

IM to know. IM to know refers to being motivated to perform an activity for the pleasure and satisfaction one experiences while learning, exploring, or understanding something new. Athletes are intrinsically motivated to know when they want to try out a new position in their sport, such as moving from the outfield to shortstop in baseball. IM to know would also be operating when athletes seek out new training techniques for the sheer pleasure of learning something new about their sport.

IM for stimulation. This should sound familiar! As discussed earlier in the chapter, people are very motivated to experience stimulating sensations, such as the fun and excitement of playing sport. When athletes play sport for the love of the game, we could say they are intrinsically motivated for stimulation. Sport provides a wonderful opportunity to get children and adults hooked on physical activity—because sport is fun!

IM for accomplishment. IM to accomplish involves engaging in an activity for the pleasure and satisfaction that we experience when we attempt to accomplish something important to us. Athletes are motivated in this way to work hard at their sport because they enjoy the *process* of striving to be more competent. IM for accomplishment is an example of playing for inner pride, which is what compels athletes to do their best even when no one is evaluating them. This is a critical type of motivation for athletes to possess, because it fuels the deep commitment and self-discipline needed to excel in sport through persistent practice.

Quotable Quote

"Nothing is interesting if you're not interested." **Helen Macinness**

Extrinsic Motivation

Extrinsic motivation (EM) refers to *behavior that is engaged in as a means to an end*. In other words, extrinsically motivated behavior is driven by the promise of some reward beyond the actual performance of the activity itself. Although EM lies toward the low end of the self-determination continuum, there actually are different types of EM that are ordered along the continuum (see Figure 3.1). Thus, EM involves less feelings of self-determination as compared to IM, but some forms of EM elicit more feelings of self-determination than others.

External regulation. External regulation as a form of EM refers to behavior that is completely controlled by external sources such as rewards, the threat of punishment, contracts, or rules. Athletes who participate in sport because they are on scholarship or because their parents insist that they do are motivated by external regulation. As shown in Figure 3.1, this form of motivation involves the least amount of feelings of self-determination, and it is below the threshold of autonomy. Thus, although externally regulated behaviors are motivated, they are not self-determined. This form of motivation is very common in sport, and coaches are typically the external forces regulating the behavior of athletes.

Internal pressure. Internal pressure is an extrinsic source of motivation, even though the pressure to act in a certain way seems to come from within the athlete. This occurs when athletes internalize external sources of motivation. The external source is no longer present to motivate behavior, but it has become internalized in the person as pressure to act in a certain way. Athletes who participate in summer weight-training workouts, because they would feel guilty if they fail to show up, are being motivated by the extrinsic form of internal pressure. Even though the guilt is internal, it comes from an external source (coaches, teammates, or parents). Internal pressure is extrinsic in nature and, like external regulation, below the threshold of autonomy (see Figure 3.1). This form of motivation is also common in sport, especially when young athletes have been forced into a demanding training regimen by overzealous parents at an early age. Often, as the athlete matures, the parents back off and innocently state that the athlete is pursuing her own goals and dreams.

Identified regulation. Identified regulation, as a form of EM, occurs when athletes come to value the pursuit of sport excellence and see it as an important goal for themselves, thus they choose to participate and work hard. The activity is still performed for extrinsic reasons (e.g., to perform well and win), but it is internally regulated. Notice that identified regulation as a form of EM is very close to IM on the continuum of self-determination and above the threshold of autonomy (Figure 3.1). This means that although identified regulation is extrinsic in terms of working towards an external goal, athletes feel that this goal pursuit is their own choice and that they are in control of their own motivation. That is, athletes feel autonomous and self-determining. Because sport offers such enticing and valued extrinsic rewards, identified regulation is a highly desirable form of motivation for athletes. It is self-fueling because the athletes themselves identify the goal as significant to them without any need for external regulation. Anson Dorrance, women's soccer coach at the University of North Carolina, tells of driving past a city park and seeing Mia Hamm running sprints *the day after* she and her teammates won the national championship at UNC.

Keeping Motivation Fine-Tuned

The behavior of athletes is typically motivated by all types of motivation along the continuum. Athletes are usually intense competitors who love the game and excitement of playing (IM), but at the same time they are motivated to win (EM) and regulated by coaches' rules and decisions (EM). Thus, in sport, intrinsic and extrinsic motivation occur simultaneously and constantly interact. Ideally, this interactive combination keeps motivation constant and fine-tuned. Think back to your development as an athlete in your sport. You probably began playing because you enjoyed it and wanted to learn more about it (IM to experience stimulation and IM to know). As you grew older, you developed pride in your accomplishments, and sport gave you an outlet to feel competent and self-determining (IM for accomplishment). Along the way, it helped to have coaches that demanded adherence in training and constant effort even when you didn't feel like working hard (external control and internal pressure). Your love for and competence in your sport helped you to internalize a commitment to the effort and dedication required to achieve your goals (identified regulation).

Thus, all sources of motivation may be useful, if used in the right way at the right time. Unfortunately, motivation becomes problematic when the continuum of self-determination tips toward the end of external control and internal pressure to the exclusion of any kind of IM. Research shows that athletes motivated by external regulation and internal pressure experienced greater competitive anxiety, concentrated less effectively, persisted less, and were less satisfied than athletes that were motivated by intrinsic reasons or identified regulation (Vallerand & Fortier, 1998). Thus, sources of motivation that enable athletes to feel self-determining have been shown to enhance their mental skills and competitive behavior more so than motivation that is extrinsic in nature. Many times coaches have the best intentions, but because of common motivational misunderstandings, they unknowingly destroy the motivation of their athletes by relying solely on external regulation as a source of motivation. In the next section, I offer some suggestions to help you understand how the various types of motivation can be used effectively.

Moving Effectively Along the Continuum of Self-Determination to Enhance Motivation

In this section, I attempt to provide a practical discussion of how motivation is best developed and enhanced by understanding and using various forms of motivation found along the self-determination continuum. It is critical that athletes develop some form of IM, or at least some form of self-determined motivation, such as internal regulation. As you will see, external control and internal pressure are sometimes good spark plugs to start up the engine, but the basic fuel for strong and enduring motivation is internally controlled motives for behavior.

Hook and Challenge

Any adult working with children should realize that the most important step in motivation is to hook kids on sport. Children get hooked on activities when they're fun, exciting, and challenging. Remember our previous discussion about motivating athletes by meeting their needs? Well, plug that in here. The

foundation for IM in sport may be set by creating an environment where participation is fun and exciting, where skills are taught to develop competence, and where personal improvement or mastery is supported as a primary goal.

In 1985, Benjamin Bloom (1985) and other researchers from the University of Chicago conducted a study of how world-class talent is developed. They interviewed 120 people who had achieved world-class success in such fields as athletics, music, and art. The results of the study indicated that these individuals had very similar phases of development in honing their talent. The first phase of talent development was labeled the romance phase, and this phase is characterized by play, exploration, and fun. This early romance phase is viewed as critical in the learning and development of talented individuals, because the resulting phases of talent development must be grounded on a love, or passion, for one's chosen activity. The individuals in the study had coaches and teachers who instilled a love of the activity in them as children, and throughout their careers their passion for sport, music, or art was the foundation for their talent development. Bloom found that moving too quickly to the next phase (precision training or systematic learning) before completing the romance phase squelched these performers' motivation. In this case, the performers had to return to the romance phase for a while to have fun with their activity before they could progress in their talent development. A great example of this is seen in the movie *Searching for Bobby Fischer*, where a young chess prodigy had to return to the romance phase to recapture his passion before he could progress with his talent development. This movie poignantly demonstrates Bloom's point that outstanding performers must fall in love with what they do before they can make the commitment to hone their talent through years of practice.

Bloom's original research has been duplicated in the study of talent development in young athletes in tennis (Côté, 1999; Monsaas, 1985), swimming (Kalinowski, 1985), and rowing (Côté, 1999). These phases of development in young athletes were labeled sampling (romance phase), specializing (more practice time or specializing in a specific sport), and investment (committed to elite levels of performance in one sport). The following quote from Bloom emphasizes the importance of enjoyment, excitement, and interest developed during the sampling or romance phase of talent development in athletes:

> "These are crucial years, even more crucial than those that follow, because it is during this period that [athletes] became interested and caught up in the sport of swimming. In time that interest became self-motivating. Had there been no excitement during the early years, and no sense that the young swimmer was very successful, there would never have been a middle [specializing] or later [investment] period" (Kalinowski, 1985, p. 141).

Thus, keep in mind the importance of developing this love of the game, which serves as motivational fuel throughout athletes' lives.

Allow Control and Demand Responsibility

All motivational theories in psychology emphasize that motivation is enhanced when individuals perceive some responsibility and control for their own lives. Wayne Gretzky, arguably the best ever at his position in ice hockey, was approached by a father with his young son who was a youth hockey player. The father said to Gretzky, "Wayne, please tell my son to practice." Gretzky looked at the father and replied, "No one *ever* had to tell me to practice." Achieving at the upper end of a person's capabilities demands the motivation that comes with being responsible for yourself. External regulation in the form of pressure to practice from parents and coaches is only a stopgap, short-term motivator of behavior. But this point is dismissed by many coaches who still subscribe to the jug-and-mug approach to motivation.

Why is that? First of all, some coaches mistakenly assume that giving athletes more responsibility totally undermines the coaches' control of their teams. It does not. Coaches assume the ultimate responsibility for any decisions made within the team. Athletes should not expect, nor be given free rein, to do anything they choose, but they should be given choices within a structured situation. The coach who allows athletes some control is not necessarily a democratic coach. All decisions need not be voted on (and should not be), as they are the responsible decisions of the coach. But the structure and rules may be arranged so it is possible for athletes to set their own goals and learn to take personal responsi-

bility for striving for them. What the coach must do is to carefully designate areas within the program where athletes can provide input, and then nurture these into important and valued responsibilities that the athletes carry out. Examples abound, such as evaluations of practice and competitive performances, input into practice plans and game strategies, leading warm-ups, and selecting team captains.

Another problem is that sometimes athletes who are given responsibilities do not use them wisely (Martens, 1987). When this occurs, coaches tend to panic and immediately withdraw any future responsibilities. However, this could be used as a teachable moment to explain how the athletes' erred in handling their responsibility and to set additional guidelines. Helping people learn responsibility is a long-term process. It's achieved by numerous events that cumulatively allow athletes to experience the consequences of various behaviors and to grow from these experiences. If coaches have credibility with and respect from their athletes, then frank, honest discussions about expectations for responsible behavior and mature decision-making will nurture important social development and self-determining motivation in athletes. Colleen Hacker, sport psychology consultant for the U.S. Women's Soccer Team that won the World Cup in 1999, introduced the acronym TRY (Take Responsibility Yourself). Coach Tony Di Cicco felt the TRY concept was essential in getting each player to individually and unselfishly commit to developing herself in the way that had the greatest impact on the team's success (DiCicco & Hacker, 2002).

A common myth about responsibility is that winning develops responsibility in athletes. Nothing could be farther from the truth. Bob Huggins, men's basketball coach at the University of Cincinnati, states, "The hard thing is to come back after wins with the same kind of intensity, the same kind of effort, the same kind of enthusiasm, the same kind of concentration. It's much harder when you win." Huggins seems to think that winning might even *decrease* athletes' responsibility for motivation to train hard! It's not the outcome of winning that develops responsibility in athletes, it's the process used in pursuing winning. Occasionally, we read about former winning athletes who have become "losers in life" because they never learned how to take control of their own lives.

Clipboard

Teaching Responsibility Using Natural or Logical Consequences

Many sport practitioners assume discipline must be the responsibility of the coach (external regulation). However, the purpose of discipline is to help athletes internalize an inner guidance system for responsible behavior (identified regulation). One effective way to teach self-discipline is by using natural and logical consequences (Nakamura, 1996). When Matt is habitually late for team bus trips, the team should leave without him, with the consequence being that Matt does not make the road trip or play. Another natural consequence of this is that Matt has now let down his teammates who cannot count on him to be responsible. The coach, in talking with Matt, must link Matt's behavior to the natural consequences that occurred, instead of allowing Matt to feel that the coach delivered the punishment by allowing the bus to leave without him. The coach should guide Matt in solving his problem and gaining credibility from his teammates, so Matt can internalize the link between his behavior and the resulting consequences. The coach must be committed to allow *natural consequences* to occur to instill discipline, which may be difficult if Matt is a key player whose absence might likely cause the team to lose the game.

Logical consequences require the coach to structure situations to link appropriate consequences to a disciplinary problem. If Lisa destroys equipment in a temper tantrum, ask her or her parents to repair or replace the item. If Cody and Josh ask to shoot baskets in the gym after hours, but then leave it in a mess, their privilege of practicing on their own is revoked. Again, what is important is that the coach clearly links the logic of the particular consequence to the athletes' behaviors when discussing the issues with them. Using consequences to force athletes to take responsibility for their actions is very different from coaches handing out random punishment in an attempt to control athletes' behavior. For example, requiring the whole team to run sprints until they are sick because one athlete swore in practice seems to be an illogical punishment that fails to emphasize logical consequences.

Coaches must stand firm to not interrupt the natural process of enabling athletes to learn from consequences. A typical natural consequence of poor study habits is failing grades and resulting ineligibility to participate in sport. Disturbingly, some coaches have resorted to requesting teachers to change grades so that athletes can become eligible. This action serves to stunt the development of self-discipline and responsibility in athletes, because they learn that there are no negative consequences for their behavior.

Caution! Extrinsic Reinforcers in Use

There are times when external regulators are useful for motivation. External regulators are termed reinforcers in psychology. **Reinforcement**, or behavior modification through rewards and punishment, is based on *the premise that rewarding a behavior increases the probability that the behavior will be repeated, and punishing a behavior decreases the probability that the behavior will be repeated*. The use of rewards and punishment as extrinsic reinforcers is sometimes very effective in motivating athletes. However, the key word is *sometimes*. There are times when extrinsic reinforcers lose their power to motivate, thus it is important to understand that reinforcers have the potential to be useful as well as destructive.

Remember that we defined motivation as a complex set of internal and external forces, and much of the complexity of motivation is the constant interaction that occurs between external motivators and people's internal perceptions of these motivators. This means that reinforcers may be interpreted differently by individuals, thus having entirely different effects on their behavior. Behavior modification began in experimental psychology using animals in stimulus-response research studies, where rewards and punishment could quickly shape the response patterns of the animals. The smaller brains of animals made the use of reinforcers more straightforward, but the use of reinforcers with humans is more complicated based on the human ability to process information at a higher level. Self-determination theory, like most social cognitive theories of motivation, is based on the idea that the motivational impact of rewards depends on the psychological meaning of these rewards to the individuals receiving them (Deci & Ryan, 1985).

Undermining effect of extrinsic reinforcers. Most people assume that when athletes receive trophies and medals, they become more motivated. This may be true *sometimes*, but it is important to understand that receiving extrinsic rewards can often undermine, or weaken, IM. To illustrate this point, consider the following motivation fable:

> *An old man lived alone on a quiet street and became annoyed one day when a group of children began playing noisily outside his house. He called the children into his house and said, "I really enjoy hearing you play outside my house, and if you come back and play tomorrow, I will pay each of you a quarter." The children enthusiastically returned the next day to play, as they were very motivated to make their money. When they came into the house for payment, the old man said, "Unfortunately, I'm running short on cash this week so I can only pay you fifteen cents." The children grumbled, but took the money and left. The next day when they came in for their money, the old man said, "Gee, I'm really sorry, but I can only pay you five cents today. And it looks like after today, I won't be able to pay you anything." The children grew indignant, retorted to the man that they refused to play for nothing, and stormed out of his house. They did not return to play there again.*

Obviously, the children in our fable were outsmarted by a master of psychology who fooled them into thinking that they were only playing for money. Somehow this made them forget that they played because it was fun!

When extrinsic rewards are offered to control or even bribe individuals, IM is likely to be undermined. This is called the **overjustification effect**, meaning that *the extrinsic reward decreases feelings of intrinsic motivation.* In our motivation fable, the old man overjustified the children's play by paying them to do something that they loved to do. Research shows that when the reward is offered prior to the activity, people's perceptions of why they are doing the activity change. In this case, the children became consciously aware that they were playing for money, and their IM to play was decreased.

A popular theory in psychology, called **cognitive evaluation theory**, explains that the overjustification effect, in which rewards decrease feelings of IM, occurs when rewards are perceived by athletes as controlling (Deci & Ryan, 1985). Research using this theory has shown that *intrinsic motivation is enhanced when athletes feel more self-determining and competent about their abilities.* Thus, any events or factors in the sport environment (such as rewards or coaching behavior) that enhance athletes' feelings of competence and self-determination will increase their IM. Conversely, any events or factors that decrease athletes' feelings of competence and self-determination will decrease their IM.

Research testing cognitive evaluation theory with athletes. An interesting pair of studies conducted in 1977 and 1980 examined the influence of scholarships on the IM of college athletes (Ryan, 1980). The results showed that college football players on scholarship had less IM than players who did not receive scholarships. However, when Ryan examined the motivation of college wrestlers and female athletes, he found the opposite. That is, the wrestlers and female athletes who were on scholarship had more IM than their respective teammates not on scholarship. Ryan interpreted these results according to cognitive evaluation theory and the nature of college athletics in the late 1970s. That is, the football players felt that their scholarships were controlling, which decreased their motivation. When asked, the football players indicated that a large percentage of good players in their sport received full scholarships to play in college. However, the wrestlers and female athletes stated that not many good athletes in their sport received *full rides* or college scholarships (typical of this time period), thus the scholarships they received were seen as informational about their competence and success. That is, the scholarships made them feel special and extremely competent to have earned something that very few people achieve in their sports. The Ryan study is a good example of how extrinsic rewards influence motivation differently depending upon how individuals interpret them (Deci & Ryan, 1985). When rewards are viewed as controlling or detrimental to athletes' feelings of autonomy and self-determination, they tend to decrease IM. Conversely, when rewards are viewed as informational and earned by athletes based on their competence and hard work, they tend to increase IM.

More recent research with college athletes indicates that it is not the actual scholarships themselves that influence IM in athletes, rather how the scholarships alter the treatment given to them by coaches (Amorose & Horn, 2000). Athletes with higher IM perceived their coaches to (a) emphasize training and instruction, (b) employ a democratic leadership style, (c) emphasize positive and informational-based feedback, and (d) deemphasize punishment and ignoring behaviors. In fact, this research showed that the behavior of coaches was more important in influencing athletes' motivation than their scholarship status. In linking these findings to cognitive evaluation theory, these coaching behaviors enhanced athletes' IM by facilitating their feelings of self-determination and perceived competence. Therefore, coaches should support their athletes' self-determinism and competence, as opposed to simply engaging in controlling behaviors with the intent of externally regulating athletes' motivation.

Importance of contingent rewards and feedback. Extrinsic reinforcers lose their power, and often backfire by decreasing IM, when they are given non-contingently, which means the reinforcement is not logically linked to or based on an expected behavior. A popular misconception is that you can never give someone too much positive reinforcement, but this can be problematic if coaches provide extensive positive reinforcement to athletes without making it contingent upon such important behaviors as performance, effort, mental toughness, sportsmanship, or teamwork. What occurs is that the positive reinforcement loses its motivational power, as the athletes discount it because it is given non-contingently, which does not make them feel it is earned or based on their achievements.

It is important to realize that extrinsic rewards are not bad, nor do they always weaken motivation. Try to recall a situation in your past when you received an important award that made you feel proud and more motivated than ever. Now consider why you felt that way—and place your feelings of motivation somewhere along the continuum of self-determination shown in Figure 3.1. Chances are your IM surged with pride and fulfillment. In this situation, receiving the award fueled your motivation to continue in the activity.

Effective use of extrinsic reinforcers. Extrinsic sources of motivation are often very useful and can be powerful motivators if used in the right ways. In fact, extrinsic rewards, when used effectively, can develop

Photo by Tim Hipps, courtesy of US Army

and strengthen IM in athletes. Following are several guidelines for using extrinsic reinforcers effectively.

1. Extrinsic rewards are useful to help develop interest in a sport when a person does not have the initial IM to participate (Martens, 1987). Parents or coaches who are skilled motivators may then gradually withdraw or deemphasize the extrinsic rewards and emphasize the intrinsic rewards inherent in the sport. For example, a young boy may initially become motivated to play soccer to get a chance to wear a cool and flashy uniform or because his mother encourages him to play (both extrinsic motivators). However, in time, he develops a love for the game of soccer and a deep intrinsic motivation to continue to play the sport.

2. It may be worthwhile for adults to help young athletes process what extrinsic rewards should mean to them. Congratulate an athlete for winning a trophy or medal, and then ask her to explain what the award means to her. Help her to understand that the trophy is nice, but the ultimate reward is pride in yourself and feelings of accomplishment. Perhaps explain that the trophy is made of metal, which will even-

tually tarnish or grow dull, but her pride in achievement and self-motivation can always burn bright within her.

3. Extrinsic rewards should be used to enable athletes, not control them. Praise should be given honestly, not in a manipulative manner. When athletes win individual honors or the attention of college recruiters, coaches and parents should try to help them feel good about earning the honors based on their competence, as opposed to feeling pressure to live up to the honor. College scholarships are awards earned through hard work and ability in high school, and are not work contracts signed as labor agreements with college coaches.

4. Extrinsic rewards must be earned and given to athletes contingent upon specific behaviors. Rewards quickly lose any motivational effect when given indiscriminately. For example, a common practice in youth sport is to give participation awards, which means if you are on the team roster and have a pulse, then you receive this award. These awards are meaningless to athletes unless they are attached to important contingencies, such as attending all practices. Rewards must be *earned* to fuel subsequent motivation. In summary, clearly link the reward to an athlete's specific behavior or performance to make it meaningful.

5. The best types of extrinsic rewards are novel, creative, and underwhelming. Simple, yet powerful, extrinsic motivators help to internalize pride in achievement and self-responsibility to produce a successful work ethic. In this age of instant gratification and exorbitant professional sports salaries and endorsements, people forget that the power of extrinsic motivators comes from their meaning, not their monetary value. John Buxton, coach at Culver Academy in Indiana, gives out lollipops to athletes for specific behaviors such as hustle, rebounding and playing well after making a mistake, and displaying emotional control (Thompson, 2003).

In the movie *A Beautiful Mind* (based on a true story), Russell Crowe portrays the character of John Nash, a brilliant scholar who suffered from a devastating mental illness. Nash went on to win the Nobel Prize for his work in economic theory, but one of the most deeply personal rewards was given to him in the faculty lunchroom at the University of Princeton. As Nash sat down to eat his lunch, his faculty colleagues walked up to his table and laid their pens down on the table in front of him in a quiet acknowledgment of his brilliance. This presenting of the pens was a ritual at Princeton; it represented the highest acclaim and respect a professor could receive from his colleagues. As an extrinsic reward, the pens held little material value, but their motivational power—symbolic in nature—was immense.

6. An important facilitator of motivation is the establishment of a motivational climate in which an individual's goals may be nurtured and supported by others. The objective is to create an environment where athletes motivate and reward each other in their shared pursuit of excellence. It is erroneous to think that all extrinsic sources of motivation must come from the coach or leader. When athletes reward each other, the coach appears less manipulative and controlling, which enhances a climate of intrinsic motivation and feelings of self-determination.

7. As a coach, be aware that your initial assumptions and expectations about individual athletes tend to influence your coaching behavior and feedback. Research has shown that teachers who were led to believe that they were working with high EM students became very controlling and autocratic in dealing with these students (Pelletier & Vallerand, 1996). Conversely, teachers who were led to believe they were working with high IM students behaved in more autonomy-supporting ways towards the students. And importantly, students' levels of IM either increased or decreased depending on whether their teachers were autonomy-supportive or controlling, respectively. Coaches should attempt to provide contingent, informative, supportive feedback to all athletes, without pigeonholing athletes as a certain motivational type. We should all keep in mind the powerful influence that we have on the IM and EM of our athletes.

Clipboard

Mission: POSSIBLE

Pat Summitt, coach of the University of Tennessee's women's basketball team, is known for her no-nonsense approach to demanding the best from her players. However, she understands that motivation takes several forms, thus every year her staff puts together highlight films with motivating music to show her players during the NCAA tournament. For the 2004 tournament, the Tennessee staff created a miniseries on tape and showed each episode as the team wove their way through the postseason tournaments. The miniseries was titled "Mission: Possible" and starred a vaguely familiar coaching legend (Summitt herself) in sunglasses and slicked-back hair offering her players a mission—if they chose to accept it. She told the team there are three tools—focus, accountability, and attitude—that, "if used properly, will guarantee a successful mission." Each episode concluded with highlight clips of each player, who were identified by secret agent code names. As you might expect, the players loved the miniseries. The motivational Mission: Possible works because it is part of a larger philosophy about motivation and excellence that permeates the Tennessee program from day one. And interestingly, Summitt has never seen Tom Cruise in the original movies—she's too busy running her program! (Summitt's Spoof, 2004)

Wrapping Up

How is your Motivation I.Q now? If the concepts are a bit fuzzy, that's OK. Understanding your own motivation and the motivation of others is a continuous and challenging task. As a review, consider how motivation works within the balanced triad philosophy espoused in Chapter 2 (see Figure 2.1). The triad of optimal performance, development, and experience is kept in balance by considering the important motivational needs of athletes, and then providing opportunities for them to experience stimulation and challenge, to feel accepted, and to develop competence and feelings of self-

worth. The triad is also kept in balance by allowing athletes some control of their sport experiences, which fosters an intrinsic motivational orientation and a sense of personal responsibility and competence. The quality of sport participation suffers when athletes are externally regulated or pressured to perform at the expense of developing their personal skills and experiencing the excitement of playing sport. Also, coaches should recognize that many popular ideas about motivation are really myths, and that helping athletes develop and enhance motivation is a complex and long-term process. Borrowed motivational gimmicks may be inadequate motivators unless they are part of an ongoing coaching philosophy based on a deeper understanding of human motivation.

Motivation is an essential building block in our journey to gain the Inner Edge. Look back at our big picture of the Inner Edge in Chapter 1 (Figure 1.2) to recall the primary place of motivation in the model. You may remember that motivation, along with a foundational coaching philosophy, forms the basis for all other parts of the Inner Edge. Athletes are unable to achieve quality sport participation unless the critical foundation of motivation is established. Understanding and harnessing the power of motivation requires continuous effort and a commitment to moving beyond popular myths, yet the payoffs are large with regard to the achievement of life goals and human potential.

Summary Points for Chapter 3

1. Research has supported that motivation in the form of commitment and self-control is the best psychological predictor of elite status in sport.
2. Motivation is defined as a set of internal and external forces that interact in complex ways to influence the choices we make, and the amount of effort and persistence that we expend.
3. Achievement behaviors that directly emanate from motivation are choice, effort, and persistence.
4. A common motivational myth is that athletes need external motivators such as pep talks, threats of punishment, gimmicks, and home crowds to perform their best.
5. Although motivation is the direct personal responsibility of each athlete, coaches can indi-

rectly develop and enhance motivation by arranging the competitive environment, so that athletes are optimally challenged to pursue their goals and meet their motivational needs.

6. An important key to motivation is understanding that athletes are motivated to fulfill their needs, which includes the need to experience stimulation/challenge, the need to be accepted, and the need to be competent and feel worthy.

7. Success-oriented athletes possess motivational orientations that enable them to make productive causal attributions for their successes and failures, to enjoy a stable sense of self-worth, and to engage in the achievement behaviors of effort and persistence.

8. Failure-oriented athletes possess motivational orientations that influence them to make dysfunctional attributions that fail to enhance motivation, and to exhibit an avoidance pattern of achievement behavior, such as inconsistent effort, lack of persistence, and preference for simple or unreasonably difficult tasks.

9. All human beings strive for the important motivational need of autonomy, which is the ability to govern oneself and be self-determining.

10. Intrinsic and extrinsic motivation differ based on their place along the continuum of self-determination, even though they often operate simultaneously and interact in complex ways.

11. To enhance feelings of self-determination, coaches must allow some control and demand personal responsibility from athletes, as opposed to rigidly regulating all facets of athletes' lives.

12. Although research supports the effectiveness of external reinforcers in shaping behavior, extrinsic rewards have the potential to undermine feelings of self-determination and motivation.

13. Research supports cognitive evaluation theory in that rewards that are informational about competence and contingent upon achievement tend to enhance motivation, while rewards that are controlling and noncontingent tend to weaken motivation.

Glossary

attributions: reasons people accept as to why they succeed and fail, which influences subsequent motivation

autonomy: the ability and opportunity to govern one's self

cognitive evaluation theory: athletes' levels of intrinsic motivation varies based on the degree to which they (a) perceive themselves to be self-determining, and (b) perceive themselves to be competent

extrinsic motivation: motivation to engage in an activity to gain some reward external to the activity itself

hardiness: a personality characteristic that enables individuals to remain committed to and invested in life pursuits, to feel personal control over life events, and to see change and problems as opportunities for growth

intrinsic motivation: motivation to engage in an activity to experience the pleasure and satisfaction inherent in doing the activity itself

motivation: a set of internal and external forces that interact in a complex way to influence the choices we make and the amount of effort and persistence that we expend

overjustification effect: a decrease in intrinsic motivation that occurs when behavior that is already intrinsically motivated is extrinsically rewarded

reinforcement: the motivational premise in which rewarding a behavior is believed to increase the probability that the behavior will be repeated, while punishing a behavior will decrease the probability that the behavior will be repeated

self-determination: being in control of one's self and life pursuits, or determining one's own course of behavior

Study Questions

1. What is motivation? Identify and explain the three key achievement behaviors related to motivation.

2. Identify several common myths about motivation, and provide a rationale to dispute each myth.

3. Why is the question "How do I motivate my athletes?" a bit narrow and naive considering the social psychological perspective of motivation?

4. Define and explain motivation as it relates to human needs. Identify the important needs of athletes and indicate how these differ from wants. Generate multiple examples of the ways in which motivation may be enhanced in sport by attempting to meet the needs of athletes.

5. Explain how the positive motivation cycle links motivation, achievement behavior, and competence in a reciprocal fashion.

6. Explain the different motivational orientations and behavioral patterns of success-oriented and failure-oriented athletes.

7. Explain the continuum of self-determination in terms of the various sources of intrinsic and extrinsic motivation. Explain why intrinsic and extrinsic motivation are not dichotomous, but separated in degree across the continuum. Provide examples for how all sources of motivation may be effectively used.

8. Why do extrinsic rewards tend to weaken intrinsic motivation? Using specific examples, explain how rewards could be structured in sport to avoid this undermining effect and enhance motivation.

Reflective Learning Activities

1. Motivation I.Q. Revisited

In groups of four, compare and discuss your answers to the Motivation I.Q. test from the chapter. Your task is to reach a consensus (or at least 3 out of 4 must agree) on the correct answer for each question. Be sure to write down your rationale or reasoning to support your answers. (10 minutes in groups)

2. Who's the Boss?

Identify some specific areas in which athletes can be given responsibility within a sports team. Examples might include:

a. designating team captains
b. setting social rules related to training (e.g., alcohol policy, curfew, diet)
c. game and practice evaluations

Determine what the coach's and the athletes' roles should be in these areas of responsibility. Discuss how your guidelines will be similar or different for various age groups.

3. Pushing the Envelope

A very popular assumption among many coaches is that motivating athletes requires the use of extreme dispraise. The rationale behind this assumption is that even if athletes want to do their best, it takes an outside force to constantly ride and berate them to maximize every last drop of motivation and ability that athletes possess. Many athletes agree with this point and state that even though they don't enjoy the yelling and dehumanizing treatment, they understand it and appreciate it because the coach is only trying to make them better.

There may well be some truth to this. Perhaps we can't drive ourselves to push the envelope to our individual limits without a strong external regulator like a coach. What do you think? Choose the statement below that best represents your position on the issue, and be prepared to give specific reasons to support your position.

a. Coaches should use any type of motivation to get the best out of their athletes.
b. Coaches have the right to motivate athletes any way they see fit, but I personally disagree with a philosophy of using dispraise and belittling to motivate athletes.
c. Coaches have no right to engage in dehumanizing dispraise no matter what their intent.

(Participants work as individuals for 5 minutes to establish the logic to support their position. Then, break participants into three subgroups representing the three position statements listed above. In subgroups, they share their rationale and build an argument for 10 minutes. Then, each group presents their argument to the total group with questions and answers afterwards for 15 minutes.)

4. How Motivated Are You?

To assess your own motivation, complete the following inventory that measures different forms of extrinsic and intrinsic motivation (Sport Motivation Scale; Pelletier et al., 1995). The inventory contains seven subscales of four items each, which assess the three types of IM (IM to know, to experience stimulation, for accomplishment), the three types of EM (external regulation, internal pressure, internal regulation), and amotivation (no IM or EM).

Why Do You Practice Your Sport?

Using the scale on the following page, please indicate to what extent each of the following items corresponds to one of the reasons for which you are presently practicing your sport.

		Does not correspond at all			Corresponds moderately			Corresponds exactly
1.	For the pleasure I feel in living exciting experiences.	1	2	3	4	5	6	7
2.	For the pleasure it gives me to know more about the sport that I practice.	1	2	3	4	5	6	7
3.	I used to have good reasons for playing sports, but now I am asking myself if I should continue doing it.	1	2	3	4	5	6	7
4.	For the pleasure of discovering new training techniques.	1	2	3	4	5	6	7
5.	I don't know anymore; I have the impression that I am incapable of succeeding in this sport.	1	2	3	4	5	6	7
6.	Because it allows me to be well regarded by people that I know.	1	2	3	4	5	6	7
7.	Because, in my opinion, it is one of the best ways to meet people.	1	2	3	4	5	6	7
8.	Because I feel a lot of personal satisfaction while mastering certain difficult training techniques.	1	2	3	4	5	6	7
9.	Because it is absolutely necessary to do sports if one wants to be in shape.	1	2	3	4	5	6	7
10.	For the prestige of being an athlete.	1	2	3	4	5	6	7
11.	Because it is one of the best ways I have chosen to develop other aspects of myself.	1	2	3	4	5	6	7
12.	For the pleasure I feel while improving some of my weak points.	1	2	3	4	5	6	7
13.	For the excitement I feel when I am really involved in the activity.	1	2	3	4	5	6	7
14.	Because I must do sports to feel good about myself.	1	2	3	4	5	6	7
15.	For the satisfaction I experience while I am perfecting my abilities.	1	2	3	4	5	6	7
16.	Because people around me think it is important to be in shape.	1	2	3	4	5	6	7
17.	Because it is a good way to learn lots of things that could be useful to me in other areas of my life.	1	2	3	4	5	6	7
18.	For the intense emotions that I feel while I am doing a sport that I like.	1	2	3	4	5	6	7
19.	It is not clear to me anymore: I don't really think my place is in sport.	1	2	3	4	5	6	7
20.	For the pleasure that I feel while executing certain difficult movements.	1	2	3	4	5	6	7
21.	Because I would feel bad if I was not taking time to do it.	1	2	3	4	5	6	7
22.	To show others how good I am at my sport.	1	2	3	4	5	6	7
23.	For the pleasure that I feel while learning training techniques that I have never tried before.	1	2	3	4	5	6	7
24.	Because it is one of the best ways to maintain good relationships with my friends.	1	2	3	4	5	6	7
25.	Because I like the feeling of being totally immersed in the activity.	1	2	3	4	5	6	7
26.	Because I must do sports regularly.	1	2	3	4	5	6	7
27.	For the pleasure of discovering new performance strategies.	1	2	3	4	5	6	7
28.	I often ask myself: I can't seem to achieve the goals that I set for myself.	1	2	3	4	5	6	7

Scoring instructions: EM-external regulation (6, 10, 16, 22), EM-internal pressure (9, 14, 21, 26), EM-internal regulation (7, 11, 17, 24, IM-for accomplishment (8, 12, 15, 20), IM-for stimulation (1, 13, 18, 25), IM-to know (2, 4, 23, 27), Amotivation (3, 5, 19, 28). Sum numbers corresponding to items in each subscale and list total subscale scores below:

EM-external regulation _____   IM-for accomplishment _____

EM-internal pressure _____   IM-for stimulation _____

EM-internal regulation _____   IM-to know _____

Amotivation _____

Plot your scores on the graph below, and connect your scores with a line to illustrate your highs and lows. Compare your scores to those represented by the dotted line which are the average scores found in research with university athletes. Reflect on your scores. Do you feel they are accurate portrayals of your motivation? Think about ways that you can refine your motivation to enhance the quality of your sport participation.

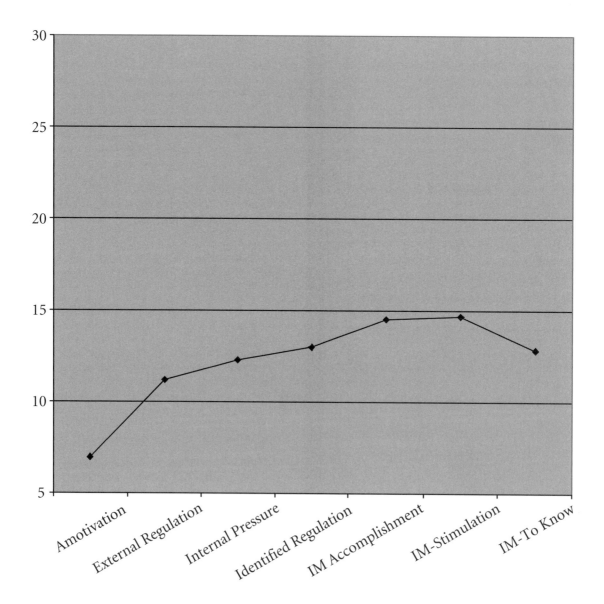

Chapter Four

Communication

Photo by Dale Sparks, All-Pro Photography

Chapter Preview

In this chapter, you'll learn:

*   the communication basics for coaches
*   that communication is a process and how it typically breaks down
*   how to become a Credible Communicator
*   how to enhance communication effectiveness within your team

"Seek first to understand, then to be understood."

Stephen Covey

"When he's calling you an _____, don't listen. But when he starts telling you why you're an _____, listen. That way you'll get better." Assistant coach **Dan Dakich** to a freshman Indiana University basketball player, describing how best to deal with Coach Bob Knight's communication style (Feinstein, 1986, p. 4)

A s a college basketball coach, I believed that I was a good communicator. One day I was working in practice with a small group of players, including my point guard Lisa. Not only was Lisa the most skilled player I had ever coached, but she was also the strongest leader and most motivated athlete I had ever coached. I respected and admired her, and was thrilled with the opportunity to coach her. As the players worked on a particular offensive drill, I complimented several players on their performance, and then gave Lisa some specific feedback about how she could perform better in the drill. To my astonishment, she uncharacteristically walked off the floor in tears. When I caught up with her and asked what was wrong, she looked at me and very quietly said, "Coach, you *never* say anything good to *me*." I was shocked. This was Lisa, my rock-steady point guard that was the heart and soul of my team, and the best and most committed athlete I had ever coached. How could this happen?

It happened because I was completely unaware of my own communication biases. I made the mistake of *assuming* that Lisa knew that I appreciated her, and *assuming* that because she was so successful and skilled that she didn't need as much positive reinforcement from me as her other teammates. I was wrong. I learned the very important lesson that even if we *know* the principles of good communication, we still have to work hard to *recognize* our own communication styles and behaviors, especially our biases or weaknesses. My intent was good with Lisa, but intent gets you nothing if you don't communicate it accurately.

The purpose of this chapter is to raise your awareness about your communication skills, including your strengths and weaknesses. You must be able to recognize and understand why interpersonal misunderstandings occur, and then learn how to minimize or avoid these communication gaps. To do this, you'll read about the nature of communication skills and interpersonal effectiveness, particularly in relation to coaching. As opposed to just reading the material in the chapter, be honestly self-reflective in assessing your communication abilities as you read. It is my hope that you will strive to internalize the material and work daily to be a better communicator. Being an effective communicator takes hustle! It requires daily practice and an open mind to constantly evaluate and understand why communication breaks down and how we can do it better.

Importance of Communication for Coaches

Communication is *the process by which we understand others, and in turn, endeavor to be understood by them* (Anderson, 1959). I can't think of anything more important for coaches than to understand their athletes, and for their athletes to understand them. Many people believe that the most important quality of coaches is knowledge about their sport. Clearly, athletes want coaches to know their stuff so they can effectively teach techniques and strategies. But if coaches aren't skilled communicators, they can't teach their stuff in effective ways to their athletes. A survey of U.S. Olympic athletes who competed from 1984 to 1998 showed that athletes ranked the ability to teach and the ability to motivate as the two most important qualities of coaches (Gibbons & Forster, 2002). Coaches' training knowledge, skill competence, and strategic knowledge of their sports were ranked third, fourth, and fifth. In another study, ten U.S. Olympic champion athletes were interviewed to determine the role that coaches played in the success of their athletes.

> ### Quotable Quote
> *"Athletes don't care how much you know until they know how much you care."* **Jim Tressell**, head football coach at Ohio State University

The most important influence identified by the athletes was the quality of the coach-athlete relationship, which was viewed as more important to the athletes' success than coaches' knowledge and skills (Dieffenbach, Gould, & Moffett, 2002).

It's important that coaches have the knowledge and skills to be effective teachers, but communication ability provides the vehicle through which coaches' knowledge and skills are transmitted to athletes. If you aren't a strong communicator, you will be less effective as a coach no matter how much you know about your sport. Consider how communication is essential to coaching for the Inner Edge. Your philosophy will only impact your athletes if it is effectively communicated to them. Your understanding of athletes' motivation and your ability to motivate them requires effective communication skills. As a leader, you must transmit your vision for others to understand and buy into, and your decision-making and reinforcement skills require expert communication skills. Great team chemistry, or cohesion, requires constant, consistent, mature, quality communication from you. And finally, implementing mental training and teaching mental skills to athletes requires you to be a skilled communicator.

> ### Quotable Quote
> *"Unless [athletes] are willing to listen to you, unless you're prepared to listen to them and understand them as people, the best coaching book in the world isn't going to help you."* **Graham Taylor**, professional soccer coach and former coach of England's national team (Jones, Armour, & Potrac, 2004)

Can you think of some examples of how coaches have communicated in innovative ways to create a productive team culture? Here are some of my favorites. In the first team meeting each year, former UCLA men's basketball coach John Wooden painstakingly demonstrated to his players the proper way to put on their socks. Coach Wooden's sock demonstration communicated to his players that no detail was too small to overlook in striving for excellence. Duke University men's basketball coach Mike Krzyzewski sets aside time in training sessions for his teams to practice time-outs. This familiarizes Duke players with the specific routine of time-outs and allows them to practice communicating so that communication is enhanced during the actual competition time-outs. Terry Hoeppner, former football coach at Miami University, posted a number on a board in the team locker room under the heading "Number of Days We've Been in the Right Place at the Right Time." Coach Hoeppner's number board is a public communication that Miami players are prioritizing their time and their decisions, and putting the team first. Each of these examples, although seemingly small, represents a practice of communication that contributes to a success-oriented, cohesive team culture.

©iStockphoto.com

In short, communication skill is as essential, and arguably *more* essential, than coaches' knowledge about their sport. In fact, communication is the most important *human*, or life, skill. Most people spend more time communicating each day than in any other activity. To help your athletes get the Inner Edge, you must be a strong communicator.

Communication Basics

Four communication basics are presented in this section. Understanding these basics is the starting point in enhancing your communication ability.

1. Communication is a process.

Communication is not simply what one says to another. It is a complex process of taking a thought, turning it into a message, and delivering the message. The process then continues as the other person receives the message, interprets it, and then responds to the message. As shown in Figure 4.1, communication can break down at any point in the process. Coaches must accurately turn their thoughts into appropriate message content and then deliver the message effectively. Athletes must be receptive to the message (listen!) and then interpret the message accurately or in the way it was intended. The ways in

which athletes interpret messages influence their behavior, which is then directly observed by the coach, who interprets their behavior, and then begins the process over again.

Consider the example of a football coach who pulls a player out for a series during a game because he believes the player needs a quick rest. As the player comes out, the coach says offhandedly, "Take a break, Evan." Evan interprets the coach's verbal and nonverbal message as "You're not doing the job, Evan." So he slams his helmet down, which the coach notices and interprets as immature behavior, and then benches Evan for the rest of the game. In this case, communication broke down between player and coach because the true intent of the coach was lost in the process. It may have been that the content of the message was unclear, the message was not delivered in a way to convey its true intent, Evan may have only heard part of it, he interpreted it as punishment and behaved emotionally and immaturely, at which point the coach's thought was, "This guy needs some discipline." Which he did!

Communication can be disrupted at any link in the process. So what can coaches do to keep communication channels running as smoothly as possible

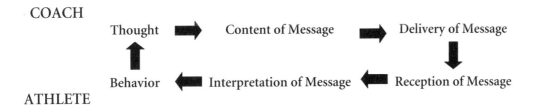

COACH

Thought ➡ Content of Message ➡ Delivery of Message

Behavior ⬅ Interpretation of Message ⬅ Reception of Message

ATHLETE

Figure 4.1 Communication as a process

within teams? First, you as the coach should continually work on your communication skills to enhance the first part of the process. How effective are you at turning your thoughts into clear, concise messages and then transmitting the messages in understandable and appropriate ways? Second, you should make your athletes aware of how important it is to communicate effectively, insisting that they be hyperaware of how they send messages, as well as how they respond to feedback. Everyone on the team should consciously work to raise their tolerance level and trust in each other to preserve the links in the communication process (Orlick, 1986). Once in while, messages will be interpreted inaccurately, and instead of becoming upset, athletes and coaches should immediately clarify things (or give each other the benefit of doubt *until* it can be clarified).

2. Communication includes content and delivery dimensions.

Most of us mistakenly assume that the content, or verbal portion, of communication is the most important aspect of the message. Actually, the verbal content of any message only makes up 7% of the total message sent to another person, leaving a whopping 93% of the message that is influenced by nonverbal behavior such as body position, tone of voice, and facial expressions (McKay, Davis, & Fanning, 1983). Thus, the second communication basic is that communication includes content and delivery dimensions, and that *how* you send the message is just as—if not more—important than what you actually say. Research examining voter perceptions during the 1988 U.S. Presidential election showed that only 10% of voter impressions were based on candidates' words. Forty percent of the voters' impressions were based on voice quality, and 50% was based on general appearance and body language (Walton, 1989).

Nonverbal communication is very important in understanding the message being delivered. That is why face-to-face communication is preferred when discussing important issues. However, nonverbal messages are more difficult to interpret accurately because of stereotypes and cultural differences. Later in the chapter, we'll discuss strategies to enhance your nonverbal communication with your athletes.

3. Coaches' communication greatly influences the behavior, performance, and psychological wellbeing of athletes.

One of the most astonishing things I realized as a coach was just how influential my words and actions were. Like it or not, your communication and behavior as a coach directly and critically impacts on the development and performance of your athletes (Horn, 2002). Moreover, as a coach, you must be careful in developing different expectations for athletes, because research has shown that coaches' expectations influence the ways in which they communicate with these athletes. This is called the self-fulfilling prophecy.

Clipboard

Pygmalion in the Classroom

A very famous research study emphasized the power of teachers' (and coaches') communication in the lives of young learners. In 1968, Rosenthal and Jacobson published the results of an experiment they had conducted with teachers and students in 18 elementary school classrooms. The purpose of the study was to see if the academic progress of students could be influenced by their teachers' expectations. The researchers told the teachers that certain children in their classes were late bloomers and thus were expected to show big gains in academic performance during that school year. In reality, the children targeted as late bloomers were selected randomly from the group of students, and had no special abilities or potential as identified by the researchers. However, at the end of the school year, the group of children that were specially targeted had made greater academic progress than the children who had not been identified as special.

Why did this happen? Rosenthal and Jacobson concluded that the false information given to the teachers led them to create higher expectations for the targeted students as compared to the other students. These higher expectancies influenced the ways in which the teachers communicated with their students, with the supposition being that they acted in ways towards the favored students to stimulate better performance from them as compared to the regular students. In summation, the teachers' expectations served as self-fulfilling prophecies by influencing communication patterns in such a way that the original expectations were fulfilled.

According to the **self-fulfilling prophecy theory**, *the expectations that coaches form about the ability of individual athletes can serve as prophecies that dictate or determine the level of achievement each athlete will ultimately reach* (Horn, Lox, & Labrador, 2001). Four steps explain how the self-fulfilling prophecy occurs with coaches and athletes (see Figure 4.2).

Step 1. The coach develops an expectation for each athlete regarding his or her ability and predicted level of performance. We all do this in sizing up individuals, and clearly part of coaches' jobs are to assess the potential of their athletes. Developing expectations for athletes is not in and of itself the problem. Problems occur when expectations are inaccurate, rigid, and inflexible, and when these expectations bias coaches' communication with athletes. Thus, coaches should avoid pigeonholing athletes based on inflexible and inaccurate beliefs about their abilities and potential. Coaches should use daily performance information to continuously assess the abilities and progress of their athletes, and make sure to keep their expectations of athletes flexible and open to change. Using personal cues in developing expectations for athletes often creates inaccurate beliefs about their abilities, based on limiting stereotypes. For example, coaches might expect different practice behaviors and performance levels of athletes based on gender, race, physical appearance such as size and body type, and even family background. The history of sport provides many examples of how athletes overcame stereotypical expectations. Doug Flutie was never expected to be a great professional quarterback because he is only 5'9", but he went on to a successful professional football career. Doug Williams was one of the first African-Americans to become a successful NFL quarterback, breaking through a decades-old stereotype that black athletes could not succeed as quarterbacks. The marathon event in track and field was not sponsored for female athletes in the Olympic Games until 1984, because of the stereotypical belief that women lacked the stamina for such events.

To avoid negative expectancy effects, coaches should rely on multiple performance-based assessments of their athletes' abilities, as these are more accurate than person cues such as size, gender, race, and reputation. Coaches should also realize that their initial assessments of an athlete's competence may be inaccurate, and thus they may need to revise it continually as the season progresses (Horn et al., 2001). A good rule of thumb is to maintain high expectancies for all of your athletes and not fall prey to stereotypes, such as "you have to treat girls differently because they have less skill," or "he's too small to succeed in that position."

Step 2. Coaches' expectations of athletes influence their communication with their athletes. Research supports that coaches often communicate differently with athletes based on the expectations that they have for these athletes (Horn et al., 2001). For

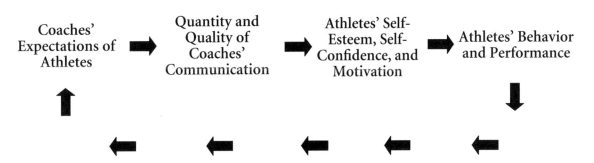

Figure 4.2 Coaches' expectations as a self-fulfilling prophecy

example, coaches may provide more specific instruction to high expectancy (as compared to low expectancy) athletes because they believe these athletes have the skills to use this feedback to improve. Another example is a tendency to over-praise low expectancy athletes for mediocre performance, which seems like a positive approach to coaching, but in reality can lower their perceived competence, motivation, and goal aspirations. Biased communication with athletes based on expectations does not happen automatically, and some coaches are able to avoid this negative expectancy effect. However, all coaches must be mindful how expectations influence their communication with others, and work to provide quality communication to all their athletes. Thoughtful practice management strategies can be used to ensure that coaches communicate directly and specifically to athletes on their teams, regardless of skill level of these athletes.

Step 3. Coaches' communication with their athletes affects how competent the athletes see themselves to be and how motivated they are to improve. Athletes who are consistently provided less effective instructional communication from coaches will not show the same levels of skill improvement as those athletes who receive high quality communication from coaches. Research has shown that different types of communication from coaches can influence athletes' self-esteem, self-confidence, intrinsic motivation, performance anxiety, and dropout behavior (Horn, 2002; Horn et al., 2001).

> ## Personal Plug-In
>
> Identify as many examples as you can for how the frequency, types, quantity, and quality of communication from coaches may be influenced by their expectations of individual athletes.

Step 4. Athletes' behavior and performance conform to coaches' expectations, completing the self-fulfilling prophecy. This final step confirms to coaches that their judgments, or expectations, of their athletes were accurate.

Research has supported the four steps in the coaching expectancy process, but it has also shown that not all coaches create self-fulfilling prophecies for their athletes. Likewise, not all athletes are susceptible to self-fulfilling prophecies created by their coaches. Overall, however, coaches should be mindful that expectations are very powerful influences on their communication with others. Follow three guidelines to avoid creating negative self-fulfilling prophecies for your athletes. First, maintain high expectations for all your athletes based on their unique skills levels (everyone can learn and improve their individual skills). Second, keep your expectations for your athletes flexible and open to constant change by creating a clean slate upon which you evaluate their performances each day of training and competition to accurately assess their developing abilities. Third, develop your communication skills so that you systematically send quality messages, provide specific, informative feedback, and listen effectively to all your athletes, regardless of expectations you have for them. Tips for enhancing your communication skills are provided later in the chapter.

4. You cannot not communicate.

The final communication basic builds upon the first three by stating a logical, but often forgotten, maxim: As a coach, you cannot *not* communicate. Communication is inevitable. You communicate to your athletes and others without even trying. If you choose not to respond to an athlete, that communicates a message to him or her. You communicate all the time through your body, your behavior, and of course your words, or lack of them. By not providing performance feedback to a low expectancy athlete, you have communicated to her that you do not choose to coach her in that situation. Knowing that communication is a process, this athlete may interpret your non-response as evidence that she is not highly skilled or worth your time, which decreases her confidence and motivation. As a human being, and particularly as a coach, you simply cannot *not* communicate!

The Credible Communicator

You now know the communication basics. The remainder of the chapter is designed to enhance your communication skills as a coach. Your most important objective as a communicator is to establish credibility. Being a credible communicator means that people listen when you talk, that they believe and value what you have to say. Who do you listen to? Why do you listen to him or her? Who is the most credible communicator you know? What makes them credible?

In Figure 4.3, the building blocks for becoming a Credible Communicator are shown. The cornerstones for credible communication are authenticity and emotional competence (Guilar, 2001). These two key interpersonal characteristics provide the foundation for all communication skills. In this section, we'll discuss the importance of the cornerstones, and then the remaining building blocks for credible communication (Power Listening, effective sending or PITCHing it, and managing conflict) are presented in the subsequent sections of the chapter.

A favorite quote of mine is by Joseph Campbell, who states that "the privilege of a lifetime is to be who you are." Society constantly pressures us to conform—to be like others. Many coaches try to emulate others, believing that success can be attained by following the ways of others. Obviously, we can learn a lot by observing other master coaches and great individuals, but fundamentally we all have to be who we are. And importantly, we need to know and understand who we are and what we're about.

Authenticity

Authenticity is being who we really are, feeling comfortable with that, and being forthright and honest about ourselves when communicating with others. Why is authenticity so important? Because it develops trust. And if you trust someone, they have credibility with you and you listen to what they say because it is believable and trustworthy. Thus, authenticity develops trust, which enhances the communication process. Coaches who attempt to be what they are not or who are superficial in their communication with athletes do not gain the trust of their athletes, and ultimately do not have credibility. I found as a coach that I gained more credibility and respect from my athletes when I admitted mistakes or apologized. They knew I was being authentic, and they realized that it takes a great deal of confidence to admit when you're wrong. In short, I attempted to be authentic—to show my athletes who I really was. When we are superficial or too proud to disclose our thoughts and feelings with our athletes, it is because of our own fear and lack of courage. So a first step in becoming a better communicator is understanding yourself and simply being who you are.

Emotional Competence

Authenticity is how well we know ourselves and how much we allow ourselves to be who we truly are. Emotional competence is how well we manage our feelings when relating to others. According to Goleman (1995), our emotional intelligence determines

Figure 4.3 The Credible Communicator

our potential for learning practical skills necessary for succeeding in life, including self-awareness, self-regulation, empathy, and adeptness in relationships with others. Our emotional competence shows how much of that potential we have realized. Goleman (1998) explains that you can be very empathic, or understanding of the perspective of others, yet fail to develop the communication skills to put that empathy to work. Emotional competence is particularly important for leaders or coaches, whose role is to influence others to perform effectively. Research with hundreds of top executives in global companies demonstrated that emotional competence made the crucial difference between mediocre and the best leaders (Goleman, 1998).

At the heart of emotional competence are two abilities: empathy, which involves reading the feelings of others, and social skills, which allow us to handle these feelings in artful ways (Goleman, 1998). **Empathy** is *the human skill of knowing how others feel, and understanding how those feelings are affecting them.* Sensing what your athletes feel without their saying so is what empathy is all about. Think of it as your interpersonal radar as a coach. You can develop your empathy skills by observing and getting to know your athletes to better understand their subtle nonverbal cues. Empathy is also enhanced by becoming more self-aware and recognizing the feelings in our own bodies. It is difficult to be empathic if you're not self-aware, because empathy is based on feelings we've already experienced.

Personal Plug-In

Can empathy ever become counter-productive for a coach? Explain when and why a coach may have to strategically and/or intentionally avoid empathy with athletes.

Emotional competence enables us to respond openly and rationally, without becoming defensive. I've observed numerous times how you can warm the climate in the room when talking to others just by taking some responsibility for the issue at hand, saying things like, "I know that you're disappointed," "I regret that this occurred," and when appropriate, "I apologize for . . ." I notice that people relax, and although it is disappointing that *they* don't always take responsibility, I feel good knowing I've done all I can

to enhance the communication process. It's almost like people *expect* you to respond defensively and not listen to them, so when you listen authentically and take some mutual responsibility for the issue at hand, you can ease the tension and open up the communication process quite a bit.

Stephen Covey (1985) provides a useful analogy of an emotional bank account in his acclaimed book *The Seven Habits of Highly Effective People.* As a coach, your emotional bank account, or EBA, is the amount of trust that you've built up in your relationship with each of your athletes. As with any bank account, the key is to build up a reserve. Building up the reserve in your EBA helps cover any withdrawals, or mistakes, you make with your athletes. If your EBA, and thus trust level, is high, communication between the two of you is easy, instant, and effective. However, if you behave in ways that create distrust (e.g., being untruthful, discourteous, disrespectful, unfair, self-centered), this will create an overdrawn EBA. The trick is to make continuous deposits to ensure a large EBA reserve. Covey explains six types of deposits that we can make in our EBAs to enhance our communication and relationships with others.

1. Understand the individual. Covey states that seeking to really understand another person is one of the most important deposits you can make. What constitutes a deposit for one of your athletes doesn't necessarily work as a deposit for another athlete. Deposits are personal, and based on knowing the person. Know what is important to each of your athletes. Develop some insights into their emotional competence, their goals and aspirations, their identities. I believe this works for teams as well. Every team you coach is a bit different, so work to understand what kind of deposits really build up the balance in your EBA with each team.

2. Attend to the little things. Details are important, and I've found that details make champions. Covey makes the important point that little things often become big things. He cautions that seemingly little forms of unkindness and disrespect often make large withdrawals from your EBA with your athletes, and little kindnesses may often create unexpectedly large deposits.

3. Keep your commitments. Promises represent major deposits or withdrawals in an EBA. Promises not kept are big withdrawals, and will erode trust. Promises kept or commitments honored are huge deposits, as athletes learn that you are true to your word.

4. Clarify expectations. Communication always flows more smoothly when expectations are clarified up front. Major EBA withdrawals occur when athletes are admonished for things coaches thought they should understand, but they didn't because it was not made clear. Covey states that almost all relationship problems are rooted in conflicting or ambiguous expectations. A terrific deposit to make in your team's EBA is to clarify your expectations and make them explicit in the beginning, and then to communicate these expectations consistently over time.

5. Show personal integrity. Personal integrity begins with authenticity, as discussed previously. It means that you are consistent in your professional and personal behavior based on your philosophy and who you say you are. It means that you are honest and forthright when talking to athletes, and it means that you are loyal to those individuals who are not present. Coaches make major EBA withdrawals by talking about others in derogatory ways when they are not present. Would you trust someone who does this?

6. Apologize sincerely when you make a withdrawal. It's easy to hurt feelings, miss a commitment, and overlook little things in your busy life as a coach and person. Covey emphasizes that people forgive mistakes, and that honest and sincere apologies buffer the effects of EBA withdrawals. However, it takes personal confidence and strength of character to apologize genuinely. Genuine, authentic apologies make deposits; apologies interpreted as insincere make withdrawals.

Overall, the foundation for being a credible communicator as a coach is to be authentic and emotionally competent. Keep in mind that all of us are continually striving to be the best we can be at these—no one ever achieves total authenticity and emotional competence! What's important is to strive to enhance your abilities in these areas, and to daily practice and work on understanding yourself and your interpersonal strengths and weaknesses.

Becoming a Power Listener

We've laid the cornerstones for becoming a credible communicator by focusing on authenticity

and emotional competence. Now, working through the model of the Credible Communicator shown in Figure 4.3, the next step on the way to communication effectiveness is to become a power listener. Revisit the quote by Stephen Covey listed at the beginning of the chapter ("Seek first to understand, then to be understood"). Think about what this means. Many people engage in constant communication to make others understand their points of view. Understanding the perspectives of others takes a back seat to their own needs to speak. However, true communication occurs when we seek first to understand, or when we listen.

Hearing is automatic; listening is not. Listening involves a deep desire to understand and connect, and it takes effort and sincere caring. True listening means that we make ourselves available to others by suspending our needs, and by giving them our complete attention. Mohandas Gandhi set aside each Monday as a day of silence. During this time, he sharpened his powers of observation and listening skills to strengthen his connections with others.

Most communication books advocate *active* or *reflective listening*, which emphasizes the continuous mutual interaction between the speaker and the listener. Active listening and reflective listening are important, but listening is so important for coaches that I like to advocate *Power Listening*. Power Listening incorporates all the principles of active and reflective listening, but also emphasizes the need for effort, for hustle, for being powerful in your ability to focus as a coach to listen to your athletes. Listening is exhausting, and becoming a Power Listener takes work, practice, self-reflection, and even feedback from trustworthy sources. Power Listening will create many deposits in your emotional bank accounts with your athletes, so it is a great use of your time, even if it is exhausting. Before we talk about how to develop your Power Listening skills, let's identify some typical blocks to listening that we all are guilty of at times.

Blocks to Listening

It's so easy not to listen. We're all very busy people, and we've all developed interpersonal habits that derail effective listening. Typical listening blocks for coaches include mind reading, prejudging, filtering, advice giving, identifying, being right/defensive, and rehearsing (McKay et al., 1983). *Mind reading* involves trying to figure out what your athletes *really* are thinking and feeling, without listening to them. This involves making assumptions, and as my college basketball coach used to tell me, "when we assume we make an 'ass' out of 'u' and 'me.'" Often, mind reading goes hand in hand with *prejudging*, which occurs when your listening is affected by your opinions (often stereotypes) of certain athletes. If you prejudge someone to be a whiner or problem athlete, it is easier to miss his true messages because you've already predetermined what he will say. And all of us (particularly those of us with small children!) learn the listening block of *filtering*, which involves half-listening while you're attending to 20 other things you have to do at that minute. Filtering happens when you hear, but don't listen, or even when you simply don't hear because your mind is on something else. Power Listening gets its power from being the main focus of your attention. To be a Power Listener, you absolutely cannot half-listen, pretend to listen, or listen to several things at once.

Probably the most common listening block practiced by coaches is *advice giving*. This occurs when you immediately jump in to fix the problem and provide helpful suggestions to your athletes. This listening block is well intentioned, because as coaches we believe our job is to help our athletes solve problems. However, while you are cooking up solutions and suggestions in your mind, you are probably missing something important. Advice giving is not listening, and athletes often feel as though you didn't listen because you were so busy giving advice. It is very frustrating when someone tries to fix your problems, when all you wanted was someone to talk to or listen to you and validate your feelings.

Another typical, and sometimes well intentioned, listening block for coaches is *identifying*. Identifying means that you jump in to your athlete's story to tell her how this reminds you of something that happened to you or that you experienced. That is, you launch into your story before she can finish hers. I believe this is often well intentioned, as when coaches attempt to empathize and share similar experiences with their athletes to show them that they understand. However, it is not listening, and it derails the focus of attention from the person speaking. Stifle the need to match stories and experiences—it blocks listening and often serves as a withdrawal in your emotional bank account with an athlete.

The final two listening blocks—*being right/defensive* and *rehearsing*—are based on people's need for power and their refusal to attempt to understand others. People using these listening blocks seek first to be understood, instead of vice versa. Not only does this block communication, but it creates conflict and serious withdrawals from one's emotional bank account. It is maddening! *Being right* means that a coach will go to any lengths to avoid being wrong (even if they are). This type of person can't take critical feedback, can't be corrected, and refuses to accept suggestions. *Defensiveness* goes along with being right and adds negative emotion to the communication process, which blocks listening even more. Defensive coaches are self-protective, emotionally reactive, and resistant to learning, all of which block listening. Defensiveness blocks people from learning and reflecting, and thus promotes incompetence. It is my belief that people get defensive when they know there is a grain of truth to what is being communicated to them. They resist true listening because they are fearful of exposing their incompetence or lack of confidence. Defensive people who have to be right often practice *rehearsing*, which means that instead of listening, their attention is focused inward on the perfect comeback or argument that they are rehearsing to bomb back to the speaker so they can "win" the discussion.

What are your typical listening blocks? It's important to do the exercise listed in the Personal Plug-In to raise awareness of listening blocks that have probably become habitual and automatic. Practice listening every day by attempting to avoid using these blocks. It takes some effort, and you'll still catch yourself advice-giving or identifying at times, but if you're aware that you're doing it, that's half the battle.

Personal Plug-In

What listening blocks do you typically engage in? Write down 4-5 groups of people or individual persons (e.g., my athletes, partner, supervisor, assistant coaches). Evaluate your listening with each set of people, and write down typical listening blocks that you use with each of them. Identify situations that trigger the use of these blocks. Consider some strategies you can practice in your daily life to stop these blocks and enhance your listening.

Clipboard

Always Being Right is Wrong

Former U.S. Women's Soccer coach Tony DiCicco describes a valuable lesson he learned about the listening block of always having to be right. In his first year coaching the U.S. team in a tournament in France, he admittedly was overcoaching from the sidelines. He was specifically over-verbalizing to one player, when Mia Hamm came over to him and said, "Tony, just let her play." DiCicco recalls that he reacted negatively to Hamm's point by yelling at her, thinking that she was being disrespectful. Hamm came in to a scheduled one-on-one meeting the next day with DiCicco, with tension still in the air between them. Coach DiCicco said to her, "I've given a lot of thought [to what happened yesterday on the field], and the bottom line is, and I need to tell you this, I think you were right. I did overcoach." DiCicco recalls that Hamm was amazed at his response, and went out and played wonderfully the next night. He learned the valuable lesson that sometimes athletes are right and can help us as coaches learn about ourselves. In admitting fault and displaying openness and vulnerability, Coach DiCicco enhanced his relationship with his star player. His support of her comment validated her feelings about being a team leader and honest communicator, which empowered her to play her best (DiCicco, Hacker, & Salzberg, 2002).

Four Steps in Power Listening

Power Listening means that you grant someone the privilege of your presence and your full attention. It *is* a privilege for other people to gain your attention, and effective communication doesn't mean that you submissively allow others to drone on and waste your time. Effective communicators are assertive communicators, which means they can start and stop conversations. Instead of pretending to listen to those who abuse the privilege of your time (e.g., phone solicitors, salespeople at your front door, negative coworkers who complain about the same thing every time, or friends who likes to gossip about others), politely tell them that you don't have

time at that moment. Power Listening doesn't mean that you have an open door to anyone at any time who wants to unload on you. Power Listening takes place when you make the conscious decision to listen by granting someone the privilege of your full attention. In this section, the four steps involved in Power Listening for coaches are outlined. They are preparing, attending, understanding, and responding.

Preparing. Just as athletic excellence begins with preparation, so does listening excellence. The first step in Power Listening is mentally preparing to do it. Take time before meetings with athletes to increase your concentration and narrow your focus of attention. Create a mindset that you will be an interested and attentive listener, no matter how much you have to do or how tired you feel. Creating the mindset and mental focus for power listening is the first important step to follow to be an effective listener. Mentally prepare to listen and communicate effectively prior to an athlete coming to your office, prior to going to practice or training, prior to meeting with your staff, and prior to meeting with your supervisor. Remind yourself to be an authentic listener, to manage your emotions appropriately, and to avoid your typical listening blocks.

Attending. The second step in Power Listening is to attend to the speaker. **Attending** is defined as *having a single-minded focus on the speaker, and actively communicating that focus to him or her during the entire conversation.* Attending is the foundation skill for all counselors and professionals for whom listening is a living, because it directly influences the speaker to talk openly, freely, and productively.

Effective attending behavior includes eye contact with the speaker that makes a meaningful, personal connection—think of it as listening with your eyes. It also includes attentive body language, such as leaning forward to show interest, an open posture

Photo courtesy of WVU Photographic Services

without crossing arms or legs, and a natural and relaxed body position. Finally, effective attending involves verbal tracking, or single-mindedly staying with the topic being discussed. Verbal tracking means you're concentrating on the words and meaning of the message being communicated, without allowing any listening blocks to interfere. Don't be afraid of silence, or long pauses, in the communication. Become comfortable with the silence, which lets the speaker know that you're not in a hurry, you're not going to jump in when they pause, and that silence is appropriate to collect thoughts and assimilate what has already been said.

Understanding. The third step of Power Listening, understanding, involves the important skill of empathy, discussed previously in the chapter. Instead of identifying, rehearsing, or advice giving, shift your thinking and feeling away from yourself and toward the speaker. Think developmentally and contextually to understand how the speaker is really feeling. If your 16-year-old team captain is telling you that he is not performing well because his girlfriend broke up with him, put yourself in his shoes and remember how if feels to be 16 and how important social acceptance and popularity is at this age. If one of your college athletes is upset because her father is pressuring her to perform better, put yourself in her shoes and remember that the need for parental approval is very powerful.

> ## Quotable Quote
> *"You can observe a lot just by watching."*
> Yogi Berra

Understanding means you listen with openness without any prejudging or mind reading. One strategy I use in listening is to click an imaginary switch in my brain that puts my current beliefs and opinions on hold, and that tunes me into a mindset where I ask, "What can I learn from this conversation?" By suspending my beliefs, I then listen freely, and take in the new information to see if indeed it may change my beliefs or opinions. Sometimes it does and sometimes I maintain my current beliefs. This is known as being open-minded, a particularly important Power Listening skill for coaches. As a college basketball coach, one of my post players gave me some feedback on the way to the locker room at

halftime that I brushed off immediately as "not a good idea." But as we talked at halftime, I realized that my player's idea was a good one. To her surprise, I made the change she suggested in our offensive formation. We won the game and she scored 20 points in the second half, because the adjustment worked so well. After the game, she thanked me for listening to her, but I admitted that my first response was to not listen to her because I was resistant to players' suggestions. She replied, "Well, coach, sometimes I think we experience things out on the floor that are more difficult for you to see." She was right, of course, and I learned an important lesson about listening openly to my players instead of letting my pride and need to be right interfere with my communication with them.

Another important part of understanding is to sift through all the information being presented to you by the speaker. When people are emotional, they often ramble, repeat themselves, go off on tangents, and even contradict themselves. In trying to understand the speaker's message, focus on the ideas they are sending you without getting hung up on the details. You don't need to remember everything they say in exact detail. It is more important to listen actively by working out the key ideas, or core of the message, from the mass of details that often are part of people's stories. Similarly, tune in to the feelings that accompany the speaker's words, which often give away the real message that is difficult to articulate. As a sport psychology consultant, I often observe that there is an issue behind the issue, meaning that the athlete talks to me about one thing, but through Power Listening it becomes apparent to me that there is a deeper, larger issue involved.

Responding. The final step in Power Listening is responding. Listening is never passive, and power listeners always realize that they're active collaborators in the communication process. When appropriate (such as when the speaker stops or asks you a question), it is helpful to clarify exactly what you perceived to be said. Typical clarifying responses are "Do you mean that . . .?" "What I hear you saying is . . .," and "In other words . . . ." Power listeners always clarify their understanding without making assumptions as to the exact nature of the message. You should be responding throughout the communication process by actively making eye contact, nodding, saying "uh huh" or other short phrases to indicate understanding. Your feedback to the sender should be honest, immediate, and supportive (McKay, Davis, & Fanning, 1983).

How much should you respond? We've talked about how advice giving blocks listening, so, is it appropriate to respond to feedback? When is it appropriate to respond with feedback? There are two guidelines you can follow to attempt to be a Power Listener and still provide feedback to those talking to you. First, speakers will often ask your advice or ask you what you think. At that point, it's obviously appropriate to honestly respond to them. The key is to wait until they ask before jumping in with your "helpful" advice. Second, and probably most important, your response should attempt to help the speakers find the best solution for themselves, *not* to give the solution to them. Consider the following excerpt from a book titled *Masterful Coaching* by Robert Hargrove (1995):

> *"When people think of a coach, they often think of someone who has all the answers or who offers advice that tells people what to do. While it's useful to know something . . . and to be able to offer advice, this kind of interaction with people can be very disempowering. A committed listener helps people think more clearly, work through unresolved issues, and discover the solutions they have inside them. This often involves listening beyond what people are saying to their deeply held beliefs and assumptions that are shaping their actions. If you listen closely enough you will discover that people's beliefs and assumptions are contained in almost everything they say and do" (pp. 56-57).*

Hargrove suggests that coaches listen for when athletes move from simple observations to arbitrary conclusions about these observations. Listen for where athletes use defensive reasoning or where they personalize something that may or may not have been personal. Listen for unsubstantiated assumptions and conclusions, as opposed to observations. The questions that you ask as a listener should challenge athletes to consider their possible flawed or irrational reasoning. Some example questions: "What made you believe that your teammate was being unsupportive? What makes this situation unfair—what is the evidence that I am being unfair—what does it mean to you that a coach is unfair?" "What do you think your teammate was thinking when she said/did that?" You

may also ask athletes to clarify what seem to you to be mixed messages by asking "How do you put these two things together?" Repeat incongruities to athletes by saying "You say . . . but it also seems that . . .", "Your words seem to say . . . but your actions say . . .", "What do you think? Do you see how it sounds to me?"

It is extremely important that your intent in asking these questions is to help the athletes find their own best solutions, and that your nonverbal behavior in responding is nonjudgmental and nonevaluative. The tone of your questions and your body language should be that of a caring, thoughtful person searching for the facts, not that of an authority figure sarcastically challenging their words and demonstrating power.

I once worked as a mental training consultant with a college golfer who wanted to become more mentally tough. In describing his style of physical training and preparation, he indicated that he preferred to hit balls on the range because he became too upset when he hit bad shots if he was practicing out on the course. He admitted that if he was playing a practice round and hit a bad shot, he would immediately quit. Can you see the flawed logic behind this golfer's practice behaviors and his intent to be mentally tough? I responded to him like this: "Mike, I hear you saying that you want to work to increase your mental toughness. But you've described how you choose to practice at the range and quit a practice round if you hit a bad shot. How do you put these things together? What might be some strategies you can use to practice being mentally tough?" My intent was to respond as a Power Listener by challenging Mike to adopt more productive practice strategies to enhance his mental toughness.

Another example is an ice hockey player named David who came to me because he was very upset by his lack of playing time. He felt he received no respect from the coaches or his teammates. He talked about how it was giving him a bad attitude and how he had begun to cruise through practices because he was being treated so unfairly. How would you respond as a Power Listener to this athlete? I followed these steps. I was prepared to give him my full attention and I did. I attended to him diligently and validated his feelings of frustration and disrespect. I responded by attempting to get him to see that how he was behaving was directly related to his lack of playing time. I paraphrased him and said, "I understand that you feel frustrated and resentful that you are not playing more. I'm sure that must be hard. You want to excel and for the coaches to believe in you and give you a chance. Is that right?" He affirmed this and I went on. "But you've also described that you lack motivation, have a 'bad attitude' in practice, and often 'go through the motions' of practice. How do you put these two things together? How might they be related?" The key point is to respond to athletes in ways that force them to think through and solve their own problems. It wouldn't be useful in this situation to tell David that he is creating this negative situation with his negative behavior, or at least contributing to it. What is important is to respond to him in ways that allow him to think more rationally and take responsibility for the situation, which empowers him to take control of his thinking and behavior.

Clipboard

Taking It On the Chin (and Relishing It!)

A key skill for Power Listeners and Credible Communicators is the ability to receive feedback in a productive manner. This is critical for coaches and athletes, because feedback is a constant type of communication used in sport to help people improve. Explain to your athletes that feedback is a resource as well as an opportunity. Urge them to value the resource and use the opportunity to learn and enhance their skills. This resource and opportunity is squandered if athletes don't accept the feedback and/or react defensively when it is given. It's difficult for all of us to receive critical feedback about ourselves, but the trick is to accept the discomfort and honestly attempt to understand the feedback being given to us. Here are some guidelines for receiving feedback:

- Don't argue with the person providing feedback—seek to understand them.
- Ask questions to clarify and allow for understanding: "How so?", "In what way?", "How often?", "When?", "How did that affect you?", "Can you be more specific?".
- Be open-minded and ask the person giving the feedback for suggestions concerning behaviors that might be more productive.

- Check for understanding by repeating what you heard and asking for confirmation.
- Thank the person for the feedback. Remember that giving feedback takes courage (especially athlete to coach) and can be just as difficult as receiving it. Also remember that the person could have withheld this information and not provided you with the opportunity to learn and improve.

PITCH It! Sending Effective Messages

Power Listening was discussed in the last section as an important key to communication based on the idea that we should seek first to understand others. However, because communication is a continuous and reciprocal process, it is also important that coaches seek to be understood. Coaches impart huge amounts of information in running their programs and interacting with athletes, so it is critical that they strive to enhance their effectiveness in speaking to others.

Thus, the next step to becoming a Credible Communicator is to be effective in speaking and sending messages to others (see Figure 4.3). To keep it simple, think of the acronym PITCH for effective sending skills. To be a Credible Communicator, your messages should be Productive, Informational, Timed, Consistent, and Honest. In other words, PITCH it! In this section, we'll talk about each component of being an effective PITCHer.

Productive

A key mental skill is productive thinking, and productive thinking stems from productive communication. Thus, the first step in sending effective messages to your athletes is to make your messages *productive*. Communicating productively means managing your emotions when talking to your athletes. It means that you communicate the attitude, commitment, and beliefs that you want the athletes in your program to have. It means that you are thoughtful in the words you use with athletes, that you choose these words carefully so that they have meaning and are credible with your athletes.

An interesting research study asked collegiate gymnasts what qualities they felt were most important for coaches to be effective leaders (Massimo, 1973). The most important quality identified by the athletes was "minimal verbiage," which was rated ahead of technical competency and understanding of team dynamics. Overcoaching, such as talking constantly, takes away from being a credible communicator. Athletes begin to use listening blocks because they've learned that overly verbal coaches talk all the time, and although there may be useful information in the communication, there is also a lot of unnecessary verbiage that is not productive for the athletes.

Personal Plug-In

Thoughtfully reflect on how productive you are at sending messages to others. Identify your strengths and weaknesses. Do you talk too fast, babble when nervous, use complicated words so that athletes lack understanding, yell when emotional, or tend to always be negative and critical? Be honest in your assessment, and then attempt to enhance your sending skills by working on your limitations.

Another block to being a productive communicator is negativity. A negative communication approach means that your typical pattern in sending messages is to focus on problems and the negative aspects of a situation. Nothing hurts team morale and athletes' motivation like a negative coach. Of course there are times when it is highly appropriate to provide critical feedback and/or to firmly confront athletes whose behavior is detrimental to their own development and the development of the team. However, coaches that are constantly negative quickly lose credibility with their athletes. Most of us prefer to be around people who are productive thinkers, who understand and acknowledge problems and setbacks, but who focus on solutions and moving forward instead of dwelling on negative issues.

Mary Harvey, goalkeeper on the U.S. Women's Soccer Team who won the 1991 World Cup, gave up an easy goal just before halftime to tie up the score 1-1. Instead of berating her or questioning her about what happened on the goal, Coach Tony DiCicco simply talked to her about the upcoming second half and what she should focus on to prepare for that half

of play. A year later, Harvey told her coach: "I never told you this, but at halftime, when you didn't mention the mistake I made and simply told me what I needed to do in the second half, well, that had an unbelievable impact on me. It gave me a lot of confidence and allowed me to focus on the second half" (DiDicco et al., 2002, p. 101). Don't point out or dwell on the obvious when athletes make dumb mistakes. It only focuses on the negative, so a better strategy is to brush the mistake aside by focusing on what the athlete can now do to perform well. A good strategy is to develop a *mistake ritual* for your team, which is a common gesture coaches and athletes make after mistakes to indicate that it's over, things are okay, and it's time to move on with the performance. Examples include conveying "no sweat" by wiping two fingers across your brow as if wiping sweat away, "brush off" by brushing your hand across your shoulder to brush away the mistake, and "wave goodbye" in softball and baseball by taking off your cap momentarily as if to wave away the mistake prior to putting the hat back on (Thompson, 2003). Ask your team to develop their own signature mistake ritual—it really works!

Productive communicators inspire athletes to think and respond more productively in their training and in competition. Modeling is a powerful process, and you'll find that by working to make your communication as productive as possible, athletes pick up on this and become productive thinkers themselves. Developing the Inner Edge in your athletes starts with the messages they hear from you every day. Your messages can inspire them and make them feel valued, which makes major deposits in your emotional bank account with them, and enhances their commitment and performance. When Jimmy Johnson took over as coach of the Dallas Cowboys following a season in which they won only one game, he instituted a policy of productive thinking and speaking that was expected of the entire team. When reporters queried Coach Johnson and players about the previous season, they refused to talk about it. Their focus was on moving forward and thinking productively about building a successful team. Three years later, they won the Super Bowl, culminating in an incredible rebuilding process that was founded upon productive thinking and attitude about preparation and success.

Informational

The second key in PITCHing to your athletes is to send messages high in *information*. Think again about whom you listen to and why you listen to them. People gain credibility with us by sending informative messages. Get right to it. Provide the information that your athletes need to learn and excel in clear and concise language. A good check for yourself is to evaluate each of your messages by asking the question, "Did this message allow the listener to learn something of value?" Effective coaches send information-rich messages to their athletes that allow them to learn and get better. Consider the following quote by a U.S. Olympian talking about the difference in the information he received from his college coach and his Olympic coach:

> *"I'm from a well-run program. If the other team was coming at you with a [certain strategy], our [college] coach would say, 'All right, they're coming at you with this, so we'll do this.' Here, you get, 'You guys are going to have to get your butts in gear.' So you're sitting there thinking, 'Okay, how should I interpret that? It's been disappointing. I expected to learn a lot and I haven't'* (Swift, 1988, pp. 54-58).

Obviously, the athlete in this example was disappointed by the lack of specific information provided to him, which prevented him from learning and excelling. Feedback is informative when it is specific and linked to observable behaviors. General praise like "good job" is common in sport, but positive reinforcement and performance feedback are more effective when they are linked to specific behaviors. Remember that your expectations of your athletes can influence your communication with them, so focus on providing all your athletes with informative instruction and feedback.

Time It

As they say, timing is everything. An important consideration in sending messages effectively is the element of *time*. Several aspects of timing should be considered in communication. You only get one chance to make a first impression. Whenever you are speaking to someone or to a group, the first minute of your message is the most important. It is within this minute that you establish credibility as a speaker. I find it helpful to plan very carefully for the first few remarks I will make and how I will say them. I focus on exactly what I want to say and how to say it, and I even practice!

A general guideline for effective communication is to deliver messages immediately. This is particularly important in providing feedback, so that information is conveyed immediately to athletes so they can improve. Communicating immediately is also a good guideline to follow when you need to deal with conflict or engage in a difficult conversation with someone. However, take your *emotional temperature* and if you cannot communicate productively, it is best to wait until you can effectively manage your emotions prior to speaking. Likewise, observe the emotional condition of your athletes. I found that after tough losses in competition, it is often better to wait until the next day at practice to expect athletes to engage in a productive discussion about their performance. Think of these as "nonteachable moments" (Thompson, 2003), which are times when it is hard for people to hear and receive criticism or technical instruction. So no matter how well-intended your comments may be, avoid giving feedback, particularly critical feedback, in nonteachable moments.

Another guideline found in the leadership literature about the timing of communication is to praise publicly and criticize privately. I agree this is a good rule of thumb for coaches, because it emphasizes that the intent of the critical feedback is to help athletes realize their potential, not to humiliate them in front of others. We've all read public accounts of coaches who use public humiliation as a means of motivation. This approach is the familiar jug-and-mug motivational myth discussed in Chapter 3, and it is based on faulty logic because it assumes that the athlete does not want to excel and needs to be publicly chastised to become motivated. Whether or not you praise and criticize in private or public, the most important point is to view your feedback as a learning resource, not as a means of coercion to get people to do things that they don't necessarily want to do. This type of "motivation" is short-lived and inefficiently fuels athletes.

Consistent

The "C" in PITCH represents the need to be a *consistent* communicator. People whose communication patterns change according to their moods and whims are ineffective communicators and leaders. Coaches should clarify expectations for their athletes and communicate consistently based on these expectations. Inconsistent feedback from coaches creates anxiety in athletes and destroys team morale. An important part of a coach's consistency is the need to repeatedly clarify the team mission and goals. Martens' (1987) notes that coaches should be optimally redundant, meaning that certain messages should be provided over and over because of their importance to the team's success. By consistently reinforcing desired athlete behaviors, you are increasing the probability that these behaviors will be repeated. Focus on catching people doing things right, as opposed to adopting a negative communication approach in which the focus is on catching people doing things wrong.

Another important part of consistent communication is to make your verbal and nonverbal messages congruent. Ask a friend or family member to describe your nonverbal tendencies to you. Often, we are unaware of our body language or facial expressions, and sometimes that communicates the

Photo by Brett Hansbauer

wrong messages to athletes. For example, if you verbally support an athlete who just made a crucial mental error, your body language and facial expression should be congruent with your supportive message. Read over the list of body language messages in Table 4.1—can you think of others? Body language in the form of body positioning and gestures makes up 55% of a message, so keep in mind that over half of what you're trying to say is being said with your body (McKay et al., 1983).

A good guideline to follow in making your communication consistent is to make your feedback contingent. Praise from the coach should be earned by athletes for such things as quality performance, outstanding effort, critical leadership, and mental toughness. Noncontingent praise given glibly, without any link to the athlete's behavior, lessens your credibility as a communicator and often makes athletes feel manipulated and less confident in their abilities.

Finally, make your messages consistent by avoiding double messages. If you're explaining to your tennis player that she will not play in the team doubles matches because of her lack of effort in practice, don't say things like, "I know you're a good player, but…" or "I hate to do this, but . . ." or "You're a terrific tennis player, but . . ." Keep the information clear and consistent by explaining the rationale for your decision. Double messages confuse athletes and block the process of communication.

Honest

The final letter "H" in PITCHing, or being an effective sender, stands for *honest* communication. The importance of authenticity as a foundation for communication effectiveness was discussed previously, and authenticity means that you are honest in the messages you send to others. Coaches who lack credibility with their athletes are often accused of having hidden agendas. Hidden agendas, termed **meta-messages,** are *messages whose real purpose is not conveyed verbally, but hidden in the nonverbal content of the message.* These messages are delivered to others when we lack the authenticity and courage to directly say what we really mean.

Meta-messages are recognized through **paralanguage,** which is *the vocal component of a person's speech, including pitch, resonance, articulation, tempo, volume, and rhythm* (McKay et al., 1983). Paralanguage refers to how you say it, not what you say.

Through paralanguage, you unintentionally betray your moods, emotions, thoughts, and the true intent of your message. Thus, a meta-message is delivered when you intentionally alter the rhythm or pitch of your voice for emphasis. Consider the following meta-messages embedded within seemingly innocent statements:

- "It's only a game."
- "Come on, relax!"
- "Are you still here?"
- "I was merely making a point."

Table 4.1 **Body Language 101 for Coaches**	
Body Position	**Body Message**
slumped	fatigue, embarrassment
tall, erect posture	confidence, enthusiasm
learn forward	interest, openness, empathy
lean away	lack of interest
closed body (legs/arms crossed)	defensiveness
hands locked behind head	superiority
rub neck	frustration
tug ear/rub nose	anxious to speak
sitting across desk from athlete	distance; separating self

What other meta-messages have you received from others?

Credible Communicators speak openly and honestly, and they are confident enough to own their own messages, without having to resort to sarcastic meta-messages. Avoid using sarcasm and directly and honestly speak your mind. Your athletes will view you as authentic and trust you and the messages you send them.

Quotable Quote

"I never give 'em hell. I just tell the truth and they think it is hell."

President Harry S. Truman

Managing Conflict

We've now identified the first four key components to becoming a Credible Communicator: authenticity, emotional competence, power listening, and PITCHING, or sending effective messages. As you can see in Figure 4.3, the final characteristic needed to be a Credible Communicator is the ability to manage conflict effectively. Conflict is uncomfortable to most people, but conflict is inevitable within sport teams. Thus, conflict should be viewed as a normal and, strangely, even *welcome* part of an athletic program, because it indicates that the group is committed to achieving difficult goals. Teams that experience little or no conflict may lack passion for their achievement goals. What is critical are the ways in which coaches, athletes, and teams resolve conflict. In this section, suggestions are provided for coaches to help them enhance their effectiveness in confrontations and managing conflict.

Approaches to Conflict Management

When dealing with conflict, there are many behavioral approaches that coaches can adopt. As shown in Figure 4.4, there are five approaches to managing conflict (adapted from Guilar, 2001). *Avoidance* is typically a disastrous approach, and as shown on the grid, it shows a lack of concern for others and yourself. Avoiding conflict only makes it fester within a team, become a bigger problem, and create other problems and discontent. Avoidance may be useful when the issue is a trivial one or when coaches feel that it would be advantageous for athletes' development to resolve conflict on their own. *Competition* is another unproductive approach to conflict management because, although one side wins, the other side does not. Competing in dealing with conflict seems antithetical to effective communication within teams, because the intent is to be right, as opposed to finding a win-win solution or at least an acceptable solution. *Accommodation* is a passive, give-in approach that often results from a lack of assertiveness. Athletes and teams will not grow and develop into mature, cohesive units using such approaches as avoidance, competition, and accommodation, although at times each of these approaches might be warranted.

Obviously, the best approach is *collaboration*, which requires (a) open and emotionally competent communication, (b) empathy, and (c) a commitment to the goals of the team by all involved. Collaboration differs from *compromise*, in which two parties simply agree to half the benefits. Compromise feels like a retreat or half-victory, whereas collabora-

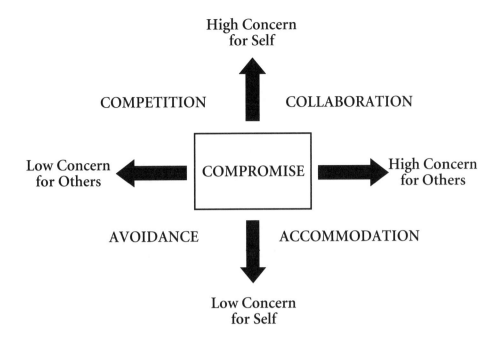

Figure 4.4 Approaches to conflict management

tion feels like working together to think outside the box to identify a new solution that serves everyone.

Consider how the different types of conflict resolution could be used in the following situation. Three seniors on a college volleyball team are resented by their teammates because they are so vocal and demanding in preseason training. The underclassmen on the team feel that the seniors are negative and too demanding. They begin to resent the seniors, which results in ineffective communication and low team morale. Avoiding the issue would be a bad choice, because it is not something that will simply go away. The coach could meet with each group (seniors and the underclassmen) to hear them out and decide which side is right. This creates competition, which could create even more resentment and divisiveness. The team could meet, air their differences, and then agree to each try to get along better. However, this type of compromise doesn't really move the team forward. A collaborative approach would be to create an honest team discussion about the ways in which teammates are communicating with each, why this occurs, and how individuals feel about it. The outcome from this collaboration is that the athletes understand each better, and realize that the conflict is simply the result of the team's commitment to their goals of winning and playing well.

It is useful to understand these different approaches, and to consider which ones work best in different situations. Avoidance, accommodation, and compromise are quicker and easier than collaboration, but collaboration can build strong team cohesion and confidence that any obstacles can be surmounted by working together. Read the stories written about the 1980 U.S. Men's Olympic Ice Hockey team that won the gold medal in Lake Placid, the 1999 U.S. Women's Soccer Team that won the World Cup, and the 1996 U.S. Women's Olympic Basketball team that won the gold medal in Atlanta. Each of these teams demonstrated outstanding communication abilities to resolve the typical and atypical conflicts that arose within their teams using collaborative methods, which made them stronger, more cohesive, and more resilient.

For conflict to be of value, your team must first consider it valuable and necessary, and then understand that they are expected to engage in effective communication to resolve conflict in collaborative ways. Does your team need or have conflict resolution strategies? Consider these questions:

- How does your team handle conflict now? Is it encouraged, accepted, understood, and expected? Or is it avoided, hushed up, buried, and feared?

- Does your team tend to always handle conflict in the same way, or do you have a variety of methods or strategies for dealing with different types of conflict that may arise?
- Are these strategies working? Why or why not? How might conflict resolution be improved within your team?

A Communication Strategy for Resolving Conflict: The Four "Olves"

A basic formula to use in resolving conflict on a team is the four "olves:" invOLVE, resOLVE, absOLVE, and evOLVE. First, *involve* team members in discussing problems or conflicts as they arise. Second, *resolve* the conflict expeditiously, professionally, rationally, and equitably. This resolution should include input from the initial involvement of athletes. Effective conflict resolution requires a quick and accurate identification of the problem, followed by an immediate shift in attention toward identifying solutions to the problem. Often, people get fixated on their problems and spend valuable time and energy complaining, as opposed to focusing on possible solutions. Spend time and energy where it counts—on considering various ways to solve problems. Third, move on with the team agenda to demonstrate that the athletes responsible for the conflict are *absolved* of any continuing guilt. Once conflict is resolved, it should be over, and athletes should not be treated like they are in the "doghouse." Finally, help the team understand that conflict can be useful to help us grow and learn, so the team should *evolve* from the conflict as stronger, smarter, more experienced, and more cohesive.

Photo courtesy of UT Lady Vol Media Relations

As a coach, discuss the inevitability of conflict, and even its value, on a team. Ask your athletes to accept conflict, and to recognize it as a necessary part of pursuing and achieving difficult goals. Explain the ways in which you would like to see conflict resolved in your team, which might include such things as the role of team captains, the involvement of all team members, the need for personal responsibility, and a commitment to open and mature communication within the team. Orlick (1986a) provides several good ideas for team conflict resolution and management, including expecting athletes to stay expressive within training and competition (no clamming up or pouting when things go wrong), stating intent to teammates prior to offering critical feedback, and focusing on the intent of the coaches to improve their skills when receiving critical feedback from them. Athletes should develop and practice specific behavioral routines for receiving critical feedback during competition (adapted from Orlick, 1986a):

1. Exhale deeply and relax your body.
2. Interpret the feedback and think "what do I need to do?" (Be receptive and learn!).
3. Visualize the correct image of performance (feel and see the correct performance).

There are many specific strategies that you can implement to fit your coaching philosophy and the motivational needs of your athletes. Overall, the intent is to plan and act systemically with regard to conflict, so that the focus is on how problems arise and how they are resolved as opposed to placing blame and personalizing conflict. Teach your athletes how to think about and respond to conflict,

---

Personal Plug-In

1. Identify a current or past conflict in which you were involved.
2. Reflect on your behavior in this conflict, and write down the name of the conflict management approach that you used.
3. Was this approach successful? If not, what other approach might have been more successful and why?
4. Brainstorm specific examples within a sport team for the effective use of each approach.

model effective conflict resolution yourself as the coach, and then set team expectations for mature, rational, personally responsible communication that is always needed to turn uncomfortable conflict into collaborative team growth.

Effective Confrontations

Effective conflict management requires effective confrontation skills. **Confrontations** are *face-to-face discussions with individuals with whom you are experiencing conflict*. Confrontation skills are the specific communication skills needed to successfully resolve conflict. Coaches must constantly confront athletes in their attempts to motivate them. However, the purpose of confrontations is not to display power or put athletes in their places, rather to help them examine their behavior and the consequences of that behavior. Confrontations occur continuously in an intense achievement culture like sport and should be viewed as necessary and even facilitative to athletes becoming the best they can be.

Most people don't enjoy confrontations, but coaches and others in leadership positions must confront athletes on a regular basis. Avoiding or delaying confrontations only aggravates the tension that needs to be resolved. Here are some guidelines to consider in enhancing your confrontation skills as a coach:

Personal Plug-In

Identify several issues that typically create confrontations in sport between coaches and athletes. Then, identify issues that often create confrontations between teammates. How should these confrontations be resolved?

Quotable Quote

"You have to be honest with people— brutally honest. You have to tell them the truth about their performance, you have to tell it to them face-to-face, and you have to tell it to them over and over again. Sometimes the truth will be painful, and sometimes saying it will lead to an uncomfortable confrontation. So be it. The only way to change people is to tell them in the clearest possible terms what they're doing wrong. And if they don't want to listen, they don't belong on the team." **Bill Parcells**, head coach of the NFL Dallas Cowboys

---

- Describe the person's behavior. Don't evaluate, command, judge, label, or accuse. Instead of telling an athlete that he is lazy and uncommitted, describe his behavior in the following way: "You've been late to practice twice this week. I've noticed also today and yesterday that you were not putting full effort into the drills. This is a real problem, because you're not fulfilling your responsibilities to the team. Can you tell me what's going on?"

- Remain calm and unemotional no matter what. Even if the other person loses their temper, becomes defensive, or even takes a cheap shot at you, stay cool. Respond professionally, and demonstrate that your intent is to help the other person, not to put them down or win an argument. If you are verbally attacked, focus on responding to the person's words, not reacting to his or her emotional outburst. Use silence effectively to keep things calm, and be deliberate and thoughtful in your responses. Attempt to move the conversation away from personal issues toward professional interests that you both have at stake (e.g., success of the team).

- Nail it. Be concrete and concise in your description of the person's behavior. Your communication approach should be assertive, not aggressive, but certainly not passive. Stick to your point.

- Communicate with empathy. Demonstrate that you understand the other person's feelings and perspective. This is not to let them off the hook, but to communicate understanding to them. However, just because you understand their feelings does not mean that you will accept or condone their behavior. It is important to be empathic, but at the same time remain tough.

- Mentally prepare for any confrontation by focusing on the proper motivation for the confrontation. We confront people to reach helpful resolutions, not to get back at them, put them down, or show them that we're right and they're wrong. Avoid sarcasm and meta-messages—be authentic and honest in your words.

Wrapping Up

Because communication is the most important human skill, it is the most important coaching skill. I hope that as you read this chapter, you were constantly reflecting on your own communication style. Communication is a fundamental human skill that we can all improve every day of our lives. It's no accident that many of the master coaches of our time are innovative communicators.

Remember the communication basics and especially that you as a coach simply cannot not communicate. The influence of your communication on your athletes is more powerful than you've probably even realized. Maintain high expectations for all your athletes, and develop your PITCHing skills by sending messages to them that are productive, informative, timely, consistent, and honest. Work on your Power Listening skills every day, even though listening is an exhaustive exercise. Remember that power listening makes large deposits in the emotional bank accounts you have established with your athletes, so it's well worth the effort. And finally, embrace and welcome conflict as a sign of personal growth and commitment to achievement. Practice your confrontation skills so that you can manage conflict effectively in your leadership role as the coach. Remain a student of effective communication your entire life—it will pay huge dividends and lead to more fulfilling relationships with others.

Summary Points for Chapter 4

1. Communication is the process by which we understand others and, in turn, seek to be understood by them.
2. Athletes rate the quality of coach-athlete relationships and the ability to communicate as more important than coaches' technical knowledge and skills.
3. Communication includes content and delivery dimensions, thus coaches should work to understand their nonverbal communication skills.
4. Coaches' expectations of and communication to their athletes can act as self-fulfilling prophecies for the performance and psychological development of their athletes.
5. Authenticity and emotional competence are the building blocks for becoming a Credible Communicator.
6. Typical blocks to listening include mind reading, prejudging, filtering, advice giving, identifying, being right, defensiveness, and rehearsing.
7. The four steps in Power Listening are preparing, attending, understanding, and responding.
8. Effective messages are productive, informative, timely, consistent, and honest.
9. Approaches to conflict management include avoidance, competition, accommodation, compromise, and collaboration.
10. Conflict is a natural, inevitable, and even valued occurrence within sport teams.
11. Effective confrontations require describing behavior, being clear and concise, remaining unemotional, displaying empathy, and motivation to help others or solve problems.

Glossary

attending: having a single-minded focus on the speaker, and actively communicating that focus to him or her during the entire conversation

communication: the process by which we understand others, and in turn, endeavor to be understood by them

confrontation: a face-to-face discussion with an individual or group with whom you are experiencing conflict

self-fulfilling prophecy theory: the expectations that coaches form about the ability of individual athletes can serve as prophecies that dictate or determine the level of achievement each athlete will ultimately reach

Study Questions

1. Why are the communication skills of coaches viewed as more important to athletes than coaches' technical knowledge and skills?
2. Explain communication as a process. Provide a positive example of how the process works, as well as a negative example of how it may break down.
3. Explain why nonverbal communication is so powerful.

4. Identify and provide examples for the four steps in the coaching expectancy process (self-fulfilling prophecy). Generate five practical guidelines that coaches can follow to avoid the negative expectancy effect with their athletes.
5. Why is the emotional competence of the coach a foundation for communication?
6. Define the seven typical listening blocks used by coaches.
7. Outline the four key steps in Power Listening, and provide examples for how you successfully complete each step.
8. What are some guidelines you should follow in receiving feedback from others?
9. What does the acronym PITCH represent? Identify and explain, using examples, each characteristic of effective sending.
10. Identify a typical or recent conflict that you experienced on a sport team. Explain how this conflict would be resolved using the five approaches discussed in the chapter. Which approach works best in this situation and why?
11. Identify a situation in which you as a coach must confront an athlete. Describe the communication behaviors you would engage in to make this confrontation successful.

Reflective Learning Activities

1. Check your Credible Communication Score! (adapted from Feldman, 1999)

a. Take a self-reflective moment and honestly respond to each of the questions below, which assess different aspects of communication important to coaches.

	not at all	rarely	some-times	often	very often	always
1. It is easy for me to recognize what emotions I am experiencing.	1	2	3	4	5	6
2. I understand and appreciate my athletes' feelings.	1	2	3	4	5	6
3. People tell me I'm hard to talk to.	1	2	3	4	5	6
4. I tend not to listen to people with whom I disagree or dislike.	1	2	3	4	5	6
5. It's hard to understand why others feel the way they do.	1	2	3	4	5	6
6. It's easy to talk honestly and openly to others about myself.	1	2	3	4	5	6
7. I am able to receive negative feedback without getting defensive.	1	2	3	4	5	6
8. I think about the emotions behind my actions.	1	2	3	4	5	6
9. I pay attention to the feelings, thoughts, and actions of others.	1	2	3	4	5	6
10. I try for a win-win solution whenever I speak or act.	1	2	3	4	5	6
11. I tend to react very emotionally when provoked.	1	2	3	4	5	6
12. I daydream when I should be listening.	1	2	3	4	5	6
13. When athletes talk to me, I always give advice or try to solve their problems.	1	2	3	4	5	6
14. I take my emotional temperature before making important decisions.	1	2	3	4	5	6
15. I am able to speak my mind without getting others upset.	1	2	3	4	5	6
16. I say what I'm feeling no matter how it will impact others.	1	2	3	4	5	6

	not at all	rarely	some-times	often	very often	always
17. When I feel angry, I can remain composed and speak rationally.	1	2	3	4	5	6
18. I am careful in conversations to present myself so that others approve of me.	1	2	3	4	5	6
19. When I feel I know the message a speaker is trying to get across, I stop listening and consider my response.	1	2	3	4	5	6
20. It's hard for me to realize when I am experiencing different emotions.	1	2	3	4	5	6
21. It's difficult for me to consider various options when I am frustrated or angry.	1	2	3	4	5	6
22. I am happy to let my athletes know the real me.	1	2	3	4	5	6
23. It is easy for me to understand how my athletes feel, and to let them know I understand.	1	2	3	4	5	6
24. My athletes would tell you that they don't really know me.	1	2	3	4	5	6

b. Score your responses by totaling the subscale scores listed below. "R" listed next to an item number means that you reverse score that item (1=6, 2=5, 3=4, 4=3, 5=2, 6=1).

Self-Awareness
(Recognizing your emotions and knowing
the reason behind them)   _____   Items 1, 8, 14, 20R

Authenticity
(Being comfortable with who you are and
in sharing that with others)   _____   Items 6, 18R, 22, 24R

Emotional Control
(Managing emotions effectively and
resisting impulses to act emotionally)   _____   Items 7, 11R, 17, 21R

Empathy
(Understanding the feelings of others)   _____   Items 2, 5R, 9, 23

Power Listening
(Attending to content and validating
speaker)   _____   Items 4R, 12R, 13R, 19R

Communicating with Flexibility
(Addressing your and others' needs;
being adaptable in conversations)   _____   Items 3R, 10, 15, 16R

c. What do you notice about your scores? Where are your communication strengths and weaknesses? Consider ways that you can specifically work to enhance your skills in areas of need.
(Complete questionnaire individually; then discuss for 10 minutes with a partner.)

2. Ask a Friend

a. Sit down with a family member, close friend, coworker, or assistant coach (someone that you trust and value) and ask them the following questions about their observations and perceptions of your communication style. This person should know that they can be completely honest without upsetting you.

1. What are my communication strengths?
2. What are things that you notice that would make me a better communicator?
3. How well do I explain things and/or send information to others?
4. How could my sending skills be enhanced?
5. Describe my typical nonverbal behavior when (speaking/listening/receiving feedback, managing conflict).
6. Describe any interpersonal habits or gestures that I have when communicating with others.
7. Thank your partner sincerely for being honest and helping you understand your communication behaviors.

b. Reflect on what you've learned from your partner in this exercise. How do the findings from this exercise relate to the self-evaluation you completed in the previous exercise?

(Discuss in groups of 3 for 15 minutes—then share insights with whole group for 10 more minutes).

3. How's Your "D"? (adapted from Guilar, 2001)

Defensiveness is an emotional reaction where one feels attacked and vulnerable. It is a natural response, but not a productive one. Defensiveness occurs when we react emotionally, instead of responding rationally. Defensiveness blocks communication!

Identify a conversation in which you acted defensively. In the space below, briefly describe this incident. Then recall your emotional and behavioral reaction. Finally, consider how you might have responded more effectively in this situation.

A critical incident where I felt attacked or vulnerable:

_____

_____

_____

Your experience of the conversation—your emotional and communicative reaction:

_____

_____

_____

How you could have responded more effectively:

_____

_____

_____

4. The Hot Seat (Hargrove, 1995)

a. The purpose of this exercise is to allow members of a group to practice giving feedback to others. Divide into groups of 8-10 people (entire teams can do it at once) and sit theatre style with one chair front and center (the hot seat). Provide some general guidelines about giving and receiving feedback:

When giving feedback:
- Be direct—don't sugar-coat.
- PITCH it.
- Focus on changeable behavior, not personalities.

When receiving feedback:
- Sit with arms and legs uncrossed.
- Be a power listener.
- Listen with the intent to learn something new.
- Acknowledge that you got the feedback and appreciate it.

b. One person from each group goes to the Hot Seat and each person in the group gives him or her feedback based on the following examples (use alternative questions to fit your needs):

1. "One thing I appreciate about you is . . ."
2. "One thing I find difficult about you is . . ."
3. "One thing I want to create with you is . . ."

c. People giving feedback should demonstrate care and generosity of spirit, and the person in the hot seat is asked not to speak except at the end to acknowledge the feedback. Once everyone in the group has had a turn in the hot seat, the groups should discuss what they experienced and what they can extract from the exercise.

5. Personal Shield *(adapted from Rohnke & Butler, 1995)*

a. The purpose of this exercise is to challenge participants to engage in authentic self-reflection as to who they are and what they are about, and to practice speaking to others in an open manner about themselves.

b. Reproduce the shields shown in Appendix 4A. Give each participant the instructions shield and the blank shield, and ask them to create their personal shield to visually represent who they are. Emphasize that artistic quality is not a necessity! Emphasize the importance of authenticity and challenge participants to put thoughtful self-reflection into the development of their shields.

c. Participants then share their personal shield with others in small groups of 4 or with the entire group if appropriate. The exercise can be done in 5-10 minutes or could take longer depending on the size of the group. It works best to give participants a day or two to create their shield before presenting them.

6. Face-Off!

a. In groups of three, identify a situation in which a coach must confront an athlete to resolve an important issue. One person acts as the athlete, the second person as the coach, and the third person as the observer. The coach confronts the athlete about the issue, attempting to use the effective confrontation skills presented in the chapter. The observer takes notes and provides feedback to the coach at the completion of the role-playing situation.

b. Choose two additional issues and rotate roles so that each group member plays the coach and practices his or her confrontation skills. Allow 20-25 minutes for the entire exercise.

Chapter

Five

Leadership

Chapter Preview

In this chapter, you'll learn:
- the meaning of transformative leadership
- myths about leadership
- the three-ring circus model of leadership
- the five essential leadership hats all coaches must wear

"Leadership . . . I'm not sure how to define it, but I know it when I see it." **Dwight D. Eisenhower**, former U.S. President and Five Star General

"If I accept you as you are, I will make you worse. However, if I treat you as though you are what you are capable of becoming, I help you become that." **Goethe**

In the previous three chapters, philosophy, motivation, and communication were presented as important building blocks in gaining the Inner Edge. In this chapter, we'll discuss leadership, which is the fourth critical foundation upon which to build and sustain optimal sport performance, development, and experiences for your athletes. In particular, we'll focus on the importance of transformative leadership, which goes beyond managerial tasks such as evaluating performance, organizing groups, and controlling resources. Transformative leaders operate outside the boundaries of organizationally defined procedures to *transform* the sport environment in innovative ways to inspire, motivate, and refresh others in the environment. Actress Marlene Dietrich spoke admiringly about the transformative leadership style of legendary director Orson Welles by saying, "When I have seen him and talked with him, I feel like a plant that has been watered."

In sport psychology, much of the theory and research on leadership is directed toward coaches, as they are the most obvious leaders in sport. Thus, much of the discussion in this chapter will focus on coaches as leaders. However, the perspectives on leadership discussed in this chapter readily apply to developing leadership in athletes, so they may help their teammates achieve the Inner Edge. And beyond coaches transforming athletes and athletes transforming teams, leadership skills are usefully applied to self-leadership. Although rarely discussed, self-leadership involves applying transformative leader-like behaviors to our own lives to achieve self-fulfillment. To use Marlene Dietrich's metaphor of the plant, skilled self-leaders water themselves daily! Effective leadership from all of these perspectives enhances the quality of sport participation by balancing the sport psychology triad to enhance athletes' performance, development, and experiences.

Leadership Lingo

Leadership may be defined as *the behavioral, psychological, and social process of influencing individuals to move toward the achievement of specific objectives.* The behavioral aspect of leadership is commonly understood—we recognize leaders because they act like leaders. Like Eisenhower said, we know it when we see it. The social aspect of leadership is probably the next most common way of recognizing leadership—leaders create a social environment whereby individuals can thrive in their pursuit of team goals. For example, a coach can establish a strong tradition of success built on commitment and effort to influence athletes to work hard even when the coach is not physically present. The psychological aspect of leadership is the least understood process and the most intriguing. This has to do with personal charisma, and how leaders get people to do what they want them to do. How did Hitler convince thousands of German citizens to participate in horrific crimes against humanity in the Holocaust? Why are some coaches so gifted in inspiring athletes to become deeply committed to achieving excellence in their sport?

Transformative vs. Transactional Leadership

The fact that our definition of leadership includes behavioral, social, and psychological processes emphasizes the transformative nature of effective leadership. **Transformative leadership** *involves altering people's frames of reference or ways of thinking so as to produce profound shifts in their perceptions and ways of being, living, and responding* (Hargrove, 1995). To transform means to change one form of energy into another, or to change the condition, nature and function of something. Electric transformers change a voltage of a certain type of electricity into a more useful form of energy. Effective leaders in sport are *transformers* (some are more electric than others!). They help athletes transform their raw, undisciplined energy into a refined focus which enables them to pursue and achieve important goals. Transformative leaders also change the isolated energies of individuals into a productive interactive group form of energy where the pursuit of goals is a shared responsibility and team commitment.

This is in contrast to traditional, or **transactional, leadership** whereby *leaders influence followers via behavioral transactions such as providing resources or doling out rewards and punishments.* Consider the following differences between transformational and transactional leaders:

- Transactional leaders have subordinates; transformative leaders attract willing followers.
- Transactional leaders are given their position; transformative leaders take the initiative to lead.
- Transactional leaders operate safely within the status quo; transformative leaders take risks to achieve great things and challenge the status quo.
- Transactional leaders have ascribed influence based on formal authority; transformative leaders develop influence based on their competence.
- Transactional leaders are concerned with the physical environment; transformative leaders are concerned with the social and psychological environments as well.
- Transactional leaders rely on tradition and bureaucratic procedure; transformative leaders rely on vision, logic, and intuition.

Traditional, or transactional leaders, are typically managers. Clearly, managerial duties are part of any coach's position in the form of organizing, scheduling, budgeting, and allocating resources. Coaches may also act like managers when they use behavior modification techniques to provide rewards and apply punishment with the intent of enhancing the performance of their subordinates. But true leadership—especially transformative leadership—involves much more than managing schedules, budgets, resources, and rewards and punishments. Successful coaches fulfill the managerial

Photo courtesy of WVU Photographic Services

duties that are part of their overall responsibilities, yet they evoke excellence in their athletes through their transformative leadership skills.

Transformative leadership involves helping people (athletes and others) transform themselves and their world. It involves significantly influencing people's visions and values as well as enhancing their performance. The key to the transformative process is that it expands people's capacity to be effective for themselves, as opposed to relying on the actions of the leader to make them effective. We all can think back to a special coach, teacher, or mentor who touched our lives by helping us envision new possibilities or choices and the ability to perform and achieve at a level we never could have imagined.

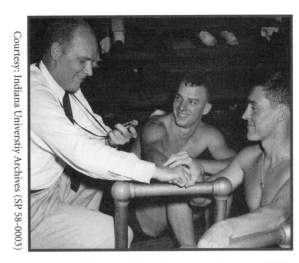

Courtesy: Indiana University Archives (SP 58-0003)

Clipboard

James "Doc" Counsilman: A Transformative Leader

James "Doc" Counsilman, legendary swimming coach at Indiana University, won 288 meets in 33 years (1958-1990) against only 37 losses. He won six straight NCAA Championships, 23 Big Ten titles, had 18 undefeated seasons, and coached two Olympic teams. He also swam the English Channel at age 58. But indisputably, what made Counsilman the consummate transformative leader was his commitment to new ideas and learning. He was the primary authority on the mechanics of his sport, writing three books on swimming technique that were translated into over 20 languages. He introduced interval training to swimming, developed pace clocks for the training, and even invented the pool bottom markers now used in pools worldwide. He studied physics to better understand principles of propulsion and employed underwater cameras to study and improve upon new swimming techniques. Counsilman personally designed each piece of equipment in the swimmer's weight room at Indiana, which were specially designed to accommodate forces like inertia and were the first of their kind based on isokinetic theory.

Counsilman's coaching philosophy was built around eight basic elements: caring for his athletes, consistency in communicating with athletes, emphasizing acceptance and belonging for all swimmers on the team, using personal goal setting and feedback to enhance athletes' sense of accomplishment, positive team spirit and commitment to team goals, rewarding and recognizing athletes, enhancing athletes' self-esteem, and challenging athletes during every workout. He became the world's best coach in swimming because he not only *developed* his philosophy, but he had a clear vision of how to *apply* the philosophy.

Bob Knight said at Counsilman's retirement, "I don't think there has ever been a coach in any American collegiate sport that has done more for his sport or more thoroughly dominated his sport than Doc Counsilman" (Isaacson, 1990, pp. 3-10). Former Indiana swimmer, Charles Hickcox, stated, "If IU had not had Doc . . . they might as well have closed the pool" (Walton, 1992, p. 98). Mark Spitz claims he would not have won seven gold medals at the 1972 Olympic Games without the coaching of Doc Counsilman. All of these accolades are ironic considering that one of Counsilman's stated coaching objectives was to avoid conveying the coach as indispensable and to work toward building self-reliance in athletes. Indeed, it is a transformative coach that could build such confidence and self-reliance in his athletes to achieve unprecedented excellence, only to have these athletes give him all the credit in the end.

Transformative leaders have changed the course of history and the world as we know it. Consider the ways that Jesus of Nazareth, Joan of Arc, Adolph Hitler, Martin Luther King, Jr., Franklin Roosevelt, Vladimir Ilyich Lenin, Elizabeth Cady Stanton, and Mohandas Gandhi transformed the world. Although transformative leaders in sport may not change the course of world history, they do strongly influence the quality of the sport experience for thousands of athletes according to their leadership abilities. Consider the transformative coaches mentioned in previous chapters: Vince Lombardi, Pat Summitt, Frosty Westering, Tara VanDerveer, Anson Dorrance, and Joe Paterno. Consider the transformative impact of athletes whose contributions to their sports have gone beyond actual performance such as Billie Jean King, Arthur Ashe, Martina Navratilova, and Jackie Robinson. Consider the impact of transformative leaders within sports teams such as Michael Jordan, Diana Taurasi, Joe Montana, Carla Overbeck, Karch Kiraly, and Wayne Gretzky, who received the highest compliment in team sport of "making everyone around them play better."

Transformative, or Triple-Loop, Learning

A useful visual model for understanding transformative leadership is illustrated in Figure 5.1 as the process of transformative learning (modified from Hargrove, 1995). The model is based on the point that transformative leadership involves helping athletes learn not only incremental improvement strategies to enhance their performance, but also enabling them to reframe how they think and to even

transform who they are in meaningful and productive ways. Hargrove calls this moving from

- **single-loop learning** (*helping people develop behavioral strategies to improve and perform better*), to
- **double-loop learning** (*helping people to fundamentally reshape the underlying patterns of their thinking and behavior so they are capable of doing different things*), and even
- **triple-loop learning** (*enabling people to create shifts in their context or point of view about themselves and their world*).

Single-loop learning is typically emphasized by transactional leaders, whereby the emphasis is on modifying behavior to gain needed skills and improve in an incremental manner. Helping athletes engage in double-loop learning is a more innovative leadership focus, because this goes beyond mere behavioral change and skill development to challenge

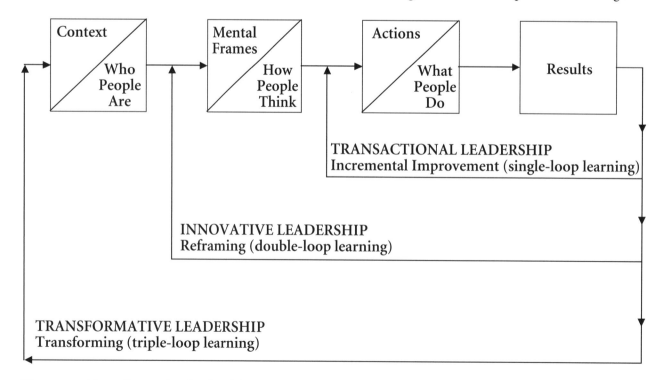

Figure 5.1 Transformative leadership

athletes' current ways of thinking (termed "mental frames") to enable them to think differently. Mental frames are internal pictures or hidden assumptions about the way the world works (Hargrove, 1995). Most people are unaware of their own mental models that shape the way they think and interact. True transformative leadership moves athletes to the level of triple-loop learning to create profound shifts in how they view themselves and the world around them, by challenging people to identify, examine, and improve their mental models.

Personal Plug-In

Can you think of leaders who moved beyond innovative and became even transformative? In considering this, think about HOW these individuals enabled people to engage in double- and triple-loop learning.

Let's use the example of building "character" or sportsmanship to illustrate this concept of single-, double-, and triple-loop learning in relation to leadership in sport. A big issue in youth sport is the development of sportsmanship or "character" in young athletes. A common method used by coaches, parents, and youth sport leaders to facilitate sportsmanship in athletes is by the use of reinforcement (using rewards and punishment) and by emphasizing positive role models who espouse and display sportsmanlike behaviors. In the learning model pictured in Figure 5.1, this would be an example of single-loop learning. Young athletes are rewarded if they display the right behaviors and punished if they display the wrong behaviors in relation to actions such as moral actions, sportsmanlike behavior, and aggression against others. The focus in single-loop learning is on shaping athletes' behavior by focusing on what they *do*. Obviously, coaches must use reinforcers wisely (discussed in Chapter 3) to shape behavior in their athletes and, of course, the behaviors that coaches and other influential adults model are clearly mimicked by young athletes. However, this is just the first step in developing sportsmanship and moral character in people.

More recent approaches to character development focus on helping young athletes reframe their ways of thinking about what is right in terms of behavior in sport (e.g., Miller, Bredemeier, & Shields, 1997). In this approach, the leader engages athletes to think about and discuss moral dilemmas when they arise (e.g., cheating to win, engaging in aggressive play with the goal of harming another), to enable them to reframe their underlying beliefs and values about what is right and wrong. What is important in this approach is that over time, the mind-frame of the children is modified so that they engage in moral actions and exhibit sportsmanship because they believe it is right—NOT to gain rewards or avoid punishment. This is an example of double-loop learning, where young athletes are challenged and enabled to reframe their thinking, which then drives their behavioral actions related to demonstrating "character" in sport.

A commitment to moral principles and integrity can then become internalized through triple-loop learning. In this approach, young athletes move from rewards and punishment (single-loop), to reframing how they think about sport and what constitutes appropriate behavior (double-loop), to now identifying who they are based on a deeply internalized set of values and moral principles (triple-loop). They choose not to cheat or intentionally hurt others, not because they're afraid of getting caught, but because they understand that this hurts other people and degrades the game, and most importantly, because they identify themselves as the type of people who believe in playing fair and upholding the integrity of the game. In this sense, they have evolved and transformed themselves and their points of view about the world and about sport.

Another example of triple-loop, or transformative learning, is seen in the development of athletes within sport programs with strong traditions and norms that enable them to excel through reframing how they think in productive ways as well as internalizing a set of values that defines who they are. The Duke men's basketball program and transformative coach Mike Krzyzewski epitomize how transformative learning occurs in athletes. Carlos Boozer, a Duke player, was asked in 2002 what it means to be a Duke player. He answered, "It means a lot of tradition, a lot of loyalty. We're like a family. The players that came before us, we're kind of representing them, so we have to be aware of the people who came before us. We want to uphold the tradition and keep the excellence of winning going . . . It's something that's bigger than ourselves, and we cherish it" (Perry, 2002, p. D4). Coach Krzyzewski built the

Duke basketball program on transformative leadership, which led Boozer to internalize pride in and commitment to being a Duke basketball player and redefine who he is in a very meaningful way.

In summary, transformative leaders enable people to not only enhance the skills they currently possess (single-loop learning), but also to think in fundamentally different ways so they gain abilities that they were not even aware existed (double-loop learning). And finally, transformative leaders help people make fundamental shifts in their beliefs about themselves and the world around them (triple-loop learning). This change in the context of who one is then influences productive and innovative thinking that leads to productive actions that bring positive results (see Figure 5.1). Consider the transformative influence of legendary coach John Wooden as described by Kareem Abdul-Jabbar: "It is a rare experience to meet an individual who affirms the positive values you were introduced to in childhood . . . You wonder if such values work, and then you encounter an individual like John Wooden and see the success he's had as a person, not just in terms of wins and losses, but as a man trying to live his life with some balance and honor, and then you know it's possible. He was the real thing. His example in my life continues to be bright and shining" (Biro, 1997, p. 157).

How can you as a coach facilitate triple-loop, or transformative, learning in your athletes? Read on. Later in the chapter, various ideas are discussed and suggestions provided to work on becoming a more transformative coach.

Power

Because power is typically associated with leadership, it seems important to define it and clarify its relationship with leadership. The term power is usually associated with force or strength such as the power of an army or a powerful hurricane. **Power** is defined as *the ability to control and influence others*. Sounds a lot like our definition of leadership, doesn't it? However, leadership is more about influence, whereas power is more about control. Power is essential for coaches to move athletes and teams toward their objectives, yet it is greatly distrusted and misunderstood because it is so often misused (Martens, 1987). Coaches often misinterpret their leadership function as being exclusively about authority and control. As discussed later in the chapter, effective

leaders must accept and maintain control, because they are appointed authority figures. But if coaches' only type of influence is their control over others based on their authority, they are not leaders. A common phrase used in sport is the need to earn respect, as opposed to demanding it. Coaches who demand respect, but who do nothing to earn it, will not have the transformer-type abilities to effectively lead their teams. Transformative coaches earn respect from their athletes by demonstrating competence through superior skills and knowledge, and by gaining credibility as a coach who is committed to the team and the well-being of her athletes. Effective coaches use power wisely, and power is then reciprocally gained through their transformative leadership (Jones, Armour, & Potrac, 2004).

Clipboard

Life Lesson

There was a rule against facial hair for players on UCLA basketball teams. Star center Bill Walton showed up one day after a break with a beard. Coach John Wooden asked him, "Bill, have you forgotten something?" Walton replied, "Coach, if you mean the beard, I think I should be allowed to wear it. It's my right." Wooden asked, "Do you believe in it that strongly?" Walton answered, "Yes, I do coach. Very much." Wooden responded very politely and calmly, "Bill, I have a great respect for individuals who stand up for those things in which they believe. I really do. And the team is going to miss you." Walton went into the locker room and shaved off the beard prior to practice (Wooden, 1997, pp. 152-153).

A productive way to think about power is to view it as something that flows from within a person with a strong sense of self (Lynn, 2002). Ultimately, this is the only true power that we have. Yes, you have authority as a coach, but your power is felt by others in the form of confidence, inner strength, or a strong presence. When leaders have this type of true power, it is very obvious to those around them and people are drawn to this power. The true roots of leadership are in this power. It is from here that vision, direction, influence, and inspiration emanate. In the previous Clipboard example, Coach Wooden drew a line in the sand for Bill Walton, and this ultimatum worked in Coach Wooden's favor not because of his authority as coach, but because of the internal power that he had developed as an outstanding coach who believed in his principles and taught his players to do the same thing. It's just that his principle was more important for the team than Walton's on this matter! I believe that Walton understood and accepted that at some level.

A term that is related to power is **empowerment**, which simply means that *you grant power to others by giving them ability or enabling them to effectively accept responsibility*. Transformative coaches empower athletes and staff members to create a collective interactive leadership group to help achieve team goals. Empowerment from transformative coaches is one of the key ways to keep the triad of sport psychology objectives in balance. When you empower athletes, they are more motivated to learn new skills to perform better, they experience more enjoyment from participation, and they develop important self-leadership skills. Peter Stanley, elite British track and field coach, talks about how he perceives his role in serving and empowering his athletes (not vice-versa!):

> *"The worse thing I think I've seen in athletics is when coaches perceive themselves to own their athletes. When I first got into coaching, I called the athletes 'my athletes', and it was only as I grew older that I realized that they were not 'my athletes' but that I was 'their coach.' They actually own me because they are the ones who choose to come and train with me. In effect, they decide whether to use the service I offer or not. So, I have a responsibility to give them everything that I can. It really bugs me when coaches have an almost stranglehold grip on their athletes and won't let them speak or listen to anybody else. I see it as an inadequacy on the behalf of the coach"* (Jones et al., 2004, p. 83).

Leadership Myths

Our society is fascinated with transformative leaders who have stood against incredible odds or took unfathomable risks to achieve great things. Along with this fascination comes the inevitable misconceptions and dogmatic beliefs about leadership that simply are not true. In this section, we'll overview three leadership myths: the Born Leader, the Rah-Rah Leader, and the Formula Leader.

The Born Leader

The Born Leader myth assumes that great leaders are born with the qualities that enable them to lead effectively. Called the "great person" theory of leadership, this myth has been fueled by our cultural fascination with heroes who are distinguished from other mere mortals by having innate superior wisdom, strength, virtue, and/or attractiveness. Individuals assumed to be Born Leaders by society include Abraham Lincoln, Daniel Boone, Susan B. Anthony, Martin Luther King, Jr., Franklin Roosevelt, and most successful, high profile coaches that you know.

But the "great person" theory doesn't hold water as research and popular evidence clearly show that individuals do not become leaders by virtue of the possession of a certain combination of traits that were established at birth. Contrary to our fascination with heroes and the myth of the Born Leader, effective leaders turn out to be normal people like the rest of us. It's just that these people have developed their skills, knowledge, and techniques to be an effective leader in their particular situations. They've worked very hard to develop their philosophy and the behavioral, social, and psychological skills needed to transform their programs into productive and cohesive climates where athletes thrive in developing their skills. Leadership is a skill, and it is a skill that may be developed. Remember, leaders are made, not born, and most typically they are *self-made*.

There is not one set of traits that make one a Born Leader. Becoming a transformative leader involves much more than "having the right stuff" as a birthright—it involves learning and experience and effort in developing leadership ability. Later in the chapter, we'll discuss the roles that leaders must fulfill, and provide suggestions about effective leadership within these roles.

The Rah-Rah Leader

The myth of the Rah-Rah Leader is similar to the jug-and-mug motivational myth described in Chapter 3. This approach to leadership assumes that effective leaders are loud and emotionally intense, and that they motivate athletes through the sheer force of their emotional cheerleading. Can you see the flawed logic behind this notion of leadership, especially as it relates to motivation? The Rah-Rah idea of leadership assumes that

Consider 4-5 famous coaches that you feel are outstanding leaders—even transformative leaders. Now consider the personality, philosophy, attitudes, values, and skills of these coaches. How are they different? Do you see any similarities?

(a) the only function of the coach is to motivate, usually by fear or emotional intensity, and

(b) that athletes have no inner motivation and must receive this from the coach.

Coaches who buy into the Rah-Rah leadership approach forget the more important aspects of leadership such as increasing their knowledge, developing their skills, relating to players, and implementing effective communication and reward structures. Many times coaches turn to the Rah-Rah leadership style because they lack the knowledge, ability, and work ethic to become a transformative leader. Research has shown that leaders must be emotionally compelling so as to create good feelings in those they lead, but that a simplistic Rah-Rah approach falls short of creating these feelings (Goleman, Boyatzis, & McKee, 2002).

Quotable Quote

"To expect to rule others by assuming a loud tone is like thinking oneself tall by putting on high heels." **John Petit-Senn**

Some transformative leaders *are* emotional and quite Rah-Rah in their leadership styles, yet this is not the basis for their leadership effectiveness. Rather, it is one part of their leadership style. For example, General George Patton was a transformative leader who as part of his leadership style used the Rah-Rah technique effectively. He was flamboyant, arrogant, and impetuous, and his emotional intensity inspired his troops to successfully streak across North Africa and Europe during the Second World War. In contrast, General Dwight Eisenhower was a transformative leader who was not Rah-Rah at all. Rather, Eisenhower led with a quiet intensity and calm manner that was important in making critical and rational decisions as the Allied Commander of the D-Day invasion of France. However, both generals shared other important requirements for their leadership positions, such as brilliant tactical strategizing, tireless commitment to and belief in their objectives, and confidence in their ability to command and lead others in a transformative way. Leaders, and coaches that rely only on Rah-Rah tactics are cheerleaders, not people-leaders. And although some individuals respond well to Rah-Rah coaches, if there is no substance behind the Rah-Rah, this influence will be short-lived.

The Formula Leader

The third myth of leadership is that there is one secret formula that great leaders follow that always works to achieve success in all situations. Young coaches flock to coaching clinics in their haste to adopt the leadership formulas of successful coaches and teachers such as Phil Jackson, Rick Pitino, David Leadbetter, and Vivian Stringer. However, it should come as no surprise that there is no secret formula that coaches can successfully adopt that will ensure leadership effectiveness and team success. In fact, the more young coaches try to force a particular formula into their leadership situation, the more likely it is that they will fail. Why is this? Can't we learn from successful leaders? Why shouldn't we pattern our leadership styles after our former coaches who were masters at transforming our energy into efficient, productive behavior and accomplishment?

We can learn from and gain insight into effective leadership from others, but we cannot copy their formulas. A movie was made about NASA's search for a group of individuals that had "the right stuff" to become America's first astronauts in the Mercury space program. Sport psychologists are interested in "the right stuff" as it pertains to effective leadership in sport. However, we know there is no exact formula to create a transformative leader. What *is* important in developing leadership is that individuals allow their own interpersonal style to emerge, which is their distinct and natural charisma. We can all try to analyze the words and styles of charismatic leaders to try to understand what gave them their masterful presence, but this should only be done within our search for greater self-understanding and the nurturing of our own personal charisma. Drama teachers emphasize to students that bringing out the actor within requires "becoming more profoundly what you already are" (Zielinski, 1998, p. 44). The essence of modern acting is authenticity, thus actors are taught to become more aware of their own identity. A famous drama coach explains, "When people ask what I do as a presentation coach, I don't say I package people. I say I unwrap them" (Zielinski, 1998, p.44).

Leadership is a *learned skill*, so we know that "the right stuff" can be developed through education, training, self-reflection, and practice. We do know that leaders influence people behaviorally, socially, and psychologically, so if we develop our abilities in these three areas, we just might measure up with "the right stuff" to be effective leaders.

Another weakness with the Formula approach to leadership is that it fails to take into account the interactional nature of leadership. In the next section, an interactional, three-ring circus model of leadership is presented as an alternative to trying to find the secret formula to be an effective coach and leader.

Three-Ring Circus Model of Leadership

Because coaches in leadership positions often feel like they're running a three-ring circus (e.g. juggling balls, taming wild beasts, dealing with clowns, walking a tight-rope, playing with fire), I thought a circus model would be particularly relevant to sport!

The Separate Rings

The first step to understanding the three-ring circus model of leadership is to identify the three rings of the circus. The rings represent the three important components that must be considered in effective leadership: coach, athletes, and context (e.g., Chelladurai, 1993). It is helpful at first to think about each of these rings independently, as shown in Figure 5.2. The first ring represents the *athletes* on the team, and this ring is made up of all their personal characteristics including age, level, ability, personalities, attitudes, and values. The second ring is the *leader's* ring, which includes all of the coach's personal characteristics including education, training, personality, skills, attitudes, experience, and values. The third ring contains the *context*, which is made up of organizational factors such as type of sport and size of the team, as well as constantly changing situational factors such as the differences between competition and practices.

The Interconnected Rings

The model of leadership is built by interconnecting the three circus rings that represent the coach, the athletes, and the context (see Figure 5.3). Thus, the model is *interactional*, which has been supported as a more viable way to study leadership as compared to the "great person" approach discussed in the previous section. The key point is that transformative leadership occurs when coaches operate within the shaded middle portion of the model. Coaches most effectively transform individuals and teams from this position, because it is the center of the interaction between the three components of leadership. If you've been to a circus, you know that the ringmaster always stands in the middle of the center ring. Thus, in our model, effective coach leaders must become skilled circus ring-masters to constantly negotiate the interactive nature of athletes' abilities and needs, situational constraints, and their own interpersonal style and abilities.

Consider alternative places where ringmasters, or coaches, might stand in attempting to effectively control the circus, which in our case is representative of their teams (see Figure 5.3). Obviously, if they

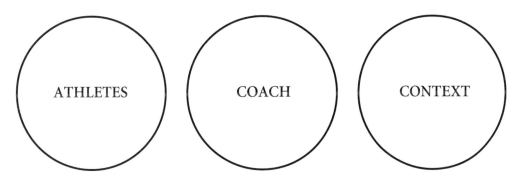

Figure 5.2 Separate rings of leadership

stand isolated in one of the rings, then they are not in position to understand and influence what is occurring in the other two rings. If they stand in Position 1, they miss what is happening in the context ring. Coaches who lead in this way consider the needs of their athletes, but they are rigid in leadership style as they behave the same way despite changing contextual factors. Research supports that different contexts and situations require different types of leadership (e.g., Horn, 2002). Grant Hill, NBA All-Star and former Duke basketball player, lauded Coach Mike Krzyzewski for his grounded, yet dynamic leadership by stating: "Every team I was on over my four years at Duke, he coached differently" (Krzyzewski, 2000, p. 16).

If the ringmasters, or coaches, stand in Position 2, they focus on the needs of their athletes in relation to contextual requirements, but they fail to provide a consistent foundational philosophy based on their personal coaching objectives, priorities, and skills. This is not an effective leadership position because it is not grounded by an established coaching philosophy through which coaches can and should exert influence (leadership) to affect the lives of their athletes. This leads to inconsistent and flighty leadership behavior, and a lack of continuity within the sport program.

If the ringmasters, or coaches, stand in Position 3, they fail to account for the specific needs, interests, and abilities of their athletes. This leadership breakdown occurs often in youth sport, where coaches may have a clear philosophy and objectives about how to coach football, but they fail to consider that their nine- and ten-year-old players really don't care to be treated like the Chicago Bears. This limitation to effective leadership often occurs when coaches fail to consider the motivational needs of their athletes, as discussed in Chapter 3. It also occurs when coaches fail to adapt to the specific abilities that athletes often bring into a program. A tennis coach at a local university required all athletes on his team to play a serve-and-volley style of tennis, even though many incoming athletes were excellent baseliners whose outstanding ground-stroke abilities were not used effectively. The coach required this style of play because it was his personal style, and because he thought male tennis players should not play a "pansy" baseline game. Obviously, there are baseline-oriented tennis players who are highly success-

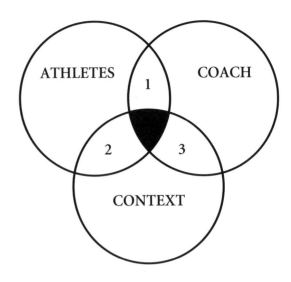

Figure 5.3 Three-ring circus model of leadership

ful in professional tennis, so it seems that this coach's leadership position, in which he ignored the unique abilities of his players, was limited in terms of optimally influencing the performance, development, and experiences of his athletes.

Transformative leadership requires that coaches situate themselves in the center of the three leadership component rings. It requires constant assessment of what is happening in all the rings, so that the most informed decisions can be made. Different situations require different leadership functions to be performed, but these functions are carried out in relation to a coach's foundational philosophy and with the best interests and need of these particular athletes in mind. Effective leaders must develop their ringmaster skills by assessing how the three rings interact in their particular situations, and then consider ways they can most effectively transform these interactions to help athletes develop skills, perform better, and enjoy sport. Research with elite coaches has supported adaptability and flexibility in leadership as a crucial factor in coaching success (Jones et al., 2004).

From Circus Ringmaster to Mad Hatter: Required Leadership Roles

At this point, I have introduced you to the study of leadership in sport psychology by suggesting that leaders become electric transformers and circus ringmasters! What could be next? Would you believe a mad hatter? Read on.

You should now understand the true nature of transformative leadership as opposed to popular myths about super-men and -women, and you should also understand that effective leadership occurs when coaches account for the interactional nature of their particular three-ring circus. It's now time to turn our attention to specific strategies that can be used to enhance leadership effectiveness. This involves learning how to wear many hats—to become a mad hatter, if you will! Transformative coaches wear many hats to fulfill their required leadership roles. In the remainder of the chapter, we'll identify the "the right stuff" for leaders in sport as related to wearing five leadership hats: the vision hat, the relationship hat, the control hat, the reinforcement hat, and the information hat (modified from Smith, 1997). Each of the required leadership roles in relation to these hats is discussed, and then suggestions to enhance leadership ability within each role are provided.

The Vision Hat

The first hat that transformative leaders must wear is the vision hat. The vision hat is your thinking cap! Just as citizens want vision from their political leaders, athletes want vision from their coaches. **Vision** is defined as *the power of imagination or the ability to perceive something not actually visible, which typically involves broad future aspirations or achievements that depart significantly from the status quo.* Think of vision as a combination telephoto and wide-angle lens of awareness. Transformative leaders use this lens to see into the future (telephoto) and envision big picture possibilities (wide-angle). Former U.S. President John F. Kennedy presented such a vision to Congress when he told them "I think we should go to the moon." Walt Disney envisioned the magical grandeur of Disneyworld in the sleepy marshland of central Florida.

For coaches, vision is necessary to build the type of program and team that they want. Vision requires three things:

- the vision of what you want to accomplish (charting your course)
- the vision of how to do it (developing an action plan)
- your ability to live your vision and inspire others to live it

These three components are discussed in the next sections to provide you with some insights as to how to better wear the vision hat as a coach.

Remember the Law of Navigation (Chart Your Course)

The Law of Navigation states that anyone can steer the ship, but it takes a leader to chart the course (Maxwell, 1998). Charting the course of your team involves not only your vision for the team's ultimate destination, but also an understanding of what it will take to get there as well as a recognition of the obstacles your team likely will face long before they appear. The secret to the Law of Navigation is freeing yourself up to think beyond the safe and accepted status quo. Bill Bowerman, the legendary track and field coach at the University of Oregon, experimented using his waffle iron to develop a prototype "waffle-soled" running shoe that led to the development of Nike, Inc. Of course, that vision turned into a billion dollar corporation!

> ### Quotable Quote
> *"You have to color outside the lines once in a while to paint your life's masterpiece."*
> **Author unknown**

Preparing to develop one's vision requires "GAP thinking," which refers to the need for leaders to move their consciousness into the GAP—a place where they

Photo by Brett Hansbauer

"gain another perspective" of awareness (Blank, 1995). Leaders enter the GAP when they seek information from multiple sources. This involves seeking out and listening to new and alternative sources of information and asking questions to broaden and deepen your understanding of the organization beyond the current status quo. People lack vision when they cling to old mental models about "how things are or should be." GAP thinking means that you gain another perspective by tuning in to insight and information that most people see as meaningless or even wacky. Tranformative leaders inform their vision by always challenging basic assumptions that most people hold as true, yet which often mask faulty, inappropriate, or short-sighted ways of thinking. Consider the message in the following quote (author unknown) which sums up the idea of GAP thinking:

Risk more than others think is safe.
Care more than others think is wise.
Dream more than others think is practical.
Expect more than others think is possible.

Overall, then, coaches begin developing their vision by tireless preparation in the form of information gathering with the goal of gaining deeper and unbiased insight into the specific context in which they are working. Following are some practical tips to consider in attempting to enhance your insight-gaining ability:

• Have courage in developing unusual ideas that diverge from current thinking. Consider that Columbus, Copernicus, and Lucy B. Anthony were all ridiculed for thinking in new ways. Consider how the GAP thinking of Dick Fosbury in the 1960s created the "Fosbury flop" high jumping technique that is used by elite jumpers across the world today. Fosbury was ridiculed by fans and his technique was resisted by coaches, but he persisted in developing his new style which resulted in an Olympic gold medal in 1968 and a biomechanical breakthrough in high jumping that is described by his name. Fosbury states,

"Within each of us lies a . . . talent or a gift that we can develop if we just pay attention . . . Perhaps you're frustrated with some requirement . . . that prevents you from reaching your full potential. Per-

haps someone who works for you wants to 'draw outside the lines' on occasion. To awaken the Olympian within, we have to look at what works now, not just at what's worked in the past. By having open-minded coaches and by focusing on what worked for me, I was able to add an innovation to the sport that has eventually pushed the world record to more than eight feet. That's how you make a winner out of a 'flop'" (Fosbury, 1999, p. 67).

• Ask questions that penetrate to the core of a problem. Continuously ask "why?" to break down entrenched yet limiting patterns. Instead of considering "what is?," consider "what can be?" Research on extraordinary leaders has shown that they spend significant time thinking about what they are trying to achieve, constantly monitor their progress, and correct their courses when necessary instead of just operating on blind faith or automatic pilot (Gardner, 1998).

• Learn rather than disagree (Blank, 1995). When you disagree with another idea, immediately adopt a learning posture. Instead of reflexively arguing for your point of view, ask "What else can you tell me about that?" Take time to think clearly about the alternative position, and learn from your analysis. You may end up still disagreeing or you may end up changing your position, but in either case, you have gained insight through learning in that situation.

• Take time to physically remove yourself from the sport environment to allow your mind to slow down and think more deeply about things.

• Insight takes time, so persistence and tenaciousness is needed in pursuing difficult problems over long periods of time.

• Use the blank page method of making visual connections between ideas. Sit down with a blank paper pad and draw or write out ideas that represent what you would like to accomplish. Go through several pages, try everything, and don't be highly evaluative. Let your thoughts flow without interruption. The emphasis should rather be on linking, connecting, integrating, stretching—it can be very messy and inconclusive. Draw up several renditions of your ideas, and then leave them alone a while. Return to them in a few days to see if they're still good ideas or if you've gained more insight since you drew up these original thoughts.

Clipboard

Now That's Vision . . .

In the late Middle Ages, a young Frenchman was walking down the street when he came upon several laborers working with large stones. "What are you doing?" he asked the first worker. "I'm trying to make this round stone square," replied the first man. "I've been working on this one stone for more than a week, and look how little progress I've made."

The young man walked a bit farther and spoke to a second worker who was hammering away at a similar block of stone. "What are you doing?" he asked the second man. The worker replied, "My job. I'm a stone mason."

Not much farther down the path the young man encountered a third laborer, also working a heavy piece of stone. "What are you doing?" he asked the third man.

The worker looked up briefly from his task and replied, "I'm building a cathedral."

Synthesize Information and Insights Into a Specific Action Plan

Information-gathering and insight development (the what of the vision) should be followed by the development and implementation of a specific action plan (the *how* of the vision). If the first step was about charting the course, this second step is about developing specific directions to successfully navigate the course. Examples include

- Key points of one's foundational coaching philosophy should be written out, and specific objectives established based on this philosophy.
- A team and individual goal mapping program should be implemented (see Chapter 8) that operationally defines key markers of success based on one's objectives. This is particularly

critical for coaches, because coaches operate in a context where objectives are often conflictual. For example, college coaches are hired and fired on the basis of winning percentages, thus coaching objectives related to optimal development and optimal experiences for athletes are often underemphasized at the expense of winning. This is also helpful for youth coaches, who get seduced by their own egos and social pressure to focus on objectives related to the coach's needs (winning and prestige) as opposed to the athletes' needs (stimulation, acceptance, competence, and worthiness).

- Activating one's vision involves overcoming complacency and establishing a sense of urgency (Kotter, 1996). This is typically the first order of business when a coach comes in to a new program that has under-achieved in the past. The norms within the program (discussed in Chapter 6) must be transformed to create an urgent, important commitment to excellence and productivity. To do this, coaches should attempt to get a renewed commitment from key leaders and performers within the team, set high expectations and specific goal achievement strategies for athletes that requires committed behavior beyond the current status quo, work to enhance all forms of intrinsic and extrinsic motivation discussed in Chapter 3, and provide constant performance feedback to clarify expectations and shape behavior. Bold moves to reduce complacency and establish urgency often create conflict and anxiety at first, but transformative leaders should accept this as normal human resistance to change from familiar, yet limiting, patterns of thinking and behaving.

Live Your Vision and Action Plan

The most critical factor related to athletes becoming transformed by the vision and action plans of their leaders is the degree to which leaders adhere to their own vision and action plan. Without qualification, coaches must behaviorally, socially, and psychologically adhere to the ideals they have set for their athletes. One of the most important ways that leaders transform individuals is by modeling. Leaders should never ask more from their followers than they are willing to do themselves. If coaches want their athletes to be intensely committed, tireless workers—and model citizens—then they must demonstrate their intense commitment, tireless work ethic, and model citizenship every day. Any inconsistencies in leadership modeling will cause you and your vision to lose credibility in the eyes of your athletes.

Clipboard

Do as I Do, Not as I Say

An Indian woman brought her small child to Gandhi and implored him, "Great wise one, please tell my child to quit eating sugar." Gandhi looked at the woman and said, "Bring the child back to me in two weeks." The woman beseeched Gandhi to admonish her child, but he refused. So in two weeks, they returned, and the woman asked Gandhi again, "Please tell my child to quit eating sugar." Gandhi looked at the child and said, "Stop eating sugar." The woman looked quizzically at Gandhi and asked, "Why could you not tell this to my child two weeks ago?" Gandhi replied, "Because two weeks ago, I was still eating sugar."

You should decide on "the right stuff" to model for transformative leadership in your particular three-ring circus, but here are some logical suggestions about effective leadership modeling.

Walk the walk. Coaches should always exude confidence—in themselves, their vision, and their athletes. It's not enough to "talk" one's vision, you must also "walk" it. Athletes want leaders who know the way. In uncertain times, athletes want leaders who can find the way. Confidence doesn't mean that leaders know all the answers. In fact, it's been my experience that the best leaders are honest when they are unsure, whereas less confident leaders put on a false front and try to act like they're sure when they're not. Athletes sniff this out right away, and the coach loses credibility by not being honest. Confi-

> ### Quotable Quote
> *"Example is not the main thing influencing others. It is the only thing."* **Albert Schweitzer**

dence means that the leader is committed and believes he or she can find the answers.

Everything about a person—your posture, how you carry yourself, your consistency in moods, your appearance, your facial expressions, and your body language—are instrumental in "walking" your vision and action plan. Transformative leaders must be able to manage the meaning of distressing situations in effective ways to maintain the confidence of athletes and the team. A team's capacity to function is related to the confidence that coaches communicate to their athletes, particularly in stressful times. A transformative leader not only keeps his or her chin up, but keeps the team's chin up in moments of great adversity. I have always viewed this leadership challenge as a great opportunity for self-development in terms of emotional management and self-regulation, and it clearly is a skill that can be developed.

> ### Quotable Quote
> *"Be more concerned with your character than your reputation, because your character is what you really are, while your reputation is merely what others think you are."*
> **John Wooden**

Take personal responsibility. Evoking excellence via transformative leadership involves setting higher standards for yourself and your athletes. John Wooden (1988), legendary basketball coach at UCLA from 1949 to 1975, said, "In all my years of coaching, I have never yelled at a player. If the player makes a mistake in a big game, my gut-level response is that I must not have given him enough coaching." This example emphasizes a great coach's philosophy and belief that he was willing to take responsibility and set high standards for himself, as well as his team. Setting high standards for athletes is the greatest compliment you can give them, even if they don't realize that at the time. The trick to doing this successfully is achieving a balance between the toughness needed to hold people to a higher standard, and the compassion and empathy for what they have to go through to achieve this standard.

A principle that I found effective as a coach is to take personal responsibility when your team fails and give credit to the athletes and others in the program (e.g., assistant coaches) when your team succeeds. This should not be done in a dishonest manner, but rather in a manner that says that you always accept responsibility when things go wrong in your program, and that your sense of leadership allows, even compels, you to credit your athletes and assistants when the team is successful. This really works, and the people in your program will respect you for taking the ultimate responsibility for failure and sharing the fruits of success.

Establish comfortable professional boundaries. Coaches should set themselves apart from their athletes by establishing appropriate psychological boundaries. Although it is important to stay closely involved in the lives of athletes to develop empathy and effective communication, leaders must remain socially and psychologically separated. A recommended guideline is to maintain a *professional* relationship with athletes, which means that even though we may know them personally very well and feel great affection for them, our relationship with them is based on our professional connection as coach and athlete. Despite athletes' attempts to become "buddy-buddy" with you, they will respect you and your vision more if you stay focused on the professional aspect of your relationship with them.

Manage time effectively. Manage your time and the time of your athletes effectively. This does not mean that you are constantly rushed, too busy to talk with athletes, or always checking your watch to go somewhere else. It means that you are focused and efficient in implementing your vision, and that you acknowledge their commitment to your vision by respecting the time they give to it.

Be flexible in driving your vision. Demonstrate your ability to be flexible as a leader and to change directions if your vision and action plan need to be modified. Be prepared and willing to admit misjudgment or mistakes. As a former coach, I found that when I honestly admitted regret over certain actions or mistakes, I gained credibility with my athletes. Such openness enhanced the trust between us, and it demonstrated that although I was the navigator and leader of the group, I was not above meeting the same interpersonal expectations that I had for my athletes.

Summing up. Transformative coaches logically organize the social environment in ways that require adherence to their vision and action plan. Their interpersonal interactions with athletes consistently convey and reinforce their vision for the team, their coaching objectives, and the specific goals that are set toward achieving their objectives (see Clipboard). Coaches should use many of the team building ideas discussed in Chapter 6 to create the type of achievement climate that nurtures their visions and allows them to flourish. Transformative coaches work to enhance their mental skills and the mental toughness that is a prerequisite for maintaining the effort and persistence needed to provide effective and consistent leadership. Chapters 7-17 of this book focus on developing mental skills in athletes, and development of these skills is highly recommended for coaches who wish to be effective leaders.

Keep in mind that athletes buy into the coach first, then the coach's vision after that (Maxwell, 1998). So your first goal is to get your athletes to buy into you; then they are more likely to buy into your vision and action plan for the program. Maxwell (1998), author of several books on leadership, emphasizes that people don't follow worthy causes. Rather, he states that they follow worthy leaders who promote worthwhile causes. The point of this is that your vision is only as powerful and effective as you are in delivering it. For example, most people buy Nike shoes because they are buying into Michael Jordan, not because of the quality of the shoes. Corporations understand this, and their use of highly credible sources to advertise their products (vision) reflects the power of the messenger over the power of the message. Your ability to advertise your vision involves building credibility, networking with key athletes in your program, building relationships, and living every day the actions that represent the vision you are building for your program. In the next section, the importance of relationship skills for leaders are discussed, which are critical for coaches in articulating and implementing their vision and action plan with athletes.

Clipboard

Visionary or Throwback? The Dee Knoblauch Dilemma

Many coaches today who attempt to provide a fresh vision and inspiring action plan are stymied by social pressures that have influenced athletes to be less intrinsically motivated and often cynical of ideals such as commitment and hard work. Because it has become more difficult to get athletes to buy into these traditional values, coaches have become more autocratic, and college and even high school sports have become characterized by professional values such as the need for lavish extrinsic reinforcers and a growing acceptance of unsportsman-like behavior as part of the game.

Not so in the case of Dee Knoblauch, former women's basketball coach at Mt. Union College in Ohio. Knoblauch was a transformative coach not because she won, but because of the *reasons why* she won and the *ways in which* she coached. Her teams were consistently successful (two Final Four appearances) because she had a strong vision for excellence and a specific action plan to carry out her vision. Talking to her is like going back in time to when athletes played sport for fun, and playing well and fairly was as important as winning games. Knoblauch had four rules for her team when she coached: (1) work hard, (2) be a team player, (3) no swearing, and (4) no whining. Of course, no one adhered to the rules more so than Knoblauch. The strongest language she used in moments of frustration is "Nuts!" Her players sprinted through every drill in practice. They sprinted to the locker room. They sprinted to the bench. During games, Knoblauch had the person running the video camera tape the players as they sprinted to the bench for time-outs, and the huddle was captured on video as well to ensure concentration and attention from all players. Knoblauch states, "It's the little things that make the difference between winning and losing."

Mt. Union is a NCAA Division III college, so no players received athletic scholarships and many paid a lot of money for the privilege of playing for Knoblauch. Their team GPA was 3.2 and their graduation rate was 100%. Knoblauch held team discussions about such issues as alcohol and nutrition, where she emphasized the need for optimal fuel and energy for performance, but she left the responsibility with the athletes for choices they would make about their lifestyles. Of course, because Knoblauch earned such respect and credibility with her athletes, a strong group norm existed for appropriate social behavior as well as for effort and intensity without the need for admonishment from Knoblauch. She empowered her athletes to become transformative leaders themselves in inspiring each other toward goal attainment, personal development, and the joy of playing sport.

Was Dee Knoblauch an out-of-touch throwback? . . . A coach in a time warp? No. Actually, she represents a coach with the courage and commitment to stand behind her values and objectives of what coaching leadership should be in an age where social forces often make a mockery of traditional ideas about sport.

===

Wrapping up the Vision Hat: Beware the Vision Killers

To wrap up the important leadership ingredient of vision, take the following "vision killer" exam (Lynn, 2002). Your behavior as the leader has a tremendous influence on how committed your athletes are to your vision. Assess your leadership behaviors in relation to the following ten vision killers. Choose the number for each item that best represents your behavior as a leader or coach.

Vision Killer	*Self-Assessment*
	never always
1. Treating athletes badly, such as not showing them you care, forgetting to say thank you, not respecting them, not making them feel valued.	1 2 3 4 5 6 7 8 9 10
2. Not setting good examples and living by the adage "do as I say, not as I do."	1 2 3 4 5 6 7 8 9 10
3. Focusing on too many things at once.	1 2 3 4 5 6 7 8 9 10

Vision Killer	*Self-Assessment*		
	never		always
4. Pushing too hard on the task and forgetting the athletes as people.	1 2 3 4 5 6 7 8 9 10		
5. Not giving clear directions.	1 2 3 4 5 6 7 8 9 10		
6. Giving inconsistent direction.	1 2 3 4 5 6 7 8 9 10		
7. Not taking responsibility for failure.	1 2 3 4 5 6 7 8 9 10		
8. Focusing on details and forgetting to tell the "whys" or the big picture.	1 2 3 4 5 6 7 8 9 10		
9. Showing little or no personal commitment to the vision.	1 2 3 4 5 6 7 8 9 10		
10. Allowing one or a few athletes to sabotage the vision through little effort, lack of performance, or negative attitudes toward you and their teammates.	1 2 3 4 5 6 7 8 9 10		

What are your three worst scores? Reflect on why you scored lower on these items, and consider ways to enhance your leadership behavior in these areas. Don't be too tough on yourself—often our strengths contribute to our weaknesses. For example, you may be a hard-driving, visionary leader with a strong plan to build your program and train your athletes to experience as much success as possible. However, you may get so busy driving the program that you forget to take the important time to validate your athletes and their progress as part of the vision. In this sense, your strength of vision and strong will contribute to your weakness of forgetting to validate the most important people in the whole vision! We're all susceptible to overlooking key leadership behaviors at times, and the point is to continually self-assess and self-reflect to remain aware of vision killers that may develop in your program, despite your best intentions.

Another good exercise is to keep a written log for a two-week period. Note at least one visible action or behavior that you engage in each day that demonstrates your commitment to and passion for your vision. Go ahead—try it! You can jot it down in your daily calendar or date-book. It's a great exercise to raise your awareness of the degree to which you're living your vision and providing examples of your commitment to your athletes. Take the test, and make sure you're walking the walk that you expect your athletes to follow!

The Relationship Hat

If vision is the first important hat that transformative leaders must wear, then the relationship hat is second, because a vision cannot be carried out without effective communication within a team. Think of this relationship hat as a nurse's cap, because the emphasis when wearing this hat is your ability to care and demonstrate that caring for your athletes. Transformative coaches foster relationships

Photo by Tim Hipps, courtesy of US Army

that enable the team to achieve its mission, which requires solid communication skills as discussed in Chapter 4. *You cannot become a transformative leader unless you are a strong communicator.* This does not require one to become a Rah-Rah leader, but rather it requires the ability to send information effectively to athletes as well as receive information by being an effective listener.

In a study of influential 20th century leaders, Howard Gardner (1998) found that these leaders possessed three key strengths. The first strength was that of vision, which we have already discussed. However, the second and third leadership strengths identified in great leaders were relationship-oriented. The second was linguistic, or the leaders' abilities to tell stories that transformed people's beliefs in productive ways. Using this perspective, leaders achieve influence through the stories they tell. These stories influence people's mental frames, because we all have stories (mental frames) in our minds, and if a leader wants to affect us, he or she must change the stories we already believe. Consider how William Wallace (made famous by Mel Gibson in the movie *Braveheart*) constantly told the story of freedom for Scotland to transform people's ways of thinking and beliefs about the possibility of their country moving beyond English oppression. Consider the "story" made famous by Rosa Parks when she refused to comply with racist laws in the 1960s. Her story was then retold numerous times by civil rights leaders and led to significant advances in civil rights in America.

Clipboard

A Transforming Swede

Pia Nilsson has been head coach of the Swedish national golf team since 1990, and she has molded such world-class players as Annika Sorenstam, Helen Alfredsson, Liselotte Neumann, and Jesper Parnevik. Her leadership style is based on what she calls the Chosen Truths:

- Human beings are always more important that their performances
- Humans have unlimited potential
- Mind and body are one system
- Golf is fun

"We develop as human beings through the game of golf," says Nilsson. "We don't do anything that might lead to lower scores, but might not be good to us in our lives as a whole. Who we are is, for us, always more important than what we do." Sorenstam, top women's golfer, says of Pilsson, "So many people try to make golf harder than it is. Pia makes it easier" (Burnett, 1997, p. 22).

The third strength identified in influential leaders was the ability to understand others and get in their mindset. Thus, to be a transformative leader, coaches must have or develop the ability to understand the perspectives of their athletes, which is a quality termed **empathy**. As defined in the last chapter, empathy involves *the important human skill of knowing how others feel, and understanding how those feelings are affecting them.* As adults, we often forget about how we felt as a young person and make the mistake of evaluating athletes' emotional and social behaviors in relation to our current levels of maturity (Nakamura, 1996). It is unrealistic to expect and demand that young athletes think and act like we do. Although coaches should have certain expectations for their athletes in terms of behavior and commitment, the skill of empathy helps coaches avoid unrealistic expectations of their athletes, which can result in frustration and a lack of communication.

Researchers in the helping professions have learned that empathy is the most vital quality for success as a helper. In his acclaimed best seller *Emotional Intelligence*, Daniel Goleman (1995) identified empathy as one of the most important keys to emotional intelligence, which is more predictive of success in life than one's actual intelligence as measured by I.Q. Goleman's more recent book (Goleman et al., 2002), titled *Primal Leadership*, explains that leadership works when leaders use key emotional intelligence skills to empathize and manage social relationships effectively to create optimism, confidence, and feelings of success in those they lead.

Thus, empathy (and other key emotional intelligence skills) is the foundation upon which a coach fulfills the relationship role. Empathy allows coaches to understand the interests and needs of their athletes, which you learned in Chapter 3 is a prerequisite for effective motivation. Also, empathy is necessary for coaches to understand both athlete and situational needs to effectively inform the development of a vision for their programs. Empathy is a critical skill needed for coaches to gain the trust and credibility of their athletes, and along with transformative storytelling, is the most basic and necessary interpersonal relationship skill for transformative leaders.

The Control Hat

The third hat to adorn the head of a transformative leader is the control hat. Envision this hat as the hard-hat worn by construction and plant workers—it represents issues that typically arise between management and workers in the union! Part of the role of a leader is assuming control and deciding how much control to delegate and relinquish to others. Transformative coaches must use their power wisely to exercise legitimate control over the team and its members. By far, the most frequent topic related to the control role of leaders is the appropriateness of various decision-making, or leadership, styles. The main issue of control revolves around the degree to which leaders allow, empower, or demand that others become involved in the decision-making process.

Decision-Making Styles

In the research literature on leadership, three decision-making styles have been identified: autocratic, democratic, and permissive. The *autocratic* decision-making style is the traditional authoritarian approach to leadership, where the coach makes all the decisions and retains total control of the team. A *de-mocratic* decision-making style (also called participative decision-making) is characterized by the leader relinquishing certain decision-making duties to team members, or at least providing them with the opportunity to voice their opinions about certain important decisions that directly affect them. *Permissive* leaders lack control of the team and are passive in providing vision and direction.

Although the effectiveness of these decision-making styles is hotly debated in relation to leadership in sport, the debate seems irrelevant if we truly believe in the soundness of our previously discussed three-ring circus model of leadership. If you remember (see Figure 5.3), effective leadership occurs in the ringmaster position, which requires that coaches make decisions based on the constant interaction of contextual factors with athletes' needs as related to the coach's skills and personality. Thus, the three traditional decision-making styles should be considered as behavioral alternatives that the ringmaster chooses from depending on what is happening in each of the rings. Consider how all three decision-making styles may be effective. If a fire breaks out in Ring 1, the ringmaster doesn't gather people around to discuss the best course of action. She makes an autocratic decision to call the fire department to control the fire. Autocratic decision-making is effective in times of crisis or stress, or when expediency is needed. However, lack of time should not be used as an excuse for using an autocratic decision-making style at all times.

There are times when a democratic decision-making style is useful for leaders. If the ringmaster wants to evaluate the success of the circus performances, particularly in relation to what happens in the three rings simultaneously, she doesn't conduct this evaluation without surveying the performers and discussing their impressions of how the show is doing. She uses a democratic process whereby group members are expected to provide information that the ringmaster can then use to make an informed decision. Democratic decision-making is useful when the leader needs to gain a broader perspective by obtaining information from those around her who are involved in the decision, or when the leader needs to gain additional expertise beyond her own to make the best decision. Obviously, a democratic style or participative decision-making enhances the feelings of ownership of decisions for everyone on

Photo courtesy of WVU Photographic Services

the team and can enhance personal growth. In this way, it may serve to enhance the intrinsic motivation of athletes as they feel more self-determining (as discussed in Chapter 3).

Contrary to popular belief, there are even times when a permissive—often termed laissez-faire—decision-making style is warranted. If the trapeze artist in the circus is deciding whether to wear a green or purple cape, the ringmaster doesn't micro-manage by insisting that he wear green. A permissive decision-making style is an effective leadership behavior when the issue at hand does not require the special skills or knowledge possessed by the leader. Also, this style is effective when the decision to be made is peripheral to the established vision and action plan of the team. Obviously, the color of the trapeze artist's cape is not central to the performance and success of the circus! As summed up by Graham Taylor, professional soccer coach and former coach of England's national soccer team, "Sometimes, by not coaching you're a good coach" (Jones et al., 2004, pp. 147-148).

Personal Plug-In

Identify three decisions or responsibilities you would consider delegating to athletes on a team. Also, identify three decisions or responsibilities that you feel the coach of the team should keep within his or her control.

Distinguishing Democratic Process From Democratic Decisions

Only a rigid, secret formula-oriented coach would choose to use one decision-making style at the exclusion of the others. Most popular literature advocates a democratic style of leadership, but that is too simplistic and idealistic to be a practical alternative. Leaders must exert control and power at times, and make stand-alone decisions. Of course, a wise and transformative leader would gather information from the context as well as her athletes prior to making the stand-alone decision. The definitive point is that the decision is hers alone, but what makes her a transformative leader is that she uses her power and control effectively to develop insight gleaned from her interaction with her athletes to make an informed decision that is in their best interests. I call this the "big picture" of decision-making,

with the point being that the coach is in a unique position as leader to understand complex and broad issues involving numerous factors and links within the athletic program and even the school, university, or organization. Kelley and Thibaut (1969) use the analogy of the difference in solving a crossword puzzle as opposed to constructing a crossword puzzle. Participative or democratic decision-making works well in solving a crossword puzzle, but the complexity in constructing a crossword puzzle requires a different sort of task focus or type of leadership.

It seems helpful to distinguish between democratic process and democratic decisions in understanding the effective use of decision-making styles. This point has been misunderstood by coaches who insist that democratic leadership behavior has no place in sport. The United States federal government is a good example to use in understanding democratic process and democratic decision-making. The United States is a democracy, but the citizens don't participate in an impromptu vote to decide the best method to repel a missile attack aimed at our major cities. The President is empowered to make autocratic *decisions* within the democratic *process*. That is, through a national vision (the Constitution) and action plan (federal laws), the United States has established a democratic process to empower leaders to best represent the interests of its citizens. In times of stress or crisis, we expect our empowered leader to exert control in the form of direct and strong autocratic decisions. In stressful times (such as the heat of competition), leaders inspire confidence in others by making firm and rational decisions to transform the situation and people's responses to it. However, when it is time to empower (elect) a new leader, the democratic process gives all citizens the right to a vote as to who that leader should be.

A democratic leadership process seems ideal for sport. In fact, I would call that transformative leadership. Research supports this point by indicating that athletes high in intrinsic motivation perceive that their coaches exhibit democratic coaching behaviors (Amorose & Horn, 2000). But to effectively wear their control hats, transformative leaders must at times make critical decisions autocratically. Athletes in this type of system feel empowered as the coach provides them with opportunities for responsible leadership and decision-making on their own. But coaches must have the courage and competence to make stand-alone, take-charge decisions in times of need to gain the confidence and respect of their athletes.

Timing is Everything

As you may have surmised from the previous discussion, timing is everything in effectively wearing the control hat of leadership. The timing of the leadership style or behavior is just as crucial as the type of leadership style or behavior. Transformative leaders recognize that *when* to lead is as important as *how* to lead. Maxwell (1998) identifies four quadrants that represent what can occur based on the action and timing of leader behavior (see Figure 5.4). I'll help you understand each quadrant by using examples of my previous experiences as a college basketball coach.

The first quadrant represents what can happen when a coach chooses the *wrong action at the wrong time*. Disaster! I once was working with the center on my basketball team, attempting to help her learn a new offensive move. As she struggled in learning the move, I said in a glib attempt to motivate her, "Come on, Mary. You can do it. It's easy!" She looked at me with frustration, defeat, and tears in her eyes and replied softly, "It's easy for you . . . " I realized I was wrong to infer that it was easy for her to learn this skill, especially at a time when she was struggling and feeling incompetent. It took some time to gain back her trust due to my lack of empathy at a time when she needed reassurance instead of my attempt at lighthearted motivation.

The second quadrant represents what can happen when a coach chooses the *right action at the wrong time*. Resistance! I learned quickly as a coach that talking to a team immediately after a heart-breaking loss requires great care. My mistake the first time this happened was to attempt to get my athletes to open up to discuss their feelings about a tough loss to our arch-rival. It wasn't a bad idea, but they just weren't ready. I met stiff resistance, which surprised me as they typically responded very openly to me. The next day at practice they were ready to discuss the loss, and they explained to me that the night before was just not a good time for them to think clearly about it. Rather, they needed some time to

ACTION

TIMING	Wrong Action Wrong Time\n\nDISASTER	Right Action Wrong Time\n\nRESISTANCE
	Wrong Action Right Time\n\nMISTAKE	Right Action Right Time\n\nSUCCESS

Figure 5.4 Leadership behavior and timing

think through what had happened in the competition. My athletes helped me learn the valuable lesson of timing, because although my actions were right, the time was wrong.

The third quadrant represents what can happen when a coach chooses the *wrong action at the right time*. Mistake! With eight seconds left in a game in which we were down by one point, I called a time-out to set up a play for my team. Instead of telling them exactly what to do, I allowed them some latitude and called for an offensive set in which they would then read the flow of the play to dictate who would take the last shot. I used a democratic style, as I thought they could make the decision on the floor as to the best option to use in getting the last shot. We failed to score, turning the ball over due to our lack of execution. After the game, I realized that I had chosen the wrong course of action for that time. It was not what my team needed from me, and it was a mistake. It was the right time to make a crucial call, but I made the wrong one.

Fortunately, I was able to rectify my mistake in a game later that season. This situation represents the final quadrant in Figure 5.4, which is where the coach chooses the *right action at the right time*. Success! Our team found ourselves in the same last-second situation we had faced earlier in the year. This time I was ready, as I had learned from my mistake. My leadership behavior was totally autocratic, which was the right action for this situation because autocratic behavior is warranted in stressful situations. I told each athlete exactly what they must do on the play, emphasized that they had one job to do, and made those jobs very clear and specific for them. The result was that we got a great shot, it went in, and I learned a valuable lesson about choosing the right leadership style to use depending on the situation.

As a transformative leader, when the right action and the right timing come together, incredible things happen. This often occurs in sport when coaches are hired to lead programs that are ripe for the unique leadership skills of that particular person. It's as if a key finally finds the lock that it was meant to open. Veteran coaches understand the crucial aspect of timing in attempting to enhance team cohesion, performance, and motivation in their athletes. Remember the three-ring circus analogy used previously in the chapter, which may help you to think about the situation or context before assuming that a certain leadership decision is a good one. Consider the emotional needs of your athletes based on the time of the season, the proximity of competition (upcoming or just completed), and the influence of good and bad performances (or wins and losses). Develop a file folder in your head of what you learn about timing and various leadership behaviors. Timing *is* everything in knowing how to expertly wear the control hat of transformative leadership.

The Reinforcement Hat

The fourth cap that leaders must wear is the reinforcement hat. Transformative coaches must understand how to shape the behavior of their athletes by harnessing the power of reinforcement in the form of rewards and punishment. Envision this as a jockey's hat to emphasize that shaping by reinforcement has traditionally used the whip or the carrot as incentives, much like with horses!

A significant line of research by Ron Smith and Frank Smoll at the University of Washington has examined the effectiveness of training youth sport coaches in appropriate reinforcement and communication techniques (Barnett, Smoll, & Smith, 1992; Smith & Smoll, 1990; Smith, Smoll, & Curtis, 1979). By developing a training program and behavioral observation system for coaches, Smith and Smoll found that the trained coaches did increase their ap-

propriate use of reinforcement and instructional behaviors as compared to untrained coaches. More importantly, the researchers found that children who played for the trained coaches enjoyed sport more, liked their coaches more, and felt their coaches were better teachers than children who played for untrained coaches. Also, children who played for trained coaches significantly increased their self-esteem and dropped out of sport at a lower rate than children who played for untrained coaches. This research demonstrates how important it is for coaches to effectively master reinforcement and communication behaviors.

It is beyond the scope of this chapter to extensively discuss reinforcement techniques. You may want to re-read the section in Chapter 3 on using extrinsic rewards with athletes to enhance their motivation. However, in relation to our discussion on transformative leadership, consider the following tips:

- Design and use reinforcers that are consistent with your vision, philosophy, and action plan. For example, leadership effectiveness is lost when coaches espouse a philosophy that values athlete development over other goals, but then they punish athletes when they give maximum effort yet lose to another team.
- Identify contingencies, or behavioral markers, that reflect your vision, philosophy, and action plan. In the previous Clipboard example of Coach Dee Knoblauch, her first objective in her action plan ("Work hard") was operationalized as demonstrating intensity in practice by sprinting through and between drills. Her second objective ("Be a team player") was operationalized in one way by expecting all athletes to be engaged and attentive in the time-out huddle. Knoblauch structured the environment so she could assess these behaviors, and by rewarding athletes for successfully meeting these contingencies, she skillfully demonstrated how effective reinforcement transformed her players and team culture.
- Emphasize encouragement and appreciation to reinforce leadership skills exhibited by athletes. Remember that transformative leaders don't wear the reinforcement hat to force athletes to comply with their rules. Rather, they wear the hat because they realize how impor-

tant it is to make athletes feel appreciated and their contributions to the team valued. They understand that the words and actions of coaches are especially significant to athletes because of the coach's position of power and control.

- Offer support and reinforcement in a way that says "You deserve it!" rather than "You need it!" (Smith, 1997).

- Use recognition as a powerful reinforcer to publicly recognize athletes' achievements. Follow these guidelines to make recognition a significant reward and motivator. First, the recognition must come as a result of some measured and valued accomplishment known by the team. Second, the recognition must come from a respected authority figure and given to the athlete in an honest and sincere manner. Third, make sure that when you recognize significant accomplishments of athletes that there are no strings attached. It is a reinforcer for achieving a past accomplishment, and should not be accompanied by admonishments such as ". . . and you better keep up the good work!" Remember: sincere recognition in a suitable public forum by a respected authority figure is a very strong reinforcer and motivator.

The Information Hat

The final hat to be worn by effective leaders is the information hat, which represents the important role of the leader as an information disseminator. Envision this hat as a Sherlock Holmes-style detective cap because a transformative coach should remain in tireless pursuit of information to allow athletes to develop and improve. Coaches fulfill this role when they choose appropriate information and effective teaching strategies for their athletes depending on level and skill. In an observational study of legendary Coach John Wooden's coaching practices, researchers found that 75 percent of his communications to his players carried information (Tharp & Gallimore, 1976). Effective leaders should strive to be like Coach Wooden, who won 10 NCAA championships, by ensuring that communication with athletes is information-dense. Here are some other suggestions to help fulfill the information role of an effective leader:

Photo by Tom Campbell/Gold & Black Illustrated

- Increase awareness and insight into how problems typically arise in groups of people, and take corrective action at an early stage before problems become full-blown. Transformative coaches work to be problem-finders to alleviate a constant need to be problem-solvers.

- Keep current with developing knowledge. A big part of having "the right stuff" is *knowing* your stuff. Effective coaches become students of their sport, as well as student's of all the sciences that inform their sport (e.g., physiology of training, mechanics, sports medicine, psychology).

- Become a bulletin board, or an internet Web site. Coaches transform team cultures by keeping everyone informed about pertinent information. In particular, athletes should be informed about their collective as well as individual accomplishments. Also, athletes should be continuously informed about issues that affect their lives such as new state guidelines for eligibility, academic requirements for scholarships, and athletic department policies. Effective coaches provide a wide range of information that demonstrates their interest in helping their athletes develop as people.

- Provide your athletes with continuous positive evaluative statements about individual and team progress in relation to your leadership vision and action plan. This reinforces and affirms athletes' commitment to the vision and plan, and enhances their motivation to achieve. Continuously providing positive information about how the vision and action plan are working enables the coach to wear many leadership hats at once: providing vision, enhancing relationships, effectively reinforcing athletes, and providing important information to help athletes focus on their pursuit of excellence.

Wearing the Hats: What Athletes Want From Coaches

That's a lot of hats! Can a coach actually wear them all? The answer is yes, because they blend together as coaches go through their days and teach, inspire, plan, explain, motivate, reinforce, empathize, mentor, decide, evaluate, listen, inform, and—well, yes—lead. You automatically wear all the hats, whether you want to or not.

What do you think athletes want from coaches? Following are lists of coach behaviors that athletes identified as *helpful* to their performance as well as *hurtful* to their performance (Gould, Greenleaf, Lauer, & Chung, 1999; Orlick, 2000; Orlick & Partington, 1988). You'll notice that the behaviors listed involve wearing all five leadership hats that we've discussed.

Coach Behaviors Athletes Feel Hurt Their Performance

1. Too uptight in final preparation phase for competition
2. Trying to get athletes "up" for competition
3. Excessive technical input at the last minute prior to competition
4. Failing to give confidence-enhancing feedback
5. Poor planning, and lack of responsibility, organization, and preparation (mental and physical)
6. Creating the impression that the coach's "neck is on the line" in terms of game outcome
7. Adding pressure by predicting where the athlete should place in competition
8. Overtraining, including failure to provide adequate recovery and rest time
9. Showing a lack of enthusiasm and lack of effort or work ethic
10. Poor communication, including failing to provide essential information to decrease uncertainty

Coach Behaviors Athletes Feel Help Their Performance

1. Providing mental preparation
2. Providing good technical training and physical conditioning
3. Being calm, relaxed, and not overly instructive when coaching
4. Allowing athletes to have time alone
5. Prepare and protect athletes from distractions
6. Good communication
7. Giving verbal support and confidence-enhancing feedback
8. Working to build team chemistry
9. Being well-organized
10. Helping athlete keep goals in perspective

Nurturing Leadership in Athletes

So far, the focus of this chapter has been on the leadership abilities of you, the coach. As just discussed, coaches have to wear many leadership hats to be transformative leaders and coach for the Inner Edge. However, as you know, teams gain the Inner Edge when they have effective leadership from athletes on the team.

An issue that coaches frequently raise with sport psychologists is what to do when a team lacks leadership. The field of sport psychology has not addressed this issue much at all, focusing instead on the leadership of coaches rather than athlete or peer leadership. It is commonly assumed that athletes with the most skill on the team are the most likely candidates for team leaders. Research supports that both athletes and coaches used skill as the primary factor in rating leadership ability in athletes on their teams (Glenn & Horn, 1993). However, in this study, athletes were rated higher in leadership ability by their teammates if they were more confident and displayed characteristics stereotypically defined as masculine leadership behaviors (e.g., assertiveness, aggressiveness). So, good team leaders seem to be athletes who are respected for their skill as well as personality characteristics related to communication, confidence, and assertiveness.

Coaches can nurture leadership on their teams in many ways. Because certain athletes have the personality characteristics that make them effective leaders, we often assume that athletes who don't have these characteristics can't step forward and lead. But leadership takes many forms, such as the quiet leader that leads by example in practice and competition, the supportive leader that validates and listens to teammates behind the scenes, and the vocal leader that publicly exhorts teammates to train hard and work together. Tony DiCicco, former coach of the U.S. Women's National Team, terms this "layers" of leadership, and feels that it is the key to a team fulfilling its mission (DiCicco & Hacker, 2002).

Coaches should focus on ways to nurture and teach leadership, as opposed to just waiting for the right leader to arrive in their programs. When meeting with team captains or upperclassmen who are likely leader candidates, discuss what leadership should be for your team. Describe what you want in a leader, and ask them what they think the team needs in a leader. In fact, this is a good team discussion to have as a whole, so that the team defines the type of leadership preferred and needed. A college team I consulted with described their optimal leader as someone who could provide both performance *urgency* and interpersonal *support*. That is, they wanted someone to create a sense of urgency for effort and intensity in training and competition, but in addition, they wanted someone who could fulfill the role of supporting teammates not only publicly but also one-on-one to make them feel important to the team and appreciated by others. The players told me that they didn't mind a leader getting in their face or challenging them to work harder, as long as they were also supportive. This discussion was productive because the players understood that the challenging and urgent behaviors displayed by the team leaders were not personal, but rather based on the team goal to excel. Interestingly, a recent book on developing leadership in athletes supports that idea that athlete leaders must be "enforcers" as well as "encouragers" (Janssen, 2004).

DiCicco fostered layered leadership on his teams by assigning players various tasks that required them to act as leaders. For example, two players were each assigned half of the team and given ten minutes to warm them up and report back to the coach. Similarly, certain players were designated as leaders of small groups in various competitive drills within practice. The idea behind these exercises is to give everyone on the team the chance to practice leadership skills and assume responsibility as a leader (Dicicco & Hacker, 2002).

Athletes assuming leadership roles should model the key leadership behaviors described previously in this chapter. These might include such things as validating teammates' contributions, involving them to feel a part of the group, clarifying the team mission and goals in terms of expectations for training focus and intensity, and attempting to be strong communicators. Well-established programs have developed socializing traditions that develop leadership within the team so when athletes move into leadership roles, they've learned what is important in terms of leadership for their teams. These traditions create team norms for acceptable behavior, effort, communication, and performance.

Coaches should be cautious in attempting to force leadership roles on certain athletes. Sometimes athletes in key tactical positions are naturally expected to demonstrate leadership (e.g., volleyball setters, basketball point guards, football quarterbacks). When athletes attempt to "force" a leadership style that is not a good fit for their personalities, it typically disrupts the team as well as the athletes who are trying to serve as leaders. Teammates become resentful, and the athletes attempting to lead in unnatural or unfamiliar ways often become distracted from their own performance. It's understandable that teams need some leadership from athletes in key positions, but coaches should allow the personality of each athlete to emerge in a leadership style that is authentic for that individual.

Wrapping Up

Leadership is a skill that can be learned. Developing leadership skills involves assessing your current ability to wear the various hats required of a coach. Coaches who want to develop their leadership skills should engage in the following self-assessment: Which hats fit well and look good on me? Which hats are more uncomfortable or ill-fitting? Which hats are outdated and remind me that I need to buy a new one that is more contemporary? It is important to evaluate your leadership skills in relation to the required roles of a coach, and to be honestly self-critical in doing so. Once this is accomplished, you can develop strategies to work on your leadership abilities in deficient areas.

In reality, a true transformative leader wears all of the hats simultaneously. Transformative coaches succeed in establishing a strong vision and action plan of success by valuing human relationships, using power wisely while empowering others, understanding the motivational value of encouragement and appreciation, and continuing to seek knowledge to continuously sustain and refine the vision. They're electric transformers, circus ringmasters, and mad hatters rolled into one!

As a coach, you should challenge yourself daily to engage in transformative leadership. The most exciting opportunity we all face in life is our opportunity to significantly influence the lives of others. In the words of former U.S. President Woodrow Wilson:

> *You are here to enable the world to live more amply, with greater vision, and with a finer spirit of hope and achievement . . . You are here to enrich the world . . . You impoverish yourself if you forget this errand.*

Summary Points for Chapter 5

1. Leadership is defined as the behavioral, psychological, and social process of influencing individuals to move toward the achievement of specific objectives.

2. Transformative leadership focuses on using innovation and vision to inspire important social change, as opposed to managerial leadership that focuses on behavioral transactions such as evaluating performance, organizing groups, and controlling resources.

3. Transformative leaders help athletes engage in triple-loop learning to reframe how they think and transform who they are in meaningful and productive ways.

4. Power, as the ability to control and influence others, is part of leadership, yet effective leaders must earn respect and credibility as opposed to relying on their designated authoritative power.

5. The "great person" concept of leadership, which states that all great leaders share a common set of characteristics, is a myth, as well as the Rah-Rah and Formula concepts of leadership.

6. Effective leadership requires a constant accounting of the interactive effects of (a) athletes on the team, (b) the characteristics of the leader/coach, and (c) contextual characteristics such as type of organization and changing situations.

7. Coaches need to develop five critical leadership skills: vision, interpersonal relationship skills, effective decision-making styles, knowledge about reinforcement techniques, and the ability to impart useful knowledge to athletes.

8. A leader's vision must be supported by a specific action plan and consistent modeling of the vision and plan by the leader.

9. The most important relationship skills for coaches are storytelling to reframe thinking, and empathy, which is the ability to adopt the perspective of other people.

10. A transformative coach uses all three decision-making styles (autocratic, democratic, and permissive) effectively by assessing the nature of the situation and the amount of input needed by others to make the best informed decision.

11. Research with youth sport coaches demonstrates that coaches trained in reinforcement and communication effectiveness influence athletes in a more positive way than untrained coaches.

Glossary

double-loop learning: helping people to fundamentally reshape the underlying patterns of their thinking and behavior so they are capable of doing different things

empathy: the human skill of knowing how others feel, and understanding how those feelings are affecting them

empowerment: granting power to others by giving them ability or enabling them to effectively accept responsibility

leadership: the behavioral, psychological, and social process of influencing individuals to move toward the achievement of specific objectives

power: the ability to control and influence others

single-loop learning: helping people develop behavioral strategies to improve and perform better

transactional leadership: leaders influence followers via behavioral transactions such as providing resources and/or doling out rewards and punishments

transformative leadership: altering people's frames of reference or ways of thinking so as to produce shifts in their perceptions and ways of being, living, and responding

triple-loop learning: enabling people to create shifts in their context or point of view about themselves and their world

vision: the ability to perceive something not actually visible, typically broad future aspirations or achievements that depart significantly from the status quo

Study Questions

1. Define leadership and explain the differences between transformative leadership, transactional leadership, managing, and power.
2. Provide examples of single-loop, double-loop, and triple-loop learning, and identify ways that coaches can help athletes move beyond single-loop to more transformative learning experiences.
3. Identify the three leadership myths and provide a rationale for why they are myths.
4. Explain the three-ring circus model of leadership and discuss why an interactional perspective is necessary for effective leadership.
5. What are the five hats, or required psychological/behavioral/social skills, that must be worn by transformative coaches? Explain why each hat must be included for effective leadership to occur.
6. What do we mean by leadership "vision," and how can coaches put their visions into motion?
7. Describe the three decision-making styles coaches need, and explain why transformative coaches use all three styles at certain times.
8. Why is democratic decision-making often confused with the democratic process? Explain how the three decision-making styles can be used in a team with a democratic process.
9. Cite some research and anecdotal evidence from the chapter that supports effective reinforcement as an important leadership requirement.

Reflective Learning Activities

1. Hypocrisy

College athletics—and to a growing extent, high school athletics—have created a tough dilemma for coaches. These sport programs were established as extracurricular activities within *educational* institutions, with the objective being the development of athletes' skills within a competitive environment. The establishment of these sport programs was based on the balanced triad philosophy presented in Chapter 2, which emphasizes the need for a congruent perspective between performance, development, and experiences in sport.

Schools and colleges continue to pay lip service to the educational nature of sports (mainly to keep their tax-exempt status), while at the same time implementing a professional model whereby performance and winning supersede all other objectives. Coaches are hired with accolades to their strength of character and their concern for individual athletes, while the bottom line is that they are expected to win—often at any cost. Many coaches will tell you that they agree with the balanced triad philosophy, but they also know that to keep their jobs they had better win. They are effective leaders, but they are constrained by the current sport structure to professionalize their attitudes and coaching practices to fulfill their ambitions in the coaching ranks.

How should leaders in sport, especially coaches, deal with this hypocritical dilemma? Discuss the coach's dilemma within this hypocritical sport structure. Identify several alternatives that could alleviate the problem. (Groups of 4 for 10 minutes; then large group discussion for 10 minutes)

2. My Way or the Highway

In the chapter, we discussed how autocratic decision-making is a useful leadership behavior, but within an overall *democratic leadership process*. However, many coaches adhere to a total *autocratic* leadership process because they believe it works. Why is this? Discuss the tendency in sports for coaches to run their programs in a totally autocratic manner. Identify why this happens, the outcomes from this approach, and why it is so difficult to change. (Groups of 3 for 10 minutes; then large group discussion for 10 minutes)

3. Your Coaching Objectives

a. Take a few minutes and write down at least five coaching objectives. These would be objectives that you feel are of primary importance for athletes in your particular coaching context.
b. Look at the objectives that you have written. For each objective, decide which component of the triad philosophy (Chapter 2) it emphasizes. Beside your objectives, write the initials

P, D, or E to represent optimal performance, development, or experience. Are your objectives skewed toward one part of the triad? Or do your objectives represent the balance needed for quality sport participation as shown in the triad?

c. Take the time now to develop additional objectives as needed to represent all three components of the triad. Remember that your coaching objectives should represent the whole model, as opposed to over-emphasizing one component over another. (Individual activity)

4. Any Leaders Out There?

Coaches are always seeking team leaders or athletes who emerge to strongly influence their teammates in productive ways. Instead of waiting for these leaders to emerge, what things can coaches do to develop leaders within a team? Identify several ways that coaches can build effective team leadership in athletes. (10 minutes in groups of 4; 10 minutes for whole group to discuss)

5. Leadership Report Card

Grade yourself on each of the following leadership skills. Use the traditional grades:
(A = excellent, B = good, C = average, D = below average, F = poor or not at all)

Scoring: (A = 4, B = 3, C = 2, D = 1, F = 0)

Sum the scores for items 1-3
for your Vision Score   _____

Sum the scores for items 4-6
for your Relationship Score   _____

Sum the scores for items 7-9
for your Control Score   _____

Sum the scores for items 10-12
for your Reinforcement Score   _____

Sum the scores for items 13-15
for your Information Score   _____

Transformative Leadership Total Score   _____

Interpreting Your Leadership Score:

60 - 55	Electric transformer, circus ringmaster, and mad hatter rolled into one!
54 - 45	Good leader—work to polish and refine your leadership skills in specific areas.
44 - 30	Typical or average leadership skills—need to become more transformative.
29 - 19	Weak leader—reread this chapter to help you get started.
18 - 0	Turn in your whistle . . . and forget about running for public office!

6. High Point and Low Point Lessons (Lynn, 2002)

Experience is often the best teacher. However, experience is worthless unless you learn from the past. Treat your past as a rich source of knowledge to help you become more effective. In this exercise, visit your past to examine your high and low points as a leader. Your frame of mind should be open to learning, not judgmental or self-critical. Don't bury your failures—learn from them and then file them away!

a. Consider a few low points related to your position as leader. Reflect deeply on these times. What can you learn about yourself from these low points? Write down at least two lessons.

_____

_____

_____

_____

b. Consider some of your high points as a leader. Reflect deeply on these times. What can you learn about yourself from these high points? Write down at least two lessons.

_____

_____

_____

_____

c. On the continuum below, place an X on the line that indicates your level of personal satisfaction with the leader you have become.

$\longleftrightarrow$

very dissatisfied   very satisfied

What would make your X move up the scale toward more satisfaction?

_____

_____

_____

_____

Chapter

Six

Team Cohesion

Photo by Brett Hansbauer

Chapter Preview

In this chapter, you'll learn:

*   the nature of task and social cohesion,
*   how cohesion influences behavior in sport,
*   how to create a HOW WE DO IT HERE culture, and
*   team building exercises to build TEAM cohesion.

"Teamwork is the essence of life . . . Great teamwork is the only way to reach our ultimate moments, to create the breakthroughs that define our careers, to fulfill our lives with a sense of lasting significance. All of us are team players, whether we know it or not. Our significance arrives through our vital connections to other people, through all the teams of our lives . . . Our best efforts, combined with those of our teammates, grow into something far greater and far more satisfying than anything we could have achieved on our own." **Pat Riley**, professional basketball coach *(Riley, 1993, pp. 15-16)*

P eak experiences in sport often occur within teams that possess just the right "chemistry." One legendary example is the magical team chemistry of the 1980 U.S. Olympic Ice Hockey Team, depicted in the movie *Miracle*, which stunned the world by defeating the powerful Soviet team on their way to a gold medal in Lake Placid. Another stunner occurred in the 1985 NCAA men's basketball championship game when Villanova beat a powerful Georgetown team led by Patrick Ewing. Villanova made 22 of 29 field goal attempts for the game, an unbelievable 79%, including 9 of 10 in the second half. Ed Pinckney, hero of the Villanova team, describes it: "I've thought about this a lot through the years. During our run, there wasn't a lot of talking on

the court. Guys just suddenly knew what other guys were going to do before they did it. The chemistry was incredible, and I still don't know what triggered it. Maybe going through so many wars over the years, three seniors getting so comfortable with each other. There was just so much . . . trust" (Layden, 2004, p. 73). A more recent example would be the U.S. Women's Soccer Team that captured the 1999 World Cup in front of a packed Rose Bowl in Pasadena, California, in a wild penalty kick shoot-out.

In a survey of 65 U.S. coaches who participated in the 1996 Atlanta and 1994 Nagano Olympic Games, team cohesion was identified by the coaches as one of the three top factors influencing success at the Olympics (Gould, Greenleaf, Guinan, & Chung,

● **105**

2002). As a coach, you know that the ability of athletes to interact effectively in pursuing team goals often influences performance more so than individual talent. As professional basketball coach Pat Riley suggests in the above quote, the cohesive forces of the team create a driving force far stronger than the sum of the individual abilities on the team. Thus, gaining the Inner Edge is important for teams, not just individual athletes.

The significant influence of team chemistry on performance and satisfaction in sport has spawned the systematic study of group dynamics in sport psychology. A **team** is *a group of individuals who are expected to work together with commitment to reach a common goal.* **Team cohesion**, the focus of this chapter, refers to *the team's ability to interact effectively in their pursuit of team goals and group satisfaction.* Popular terms for team cohesion include team unity, togetherness, and "team chemistry." Cohesion is an important social-psychological objective for sport teams because it enhances performance and also makes team membership more enjoyable. **Team culture** refers to *the formal and informal social and organizational systems within the team* that ultimately influence team cohesion and performance. **Team building** refers to *a deliberate process or attempt to develop an effective team culture that will nurture and support team cohesion and performance.* In this chapter, these three terms are discussed extensively to

- provide you with a basic understanding of group cohesion, and
- identify team building strategies that you can use to develop a productive and enjoyable team culture and greater team cohesion.

A Case Study on Team Cohesion

To assist you in understanding the many factors that influence team cohesion, the 1996 U.S. Olympic women's basketball team will serve as a case study for this chapter. The following case description frames the team situation from which examples will be drawn throughout the chapter.

The 1996 U.S. Olympic women's basketball team spent 14 months together, traveling more than 100,000 miles, playing 52 games, prior to the start of the Olympic Games in Atlanta. Their global barn-storming tour included a game in Siberia, where the court was so cold that the play-

ers wore coats and gloves when they weren't in the game. And part of the women's responsibility as a team member was the caretaking of a mechanical pig mascot named Babe.

The team culture was interesting. Point guard Teresa Edwards had played in the last three Olympic Games, and she had a chance in Atlanta of becoming the first basketball player to ever win three Olympic gold medals. Power forward Katrina McClain turned down a contract offer of $300,000 from a team in Hungary so she could play on the U.S. Olympic Team (where she made $50,000). Rebecca Lobo joined the U.S. team after leading her University of Connecticut team to an undefeated season and national championship, ultimately being named college player of the year. Although she was an outstanding player in the college ranks, she was slow in comparison to the rest of the U.S. squad, yet she was assured a place on the team due to her marketing appeal. Only with the support of her teammate Jennifer Azzi (another former player of the year from Stanford) was Lobo able to meet the speed and endurance requirements to stay on the team. Although she lacked the performance ability of Edwards, McClain, Lisa Leslie, and Sheryl Swoopes, Lobo was the fan favorite of the touring U.S. Team. "How would you feel," Lobo asked Azzi, "if you were playing the worst of any player on the team and got the most attention?" (Wolff, 1996b, p. 96). Lobo, Swoopes, and Leslie received the most commercial endorsement opportunities. Reserve forward Carla McGhee spoke of this attention, "I would love to have a contract . . . but there's no room for jealousy" (Wolff, 1996b, p. 97).

Added to this mix of team culture was coach Tara VanDerveer, who took a leave of absence from her coaching position at Stanford University to reestablish American superiority in women's basketball. The U.S. team had finished third at the 1992 Barcelona Games and had suffered another painful loss to Brazil in the 1994 World Championships. VanDerveer is a tough and demanding coach who was not dazzled by the outstanding credentials of her players. "Performance is the basis for being on this team, not reputation or who's popular," she stated (Wolff, 1996b, p. 96). VanDerveer was also concerned about Edwards and McClain, as national team veterans, buying into her system of play. She stated, "I didn't want to get into a yearlong fight with a player who was bucking the system . . . But they bought into it. And if they were going to buy into it, it was going to work. Your best players have to be your leaders. And they both decided very early that they were going to be our leaders" (Wolff, 1996a, p. 60).

The team committed to two clear objectives from the beginning. First, their goal was to win the gold medal at the 1996 Olympics to restore American women's basketball back to international prominence. Their second goal was to create excitement, acceptance, and support for girls' and women's basketball in the United States and across the world. Throughout their 14-month tour, they would painstakingly make public appearances and sign autographs for hours as they honored their commitment to serve as tireless ambassadors for the women's game. On the final day of the Olympics in Atlanta, the U.S. team completed a perfect 60-0 record by defeating Brazil 111-87 to win the gold medal. Their gold medal performance was their best ever with a team record 30 assists. The players mounted the medal stand holding hands as a gesture of the cohesion that had taken them to this final crowning moment.

Photo: Miami University IT Communications

What important aspects of team culture and cohesion can you identify from the case study? Identify obstacles that had to be overcome for the U.S. team to achieve cohesion, and then identify some key occurrences that may have facilitated the team's development of cohesion and outstanding success. Then, check your ideas against those presented in the chapter as you read on.

Cohesion Basics

In this section, the basics of cohesion are presented including the difference between task and social cohesion, the dynamic nature of cohesion, and the ways in which cohesion influences behavior in sport.

Task and Social Cohesion

As defined previously, cohesion is the ability of team members to interact effectively in pursuing group goals and attaining group satisfaction. The first cohesion basic to understand is the difference between task and social cohesion. **Task cohesion** refers to *the team's ability to interact effectively to successfully achieve performance or task goals.* Consider the obstacles faced by the U.S. Basketball Team in their pursuit of task cohesion. As any coach or athlete can tell you, an All-Star-type team such as the Olympic team often struggles in achieving task cohesion due to unfamiliarity with each other's tendencies and playing styles. Also, because everyone on the U.S. team was a star in college (most were All-

Americans and several were Players of the Year), some players had to accept and fulfill less glamorous roles than they were accustomed to. The U.S. team was successful because outstanding players like Jennifer Azzi, Don Staley, and Rebecca Lobo accepted and competently fulfilled their roles on the team. The best indicator of task cohesion was their perfect 60-0 win-loss record and the 30 total team assists statistic achieved in the gold medal win over Brazil. This stat in basketball is indicative of players' abilities and willingness to pass the ball effectively and unselfishly to set up a score for a teammate.

Quotable Quote

"To be the best in the world. . . it's even more satisfying as a team, because that's more difficult. If I play well, that's one thing. But to make others play better. . ." **Bill Russell**, winner of two NCAA championships, over 50 college games in a row, the 1956 Olympic gold medal, and 11 NBA championships in 13 years *(Deford, 1999, p. 102)*

Social cohesion refers to *the team's ability to get along interpersonally or socially.* The focus of social cohesion is about how people get along with each other, as opposed to how well people work together as in task cohesion. A team is socially cohesive if they like each other and enjoy spending time together. However, it is a mistake to mandate social cohesion, or to mistakenly equate social with task cohesion. Many coaches confuse these concepts, thus they believe that a team can only be effective if social cohesion is high. Thus, social cohesion is sometimes forced on athletes who are expected to room together or spend time together socially as if these mandatory social requirements will automatically transfer into better group performance. Attempting to force social cohesion onto a team is often rebuffed by team members who may resent coaches who seem as if they're policing choices about friends and social activities. Also, emphasizing social cohesion can sometimes interfere with task cohesion or other aspects of team sports that are important for performance. For example, athletes may spend valuable practice time "cutting up" with their friends, which interferes with the development of task cohesion or effective team performance. Also, extreme social cohesion may influence the intra-team competitiveness that is needed to push teammates to achieve goals and maximize their potential.

This is not to say that social cohesion should not be valued as it is an enjoyable occurrence within a team. Life is much easier when we work with people that we like and enjoy being around. Often, teammates become socially cohesive as they share interests and values related to their sport participation. As discussed in Chapter 3, an important motivational need of athletes is to be accepted or belong to a group, so a certain amount of social cohesion is important to meet this need. This could take the form of emphasizing that athletes should be supportive and respectful of teammates to build a sense of "team," which creates pride in group membership and feelings of being a part of something significant. Fortunately, the U.S. team possessed social as well as task cohesion, which probably made their thousand-mile journey, numerous hotel rooms, and travel fatigue much less onerous.

Dynamic Nature of Cohesion

Another important factor to consider about cohesion is that it constantly ebbs and flows throughout a competitive season. That is, cohesion is dynamic and constantly changing, as opposed to being a static quality that remains firm within a team. The dynamic ups and downs in cohesion are a natural process of human interaction in groups. Often, conflict arises within teams for any number of reasons and coaches and athletes often panic or overreact to this conflict as a threat to team cohesion. Yet, *interpersonal conflict is inevitable* where human beings are involved, and conflict typically occurs even within the most cohesive teams. In minimal or moderate quantities, conflict can even be viewed as a result of intensity and commitment in goal pursuits or as a natural offshoot of personal or team growth. What is critical for strong

and enduring team cohesion are the ways in which teams *resolve* conflict. Athletes should be encouraged to resolve inter-team conflict in productive, non-emotional ways on their own, without intervention from coaches. Coaches should step in to arbitrate conflict resolution when the conflict begins to interfere with the pursuit of team goals.

Quotable Quote

"We must all hang together, else we shall all hang separately."

Benjamin Franklin, upon the signing of the Declaration of Independence

---

One popular description of the dynamic nature of cohesion is the idea that sport teams endure four developmental stages in pursuing task and social cohesion: *forming, storming, norming,* and *performing* (Tuckman, 1965). Consider the 14-month experience of the U.S. basketball team in negotiating these four stages. First, the team was formed as the result of tryouts from which the coaching staff chose team members. At this point, the players made an initial assessment of their possible roles on the team. The storming stage involved the typical conflicts that arise in adjusting to various roles. Perhaps some storming occurred due to the inescapable prestige afforded to certain athletes (e.g., Lobo and Swoopes) to the exclusion of the others. Storming also may have occurred due to the fact that all members of the team were once the best player on their college teams, so new roles had to be considered and accepted, which often precipitates some interpersonal conflict. The team reached the norming stage when team roles become somewhat stable and accepted, and respect developed for each player's unique contribution to the team. For example, Teresa Edwards rose to defend the much maligned play of Lobo and Nikki McCray by saying, "A team . . . needs a dose of everything—experience, youth, competitiveness. Rebecca and Nikki represent youth. They only needed time and patience" (Wolff, 1996b, p. 97). Obviously, teams reach the performing stage when most structural issues are resolved, roles are clear, valued, and accepted, and when task cohesion has reached its highest point. From all acounts of the U.S. team, they peaked at just the right time at the Olympic Games where their gold medal performance was lauded as the best ever by an American team.

The forming, storming, norming, and performing sequence of developing cohesion may occur several times across a season. Cohesion does not follow a linear path that builds to the final solid achievement of team cohesion. Team cohesion has been compared to the swing of a pendulum, which moves back and forth in constant motion. Thus, coaches and athletes should be prepared for the dynamic, often conflictual merging of personalities that constantly influences team cohesion. Later in the chapter, we'll talk about team building ideas to help you nurture an effective team culture and build strong cohesion within your team.

Clipboard

What's Good for the Goose . . .

"When you see geese . . . flying in a 'V' formation, think about what science has learned about why they fly that way. As each bird flaps its wings, it creates uplift for the bird immediately following it. By flying in a 'V' formation, the whole flock can fly at least 71% farther than if each bird flew on its own. Perhaps people who share a common direction can get where they are going quicker and easier if they cooperate.

Whenever a goose falls out of formation, it feels the resistance of trying to go it alone and quickly gets back . . . to take advantage of flying with the flock. If we have as much sense as a goose, we will work with others who are going the same way as we are. When the lead goose gets tired, he rotates back . . . and another goose flies on point. It pays to take turns doing hard jobs from our group. Perhaps the geese honking from behind are even the 'cheering squad' to encourage those up front to keep up their speed.

Finally, if a goose weakens or is wounded and falls out of formation, two geese fall out and follow him down to help and protect him. They stay with him until he is either able to fly or until he is dead. Then they set out on their own, or with another formation until they catch up with their group. If we had the sense of a goose, we would stand by each other like that" (Mears & Voehl, 1994, p. 2).

How Cohesion Influences Behavior in Sport

While cohesion sounds like a good thing, where's the proof? Is cohesion really important for teams to perform better, or is it just a "warm fuzzy" type of concept that sounds good but doesn't really matter? What is it about cohesion that influences athletes to work together in a more productive way? And can too much cohesion ever become a bad thing for teams? Let's address these questions.

Cohesion enhances team performance. Research has shown that cohesive teams do perform better than less cohesive teams (Carron, Colman, Wheeler, & Stevens, 2002). In fact, cohesion is a more important factor in influencing performance in sport than any other type of team or group (e.g., military groups, unions). Both task and social cohesion are related to performance success in sport, indicating that coaches should be aware of both types of cohesion and their effects on team performance. The research also shows that cohesion in female teams is more strongly related to performance than on male teams (Carron et al., 2002). This suggests that females, who are socialized in society to be more relationship-oriented and nurturing of others, perform better in team situations when there is a high level of cohesion. Thus, a drop in cohesion in a female team might be more disruptive to performance and team success as compared to male teams.

Photo by Brett Hansbauer

As you might expect, cohesion has been found to be stronger in interactive teams (e.g., volleyball, basketball, field hockey) as compared to coactive teams (e.g., swimming, track and field, golf). It seems logical that cohesion would be strongly emphasized in sports that require extensive tactical interaction and interpersonal cooperation. For example, volleyball teams require constant communication between the setter and hitters regarding the type and placement of various sets along the net. When cohesion breaks down in volleyball team, performance suffers greatly due to the highly interactive nature of volleyball, where different teammates are required by the rules to touch the ball and communication is constantly required on court.However, cohesion is related to success in both interactive and coactive teams, even though the absolute levels of cohesion between the types of teams are different. For example, highly cohesive golf teams spent more time giving each other tips regarding technique and strategy and were more committed to achieving team goals than less cohesive teams (Williams & Widmeyer, 1991). Thus, cohesion may enhance performance in all types of sport teams by facilitating intra-team communication and commitment to team goals.

How cohesion can become negative. Can cohesion ever have negative effects on athletes' behavior? The answer is yes—if cohesion is narrowly defined or twisted to mandate conformity. There are times when extreme cohesion is hazardous for youth, like when they are urged to "go along with the crowd" even if this leads to aggression, violence, or harmful personal behavior such as abusing drugs or taking insane risks. This hyperconformity, discussed previously in Chapter 2, involves a rigid and typically harmful code of behavior expected of group members. Several years ago in Glen Ridge, New Jersey, a group of upper-middle class high school athletes sodomized a mentally retarded girl with a baseball bat in a horrifying distortion of male bonding and hyperconformity to demonstrate their power over and disdain for weak individuals. Often, violent group behavior occurs in cohesive groups due to a diffused sense of responsibility. This emphasizes the importance of athletes retaining their individuality and independent sense of self when making important life decisions.

Hyperconformity can also lead to crossing the line in team hazing rituals, where athletes can be seriously hurt and even killed, all in the name of "fitting in" with the team. In a 2003 preseason training camp, teammates brutally sodomized three football players from Mepham (NY) High School using broom sticks, pine cones, and golf balls (Wahl & Wertheim, 2003). As you might expect, all three athletes experienced extensive physical and emotional damage, and were subjected to taunts from classmates after they reluctantly told the truth about the hazing incident. The original idea behind hazing, to "initiate" new team members in silly yet harmless ways to bond them to the team, has expanded to offer an excuse for bullying, ignorant behavior that destroys lives, as well as teams. Hyperconformity and negative hazing rituals are serious problems in sport, and coaches are ultimately responsible for a team culture and the behavior of individual athletes within that culture who would allow such things to occur.

Cohesion could also be problematic if a team falls into the trap of **"groupthink,"** which is the *tendency for members of a group to reach consensus and make decisions too superficially and too quickly* (Janis, 1972). This happens because group members do not wish to endanger the group's sense of cohesion by questioning commonly held, though often unspoken, assumptions. This is popularly known as "peer pressure," something we all warn our children against! Groupthink has contributed to several historical disasters, such as the consensus to commit mass group suicide by 914 members of the People's Temple, a destructive doomsday cult in Jonestown in 1978, as well as the 1986 *Challenger* space shuttle explosion that killed seven crew members. Prior to the launch of the *Challenger*, there was much speculation among engineers and consultants as to the effects the unseasonably cold Florida temperature would have on the shuttle. The shuttle exploded when the O-ring seals on the rocket failed due to the cold temperature. However, the decision to launch was made based on the pressure of groupthink, even though individuals later admitted that they had misgivings about the decision, but agreed to the launch.

In my work as a sport psychology consultant with a college volleyball team, the groupthink problem was identified in a team building exercise as an obstacle to the team's performance. Because the previous year's team had many interpersonal conflicts, the players on this particular team really focused on everyone liking each other and avoiding conflict.

However, they soon realized that this pressure to conform and avoid conflict interfered with their ability to be honest with each other and resolve important performance-related issues. This included disagreeing, giving teammates critical feedback, and being intense on the court. By identifying the groupthink problem, reaching an understanding that conflict was not a bad thing, and agreeing on interpersonal guidelines for giving feedback and resolving conflict with teammates, the team got rid of the groupthink attitude that was holding them back from becoming the best team they could be. They realized that social cohesion in the form of groupthink was definitely not as important as pushing each other to compete at a level that could win a championship and stretch the performance levels of each other and the team.

Consider the following quote by Tisha Venturini, professional soccer player, on how important competition within the team was during her development at the University of North Carolina: "The great thing about our team is that it gets nasty at times, but we all understand that's what is making us better. Let's say I am going against Mia in one-v-ones. The harder we go, the more we are helping each other. If I am going fifty percent on defense, that doesn't make her any better. Sure, you can get angry. I get angry, but once the practice is over that's it. It's healthy. It gets bad at times, but the personalities on the team won't let it carry off the field. Everyone understands that to be the best in the world, this is how we have to train" (Gregg, 1999, p. 9).

Cliques, which are *subgroups of cohesion within a team*, can also be problematic if they are allowed to disrupt team cohesion. The social aspects of cliques are not necessarily disruptive for teams, as people typically prefer the company of certain individuals for social activities. Cliques, however, should be considered a threat to team cohesion and performance if (a) they become exclusionary to the point of making others feel that they are not wanted or less valued, and/or (b) if team cohesion is in any way compromised by the dynamics of the clique. This latter case could occur if athletes were less supportive of or cooperative with teammates outside of their social clique, or if competitive performance decisions become influenced by clique membership. Overall, athletes should be given free rein to develop friendships and social links with whomever they wish, but they should provide unconditional support to teammates and engage in unbiased performance behavior that is unrelated to any social concerns.

In summary, cohesion in a sport team is a positive group psychosocial state, which all teams should strive toward. However, all athletes should maintain a strong self-concept and personal identity to avoid falling into the hyperconformity or groupthink trap. Diversity in ethnicity, race, attitudes, values, and personalities should be supported and valued in teams, as they provide a wide range of resources with which to solve problems and pursue group goals. Coaches should educate their athletes that conflict and disagreements are okay as long as they are resolved in an appropriate manner (this is discussed later in the chapter).

Team Building (TB) for Cohesion: HOW WE DO IT HERE!

As defined at the beginning of the chapter, team building (TB) refers to a deliberate attempt to build an effective team culture that nurtures and supports team cohesion and performance. A team's culture includes the formal and informal social and organizational systems within the team that affect its cohesion and performance. Basically, you want to use TB to build the type of team culture that creates cohesion and leads to outstanding team performance.

Think of your team culture as "HOW WE DO IT HERE" (Thompson, 2003). Your task as coach is to engineer the team climate that you want for HOW WE DO IT HERE. Once the HOW WE DO IT HERE climate gets established and accepted by your athletes, you'll find that they actually carry it out themselves. Examples of HOW WE DO IT HERE abound in popular books written by coaches and athletes who have been involved in many outstanding and cohesive programs.

Quotable Quote

"The entire aim of our policies at Tennessee is to get our players to discipline each other. . . We have evolved a system in which. . . I don't have to do a whole lot of punishing, penalizing, or pushing them. Our upperclassmen become the disciplinarians of our team instead of me." **Pat Summitt**, University of Tennessee women's basketball coach (Janssen, 2004, p. 123)

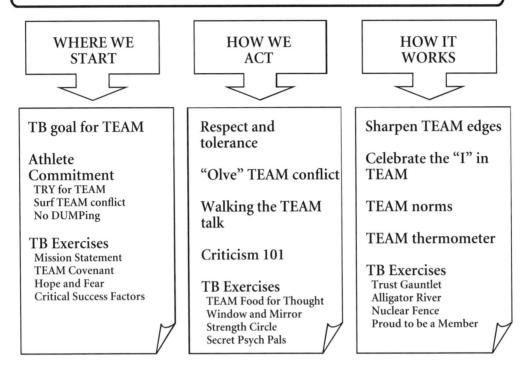

Figure 6.1 Building the TEAM

In this section, a HOW WE DO IT HERE framework is provided to help you engage in TB with your team (see Figure 6.1). Three steps to TB are outlined including where we start, how we act, and how it works. Within each step, practical TB suggestions are presented about ways in which a productive, cohesive, motivational climate may be developed within sport teams. The section ends with some examples of TB exercises, all of which are described at the end of the chapter. These TB exercises are listed in Figure 6.1 based on where they might fit in your overall TB program. Obviously, you can use these exercises in many ways and also find additional exercises to build your team's sense of HOW WE DO IT HERE.

As a starting point, I've used the acronym TEAM to represent the popular phrase Together Everyone Achieves More. The idea is to introduce TB based on a concept such as TEAM, so your athletes readily understand the importance of team cohesion and TB. There are other examples of popular TB themes, such as the Power of One (DiCicco & Hacker, 2002), and I encourage you to develop your own for your team.

Step 1: Where We Start

A cohesive team culture is like a geranium: it must be nurtured in the right environment to thrive. Thus, Step 1 in TB is to establish the necessary conditions for which a cohesive team culture can thrive. Basically, this is where we start on our way to creating the HOW WE DO IT HERE climate that we want and need (see Figure 6.1).

Specifically, where we start involves two foundation steps for TB:

- clarifying the goal of TB
- gaining a commitment to TB by all team members

Clarifying the TB goal for TEAM. All athletes on the team must understand the TB goal for TEAM. The goal is not to create a "warm fuzzy" feeling among teammates. Nor is the goal to foster similarity or total agreement among teammates. The goal of TB is *to develop and maintain effective intra-team interactions to facilitate cohesion and the spirit of TEAM (Together Everyone Achieves More).* Differences can be accepted and even celebrated, but they must exist within an atmosphere of mutual respect and unconditional support for members of the team.

Athlete commitment to TB. Athletes cannot be indifferent to or cynical about participating in TB, or it simply will not work. Many athletes state that they are interested in developing the Inner Edge, yet they balk when they find out that techniques like TB do not work by magic. TB works and cohesion develops when athletes become deeply committed to engaging in the self-reflection, honest and open dialogue, and behavioral change necessary to sustain an optimal team culture. It is helpful to gain a commitment from formal leaders (captains) and emergent leaders (athletes on the team who have influence and lead by example) to TB, which serves to model commitment to others.

All team members should understand that a cohesive team culture does not occur in one meeting, and they must commit to a continuous TB process of team meetings, activities, and discussions. Team cohesion is attained by effort and persistence over time to create a consistent and stable team culture. The best time to begin TB is in the initial stages of team development, such as the beginning of preseason. The worst time to try TB is when things are going wrong, such as when the team is mired in a slump or losing streak. If TB is attempted as a quick fix for problems, the result is most often failure and a lot of cynical and distrusting athletes. TB should be an integral part of a team's experience from day one; otherwise, its effects will be superficial and short-lived.

Clipboard

Playing for Each Other

The University of North Carolina women's soccer program has won 18 national championships in the last 23 years, giving new meaning to the term sports dynasty. Prior to the 1997 national championship game, coach Anson Dorrance read three deeply personal letters written to the team by the seniors who were about to play their last game for the Tarheels. Dorrance summed up how the players' commitment to each other created a powerfully cohesive team: "You would think they are playing for a national championship, but they aren't. Every one of those girls is playing for the people around her."

As shown in Figure 6.1, three key points can be made about the commitment required of athletes in TB:

1. Athletes have to TRY for the TEAM. TRY stands for "take responsibility yourself" (DiCicco & Hacker, 2002). All team members must be willing to accept personal responsibility for their own physical training, mental training, and commitment to TB for the TEAM. With regard to TB, personal responsibility involves many things that can be identified for athletes, such as shedding pretense to be honest and sincere with teammates, and actively engaging in discussions as opposed to only listening. Sometimes athletes tell me that they'll sit in on TB meetings, but they would prefer not to talk openly in front of the group. This is unacceptable and is really just an excuse to avoid accepting personal responsibility for team cohesion. There is an "I" in TEAM, and that "I" involves each athlete doing his or her part to nurture a cohesive team culture or accept responsibility for achieving TEAM. *Every* athlete on the team must TRY for TEAM to happen.

Clipboard

TRY It!

The year prior to the 1999 World Cup, the U.S. Women's Soccer team was on an exhausting international playing tour. After arriving at the hotel in Brazil after an all-night flight, star player Julie Foudy unloaded her personal gear in her room and then told her astonished and dead-tired roommate, "I'm going downstairs to help unload the bus." No one asked Foudy to help with the team gear and it wasn't her responsibility, yet she took on the responsibility herself to make the TEAM work. And interestingly, her teammate followed her downstairs, showing that when we TRY, our teammates notice and will TRY harder as well!

On the same trip, the team was doing fitness training on the field on a very hot day. The last fitness drill was very demanding, and required the players to completely cross the line (not just touch it) before the whistle was blown by the coach. Superstar Mia Hamm hit the line (but was not across it) just as the last whistle blew. Coach Tony DiCicco saw it, but didn't say anything because of the intolerable heat conditions. As the players walked off the field, Hamm approached her coach and said, "Tony, will you time me again? I want to do it right." Hamm met the fitness standard the second time by crossing the line prior the whistle. As her coach explained, it wasn't acceptable to Mia Hamm that she had completed the fitness drill properly, even though nobody else knew it. She took the TRY route to be responsible for her own training, and set a powerful TRY example for her teammates as they watched her rerun the fitness drill.

Little wonder that this team won the gold medal in the 1996 Olympics and the World Cup in 1999! TRYing for your team makes all the difference (Di-Cicco & Hacker, 2002, p. 84).

━━━━━━━━━━━━━━━━━━

2. Surf TEAM conflict. Conflict is like a wave. It has the potential to crash on top of us and knock us down, or to sweep us forward. Help your athletes understand the potential of conflict as a source of learning and growing, and focus them on using conflict when it occurs within teams to "surf" forward and get better.

Athletes and coaches must accept the idea that in building an effective team culture, hidden conflicts and feelings can emerge that at times do not feel very positive. However, these short-term negative feelings are far outweighed by the long-term benefits of "clearing" issues by openly and honestly expressing thoughts and feelings to each other. What is important is that thoughts and feelings are expressed in a climate of mutual respect and in a rational, mature manner. TB is not designed to air out petty grievances or immature outbursts that are often based on personal wants as opposed to team needs. An arbitrator (such as a sport psychology consultant) is often effective in channeling discussion appropriately, but in the absence of this, team leaders can clearly explain ground rules and enforce them. All team members should keep in mind that conflict is not necessarily bad, and that an argument that is appropriately resolved results in greater team growth than if the issue was swept under the carpet.

Music is a good metaphor to use to understand how conflict influences team cohesion (Heerman, 1997). Music involves harmonics that combines both consonant factors and dissonant factors. Just as

in great music, great teams are animated and enlivened by drawing upon *both* consonances and dissonances. Teams always welcome the consonant, such as agreement over roles and the alignment of team energies in pursuing goals. However, many teams attempt to avoid or ignore the dissonant, such as disagreements, conflicts, and negative feelings. In music, dissonance leads to resolution. In teams, embracing the dissonant can enable the team to grow, mature, and evolve into a more trusting, open, and cohesive unit. Remember that cohesion is dynamic, with continual ebb and flow, and the team should embrace and build upon consonances while acknowledging and working through dissonances. Although you may not welcome or enjoy conflict within your team, it is necessary and healthy. Surf it—don't avoid it!

Quotable Quote

"Not everything that is faced can be changed, but nothing can be changed until it is faced."

James Baldwin

3. No DUMPing is allowed. All members of the team must agree that their inputs and feedback in TB sessions will be put forward for the purpose of making things better, perhaps by clarifying a situation or helping to solve a problem. TB sessions are not for dumping or venting feelings in a non-constructive manner. In fact, I tell athletes that DUMPing stands for Distracting, Unproductive, Me-oriented, Petty statements that destroy the TEAM concept. A popular assumption is that team meetings are needed to "blow off steam" or "clear the air," but DUMPing in the form of emotional venting does not enhance cohesion or facilitate problem-solving or conflict resolution. DUMPing typically results from frustration or defensiveness, and team members should talk about and commit to the need to avoid this immature behavior.

Step 2: How We Act

After the necessary conditions are set for effective TB, the second step in creating a cohesive team culture (TEAM) is to clarify expected interpersonal behaviors among team members. That is, you must begin to shape your HOW WE DO IT HERE culture in terms of how athletes act within the program (see Figure 6.1). These guidelines will shape the nature of task and social interactions toward establishing a cohesive unit. Interpersonal guidelines should logically emanate from your coaching philosophy and should be appropriate for the age and level of team members. Following are some examples of interaction guidelines that I believe are important, but I urge you to think creatively about innovative ways to shape interpersonal behaviors among team members.

1. Request mutual respect and tolerance of others. Mutual respect for each other is the most basic and necessary component of a productive team culture. Team members should follow the Golden Rule: treat others as you would like to be treated. This means that when athletes are in conflict with a teammate, they don't resort to emotional outbursts or sarcastic put-downs. This means that if they don't agree with another person, they voice their disagreement in a respectful manner. This means that a teammate is a teammate—which gives her special status and gives others the *responsibility* of supporting and respecting her as a teammate. This doesn't require friendship, but rather a professional attitude of support for her as a teammate. Personal feelings toward others are basically inconsequential in relation to the importance of striving for team goals.

Because sport is so challenging and the goals so important and valued, stress levels get high and individuals tend to overreact and complain about inconsequential things. Team members should keep in mind that at times even our best friends get on our nerves, so the focus should be on being tolerant when teammates engage in behavior that is irritating. Being tolerant is an important mental skill, because tolerance comes from the mature understanding that we can't control the behavior of others. Teams face enough important challenges and need to avoid wasting energy in trying to settle inconsequential problems that naturally occur when humans spend time together. Each athlete should always interact with teammates in a mutually respectful manner, and everyone should be prepared to tolerate small issues and focus attention on team goals as opposed to minor irritations. If we choose to spend our lives looking for the worst in people, then our lives will be preoccupied with small-minded objectives such as gossip. Athletes should

search for the positives in their teammates and focus on their strengths and what they add to the team. These good qualities may be nurtured by expressing appreciation for them, which serves to build a mutually appreciative team culture.

2. Involve, resolve, absolve, evolve. A specific formula for effective conflict management focusing on the "olves" was presented in Chapter 4 on communication. Teach and lead your athletes to follow the four "olves" in conflict resolution, including *involving* your athletes in the decision-making, *resolving* the issue directly and expediently, *absolving* team members of any guilt or bad feelings ("it's over"), and *evolving* as a collaborative team that grows and learns from conflict.

In our case study of the U.S. Basketball Team, conflict came in the form of endorsements and fan support, which was given to certain athletes while excluding others. This could have blocked the development of task and social cohesion within the team, particularly because the attention was unrelated to performance and ability. Using our formula, we would talk initially to the players who were receiving the attention (invOLVE). As in the case of Rebecca Lobo, it seems that this approach would ease the pressure she felt in receiving what she perceived as undue attention. In fact, Lobo could be reminded that she does deserve the attention based on her college accomplishments, and that she can use her forum to promote the rest of the team and women's basketball (absOLVE). Then, the rest of the team could be involved in a group discussion of fan and media support for the team, emphasizing the reality of marketing and endorsement appeal as being beyond the control of the athletes. The resolution could be based on (a) USA Basketball promoting all of the individual athletes in such ways as playing exhibition games in each person's home or university town, (b) players understanding the nature of media and fan support as based on public perception, and (c) the players receiving the most attention keeping this in perspective without guilt, while continuing to support the team's goals and mission (resOLVE). These players could then be absolved of any guilt they are feeling, and the team evolves into a cohesive and mature group, which now has experience in dealing with the media and the fickle nature of public perception (evOLVE).

3. Walk the TEAM talk. Like most things in life, it is far easier to talk about TEAM and HOW WE DO IT HERE than it is to actually *live* it on a day-to-day basis. Challenge your athletes to walk the TEAM talk and lead team discussions as to how to do this. Social support often becomes a buzz word that athletes admit is important for a team, but which in reality they fail to demonstrate because they don't know exactly how to provide social support to teammates. Social support can take many forms, so coaches should explain exactly what forms are needed within a team. Researchers have identified these types of social support as important for sport teams (Rosenfeld & Richman, 1997):

Listening support listen without giving advice or being judgmental

Task appreciation acknowledge teammates' efforts and abilities in training and performance

Task challenge challenge teammates to get better, which builds competence and motivation

Emotional support comfort teammates; let them know you care about them and are with them

Emotional challenge challenge teammates to evaluate their attitudes about team issues

Shared reality make teammates feel you understand their concerns as a teammate going through the same or similar issues

Personal assistance help teammates out by working together after practice or doing them a favor, such as running an errand for them

Clipboard

Winning and Losing Together

As a freshman basketball player for Duke University, Christian Laett-ner stood at the free throw line in front of a huge Meadowlands arena crowd in New Jersey and a national television audience. There was one second left on the clock, and Duke was down by two points. Laettner, all alone at the free throw line with the game seemingly on his shoulders, missed the first shot, the opposing team got the rebound, and the game was over. Duke lost. As the buzzer sounded, Duke's two senior captains (Danny Ferry and Quin Snyder) rushed over to Laettner and put their arms around him. Suddenly, the whole Duke team wrapped themselves around Laettner to console him. Snyder spoke to Laettner, "Laett, don't worry about it, man. We win and lose together."

Two years later playing in the Final Four against powerful #1-ranked Nevada-Las Vegas, Laettner was faced with two free throws with the score tied and 12 seconds left on the clock. Just before shooting, Laettner grinned at his coach, Mike Krzyzewski, and said, "I got 'em, Coach. I got 'em." Krzyzewski remembers: "Forty-seven thousand people in the stands, millions more watching at home, tie score—and Laettner smiles and says, 'I got 'em.'" Laettner made both free throws, and Duke went on to capture their first national championship in the Krzyzewski era. Krzyzewski believes it was his teammates' social support early in his career and the shared responsibility for team success and failure that enabled Laettner to have such extraordinary confidence. Krzyzewski states, "He was able to put that early loss behind him . . . because of what he saw in his teammates' eyes. If, after a failure, a group of people are always able to look at one another and see compassion and empathy in one another's eyes, then they are going to be looking at a winning team" (Krzyzewski, 2000).

Open discussions are useful for teams to identify specific behaviors that promote social support and cohesion within the team. These often are very simple, yet in stating them publicly, athletes are reminded to habitually engage in them. Examples might include the following:

- Say hello, smile, and project an enthusiastic and motivated mood when you walk into practice.
- Ensure that a teammate has unqualified support and encouragement when working to master a new task.
- Take responsibility to fix problems when they arise in team drills instead of expressing frustration, displaying moodiness, or making negative comments.
- Athletes can listen intently and make eye contact when receiving feedback and informa-

tion from coaches. Coaches can do likewise when athletes are talking to them.

> ## Personal Plug-In
>
> Can you think of other specific behaviors that could be specified to promote social support and cohesion for sport teams? Choose a specific age group and sport, so you can tailor your ideas to the specific nature of each situation.

4. All team members must pass Criticism 101. Because sport is an achievement activity, criticism in the form of critical performance evaluation is necessary and even valuable in helping athletes to improve their skills. However, not many people like to receive critical feedback. Thus, I recommend that all coaches spend some time talking with athletes about the importance and productive use of criticism. Call it Criticism 101!

The theme of Criticism 101 is to become aware of the best way to deliver criticism as well as the most productive way to interpret it when received from others. The person offering the criticism should attempt to phrase it constructively, and the person on the receiving end should try to receive it in a constructive manner. Also, both parties should focus on the intent of the message (Orlick, 1986a). It is helpful if the person offering the criticism explains her intent when offering the criticism. For example, a teammate could say in a team meeting, "I'm saying this because I think it will help us perform better." A coach could remind an athlete to whom she is providing critical feedback, "I'm telling you this so you can make improvements to get better."

Athletes should try to understand the intent of coaches' critical comments even when they don't explain it, and to take it as a compliment because they wouldn't be criticized unless the coach felt they had the ability to use the criticism to improve. Everyone on the team (including the coach) should agree to raise their "defensiveness threshold," meaning that criticism should be accepted as an important extrinsic reinforcer to provide information that we all need to change our behavior in productive ways. Knee-jerk defensive reactions to criticism are immature and only serve to stifle athlete development and team cohesion.

Step 3: How It Works

If you've gotten this far in your program, you're doing great. You've gotten your athletes to buy into the TEAM concept and to consistently act in ways that represent HOW WE DO IT HERE. There are some additional things you can do to keep the TEAM working to maximize team cohesion and performance, representing "how it works" now that you're at this point (see Figure 6.1).

1. Sharpen the TEAM edges. Good coaches know that successful team performance is based on sharpening athletes' skills through focused training and instruction. The "outer" performance edge must be achieved by repetitive and intense training, constantly sharpening this edge to create a fit, skilled, task-cohesive team. Thus, coaches manage, organize, and teach effectively to reduce the probability of team breakdowns due to a lack of task cohesion. The best coaches are able to quickly diagnose performance breakdowns that result from a lack of team coordination, and then organize a specific training technique to correct the coordination problem. For example, if a volleyball team tends to break down defensively during one specific rotation (position of players on the floor), the coach can simulate different types of attack against this particular rotation. This is an important step in TB, which provides a sound foundation of correct performance interaction through repetitive drilling and practice. Athletes should be aware that the over-learning that occurs through the many hours of practice is an essential part of TB. Coaches should closely observe team performance to note the exact precipitating factors that disrupt task cohesion and create breakdown drills that smooth over the disruptive factor. For example, a basketball team's inability to execute a full court press could be the result of players not communicating to each other the movements of their opponents.

Of course, the Inner Edge of athletes must be sharpened as well, and if you're reading this book, I know that you are a coach who is committed to this edge as well as the physical training edge. Incorporating different types of mental training sharpens the Inner Edge not only of individual athletes, but of the team as a whole. In particular, Parts 2 and 3 of this book provide you with many examples of how to coach for this Inner Edge with your team.

2. Celebrate the I in team. A common saying in sport is "there is no *I* in *team*." Well, actually there is, or at least there needs to be. Research with groups of people has substantiated an occurrence termed **social loafing**, which means that *individuals tend to exert less effort as the size of the group increases* (Latane, Williams, & Harkins, 1979). Social loafing in a team occurs due to a sense of diffused responsibility with athletes feeling that teammates will pick up their slack. However, effective team management can totally eliminate social loafing. The key is to make sure that each athlete's performance is monitored and evaluated. When the behavior and performance of individual athletes are identified, social loafing disappears. Coaches should use filming, behavioral checklists, practice statistics, or any other methods to ensure that each athlete on the team understands that his or her individual behavior is being evaluated. Social loafing may also be stymied by convincing athletes that their input is essential for team success. When athletes accept their role on the team as essential for the team to reach its goals, then they are likely to fulfill their role with great motivation.

So you see, there *is* an I in team, or at least there should be if you want to maximize individual contributions to task cohesion. Actually, this traditional saying has been used by coaches to indicate that team goals should override individual goals. (The relationship between team and individual goals is discussed in greater detail in Chapter 8.) Obviously, individuals cannot pursue their personal goals at the expense of team productivity. But don't misunderstand this as saying there is no I in team. There has to be! Individual athletes will buy into the team, commit to its goals, and accept and fulfill needed roles on the team *if and only if* they receive individual attention and reinforcement for doing these things.

To keep the I in team, the dynamic duo of *goals and roles* should be emphasized. Each athlete should set personal goals that are congruent with the broader team objectives. Sometimes these goals need to be modified from the athlete's original personal objectives (e.g., starting setter on the volleyball team) into goals that fit needed roles on the team (e.g., back-up setter, defensive specialist, and team sparkplug when she comes onto the floor). What is critical—and I mean critical—is that the goals and roles of all team members must be supported and valued by the coaches and players on the team. Coaches de-

Photo by Sgt. Jim Goodwon, courtesy of USMC

stroy cohesion when they persuade athletes to accept particular roles, and then fail to reinforce athletes for effectively fulfilling these roles. If it is true that a team is only as strong as its weakest link, then all links should be equally valued and rewarded.

Clipboard

Starburst Power!

At the end of an extended road trip to Florida, swim coach Roch King of Bloomsburg University (PA) gave each of the swimmers on his team three Starburst candies. He told them that the first one was from him to them as thanks for their hard work and focus on the trip. The other two candies, he told them, were for them to give to teammates to thank them for something they did to make the trip successful. Coach King was pleased to get several Starbursts from his swimmers thanking him for all he did to make the trip a success. However, he was even more pleased when many swimmers came to him asking for more Starbursts because there were additional people on the team they wanted to thank (Thompson, 2003).

How can you use this concept with your team? Think of ways you can create situations where your athletes focus on the "I" in TEAM, in terms of appreciating their teammates and recognizing their individual contributions to the team's success.

3. Nurture TEAM norms. Norms are commonly accepted social practices within a team—they represent what is "normal" behavior for that team. All of a team's norms represent HOW WE DO IT HERE, so they're very important in creating the team culture that you desire for your program.

A big part of TB is to create and nurture an effective **team norm for productivity**, which is *the standard for effort and performance accepted by the team.* To build a successful program based on a sound philosophy, coaches must create and perpetuate a high-level team norm for productivity, so that this high performance "work ethic" becomes traditionally accepted as athletes move in and out of the program. First-year coaches who have moved to programs that lack winning traditions know that their first task is to change the attitudes and belief structure of the athletes on the team. An old sports adage is that losing becomes a habit, which in social-psychological terms means that the team accepts a lower level of effort and performance as being acceptable when they repeatedly lose.

Quotable Quote

"No one would have dared to give any less than one hundred percent when that Carolina shirt was on her back." **Angela Kelly**, former University of North Carolina soccer player (Dorrance & Averbuch, 2002)

Tara VanDerveer was confronted with this task when she was chosen as coach of the 1996 U.S. Olympic Basketball Team. Confidence had fallen in the U.S. program due to a 3rd place finish at the 1991 Pan American Games, a bronze medal in the 1992 Olympic Games, and a loss to Brazil in the 1994 World Championships. VanDerveer knew that she was hired to reverse this trend, and she had to quickly establish a strong productivity norm and a positive belief structure within the newly created Olympic Team. To program her own goal for the team, every day VanDerveer would visualize her players receiving their gold medals in Atlanta. Nine months prior to the Olympics, VanDerveer took her team inside the Georgia Dome for a mock medal ceremony. As an inspirational Olympic video played on the big screen, each player practiced receiving a gold medal around her neck (they used Teresa Edwards' gold medal from the 1988 Games). And VanDerveer's training demands clearly indicated the effort that she believed was required to win the gold medal. Star center Lisa

Leslie said, "With Tara giving us such hard workouts, we had to pick each other up. We became so close [as a result]" (Wolff, 1996b, p. 97).

Leslie's comment emphasizes the need to establish a feeling of unity and distinctiveness that enhances task and social cohesion, which at the same time raises the group norm for productivity. Over time, this sense of unity and distinctiveness evolves into team tradition, or team codes, which can become so entrenched that players themselves enforce it. Consider popular examples of strong team success traditions or codes such as the University of Tennessee Lady Volunteers basketball, University of Notre Dame football, or the women's soccer program at the University of North Carolina. Over the years, strong leadership from coaches and players has created what becomes a mystique about these programs, and they become perceived by others as perennial powers. By creating feelings of unity and distinctiveness, athletes develop pride in a program which makes them want to preserve a strong team norm for success. Small details are important in developing and perpetuating a strong group norm for productivity. Examples might include furnishing practice t-shirts with inspiring words or slogans (see Clipboard example), sprucing up the locker room area by establishing a team record board, and creating a Hall of Fame for previous players.

Clipboard

Wearing It on Your Sleeve

A college volleyball team wore practice jerseys with the following TB theme scripted on the back:

DETAILS MAKE CHAMPIONS
(I see me)

This TB theme revolved around the idea that by taking care of the smallest details in preparation and training, the team would emerge as conference champions. The players agreed that they had the talent to win, but that they had to clarify the effort needed to use their talent in a task-cohesive manner. The "I see me" phrase was an offshoot of a social support phrase used among teammates. When players saw their teammates working extra hard on a difficult drill, they would say, "I see you, Lori" or "I see you, Molly." It was a nice way to acknowledge or show appreciation for a teammate's hard work or extra effort. The players decided to modify this slightly for their t-shirts to emphasize the importance of everyone taking personal responsibility for the details of becoming champions. Thus, the phrase "I see me" represented each player's personal commitment to the team goal of doing every little thing right toward winning a championship.

━━━━━━━━

When attempting to establish a team norm for productivity and success, key team members, including team captains, can be useful models and enforcers of team norms. Coaches can present their philosophy and target goals along with a code of behavior and examples of the commitment that they feel are needed to achieve these goals. When strong leaders within teams accept and commit to a certain team norm for productivity, productive social norms for desirable behaviors are typically enforced and followed. Coach VanDerveer understood this when choosing the members of her Olympic squad. She knew that it was critical for Edwards and McClain, as national team veterans and two of the best players in the world, to accept her philosophy and group norm for productivity. And as VanDerveer admitted, "They bought into it. And if *they* were going to buy into it, it was going to work" (Wolff, 1996b, p. 97).

4. Use your TEAM thermometer. It's important to constantly take your team's "temperature" to know how best to interact with them. Use your TEAM thermometer to assess whether and/or when you should meet with the team, how you should approach discussions with them, and how you will seek input from them. A good way to get an initial reading on your TEAM thermometer is to begin a team conversation with a question, such as "what is the focus we need in today's practice?" or "what is the most important thing to focus on this week in preparation for Saturday's competition?" (Thompson, 2003).

With regard to team meetings, most athletes *hate* meetings. But to build an effective team culture, meetings and group discussions are necessary. However, read your team using your thermometer to consider the best approach in providing feedback, resolving issues, and evaluating practice and competitive performances. Sometimes athletes are ready to talk, and other times they need time to sort out their emotions prior to analyzing and discussing the team's performance. Instead of starting practice with a team meeting or conversation, begin with physical activity, and then have a team conversation following a conditioning drill (Thompson, 2003). Also, occasionally forego scheduled team meetings when your athletes need rest or some down time alone. They will appreciate your willingness to meet their needs, and their focus and engagement should be much sharper when meetings and conversations are well-planned and carefully scheduled by using your TEAM thermometer.

TB is compromised when leaders fail to run efficient, productive meetings. An important rule of thumb to follow in TB is to always use other people's time effectively. If coaches expect their athletes to accept personal responsibility for team goals, then they must accept personal responsibility to use the athletes' time efficiently. TB works best by using frequent yet short and concise group meetings to consistently reinforce productive interpersonal patterns and norms for productivity within the team. For example, 5 minutes at the end of each training session could be effective for team members to give feedback and evaluate the quality of the workout as well as the team's progress toward group goals. Orlick (1986a) suggests spending this time answering these questions:

- What went well?
- What needs work?
- What would you like more of from your coach, fellow athletes, or yourself?
- What would you like less of from your coach, fellow athletes, or yourself?

Similar concise evaluative discussions could be worked in after competitive events to evaluate and share feedback about individual and team performance.

Group TB sessions held at the beginning of the year should also have a specific focus and time limit. As a sport psychology consultant, I always attempt to be as organized and efficient as possible in presenting ideas or leading discussions in groups. I find it is helpful to bring worksheets that help athletes to engage in the activity in a meaningful way. No one likes to sit in meetings where they are talked *at*, and effective TB is not achieved by lecturing to athletes. In fact, it may be useful for team leaders to run certain meetings. It is critical that athletes feel that things are being accomplished when they meet, as opposed to their time being wasted. Clear objectives should be set for each group meeting, and the meeting may then be run efficiently by keeping this objective in mind.

TB disintegrates when meetings turn into gripe sessions. The strategy of identifying problems and focusing on solutions should be followed in TB sessions as a form of conflict management. Also, an effective moderator helps by limiting discussion points to new ideas or thoughts instead of letting athletes beat the same dead horse over and over. Once group interaction standards and guidelines have been established (an earlier step in TB), discussions should be much more efficient and productive.

Example TB Exercises

Hopefully, the three-step approach to TB discussed in this section has given you some insight about ways to enhance cohesion and build a commitment to TEAM in your program. Because TB is very popular in business as well as sport, many books and resources are available that identify specific TB strategies. Following are some example exercises for TB with athletes (also listed in Figure 6.1):

1. Mission Statement

A mission statement is a written agreement among team members that establishes and clarifies the purpose and objectives of the team for that year. Professional basketball coach Pat Riley (Riley, 1993) used a mission statement as part of his attempt to move his players beyond what he called their "disease of me." He developed a mission statement called "Success Through Unselfishness" and worked to get the players to commit to the mission. They did, and were quite successful, thanks to a new emphasis on teamwork, a solid work ethic, and an aggressive and persistent defense that won many games for them.

A mission statement should be clear and understandable to all team members, as well as brief enough for all members to keep in mind. The mission statement should focus primarily on a single thrust of team effort or focus, and should reflect the team's distinctive personality and competencies. That is, the mission should play to the team's strength(s). Finally, the mission statement should be worded to serve as an energy source and rallying point for the team.

Another variation of this exercise is "Developing a Team Covenant." A Team Covenant is more involved than a mission statement, as the covenant spells out specific behaviors that the team agrees to engage in to fulfill its mission (see Clipboard).

Clipborad

Developing a Team Covenant

One team building strategy that works in many situations is the development of a team covenant. A covenant is a sincere unconditional agreement among team members that they will engage in specified behaviors to help the team achieve its goals and mission. Following is an example of a team covenant developed by a college basketball team with the help of a sport psychology consultant. The players mapped out the specific ways that they wanted to operationalize their commitment to a successful season. The ideas in the covenant represent their thoughts—the consultant helped to refine these thoughts and capture them in an organized way for the final written covenant. Each player was given two copies to sign and display prominently at home and in her locker. Throughout the season and as problems arose, the team reviewed different points in the covenant to remind themselves of their affirmation to the team.

Eastern University Basketball

2004-2005

Team Covenant

GOAL: Our goal is to **get the edge** by building the best team we can be. To get the edge we need, we will do the following:

I.   MATURITY
   I will work to be **secure and comfortable with myself** so I can interact productively with my teammates and coaches no matter what.
   I am **not "too cool"** to take an active role in building this team.
   Although honesty and openness make me vulnerable, I will be **honest and open**.

II. PERSONAL RESPONSIBILITY

I take personal responsibility for the **quality and intensity of our practices every day** no matter what else is happening in my life.

I take personal responsibility for the achievement of our **team goals** and our **team attitude**.

I take personal responsibility to **support my teammates** in the pursuit of their goals and to maintain a **productive, professional relationship** with each of them.

I take personal responsibility to **manage my life productively** during the season to make basketball a high priority.

III. COMMITMENT

We are committed to **out-prepare our opponents**, which gives us confidence every time we take the floor. Knowing we haven't cheated in our workouts gives us the edge no matter who we're playing.

We are committed to **outwork our opponents during games** no matter what the score or final outcome. We know that one-time effort is easy, but sustained effort over time gives us the edge.

We are committed to **"strengthen our grip,"** which means that we will not become apathetic or negative when we encounter adversity, either personally or as a team. We realize that it is easy to be committed when everything is going great, but we get the edge from bouncing back after setbacks and disappointment.

IV. ENJOYMENT

We will not lose sight of the fact that we are playing because we enjoy the game of basketball. We know that when we **focus on the enjoyment of playing**, we perform better. We resolve to have fun, be enthusiastic, and let our love of the game make us true winners.

As a member of this team, I affirm my commitment to this team covenant. I realize that this covenant is meaningless unless I **put these ideas into practice every day through my actions** as a member of this team. The way I practice, the way I manage my life, and the way I interact with my teammates and coaches will demonstrate my acceptance of this contract.

_____

Signature

2. Hope and Fear Exercise

This exercise works well near the beginning of the preseason or before beginning a major tournament or championship. Assemble the group and pass out a blank 3x5 index card and pencil to each athlete and coach (or coaches can conduct the exercise and not participate). Participants should think about one *hope* that they have for the upcoming season or tournament and write this on the *front* of the card. Then, they should think of one *fear* that they

have for the same time frame or event and write it on the *back* of the card.

When all participants have completed their cards, the leader should collect the cards, shuffle them, and then redistribute them randomly so that each participant receives one card. Each participant in turn reads the hope and fear listed on her card, and the group can discuss/interpret the hopes and fears as the exercise continues. Sometimes participants break the anonymity by explaining their reasoning when their card is read—this is okay, but make it clear that it is not mandatory. Set up the exercise by emphasizing that who says what is not important, rather the significance of the exercise lies in teammates understanding each other's thoughts and concerns about the upcoming event or season.

3. TEAM Food for Thought (modified from Yukelson, 1997)

Many different questions can be used to stimulate a team "food for thought" session. Team leaders should try to choose or develop a question that will generate discussion, and mutual understanding, on important issues affecting the team culture and task and/or social cohesion. Examples might include the following:

a. If your coach were speaking at an end of the year banquet about the character, personality, and/or accomplishments of this year's team, what would you want to be said?

b. What can and what do you want to accomplish this season, and what will it take to get there?

c. What would make our team environment a more enjoyable and productive place to be?

d. If you could change anything about our practices, what would it be?

e. When your coach is at her best, what does she do? When your coach is at her worst, what does she do?

f. What behaviors (or attitudes) displayed by other athletes impress you the most?

g. I would like to be known as the type of athlete who . . .

h. When other teams observe you, what do they see? What kind of image do you want to project as a team? What things must be done to create this image?

4. Window and Mirror

With the group sitting in a circle, each participant discloses how she thinks the others on the team perceive her. This is the window—how the athlete thinks teammates see her when they look from the outside. Then, the participant discloses how she sees herself, which is the mirror (representing the true self). Group members can make comments and/or ask questions regarding each participant's description of their window and the mirror selves. Conclude the exercise by emphasizing that we often misunderstand the behavior of others through our cursory glances at windows. Teammates should be encouraged to get to know the "mirror selves" of their teammates to better understand them.

5. Trust Gauntlet (Meeker, 1994)

This exercise works well with large teams. Team members stand shoulder to shoulder, forming two lines. The two lines face each other, with enough space between the lines for a person to pass. As you have the group form the two lines, you, as the facilitator, can be walking between the two lines. This will gauge the space that they are allowing for the runner. Make sure there is sufficient room for the runners to accelerate and decelerate about 15-20 feet on each end of the line.

Members of each line extend their arms out in front of them. The arms are interwoven in a zipper pattern (i.e., every other arm is someone else's). Team members then run the gauntlet, one at a time. As the person runs, the extended arms are quickly raised, just in time to allow the member to pass, and then just as quickly brought back down behind the team member. Once the lines are set at the right distance, lead the members in practicing lifting their arms rapidly.

The exercise should be "challenge by choice," with no one being forced to run the gauntlet. The goal of the exercise is to teach team members to have trust and confidence in their teammates. Trusting each other in this physical activity provides a great opportunity to discuss issues of trust as they apply to the team in practice and competition.

6. Proud to be a Member (Bendaly, 1996)

This is a short and to-the-point exercise designed to enhance team commitment by asking individuals to share why they are proud to be a member of the team. Ask team members to individually complete the following sentence:

Being a member of this team is important to me because . . .   OR

I am proud to be a member of this team because . . .

There really is no need to discuss responses, unless team members do so spontaneously. Discussion is often anticlimactic, as the statements are more powerful if they stand alone.

7. I'll Bet You Didn't Know (Bendaly, 1996)

The objective of this activity is to have fun and get to know each other. Ask team members to think of something about themselves (preferably something unusual) that other team members don't know—OR to invent something about themselves. Each team member shares his or her piece of information with the team and the team members must decide if the information is true or false.

a. Each team member should develop a personal statement starting with "I'll bet you didn't know that I . . ."
b. Invite team members to share their statements one by one.
c. After each statement, ask each team member to vote true or false. Then ask the owner of the statement to declare whether the statement was true or false.
d. All team members should keep a tally of their scores. Each time a member guesses correctly, she or he receives +1. Incorrect guesses are scored as -1.
e. At the completion of the activity, award some prize to the "Athlete Who Best Knows Her/His Teammates."

8. Critical Success Factors (Bendaly, 1996)

Explain what is meant by "critical success factors," or CSF. CSF are **the limited number of areas to which a team must give full attention and achieve success if it is to reach its goals and fulfill its potential.**

a. Ask team members to write down what they feel are the CSF for this team. (This can be done individually, in small groups, or in brainstorming fashion as a large group.)
b. On a board or flipchart, write out all CSF identified. Then, as a group, discuss these to

Central High School Soccer
Critical Success Factors for 2001

Critical Success Factor	Attention presently given to this CSF (Rate on 1 to 10 scale where 1=low and 10=high)	Recommendations for strengthening this CSF

reach a consensus on what all team members accept as CSF for the team.

c. The group leader takes the list and develops a worksheet for all team members that lists the identified CSF along with a rating scale and a space for recommendations to strengthen each CSF (see format above):

9. Alligator River

Set-Up: Use tape to make "banks of river" about 4 yards apart
Paper to serve as "rocks" per team (4 per team)
One blindfold for each group

Rules:

a. One person is mute, one is blind (blindfolded), and one does not have the use of their legs. (Pick biggest person to be blind.)

b. All team members start on one side. Their mission is to get their whole team across Alligator River. The pieces of paper are "rocks" and can be used to cross the river.

c. If anyone touches the river instead of a rock, they're dead.

d. If a team member touches the other bank, they cannot come back.

Debrief: The purpose of the exercise is group problem-solving and to use team resources to think in different ways. Did the team listen to your ideas? Did you develop a strategy or just plunge in? How did the mutes feel? Did the limited people feel supported and informed by the team? Use this to emphasize roles and using strengths of people unlike us.

10. Nuclear Fence

Set-Up: Tie rope or bungee cord between two objects about waist height (several feet in length)

a. All team members start on one side of fence. Mission is to get whole team across fence without touching the fence or breaking the plane between the fence and the floor.

b. Two team members don't speak or understand English. One other team member has a broken leg (tie bandana to this leg).

c. There must be constant physical connection between all participants until everyone is across the fence (everyone must maintain physical contact with a teammate). If contact is broken by anyone, everyone must start over on one side of the fence.

d. If anyone touches fence breaks plane underneath fence, everyone must start over on one side of the fence.

Debrief: The purpose of the activity is group problem-solving. How did you convey information to the non-English speaking teammate? How did this teammate feel? How did you take care of your injured teammate? Did this teammate feel a part of things? How did you develop your strategy? Did everyone's opinion count?

11. Secret Psych Pals (Janssen, 2002)

a. Each athlete draws a name of a teammate and becomes this person's Secret Psych Pal for an upcoming competition.

b. Athletes then secretly do special things for their Secret Psych Pals in the days leading up to the competition (like writing notes, leaving "treats" in their locker, or any well-meaning gestures) to psych up their Pal!

c. Secret Psych Pals then reveal themselves right before the competition.

12. Strength Circle
   a. The team sits in chairs in a circle with one chair in the middle of the circle.
   b. Each athlete on the team takes a turn sitting in the middle of the circle. During each athlete's turn in the middle, teammates go around the circle in turn and verbalize a compliment or statement of appreciation directly to that athlete. When the statement is being made, the teammate should make eye contact with the athlete in the middle of the circle.
   c. Ask your athletes to make thoughtful, honest comments to their teammates. The key is to recognize each athlete on the team for his or her strengths, what he or she brings to the team, and why he or she is appreciated by his or her teammates. Coaches may be included in the circle as well!

Wrapping Up

A better understanding of team dynamics was rated by coaches as their biggest need in a survey conducted by the United States Olympic Committee. Obviously, coaches realize that team cohesion is critical for the Inner Edge. Consider the ways that cohesion may serve to "balance the triad" of sport psychology objectives identified in Chapter 2 (see Figure 2.1). First, through the development of task cohesion and control over social loafing, team *performance* may be enhanced, and individual performance may also be enhanced as the team culture provides a supportive and organized environment for individual athletes to develop skills and perform effectively. Second, being a part of a cohesive team facilitates the *development* of athletes as they are mentored into the team, expected to take responsibility for team obligations, and requested to demonstrate leadership within the team. Third, team cohesion makes the sport *experience* more satisfying for athletes as they affiliate and identify with an enjoyable group of people. Intrinsic motivation for the sport experience is nurtured as team membership fulfills the important athlete need of acceptance and belonging to a group. Remind your athletes to have the sense of a goose—to work together to achieve more than you could on your own, to take individual responsibility to keep your group going, and to stand by each other with unconditional support.

Summary Points for Chapter 6

1. Team cohesion is the ability of team members to interact effectively in their pursuit of team goals and group satisfaction.

2. Team culture refers to the formal and informal social and organizational systems within the team that influence team cohesion and performance.

3. Team building is a deliberate process or attempt to develop an effective team culture that will nurture and support team cohesion and performance.

4. Task cohesion refers to the team's ability to interact successfully to achieve performance or task goals, whereas social cohesion refers to the team's ability to get along interpersonally and socially.

5. Cohesion is dynamic in nature and constantly changes across competitive seasons as teams evolve and resolve internal conflicts.

6. Research has shown that cohesion is related to success in sport teams, and that this relationship is stronger in female teams as compared to male teams.

7. Cohesion can have negative effects when it creates hyperconformity, or a rigid and harmful code of behavior expected of group members.

8. Team building requires a commitment to a continuous process whereby all team members must accept personal responsibility for team cohesion and adhere to specified interpersonal behaviors.

9. Social loafing, or the tendency for individuals to exert less effort as the size of the group increases, occurs due to a sense of diffused responsibility within the team.

10. Social loafing can be eliminated by monitoring and evaluating each team member's performance, and by convincing athletes that their individual input is essential for team success.

11. A strong and effective team norm for productivity, which is the standard for effort and performance accepted by group members, is essential for team success.

12. Conflict resolution should follow the steps of involving team members, resolving the conflict in an expeditious and equitable manner,

absolving athletes from any prolonged guilt, and transforming the team into a more experienced and cohesive group.

Glossary

cliques: subgroups of cohesion within a team

groupthink: tendency for members of a group to reach consensus and make decisions too superficially and too quickly

social cohesion: the team's ability to get along interpersonally or socially

social loafing: a social phenomenon in which individuals exert less effort as the size of the group increases

task cohesion: the team's ability to interact effectively to successfully achieve performance or task goals

team: a group of individuals who are expected to work together with commitment to reach a common goal

team building: a deliberate process or attempt to develop an effective team culture that will nurture and support team cohesion and performance

team cohesion: the team's ability to interact effectively in their pursuit of team goals and group satisfaction

team culture: the formal and informal social and organizational systems within the team that ultimately influence team cohesion and performance

team norm for productivity: the standard for effort and performance accepted by the group

Study Questions

1. Explain the difference between task and social cohesion, and how both of these constructs are related to successful performance in sport.

2. Why is cohesion in sport teams so dynamic and changing, particularly in relation to the social and evaluative nature of competitive sport?

3. Identify the key steps you would take in beginning a team building program.

4. Conflict is inevitable in any group, so describe how you would recommend that a sport team resolve conflict when it arises.

5. How can social support within a team become more concrete and systematic?

6. With regard to social loafing, explain why there really is an "I" in TEAM.

7. Define team norm for productivity, and discuss the ways in which this can be nurtured in a sport team.

Reflective Learning Activities

1. Rate Your Team Cohesion

Listed below are strengths that are commonly found in a cohesive team. To assess your team, consider the degree to which you think that each statement is true for your team. (This questionnaire could also be used in a mini-research study where students ask athletes within one or more teams to complete the questions, and then the results are examined and shared with participating teams.)

Scoring:

75-66 Congratulations! You have a cohesive team. But remember that cohesiveness is a continuous process, so be sure to continue to nurture your team culture so it remains cohesive, productive, and enjoyable.

65-50 Your team is average in terms of cohesion. They have certain strengths, but their weaknesses in cohesion are enough to threaten group performance and the value of team membership. Assess your weakest points, and plan out how to strengthen these areas.

Below 50 Your score indicates below-average team cohesion, which means there is a lot of work to do. Take a look at your weakest points, assess the root causes of these obstacles to cohesion, and plan structural and behavioral interventions to improve your team culture.

2. Issues and Answers

Team forums are often useful to discuss conflictual issues that arise within teams. But should all issues be discussed by the entire team? Identify issues that may occur within sports teams and decide whether they should be discussed in a team forum. If not, what would be the alternative way to resolve the issue or conflict? (Groups of 3-4; 10 minutes; then 10 minutes for entire group to discuss)

3. Dealing with the "Prima Donna" (modified from Nakamura, 1996)

Jason, the top sprinter in the state, is on your high school track team. He has developed quite the "big head" due to his success. He assumes he knows it all and is constantly telling teammates what to do, but never listens to them in return. Behind the back of certain teammates, Jason makes fun of what he perceives as their pitiful lack of athletic ability. At meets, he doesn't bother to cheer for teammates in other events because he says he needs to relax and "psych up" for his own events. His teammates feel that he just doesn't care and is selfish. He puts on a big act around the coach, so the coach is not as aware of the problem as the athletes on the team are. Finally, Jason's behavior gets so annoying that two team members are delegated by the group to talk to the coach about it. The athletes explain to the coach that Jason is a royal pain in the posterior, and if the coach doesn't do something, they're going to drown him in the steeple-chase pit.

What should the coach do in this situation? Discuss the merits of each of the choices below and decide what course of action you think would be best.

  a. The coach decides to have a private talk with Jason to straighten him out.
  b. The coach tells team members they have to learn to be tolerant of others, even jerks like Jason.
  c. The coach tells the athletes that they should talk to Jason themselves to make him aware of his behavior.
  d. The coach calls a team meeting and confronts Jason with the problem.

4. Building the HOW WE DO IT HERE (modified from Bump, 1989)

For each area, identify two things you could do as a coach to enhance team cohesion.

Team tradition and pride in team membership:

_____

_____

_____

_____

_____

Communication during competition:

_____

_____

_____

_____

Rules and policies:

_____

_____

_____

_____

_____

Communication outside of competition:

_____

_____

_____

_____

_____

Leadership from athletes:

_____

_____

_____

_____

_____

Leadership style of coach:

_____

_____

_____

_____

_____

Mutual respect and trust among team members:

_____

_____

_____

_____

_____

Clarity and pursuit of team goals:

_____

_____

_____

_____

_____

Abilities to resolve conflicts:

_____

_____

_____

_____

_____

Honest disclosure within the team:

_____

_____

_____

_____

_____

_____

Part Two

Mental Training Tools

You now have a solid foundation of sport psychology knowledge from Part 1 of the book to gain the Inner Edge. It's now time to get equipped with your mental training tool box to help your athletes get an even bigger edge. In Part 2, you'll learn how to use four basic mental training tools with athletes. To keep you focused on the "big picture," note the shaded portion in Figure 7.1, which shows how the mental training tool box is related to all other aspects of the Inner Edge. The tools in the tool box are used in many combinations to build the mental skills upon which the Inner Edge is balanced.

This part of the book begins with Chapter 7, which introduces you to the concept of mental training and what it's all about—and not about! Then, in Chapters 8-11, the four basic mental training tools of goal mapping, imagery, P³ Thinking, and physical relaxation are presented. As you'll see, it works best to use tools in the mental training tool box along with the tools in your physical training toolbox. You'll learn ways to use goal mapping to enhance physical training, imagery to help develop skills and learn tactics, and how physical relaxation techniques are useful in physical stretching and flexibility exercises.

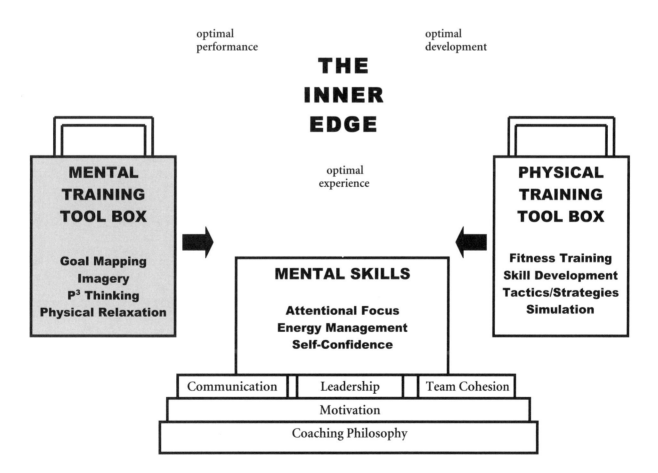

Figure 7.1 Where the mental training tool box fits into the "big picture" of the Inner Edge

Start small in using these mental training tools. But make your mental training efforts, however small in scope, a systematic part of your program and the day-to-day training of your athletes. Work to incorporate these training methods into your physical practice schedule and your normal competitive preparation. Mental and physical training should be all mixed together —don't make a big deal out of mental training as "something special we're doing today." Successful coaches utilize these techniques constantly in innovative ways. So pick up your tool box, and get going!

Seven

Beyond Shrinks: What Coaches Should Know About Mental Training

Photo by Sally Mendez, courtesy of US Navy.

Chapter Preview

In this chapter, you'll learn:
- what mental training in sport is all about
- that mental training is about stretching, not shrinking
- that mental training helps normal athletes become supernormal
- the role of coaches in mental training

"I won this week with my mind. I didn't drive the ball particularly well . . . My putting came in spurts. So it's nice to win a tournament with your mind because that's what wins majors." **Tiger Woods**

"This sport is about pain. Your legs, your chest, everywhere . . . You fall apart. In the Tour de France you push yourself to where you think you can't go. The key is to be able to endure psychologically." **Greg LeMond**

"An intense, rock-hard mentality is the cornerstone of our program . . . Above all other qualities, mentality must be present for achievement. We've had some incredibly talented or fit athletes without this mentality, and in the most important games, they've been useless to us." **Anson Dorrance**, coach of the University of North Carolina women's soccer dynasty *(Dorrance & Averbuch, 2002, p. 243)*

C hapters 2-6 have provided you with information on how to practically use philosophy, motivation, communication, leadership, and team cohesion as vital building blocks to gain the Inner Edge for your athletes and your program. Now that the building blocks are in place, the rest of the book is devoted to presenting ways for you as a coach to help athletes develop the mental skills they need to excel in sport as well as life.

In this chapter, I'll introduce the basics behind **mental training**, which is simply *the use of cognitive-behavioral strategies and techniques to enhance ath-*

letes' mental skills such as confidence, concentration, and dealing with pressure. The foundation for solid and effective mental skills in athletes is a philosophy based on the balanced triad of optimal performance, development, and experiences in sport (see Figure 2.1 in Chapter 2). Obviously, mental training focuses on helping athletes perform better, but it is also concerned with helping athletes develop their physical and mental skills and keeping sport in perspective, so that they may enjoy their competitive experiences.

Mental training is often misunderstood, so the purpose of this chapter is to

- provide you with a clear and accurate description of what mental training is about,
- convince you that mental training is effective and useful, although it does require commitment and hard work, just like physical training, and
- make it clear what the coach's role can and should be in mental training.

To get started, read the following true story of a high school athlete who discovered mental training when she encountered overwhelming expectations and pressure during her senior year.

Jordan is a high school cross-country/distance runner who experienced much success as a junior by qualifying for the state finals in both cross-country and track. As her senior year begins, her picture appears in the paper along with an article that describes her as a sure thing for a Division I track and cross-country scholarship. Then a strange thing happens. Jordan fails to place in the top ten at the first cross-country meet in the fall. She continues to struggle in the next two meets. Her coach has no explanation for why Jordan's performance has fallen off so drastically, although she suspects it's because of the attention and pressure. She tries to help Jordan by encouraging her and telling her not to worry about winning or pleasing others—just to run for fun—but it doesn't help. Everyone is frustrated and concerned—Jordan, her coach, her parents, and her teammates. What is going on here?

Jordan is choking. She is experiencing a major decrement in performance due to the building pressure of being a top runner in the state and of wanting (and needing) an athletic scholarship to college.

She feels constrained by the weight of everyone's expectations, and she begins to doubt whether she can meet these expectations. Jordan is an athlete who has all the foundations—physical talent, motivation to succeed, an excellent team program, and a knowledgeable and positive coach—but she needs help in the form of mental training to deal with the mounting pressure inside her head and outside in her social environment.

Jordan can be helped, and in fact, she was. By learning some basic mental training strategies, Jordan began to think more productively and slowly recovered her confidence. A key for Jordan was to reclaim running for herself and to stay focused on the joy she felt in running, which in turn freed her up to relax and perform better. She learned how to "park" the negative thoughts and feelings that emerged from others' expectations of her. By the end of the season, she was winning races again, although she continued to work hard at mental training because she wanted to stay mentally strong to prepare for the new pressures of running at the collegiate level. Jordan's story has a happy ending because she chose to do something proactive to turn herself around. She made a commitment to mental training along with her physical training. Jordan realized that she needed help in mental training, she was open and receptive to help, she worked hard at it without expecting miracles, and she strongly believed that it could help her. It did—by teaching her to help herself.

Personal Plug-In

What competitive obstacles have you or someone you know faced that may have been facilitated by mental training? Consider the specific nature of the obstacle and how it made the person think, act, and feel in dysfunctional ways.

Not everyone is like Jordan. Many people view sport psychology as akin to voodoo, or see it as some kind of psycho-babble. Nothing could be further from the truth, as you will learn in this chapter. Many athletes are embarrassed to admit they use sport psychology in their training because of the stigma attached to mental training. This amazes me because many of the best athletes in the world attest to the power of sport psychology and mental training. Research has shown that mental training techniques can help athletes respond to pressure more effectively and perform better. Yet fear and ignorance remain, largely the result of a lack of education and exposure to the realities of sport psychology. Thus, my goal in this chapter (and remaining chapters) is to erase this stigma by educating you about mental training and providing you with ideas about how to use it.

The chapter is organized around six common statements or questions about sport psychology and mental training:

1. "You either have it or you don't." (why mental training is often neglected)
2. "I don't need a shrink." (how mental training is misunderstood)
3. "What do you actually DO in mental training?" (what mental training is)
4. "Where's the proof?" (does mental training work?)
5. "What if they listen to you—and not to me?" (how coaches should approach mental training)
6. "I'll do it if you guarantee success." (what mental training can guarantee)

Photo by Brett Hansbauer

"You Either Have It or You Don't"

Consider the following two cases:

Case 1: Grant, a promising tight end on a high school football team, draws the attention of college recruiters. Several Big Ten coaches watch Grant play to evaluate his abilities. They tell Grant's high school coach that he has good hands and the necessary speed, footwork, and blocking technique, but that he lacks the upper body strength needed to play at the Big Ten level. They suggest that the coach help Grant develop his upper body through a prescribed weight lifting program, which will ensure his goal of receiving a Big Ten scholarship.

Case 2: Grant, a promising tight end on a high school football team, draws the attention of college recruiters. Several Big Ten coaches watch Grant play to evaluate his abilities. They tell Grant's high school coach that he has good hands and the necessary speed, footwork, and blocking ability, but that he lacks the aggressiveness and mental toughness to make the big plays under pressure needed to play at the Big Ten level. They suggest that the coach help

Grant consider other alternatives to playing in the Big Ten.

Why is Grant's problem in Case 1 viewed as fixable, while his problem in Case 2 is viewed as unfixable? In Case 2, the coaches decided that he just didn't have it. But wait a minute—he didn't have it in Case 1 either, but a remedy was quickly prescribed to help him get it. Why the difference? The difference lies in what we believe is changeable versus what we believe is fixed. Most people would agree that physical fitness and skills such as strength, endurance, and accuracy may be enhanced through practice. But when it comes to mental skills like confidence and performing under pressure, most people assume that these skills are innate and fixed. That is, you either have it or you don't.

Mental Skills Are Learnable

Mental training is based on the premise that mental skills are like physical skills—they can be taught and learned to a certain degree. Athletes can and do develop their mental skills over time (e.g., Durand-Bush, Salmela, & Green-Demers, 2001; Orlick, 2000;

Orlick & Partington, 1988). Although some coaches resist mental training because they feel mental skills cannot be trained, many coaches recognize its importance. However, they don't know how to implement such training with their athletes because the traditional coaching focus is on teaching physical skills and strategies of the sport. A common perception is that athletes develop their mental skills through experience, which is true in many cases. But this is trial and error learning, where athletes have to *make* the mistakes before they learn from them to improve their mental skills. The purpose of this book is to provide you with the knowledge and skills that coaches need to help athletes develop the mental skills needed for competition without having to go through the trial and error method of learning from mistakes.

Clipboard

Making a Difference

Consider the following testimonial from a Canadian Olympic pairs skater about the importance of mental training for her and her partner (Orlick & Partington, 1988):

> *"I look at what we won with this year, and we did virtually the same stuff technically that we did five years ago. We did no other major triples or anything, but we learned how to mentally get ourselves through the program. I think a lot more time has to be spent on getting kids ready mentally, finding out what they need to do mentally to be successful. I think a lot of kids have the physical skills to skate with the best of them. But whether or not they've got the mental skills is another question. They need to know what will work for them and what they need to do to make it work for them. Everyone keeps . . . physically pushing. But are they mentally pushing as well? I don't think they are . . . People [develop these skills] over time, but there has to be a faster way" (pp. 119-120).*

Quotable Quote

"The greatest barriers in our pursuit of excellence are psychological barriers that we impose on ourselves, sometimes unknowingly." Terry Orlick

Mental Training is Necessary and Worthwhile

The other reason most frequently cited as to why mental training is ignored by many coaches is time. Coaches say they don't have time for mental training. The line typically goes like this: "Hey, I think it's real important, and I believe it's helpful. Unfortunately, we just don't have the time to do it—it's a luxury we can't afford in terms of the physical work we have to do." I understand the time constraints under which coaches work. But I can't help but think that the real reason behind this logic is that coaches don't truly believe that mental training *makes a difference*. It has been my experience that if coaches believed that peanut butter and jelly tacos improved performance, then *everyone* would be eating PB&J tacos! If coaches really believed that mental training would make a difference in their team, they would take the time to do it.

To be fair, the field of sport psychology has been slow to package mental training in concise and useful ways for coaches and athletes. One of my goals for this book is to help you make simple and easy applications of mental training to meet your specific goals and needs as a coach. I hope that by reading this book, you will become convinced that

(a) mental skills are critical for successful sport performance,
(b) it is necessary and worthwhile to spend time using mental training techniques, and
(c) you have the knowledge and ability to successfully implement mental training with your athletes.

In Chapter 5, we identified several hats that an effective leader must wear. Well, here's another one! An objective of this book is to empower you—the coach—to wear the hat of sport psychologist so that you can incorporate mental training to help your athletes get the Inner Edge.

In summary, here are the key points from this section:

- Mental skills are like physical skills—they can be taught and learned.
- Many athletes have developed mental skills from trial and error, but mental training attempts to help athletes develop mental skills without having to wait for experience.

- Coaches that say they don't have time for mental training really don't believe that it makes a difference.

"I Don't Need a Shrink"

Are you normal? Here's a great two-step test to find out:

Step 1: Find a board that is one foot wide and twenty feet long. Lay the board flat on the ground, and attempt to walk the length of the board without falling off. Could you do it? If so, you're normal.

Step 2: Place the board across a steep ravine where 300 feet below lay jagged rocks and rushing water. Attempt to walk the length of the board without falling off. Could you do it? If you broke into a sweat at the thought of taking such a risk, you're normal.

What changed between the two steps in our normalcy test? The only thing that differed between the steps was the risk and pressure involved in Step 2. It was the same task as in Step 1, but the consequences of failure in Step 2 were much direr. Performing the task correctly became significantly more important in Step 2, and this increased importance created fear of physical harm, fear of failure, anxiety, and a loss of confidence to complete a task that was easy in Step 1.

Becoming Supernormal

This normalcy test was provided here to help you understand an important point about mental training. A common misperception is that athletes who practice mental training are abnormal. Often, when a visit to a sport psychologist is suggested, athletes laugh and say, "I don't need a shrink." The connotation is that mental training is a psychotherapy technique targeted to alleviate mental illness in abnormal people. But mental training is designed for very normal athletes. In fact, it is designed for the athletes that are so normal that they respond to pressure very much like you did in Step 2 of our normalcy test. Mental training attempts to help *normal* athletes develop *supernormal* responses to situations that are *abnormal* in the amount of stress and risk involved (Martens, 1987). An eighteen-year-old place kicker for the Ohio State Buckeyes has to be supernormal to run onto the field in Ohio Stadium in front of 100,000 screaming fans and a national television audience to attempt the game-winning field goal that could send his team to the Rose Bowl. Not many people face such abnormal amounts of stress in their lifetime. At the moment of that kick, the consequences of failing are as grave in the mind of this athlete as the consequences you faced in traversing a narrow board above a rocky gorge.

Coaches spend a lot of time helping athletes become supernormal through repetitive practice, intense physical training, and appropriate nutrition. Mental training is just one more way to help athletes become supernormal in preparation for the pressure of competition. In fact, mental training doesn't work to "shrink" athletes. If anything, it's designed to "stretch" the potential of athletes or to "enlarge" their capacity to perform better, to develop more fully, and to enjoy sport more. Sport competition challenges participants to move beyond their normal comfort zones. Keep in mind the adage that says, "You don't have to be sick to get better!"

Achieving optimal performance, development, and experience in sport may only be achieved when we venture beyond our normal comfort zones. Mental training helps athletes stretch (definitely not shrink) their comfort zones, while at the same time it helps athletes effectively cope with the natural discomfort that is a normal result of pursuing important goals. Interestingly, research indicates that mentally skilled athletes experience anxiety and mental distractions just like other athletes. The key is that the mentally skilled athletes respond more productively by refocusing, reframing, and coping when their comfort zone is stretched.

Clipboard

Now THAT'S Supernormal!

Lance Armstrong's claim to fame is not that he's won six Tour de France bike races—perhaps the most grueling sport challenge in the world. Rather, he feels his defining characteristic is that of a cancer survivor. In his acclaimed book "It's Not About the Bike," Armstrong (2001) describes how he used his supernormal mental skills to fight back during his cancer treatment: "To cope with [chemotherapy], I imagined I was coughing out the burned-up tumors. I envisioned the chemo working on them, singeing them, and expelling them from my system. When I went to the bathroom I endured the acid sting in my groin by telling myself I was peeing out dead cancer cells . . . I began to think of my recovery like a time trial in the Tour. It made me want to go even faster. I began to set goals with my blood, and I would get psyched up when I met them. [My doctor] would tell me what they hoped to see in the next blood test, say a 50 percent drop. I would concentrate on that number, as if I could make the counts by mentally willing it. I wanted to tear the legs off cancer, the way I tore the legs off other riders on a hill. 'Cancer picked the wrong guy,' I bragged. 'When it looked around for a body to hang out in, it made a big mistake when it chose mine. Big mistake'" (pp. 127, 141).

Photo by Robin Vealey

An Educational Focus on Skill Development

It's easy to get confused about the nature of mental training because some professionals that offer sport psychology services have been trained in clinical or counseling psychology. These professionals are licensed to provide clinical services to individuals who are in need of psychotherapy and emotional counseling. Often, licensed psychologists are retained by professional sports teams and engage as consultants with athletes regarding issues such as drug and alcohol rehabilitation, depression, and relationship counseling. Licensed psychologists that have specialized in sport psychology may also offer educational services similar to the mental training strategies presented in this book. If you seek the expertise of a sport psychologist, the first step might be to clarify the background and training of that individual, as well as to clarify the nature of what they can offer you and your athletes.

Many sport psychology professionals have been trained as sport scientists/practitioners and are not licensed psychologists. These professionals base their interventions with athletes on an *educational approach* with an emphasis on *teaching skills* that the athlete needs to become supernormal in handling the pressure of competition (Martens, 1987). The mental training program presented in this book is an educational program based on my training as a sport science professional. I am an educator, and my focus in this book is on teaching skills to athletes much like coaches teach physical skills. I fill the role of "mental coach," and often in my work with teams the athletes fall into the routine of calling me "Coach." I consider it quite a compliment!

However, sometimes in my individual consultations with athletes, it becomes clear that the performance problem the athlete is experiencing is really a symptom of a deeper emotional problem. In this case, I have been trained to recognize such symptoms and refer the athlete to one of my clinical or counseling psychology colleagues for more psychotherapy-type intervention. I suggest that you contact some appropriately trained professionals in this area and interview them to establish a referral list to be used when problems arise. Following are some guidelines that may help you understand how to recognize deeper emotional problems in athletes, which requires referring them to a school psychologist or clinical/counseling psychologist on campus or in your community (Andersen, 2001):

1. Problems that exist over a long period of time and/or interfere severely with daily life and normal functioning should typically be referred to a mental health professional such as licensed psychologist or social worker.

2. Problems that seem to threaten the core identity and total sense of self of an athlete should be referred. An athlete who becomes very anxious and engages in negative self-statements and behavioral "flightiness" before a major competition is experiencing normal reactions to the pressure of competition. However, an athlete whose total sense of self and positive identity is threatened by the possibility of losing a game and/or an athlete who becomes emotionally despondent after failure should be referred to counseling. Eating disorders, a growing problem in girls and women athletes,

is related to identity and self-esteem issues emanating from oppressive societal ideals about female attractiveness, and should be referred to a licensed mental health specialist.

3. Unusual and out-of-the-ordinary emotional reactions by athletes are often symptoms of a problem requiring clinical counseling. This may include depression, personal and social withdrawal, anger and aggression, and hopelessness.

It is important for you, as a respected and trusted coach, to help the athlete understand that these professionals help people develop life skills to productively deal with problems in living that we all face as human beings. The goal is to help the athlete see that seeking help from a mental health professional is a proactive step toward enhancing their daily living skills, and does not necessarily mean they have a profound medical or mental condition that makes them abnormal or vastly different from their peers. It is helpful if you know the individual you are referring your athletes to and can reassure them that the counselor is competent and will sympathize with their situation.

In summary, here are key points for this section:

- Mental training helps normal athletes develop supernormal responses to situations that are abnormal in the amount of stress and risk involved.
- Mental training is not a "shrink" program. Rather it is designed to "stretch" the potential of athletes or to "enlarge" their capacity to perform better.
- The mental training approach offered in this book is an educational program that emphasizes teaching skills to athletes
- Coaches must differentiate between typical performance problems of athletes and deeper emotional problems that require referral to clinical mental health specialists.

"What Do You Actually DO in Mental Training?"

So what's it all about? What do you actually DO in mental training? Basically, the focus boils down to helping people learn how to think better. Bob

Rotella (1995), a mental coach for several PGA golfers, likes to say that people by and large become what they think about themselves. He uses the example of Nick Price, PGA golfer, who sought out Rotella's services in an attempt to become more consistent and confident in his play. Rotella quickly observed that Price made the mistake of letting events control the way he thought, rather than taking control of his thoughts and using them to influence events. For example, if Price played poorly on the first few holes, he would lose his concentration and confidence and begin second-guessing his swing technique. Rotella worked with Price to enable him to plan before the round how he was going to think, and then to choose to think *productively* and *consistently* on every shot no matter what the outcome. Thinking well is a choice, even though we mistakenly believe that our thoughts are automatic and uncontrollable. Mental training teaches you how to think more productively and provides ways for you to practice productive thinking so that it becomes habitual. By practicing productive thinking, athletes can become more mentally skilled and more mentally tough. That is, they can become supernormal!

Using the Mental Training Tool Box to Build Mental Skills

Chapters 8-14 in this book are all devoted to describing specific mental training techniques and strategies in ways that will make it easy for you to use them. In Chapters 8-11, you'll be introduced to the four basic **mental training tools**: goal mapping, imagery, P³ Thinking, and physical relaxation. These mental training tools are *cognitive-behavioral techniques or procedures that athletes engage in to develop physical and mental skill.* Cognitive-behavioral refers to thoughts and feelings (cognitive) and actions (behavior), thus the mental training tools are used to enhance how athletes think, feel, and act. Even though athletes may know how they *want* to think, feel, and act, and how they *should* think, feel, and act in critical situations in sport, it takes practice to undo the automatic thinking and behavior patterns that they have developed over time in response to competitive pressures. Thus, these methods are used to develop the right strategies for each athlete based on his or her unique mental and physical needs, and then practiced over time to become automated.

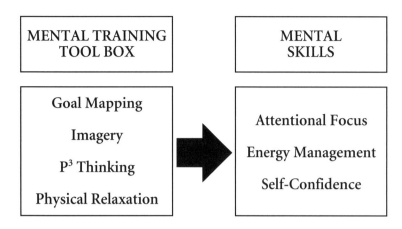

Figure 7.2 Using the mental training tool box to build mental skills

In Chapters 12-14 of the book, we'll discuss the three critical mental skills that athletes need to pursue and achieve excellence: attentional focus, energy management, and self-confidence. **Mental skills** are psychological abilities that facilitate athletes' performance and personal development. Athletes who are confident and focused will obviously perform more optimally than athletes who are not. Athletes who learn to manage their emotions have achieved an important developmental marker of maturity.

The basic premise of mental training is that the mental training tools are used to build athletes' mental skills (see Figure 7.2). Once you've learned the basics of goal mapping, imagery, P³ Thinking, and physical relaxation, then these four tools can serve as a menu of available options in building athletes' mental skills. They serve as your tool box that you and your athletes can carry around for developing and enhancing mental and physical skills. For example, athletes can use imagery to build confidence, to practice an optimal competition focus, and to mentally practice shooting jump shots, running the offense, or breaking a full-court press. If you have an athlete who tends to choke in pressure situations, then you need to decide what combination of mental training tools you can use to help build her confidence and control her focus during competition. In Part 4 of the book, I'll help you "put it all together" in using different combinations from your tool box to develop mental plans for athletes and implement mental training for different situational needs. We'll also discuss common challenges faced by coaches such as burnout, slumps, and inconsistency, and then offer suggestions about ways to effectively deal with these common sport challenges.

Interdependence of Physical and Mental Training

Figure 7.3 illustrates the critical interdependence between physical and mental training. In reality, there is no way to separate these concepts, as they are interdependent and symbiotic. Physical and mental training feed off of each other, and attempts to think about and train them separately are foolish and counterproductive. As shown in Figure 7.3, the interdependence of physical and mental training serves as the foundation for the development of physical fitness, physical skills, and mental skills in athletes. Mental training will *never* take the place of physical training and appropriate education about the techniques and strategies of your sport. It is my experience that mental training tools are only useful when they are used in conjunction with physical training. For example, athletes often learn to use imagery in quiet, relaxed settings, but imagery should be incorporated into the actual physical training sessions so that athletes learn to use it habitually.

The triangular relationship between physical skills, physical fitness, and mental skills shows that they are interdependent and constantly interacting. It would make no sense to attempt to rebuild the confidence of an athlete coming off of a serious knee injury if we were not working in concert with his trainer and doctor to understand his physical condition. Many coaches are innovative sport psychologists because they understand that mental skills can be built through the development of sound physical skills and solid physical training to prepare for com-

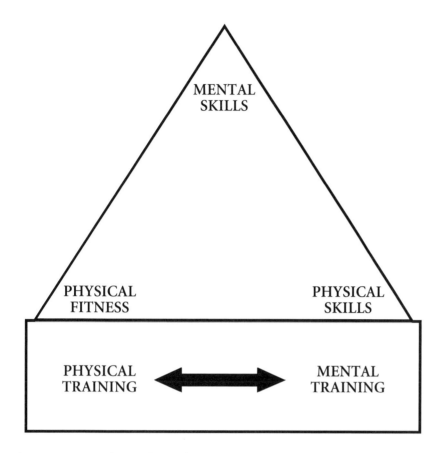

MENTAL SKILLS

PHYSICAL FITNESS

PHYSICAL SKILLS

PHYSICAL TRAINING

MENTAL TRAINING

Figure 7.3 Interdependence between physical and mental training

petition. For example, the first step to being confident is to earn the right to be confident by ensuring that your preparation is complete and that no shortcuts have been taken. If athletes cheat in their physical training, then their confidence is based on quicksand in the form of hope that they'll get by without adequate preparation.

It has always amazed me that popular sport stars known for their mental toughness are perceived by many as having been born with such strong confidence and mental skill. Ken Griffey Jr. is hailed as one the purest talents in baseball and a mentally tough athlete who thrives under pressure to perform amazing feats. But few people are aware of Griffey's outstanding work ethic in terms of taking extra batting practice, watching videotapes to improve his mechanics, and his serious study of opposing pitchers.

Physical and mental training are like having two-year-old twins. You'd like to be able to diaper one twin while the other one plays quietly, but it doesn't usually work that way. They typically need and want attention at the same time. As a coach I want you to understand how to incorporate mental

Personal Plug-In

Brainstorm some specific ways that mental training techniques could be used in conjunction with physical training.

training into the physical training of athletes, because unless you do that, you won't have much of an impact. Therefore, examples are provided in each remaining chapter as to how particular mental training tools may be incorporated into physical practice routines.

In summary, here are the key points for this section:

- Most basically, mental training teaches athletes how to think more productively.
- Mental training tools are basic methods that can be used separately or in combination to enhance various physical and mental skills.
- Mental skills such as confidence and attentional control are enhanced by physical practice and the use of mental training tools.

- Physical and mental training are interdependent, thus mental training should and can be incorporated into physical training programs.

"Where's the Proof?"

Does mental training work? Do athletes with superior mental skills perform better than those with less skill in this area? A growing body of evidence supports a "yes" answer to each of these questions. Evidence to support the use of mental training as an effective performance enhancement technique can be divided into four areas.

The first body of evidence is the large number of research studies that have introduced a mental training intervention with athletes and demonstrated that this intervention enhanced athletes' performance. Many studies have been published in sport psychology literature demonstrating that mental training interventions of various types do enhance performance and the cognitive-behavioral functioning of athletes (see Greenspan & Feltz, 1989; Patrick & Hrycaiko, 1998; Thelwell & Greenlees, 2001; Vealey, 1994 as examples). Specific examples of this research will be provided throughout the remainder of the book in appropriate chapters.

The second area of support for mental training is the consistent finding that successful athletes engage in systematic mental preparation more so than less successful athletes (Greenleaf et al., 2001; Gould et al., 1992a, 1992b, 1993; Gould et al., 1999). These studies all examined the performances of Olympic athletes at the Games and compared characteristics between successful and less successful Olympians (see Clipboard for detailed explanation).

Clipboard

Olympian Mental Skills

Do Olympic athletes use mental training? That's like asking whether the ocean is salty! Gould and colleagues (1992a, 1992b, 1993) examined the mental strategies used in the 1988 Olympic Games by the U.S. wrestling team. The wrestlers used a variety of mental training techniques including

- imagery to create positive images, rehearse tactics and techniques, and program goals,

- P³ thinking techniques such as parking and rational self-talk,
- emotional control skills to regulate activation and create feelings associated with peak performances, and
- mental preparation routines to maintain control and focus their thoughts and behavior appropriately.

Interesting, the more successful Olympic wrestlers were better able to cope with distractions and adhered more closely to their pre-competition routines as compared to less successful wrestlers. The most significant difference between medalists and nonmedalists was the extent to which mental skills and coping strategies were practiced and internalized. The medalists had highly developed techniques for coping with distractions, while the less successful wrestlers abandoned competitive plans under pressure or failed to rigorously adhere to their mental preparation plans. These findings emphasize the importance of systematic mental training over time so that productive thinking, responding, and coping become habitual and unshakable even under Olympic pressure.

The third area of evidence to support the effectiveness of mental training is the research finding that successful, elite athletes have better mental skills than less elite athletes (Durand-Bush et al., 2001). As mentioned in Chapter 1, mental skills were just as predictive of the batting averages of professional baseball players as were players' physical skills (Smith et al., 1995). For professional pitchers, mental skills were more important in predicting their success than physical skills. In addition, mental skills were predictive of players' survival in professional baseball two and three years later (Smith & Christensen, 1995).

The final area of evidence to support the effectiveness of mental training is the anecdotal accounts of athletes who provide rich and detailed accounts of how mental training and preparation helped them to perform better. There are numerous examples throughout this book, and other published accounts are available that could be used to introduce athletes to mental training (e.g., Naber, 1999; Orlick, 2000; Orlick & Partington, 1988; Rotella, 1995). It is this personal testimony from highly successful athletes that seems to make an impression on younger athletes about the efficacy of mental training. Coaches should consider using examples of successful athletes in their respective sports who can attest to the power and usefulness of mental training and preparation.

Clipboard

Third Time's the Charm

Most everyone knows the Dan Jansen story. In pursuit of a speed skating gold medal at the 1988 Calgary Olympic Games, he fell in both of his races after learning that his sister Jane had died from cancer. With all of America watching and willing him to win, he saw his Olympic medal dreams dashed at the same time that he tragically lost a loved one. Four years later, he arrived at Albertville, France, as the top ranked male speed skating sprinter in the world. Like a bad dream repeating his performance in Calgary, he failed to win in his specialty, the 500 meters, as well as the other sprint event, the 1000 meters.

Almost unbelievably, at the 1994 Games in Lillehammer, Norway, Jansen slipped during the 500 meter race and again failed to win the Olympic gold medal that he so desired. But as Jansen prepared himself for the 1000 meter race, his last chance to win an Olympic gold medal, he knew that he had an advantage. Jansen had begun work with Dr. Jim Loehr, a top sport psychologist, who helped him learn a new approach to competition. As Jansen (1994) explained it, Loehr was able to get him to put less pressure on himself about winning. Jansen states, "Loehr helped me realize that, whatever happens, deep in my mind I know I'm the best out there and I can be proud of myself. I have a family and friends . . . who will be there no matter what. That really eases things for a person" (p. 4). And even though Jansen considered the 500 his best race, Loehr had urged him to become more committed to the 1000 meter race by writing "I love the 1000 meters" over and over again. Jansen even taped it on his bathroom mirror. Jansen admits that working on "loving" the 1000 meters really did improve his ability in the race.

And it's a good thing. Jansen stood poised at the start of the 1000 meter sprint race in Lillehammer, facing his last chance for an Olympic gold medal.

Jansen explains that his mental training all came together in that one race in which he got into the total "zone" of optimal performance. He won his gold medal in the 1000 meters, the race that he learned to "love." It took three Olympic Games, but Jansen demonstrated how mental training freed him up to finally achieve the goal that had eluded him for so long.

In summary, here are key points for this section:

- Controlled intervention studies have shown the mental training does enhance the cognitive-behavioral functioning and performance of athletes.
- Successful athletes possess more refined mental skills and engage in systematic mental preparation more so than less successful athletes.
- Sell your athletes on the effectiveness of mental training by sharing with them the many popular examples of famous and successful athletes who engage in mental training.

"What If They Listen to You— and Not to Me?"

Mental training is sometimes threatening to coaches who lack knowledge about sport psychology. A common question that I get as a sport psychology consultant when I work with athletes is, "What if they listen to you—and not to me?" Of course this question comes from the coach, and it makes sense to ask the question. As a former coach, I would have asked the same question as I would not want someone to come in and influence my team in counterproductive ways. Thus, an important premise to remember about mental training is that it must involve the coach.

The purpose of this book is to help you gain the Inner Edge, or to implement sport psychology principles and mental training within your own team. However, if you are in the position to have a sport psychology expert work with your team in mental training, keep in mind that the objective of mental training is to empower coaches, as opposed to undermining their authority. By reading this book, you'll be well-informed about the philosophy and content of mental training, so you have the knowledge to interview any prospective sport psychology consultants at length to better understand their objectives and particular approaches. However, coaches should stay directly involved in any mental training inventions with their teams.

In Chapter 5, we emphasized the need for transformative leaders to "walk" their vision if they expect their athletes to respect them and commit to their visions and objectives. The same principle applies to mental training. If you are a coach attempting to implement mental training with your athletes, you should ensure that you are modeling the mental skills that you are trying to help them develop. If you are a coach with an outside sport psychology consultant working with your team, you should be the strongest adherer to the program, so that you can model your commitment to mental training for your athletes. If you choose not to participate in mental training with your team, the program results are typically less productive. It really helps when the coach is a central, committed figure in any mental training program.

In summary, here are the key points for this section:

- The objective of mental training is to empower coaches, not to undermine their authority.
- Coaches should demonstrate their commitment and enthusiasm for mental training, and they should remain a part of the mental training program if an outside sport psychology consultant works with their team.

"I'll Do It If You Guarantee Success"

A megatrend in our society is the growing need and expectation for instant gratification. People want fast money, fast food, and fast success. With regard to sport psychology and mental training, many coaches and athletes expect fast results. And incredibly, they expect fast results with minimal effort. I received a phone call one day from a young man on the collegiate tennis team. "I hear that you're a sport psychologist," he said excitedly. "I would really like to talk to you about building my confidence." After an initial meeting with the player for about 45 minutes, he became upset when asked about a weekly meeting

schedule with some personal assignments to be completed between meetings. He retorted, "You've

US Air Force Photo, courtesy of Geekphilosopher.com

Personal Plug-In

What are some pros and cons to having coaches implement mental training with their athletes? How do you think coaches should be involved in mental training?

got to be kidding! How do you expect me to do all this work and meet all those times. I don't have time for that! I can't believe that you can't do anything about my confidence today."

Mental Skills, Like Physical Ability, Are Developed Over Time

The athlete just described expected that a decent sport psychologist should be able to outfit him with total confidence in about 45 minutes. Of course, this is absurd. He certainly wouldn't expect to become a world-class tennis player after 45 minutes of practice. Athletes know that it takes years to develop the physical skills needed to excel at elite levels. Michael Jordan, widely considered the best basketball player in the world at the time of his retirement, was unable to quickly build the swing mechanics and develop the bat speed necessary to make any substantial improvement as a hitter in two years in professional baseball. Of course, this was a next to impossible goal for Jordan due to his lack of early physical training in baseball (Klawans, 1996). If we understand that physical skills take time to develop, why then, do athletes and coaches expect such quick results from sport psychology?

The answer lies in misperceptions about the nature of sport psychology and mental training. Many athletes and coaches erroneously believe that mental training is something that sport psychologists do *to* athletes. Because we're thought to do something mysterious *to* people, like hypnotizing them, the logic is that it shouldn't take that long to do it! In reality, mental training is something that sport psychologists help athletes and coaches learn to do *for themselves*, and it takes as long to develop mental skills as it does to develop the physical ones. Physical coaches teach basic skills and strategies, and then provide huge amounts of time for athletes to practice and perfect these skills and strategies. Similarly, mental coaches teach basic skills and strategies related to mental skills, then over time provide feedback and meet periodically with athletes to monitor their progress as they practice and perfect their mental skills.

Objectives of Mental Training

Upon explaining mental training to coaches and athletes, many state that they are only interested in it if we can guarantee success. Okay—I'll go out on a limb and guarantee it. You read it here—mental training guarantees success for athletes and coaches who use it . . . with the following qualifications:

- Participants must sincerely believe in mental training and behaviorally commit to practicing and implementing its techniques and methods for the duration of their sport participation.
- Participants must define success as an optimal balance in performance, development, and experience as shown in our balanced triad model of quality sport participation in Chapter 2 (see Figure 2.1).

Of course, what many coaches and athletes mean is that they will only participate in mental training if it guarantees that they will win. Mental training cannot guarantee winning, any more than a pre-event meal or type of strategy can guarantee winning. The objective of mental training is to help athletes perform and develop optimally, as well as to enrich their sport experience, which balances the important sport psychology triad. The irony is that if mental training helps athletes to do these things, then it also increases the probability that they *will*

win. But it doesn't guarantee it, because nothing guarantees winning—not even talent. What makes sport exciting is that any team can win or lose, because the outcome is always uncertain.

Highly skilled elite athletes often use the phrase that they want to put themselves in "a position to win." Their intent is to do everything right in preparing themselves for and situating themselves at the point where winning occurs. Mental training puts athletes in that "position to win." Athletes can mentally prepare to successfully negotiate the pressures and distractions that typically block less mentally focused athletes from being in the position to win. Mental training also allows athletes to successfully "grind." Grinding is a term that golfers use that refers to playing on days when they are not quite "on" their game and they have to struggle to play well. Often, athletes begin competition hoping to get "in the zone" that day, and when they realize that they are not, they fold mentally and their performance deteriorates. The goal of mental training is to enable athletes to take back some control on those days when they're not in the zone, and to use their mental toughness to work hard, focus, and think clearly even when it isn't happening automatically. Thus, although a main objective of mental training is to maximize the chances of athletes attaining peak performance ("position to win"), the other less stated (and maybe more important) objective is to give athletes the mental toughness and skill to perform well during those competitions when their physical and mental skills are not at their best ("grind").

A useful analogy is to compare mental training to a lawn treatment program. Periodic applications of fertilizer and herbicide keep a suburban lawn green, healthy, and weed-free (very important in competing with your neighbor!). It's a continuous process whereby the lawn is periodically treated at different times during the year, depending on seasonal needs. You could cancel the program, and your lawn would

---

Quotable Quote

"Maybe five times a year, you're going to go out and be magic. And five times a year, you're going to go out there and feel like crap. And all the rest of the matches, those are what make you a tennis player." **Brad Gilbert**, former professional player and current coach

look fine for a while, but over time weeds would begin to pop up as the overall quality of the lawn deteriorated. Grass can obviously grow without the fertilizer provided in the program, but the overall quality of the grass is much better when fertilizer is used.

In normal circumstances, athletes can perform just fine without mental training. Like the grass, they can function well without mental fertilization and weed control. But when a weed starts to creep through such as a performance slump, or fear of failure before a championship event, or self-doubt in the face of increased performance expectations, there is no mental lawn program in place to deal with it. Some athletes have strong mental skills that they have developed through years of performance success, like grass that is thick and lush with deep roots. These athletes, like the strongly rooted and mature grass, may not need additional mental training fertilization. These athletes already have strong mental skills to go with their great physical talents. However, most athletes reach a competitive point where they face abnormally high amounts of stress, and they need the mental training lawn program to help them gain supernormal skills to withstand the stress.

In summary, here are the key points for this section:

- Mental skills are not magically developed through the action of a sport psychologist. Rather, mental skills, like physical skills, are developed over time as athletes become more proficient in their use.
- The objective of mental training is to help athletes achieve optimal development and performance, which should maximize their chances of achieving successful outcomes (such as winning).
- Athletes can function well without mental training under normal conditions. However, in abnormal stress conditions, they need mental training to help them gain the supernormal skills needed to withstand the stress.
- Mental skills are life skills.

Wrapping Up

A growing body of research in sport psychology supports the effectiveness of mental training with athletes. Some examples of this research are presented in later chapters. As in any field, there are dis-

putes in sport psychology as to the most effective way to do mental training. This is analogous to disputes in education as to the most effective way to teach children to read. The mental training approach presented in this book represents one approach—*my* approach—to mental training with athletes; other approaches may emphasize different components. However, typically most all approaches use the same basic techniques, and the main differences lie in how the techniques are packaged. The applied literature in sport psychology is booming, and I encourage you to increase your knowledge by reading other sources when you've completed this book (see the Resource Guide for Coaches at the end of the book).

Is mental training for you and your athletes? I think so, because mental skills are life skills. The principles and strategies presented in the remaining chapters will not only enhance the sport experiences of your athletes, but also their endeavors in all areas of life. All of the athletes I have worked with in mental training admit that developing mental skills for sport transfers into useful ways to develop life skills for the future.

The remainder of the book provides specific information for using various mental training techniques to coach for the Inner Edge. Have confidence in your abilities as a coach—most coaches know far more about mental training than they realize. Most good coaches train their athletes mentally and physically without even considering that they are doing something special by building mental skill in their athletes. However, the purpose of this book is to deepen coaches' understanding of the mental aspects of sport, and to provide coaches with some ideas about how to more systematically enhance the mental skills of their athletes. Good luck!

Summary Points for Chapter 7

1. Mental training refers to techniques used to enhance athletes' mental skills such as confidence, concentration, and relaxation.
2. Many coaches ignore mental training because they believe that mental skills are innate and cannot be taught.
3. Mental skills are learnable, but like physical skills, require repetition to become useful and automatic.

4. Mental training focuses on helping "normal" athletes become "supernormal" in facing "abnormal" amounts of stress in the competitive environment.

5. Mental training focuses on teaching athletes skills within an educational approach, as opposed to psychotherapy, which focuses on alleviating more serious clinical conditions such as depression.

6. Mental training tools are the techniques or strategies (e.g., imagery, relaxation) used by athletes to develop their physical and mental skills.

7. Mental skills are psychological abilities that facilitate athletes' performance and personal development (e.g., self-confidence, concentration).

8. Physical and mental training are interdependent, and mental training should always be incorporated into physical training programs.

9. Research supports that mental training interventions can enhance athletic performance, and that athletes who possess superior mental skills and engage in systematic preparation are more successful than those with less skill and who fail to engage in mental preparation.

10. For best results, coaches should be directly involved in mental training with their athletes to model commitment and enthusiasm.

11. The objective of mental training is to enable athletes to perform and develop optimally, but it does not guarantee uncontrollable outcomes such as winning.

Glossary

mental skills: psychological abilities that facilitate athletes' sport performance and personal development

mental training: the use of cognitive-behavioral strategies and techniques to enhance athletes' mental skills such as confidence, concentration, and dealing with pressure

mental training tools: cognitive-behavioral techniques or procedures that athletes engage in to develop physical and mental skill

Study Questions

1. Explain what mental training is and discuss the reasons why many coaches do not use it.

2. What is the difference between mental training and clinical psychotherapy?

3. Identify several guidelines that coaches can use to help them recognize emotional problems in athletes and refer them to clinical or counseling psychologists.

4. Explain the relationship between mental training tools and mental skills, and discuss the interdependent relationship between physical and mental practice.

5. What should be the role of the coach in mental training? Provide some specific examples of the ways in which you think coaches can work within a mental training program.

6. Discuss the main objectives of mental training, and explain why it cannot guarantee winning.

Reflective Learning Activities

1. Roadblocks

In the left column, list the reasons why you have not used mental training with your athletes in the past. In the right column, note at least one solution to help you get past each roadblock.

Roadblocks to PST	Solutions

2. Stigma

As discussed in the chapter, many athletes and coaches shy away from sport psychologists and the use of sport psychology techniques because of the social stigma attached to mental illness. Why does this persist even though many elite athletes are practicing mental training techniques and lauding their usefulness? Attempt to identify deeper reasons why sport psychology is still ridiculed and distrusted in many sport circles. (Groups of 3 for 10 minutes; 15 minutes for total group discussion)

3. What's Normal?

Identify several situations that you have been in that were abnormal in the amount of stress or risk involved (these could be sport or non-sport situations). Share with a partner how you responded in this abnormally stressful situation. Were you normal or supernormal? What could have been done or what would it have taken for you to respond supernormally in that situation? (In pairs for 12 minutes).

Chapter

Eight

Goal Mapping

Chapter Preview

In this chapter, you'll learn:
- the steps involved in goal mapping
- why goal mapping is important and often taken for granted by athletes
- about different types of goals that are useful for athletes
- why a meaningful sense of purpose must guide athletes' goal maps

"I've always had those little goals that I've worked toward—they add up." **Stacy Allison**, first American woman to climb Mt. Everest

"The secret of getting ahead is getting started. The secret of getting started is breaking your complex overwhelming tasks into small manageable tasks, and then starting on the first one." **Mark Twain**

"We are not born with maps; we have to make them, and the making requires effort. The more effort we make . . . the larger and more accurate our maps will be. But many do not want to make this effort. Their maps are small and sketchy, their views of the world narrow and misleading." **M. Scott Peck** in *The Road Less Traveled*

W hen you ask athletes to identify important personal goals, they typically can do so. But if you ask them what plan they have in place to reach their goals, or what they have done *today* to pursue these goals, they typically struggle to answer. A **goal** is *a specific standard or accomplishment that one strives to attain.* Setting goals is a common human practice—most people develop ideas about where they want to go and what they want to accomplish in their lives. But this is where goal setting gets misunderstood. The term "goal setting" falsely implies that simply by *setting* goals, individuals gain some benefit in terms of motivation and increased effort and persistence. Setting goals is easy— it takes little effort to sit around and dream about lofty accomplishments and personal triumphs. But organizing and regulating your life each day in a disciplined and committed manner to actively pursue your goals is much more difficult.

In this chapter, **goal mapping** is presented as *a systematic approach to acting and thinking in purposeful ways to achieve specific accomplishments and personal fulfillment.* Goal mapping goes beyond the basic task of *setting* goals, as it involves planning, setting, evaluating, and resetting many types of goals, as well as developing strategies to pursue and focus on certain goals at certain times. Goal mapping also involves the development and expression of a meaningful sense of purpose, from which goals automatically flow. As discussed later in the chapter, without a sense of purpose or "passion" as the driving force, goals are much less effective and fail to sustain motivation.

Goal mapping enables athletes to consistently regulate their thoughts, feelings, and behavior to enhance the pursuit of their goals. A goal map is a guide—a guide to peak performance, optimal development, and meaningful experiences in sport. Consider how you use a map in your car. A goal map is used the same way: to provide a plan of direction that you constantly refer to when driving to your destination. When you encounter an obstacle in driving your car, such as a road closed for repairs or an emergency blocking traffic, you redirect your attention to your map to revise your course in relation to your destination. It would be silly to leave your choice of direction to chance and say, "I'll do my best and just hope that I arrive where I want to eventually."

Goal mapping is the most basic mental training tool in the toolbox (refresh your memory by revisiting the mental training toolbox pictured in Figure 7.1). An understanding about goals and an effective goal map is the critical first step in developing mental skills. Goals don't sound exciting, but in my experience as a sport psychology consultant, inappropriate goals are the root of most problems that disrupt the performance of athletes and teams. Athletes cannot take this important mental training step for granted in their pursuit of optimal performance, personal development, and meaningful sport experiences. And by enhancing your knowledge of goal mapping, you can customize your use of this mental training tool to fit your needs as a coach and the needs of your athletes.

Here's how the chapter is organized to help you learn how to use goal mapping as a mental training tool. First, the importance and relevance of goal mapping is explained so that you and your athletes understand *how and why* goal maps help athletes think, act, and feel better. Second, various types of goals are discussed, because a key aspect in goal mapping (and mental training) is to focus on the right goal at the right time! Third, SMAART goal mapping is presented as a recipe for developing useful and challenging goal maps. Fourth, using the analogy of a car trip, the four essential steps of goal mapping are presented. And finally, some tips for implementing goal mapping with athletes and teams are provided to help get you started.

Why are Goal Maps Important?

Sport psychology focuses on how athletes think, feel, and act, thus goal mapping is important because it provides athletes with a plan for how to think, feel, and act. If motivation is the *source* of behavior, then purposeful goals are the *regulators* of behavior. Motivation is unharnessed energy, so an effective goal map is needed to harness motivation in productive ways so athletes can use their motivational energy most efficiently.

Quotable Quote

"Quality is never an accident; it is always the result of high intention, sincere effort, intelligent direction, and skillful execution." **Will A. Foster**

A Map for How to Act

Think back to when you were encouraged to "just do your best." Did you? How did you know what your best was? And if you achieved it, how did you know it was your best? Or was it just what you accepted as your best without extending yourself, pushing your personal envelope, making yourself uncomfortable to stretch your limits? Research in sport psychology shows that setting and focusing on challenging goals stimulates athletes to perform better than simply requesting that they do their best. Using goal mapping in mental training has improved performance in speed skating, swimming, ice hockey, basketball, lacrosse, wrestling, gymnastics, and golf (Gould, 2001; Kane, Baltes, & Moss, 2001).

A goal map is a plan for how to act. Think about the most important goal you have ever had for yourself. Consider how your behavior was affected by this goal. I'm sure that this goal totally energized you and

© Eyewire Images

shaped your behavior in amazing ways, almost to the level of obsession. According to goal theorists Locke and Latham (1990), goals affect our behavior by

- directing our attention to relevant things,
- increasing the effort we expend,
- increasing our persistence over time and in the face of obstacles, and
- motivating strategy development.

So goals initiate actions in us that lead to goal attainment. Recall your most important goal again and consider how your behavior was affected in the four ways identified by Locke and Latham. Research supports that goal mapping interventions motivate athletes to work harder and to spend more time on relevant tasks (Wanlin, Hrycaiko, Martin, & Mahon, 1997). Consider how the goal map of Pete Rose Jr. fueled his behavior across time and through many obstacles (see Clipboard).

Clipboard

Eyes on the Prize

On September 1, 1997, in Cincinnati, Pete Rose Jr. got his first major league hit. The capacity crowd in Riverfront Stadium, most who were there to share the moment with him, went bonkers. For most young players trying to break into "The Show," this would be a significant milestone. But for Rose, it was a climactic culmination of a personal goal map that represented extreme commitment and perseverance. Pete Rose Jr. is the son of Pete Rose Sr. the all time major league baseball "Hit King," who amassed 4,256 hits in his professional career, a record considered by many to be unbreakable.

Rose Jr. had toiled for nine seasons in the minor leagues batting .254, where many coaches saw him as a journeyman utility player, as opposed to a young prospect. After a few years in the minors without a major league call-up, most players give up the dream of playing major league baseball. Not Rose. A scout for the Reds said, "A guy like Pete, you can't ever count him out." He endured the scorn of fans for being the son of Rose Sr. who spent five months in prison and was banned from baseball for gambling. In the off-season, Rose Jr. worked construction and as a stock boy in a sporting goods store to make ends meet, when he wasn't playing winter ball to hone his skills. His dream was to make it to the majors and to play in his hometown for the Cincinnati Reds in Riverfront Stadium, where he had romped as a child when his Dad was a member of the famous "Big Red Machine" that won two World Series. He accepted all those years in the low minors as part of his goal map to fulfill his dream, which he knew he would achieve one day. Fittingly, Rose Jr. was taking extra batting practice when the call came to inform him of his call-up to the Reds. Rose Jr. made his successful debut in Riverfront Stadium and stayed with the big club through September. However, the next year, he was back in the minors, again pursuing his goal map, even though he had experienced his one great moment at Riverfront.

Although many ridicule Pete Rose Jr.'s dogged persistence of a major league career, his commitment to a single-minded goal map merits appreciation and respect. Rose's story exemplifies the powerful effect that having a personally meaningful goal can have on human behavior. Most people retain only fleeting glimpses of their dream goals of youth, while Pete Rose Jr. continues to pursue his and can always say that he had his one moment when the dream came true.

Consider the case of Virginia Wade, a British tennis star who was hugely successful, yet had never won Wimbledon, her most coveted title. She describes how prior to finally becoming Wimbledon champion in 1977, she made a focused effort to change from wishing to win the title to actively wanting and seeking the title. Wade stated,

> *"If you waste time wishing, you can't be alert to any of the practical solutions marching by you. I was more than ready to want Wimbledon for myself. I thought about it every day with that goal uppermost in my mind. New ideas came to me. How to do it. Why I deserved it. Soon I had a realistic picture of myself winning Wimbledon. It was not merely a dream. I knew exactly what I wanted and how to get it"* (Dorfman & Kuehl, 1995, p. 7).

Everyone wants to "get there," but few people have the mental skill to map out *how* to get there and the mental toughness to act purposefully in following their map every day. Thus, motivation and goal maps are critically related. Motivation provides the raw materials that are refined into a sense of purpose (the fuel), and then goals provide the plan to expend the fuel in the most economic way. Encourage your athletes to improve their fuel efficiency by harnessing their motivation to an exciting and purposeful goal map that moves them toward their dreams.

A Map for How to Think and Feel

Along with serving as a map for how to act, where to go, and what to do, goal maps also serve the important role of helping athletes think and feel in more productive and enjoyable ways. Goal mapping is critical in helping athletes achieve the perspective needed to balance the triad of optimal performance, development, and experience in sport (see Figure 2.1 for review of the triad).

Focus. Most maladaptive responses to competition (e.g., choking, feeling worthless, giving up) result from inappropriate goals. Choking in sport occurs when athletes focus their attention on the wrong goal, such as pleasing their parents, being the hero, or the pressure to win. Peak experiences and performances occur when athletes focus on the present—the immediate goal of "right now"—as opposed to thinking of some important future goal such as winning a medal. Consider the following quote by an Olympic gold medalist, a Canadian diver:

> *"I started to shift away from the scoreboard a year and half before the Olympics because I knew that every time I looked at the scoreboard, my heart went crazy. I couldn't control it . . . It was harder to get ready for 10 dives than for 1 dive so I decided to stop looking at everyone else, just be myself and focus on preparing for my next dive. I knew I could win, but I had to dive well" (Orlick & Partington, 1988, p. 117).*

Goal mapping helps athletes to not only plan for and set appropriate and energizing goals, but also learn how to *focus* on the right goals at the right time. Thus, goals help athletes compartmentalize their thoughts to focus in on certain key things, which decrease the amount of attention available for distractions. Research shows that expert performers in sport focus on specific goals and process-oriented, technique-related strategies (e.g., "bend my knees" or "follow through"), as compared to non-

experts who tend to set more general goals and fail to utilize goal-oriented technique strategies (Cleary & Zimmerman, 2001). Goals can be effectively used by athletes to occupy their minds with present-tense thoughts about their immediate performance, such as the strategy used by the Olympic diver in the previous example. Proper focusing (discussed in more detail in Chapter 12) is the result of properly set goals and a good goal map.

Personal Plug-In

Identify some goals that have been set for you based on society's or other people's unrealistic expectations. Also, think deeply about expectations or goals you have for yourself that may be irrational or unrealistic.

Establishing personal standards of success. An effective goal map also is important to help athletes set a personal standard that they can accept for themselves, as opposed to being controlled by the often unrealistic standards of society. Consider the following quote by an Australian Olympic gold medalist: "I learned that unless you win, you're nobody . . . Like 100 people come second or third . . . but it's only the gold medal that really counts . . ." (Jackson, Mayocchi, & Dover, 1998, p. 145). This athlete was sarcastically referring to public perceptions of Olympic performances, and the pressures that athletes face to keep competition in perspective and focus on appropriate goals. Several examples of unrealistic goals based on inappropriate philosophies were presented in Chapter 2. Thus, it's clear that an effective coaching philosophy and philosophy about competition serve as important foundations for effective goal maps. The bottom line: challenge yourself and your athletes to set and focus on your own goals and your personal goal map, despite the crazy and irrational goals that society and the media glorify and expect others to attain. Own your own goals, and own your own life.

From problem to effective action. Effective goals also help athletes think better by changing negatively worded problem statements into productive action-oriented statements. Consider the following comparison list of athlete statements:

"I hope I don't pop up."

"Stroke a solid line drive."

"Now don't hit it in the water."

"Stroke a smooth, aggressive seven iron at the pin."

"Don't be so uptight."

"Use your energy to focus on your task."

The statements on the left represent typical thoughts and statements that we have as competitors—these thoughts occur because of our focus on what we *don't* want to happen. An effective goal map includes process-oriented focus goals that athletes can substitute for the negative thoughts that typically occur during competition. The statements on the right represent the action that you want your brain to fixate on. Our performance is best controlled by thoughts that create positive images of performance, such as stroking a line drive, hitting a solid approach shot over water, and channeling our competitive energy into a task focus. Therefore, designing a goal map involves identifying problems or negative thoughts that interfere with performance, and then breaking these problems down into manageable goals.

Managing emotions. Emotion is a huge part of sport, and obviously athletes experience negative feelings such as sadness, anger, anxiety, and frustration. Having an effective goal map, however, gives athletes some control over the roller-coaster of emotions that is sport participation. No one likes to lose in sport, yet mentally skilled athletes clearly understand that the amount of pride and satisfaction they feel in their performance can be gauged in many ways other than winning. Effective goal maps include many types of goals, and the best athletes know when to focus on which goals to keep an optimal mental focus and to manage their emotions.

Wrap-up. In summary, goal maps serve as the foundation for all mental training because they serve as a guide for how to act, think, and feel in the most productive ways. They energize our behavior in task-relevant ways, and they sharpen our focus on the process of performing, which is a prerequisite to flow and peak performance. Effective goal maps also allow athletes to take control of their sport participation by establishing their own personal standards of success, moving from a problem-focused to an action-focused way of thinking, and managing their emotions productively.

Types of Goals

By now, you should have a basic understanding of how goals help athletes to think, behave, and perform better in sport. It's now time to think about the *types* of goals that athletes should include in their goal map. As you know, simply having goals does not automatically enhance performance. The term "goal mapping" is based on the idea that coaches and athletes must use insight and skill in developing their goal maps so that these maps lead them in the right directions at the right times. This requires knowledge about different types of goals and how they can be used most effectively by athletes.

Outcome, Performance, and Process Goals

The goal setting literature in sport psychology makes the important distinction between outcome, performance, and process goals (e.g., Gould, 2001). **Outcome goals** are *standards based on uncontrollable results or outcomes*, such as winning the championship or making an All-Star team. These are the most common type of goals set by athletes, and they are the easiest goals to understand and set. **Performance goals** are *standards based on performance accomplishments that are usually self-referenced* (e.g., swimming or running a certain time, shooting a specific free throw percentage, hitting a certain number of greens in regulation). **Process goals** are *standards that are based on controllable thoughts or actions related to performance execution* (e.g., slow backswing, proper footwork on blocking, a softball hitter "throwing" her hands). Process goals have been shown to improve performance and also enhance confidence, concentration, and help control anxiety in golfers (Kingston & Hardy, 1997). Research has also demonstrated that swimmers who set and focus on performance goals performed better and were more confident and less anxious than swimmers who were more outcome-oriented (Burton, 1989).

Does this mean that outcome goals are bad and should never be used? Not at all. Athletes perform most effectively by *using various types of goals and knowing when to use each type* (Kingston & Hardy, 1997). Outcome goals are typically very exciting and motivational, and they can be used to energize athletes to work hard toward attaining important championships and major achievements. Performance goals are good standards to use to map out the key performance attainments that athletes need to achieve in order to lead them toward their outcome goal. Process goals are critical for actual competitive performance, and they should be used to focus attention on key aspects of performance and to occupy athletes' minds with relevant thoughts and images.

For example, a high jumper may set an exciting outcome goal of qualifying for the state track meet. The anticipation of qualifying is exciting and energizing, and he uses it to remind himself to effectively utilize his practice time and not take any shortcuts in training. He sets performance goals of increasing his leg strength through weight training, hitting his take-off point on stride each jump, and achieving a progressive set of jump heights throughout the season. He works with his coach to set process goals that focus his attention optimally for each jump, such as creating a mental state of relaxed intensity and using the trigger words of "smooth, explode, kick!" to visualize perfect technique prior to each jump. The key to this example is that the high jumper prioritizes his thinking about certain goals depending upon the situation. If he focuses on the height he must jump to qualify during his actual performance, he is certain to miss. He can use the motivation of qualifying for the state meet to energize him, but he has to focus on performance goals to train effectively, and then narrow his attention to controllable, relevant, process-oriented thoughts and images at the actual time of competition.

A problem that typically arises is that the importance and popularity of outcome goals often tend to override all other thinking about performance and process goals. Consider athletes who have trained for years, perhaps their entire lives, in their quest for Olympic gold medals. Of COURSE their goal is to win—that is the inherent goal in any sport contest. (I call it the "Duh" goal because it's so obvious.) However, over and over you read personal testimonies from athletes who focused on winning medals only to *lose* them, as well as testimonies from successful Olympic athletes who put the medals in the back of their mind, and focused on controllable aspects of their performance (Orlick, 2000). The best athletes in the world have learned how to plan and use their goal maps efficiently, to allow themselves to optimally focus and "park" the pressure by becoming very process-oriented at the time that they compete. They understand that outcome goals are uncontrollable,

US Army Photo, courtesy of GeekPhilosopher.com

Personal Plug-In

Consider an important achievement that you would like to accomplish. Specifically identify the outcome goal, performance goals, and process goals that you can use together in your goal map to facilitate your pursuit of this important achievement.

Quotable Quote

"You, and you alone, are the person who should take the measure of your own success. I do not try to be better than anyone else. I only try to be better than myself." **Dan Jansen**, Olympic gold-medalist in speed skating (Jansen, 1999).

no matter how skilled you are. There is never a "sure thing" in sport, and that is what makes sport so compelling to watch and so exciting for athletes. Thus, I don't discourage athletes from setting outcome goals within their goal maps, but I encourage them to include many other types of goals within their maps so as to have some personal standards and focus points upon which they can base their performance and their evaluation of themselves.

Long-Term and Short-Term Goals

Similar to the distinction between outcome, performance, and process goals, coaches and athletes should also include both long-term and short-term goals in their goal maps. Although this point seems intuitive, many coaches and athletes set only long-term goals (typically outcome goals), and fail to use short-term goals (often performance and process goals) to focus them on the day-to-day progression toward their long-term goals. The analogy typically used for the relationship between long-term and short-term goals is that of a staircase. No one jumps to the top of the staircase without traversing each of the steps. The staircase should be represented by a goal map, consisting of short-term process and performance goals that lead to more long-term performance goals that ultimately lead to a long-term exciting outcome goal.

Clipboard

Staircase Goals

Shannon Miller is the most decorated gymnast in American history, with seven Olympic medals and nine World Championship medals. She is a self-described perfectionist, and here is her goal mapping strategy: "I have to have a goal, whether it's in school, in my personal life, or in the gym . . . If I have a competition coming up, that's always a big motivator. But I don't have winning the competition as the goal. I try to start with that big goal, then back up from there. I say, 'OK, within six months, where do I need to be to achieve that goal?' and I make a list. Then I say, 'Within three months, where do I need to be to achieve that goal?' And then you have to remember that no matter how big your goals or how many you have, there are going to be times when you miss it by a little bit. You have to be realistic and flexible. One reason I have so many smaller goals is that even if my big goal doesn't happen, I've still achieved so much along the way, I don't feel the loss" (Compton, 1998, p. 61).

In summary, good goal maps include many different types of goals that are personally relevant and motivational for athletes. Athletes should have a clear understanding of how and when to use various goals to enable them to get the Inner Edge.

SMAART Goal Mapping

You've probably heard of the importance of working smarter, instead of just working harder. This is good advice in pursuing purposeful goals! The acronym SMAART (Smith, 1999) can be used to remember *how* to be smart in developing your goal map. Goals are SMAART when they are Specific, Measurable, Aggressive yet Achievable, Relevant, and Time-bound. In this section, the specific ideas behind SMAART goal mapping are explained.

Specific

The more specific your goals, the better. General goals to "play well" or "give one hundred percent" fail to establish *what exactly it means* to "play well" or *what behaviors a player must exhibit* to "give one hundred percent!" Athletes must specify the exact behaviors that they want to engage in that will lead to success in that situation. For example, a general goal is, "I want to keep optimal concentration during the game" (basketball). Of course you do, but how do you do that? As a coach, I was always admonishing players to "concentrate out there!" However, now I realize that I needed to help them understand *what* to concentrate on and *how to do this* effectively. This general goal should be divided into more specific goals that define ways of behaving related to optimal concentration in basketball such as (a) use my pre-shot routine prior to each free throw, (b) maintain the ball-you-opponent triangle on individual defense, and (c) sustain physical contact with my opponent in a strong box-out position when a shot is taken. Be specific for SMAART goal mapping.

Measurable

Goals must be measurable so that progress can be evaluated. Some goals in sport are easily quantifiable, such as times and other numbers that represent speed, accuracy, or frequencies of positive behaviors. However, some sports require actions by athletes that are not easily quantifiable, such as effective marking in soccer or effective decision-making by a volleyball setter. As coaches, you must find ways to help athletes quantify and assess their progress on goals, especially on those goals that are not easily quantifiable. Specify the goal in terms of how many, how often, and under what conditions. Make sure that the goal statement specifies some action that the athlete is taking. Instead of a softball player saying, "I want to concentrate consistently," she could set the following goal: "Prior to each pitch, I will repeat to myself my defensive play for that situation in the game." By making goals specific, they typically become more assessable. It's when goals are abstract, subjective, or ambiguous that assessment becomes a problem. Be SMAART—set goals that you can clearly assess to analyze your progress.

Personal Plug-In

Write down three goals that are important for you or for the athletes you are coaching. Attempt to make these goals as measurable as possible by specifying how many, how often, and/or under what conditions.

Aggressive yet Achievable

Aggressive goals make athletes stretch and push their limits. However, at the same time, if goals are ridiculously unrealistic, they are not credible goals at all, and thus do not provide direction or inspiration. Thus, we need both of the A's to make the point that the best goals are difficult, extremely challenging, and very aggressive to inspire athletes, yet they must be achievable at the upper limits of athletes' ability (Locke & Latham, 1990). These A/A goals push athletes to make themselves "uncomfortable," because if they're feeling comfortable and secure, they are not pushing their personal performance envelope. As the subtitle of the book indicates, we want to evoke excellence in athletes, and one way to do that is through A/A goals and SMAART goal mapping.

Relevant

Goals are relevant when they are individualized and personally meaningful for athletes, thus capturing their attention and invigorating their motivation. Relevancy also means that within teams, athletes must set and focus on goals that help the team's performance, not take away from it. This causes a great deal of conflict in sport, because many times coaches and athletes do not agree on the roles athletes need to accept to make the team better. Coaches should not set goals for athletes without any input from them, and likewise athletes in team sports cannot set individual goals that detract from what the team is trying to accomplish as a group. What is

needed in any team is a lot of frank and open discussion about the purpose and mission of the team, so that athletes are aware of how their individual goals should feed into this purpose. At the same time, coaches should be receptive to the goals athletes set and work with them to carefully adjust these goals so that they fit within the team concept. This was discussed in Chapter 6 with regards to team cohesion, and a critical point was made that coaches must value and reinforce all roles within the team if they expect athletes to accept and fulfill their roles.

Along with working to make team and individual goals congruent and relevant to each other, coaches and athletes should include relevant goals for practice as well as competition within their goal maps. Many times athletes set goals they wish to achieve in competition, but they forget that it's in practice and training that they make the most progress. Challenge athletes to set, focus on, and evaluate both practice and competition goals as part of their goal map.

Similarly, encourage athletes to set goals related to their physical performances as well as their mental performances. Athletes can begin by identifying a mental skill that they would like to improve and then developing goals to help break down this skill into a staircase of attainable process, performance, and outcome goals. For example, a golfer may discover that he becomes tense and loses focus and confidence after performing poorly on a hole. He could set the outcome goal of playing well after having a bad hole, and attempt to break this down into relevant performance and process goals to help him achieve this desirable outcome. Performance goals might be (a) to strike a solid, not spectacular drive, (b) to engage in productive thoughts no matter what happens, and (c) to score a par on the hole. Process goals could include (a) to behaviorally and mentally slow down his pace of play and swing thoughts, (b) to manage his thoughts by using a pre-planned focusing routine prior to each shot, and (c) to use a performance cue like ripping the velcro on his golf glove to "change the channel" or reframe his thinking to the present in terms of the immediate thoughts he should be focusing on for his next swing.

Goals are relevant when they are used to focus energy on both the "green" and "gold" zones of athletes' and coaches' lives. Orlick (1998) defines the gold zone as that part of athletes' lives that involves pursuing competitive goals, while the green zone represents athletes' lives away from the competitive arena. By focusing on purposeful living in both zones, athletes achieve a healthy sense of perspective and balance that keeps them fresh and invigorated. Because the gold zone tends to overwhelm the green zone in many people, goal maps that include relevant goals to enhance personal fulfillment outside of sport as well as personal performance are effective mental training tools. This is especially important for coaches who need purposeful goals related to living in the green zone to maintain their health and well-being. Being an effective gold and green zone model for your athletes helps them to keep their sport participation in perspective so that they can enjoy optimal performance, experience, and development in sport as well as life.

Personal Plug-In

Identify at least two "green zone" goals that can help you focus on keeping perspective and balance in your life. Don't skip this exercise—coaches need time in the "green zone!"

Time-bound

The final principle of SMAART goal mapping is that goals should be time-bound, which involves specifying a target date for goal attainment. Goals that are completely open-ended with no timeframe for achievement do not facilitate focused behavior. Specifying the timeframe for achieving goals ensures that they are Aggressive/Achievable. I have found that athletes tend to set unrealistic, dream-oriented goals when they are not required to set a timeline for accomplishing those goals. You may notice that some of your most creative moments occur when you have a deadline looming for the completion of a goal, because your focus sharpens and your brain kicks in based on the urgency of the goal. This should be a positive urgency, because we're all too familiar with the negative stress of constant deadlines that saps our creativity. Athletes need time-bound goals with manageable timelines that create a focused sense of urgency, which stimulates them to think productively and act efficiently. This is where short-term goals with deadlines can be used as stepping stones on the way to achieving an important long-term goal.

Quotable Quote

"Goals are dreams with deadlines." Ben Franklin

So there you have the SMAART way to plan and develop your goal map. Good goal maps include goals that are Specific, Measurable, Aggressive yet Achievable, Relevant, and Time-bound. These general principles will hopefully guide you in developing effective goals and useful goal maps.

Four Steps of Goal Mapping

In this section, one approach to goal mapping is presented as an example of how to use this basic mental training tool in a practical way with athletes. Of course, you can develop your own innovative ways of goal mapping as you gain experience with the process. The key is to make goal mapping as meaningful and useful as possible for athletes so they can and will use it.

Visualize yourself preparing to take a journey in an automobile to work through the four steps of goal mapping listed below:

(1) Identify your purpose—understand why your destination is your destination.
(2) Plan and develop your goal map.
(3) Act "on purpose" by hitting the GAS, downshifting and choosing effective detours, and committing to a habitual and systematic goal mapping system.
(4) Put the top down and turn up the music to invigorate your journey, refresh your goal map, and focus on the road instead of your final destination!

The first two steps involve the reflection and planning phases of goal mapping, as you prepare to begin your journey. Abraham Lincoln once said that if he had eight hours to chop down a tree, he would spend six of those hours sharpening the axe. Lincoln's advice is well taken. The first important steps in goal mapping involve preparation in the form of reflection and analysis to ensure that when the car starts moving, it moves most efficiently and in the right direction for you. Then, it's time to buckle up as Steps 3 and 4 get you moving down the road toward personal fulfillment as your goal map springs into a personal action plan.

Step 1: Identify Your Purpose

As mentioned previously in the chapter, goal mapping is incomplete without a sense of purpose to provide the passion or energy needed to pursue difficult goals. In the poignant movie "Dead Poets Society," Robin Williams plays a teacher who succeeds in challenging his students to sense and seize their purpose, instead of mindlessly pursuing goals (typically set for them by their parents) without tapping into their passion. The teacher portrayed in the movie understood that an effective goal map of one's life doesn't begin with goals. Rather, one's goal map has to begin with a clear sense of and commitment to a purpose.

Think about some big goals that you have achieved in your life. How did you feel immediately after you had achieved these significant goals? I would guess that you were very happy, perhaps even immediately ecstatic, after which you quickly turned your thoughts to the next goal in front of you. Sometimes, achieving major goals is anti-climactic for people, as if they expected to feel more as the result of the achievement. The reason for this is that our passion, or purpose, is what fulfills us, makes us feel alive, and creates the larger meaning as compared to our goals (Newburg, Kimiecik, Durand-Bush, & Doell, 2002). In my life, I have achieved major personal goals, such as winning championships as a player and coach, completing a doctorate, and publishing my work as an author. Although achieving these goals was deeply satisfying, it has always been my passion, or purpose, in doing what I feel defines me and lights me up that drives my behavior and fulfills my everyday life. My passion to play and coach the game of basketball, as well as my passion to dedicate my career to understanding sport psychology at a level where I could creatively work with athletes and coaches, has fueled my purposeful behavior and set me on my goal map journey. Thus, it is imperative to begin your goal maps with a clear sense of purpose because it is this purpose that leads to human fulfillment, *not* the achievement of goals.

Purpose is the "why" of behavior; goals are the "what" (Wright, 1997). In goal mapping, the first step to identifying your purpose requires you to understand why your destination is your destination. If this isn't clear to you, your goals will lack meaning, coherence, power, and direction. A well thought out and accurate sense of purpose brings your goals into clear vision and serves as the ultimate guide for fulfillment and success. It is no accident that the greatest athletes of all time possessed a keen sense of purpose and an absolute passion for their sport. Legendary Alabama football coach Bear Bryant died within a year of retiring, just as he had predicted by stating that "his reason for living" (working with young college athletes) was complete (Wright, 1997). Since it flows from intrinsic motivation, a sense of purpose energizes our behavior, which, as discussed in Chapter 3, is the best source of motivation because it is self-fueling. Similarly, a passionate sense of purpose enables athletes to easily get into flow, that feeling of total immersion and quality performance discussed in Chapter 1.

Consider the following quote to better understand how a sense of purpose can lead to greater accomplishment than mere goal setting:

> "I realized that I wanted to focus my attention more on the climbing and on having a great experience . . . We climb these peaks because we love them, we love the places they take us, and we love the process of learning about ourselves along the way . . . The purpose of risking your neck in an adventure is to attain some sort of spiritual or personal growth. This will not happen if you are so fixated on the goal that you compromise the process along the way." **Ed Viesturs**, world-class mountain climber (*Viesturs, 2000, p. 72-77*)

Recall our discussion in Chapter 3 about how talented individuals all began their talent development by developing an intense love or passion for their chosen activity (Bloom, 1985). Bloom found that the passion that develops during the "romance phase" of talent development was necessary to fuel performers through the next phase of systematic training. The importance of developing a passion in Bloom's work is similar to the first step in goal mapping of sensing and seizing a passionate sense of purpose. The goals in the map flow from one's purpose in the same way that talented individuals move into systematic precision training from the romance phase of playful exploration that created their love of the activity. Bloom found that attempts to move too quickly from the romance phase into precision

Quotable Quote

"You need to think about the true way of being a human being, not merely to be someone who has knowledge or is clever in what he does; but to be somebody who knows what he wants to do. Be one who knows that for life you require the truth."

Albert Schweitzer

training destroyed the performers' motivation, and this is also the case if athletes focus only on goals, and not the purpose or passion driving the goals. Goals are important, but a passionate sense of purpose is the key to performance excellence.

The distinction between goals and sense of purpose, or passion, is eloquently stated by Dawn Staley, professional basketball player and Olympic gold medalist on the U.S. Women's Basketball team in 1996. She uses the terms "dream" and "resonance" (Newburg et al., 2002) to describe her passion or sense of purpose:

"Winning the gold medal is my goal, not my dream. My dream is about playing to win as often as possible with and against the best women's basketball players in the world. Winning the gold medal as a goal gives me some direction, but my dream is something I need to live every day. And I'm doing that each time I play to win. When I'm playing to win, that's when I feel resonance. If I win, that's great. I want to win, and having the gold medal as my goal forces me to play to win. But what I love to do, what my dream is, is to play to win" (Newburg et al., 2002).

This first goal mapping step of identifying your purpose is sometimes hard to get across to young athletes. We live in a very goal-oriented society, and the goals of sport are public and highly valued by society. It's no wonder, then, that many athletes put the cart before the horse, and focus their sport involve-

ment on the achievement of goals, as if these goals will provide them with fulfillment. As a coach, then, it is your challenge to find ways, like Robin Williams in "Dead Poets Society," to get your athletes to develop a passionate sense of purpose from which goal-directed behavior such as effort, commitment, and responsibility will flow.

Several strategies discussed in previous chapters can be used in challenging athletes to sense and seize a strong sense of purpose. Emphasizing intrinsic motivation as opposed to using rigid extrinsic reinforcers, practicing transformative leadership, and working toward a strong team culture and sense of cohesion are all examples of facilitating a purposeful climate within a team. I recommend that teams take time to develop a purpose or mission statement. This could be an extension of the vision that you have developed as a coach for your program (discussed in Chapter 5). At the very least, teams should have frank discussions about what their ultimate purpose is and what they feel defines them as a team.

Individual athletes should consider their sense of purpose to understand what moves them and what energizes them to pursue their goals. Consider how Nancy Hogshead's sense of purpose fueled her success as an athlete and person, well beyond simply focusing on her status as an Olympic champion (see Clipboard).

Clipboard

A Purposeful Experience

At the 1984 Olympic Games in Los Angeles, Nancy Hogshead concluded eight years as a world-class swimmer with three gold medals and one silver medal—the most decorated swimmer at the Games. In 1992, she became president of the Women's Sport

Foundation, tripling its budget and building a Hall of Fame. She is currently an attorney at one of the world's largest law firms, and she speaks regularly to corporate and civic groups, emphasizing her fundamentals of success. As you read the following comments from Hogshead, consider how she wrapped her personal goal map within an unshakable and personally meaningful sense of purpose:

> *"Why should you push yourself? Because the rewards of reaching for excellence truly are profound. I'm not talking about a plaque or even a gold medal. It's living into a purpose or a calling that enlivens even the most mundane tasks.*
>
> *For me, the honor and glory of the Olympics come from the journey, not from any one event. Throughout my career I probably swam with a thousand other swimmers from some of the country's best teams, and only a handful of us made it to the Olympics. But all 1,000 of us went through a process that taught us the fundamentals of success and prepared us for the big challenges in life. I am altered by the Olympic experience, not because I stood on a victory platform, but because I went for it without holding anything in reserve. There was no 'What if?' because I knew I had gone through the struggle and had done everything I could do. Throughout this journey of years of workouts and competitions, there were moments of true mastery, of bliss, of a oneness with myself and the world. All the splashing and chaos of workout life were muted and my soul was very still. Truly effortless. During these times, it felt like my soul hovered about two feet above my body and it condensed into a sliver, a needle . . .*
>
> *In the yin and yang of life, I don't know whether I could have had such spiritual moments without also experiencing the downside of going for a big goal: the slumps and discouragements, the agonizing questions about whether this was the right path, the feeling that my goal was dominating my life, rather than vice versa. I endured a two-and-one-half year period in which I did not improve a single time. And still, I got back in the water every day.*
>
> *Ultimately, I felt that developing the talents God gave me was a noble purpose. I was proud of what I was doing . . . That sense of purpose gives us the ability to move beyond what we otherwise might have thought possible. To awaken the Olympian within, we must have faith in the noble purpose of our life's goals . . . We'll be amazed at what we are capable of achieving"* (Hogshead, 1999, pp. 133-140).

To be ultimately effective, goal maps should begin with a strong sense of purpose. Urge your athletes to focus on the journey and to understand why they are pushing for a certain destination, because the motivational energy that fuels their goals is not the goals themselves, but the power of purposeful and passionate living.

Step 2: Plan and Develop Your Goal Map

Once you have helped your team and/or your athletes identify a sense of purpose, you can then move on with your goal map. Identifying the different types of goals and understanding how to be SMAART in setting goals provided us with guidelines for how to set and monitor effective goals in our goal map. But how do we actually develop a goal map? Do we just start writing down goals that are SMAART? We know we need to use short-term and long-term goals as well as outcome, performance, and process goals, but how do we integrate these together in a systematic goal map?

An example goal map is shown in Figure 8.1. Athletes identify their purpose and set their goals in the top part of the goal map, and then identify and monitor their strategies to achieve their goals in the bottom part of the map. Take a look at the top part of the goal map. Notice that it is like a tree (Smith, 1999), with trunk, limbs, and branches, although it is horizontal (laying on its side) as opposed to vertical like trees look when they are growing. The tree incorporates one's purpose and goals (outcome, performance, process, short-term, and long-term) into one big goal map.

Athletes' sense of purpose or passion should be thought of as the roots of the tree. Our purpose must be strongly rooted, and these roots provide life and nutrients to the trunk and branches of the tree (goals). Without the deeply rooted purpose, the goals (like the tree) would die. Thus, the first step in goal mapping is identifying one's purpose that serves to fuel the goals in the goal map. Athletes then move left to right (think of "climbing the tree") to fill in their goal map by using different kinds of goals to get them moving and thinking productively. **Milestone goals** are *significant attainments that athletes achieve as they follow their sense of purpose.* These can be outcome or performance goals that represent meaningful personal achievements for athletes.

Figure 8.1 Goal Map

Purpose _____

Milestone Goal _____

Challenge Goal _____

Challenge Goal _____

Focus Goal _____

Focus Goal _____

Focus Goal _____

Focus Goal _____

Progress Log

	Week 1	Week 2	Week 3	Week 4

Goal Achievement Strategies (Hit the GAS!)

1. _____

2. _____

3. _____

4. _____

Moving from left to right, the performance tree becomes increasingly dense as we reach the branches representing challenge goals. Challenge is defined in the dictionary as "anything, as a demanding task, that calls for special effort or dedication." Thus, **challenge goals** are *performance standards that explicitly specify behavioral actions that are critical to reaching milestone goals*. Challenge goals are typically performance goals, and they typically represent the specific aspects of performance that must occur for athletes to be in the position for successful outcomes. Finally, the top branches of the performance tree are represented by **focus goals**, which are *specific thought and behavioral patterns that enhance focus and automaticity during competitive performance*. If focus goals remind you of process goals, you're right— they are one and the same.

Athletes can extend their goal maps to include multiple milestone goals, and "grow" their goal map in different ways. However, the goal map shown in Figure 8.1 attempts to simply things for athletes by starting with one outcome goal, and then working through the map to develop challenge and focus goals that will help them achieve the important milestone goal. The section on Goal Achievement Strategies is discussed later in the chapter, but it seems important to have these strategies listed with athletes' actual goals to provide them with a comprehensive goal map that they can use every day.

Goal map for a college golfer (Hunter). In Figure 8.2, a performance tree developed by a college golfer named Hunter is shown. Hunter's sense of purpose is based on the feeling and enjoyment of *"pure skill"* that comes when she strikes a golf shot perfectly. She enjoys the challenge of attempting to "pure" every shot, and thinks of every shot as an opportunity to enjoy pure skill. It's why she loves the game—and why she plays. The milestone goal Hunter is focusing on in this goal map is to be the *top golfer in her conference and in the top 30 nationally.*

In building this goal map, Hunter identified specific challenge goals to enhance the achievement of her milestone goal. Keep in mind that these are very individualized goals that represent key aspects of her performance that she needs to improve. Thus, she set a specific performance-oriented challenge goal to improve her short game (*up and down on chips 90% of the time*) and a mental challenge goal of *working her mental plan to recover from bad holes*. In addition,

Hunter's focus goals represent the ways she wanted to think to enhance the probability of achieving her challenge goals. For example, she used the focus goal cues of "accelerate" and "crisp" to remind her of key performance strategies to successfully execute the needed touch on chips shots around the greens. Her focus goals for mentally recovering from a bad hole included a focus on *"setting the tone" by making a solid, smooth drive off the next tee* as well as flipping her "trust switch" to autopilot. This last focus goal reminds her to avoid thinking about mechanics and just swing automatically, trusting the swing that she has developed through practice. Both of Hunter's focus goals attempted to create a productive and intentional thought pattern for different competitive demands. These focus goals were important to occupy her thoughts and to provide specific ways to achieve her challenge goals.

Goal map for a high school basketball player (Dean). A goal map developed by Dean, a high school basketball player, is shown in Figure 8.3. Dean described a passionate sense of purpose that focused on his absolute *love of competition*. He explained that he enjoyed basketball, but competing in basketball was what drove him to be his best and motivated him to develop his skills so he could test himself under pressure-filled competitive situations. Dean set a very typical milestone goal for a high school athlete, which was to *win the starting point guard position* his junior year.

As you can see in Figure 8.3, Dean set a performance-oriented challenge goal of a *90% free-throw shooting percentage*. He knew that a point guard must be a great free throw shooter, especially late in the game. He also identified a challenge goal that maximized his physical abilities to *aggressively penetrate to score or dish*. Dean knew his ability to penetrate defenses with his dribble to either score or pass to a teammate was a critical need for the team's point guard. Dean's focus goals represent key thought patterns that enabled him to optimally focus on specific performance demands. For example, focusing on being "hard to guard" means that he was active with and without the ball on offense. He also focused on "pushing" the ball to keep pressure on the opposing defense. His focus goals to enhance his free-throw shooting included the attentional cues of *"strong and soft"* to remind him to create a steady base, feel strong in his legs and stance as a shooter, and then

Figure 8.2 Goal map for college golfer

Purpose
play with/enjoy PURE SKILL

Milestone Goal
#1 in conference and top 30 in NCAA

Challenge Goal
up and down on chips 90% of the time

Focus Goal
"accelerate"

Focus Goal
"crisp"

Challenge Goal
work mental plan for bad hole recovery

Focus Goal
solid, smooth drive (set the tone)

Focus Goal
trust switch; go to autopilot

Goal Achievement Strategies (Hit the GAS!)

		Progress Log		
	Week 1	Week 2	Week 3	Week 4
1. 20 chips x 5 positions around green daily	___	___	___	___
2. 20 putts from 12, 10, 8, 6, and 4 feet daily	___	___	___	___
3. practice focus goal cues in preshot routine	___	___	___	___
4. keep bad hole recovery score (hole after blowup)	___	___	___	___

drop the ball softly over the front of the rim. "Strong and soft" became his mantra as soon as he approached the free throw line, where he would envision himself *wrapped in a cocoon* with his focus solely on his body, the ball, and the rim. Overall, Dean's focus goals were developed to get him to think intentionally in the most productive ways to enhance the focus he needed to perform successfully in relation to his challenge goals.

Goal map for high school softball team. Goal maps can also be drawn for teams, such as the example goal map for a high school softball team shown in Figure 8.4. This team identified their purpose as the *"Power of One = TEAM,"* meaning that their purpose was to play together to create the Power of One, which in turn creates greater success (Together Everyone Achieves More, or TEAM). Their purpose of improving and achieving great things together energizes their pursuit of their goals. They set the milestone goals of *challenging for the conference championship* and *winning 20 games.*

In discussing what they needed to do to make their milestone goals happen, they identified three challenge goals. The goal of achieving a *higher batting average (BA) with runners in scoring position* was a difficult goal that motivated them to achieve quality at-bats when it counted the most. They also set a challenge goal of *putting teams away,* based on their tendency last year to let teams creep back and tie the score in later innings. Their third challenge goal set their defensive philosophy of wanting the ball to be *put in play.* This goal meant that pitchers were not trying to overpower hitters and strike them out, but rather throw strikes and make the hitters hit a fieldable ball to a teammate. The specific goal statistics associated with this challenge goal are *less than 2 walks and less than 2 errors per game.*

The focus goals that helped the players meet their challenge goals included feeling *"aggressive and loose"* and maintaining a present focus or *one pitch focus* in the batter's box. Pitchers focus on one pitch at a time and think about *hitting their spots* as set up by the catcher. Defensive players use the cue *"load and lock"* as an attentional focusing strategy before every pitch. "Load" means that they repeat to themselves what they will do if the ball is hit to them, and "lock" means that once they've loaded their mind with the correct strategy to be used, they touch their gloves to the ground and "lock in" on the batter and

the ball. After each pitch, they relax momentarily, and then "load and lock" again.

Step 3: Act "On Purpose"

The first two steps in the goal mapping process involved planning and reflection to identify one's purpose and then develop one's goal map. Now it's time for action, as the rubber hits the road in Steps 3 and 4 to get athletes behaviorally energized in the pursuit of their goals.

In Step 3, athletes must now "walk the walk" by engaging in productive and intentional behaviors to "live" their goal map. The main objective in this step of goal mapping is for athletes to act "on purpose" to consciously and intentionally manage their lives to pursue their goals. This is a crucial step, for it is the point at which the process typically breaks down in terms of whether or not goal mapping is successful. That is, many athletes like to sit and plan out their dreams and goals, yet they fail to effectively manage their lives to act "on purpose" each day as part of their goal map. This is the step that ultimately separates those athletes who are intrinsically motivated and willing to persist in the face of the many obstacles from those who are not. To act "on purpose," athletes should follow the following substeps: (a) hit the GAS, or develop Goal Achievement Strategies, (b) know when to downshift and follow detours, and (c) commit to a system that makes their goal mapping practice habitual and systematic.

Hit the GAS. After athletes identify their goals within their goal map, they then should develop some Goal Achievement Strategies (GAS), which are simple behavioral plans to engage in behaviors that lead to goal attainment. You as the coach are an important resource in this stage of goal mapping to help the athletes develop GASes that are personally relevant and useful for them.

As an example, Hunter used the GAS of hitting 20 chips from 5 different positions around the green into a target area close to the pin to help her achieve her challenge goal of getting up and down on chips 90% of the time (see Figure 8.2). Hunter should practice her focus goals over and over as she engages in repetitive chipping practice. She developed a similar GAS to practice her putting to complete the "up and down" chip and one putt that is her challenge goal. Hunter also created a GAS of computing a recovery hole score in all of her practice and competi-

Figure 8.3 Goal map for high school point guard

			"be hard to guard"
			Focus Goal
			"push" the ball
			Focus Goal
		aggressively penetrate	
		to dish or score	"strong and soft"
		Challenge Goal	**Focus Goal**
		90% free throw %	"in the cocoon"
		Challenge Goal	**Focus Goal**

COMPETE to be
my best

starting point guard

Purpose   **Milestone Goal**

Goal Achievement Strategies (Hit the GAS!)

	Progress Log			
	Week 1	Week 2	Week 3	Week 4
1. dribble drills daily (one on one pressure)	_____	_____	_____	_____
2. play pick-up daily against faster opponents	_____	_____	_____	_____
3. 300 free throws daily (log % for each 100)	_____	_____	_____	_____
4. practice preshot routine with focus goal cues daily	_____	_____	_____	_____

tive rounds, which prompted her to practice refocusing after a bad hole (one of her challenge goals as shown in Figure 8.2).

Hunter then monitors each GAS using the Progress Log. This log can be used in several ways, such as simply recording the date on which she completed each GAS, noting the percentage of successful chips and putts she hit each day, and listing her bad hole recovery scores for each practice round.

As shown in Figure 8.3, Dean set a GAS of shooting 300 free throws a day using his focus goals to enhance concentration and automaticity in performance. Also, he and his coach worked out a sequence of dribbling drills that he practiced daily, all against an opponent (one on one). His final GAS was simply to seek out high caliber pick-up games so he could play and work on his ball-handling against faster and quicker opponents. His Progress Log would include his free throw percentage for every 100 shots, a personal grade and assessment on his dribbling drills performance, and a check-off that he practiced his preshot routine and played pick-up (including key things that went well along with areas needing improvement).

The GAS needed for our high school softball team's goal map (see Figure 8.4) includes a commitment to focused batting practice (BP) that the players know then translate into quality at bats (AB) in games. The coach also has designed various simulated pressure drills that are used in practice to prepare them for competitive pressure. The players practice their "load and lock" focus strategy in all practice situations, and they also create and mentally practice personal focus and refocus plans to use during competition (discussed in Chapter 12).

Overall, the objective is to develop systematic GASs that create behavioral plans for athletes to pursue and practice the goals they've set in their goal maps. The Progress Log is set up for one month, and I recommend that athletes then complete another goal map, which can then be modified based on their progress the previous month. The example goal mapping format shown in this chapter is just an example. Coaches and athletes can modify these in many ways to create the most personalized goal map for their needs.

Downshifting and detours. After hitting the GAS by developing personalized and specific goal achievement strategies, the next substep in acting

"on purpose" is to understand how and when to "downshift" and take "detours" on your goal map. *Every* athlete will at some time hit a performance plateau or slump, incur an injury, experience failure, and/or hit an unforeseen obstacle. All of these factors influence performance, and require either some additional goals or the revision of current goals. It is very difficult for athletes to lower or change their goals based on extenuating circumstances, but it is critical that they do so.

Quotable Quote

"First and foremost, you are accountable for yourself . . . Remember, this is what sets champions apart. They do what it takes to be the best no matter how painful, how boring, or how difficult it is to find the time."
Mia Hamm

Help your athletes understand that the best goal maps are flexible and change constantly based on the many factors that influence athletes' lives. When athletes are experiencing a performance slump or decrement, they should "downshift" a bit to back off, relax, and allow their physical and mental skills to surface—they always do! They should set some new challenge and focus goals that will help them think productively in working through their slump. Similarly, when athletes experience injuries or changes in their roles as decided by coaches, they should view this as a "detour" on their goal map. We all hate detours when driving on the highway, because they typically take more time than the most direct route. However, detours still get us to where we want to go, and athletes must keep this in mind! A detour, or change in one's goal map, is simply a temporary change of direction, which will add some time to the ultimate attainment of one's challenge or milestone goal. The most important thing is to keep the car moving, or to keep the goal map dynamic and active, so that it is something that athletes live every day, even if they are "downshifting" to get over a performance problem or "detouring" to take an alternative route to reach their ultimate goal.

Commit to an evaluation system. The final substep in acting "on purpose" in goal mapping requires athletes (and coaches) to commit to a system to evaluate goals. Research has indicated that goals are

Figure 8.4 Goal map for high school softball team

Power of One=
TEAM

Purpose

Challenge for
conference championship
_____
Milestone Goal

Win 20 games
_____
Milestone Goal

Higher BA with runners
in scoring position
_____
Challenge Goal

Put teams away
_____
Challenge Goal

Put ball in play
(<2 walks, <2 errors)
_____
Challenge Goal

aggressive and loose
_____
Focus Goal

one pitch focus
_____
Focus Goal

hit spots
_____
Focus Goal

"load and lock"
_____
Focus Goal

		Progress Log		
	Week 1	Week 2	Week 3	Week 4

Goal Achievement Strategies (Hit the GAS!)

1. Focused BP = Quality AB
   _____

2. Pressure drills in practice - win here!
   _____

3. Work "load and lock" in practice
   _____

4. Practice focus and refocus plans
   _____

most effective when they are monitored or evaluated (Locke & Latham, 1990). Thus, athletes and coaches should agree on how their specific goal maps can be evaluated and constantly updated. This can be very simple, yet it must be systematic. The Progress Log on the goal maps shown previously is an example of a way to evaluate both individual and team goals within a goal map.

Another way to evaluate athletes' goals is to implement a card evaluation system, where the athlete sets goals for a specified week of practice or for an upcoming competition, and then evaluates their goals at the completion of the week or event. These cards can be small (4 x 6 or 5 x 7 index cards work well) and made out of cardboard with team logos or inspirational quotes. An example of a goal evaluation card for competition is shown in Figure 8.5. The top picture is of the front of the card on which athletes set two challenge goals and then two focus goals for each challenge goal for this particular opponent. The bottom picture is the back of the card, which is completed after the competitive event, and includes evaluative comments from both athletes and coaches.

Coaches should consider evaluating individual goals for practices as well as competition, and also should consider how best to systematically monitor team goals. A common way to evaluate team goals is to use a large goal board with all team goals listed on one side, and the weeks of the season or names of opponents listed across the top. Then, each week or after each competition, the team should examine their goal board to see which goals they have achieved and to discuss why they failed to achieve certain goals. You can use team mascot stickers to denote the categories in which the goals were achieved. Over a number of weeks or competitions, the goal board will begin to show trends in terms of which goals are readily achieved and which are not being achieved. At this point, team goals can and should be adjusted, and new goals can be added as the season progresses.

There are many ways that athletes and coaches can systematically monitor progress toward their goals. Be resourceful and creative in determining what type of system will work best in your situation. It doesn't have to be complicated or flashy—it just needs to be systematic and simple.

Step 4: Put the Top Down and Turn Up the Music

The first step of goal mapping discussed earlier in this chapter involved sensing and seizing a sense of purpose. This required athletes to be self-reflective, to understand why they participate in sport, and to be "in touch" with this meaningful and energizing feeling. Steps 2 and 3 that were just discussed involved the mechanics of goal mapping, by suggesting that athletes climb the performance tree and set personal milestone, challenge, and focus goals, and then act "on purpose" by systematically living their lives in an intentional manner to behaviorally pursue their goals every day. Now, it is important at Step 4 to identify ways to revisit Step 1, so that athletes process on a daily basis just why they are engaging in sport.

So, again using our analogy of a car journey, the point is that driving one's goal map should not be an emotionless form of drudgery, but rather a journey in which one's sense of purpose or passion is kept in sight and mind to energize the ride. So now that athletes have set their goals and painstakingly planned goal achievement strategies and evaluation systems, they should get the car moving, put the top down, and turn up the music! Athletes should understand that while driving along in pursuit of their goals, they should focus on the journey and the great scenery, because focusing solely on the destination (milestone goal) gets in the way of the focus they need to drive efficiently. When people travel, they have determined their final destination and planned their journey with a map to ensure that they get there. However, during the journey, they must focus on driving their car and the experience of the journey; constantly thinking about the final destination would interfere with their driving performance as well as the quality of the trip. Athletes should do the same. Research has shown that outstanding performers not only set useful goals, but they keep their purpose or passion in sight as they pursue these goals (Newburg et al., 2002). These performers indicate that they do not wait until a goal is attained to feel the way they want to feel. Rather, their sense of purpose is their energy source, which they use as fuel to relentlessly pursue their goals.

This sounds great, but how can we help athletes achieve this important step, and not get bogged down in the drudgery of goals without meaning and purpose? Let's start with the case of Hunter, the col-

Figure 8.5 Goal evaluation card

WESTERN HILLS WILDCATS SOFTBALL 2005

NAME _____ DATE _____ OPPONENT _____

1. Challenge Goal 1: _____

    Focus Goal 1a: _____

    Focus Goal 1b: _____

2. Challenge Goal 2: _____

    Focus Goal 2a: _____

    Focus Goal 2b: _____

Athlete Goal Evaluation

1. Did you achieve your goals? Why or why not?

2. How might you revise your goal(s) to make you mentally tough and focused as well as to perform better?

Coach Goal Evaluation and Feedback

_____

_____

legiate golfer whose goal map was depicted in Figure 8.2. Hunter's passion for golf came from the "pure skill" she feels when hitting the ball well. Hunter was encouraged to take some time during practice each week just to play a few holes with the sole goal of enjoyment and experiencing this sense of "pure skill." Part of her refocusing plan when playing poorly was to get in touch with this feeling of "pure skill" by visualizing playing alone on a beautiful course and experiencing "pure skill." This refocusing technique provided the perspective that Hunter needed to relax on the course and remember why she was playing. Hunter learned to apply her passion of playing with pure skill to many of the drills that she practiced to hone her game.

In the case of Dean, the point guard whose goal map is shown in Figure 8.3, he needed to revisit his feelings of competitive passion to revitalize the pursuit of his goals. For example, his coaches ensured that Dean and other team members could experience the fun of competition each day in practice via short scrimmages or competitive drills that they enjoy. When Dean experienced apprehension and nervousness prior to games, he reframed his anxiety into exhilaration and focused on thriving on the pressure that competition creates. For the softball team represented by the goal map in Figure 8.4, they played best when they focused on the Power of One, or playing together as a team and trusting each other. The joy of the team experience was why they played, and they could develop different team strategies to maximize the Power of One feeling, such as team traditions and team building activities.

These examples may seem naive or unrealistic, but they are not if athletes possess true intrinsic motivation and a keen sense of purpose for their sport. Research substantiates that people who focus on goals without paying attention to their passion or sense of purpose struggle to achieve their goals. That is, without the purpose and passion, goal mapping is an unsustainable process. It is like a tree without the roots. The goals set in the tree trunk and branches must be sustained and provided nutrients through the roots that represent athletes' sense of purpose or passion for what they do. Coaches should help athletes to clarify their sense of purpose by asking them why they choose to practice and compete in their sport. If athletes are unclear about their reasons, coaches should encourage them to reflect upon and identify their purpose or passion for what they do.

Why I Play

A great exercise for athletes is to write in their own words why they play their sport. Consider the power in the following words [abridged] written by Colleen Day, senior leader, team captain, 1st team All-Conference, runner-up conference Player of the Year, Academic All-American, and heart and soul of the 2003-04 Miami University Redhawks women's basketball team, who won the Mid-American Conference championship:

"This is who I am.

I was born to play this game.

I play because it's the greatest game on earth.

I play because nothing else matters once on the hardwood.

I play because of locker room dances and hoop-phi chants.

I play to separate myself from the average student, the non-er.

I play to compete with my teammates for the biggest, baddest bruise.

For the unique satisfaction that follows grinding out sprint after time sprint.

To know what it's like to not feel your legs but to keep running.

To understand that injuries are the norm and,

To finally realize there is no off-season.

I play for the silly bus ride talks of procrastination, and the random topics of conversation.

For that moment when I look into my teammates' eyes and

without speaking a word know that a game is won.

I play to get strong!

I play to learn that my heart is the only real critic that counts.

To understand that winning a championship requires a lot more than talent and X's and O's.

To know the true meaning of the 'long bus ride home.'

To experience grins after wins and pitted stomachs after losses.

To learn that 'chemistry' refers more to the game than it does to school.

To guarantee playtime with my best friends almost every day.

For the connection and finish on the perfect no-look pass.

For the buzzer-beaters and game-winners.

I play for the girl sitting in the stands who has a dream.

I play to feel the pride in my parents' hugs and to see the twinkle in their eyes.

I play because my teammates not only make me a better player with each practice battle, but

also a better person with each critical comment and encouraging word.

I play because the game has molded me into someone who will make a difference in this world.

I play because I was born to play this game.

I play because the game is who I am."

Goal Mapping Tips for Coaches

You now should have some ideas about how you could implement goal mapping with your athletes or team. You may have other ideas about how to help athletes with their goal maps, which is terrific because any mental training intervention must be tailored to the exact needs of specific athletes. However, no matter what goal mapping methods you choose to use in your program, keep in mind the following tips. These tips all begin with the letter "S," the idea being that coaches should always follow three Ss in goal mapping with athletes and teams.

Simple

The first "S" tip is to keep it SIMPLE. The biggest mistake we all make in implementing any type of mental training is that we attempt to do too much too soon. Follow the KISS principle in goal mapping and other mental training exercises: keep it simple and smart. You may want to begin by asking athletes to set one milestone goal, one challenge goal, and one focus goal. Once they get the idea, they can then begin to fill out their goal maps. Obviously, you should adapt your goal mapping plans to the ages and levels of athletes you are coaching. Regardless of age, it is better to start off with too little as opposed to too much. If athletes become overwhelmed or do not understand the complexities of goal mapping,

---

Quotable Quote

"Yard by yard, life is hard; but inch by inch, it's a cinch." **Robert Schuller**

---

they will quickly lose interest and remain skeptical when you try again.

Systematic

The second "S" stands for SYSTEMATIC. No matter how simple your goal mapping program is for your athletes, it must be systematic. That is, it must follow a sequence of reflection, goal setting, development of goal achievement strategies, and goal evaluation and monitoring. The Progress Log and goal card evaluation system presented in the last section are examples of methods that can be used to systematically monitor goals. Gould (2001) suggests that coaches set up their goal mapping program into a planning phase, meeting phase, and follow-up/evaluation phase.

Planning phase. Before discussing goals with your athletes, coaches should reflect on individual and team needs and strengths. Following this needs analysis, coaches should identify some potential goals for both the team and for individual athletes. This is really an assessment phase, where the coach carefully assesses individual and team skills to initiate the goal mapping process with the team.

Team meeting phase. Gould (2001) suggests that coaches then conduct a series of meetings with their athletes regarding goal mapping. Coaches could first schedule a team meeting at which goal mapping is discussed by the team. This meeting should be informational and outline exactly how the team will use goal maps to help pursue and achieve their goals. In this meeting, the coach should emphasize whatever aspects of goal mapping he or she wants the athletes to understand, such as SMAART goal mapping or the tree analogy in building a goal map. No actual goals should be set at this meeting, as it should be used to make the athletes think about and identify important goals for themselves and the team as a whole.

A few days later, a second meeting should then be scheduled, at which some preliminary team goals should be identified as well as some goal achievement strategies. It might be useful to identify the milestone and challenge goals for the team, and then ask athletes to reflect on focus goals that would facilitate the achievement of their challenge and milestone goals. Then, at a third meeting, the team and coaches could identify some specific focus goals that can be practiced daily and revised as the team matures and progresses.

Individual meeting phase. It is important, although time-consuming, for coaches to meet with each individual athlete to discuss the athlete's goals and to help him or her develop a goal map. The coach can also be instrumental in helping each athlete develop their goal achievement strategies, so they realistically can see what is needed to accomplish the goals they've set.

Follow-up/evaluation phase. The follow-up or evaluation phase is the most overlooked aspect of goal mapping, but, as research has shown, it is critical for the success of any goal mapping program. Coaches should first decide how the team goals will be systematically monitored and evaluated, and then stick to a schedule or procedure to make sure this happens. Remember that goals are flexible and dynamic, and can be revised, expanded, deleted, and/or replaced with new goals throughout the preseason, season, and off-season. Consider different options for how you will present and monitor your team goals (e.g., board in the locker room, handouts for individual lockers, etc.), and choose some method that keeps the goals fresh in the athletes' minds. Coaches should also decide on the system that they will use to monitor and evaluate individual athlete goals. I suggest that coaches customize the example goal card shown in Figure 8.5 in a way that meets their needs.

Once athletes' goal cards are completed, coaches should discuss with athletes how they will be used in a systematic way to provide feedback and evaluation. A note of caution is in order here. Clearly, coaches should be involved in monitoring the progress of their athletes, and the assessment of goal cards is one way to do this. However, you should avoid creating a negative climate or attitude about goal mapping when athletes begin to feel that they don't own their own goals or that the coach is being heavy-handed in criticizing their pursuit of their goals. This is a fine line to walk, but you should strive from the beginning to get your athletes to buy into the program and understand that it is their personal goal maps that enable them to be successful. You as the coach can decide how much you want to monitor progress, as in some cases with mature athletes, they can evaluate their own goal progress and discuss it with you intermittently, instead of weekly. Research has

Photo by Brett Hansbauer

shown that personality differences in athletes contribute to whether they prefer self-set or coach-set goals (Lambert, Moore, & Dixon, 1999). However, for goal maps to be sustained over time, coaches should attempt to convince athletes to accept personal responsibility for their own goal maps.

Synergistic

The final S is to make your goal mapping program SYNERGISTIC. Synergy refers to a type of energy within a group enabling them to achieve goals beyond the capabilities of the individual members represented in the group. Synergy occurs when athletes accept team roles and set their challenge and focus goals based on the fulfillment of these roles. Synergy also occurs when the team is clear about their purpose, and this sense of purpose flows into the types of goals set, goal achievement strategies, and the overall attitude that prevails within a team. Effective goal mapping can help create a strong team norm for productivity (discussed in Chapter 6), which involves the standard for effort and other achievement behaviors accepted by team members.

In my years as a professor at Miami University, I observed two future professional (NBA) men's basketball players as members of different Miami teams. Ron Harper enjoyed a stellar professional career and won championships with the Chicago Bulls and Los Angeles Lakers, and Wally Szczerbiak has achieved All-Star status with the Minnesota Timberwolves. Not only were these individuals personally successful at Miami, but they worked with the coaches and their teammates to ensure that their personal goals were congruent with what the team was trying to accomplish. The teams these individuals belonged to were the most successful in Miami history, and this success was because of the synergistic effect these players' goals had on their teammates and the program as a whole.

Coaches can create synergistic goal mapping programs by communicating extensively with individual athletes about their contributions to the team effort, by ensuring that athletes feel some ownership over their personal and team goal maps, and by continually inviting team discussion and assessment of team progress and the goal mapping program. Goal maps should be exciting and useful for athletes to create a positive synergy regarding the Inner Edge.

Wrapping Up

All athletes have goals. However, very few athletes engage in the systematic goal mapping that would chart their course and provide them the road map for how to get to their destinations. Although dreams and goals are very different, some people make their dreams come true by harnessing them within long-term, systematic goal maps. Athletes should be encouraged to dream big dreams, and to allow their sense of purpose or passion to flow from these dreams. And they should also be encouraged to follow the steps of goal mapping to give their dreams their best shot, instead of standing by and hoping that their dreams come true on their own.

Help your athletes to understand that the most basic mental skill needed in sport is to think well, and that effective goal maps set athletes up to act, feel, and think productively in competitive situations. Teach your athletes to be SMAART goal mappers, and to use many types of goals in the most effective ways. Challenge your athletes to develop goal maps that are strongly rooted in their own sense of purpose or passion for their sport. Expect your athletes to act "on purpose" by not only working hard, but by working smart to achieve their goals. And finally, encourage your athletes to use their passion for their sport to keep their goals and goal striving in perspective, and to allow them to enjoy not only the achievement of goals, but the pursuit of their goals as well.

Summary Points for Chapter 8

1. Goals are specific standards or accomplishments that athletes strive to attain.

2. Goal mapping is a systematic approach to acting and thinking in purposeful ways to achieve specific accomplishments and personal fulfillment.

3. Goal mapping, as a mental training tool, has improved performance in a variety of sports.

4. Goals affect our behavior by directing our attention to relevant things, increasing our effort and persistence, and motivating the development of new strategies.

5. Goal mapping enhances athletes' focus, establishes personal standards of success, changes problems into productive action statements, and helps manage emotions.

6. Athletes should set outcome, performance, and process goals, and know when to use each type of goal to facilitate their training and performance.

7. Athletes should practice SMAART goal mapping by setting goals that are specific, measurable, aggressive yet achievable, relevant, and time-bound.

8. Athletes can follow a goal mapping program that requires them to sense and seize their purpose, set milestone, challenge, and focus goals, and act "on purpose" to behaviorally commit to their goals.

9. Coaches should ensure that goal mapping programs used with athletes are simple, systematic, and synergistic.

Glossary

challenge goals: performance standards that explicitly specify behavioral actions that are critical to reaching milestone goals

focus goals: specific thought and behavioral patterns that enhance focus and automaticity during competitive performance

goal: a specific standard or accomplishment that one strives to attain

goal mapping: a systematic approach to acting and thinking in purposeful ways to achieve specific accomplishments and personal fulfillment

milestone goals: significant attainments that athletes achieve as they follow their sense of purpose

outcome goals: standards based on uncontrollable results or outcomes

performance goals: standards based on performance accomplishments that are usually self-referenced

process goals: standards that are based on controllable thoughts or actions related to performance execution

Study Questions

1. How does the concept of goal mapping differ from the more traditional idea of goal setting?

2. Identify five reasons why goal maps are important, or ways that goal maps facilitate athletes' training and performance.

3. What is a goal? Distinguish between the various types of goals, such as outcome, performance, and process goals. When and how should each type of goal be used by athletes and coaches?

4. Explain what SMAART goal mapping means. Give an example goal for each letter in SMAART.

5. Why is sensing and seizing a purpose the foundation for all goal maps? Provide an example of a sense of purpose, and discuss how an athlete's goal map would flow from this sense of purpose.

6. Why is the analogy of a tree with strong roots an effective way to describe goal maps? Describe each part of a goal map as presented in this chapter.

7. What are the three substeps athletes must follow to act "on purpose" in pursuing their goal maps?

8. Explain how coaches can implement a systematic goal mapping program that is evaluated by both athletes and coaches.

Reflective Learning Activities

1. Goal Mapping Workbook

The purposes of this exercise are to (a) provide practice at identifying and writing specific and measurable goals, and (b) get you to reflect on negative goals that could be influencing your thoughts and behavior. Complete the following goal mapping exercises individually. Then at a subsequent meeting, share your responses in groups of three. In your groups, provide feedback to each other about the effectiveness of the goals set by members of your group.

Part A: Goal Statements. Identify three positively stated goals for yourself (see sample).

SAMPLE: I want to maintain optimal concentration during competition.

1. _____

2. _____

3. _____

Part B: Specifying Goal-Oriented Behaviors. For each goal identified in Exercise 1, develop a statement to describe specific, concrete behaviors associated with the goal.

SAMPLE: Prior to each free throw, I will focus on "steady" (base), "strong" (legs and body), and "soft" (over the front of the rim).

1. _____

2. _____

3. _____

Part C: Recognizing Negative/Self-Defeating Goals. Being totally honest with yourself, identify the following goals in relation to yourself.

1. Goals based on others' expectations of you.

_____

_____

2. Goals based on your irrational needs or unrealistic expectations.

_____

_____

In your small groups, discuss with others why these goals developed, and how they influence your behavior. Then, identify more productive and appropriate goals to replace these negative, self-defeating goals.

2. Making Your Map

Make a copy or draw a replica of Figure 8.1, and then develop a basic goal map for yourself in relation to an important achievement area. Then, pair up with a partner and explain your goal map.

3. How Aggressive and How Achievable?

As part of the SMAART goal mapping philosophy, you learned in the chapter that goals should be Aggressive yet Achievable. However, some people argue that goals should be set extremely high, even if they are unrealistic for a team or individual.

Consider the case in which you are the coach of a high school volleyball team that is young and lacks individual talent. Your personal assessment as coach is that an aggressive yet achievable goal would be to finish within the top five in your conference. However, your athletes want to set the goal of winning the conference championship. Although you privately know that there is almost no chance of this occurring, what do you tell your team?

In groups of three, attempt to answer this question, and discuss HOW aggressive and HOW achievable team and individual goals should be within a goal mapping program.

4. Embracing Your Passion

As discussed in the chapter, all goals must emanate from a meaningful sense of purpose or passion for an activity. Take some time to reflect on why you coach, and attempt to verbalize this in terms of explaining what your ultimate purpose or passion is in coaching. It helps to write this down to make it clearer and more concrete.

Sit down with a partner and share your sense of purpose as a coach. Then, try to extend this to explain how you think your goals and daily behaviors flow from this sense of purpose. What things do you/can you do to maintain passion in your coaching or to keep the meaning in the job for you?

Chapter Nine

Imagery

Chapter Preview

In this chapter, you'll learn:
*   what imagery is and how athletes can use it
*   how and why imagery works to enhance sport performance
*   tips for helping athletes use imagery in the most effective ways

"We taped a lot of famous pictures on the locker room door: Bobby Orr, Potvin, Beliveau, all holding the Stanley Cup. We'd stand back and look at them and envision ourselves doing it. I really believe if you visualize yourself doing something, you can make that image come true . . . I must have rehearsed it ten thousand times. And when it came true it was like an electric jolt went up my spine."
Wayne Gretzky *(as quoted in Orlick, 1998, p. 67)*

"**I**mage is everything." Andre Agassi, the outstanding tennis champion, made this line famous in television advertisements for a popular camera. The point of the ad was that images influence how we perceive and interpret the world around us. Images are mental pictures that we store away as vivid snapshot memories. Images are also powerful visions that we create for ourselves, based on what we hope to accomplish. As portrayed in the quote at the top of the page, Wayne Gretzky used the powerful image of winning the Stanley Cup, the most coveted prize in ice hockey, to

energize him with the vision needed to win multiple National Hockey League championships.

Thus, "image is everything" because the images that we create and store and focus on each day guide our beliefs, which in turn guide our behavior and performance. Consider the most important image of all—self-image. What is your personal image of yourself? What beliefs do you hold about yourself as a person and/or coach? Now consider the ways in which these images and beliefs that you have about yourself influence your behavior. For example, my self-image includes the belief that I have good interpersonal skills, which has influenced me to be confident and outgoing in social situations, to take on leadership roles, and to pursue a career in teaching. However, if my self-image included the belief that I am a poor public speaker, I would probably have chosen a different career and would experience anxiety when forced to talk in front of groups. Truly,

Quotable Quote

"The greatest discovery . . . is that human beings, by changing the inner attitudes of their minds, can change the outer aspects of their lives." **William James**

image IS everything when it comes to self-image, because the beliefs that we hold about ourselves turn into self-fulfilling prophecies when we live in ways that support these beliefs.

Athletes must learn to develop and focus on productive images about themselves and their performances in sport, to provide the vision they need to reach the upper limits of their performance potential. All athletes possess images about themselves and engage in imagery frequently, even if they don't realize it. However, most athletes don't use imagery systematically, and often are unable to control their images. Research shows that imagery can improve sport performance, but only when it is used in a systematic and controlled fashion. Thus, the purpose of this chapter is to introduce imagery as a basic mental training tool that coaches can help athletes use in some simple, systematic ways to better their performance.

What is Imagery?

Imagery may be defined as *using all the senses to recreate or create an experience in the mind*. Research indicates that when individuals engage in vivid imagery, their brains interpret these images as identical to the actual external stimulus situation (Marks, 1983). This is what makes imagery so powerful. The power of imagery allows athletes to practice sport skills and strategies without physically being in the practice environment (e.g., pool, gymnasium, track, field). Suinn (1980) tested this phenomenon by having a downhill skier imagine skiing a downhill run on a familiar course. Suinn monitored the electrical activity in the skier's leg muscles as he imagined the downhill run. Suinn found that the printed output of muscle firings in the skier's leg muscles mirrored the terrain of the ski course. Muscle firings peaked at certain points during imagery that corresponded to times in which greater muscle contraction would be expected due to turns and rough sections on the course. Thus, whether athletes actually perform movements or vividly imagine performing them, similar neural pathways to the muscles are used. Athletes are always amazed and intrigued when they hear this example and explanation of imagery.

To help you understand what imagery is, four defining features of imagery are presented in this section. The first section explains how imagery is about recreating as well as creating experiences in our minds. The second section describes how imagery is a polysensory experience. The third section explains the basic imagery concepts of vividness and controllability, and emphasizes that imagery must be systematically practiced to qualify as a mental training tool. The fourth section discusses what is meant by internal and external imagery, and how athletes may use both of these imagery perspectives in their mental training.

Imagery as Recreating and Creating

Imagery can be used to recreate and create many types of experiences that benefit athletes. Consider the power of being able to *recreate* experiences in your mind. Have you ever watched someone perform a certain sport skill, and then gone out and done it yourself? Or have you ever improved a fundamental aspect of a sport skill after spending hours teaching it to your athletes or to youngsters at a sports camp? We are able to imitate the action of others because our mind takes a picture of the skill that we use as a blueprint for our performance. That's what imagery is— a picture in our mind that serves as a mental blueprint for performance. Imagery is based on memory, and we experience it internally by reconstructing external events in our minds.

Athletes spend a lot of time recreating their performances in their minds. We all can remember the nights after competition when we went over and over our performances in our heads. Often athletes get stuck in this type of imagery by focusing on their mistakes and failures, and they replay these miscues without any type of planned strategy for dealing with these negative images. The key for athletes is to learn to use imagery in a productive and controlled manner to learn from performance mistakes and to program their minds and bodies to respond optimally. A good example of productive creating using imagery comes from Bob Rotella's book *Golf is Not a Game of Perfect* (1996). Rotella, a renowned mental training consultant for professional golfers, was questioned by Fred Couples about whether the mental strategy he (Couples) was using prior to each shot was effective. Couples explained that prior to hitting a six-iron, he simply visualized in his mind the best six-iron shot he had ever hit. Rotella applauded Couples' strategy, which although sounds simple, is actually the best strategy you could use! Imagery doesn't have to be complicated or lengthy, but should be simple and easily used in competitive conditions, such as the strategy used by Fred Couples. In his mind, he recreated his best-ever performances to program his body to flawlessly execute a perfect golf shot.

As stated in the definition of imagery, imagery also involves using our senses to *create* experiences in our minds. Although imagery is essentially a product of memory, our brain is able to put pieces of the internal picture together in different ways. As programmers of their own imagery programs, athletes can build images from whatever pieces of memory they choose. Nancy Kerrigan developed an imagery script to prepare for her figure skating performance in the 1994 Olympic Games. In her mind, Kerrigan created and rehearsed her ideal performance from the dressing room, through her entire routine, to the exhilarating moments after leaving the ice in which she felt intense joy and pride in her accomplishment.

Football quarterbacks use imagery in this way to create offensive game plans based on the defensive tactics of upcoming opponents. By viewing films of the opponent's defense, a quarterback can create an offensive game plan and visualize the successful execution of this strategy without having previously played against that particular opponent. As discussed in Chapter 6, Coach Tara Van Derveer of the U.S. Women's Basketball Team conducted a mock medal ceremony at the Olympic basketball arena in Atlanta (months prior to the Olympic Games) so that each player experienced the gold medal being placed around her neck. Van Derveer wanted her athletes to create in their minds the emotional exhilaration of winning the gold medal to enhance their motivational drive and commitment. Of course, several months later, they all got to experience the thrill of winning the gold medal for real!

At the elite levels of international competition, athletes view photographs or videotapes of upcoming competition sites for world championships or the Olympic Games. Athletes study these photographs of the various pools, fields, arenas, dressing rooms, and warm-up areas so they can create effective images of themselves performing in those contexts. Creating these types of images serves to familiarize athletes with the sport environment far in advance of actual competition. In my work as a mental training consultant, I am always asking athletes "What will it be like?" and "How will you respond?" when they are facing hostile crowds on the road or difficult travel conditions. Research shows that elite athletes create mental focus plans for competition and regularly practice these plans mentally to better respond to various competitive stressors.

Imagery as a Polysensory Experience

The second key aspect in understanding imagery is realizing that imagery can and should involve all the senses, or that it is a polysensory experience. Although imagery is sometimes called "visualization" or "seeing with the mind's eye," sight is not the only significant sense. All of our senses are important in experiencing events. Images can and should include as many senses as possible, including visual, auditory, olfactory, tactile, and kinesthetic senses. Auditory refers to sound, such as hearing the sound of a golf ball exploding off the sweet spot of a driver. Olfactory refers to smell, such as a swimmer smelling chlorine in the pool. Tactile is the sensation of touch, such as feeling the grip of a golf club or the textured leather of a basketball.

One of the most important senses for athletes to use in their imagery is **kinesthetic sense**, or the *feel or sensation of the body as it moves in different positions.* Kinesthetic imagery would be useful for a gymnast practicing a balance beam routine or a diver attempting to feel the rotations of his body in space before reaching for the water. Professional golfer Bob Tway states that a consistent golf swing requires turning all of your mechanical thoughts into a feeling, which is simply a kinesthetic image of the perfect golf swing.

Using as many senses as possible in imagery makes images more vivid. This is important because the more vivid an image is, the more effective it is in enhancing performance. Consider how a wide receiver in football can create polysensory images for himself. The receiver uses his visual sense to read the defense and focus on the ball before catching it. He uses his auditory sense to listen to the snap count barked by the quarterback. He uses his tactile and kinesthetic senses to run his pattern, jump in the air, catch a hard thrown ball, and touch both feet inbounds. He might also smell freshly mown grass and the sweat on his opponent's jersey when he is tackled. He might even taste the saltiness of his own sweat. All of these sensory cues serve to make the image "live" and vivid, thus preparing the receiver to perform optimally when he performs for real.

Imagery as a Mental Training Tool

As just discussed, imagery is simply a polysensory experience in one's mind. Dreaming and daydreaming qualify as forms of imagery, as most of us can attest based on vivid dreams that we have experienced. However, the focus in this chapter is on understanding and using imagery as a mental training tool with athletes. Recall that in Chapter 7 we outlined four mental training tools that coaches can use to help athletes perform better. Imagery is one of those tools. Dreaming is a form of imagery, but it is not a mental training tool.

Athletes must use imagery in a continuous and systematic manner for it to qualify as mental training. Dreaming or random imagery is not systematic, and there is no evidence that these forms of imagery enhance athletes' performance. This doesn't mean that athletes have to spend numerous hours a day engaged in imagery for it to help their performance. However, there must be some sort of systematic, continuing use of imagery in an organized manner, even if it is in small doses, for it to have the desired effect on one's performance. This is similar to physical training, where random, occasional physical practice won't do much to increase an athlete's skills. However, systematic, repetitive physical (and mental) practice clearly improves performance in any sport.

Athletes must learn to control their imagery to use it effectively as a mental training tool. Controllability is the ability of athletes to imagine exactly what they intend to imagine, and also the ability to manipulate aspects of the images that they wish to change. Dreams are for the most part uncontrollable—we simply experience them during sleep. Imagery, on the other hand, must be controllable so that athletes can manipulate images in productive ways to program themselves for optimal performance. As we all remember as athletes, often our images become uncontrollable, such as when we "choke" under pressure or experience dreaded performance slumps. Thus, coaches and sport psychology consultants must help athletes gain control of their images so that imagery can be used effectively in mental training. In addition to controllability, the other key to using imagery effectively in mental training is vividness. Vividness refers to how clearly athletes can see an image and how detailed the image appears to them. Vividness involves such features as whether the image is in color, how many senses are being used, and the emotion or physical sensations experienced when engaging in imagery.

Overall, imagery as a mental training tool involves the systematic practice and use of imagery to engage in vivid and controllable polysensory images to enhance performance. When athletes first begin using imagery, it is typical to lack vividness and especially controllability of images. However, systematic practice has been shown to be very effective in increasing imagery ability (Rodgers, Hall, & Buckolz, 1991). Also, imagery has been shown to be more effective in helping athletes perform better when they have more imagery ability (Isaac, 1992). It is important to encourage athletes if they are not skilled in their initial attempts at imagery. Let them know that imagery is a skill that takes time to train, but it is a learnable skill that they can improve with

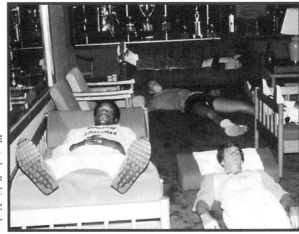

Photo by Robin Vealey

practice. This is true with even world-class athletes, as seen in the following quote:

> "It took me a long time to control my images and perfect my imagery, maybe a year, doing it every day. At first I couldn't see myself, I always saw everyone else, or I would see my dives wrong all the time. I would get an image of hurting myself, or tripping on the board, or I would 'see' something done really bad. As I continued to work at it, I got to the point where I could see myself doing a perfect dive and the crowd yelling at the Olympics. But it took me a long time . . . I started to see myself on the board doing my perfect dive. But some days I couldn't see it, or it was a bad dive in my head. I worked at it so much it got to the point that I could do all my dives easily. Sometimes I would even be in the middle of a conversation with someone and I would think of one of my dives and 'see' it." Olympic gold medalist, springboard diving (Orlick & Partington, 1988, p. 114).

Internal and External Imagery Perspectives

When you spontaneously engage in imagery, do you see yourself as if you're watching a videotape or do you see yourself from behind your own eyes? This question differentiates between an external imagery perspective and an internal imagery perspective. Athletes who use an **external imagery perspective** see the image from outside their bodies as if they are viewing themselves from behind a video camera. When athletes use an **internal imagery perspective**, they see the image from behind their own eyes as if they were inside their bodies. When your athletes begin using imagery, some of them will primarily use an internal perspective, some an external perspective, and some a combination of both. Athletes should be encouraged to use the imagery perspective with which they are most comfortable. As they become more skilled in their imagery, athletes should be encouraged to enhance their ability to use both imagery perspectives. In addition, athletes should attempt to combine the different senses used in imagery with the different perspectives to see which works best for them. Consider the different imagery perspectives used in the following examples:

> "My imagery is more just feel. I don't think it is visual at all. When I'm watching it on video I look visually at it and then I get this internal feeling. When I'm actually doing it I get the same feeling inside. It is a very internal feeling that is hard to explain. You have to experience it, and once you

> do, then you know what you are going after. I can even get a feeling for an entire program . . . I get this internal feeling . . . and usually I'm fresh and usually it will be a perfect program. I just don't step out there in training and just say, here we go, another program." Canadian Olympic figure skater (Orlick & Partington, 1988, p. 113)

> "In mental imagery . . . I would think about the last time I actually did it, 'Why did I miss that one move? Okay, I know what happened, I pulled my body in too close to the apparatus and it . . . went off. Okay, now how do I avoid that?' Then I try to see myself doing it correctly in imagery. Sometimes you look at it from a camera view, but most of the time I look at it as what I see from within, because that's the way it's going to be in competition. It is natural [that way] because I do the routines so many times that it's drilled in my head, what I see and how I do it . . . I think of it as the way I've done it so many times, and that's from within my body." Olympic rhythmic gymnast (Orlick & Partington, 1988, p. 114)

Research has shown that both imagery perspectives can enhance performance. For example, the combination of external visual imagery with kinesthetic imagery was shown to enhance performance for tasks that depend on form for successful execution (e.g., karate, gymnastics, rock climbing) (Hardy & Callow, 1999). Thus, athletes should experiment to find the imagery perspective and sensory type that is most helpful to them for specific situations. A golfer might prefer to use internal kinesthetic imagery to become more aware of how her body feels during the swing. However, she could use external visual imagery to check the mechanics of the various parts of her swing while making the shot. Research suggests that skilled performers may be able to combine external visual imagery with kinesthetic imagery because their mental blueprint is so ingrained and refined (Holmes & Collins, 2001). An external imagery perspective might be a powerful motivational tool or confidence builder to recreate past peak performance in one's mind. Many athletes shift back and forth between perspectives continuously in using imagery, and you should encourage your athletes to practice both perspectives to be competent and comfortable with each.

Does Imagery Work to Enhance Athletes' Performance?

Now that you have a basic understanding about imagery, your next question should be: "That's great, but does it work?" A good question, and every coach should have an answer to the question. Many people are skeptical that mental training techniques such as imagery can actually help athletes perform better. Imagery is often ridiculed by coaches as a new-fangled type of snake oil, and they resist learning about it because it seems like a far-fetched means of training athletes. However, imagery isn't far-fetched or even new. Everyone visualizes—it's a basic way that we think—and the point of using imagery as a part of mental training is simply to help athletes learn to control what they visualize in some basic productive ways to aid their performance. But don't take my word for it—read on as this section presents scientific evidence that supports the effectiveness of imagery as a mental training tool (see Figure 9.1). In this section, I'll provide evidence that imagery

- enhances sport performance,
- enhances competition-related thoughts and emotions such as confidence and motivation, and
- is systematically used by successful, world-class athletes who attest to its importance.

Enhancing Sport Performance and Learning

The primary question asked by most coaches and athletes is whether imagery actually does help athletes perform and learn better. It is intriguing to think that a sensory experience in an athlete's mind has the power to help him or her perform better. The research in this area is divided into three sections: mental practice research, preparatory imagery research, and mental training research (see Figure 9.1).

Mental practice research. *Using imagery to perform a specific sport skill repetitively in the mind* is called **mental practice**. Typically, mental practice occurs across a period of time in an intermittent learning style similar to a distributed physical practice schedule. Literally hundreds of studies have been conducted on mental practice, with the conclusion being that mental practice enhances performance and is better than no practice at all (e.g., Martin, Moritz, & Hall, 1999). Improvement in the following sport skills using mental practice has been documented:

basketball shooting	volleyball serving
tennis serving	golf
football placekicking	figure skating
swimming starts	dart throwing
alpine skiing	karate skills
diving	trampoline skills
competitive running	dance
rock climbing	

Keep in mind that this research is not saying that mental practice is better than physical practice. It certainly is not, as nothing takes the place of deliberate,

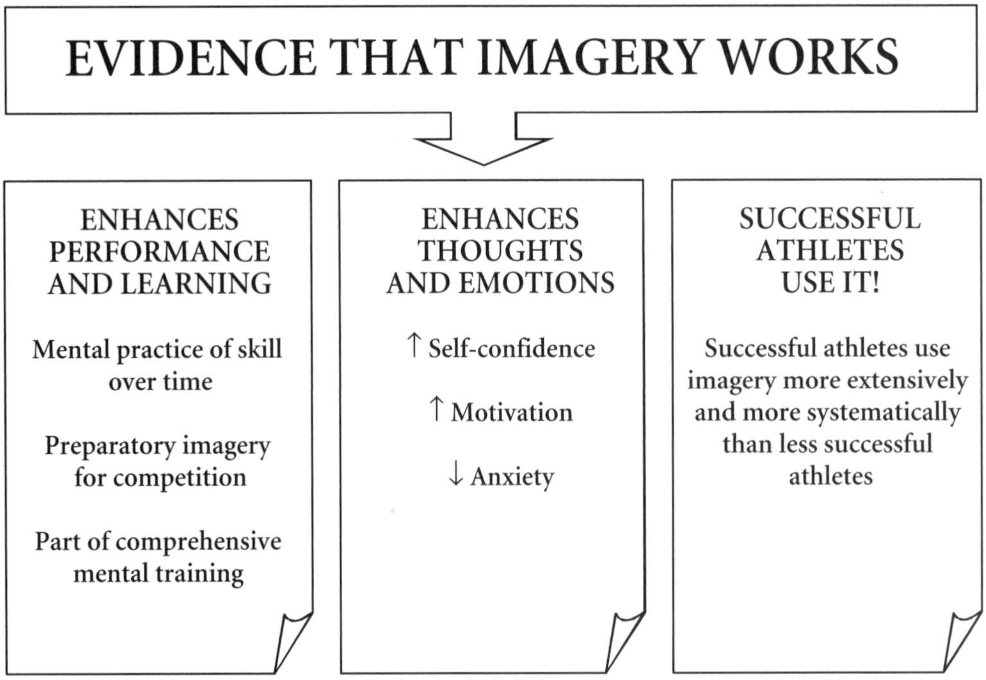

EVIDENCE THAT IMAGERY WORKS

ENHANCES PERFORMANCE AND LEARNING	ENHANCES THOUGHTS AND EMOTIONS	SUCCESSFUL ATHLETES USE IT!
Mental practice of skill over time	↑ Self-confidence	Successful athletes use imagery more extensively and more systematically than less successful athletes
Preparatory imagery for competition	↑ Motivation	
Part of comprehensive mental training	↓ Anxiety	

Figure 9.1 Research evidence supporting imagery use by athletes

> *"In bobsledding, you can only do two or three runs per day. I would have liked to do 20 of them but I couldn't. The physical demands were too high . . . So I did a lot of imagery instead and it was a real learning process . . . Each track filled up a videotape in my head."* Canadian Olympic gold medalist (*Durand-Bush & Salmela, 2002*)

repetitive physical practice in refining sport skills! However, mental practice is better than no practice, and is useful in complementing the rigorous physical practice schedules of athletes. Athletes can only engage in physical practice for finite periods of time, due to fatigue and attentional overload. Mental practice allows athletes to refine their mental blueprints of sport skills without having to physically engage in the activity. Thus, athletes should augment their physical training through mental practice to build strong and clear mental blueprints to program their minds and bodies for automatic and flawless skill execution.

Preparatory imagery research. Research has also shown that using imagery immediately before performance can help athletes perform better. Often, imagery is just used just prior to performing to "psych up," calm down, and/or to focus on relevant aspects of the task. Consider how Larry Bird, three-time NBA champion and MVP, used imagery during the playing of the national anthem just prior to games:

> *"People have noticed that during the national anthem at home games I am always looking up to the Boston Garden ceiling . . . The thing I look at up there are our championship flags. I focus on the three championships my teams have won and I always look at them in order. I start at 1981, move to 1984, and shift over to 1986. I try to capture how I felt when we won each one and play the championship through my mind. It doesn't take very long to zip through that . . ."* (*Bird, 1989*).

Imagery as a preparatory strategy used prior to performance has improved performance on strength tasks, muscular endurance tasks, and golf putting (see Vealey & Greenleaf, 2001). Imagery has also been shown to be an effective part of athletes' pre-performance routines, which involve a planned sequence of thoughts and behaviors that lead to automatic performance execution. (Pre-performance routines are discussed more fully in Chapter 12.)

Mental training research. A growing body of research in sport psychology has shown that mental training programs can enhance athletes' performance. Many of these programs include imagery as a mental training tool. For example, a mental training program consisting of imagery, relaxation, and self-talk training with college basketball players was shown to improve their defensive skills during the season (Kendall, Hrycaiko, Martin, & Kendall, 1990). Similar programs have improved performance in swimming, gymnastics, figure skating, tennis, golf, and basketball.

Clipboard

Imagery Research in the Field: An Example

Kendall et al. (1990) examined the effects an imagery training program had on the defensive performance of four collegiate basketball players. The intervention with the players was set up as follows:

Day 1: 30 minute introduction to mental preparation; introduction to imagery training by watching a professional videotape; 15 minutes of relaxation exercises.

Day 2: 45 minutes practicing a variety of imagery rehearsal techniques to enhance their imagery skill and become familiar with using imagery.

Day 3: 45 minutes of relaxation training, imagery rehearsal, and use of cue words to enhance imagery in relation to the competitive demands of basketball.

Day 4: 30 minutes of relaxation and imagery rehearsal of correctly performing specific defensive skills; using an audiotape with a personalized mental preparation script to focus on the correct defensive behaviors.

Day 5: Game day; 15-20 minutes of relaxation and imagery rehearsal followed by using the audiotape with the specific mental preparation script for optimal defensive performance.

Remainder of season: Mentally trained a minimum of 15 minutes per day using imagery and relaxation mental rehearsal coupled with the audiotape mental preparation script; kept logbooks to monitor their mental training practice each day.

The players were videotaped in all games, their defensive skills were independently analyzed and rated by two basketball experts, and reliability was established as the two raters were congruent in their analyses over 90% of the time. The intervention was clearly effective for all the players as their defensive skills increased after the intervention. The players indicated that the imagery rehearsal made them more confident, relaxed, and focused in their performance.

Enhancing Competition-Related Thoughts and Emotions

Besides helping athletes perform better, imagery has also been shown to enhance the competition-related thoughts and emotions of athletes (e.g., Vealey & Greenleaf, 2001). This is important because a basic objective of sport psychology is to help athletes think better—to enable them to effectively manage their thoughts and emotions to create a productive competitive focus. Imagery can help athletes do this!

Research has shown that imagery can enhance the self-confidence and motivation of athletes, as well as help them decrease or control precompetitive anxiety. Also, specific types of imagery have been used by athletes to change their perceptions of precompetitive anxiety from negative and harmful to facilitative and challenging. A highly successful Olympic pistol shooter states, "As for success imagery, I would imagine to myself, 'How would a champion act? How would a champion feel? How would she perform on the line?' This helped me find out about myself, what worked and didn't work for me . . . That helped me believe that I would be the Olympic champion" (Orlick & Partington, 1988, p. 113). Professional golfer Bob Ford, admired by peers for his ability to clear his mind for competition, describes his unique imagery practice of picturing himself on an elevator as he walks to the 1st tee at a tournament. When he gets to the 1st tee, the doors open and he envisions being on a "whole new floor." Ford explains this image allows him to leave all problems and extraneous thoughts behind on another "floor," and enables him to focus in on the "competition floor." Thus, imagery has been shown to help athletes create a productive and motivational competitive focus for how they want to think and feel in responding to the challenge of competition.

Incidence of Imagery Use

A lot of really successful people in sport use imagery! Of 235 Canadian Olympic athletes who participated in the 1984 Olympic Games, 99% reported using imagery (Orlick & Partington, 1988). These athletes estimated that during training they engaged in preplanned systematic imagery at least once a day, 4 days per week, for about 12 minutes each time. At the Olympic site, some reported engaging in imagery for 2 to 3 hours in preparation for their events. An analysis of the mental preparation strategies of U.S. wrestlers during the 1988 Olympics found that the wrestlers' best performances involved adherence to mental routines, including positive imagery before the matches (Gould, Eklund, & Jackson, 1992a). Mental training, including imagery, used to develop and practice systematic competitive routines and focus plans was found to be a critical factor in the successful performances of U.S. athletes at the 1996 Olympic Games (Gould et al., 1999).

Research has also examined *how* and *why* athletes use imagery. Elite gymnasts and canoeists report using imagery extensively to rehearse skills and difficult moves, to optimize concentration and quality of training, and to enhance self-confidence and motivation (White & Hardy, 1998). More successful, elite athletes use imagery more extensively and systematically as compared to less successful and accomplished athletes (e.g., Cumming & Hall, 2002).

Experiential Evidence that Imagery Works

So far, I've presented you with a lot of evidence that imagery helps athletes. However, probably the most compelling evidence for you and your athletes is the testimonials from athletes who have used imagery and believe in its effectiveness. Several athletes who have at one time been the best in the world at their sport advocate the use of imagery. Jack Nicklaus, perhaps the greatest golfer of all time, says that playing the ball to a certain place in a certain way is 50% mental picture:

> *"I never hit a shot, not even in practice, without having a very sharp, in-focus picture of it in my head. It's like a color movie. First, I 'see' the ball where I want it to finish, nice and white and sitting up high on bright green grass. Then the scene quickly changes and I 'see' the ball going there; its path, trajectory and shape, even its behavior on landing. Then there is sort of a fade-out, and the next scene shows me making the kind of swing that will turn the images into reality" (Nicklaus, 1974, p. 79).*

Certainly, Jack Nicklaus has won more major championships than anyone else because of his enormous physical talent. Yet experts feel that his concentration skills carried him to a level above all other golfers. It may be that Nicklaus's systematic practice of imagery facilitates the concentration that has been the key to his success. Similarly, observe the commitment to imagery by Alex Baumann, Olympic double gold medalist in swimming:

> *"The best way I have learned to prepare mentally for competition is to visualize the race in my mind . . . In my imagery I concentrate on attaining the splits I have set out to do. About 15 minutes before the race I visualize the race in my mind. I think about my own race and nothing else. I try to get those splits in my mind, and after that I am ready to go. My visualization has been refined more and more over the years. That is what really got me the world record and Olympic medals"* (Orlick, 1998, p. 70).

A gold medalist in diving at the 1984 Olympic Games describes her commitment to imagery:

> *"I did my dives in my head all the time. At night, before going to sleep, I always did my dives. Ten dives. I started with a front dive, the first one that I had to do at the Olympics, and I did everything as if I was actually there. I saw myself on the board with the same bathing suit. Everything was the same . . . If the dive was wrong, I went back and started over again. It takes a good hour to do perfect imagery of all my dives, but for me it was better than a workout. Sometimes I would take the weekend off and do imagery five times a day"* (Orlick & Partington, 1988, p. 112).

Colleen Hacker, sport psychology consultant for the 1996 Olympic champion and 1999 World Cup champion U.S. women's soccer team, created individualized audio and video imagery tapes before the 1996 Olympic Games and the 1999 World Cup. The tapes are full of confidence-building trigger words, phrases, and images, all set to each player's favorite songs. The tapes became a powerful source of team chemistry when the players ended up watching the tapes as a group. Kristine Lilly, who made a key header save in the World Cup final against China, stated, "The tapes give me that little extra confidence, remind me about who I am and what I can give. I'm inspired watching my teammates' tapes. And I'm reminded of what they do well, so I'll never second-guess them" (Lieber, 1999, p. 2c).

Overall, there is a great deal of research and experiential evidence that imagery is a powerful mental training tool that athletes can use to help them perform better. This leads to the next question you should be asking. HOW can a sensory experience in our mind enhance our ability to perform in sport? How can imagining clearing a high jump bar, shooting a slap shot, or swimming a race help us to perform these skills better? In the next section, I'll present the scientific explanations that explain how imagery works to enhance performance.

How Does Imagery Enhance Athletes' Performance?

Several theoretical explanations for how imagery helps athletes' performance may be found in scientific journals. To boil all these explanations down to one key phrase, research supports that imagery works as a *"mental blueprint for perfect responses."* That's it. It means that by practicing imagery systematically, athletes create and refine mental blueprints for the skills that they must perform in competition. Each blueprint contains the physical and mental responses that represent perfect performance, and through imagery practice, athletes program their brains to respond perfectly. To better understand how imagery enhances performance by serving as a mental blueprint for perfect responses, you need to understand two theories that support this idea.

Symbolic Learning Theory

The first theory, called symbolic learning theory, says that imagery acts as a coding system to help athletes learn or refine movement patterns (Sackett, 1934). All performance movements that athletes make must be encoded in their central nervous system—that is, their brains create blueprints or plans to direct and control these movements. **Symbolic learning theory** states that *imagery enables athletes to blueprint or code their movements into useful or logical symbolic components in their brains, thus making the movements that make up their performances more familiar and more automatic.* This seems logical when you consider the automatic skill demonstrated by elite athletes—they don't have to analyze or think about how to perform because their mental blueprints are highly refined for automated, skilled performances. By mentally rehearsing performance, athletes build and strengthen their mental blueprints (or the mental codes they use to execute their skills) to make their performance more automatic. For example, a gymnast can use imagery to cue herself on the temporal and spatial elements involved in performing a floor exercise routine. She can mentally rehearse her routine while listening to the music that accompanies her performance, and this music cues her for certain movements and sequences.

Symbolic learning theory has been supported by sport psychology research that has demonstrated greater performance improvement via imagery on physical tasks that require a lot of cognitive processing as opposed to pure motor tasks (e.g., Vealey & Greenleaf, 2001). That is, imagery seems to be more helpful on tasks that require mental processing. Of course, this makes imagery useful for practically all sport skills, which are defined as perceptual-motor skills, meaning that most all sport skills have a mental or perceptual component as well as a motoric component. Research has supported symbolic learning theory by showing that collegiate basketball players' free throw shooting was improved when they used imagery to mentally encode excellent free throw shooting form as modeled by expert perform-

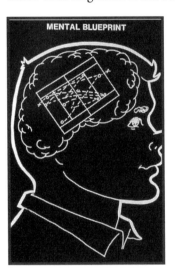

MENTAL BLUEPRINT

ers (Hall & Erffmeyer, 1983). In short, imagery helps athletes *think better*, because it enables them to code their thoughts into useful mental blueprints that serve as their guides to optimal performance.

Bio-informational Theory

The second theory that supports the idea that imagery serves as a *mental blueprint for perfect responses* is bio-informational theory. Bio- informational theory says that a mental image is an organized set of knowledge units or characteristics stored in the brain (Lang, 1979). When athletes engage in imagery, they activate *stimulus characteristics* that describe the content of the image for them and *response characteristics* that describe what their responses are to the stimuli in the situation. For example, imagining shooting a pressurized penalty kick at the end of a championship soccer game would involve the stimulus characteristics of the sound of the crowd, the position of the opposing goalkeeper, and the sight of the goal itself. The response characteristics for this image might include feeling strong legs, quick and deceptive feet, and feel-

ings of confidence and focused attention on the ball going into the goal.

The key point of this theory is that athletes must systematically practice "perfect response" imagery. According to **bio-informational theory**, *by repeatedly accessing response characteristics and modifying these responses to represent perfect control and execution of sport skills (or practicing perfect responses), imagery can enhance athletes' performances*. So the theory says that simply imaging the characteristics of the situation (stimulus characteristics) won't do it. Rather, athletes must imagine intense and perfect *behavioral*, *mental*, and *physiological responses* to various competitive challenges. Thus, a swimmer should imagine not only the conditions of the situation (swimming in a pool, water is choppy, championship meet), but also his behavioral (swimming strong and relaxed, right on pace, knifing through the choppy water), mental (confident and focused), and physiological (energy flowing into legs and arms, strong lungs) responses to the situation. Imagining these perfect responses creates psychophysiological changes in the swimmer's mind and body, thus improving his performance. Also, it is important to use kinesthetic imagery to emphasize feeling the physical sensations of performing a specific skill, which will further strengthen effective responses in athletes.

Research has shown that response-oriented imagery results in greater physiological reactivity than stimulus-oriented imagery (Bakker, Boschker, & Chung, 1996) and also that images of situations with which athletes have personal experience create greater physiological reactivity than less familiar images (Hecker & Kaczor, 1988). In addition, bioinformational theory is supported by findings that experienced athletes benefit more from imagery than do novices, which indicates that experienced athletes have a network of successful response characteristics stored in memory that they can activate during imagery.

Clipboard

The Power of Emotional Imagery

The most powerful way of increasing the power and intensity of your imagery is to infuse your images with emotion. Emotion stimulates strong responses in our brains that activate our bodies to accomplish incredible feats. Consider the following example of the power of emotional imagery:

U.S. swimmer Pablo Morales was the world record holder and strong favorite to win his specialty, the 100-meter butterfly, at the 1984 Olympic Games. However, Morales tightened up during his last few strokes and was touched out at the wall by West Germany's Michael Gross, who won the gold medal and set a new world record. This bitter disappointment for Morales only continued when in a shocking upset, he failed to qualify at the Olympic Trials for the U.S. Olympic Swim Team headed to Seoul in 1988. He retired from swimming and entered law school at Cornell University.

However, in the summer of 1991, Morales' mother lost a lengthy battle with cancer and passed away. Morales made the decision to try again for an Olympic gold medal, and dedicated his comeback to his mom. He engaged in constant visualization of his mom cheering for him and expressing pride in his comeback. At the 1992 Olympic Trials and in Barcelona prior to the start of his race, he vividly visualized the image of his mother filled with joy at his accomplishments. Ahead of the field in the Olympic final, Morales felt his muscles tightening up at the end of the race, similar to what had happened to him eight years earlier in Los Angeles. However, he put his head down and stroked fiercely into the wall with all the strength left in his body. He did it. He capped one of the most amazing comebacks in sport history by winning the gold medal, and he did it by emotionally charging his visualization of dedication and ultimate victory with the joyous memory of his mom (Biro, 1997).

Practically, imagery can be explained to your athletes as a way of enhancing performance by programming personalized and appropriate responses to specific competitive challenges. Or more simply, *imagery creates a mental blueprint for perfect responses.* Emphasize to your athletes that their images should be loaded with behavioral, mental, and even physiological responses. Tell them the Pablo Morales story so they can see how emotionally charged competitive responses can program an athlete's mind and body to achieve incredible performances.

Can Imagery Hurt Athletes' Performance?

Many coaches over the years have asked me a really important question: "Can imagery ever hurt my athletes' performance?" It's a great question. No coach would ever allow his or her athletes to experiment with untested or questionable drugs. Similarly, coaches should consider not only how mental training can help athletes, but also if there are ways in which it can hurt athletes. As discussed in the previous chapter on goal mapping, athletes' focus on the wrong goals at the wrong time certainly can hurt their performance. Similarly, athletes' focus on the wrong images at the wrong time can also hurt their performance!

When individuals used negative imagery, or imagined performing unsuccessful putts, their golf putting accuracy declined (Short et al., 2002). This research indicates that imagery can hurt athletes' performance if they systematically imagine bad performance. This doesn't mean that athletes should not use imagery, as the point of imagery training is to enable athletes to control their previously uncontrollable images. Athletes are going to experience images whether they engage in mental training or not, so it seems productive to enable them to become more skillful in their use of imagery to avoid the debilitating effects of negative imagery. The point is for athletes to create a mental blueprint for perfect responses, NOT create a mental blueprint for disastrous responses! Consider how Ken Dryden, then a 23-year-old rookie goalie for the Montreal Canadiens, created the wrong mental blueprint the night before he was to face the Boston Bruins in Game 7 of the quarterfinals at hostile Boston Garden: ["I turned on the television in my hotel, and] the only thing I could find was *The Bruins Week in Review*. All they kept showing was the Bruins' scoring goal after goal. 'Esposito scores! Orr scores! Esposito scores again!' I was already nervous, and I turned downright depressed. I went to bed and dreamed about those goals" (McCallum, 2004, p. 56).

Additional research has shown that constant attempts to suppress negative thoughts and images from conscious awareness can increase the probability that these negative thoughts and images will influence performance (Beilock, Afremow, Rabe, & Carr, 2001). In this study, individuals in a golf putting task were told, "Be careful to try not to image hitting the ball short of the target. Don't image undershooting the target!" When individuals were given "negative" image instructions (told what not to image), they performed poorly, even when they attempted to suppress these negative images. From a practical perspective, this indicates that athletes should not program themselves to NOT do something, or constantly focus on negative images and attempt to suppress them. Likewise, coaches should refrain from "negative coaching," or giving verbal feedback such as "Don't pop up!" or "Watch out for the out-of-bounds on the left". These well-meaning, yet negative, coaching comments often create mental blueprints in athletes' heads of the exact performance the coach is suggesting that they NOT do.

So there is a grain of truth in the popular notion that "thinking too much" can hurt an athlete's performance. The key is to think productively and to simplify one's thinking to the point of automatic performance. This may be difficult during a performance slump, where one's controllability of images slips a bit and negative images pop up during competition. However, the goal of systematic mental training—and imagery training in particular—is to develop more and more skill in controlling one's thoughts and images. I typically tell coaches and athletes that to resist mental training because it causes athletes to "think too much" is like an ostrich putting its head in the sand when confronted with danger. It's not a proactive way to confront competitive demands and mental obstacles that all athletes at one time will face.

How Coaches and Athletes Can Use Imagery

Now that you understand what imagery is, why it works, and hopefully believe that it *does* work to enhance sport performance, it's time for you to consider how to use imagery with your athletes. In this section, specific ways that coaches and athletes can use imagery for training and competition are provided. These are simply suggestions—as a coach, you know better than anyone how imagery might work best in your situation, and I encourage you to be innovative to meet your athletes' needs and interests.

1. Create a Productive Team Image and Model Your Belief in Imagery

We began the chapter with the idea that "image is everything." This should be applied to your team and program, because this is where imagery starts with your athletes. The "image" that you establish about your program becomes your athletes' "team image," which will definitely influence their confidence, motivation, and even performance. The way that you create a productive team image is based on all the previous chapters of this book, because your program's image emanates from your philosophy as a coach, your understanding of motivation, your

leadership, vision, and decision-making behaviors, the dynamics and cohesion within your program, the communication within the team, and the goal map the team uses to pursue excellence. Before you involve your athletes in individual imagery as a mental training tool, be sure that you have created a self-image for the team and your program that provides your athletes with a strong and productive set of beliefs and sense of team pride.

The second most important thing that you can do as a coach is to demonstrate your belief in, commitment to, and enthusiasm for imagery as a mental training tool. Include imagery as a natural part of your athletes' overall physical training and preparation, as opposed to introducing it as special, new type of mental training that is seen as separate from their "real" training. Any mental training techniques that you implement should be integrated into your athletes' habitual training and competition routines, and should be established by you as an integral part of your overall program and philosophy, not as something extra, special, or optional for your athletes. And as with all mental training techniques, start small and focus on one or two ways that your athletes can easily use imagery.

2. Teach, Learn, and Practice Sport Skills

One of the best places to start helping your athletes use imagery is mental practice, or the repetitive practice of a sport skill in the mind. Pick one or two skills in your sport, and build in ways for athletes to mentally practice these skills. Implement a volleyball serving drill in which athletes serve ten balls and mentally practice each serve prior to physically performing it. This could also be applied to shooting free throws, executing wrestling moves, serving in tennis, sprinting over a set of hurdles, or hitting a baseball. Athletes should be urged to mentally practice on their own, but they will be more inclined to do so if you incorporate mental practice as part of their regular training. Mental practice is also useful to aid beginners in learning sport skills by helping them to develop a "mental blueprint for perfect responses."

To help athletes strengthen or build their mental blueprints for perfect responses, you as a coach can guide them with verbal triggers and symbolic images. **Triggers** are *words or phrases that help athletes focus on key aspects in an image to make the mental blueprint correct and the response perfect.* Triggers are used to program the proper image. Coaches use triggers all the time in teaching skills or as points of emphasis they want athletes to think about when performing. Softball players are told to *"throw their hands"* and focus on a *"quick bat."* Volleyball serving is taught by having athletes focus on the *"bow and arrow"* technique. Basketball players are taught to *"plant"* their inside foot and *"square up"* for perfect jump shot form. Cross-country skiers think *"quick"* for their uphill technique to trigger the quick, short kick technique needed on hills. Golfers use simple triggers such as *steady head*, *balance*, and *rhythm* to create the image of a perfect golf swing in their minds prior to hitting a shot. A professional golfer kept the word *oooom-PAH* written on her driver to program the image of an easy slow backswing and a strong and vigorous downswing.

Symbolic images are *mental symbols or models for desired components of performance*. Archers can envision a *string extending from the center of the target* that pulls their arrows directly into the bull's-eye. Sprinters may imagine the explosive energy in their legs as *coiled springs* that will catapult them from the starting blocks. U.S. biathletes have used the symbolic image of the *Rock of Gibraltar* to program the steady body state they need to shoot effectively. Golfers can imagine *turning their body inside a barrel* to ensure proper body rotation on the swing and can imagine their *arms as a pendulum* swinging from the shoulders for the proper putting stroke. A gymnast may visualize her back against a *cold, steel wall* to perfect the image and movement of a perfectly straight body during a floor exercise routine.

Coaches are experts at using triggers and symbolic images in their teaching and coaching. As you read earlier in the chapter, imagery can only hurt performance if athletes imagine the wrong responses. Triggers and symbolic images help athletes lock in the proper responses so that the imagery is "programmed" in the right way. Mental practice using triggers and symbolic images may be helpful for athletes who are mired in a slump or who are

---

Personal Plug-In

Jot down several verbal triggers and symbolic images that can be used in your sport to program "mental blueprints of perfect responses." Be innovative and attempt to think beyond the traditional, typical triggers that are used by all coaches in your sport. The key is finding triggers and symbolic images that help athletes really "feel" the image. Develop new or individualized ones for specific athletes' needs.

---

having technique problems. They should imagine themselves performing perfectly and analyze how their present technique is different from their perfect performance. It may be helpful for athletes to view videotapes of themselves performing well and then internalize that performance by using kinesthetic imagery. Always keep in mind that imagery helps athletes when it gives them "a mental blueprint for perfect responses." As coaches, you want to help your athletes identify the triggers and symbolic images that really lock in those perfect responses within a sound performance mental blueprint.

As discussed previously in the chapter, athletes can use whichever imagery perspective (internal or external) feels most comfortable to them. However, as they enhance their imagery ability and use it more, I would recommend that they practice both internal and external imagery until they are competent and comfortable with both perspectives. One way to help athletes develop their internal imagery perspectives is to have them physically perform a skill, and then immediately close their eyes and try to replay the way the skill looked and felt from inside their body. This physical-mental practice routine should be repeated several times to strengthen athletes' internal imagery perspective.

3. Teach, Learn, and Practice Performance Strategies

Imagery is very useful in helping coaches teach and athletes learn and practice performance strategies, such as tactics, systems of play, and decision-making. For example, football quarterbacks can mentally rehearse various plays in relation to specific defenses, even imagining their reaction to blitzes and changing defensive formations in order to audibly and successfully complete the play. When introducing a new basketball offense or out-of-bounds play, coaches can direct athletes to walk through the new pattern and then immediately follow this physical practice by imagining their movements through the patterns. Then, prior to competition, coaches can lead athletes in the mental rehearsal of these previously learned offensive and defensive strategies and plays. Similarly, skiers may ski over a particular course in their mind to prepare for an upcoming downhill race. Softball outfielders may use imagery to practice throws from the outfield based on various situations that may arise in a game. Tennis players can mentally rehearse their planned strategy against a particular opponent. Tennis champion Chris Evert prepared for upcoming matches by mentally rehearsing planned strategies based on the tendencies of specific opponents. Coaches frequently use imagery in this way as they think through strategies and formations. You will find that by relaxing your mind and imagining the situation, you can often gain clearer insight and successfully determine how to correct problems.

4. Create and Practice a Mental Focus for Competition

Coaches typically prefer to have experienced athletes on their teams, because experienced athletes "have been there before" and thus are assumed to be more adept at handling the competitive pressures and distractions they will face. Experience gives them the advantage of having gone through competition before, so now they know what it's like. Although experience can be a strong mental advantage, imagery can be used to help athletes gain "experience" when they haven't actually "been there before."

Imagery can be used by athletes to create and practice in their heads the strong, unshakable mental focus needed for specific competitions. Coaches should help athletes answer two questions: What will it be like? How will I respond? "What will it be like?" refers to the external factors of competition, or the physical and social environment. Research has shown that huge championship events such as the Olympic Games create an environment full of distractions that athletes have never faced before (Greenleaf et al., 2001). For each competitive situation that your athletes face, help them to vividly imagine what it will be like in terms of the facilities, crowd, potential distracters, officials, weather, etc.

The second question, "How will I respond?" is by far the most important question for athletes. Explain to athletes that they should always respond, not react. Responding requires mental skill and toughness to manage one's thoughts and emotions and performance when faced with obstacles, surprises, and disappointments. Reacting doesn't take any skill at all—it is typically a raw emission of emotion (anger, anxiety, fear) in which athletes allow the competitive environment to control them and make them reactive. Imagery is the tool athletes can use to practice over and over in their heads the ways in which they will respond to any type of competitive pressure, even those that they can't anticipate. Think of these as "emotional fire-drills" (Lazarus, 1984) because using imagery in this way allows athletes time to practice rational and logical responses for situations that are unexpected and stressful.

Coaches should help athletes program the answers to the two questions ("What will it be like?" and "How will I respond?") into a short imagery routine that the athletes practice over and over in their heads in the days and weeks leading up to a particular competition. Imagery used in this way is an attempt to help athletes gain "experience" in responding to competitive challenges. The idea is to create a sense of expectancy, so that athletes expect certain obstacles and pressures, and that they even expect the unexpected. If they have been mentally trained to expect the unexpected and to respond productively to the unexpected, they will be less likely to react emotionally in ways that will hurt their performances. Coaches should attempt to simulate competitive conditions at times in practice so that athletes can practice their mental focus plan for competition. The best coaches are masters at simulation by creating all types of situations that athletes might face in competition. These "dress rehearsals" might include wearing uniforms, using clocks and officials, and simulating environmental conditions such as noise/distractions, heat, cold, and pressure. Peter Vidmar, collegiate national champion gymnast and Olympic gold medalist, describes how he and his teammates would simulate competition during practice:

"The team did really weird things to prepare for [the Olympics]. In practice, we would turn off the radio so it was silent in the gym. We would go through the dialogues, like this next routine is the Olympic Games and it's the team finals. It's the last event, and we were neck-and-neck with the Chinese. It was only make-believe when we did it, but what if we really were neck-and-neck with the Chinese during the Games and this routine was our only chance to beat them and win the gold? We'd set the whole thing up, and my heart would be pounding and I would be imagining I was in Pauley Pavilion at the Olympic Games with all the pressure and people watching. I would get really nervous, take those few deep breaths, and imagine I was there at the meet and [Coach] was the head judge. Tim [Daggett] would be Mr. Loudspeaker. 'Okay. Next up for the USA,' he would say, 'Mr. Peter Vidmar.' We were dead serious when we were doing this.

"During the Olympics, a funny thing happened. It was the last event and the USA just happened to be on the high bar and . . . I just happened to be the last up. We just happened to be neck-and-neck with the Chinese. It's the same scenario we had gone through every day for the last six months and here we were actually living it. [Coach] said, 'Okay, Pete. Let's go do it just like in the gym.' So I imagined I was in the UCLA gym. Consciously, I knew I was at the Olympics, but I was able to put

myself in the frame of mind that I was back at the gym. I was even able to geographically orient that bar to the gym as if there was a pit over there and the wall there, etc. I did my routine and landed successfully . . . We won the gold" (Ravizza, 1993, p. 94-95).

5. Create and Practice Pre-performance Routines

A **pre-performance routine** is *a preplanned, systematic sequence of thoughts and behaviors that an athlete engages in prior to performing a specific skill.* Pre-performance routines are typically used by athletes prior to the execution of specific sport skills, such as a golf shot, basketball free throw, gymnastics vault, volleyball or tennis serve, field goal kick in football, start in swimming, or any of the jumping and throwing events in track and field. Research has supported pre-performance routines as facilitative to athletes' performances.

Athletes should keep their routines simple and flexible, so that they are easily repeatable yet open to some change if competitive conditions dictate this. Pre-performance routines help athletes lock in a sense of automaticity, so that once they begin their routine they kick in their automatic pilot, which is where the best performances occur. Pre-performance routines also give athletes something to think about besides the pressures of kicking the game-winning field goal or shooting the game-winning

---

Quotable Quote

"When I see a shot, I see in my mind's eye a 'window' I want the ball to pass through at the apex of its flight." **Phil Mickelson**, professional golfer *(Best Tip, 2004)*

Photo by Robin Vealey

free throw. The key is for athletes to develop a routine and then practice it through imagery, in their physical training sessions, and then use it habitually in competition so that it becomes second nature. Hopefully, this will help their performance become second nature!

Most athletes also have pre-performance routines that they like to engage in prior to the start of competitive events. These routines typically include simple things like putting the uniform on a certain way, warming up a certain way, or listening to a particular song. It is important that each athlete identifies and then adheres to a precompetitive routine that works best for them. Some athletes prefer to spend some time in a quiet room focusing on the upcoming competition and their planned responses to the competitive challenges. Other athletes prefer to chat socially with teammates and not "overthink" about the upcoming competition. Coaches should help athletes identify what approach is best for them and to provide time and space for athletes to engage in whatever pre-performance routines they wish. Pre-performance routines are helpful mental skills, and they work best when they are systematically used in physical training and practiced via imagery in mental training. However, help your athletes understand that all routines should have some flexibility, because the nature of competition is such that times and conditions vary in ways that sometimes interfere with athletes' preferred routines.

6. Correct Mistakes

A very simple use of imagery for athletes is in correcting mistakes. Athletes receive constant feedback and corrections from coaches that are provided to enhance their performance. Imagery is a great tool that athletes can use to gain the most benefit from corrections provided by their coaches. Athletes should listen to the feedback or correction provided by their coaches and then run it through their minds in a brief image of the skill now performed correctly. That is, athletes should receive the feedback, and then see it and feel it as they incorporate the information from the coach into their image and execution of the skill.

Remember how bio-informational theory says that imagery works to help athletes perform better? It does so by creating a mental blueprint for perfect responses. By using imagery to see and feel the correction in performance, athletes are retooling their mental blueprint for more perfect responses. Coaches should teach and expect athletes to use imagery each time they receive feedback by requesting them to imagine the desired correction in performance in terms of seeing it and feeling it. Coaches should ask each time: Can you see it? Can you feel it? Using imagery to correct mistakes is also helpful when watching videotape of performances. When athletes and coaches identify flaws or mistakes in athletes' performance while watching tape, athletes should be immediately cued to imagine the correction by seeing it and feeling it. Coaches can also help athletes build in triggers or symbolic images to help athletes lock in the mental blueprint for perfect responses.

Coaches can help athletes "calibrate" their images by observing athletes perform and then comparing their observations with what the athletes perceive is occurring in their performance (Simons, 2001). Simons describes how a high jumper attempts to recall the image of her jump immediately after each attempt. She describes her image of the jump to her coach, who then describes her observations of the jump. In this way, the coach is calibrating the athlete's image of the jump to ensure that the athlete's perception and image of what she is doing is indeed correct in form. Helping your athletes calibrate their images enables them to create optimal mental blueprints for perfect responses.

7. Build and Enhance Mental Skills

As you will see throughout the remainder of this book, imagery is a mental training tool that can be used to build and enhance all types of mental skills important to an athlete's performance. A few are mentioned here, with greater detail provided in Chapters 12, 13, and 14.

Self-Confidence. With regards to athletes' self-confidence, imagery is critical to their self-image and shaping the way they think and act. Obviously, athletes should nurture a self-image of competence and success, and this can be done by recreating past successful performances and the positive feelings associated with these successes. An imagery exercise called Ideal Self-Image (ISI) is useful to work on confidence. To practice the ISI exercise, athletes should imagine themselves displaying the skills and qualities that they would most like to have, such as more assertive communication skills, a confident posture after performance errors, or the ability to manage emotions during competition. Then, they should compare their ISI with their current self-image. This should enable them to understand specific behaviors

and thoughts that they can actively engage in to begin to move toward their ISI. The ISI exercise should be used continuously to understand differences between their real and ideal selves. Imagery can then be used to practice new behaviors and ways of responding that move athletes toward their ISI.

Energy Management. Athletes who need to increase their energy (arousal) to psych up for competition can imagine playing intensely and aggressively in front of a roaring crowd. Athletes who need to decrease their energy, or arousal, before competition can mentally recall their preparation and good performances in practice and previous competitions and then visualize handling the pressure and performing successfully in the upcoming competition.

An imagery exercise called the Energy Room can help athletes regulate arousal from different competitive demands. The Energy Room image involves athletes walking down a dark tunnel to a door that leads them into a room that is very comfortable and pleasing. (You can create whatever type of room you wish.) The room is sealed and the idea is that special air is piped into the room that creates the type of energy that is needed for this specific athlete in his or her event. The athletes feel themselves become more *energized/relaxed* with each inhalation and feel increasing *focus/intensity/relaxation*. The breathing continues until the athletes feel appropriately energized and walk back through the tunnel feeling *relaxed, focused, intense, centered/confidence.* Whatever variation is used in this image, the main objective is for athletes to have an imaginary place that they can go to create optimal energy and use any mental strategies they want to employ. The room should become comfortable and familiar so it is an easy place for athletes to go in their minds to manage and control their physical and mental arousal levels.

Stress management. Energy management is usually needed just prior to or during competition. Imagery may also help reduce stress that occurs due to an overload of life demands (e.g., job pressure, exams, deadlines). Coaches and athletes both should have two or three relaxing images that they can use when they need to reduce stress and help them to relax and unwind. These images might be of a favorite place or a warm beach. An example stress reduction imagery script is shown in the Clipboard below.

Clipboard

Sample Imagery Script for Relaxation/Stress Reduction

1. Get into a comfortable position and close your eyes. Take several deep, cleansing breaths to relax and center yourself. Take a moment to scan your muscles. If you feel tension anywhere, gently remind yourself to "let it go." Continue to scan the muscles of your body. Wherever you feel any tension, allow yourself to consciously "let it go." As you do this, repeat the words "let it go" to yourself.

2. I would like you to visualize a very thick rope that is tied into a big knot. See the knot in your mind's eye. Notice the tightly intertwined pieces of the rope that are stretched taut against each other. Now visualize the knot slowly loosening, slowly loosening—a little bit of slack at a time until it is slack, limp, and completely uncoiled.

3. Now visualize a candle that has burned out. Focus on the cold and hard wax that has accumulated at the base of the candle. Now visualize the wax slowly softening—becoming first gooey, then soft like butter, then totally liquid as the wax warms and melts.

4. Visualize yourself on a loud city corner. It's windy and cold, very busy, and very noisy. Feel people buffet you as they rush by, hear the noise of cars and trucks, and smell the exhaust fumes as bus drives by. Right beside you is a construction site, and a jack-hammer goes off without warning. It is so loud that your ears hurt and your body vibrates with the noise and concussions as it tears up the concrete. Slowly, ease yourself away so you are lying on your back on a grassy knoll by a sparkling blue lake. The sun warms your face and body, and a gentle breeze creates small ripples on the water. Listen as the jackhammer fades into a woodpecker gently rapping on a tree.

5. Now focus inward on yourself. You have released the knots and relaxed your body. You have softened and then melted the tension of your day. You have transformed the bustle and noise in your life into pleasant sounds of nature. By doing this, you have gained control over your mind and body. Remind yourself now that you have the ability to gain control of your thoughts and feelings through creative visualization. Affirm your personal power to choose to think and feel well, and to believe in your ability to transform your life in productive ways.

6. Refocus now on your breathing, and repeat the following affirmation each time you exhale: "My body is relaxed and open." (Wait 30 seconds.) Now change that affirmation (each time you exhale) to: "I choose to think and be well." (Wait 30-50 seconds.) Feel pride in yourself and your abilities, and reinforce to yourself now that you have the power each day to manage how you think and feel. Take time each day to relax your body, melt away the tension, and quiet the noise in your life.

Increasing self-awareness. By systematically practicing imagery, athletes can become more aware of what is taking place within and around them by relaxing and paying attention to sensory details. A runner may learn much about a previously run race by vividly recreating it in her mind. A Nordic skier that I worked with was having problems sustaining the level of concentration she needed throughout her races. By imagining her past races in vivid detail, she suddenly became aware that she was shifting attention to the wrong things at the end of her races.

8. Aid in Recovery from Injury

Because injured athletes typically cannot participate in physical training, imagery allows them to mentally practice skills and strategies during their recovery. Injured athletes should attend team training sessions and imagine themselves running through the drills and workouts just as though they were physically performing them. Challenge your athletes to use their time recovering from their injuries to engage in mental training, and to maintain a focused, productive, strong-willed mindset toward recovery. Among other things, athletes can set progressive rehabilitation goals using the performance tree (discussed in Chapter 8) and vividly imagine the attainment of these goals. They can also use the ISI exercise to work toward full recovery of their competitive self-image. Productive, goal-oriented imagery is essential to facilitate the critical mind-body link that has been shown to enhance the healing process. Consider the following quote from Craig Billington, professional (NHL) hockey goalie: "The best example I've had . . . of the effects of positive imagery was the season with the lockout and then, being injured for eight weeks, and coming back, having to play in midseason form after a layoff of close to eight months. I came back and immediately played well that year, largely due to the visualization and my belief that I was going to be ready and I was going to play well with very little practice time. There is really no better proof than that. So I know it works . . . and if you start off slow, I know it will work for you" (Orlick, 1998, p. 74).

Tips to Make Imagery More Effective

You've now read several suggestions for how you can help your athletes use imagery in various ways. Remember to start small, keep it simple, but make it systematic and a continual part of athletes' overall training. Here are a few tips to give you even more insight into the use of imagery with athletes.

1. Imagine vivid mental, physiological, and behavioral responses to situations. Make sure your athletes load their images with *vivid responses*. Remember that imagery works by helping athletes build and refine mental blueprints for perfect responses. Repeatedly tell them that their images should include their mental, physiological, and behavioral responses to competition—not just the stimulus characteristics of the situation. That is, when they imagine a big crowd and lots of noise and distractions, make sure they image how they will respond to this (e.g., using the energy as positive fuel, keeping focused in the "cocoon," and exuding confidence as they physically warm up for competition).

2. Image performance and outcome. Tennis players should imagine executing sharply-paced passing shots and then see these shots hit in the corners of their opponent's court. Baseball players should imagine a strong and compact swing, and then see the ball driven as a line-drive through the outfield. Golfers should envision and feel the swing they will use, and then "see" the trajectory the ball will take as well as exactly where it will land. Remind athletes to follow through on their imagery to see not only perfect performances, but also perfect outcomes.

3. Be specific in all uses of imagery. Help your athletes specifically tailor their imagery to fit their individual needs. For example, consider a softball pitcher who generally pitches well until there are runners on base, which seems to distract her from throwing strikes. Although it would be somewhat helpful for her to engage in the repetitive mental practice of pitching, it would be better for her to set up many different situations in her imagery, so that she can build her confidence and concentration to pitch effectively in changing game situations. She should repeatedly envision herself in various situations with base-runners, different counts and number of outs, and different game scores to groove strong and consistent mental and physical responses to the pressure of these situations. Athletes must consider their exact performance needs, so that their imagery practice is specific in helping them develop thoughts and behaviors that can overcome performance problems. The mark of effective mental training using imagery is the systematic and controlled visualization that enables athletes to develop strong and competent behaviors that hold up under pressure.

For example, a tennis player could customize his uses of imagery to meet his specific needs to create the Inner Edge. As shown in Figure 9.2, he uses daily mental practice to create perfect serves of different types, uses verbal triggers to groove perfect blueprints of ground strokes and serves, and feels and sees correct execution when correcting mistakes. During mental preparation, he also uses imagery to rehearse tactics for upcoming opponents, match preparation and focus, and refocus strategies for typical distractions in his game. Finally, he incorporates imagery into the pre-shot routine he uses prior to serving, and he spends time recreating key points from previous matches to evaluate his performance and improve.

4. Athletes should practice imagery in many different places and positions. Most people envision mental training as something an athlete does while lying on a couch. Athletes may want to spend time developing their imagery skills in quiet, less distracting settings, but once they have become proficient at imagery, they should engage in it in many different settings and positions. Athletes should be able to engage in imagery in the locker room, on the field, in the pool, during practice, during competition—in any type of setting! It helps if you as the coach incorporate imagery into practice sessions, as it will then become second nature to your athletes. Also, encourage athletes to practice imagery in many different positions. If they are mentally practicing a sport skill such as a gymnastics routine or high jump, it might be useful for them to stand up or even walk

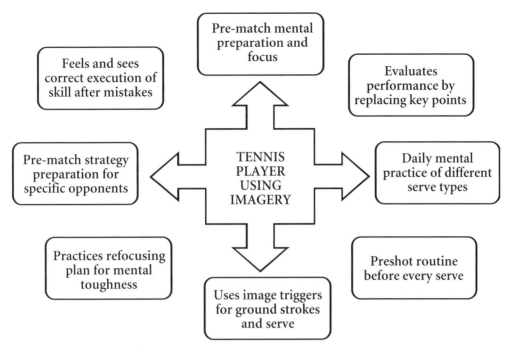

Figure 9.2 How a tennis player can use imagery

through and move their body in certain ways that match the different segments of their images. They may want to hold the bat, club, or ball in their hands to facilitate their images, repeating their imagery triggers to themselves to cue in perfect responses.

Clipboard

Training the Inner Winner

Tony DiCicco, former coach of the U.S. Women's Soccer national team, talks about the importance of developing the "inner winner" in athletes. He describes how he attempted to boost his athletes' confidence by helping them feel themselves being successful by using imagery:

"In the middle of the day, with the sun beaming down after a hard training session, I would have the players lie down on the grass, relax, and do imagery training. I had them visualize performing their unique abilities on the soccer field over and over again. I would say, 'Imagine in your mind what you do well. If you're a great header, visualize yourself winning headers. If you're a great defender, visualize yourself stripping the ball from an attacking player. If you're a great passer of the ball, visualize yourself playing balls in. If you've got great speed, visualize yourself running by players and receiving the ball.' I made a special point of

saying, 'Visualize the special skills that separate you from the rest—the skills that make your team better because you possess them.'" (DiCicco & Hacker, 2002, p. 112)

5. The timing in imagery should be the same as in the actual physical execution of the skill. Forget about slow motion and fast forward—imagery shouldn't be used for slow motion analysis nor should it be rushed. Advise your athletes to make their images as realistic as possible in relation to the actual timing of their physical performance. Timing is a critical performance factor in many sports, thus it becomes a key response characteristic that athletes want to stamp into their mental blueprint as a perfect timing response. Elite swimmers and runners are typically able to imagine their races down to the second in terms of their splits and final times.

6. Using technology to enhance athletes' images. Some athletes find it useful to buy commercially produced imagery cassette tapes or make their own imagery tapes. Sport psychology consultants can make cassette tapes for athletes that combine the practice of physical and mental skills. When making imagery tapes for athletes, they should be highly individualized with specific verbal triggers and symbolic images that are meaningful to each athlete.

The use of personal highlight videotapes has been shown to enhance the confidence and performance of basketball, ice hockey, and soccer athletes (e.g., Vealey & Greenleaf, 2001). Athletes' peak performance moments are edited from competitive videotape and integrated with special effects and motivational music. These highlight videos can then be used in conjunction with imagery to enhance confidence in returning from injury or slumps. Clearly, the equipment to produce these videotapes is not available to everyone, but as technology advances, this powerful "image producer" should become more accessible.

Example Imagery Exercises

A few example imagery exercises for athletes are provided for you in this section. These are generic examples, so I encourage you to build from these to create personalized, sport-specific images loaded with perfect response characteristics for your athletes.

Exercise 1: Place yourself in a familiar place where you usually perform your sport (gym, pool, rink, field, track, etc.). It is empty except for you. Stand in the middle of this place and look all around. Notice the quiet emptiness. Pick out as many details as you can. What does it smell like? What are the colors, shapes, and forms that you see? Now imagine yourself in the same setting, but this time there are many spectators there. Imagine yourself getting ready to perform. Try to experience this image from inside your body. See the spectators, your teammates, your coach, and the opponents. Try to hear the sounds of the noisy crowd, your teammates' chatter, your coach yelling encouragement, and the particular sounds of your sport (e.g., ball swishing through the net, volleyball spike hitting the floor). Recreate the feelings of nervous anticipation and excitement that you have prior to competing. How do you feel? How will you respond when the competition begins?

Exercise 2: Pick a very simple skill in your sport. Perform the skill over and over in your mind and imagine every feeling and movement in your muscles as you perform that skill. Try to feel this image as if you were inside your own body. Concentrate on how the different parts of your body feel as you stretch and contract the various muscles associated with the skill. Think about creating a "mental blueprint for perfect responses" as you perform the skill flawlessly over and over again and concentrate on the feeling of the movement. Now try to combine all of your senses, but particularly those of feeling, seeing, and hearing yourself perform the skill over and over. Do not concentrate too hard on any one sense. Instead try to imagine the total experience using all of your senses.

Exercise 3: Choose a particular sport skill that you have trouble performing. Begin practicing the skill over and over. See and feel yourself doing this from inside your body. If you make a mistake or perform the skill incorrectly, stop the image and repeat it, attempting to perform perfectly every time. Recreate past experiences in which you have not performed the skill well. Take careful notice of what you are doing wrong. Now imagine yourself performing the skill correctly. Focus on how your body feels as you go through different positions in performing the skill correctly. Attempt to switch back and forth from the inside your body perspective to an outside your body perspective, as if you were watching yourself on tape. Which is more comfortable and which can you see more clearly? Continue experimenting so that you can use both perspectives in your imagery.

Exercise 4: Think back and choose a past performance in which you performed very well. Using all your senses, recreate that situation in your mind. See yourself as you were succeeding, hear the sounds involved, feel your body as you performed the movements, and re-experience the positive emotions. Try to pick out the characteristics that made you perform so well (e.g., intense concentration, feelings of confidence, optimal arousal). After identifying these characteristics, determine why they were present in this situation. Think about the things you did in preparation for this particular event. What are some things that may have contributed to this great performance?

Repeat this exercise imagining a situation in which you performed very poorly. Make sure you are very relaxed to practice this image as your mind will subconsciously resist your imagery attempts to recreate unpleasant thoughts, images, and feelings. Attempt to become more self-aware of how you reacted to different stimuli (e.g., coaches, opponents, officials, fear of failure, needing approval from others) and how these thoughts and feelings may have interfered with your performance.

Exercise 5: Think back to a sport situation in which you experienced a great deal of anxiety. Recreate that situation in your head, seeing and hearing yourself. Especially recreate the feeling of anxiety. Try to feel the physical responses of your body to the emotion, and also try to recall the thoughts going through your mind that may have caused the anxiety.

Now attempt to let go of the anxiety and relax your body. Breathe slowly and deeply and focus on your body as you exhale. Imagine all of the tension being pulled into your lungs and exhaled from your body. Continue breathing slowly and exhaling tension until you are deeply relaxed.

Exercise 6: Think about the times when your performance suddenly went from good to bad. Recreate several of these experiences in your mind. Try to pinpoint the specific factors that negatively influenced your performance (e.g., officials, performance errors, opponents' remarks, opponent started to play really well). After becoming aware of these factors that negatively affected your performance, take several minutes to recreate the situations, develop appropriate strategies to deal with the negative factors, and imagine the situations again but this time imagine yourself using your strategies to keep the negative factors from interfering with your performance. Reinforce yourself by feeling proud and confident that you were able to control the negative factors and perform well.

Wrapping Up

Everyone engages in imagery. It's not something that sport psychology consultants have invented. Rather, it's a way that we all think, wonder, plan, rehash, and dream. Your athletes engage in imagery all the time, even if they're unaware of it. The purpose of this chapter was to give you the insight needed to help them use imagery productively, improving how they view and think about themselves, their performances, and competition. Imagery can be used as a powerful mental training tool to create mental blueprints for athletes of perfect physical and mental responses. Encourage and train your athletes to use imagery to their advantage, and to understand why "image is everything."

Summary Points for Chapter 9

1. Imagery is using all the senses to recreate or create an experience in the mind.
2. Research indicates that when individuals engage in vivid imagery, their brains interpret images as identical to the actual external stimulus situation.
3. Imagery can and should be a polysensory experience, including visual, auditory, olfactory, tactile, and kinesthetic senses.

4. Kinesthetic sense, or feeling the body as it moves in different positions, is a crucial sense for athletes to master in their imagery.
5. Imagery may be used as a mental training tool to systematically engage in vivid and controllable polysensory images to enhance performance.
6. An external imagery perspective refers to when athletes see the image from outside of their bodies, while an internal imagery perspective involves seeing the image from behind their own eyes as if they were inside their bodies.
7. Research supports that imagery enhances sport performance, enhances competition-related thoughts and emotions such as confidence and motivation, and is systematically used by successful, world-class athletes who attest to its importance.
8. Theory and research indicate that imagery enhances athletes' performance by creating a "mental blueprint for perfect responses."
9. Symbolic learning theory states that imagery enables athletes to code their movements into useful or logical symbolic components in their brains, thus making the movements that make up their performances more familiar and more automatic.
10. Bio-informational theory states that by repeatedly accessing response characteristics and modifying these responses to represent perfect control and execution of sport skills (or practicing perfect responses), imagery can enhance athletes' performances.
11. Imagery can hurt athletes' performance if they systematically imagine incorrect responses or constantly attempt to suppress negative thoughts and images from conscious awareness.
12. Coaches can help athletes use imagery to learn and practice sport skills and performance strategies, create and practice mental focus plans for competition, create and practice pre-performance routines, correct mistakes, build and enhance mental skills, and aid in the their recovery from injury.
13. Athletes should imagine vivid and controllable responses to competitive situations, including both performance and outcomes, using realistic timing in their images.
14. Imagery should be practiced and used in different competitive settings and positions to

make it as practical and real for the athletes as possible.

Glossary

bio-informational theory: by repeatedly accessing response characteristics and modifying these responses to represent perfect control and execution of sport skills (or practicing perfect responses), imagery can enhance athletes' performances

external imagery perspective: athletes see the image from outside their bodies as if they are viewing themselves from behind a video camera

imagery: using all the senses to recreate or create an experience in the mind

internal imagery perspective: athletes see the image from behind their own eyes as if they were inside their bodies.

kinesthetic sense: the feel or sensation of the body as it moves in different positions

mental practice: using imagery to perform a specific sport skill repetitively in the mind

symbolic images: mental symbols or models for desired components of performance

symbolic learning theory: imagery enables athletes to blueprint or code their movements into useful or logical symbolic components in their brains, thus making the movements that make up their performances more familiar and more automatic

triggers: words or phrases that help athletes focus on key aspects of a thought or image to make the mental blueprint correct and the response perfect

Study Questions

1. Define imagery and explain how it works to enhance athletes' performance. In your explanation, describe both bio-informational and symbolic coding theory.

2. Write out an imagery script filled with response characteristics that should enhance performance as prescribed by bio-informational theory.

3. Provide examples of how various senses could be used to make images more vivid for athletes.

4. Explain the difference between internal and external imagery perspective. Which perspective should athletes use, and when should they use each?

5. Identify three areas of research that support the effectiveness of imagery as a mental training tool with athletes. Provide some specific examples of research in each area.

6. Research has shown that imagery can hurt athletes' performance. Explain this research, and then explain why or why not athletes should use imagery based on these findings.

7. Identify at least six specific uses of imagery for coaches and athletes.

Reflective Learning Activities

1. Sensory Overload

Identify two ways each that athletes can use imagery in mental training to create and recreate experiences. For each image, describe how the various senses should be emphasized to enhance the vividness of each image. (10 minutes in groups of 3 divided by sport.)

2. Follow the Script

Develop an imagery script for an athlete in a specific sport (or event) for the following situations:
   a. Pre-competition focus and readiness script (to be used prior to competition)
   b. Competition focus script (to be used during competition for specific needs)
   c. Practice or training script (to enhance focus, confidence, and motivation for training)
   d. Relaxation or stress-reducer script
(Completed as homework individually.)

3. Stinking Thinking

Research shows that negative imagery can hurt performance. How can you help an athlete who comes to you with the problem of uncontrollable, negative images of performance. He is in a slump, and can't seem to get out of it, and he can only see himself performing poorly. Devise an action plan that would enable this athlete to gain control of his images and his performance. (Discuss in groups of 4 for 12 minutes; then share action plans with entire group).

4. Teach with Triggers

Demonstrate and explain precisely how you could teach a simple skill in your sport to a beginner using imagery along with verbal triggers and/or symbolic images. How will the learner use imagery and what imagery perspective will you ask them to use in their mental practice? (Individual assignment that is shared with the entire group.)

Chapter
Ten

P³ Thinking

Chapter Preview

In this chapter, you'll learn:
- that successful athletes think differently than unsuccessful athletes
- that mental toughness requires Purposeful, Productive, and Possibility Thinking
- how athletes' dysfunctional belief systems lead to Reactive Thinking
- strategies to help athletes effectively manage their thinking

"The difference between an ordinary player and a champion is in the way they think." **Patty Berg**

"If you don't want to get into positive thinking, that's okay. Just eliminate all the negative thoughts from your mind, and whatever's left will be fine." **Bob Rotella**, sport psychology consultant

"We are what we think." **The Dhammapada**

Tiger Woods' father recalls asking his son, then a second-grader playing in his first international tournament, what he was thinking about on the first tee as he stood with all the other nervous young golfers and prepared to hit his first shot. Tiger's answer was simple: "Where I wanted the ball to go, Daddy." Earl Woods, the father, said, "That's when I knew how good he was going to be" (Reilly, 1995, p. 65).

As a second-grader, Tiger Woods demonstrated the most important mental tool required of an athlete: the ability to think well. Thinking well allows athletes to focus on the right things, to visualize what they want to happen, and to mentally manage emotions, distractions, obstacles, and setbacks. In sport, as in other achievement areas, good thinking separates successful people from unsuccessful people. Consider the thinking of the following successful people:

"You're going to make mistakes in life. It's what you do after those mistakes that counts." **Brandi Chastain**, U.S. Soccer team star, after inadvertently scoring a goal for Germany and then scoring for the U.S.

"I don't know what the big deal is about playing on the road. I've never seen fans scream loud enough to block my jump shot." **Kobe Bryant**, Los Angeles Lakers' shooting guard

"Pain is weakness leaving the body." Caption on t-shirt worn by Laura Wilkinson at the 2000 Olympic Games, where she won the gold medal for 10-meter platform diving with a broken foot

Research has substantiated that successful athletes think differently from less successful athletes prior to and while competing. Successful athletes focus more on task-relevant thoughts, are less likely to be distracted, and manage anxiety more productively than less successful athletes (e.g., Williams & Krane, 2001). U.S. Olympic champions were found to be "positive perfectionists" by establishing high personal standards and developing effective organizational skills, but not "negative perfectionists" in terms of being concerned about making mistakes and having doubts about action (Gould, Dieffenbach, & Moffett, 2002). These champion Olympians were also high in **hope**, defined as *a thinking process in which people have a sense of personal agency and goal-directedness* (Curry & Snyder, 2000). Finally, these athletes showed high levels of **optimism**, or *a general expectancy that good things will happen* (Sheier & Carver, 1992). Optimism is an important characteristic of effective thinking, because optimists approach problems and handle adversity with confidence and persistence—as opposed to pessimists, whose thinking makes them doubtful and hesitant.

A unique study conducted by McPherson (2000) examined the thinking of collegiate tennis players by recording their thoughts during and after each point in a tennis match based on the questions "What were you thinking during that point?" and "What are you thinking now?" The elite athletes' thoughts were task-oriented, involved planning strategies, focused on problem-solving, and focused confidently on enabling feelings and beliefs about their competence and ability to succeed. The novice athletes' thoughts included more expressions of frustration and emotion, and were indicative of low confidence, having negative expectations and a consistent desire to quit.

Overall, the ability to think well is related to achieving the Inner Edge. However, when you read the personal accounts of successful, elite athletes, it is clear that they had to work very hard to develop their thinking skills along with their physical talents. Good thinking can be learned—all athletes can change the way they think to become more effective thinkers. In this chapter, the mental training tool of P³ Thinking is introduced. The chapter is divided into five sections. First, the concept of P³ Thinking is introduced as a basic mental training tool for athletes. The second, third, and fourth sections provide evidence to support the importance of each of the P's that make up P³ Thinking: Purposeful, Productive, and Possibility thinking. In the final section, specific strategies are provided for coaches to teach P³ Thinking to their athletes.

What is P³ Thinking?

P³ Thinking is a mental training tool designed to help athletes think better. It is a way of thinking that focuses on three important P-words: Purposeful, Productive, and Possibility. That is, thinking is effective if it is purposeful, productive, and focused on possibilities. In Figure 10.1, the three keys to P³ Thinking are shown on the left. The three R's that make up R³ Thinking are shown to the right of the three P's. Each R represents a destructive thinking alternative to each of the P's listed to the left. The main premise of Figure 10.1 is that athletes, like all of us, should focus on P³ Thinking, and should avoid the destructive aspects of R³ Thinking.

So, what is P³ Thinking and why is it preferred over R³ Thinking? The first P stands for Purposeful, which means athletes must learn to be intentional and deliberate in how they think about themselves and their sport performance. Athletes who do not think well engage in Random Thinking, leaving their thinking up to chance and hoping that they will magically and automatically engage in the right thoughts at the right time. The second P is Productive Thinking, which means athletes' thoughts are proactive, rational, and facilitative, *no matter what the situation*. A common problem in sport is Reactive Thinking, in which athletes fail to control negative thoughts, base their thinking on irrational beliefs, or allow distractions and performance errors to dictate the way they think. Choking, one of the most dreaded mental glitches in sport, is the result of Reactive Thinking.

The third P in P³ is Possibility Thinking, or thinking that is not restricted by the current status

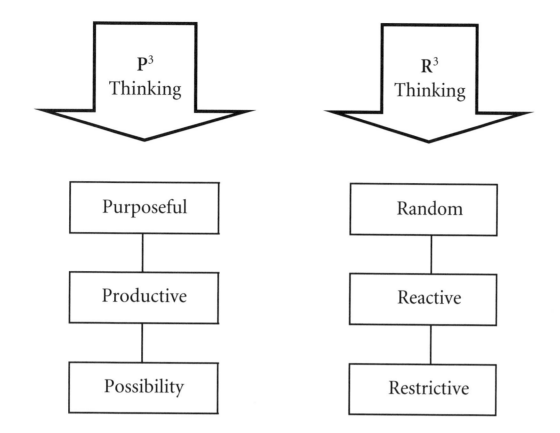

Figure 10.1 P³ vs. R³ Thinking

quo or the limitations of popular thinking. Historical accounts of great thinkers in the world demonstrate one common thread to their thinking—they bucked the status quo in going beyond the comfortable, accepted thoughts and beliefs of their times to think of innovative possibilities. As shown in Figure 10.1, the opposite of Possibility Thinking is Restrictive Thinking, in which people limit themselves without even realizing it. Dick Fosbury remained steadfast in his thinking that the new high-jump technique he developed was superior to the traditional straddle and scissors jumping styles of his time, despite the attempts by many coaches and other experts who attempted to talk him out of it. Today, all high jumpers in the world use the "Fosbury flop" technique, which was the result of Possibility Thinking.

Each of the three P's are necessary for P³ Thinking to work. Purposeful thoughts are only effective if they are Productive in nature. Purposeful and Productive thoughts need the key element of Possibility thinking to ensure that athletes are "pushing the en-

velope" to engage in unrestricted goal mapping. Thus, each P represents a key aspect of the P³ formula for effective, managed thinking. P³ Thinking is not automatic, it is difficult, and it takes time to master. Athletes have ingrained thinking habits, and the first step in P³ Thinking is for them to listen to their thoughts to understand how and when they are P³ as well as how and when they are R³. Once they gain some awareness about their thinking, then they can use the strategies offered in this chapter to enhance their thinking. Your challenge as a coach is to help your athletes commit to P³ Thinking, and then to help them engage in the mental training practice that it takes to become a habitual P³ thinker. Why? Because without a doubt, P³ Thinkers have the Inner Edge!

Purposeful Thinking

In this section, Purposeful Thinking is discussed as the first key characteristic in P³ Thinking. Purposeful Thinking requires athletes to know *what* they should think about and *when* they should think about it, and to develop the skills to engage in Purposeful Thinking despite pressure and distractions. It is helpful to begin by considering why athletes, and all of us, tend *not* to think "on purpose."

Why Athletes Don't Think "On Purpose"

Athletes go to amazing lengths to be purposeful about their physical training. They engage in specific strength and endurance training, carefully taper their physical training prior to competition, and painstakingly ingest certain foods and liquids prior to competition. Why, then, are they not as purposeful in planning how they will *think* prior to and during competition? Probably the biggest reason is that athletes, like most of us, believe that their thoughts are involuntary and just "happen." Because their specific patterns of thinking are automatic and habitual, they accept that their thoughts occur spontaneously and involuntarily. So the first reason athletes don't think on purpose is that they take thinking for granted as something that "just happens" as opposed to something they should plan and work to control.

The second reason that athletes don't think "on purpose" is that they don't know what to think about! Coaches are not helpful in this regard when they tell athletes to "think out there," "get your head in the game," or "come on, concentrate!" Athletes may not know *what* to think about or *how* to get their head in the game, and they may *try* to concentrate but fail because they don't know what to concentrate on! Another popular piece of advice given to athletes is "Don't think." What is really meant by this phrase is "Make your thinking automatic and focused," but athletes often misinterpret this advice and try to think about nothing. Have you ever tried to think about nothing? Try it right now—for the next few seconds empty your mind and think about nothing at all. How effective were you? Unless you're under the influence of a powerful drug, it is impossible to think about nothing! So it's not very helpful advice for athletes.

What might be helpful to them is specific advice on how to think and what to think about. Athletes don't concentrate in sport—they concentrate *on* something. So instead of admonishing your baseball pitcher to "concentrate," remind him to work one pitch at a time and funnel his attention on the catcher's mitt. A big part of mental training involves planning and practicing what to think about and how and when to think specific thoughts that are helpful to each athlete's performance. Many athletes learn this through trial and error, but high-level athletes do this systematically as part of their mental training. Research has shown the Olympic medalists had highly developed purposeful thinking plans and techniques for dealing with distractions, while non-medalists were less purposeful in their thinking or abandoned their thinking plans under pressure (Gould et al., 1992a, 1992b; Gould et al., 1999; Greenleaf et al., 2001).

The third reason that athletes don't "think on purpose" is that they allow the events in the environment to dictate how they think and feel. Thinking "on purpose" becomes much more difficult in the pressure of competition. Pressure leads to poor thinking by inducing worry, focus on distractions or outcomes, concern with mistakes, and fear of failure. Mentally skilled athletes have learned to manage their thoughts and feelings, no matter what is occurring in the environment. This is very difficult, but it can be learned through a strong commitment

© Eyewire Images

to mental practice. Mental skill or mental toughness is the result of P³ Thinking that has been consistently practiced to become automatic and natural. Challenge your athletes by saying, "You can allow the events in your lives to control your thinking, or you can choose to think in ways to control the events in your lives." Strongly recommend the second option to them!

Why Athletes Should Think "On Purpose"

Does Purposeful Thinking really help athletes perform better? The answer is yes, and coaches know this because they teach Purposeful Thinking every day! The term self-talk is used in the field of sport psychology as a synonym for athletes' thoughts. However, unlike imagery in which athletes' thoughts occur in sensory images, **self-talk** is *a verbal dialogue in which athletes interpret their feelings and perceptions, evaluate themselves, and give themselves instructions or reinforcement* (Hackfort & Schwenkmezger, 1993). So technically, self-talk refers to verbal thoughts (the "voice in your head") or what you say out loud to yourself, but for the practical purposes of this book, P³ Thinking may and should incorporate imagery as a way of thinking as well. In this chapter, we'll focus on verbal thoughts (self-talk) when describing P³ Thinking, but keep in mind that the four mental training tools presented in the book (goal mapping, imagery, P³ Thinking, physical relaxation) become automatically integrated in mental training.

Coaches are probably most familiar with using self-talk to help athletes learn and refine sport skills. In this use of self-talk, athletes repeat cue words or phrases to program their minds to produce the correct motor patterns for the skill they are performing

(e.g., "throw your hands," "square up," "bow and arrow"). Research has demonstrated that self-talk used to focus attention on task-relevant cues has enhanced learning and/or performance in golf, bowling, tennis, figure skating, track and field, skiing, diving, and basketball (e.g., Hardy, Gammage, & Hall, 2001; Perkos, Theodorakis, & Chroni, 2002). High school distance runners who listened to an audiotape containing personalized scripts of running technique and motivational statements performed better than runners who either listened to music or used no self-talk strategy (Miller & Donohue, 2003). Another interesting study demonstrated that using positively worded performance reminders at the end of brief rest intervals enabled athletes to perform better than athletes who viewed negatively worded performance reminders or athletes who did not view any performance reminders (Wrisberg & Anshel, 1997). For athletes who are encouraged to engage in systematic self-talk, this research indicates that focusing on positive performance reminders helps them perform better after periods of inactivity (time outs, rest periods, coming off the bench).

Systematic self-talk has also been shown to enhance athletes' confidence and motivation, so it is useful in improving mental skills as well as physical skills. One of the most common coping strategies used by U.S. national champion figure skaters was rational thinking and self-talk (Gould, Finch, & Jackson, 1993). In Table 10.1, a menu of the ways in which athletes can use self-talk as a form of Purposeful Thinking is provided, along with an example self-statement or thought for each. Research has substantiated that athletes use self-talk for all of the reasons listed in Table 10.1 (Hardy et al., 2001).

Table 10.1 Menu of Uses for Self-Talk (Purposeful Thinking) and Example Statements

Use	Example Statement
skill development and execution	"Turn in a barrel"
strategy	"One pitch at a time"
psych up for emotion and effort	"Be strong—I can do it!"
relaxation and calm down	"Slow down—deep breath"
self-evaluation/self-reinforcement	"Nice recovery on that hole—I'm tough"
focus	"Steady, strong, soft over the rim"
confidence	"I'm the best—let it happen"

However, task-specific self-talk for the purpose of skill development and execution has been shown to be the most effective in enhancing performance (Rushall, Hall, Roux, Sasseville, & Rushall, 1988; Rushall & Shewchuk, 1989).

Can Purposeful Thinking Ever Hurt Athletes' Performance?

Many athletes will tell you that they perform better when they're not thinking. Actually, they *are* thinking, even when they believe they are not. It's just that their thoughts are occurring automatically without any need for conscious control. Automatic thinking occurs when athletes are in "the zone," or the state of flow that we discussed in Chapter 1. Athletes feel invincible in the zone by performing on "automatic pilot," feeling in complete control, and thinking and performing effortlessly. Why, then, do they need Purposeful Thinking? If flow occurs when they're not thinking "on purpose," then shouldn't they avoid Purposeful Thinking? The answer is no, because it is rare for athletes to perform in the zone where their thinking is automatic and effortless. It's great when this happens, and when it does, conscious Purposeful Thinking isn't needed—it just happens automatically! However, athletes spend the vast majority of their competition time *not* in the zone or at least attempting to *get* into the zone. That is why they need Purposeful Thinking! Purposeful Thinking can help put them in the position to allow flow to occur, which is a much more proactive mental approach than hoping that one's Random Thinking will lead to flow.

There is some research that indicates that purposeful efforts to NOT think about something, in fact, causes athletes to think about the one thing they're trying not to think about (Wegner, 1994; see Clipboard below). As discussed previously, it is hard to "clear your mind" and not think about something. Also, when athletes are under the stress of competition, they are even more susceptible to thinking unwanted thoughts, and the more they try to purposely "clear their minds," the more the unwanted thoughts pop up (Wegner, 1994). Doesn't this indicate that Purposeful Thinking can be harmful? The answer is no, with one key qualification.

The key to Purposeful Thinking is for athletes to identify in advance the exact thinking or replacement thoughts that they will use to suppress their negative thoughts. Indeed, that is what Purposeful Thinking is! Research shows that when athletes focus on preplanned specific thoughts or cue words to combat negative thinking, they are much more likely to be successful in eliminating the negative thoughts than if they simply try to clear their minds or not think about it (Dugdale & Eklund, 2002). Thus, Purposeful Thinking is an effective mental strategy if done correctly by planning, practicing, and making P³ thoughts as habitual and automatic as possible.

Clipboard

Isn't It Ironic? Beware the White Bear

The theory of ironic processes of mental control (Wegner, 1994) provides insight into why Purposeful Thinking is so difficult. **Ironic processes** refer to *the tendency for athletes to think in ways that are opposite to the way that they intend to think.* That is, by deliberately attempting to suppress a negative thought, athletes can become preoccupied with the very negative thought they're trying to avoid! According to the theory of ironic processes of mental control, the tendency to experience ironic processes is greatest when individuals are in mentally demanding situations that require focused concentration. Thus, it seems likely that the mentally demanding nature of sport may cause athletes to be susceptible to ironic processes (Janelle, 1999).

The famous "white bear" study tested the theory of ironic processes of mental control by seeing how many times people who were told not to think about a white bear did so under different conditions (Wegner, Schneider, Carter, & White, 1987). Some were told to think about a white bear, some were told to NOT think about a white bear (suppress this thought), and some were told to distract themselves from thinking about a white bear. Those who tried to suppress it (DON'T think about it) actually thought more about the white bear than any other group, particular in mentally demanding situations. This same finding occurred in research asking individuals to NOT think about the umpires and to NOT putt a golf ball past the cup. As you might expect, individuals told NOT to think about the umpires thought about them more than the other groups, and those told NOT to putt the ball past the cup of course did so more than others, particular when attentional demands were increased (Dugdale & Eklund, 2002; Wegner, Ansfield, & Pilloff, 1998).

What does this research mean for coaches? First, athletes should refrain from trying to NOT do something (e.g., volleyball player saying, "Don't blow this pass"). If they have thoughts about what NOT to do, they should immediately "let go" of these thoughts and run through their minds the correct movements they wish to make. Athletes should see and think about what they want to happen, not what they fear or hope won't happen. Tell athletes not to "freak out" about having the negative thoughts—we all do. The key is to not allow them to linger in their minds prior to performance. Athletes should allow the negative thought to "pass through," focus on a task-relevant cue, and then perform. The volleyball player mentioned above should shake off the thought about not blowing the pass, and cue herself in (e.g., "stay low, meet the ball") for an effective pass to the setter. Help athletes learn task-relevant thinking for key situations, and insist that they practice this thinking in training sessions to make it as automatic as possible. Athletes should also use imagery to visualize the perfect response they will make, and replace any negative images with correct ones. Second, coaches should also be thoughtful in their communication with athletes and avoid "negative coaching," or telling athletes what NOT to do. Instead of saying "Don't pop up," say "Cut the ball in half!" provide specific feedback, instructions, and encouragement that locks in the mental picture of what the athlete *should* do.

A third strategy for coaches is to use what Janelle (1999) calls a "paradoxical intervention"—meaning it seems contradictory to common sense! The idea is to focus on the unwanted thoughts—to give them your attention—which may work according to the theory by reducing their threatening nature (reversing the ironic process). For example, I find it extremely helpful to have athletes think about the pressure they're feeling, to drink it in, to make friends with it, to believe it can become their ally. The idea is to get them used to pressure, and to begin thinking that pressure is good, that they perform better with it, and even though it doesn't always feel good, it is a necessary part of competitive excellence. This type of paradoxical thinking has not been supported by research, but I find it helps those athletes who simply cannot replace their negative thoughts. So, go with the pressure and use it, instead of desperately trying to get rid of the feeling.

Tell your athletes the white bear story so they understand that effective thinking is much more than simply trying NOT to think about something. To keep the white bear in check, help them learn brief mental focus words or phrases that cue them in to what they should be thinking about. Thinking "on purpose" helps keep the white bear away!

Summary: Purposeful Thinking as the First P

In studying several extraordinary people of the 20th century, Howard Gardner (1998) found that they spent significant time in their lives engaging in Purposeful Thinking. They were reflective, spent time thinking about what they were trying to achieve, and continuously evaluated their progress. None of these individuals operated on blind faith or automatic pilot. Instead, they engaged in Purposeful Thinking so as not to waste the opportunities that life presented to them.

As the first P in P³ Thinking, Productive Thinking requires discipline, commitment, and planning. It requires athletes to overcome life-long thinking habits and to practice intentional thinking until it becomes automatic and bulletproof under competitive pressure. Purposeful Thinking is disciplined thinking, and it works when athletes become mentally tough enough to use their thoughts to control what happens in their world, instead of letting what happens in their world control their thoughts.

Quotable Quote

"Keep your mind off the things you don't want by keeping it on the things you do want." W. Clement Stone

Productive Thinking

The second P in P³ Thinking stands for Productive Thinking (see Figure 10.1). Productive Thinking builds on Purposeful Thinking by helping athletes understand how to productively think "on purpose."

Productive thoughts are those that help athletes fulfill the goals of the sport psychology triad discussed in Chapters 1 and 2 (achieve optimal performance, development, and experiences in sport). I've never been big on telling athletes they should think "positively," because as an athlete I resented people telling me to be positive when I didn't feel like it. "Positive" has a Pollyana connotation to it, meaning that it sounds falsely naive and unrealistically cheerful. In fact, research has shown that athletes' self-talk is very personal and individualistic, and what is often perceived as "negative" self-talk by athletes can be very motivational for some individuals (Van Raalte, Cornelius, Brewer, & Hatten, 2000). However, athletes should not use this as an excuse for their uncontrollable emotional outbursts, without doing the self-reflective work required to truly understand what is productive thinking and feeling for them.

Choose to RESPOND

Productive Thinking means that athletes *choose to respond*, as opposed to simply reacting. Reacting usually involves "hot thoughts," or thinking that is emotionally driven and counter-productive (Ellis & Harper, 1997). Responding represents "cool thinking," which is relatively calm, less biased, and more reflective than hot thoughts. Reactive Thinking occurs because athletes allow the competitive environment to control them, while responding involves the important step of using mental skill to interpret and manage the competitive environment in advantageous ways. Bob Rotella (1995) recounts the productive thinking of Tom Watson in the 1982 U.S. Open. Watson, who went on to win the Open, missed a straight-on two-foot putt on the seventh hole on the last day of the tournament. On the next hole, he made an 18-footer for birdie, which put him back into a tie for the lead. Rotella recalls how Watson *chose to respond* to missing such an easy putt in such a big tournament: "He told me that his miss only showed that even great putters miss an occasional easy one. He acknowledged that it was disappointing and unfortunate to miss one in the final round of the U.S. Open. But he reminded himself that if he wanted to continue to be a great putter, he had to give himself a chance on the next hole and the ones after that" (Rotella, 1995, p. 163).

Athletes need to understand that they have responsibility, or response-ability, which is the ability to choose their responses (Covey, 1989). One of the biggest myths about human behavior is that the things that happen to us cause our reactions. This is completely false, because humans have the ultimate capacity to think, and thinking serves as the mediator between stimuli (bad call by the referee) and our responses (cursing the referee and receiving a technical foul). I repeatedly tell athletes that what happens to you is not near as important as how you *respond* to what happens to you. Athletes must learn that their response-ability is their responsibility! Another "ability" related to productive thinking is coachability, or the quality in athletes that enables them to absorb teaching and mentoring from their coaches. Actually, coachability is a thinking skill because it is an attitude or mindset that says, "No matter how much I know (or think I know), I can learn from this situation." Productive Thinking allows athletes to be coachable, and more broadly teachable, to always be open to and hunger for insight and knowledge.

Productive Thinking also requires athletes to accept that they will have negative thoughts. The greatest athletes in the world have occasional negative thoughts, but they don't focus on these thoughts or allow them to remain in their minds for long. They key is not to store negative thoughts away, to give them your attention, or to allow them to remain in your mind. Athletes should let their negative thoughts "pass through" their minds, and then immediately focus on a Purposeful, Productive thought. Thus, part of Productive Thinking is to engage in productive responses to negative or anxious thoughts.

Characteristics of Productive Thoughts

So what makes thoughts Productive? Coaches and athletes should consider four key characteristics of Productive thoughts.

Focused on the present. First, Productive thoughts are focused on the present. Athletes should "stay in the present" or "be in the now" in their thinking. Anxiety, choking, overconfidence—all of these things occur in sport when athletes either are thinking about the past or the future. Wherever you are—be there (Maxwell, 2002)! Larry Mize, professional golfer, states this as his goal: "I'm trying to stay in the present tense. Be mentally tough. Don't get ahead of yourself. And enjoy playing golf. You're not

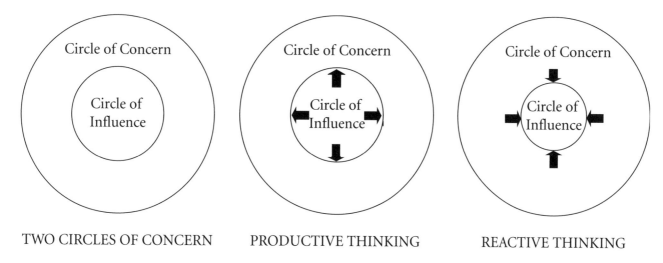

TWO CIRCLES OF CONCERN   PRODUCTIVE THINKING   REACTIVE THINKING

Figure 10.2 Productive thinking means expanding your Circle of Influence

going to hit every shot perfect, so you need to be in a frame of mind to be able to enjoy playing the trouble shots." Now that's Productive Thinking!

Quotable Quote

"Confine yourself to the present."
Marcus Aurelius

Personally controllable. A second characteristic of Productive thoughts is that they are personally controllable. In Chapter 8, we talked about how outcome (milestone), performance (challenge), and process (focus) goals are all useful in athletes' goal maps. An outcome goal of winning the conference championship in the 400 meters might be very motivational in training and preparation, but can be very anxiety-provoking the day of the race. At the time of competition, athletes should focus on performance and process goals that are within their personal control. Remember the quote by Picabo Street at the beginning of the chapter—she focused on skiing fast, not winning races. Skiing fast was within her personal control, and it was also a Productive thought.

To be Productive thinkers, athletes should focus their thoughts within their "Circle of Influence," as opposed to their "Circle of Concern" (Covey, 1989). As shown in Figure 10.2, we have two circles that represent where we choose to focus our thoughts. Our Circle of Concern contains the things in our

lives in which we're mentally and emotionally involved (e.g., our health, our families, winning the championship, problems with teammates). Our Circle of Influence contains those things in our lives over which we have some degree of control.

When we engage in Productive Thinking, we focus our attention and efforts on our Circle of Influence, or the things over which we have some control and can do something about. Productive Thinking enlarges our Circle of Influence in relation to our Circle of Concern (the middle circle in Figure 10.2). When we engage in Reactive Thinking, we focus our thoughts on our Circle of Concern and problems and circumstances over which we have no control. Reactive Thinking shrinks our Circle of Influence and increases our focus on events and issues in our Circle of Concern over which we lack control (the far right circle in Figure 10.2). Athletes should attempt to focus on how they can *influence* the conditions that cause them to think negatively, instead of worrying about the conditions themselves. Following is an example of an athlete thinking productively to enlarge his Circle of Influence, as opposed to reacting to uncontrollable factors in his Circle of Concern:

Jason was very concerned about performing in the high jump at the regional track meet. He was worried about how his opponents would do, the forecasted rainy weather, and the fact that all of his family and friends would be at the meet watching him (Circle of Concern). These were all legitimate concerns. However,

Jason mentally prepared for the meet by focusing on his Circle of Influence. He focused on the fact that he had trained tirelessly, even in wet and cold weather, thus he was prepared to execute in whatever conditions were present. He allowed his thoughts about his opponents to "pass through" his mind, and quickly replaced these thoughts using trigger words to emphasize proper form ("calm mind, explosive legs; deliberate approach, strong PLANT; EXPLODE; and kick out for an extra inch"). He engaged in repetitive mental practice in which he visualized his jump technique using his trigger words. He also visualized missing at certain heights, and then practiced his Purposeful and Productive Thinking that prepared him for his next jump after the miss. He planned Productive, Purposeful Thinking for the time he would spend waiting between jumps. He chose to view the pressure from his family and friends watching him as an extra source of energy and inspiration, focused on enjoying the attention, and used it to energize easily. He focused on the unconditional love and acceptance that he receives from his family and friends, and reminded himself that how he performs as an athlete has nothing to do with that. Finally, Jason reminded himself to expect anything and everything, and to think productively NO MATTER WHAT happened at the meet. He chose to think on purpose and productively, and thus expanded his Circle of Influence to shrink his Circle of Concern.

Task-related. The third characteristic of Productive thoughts is that they are performance-specific and task-related. The best thoughts to trigger good performance are brief verbal triggers or cues that create a clear picture and feeling of perfect performance. Coaches can help athletes identify the right verbal cues to lock in automatic execution of skills. These cues should be brief and simple, such as the triggers used by the high jumper in the previous example ("explosive legs," "strong and deliberate approach"). The trigger words can be integrated into vivid performance images, such as feeling "coiled like a spring" in the starting blocks ready to "explode" and "drive low" into a full sprint to the finish line. Whenever negative thoughts creep in just prior to performance, athletes should simply go over in

their minds what they will do, using preplanned trigger words and strong images of perfect performance.

Personally relevant. The fourth characteristic of Productive thoughts is that they are personally meaningful and relevant for each athlete. A collegiate volleyball player once told me that, in warm-ups prior to each match, she liked to think about how her teammates were counting on her and how she couldn't let them down. My initial thought was that this wasn't a particularly good thing to think about, but she explained that the thought really energized her and focused her in the warm-up period. She liked feeling the pressure and responsibility of playing well for her teammates. Thus, this thought was productive for this athlete, although for someone else the pressure could be Reactive and negative.

Personal Plug-In

For each of the following situations, identify a Productive Thinking response for an athlete:
- Athlete receives unjustified criticism from the coach
- Bus breaks down and the team is late for competition
- An athlete starts out competition playing badly
- An athlete is returning to competition for the first time after a serious injury

Countering to Defeat Irrational Thinking by Athletes

We've established that Productive Thinking requires athletes to respond with cool thinking, as opposed to reacting with hot thoughts. We've also identified some key characteristics of Productive thoughts. However, some athletes will continue to engage in negative thinking despite your best efforts to get them thinking more purposefully and productively. These athletes have deeply ingrained belief systems that create self-defeating and irrational thoughts, without them even realizing it. To help these athletes become better thinkers, coaches have to help them make profound, philosophical changes in how they think about the world, their sport, other people, and their performance.

The ABCs of REBT. Although coaches aren't therapists, you can help athletes think better by understanding Rational Emotive Behavior Therapy, or

REBT (Ellis, 1996). REBT attempts to help people become more rational and productive in their thinking by challenging their dysfunctional philosophies, which lead to Reactive Thinking. Here are the ABCs of REBT:

A   Athletes encounter Adversity or an Activating Event that blocks the pursuit of their goals.

B   Athletes' Beliefs influence them to interpret the Adversity or Activating Event in a particular way (these Beliefs may be rational or irrational).

C   Athletes experience both behavioral and emotional Consequences as the result of their Beliefs (these Consequences may be appropriate/healthy or inappropriate/unhealthy).

Athletes, like all of us, typically believe that A causes C. When a figure skater performs poorly in an important competition (A), she feels depressed and despondent (C). When an ice hockey player is slashed by an opponent (A), he drops his gloves, instigates a fight, and is penalized (C). Both of these athletes would tell you that they reacted the way they did (C)

Table 10.2 Irrational vs. Rational Beliefs and Consequences
(adapted from Ellis, 1996)

Example 1: Rational Thinking, Feeling, and Acting (Productive)
Adversity or Activating Event
- Athlete misses free throw at end of the game and team loses.

Rational (Productive) Beliefs
- How frustrating and demoralizing!
- I feel like I let the team down.
- What a horrible time to miss!

Rational Emotional Consequences (appropriate bad feelings)
- Embarrassment, sorrow, frustration, regret

Rational Behavioral Consequences (Productive behaviors)
- Ask coach for more practice in pressure situations
- Remind self that Michael Jordan missed more crucial shots than he made—but still wanted to take them ("Be like Mike—I want the ball!")
- Continue normal practice routine and pre-shot routine (focus on all my makes, not on one miss)

Example 2: Irrational Thinking, Feeling, and Acting (Reactive)
Adversity or Activating Event
- Athlete misses free throw at end of the game and team loses.

Irrational (Reactive) Beliefs
- I'm a choker.
- I should never miss in that situation.
- I'll never be a clutch shooter.
- I'm devastated and can't face my teammates.

Irrational Emotional Consequences (inappropriate bad feelings)
- Depression, feeling worthless, unaccepted by teammates, ridiculed

Irrational Behavioral Consequences (Reactive behaviors)
- Less aggressive on offense to avoid going to the free throw line
- Develops free throw shooting slump due to lack of confidence and focus

because of the situation (A). The figure skater would say: "I blew it when it counted—don't you understand?" The hockey player would say, "Of course I decked the guy—he slashed me!" Actually, both of these athletes reacted based on their B's or Beliefs about the situation and the world. And, as Ellis (1996) emphasizes, faulty beliefs based on dysfunctional philosophies are what creates negative consequences for us. That is, A contributes to C, but A does not exclusively "cause" C. B interacts with A to bring about C. To become a better thinker, athletes must come to grips with their B's, especially those B's that are Reactive, irrational, and self-defeating.

Quotable Quote

"[People] are disturbed not by things that happen, but by their opinion of the things that happen". **Epictetus**

Healthy vs. unhealthy beliefs and consequences. What is actually meant by the term "rational" in REBT? Rational refers to "what leads to good or beneficial results" or "what is effective and sensible for you" (Ellis, 1996). Beliefs and Consequences are rational if they are "normal" and helpful to athletes in reaching their goals. Beliefs and Consequences are irrational if they prevent athletes from achieving their goals. Thus, irrational beliefs are inefficient and Reactive. However, this doesn't mean that irrational beliefs are negative and rational beliefs are positive. What distinguishes rational from irrational is the degree to which the athlete uses rigid and absolute language such as *should, must, have to, never, always,* or *can't stand it.* The figure skater in the above example is depressed and despondent because she believes she must perform well. The hockey player decked his opponent because he believed that others must treat him nicely at all times. Irrational thinking is full of demands. Rational thinking, as a form of Productive Thinking, is about preferences, or what athletes want to happen.

An example of rational (Productive) as opposed to irrational (Reactive) thinking, feeling, and acting is shown in Table 10.2. In Example 1 (Productive Thinking), the player who missed the free throw feels badly, is highly frustrated, demoralized, and feels like he let his team down. These are very normal and rational thoughts! He is embarrassed, frustrated, regretful, and probably pretty darn mad at himself. Although the player doesn't feel particularly good or positive, these thoughts and feelings are highly rational and productive, and they lead him to engage in self-helping, productive behaviors such as practicing more in pressure situations, reminding himself to stay aggressive, and focusing on the fact that he is a good free throw shooter who unfortunately missed a big shot.

Now notice the difference in the thinking, feelings, and actions of the athlete in Example 2. The athlete ascribes permanence ("I'm a choker" and "I'm not a clutch shooter") to one episode of behavior, rather than seeing it as temporary and changeable. He believes he *should never* miss. Of course he's not happy that he missed, but to believe that you should *never* miss in this situation is unrealistic and irrational. Based on these thoughts, the player feels devastated, worthless, and ridiculed. These feelings lead to the Reactive behaviors of avoiding going to the free throw line and developing a shooting slump.

Clipboard

Seeing Life Like It Is: Temporary—Not Permanent!

One key aspect of Productive Thinking is to view setbacks and performance difficulties as temporary, not permanent. Consider the words of John Naber, winner of four Olympic gold medals in swimming (1999, p. 58): "To awaken the Olympian in each of us, we have to look at negative evidence as temporary. Just because I can't swim the 100 meters in less than a minute doesn't mean I'll never do so. Just because this job seems beyond me now doesn't mean it always will be."

Similarly, consider the Productive Thinking practiced by gymnast Kim Zmeskal at the 1991 U.S. National Championship meet. In warming up for her uneven bars routine, she fell three times on a critical release move. Tim Daggett, fellow U.S. gymnast, witnessed what happened (1999, p. 147): "Minutes before she attempted to become the best in the country, she could not make the move work. She struggled . . . and just couldn't do it. But that didn't mandate that she would fall in competition. A gymnast with less desire would have let the falls . . . take away her confidence, but not Kim. At the end of the day, Kim Zmeskal was crowned the best performer in the country on that apparatus, earning her first-ever national title. Her difficulty in the warm-up was real, but she refused to see it as permanent."

The three most common irrational beliefs, or dysfunctional philosophies, held by athletes are as follows (adapted from Ellis, 1996):

1. I must/have to perform perfectly (or well).
2. You (coaches, teammates, opponents, officials) must always treat me nicely and fairly.
3. Training and competition conditions must always be favorable for me.

These beliefs occur frequently in sport, because our society (media, fans, parents) creates unrealistic expectations for athletes. Sport performance is so glorified that young athletes quickly learn that they gain unparalleled status, attention, and rewards simply by performing well in a game. They lose sight of the fact that it is a game, and that it is irrational to believe that they should always perform perfectly, be treated exactly like they want, and that things should always go their way. Thus athletes learn to think in certain ways based on powerful messages they receive from a sports-crazed, perfectionist, winning-obsessed, unrealistic society. So it's not entirely their fault that they've developed Reactive Thinking patterns. However, it is their responsibility to develop the mental skills and toughness required to think productively, if they want to be successful. And as their coach, you are in the perfect position to help them recognize and change their irrational or Reactive thinking into Productive Thinking.

Countering athletes' irrational thinking. If athletes want to think better, they must make profound philosophical changes in the way they view their world. Specifically, they must give up their rigid, self-defeating thoughts that focus on how they never or always should do things (e.g., *never* lose, *always* play perfect, *must* win). Because athletes created their irrational thinking patterns, they have the ability to reshape them into Productive Thinking patterns. But this takes work as they must observe, analyze, dispute, and modify their Reactive thoughts. A tough job—

but doable! This is where countering comes in as a way to break down irrational and Reactive Thinking to move toward more Productive Thinking.

Countering involves *using productive reasoning to refute the underlying irrational assumptions that lead to negative thinking.* Countering can be practiced by athletes in an internal dialogue, and it also can occur in conversations between athletes and coaches. To add to the ABCs of REBT, countering requires the addition of D and E. D stands for Disputing, which leads to E, or an Effective new philosophy or way of thinking (Ellis, 1996).

> ## Personal Plug-In
> Identify several irrational (or Reactive) beliefs often held by athletes. Remember that these beliefs may have been developed by society's attitudes, norms, and values. Consider why each of these beliefs is so powerful and why athletes have learned to automatically accept each belief as truth.

Athletes (and their coaches) must logically argue against their irrational thoughts and change them to more functional, Productive thoughts. Here are some Disputing questions that could be applied to athletes: "Am I really a worthless person if I don't win?", "Is this championship really the most important thing in my life?", "Do I *have* to win, or do I just want to win very badly?", and "Do I really believe that the umpires will *always* make perfect calls that turn out in my favor?" Other more general Disputing questions include "Is it helpful for you to think this way?" or "How is continuing to think this way affecting your life?"

Athletes are known for believing that things "aren't fair," describing such Activating Events as poor calls by officials, biased judging in gymnastics or skating, or adverse weather conditions on the one day they're scheduled for the downhill at the Olympics. As a coach, I'm sure you've responded at some point in your career by saying, "Life isn't fair." That's exactly right. To assume that human sports officials will never make mistakes, that environmental conditions will always be favorable to you, and that you will always be fairly judged is irrational! It just isn't so. In fact, experienced Olympic athletes understand that medaling at the Olympic Games

takes a great deal of talent, preparation, persistence in the face of obstacles, and luck (Gould et al., 2001). Yes, luck. These athletes understand that many factors beyond their control (Circle of Influence) affect their medal chances, so they rationally and productively focus on what is within their control.

The driving force behind Disputing as a method of countering is that athletes need to be pushed to question the beliefs they have developed throughout their lives. Once our beliefs become ingrained, we rarely question them even though they may be illogical and self-defeating. As discussed in Chapter 4, coaches need to communicate with athletes in ways that enable them to identify irrational or reactive thoughts or beliefs. Using the D (Disputing) to follow the ABCs in REBT then leads to E, or Effective new thoughts, feelings, and behaviors.

No matter how much athletes might try to think better by superficially "parroting" productive statements, if their underlying thinking is dysfunctional, they'll never be able to undo their Reactive Thinking and move to Productive Thinking. Research has supported REBT as an effective intervention in hundreds of studies published in psychology literature (Ellis, 1996). Research has shown that REBT can effectively reduce precompetitive anxiety in gymnasts (Elkko & Ostrow, 1991) and, as part of a comprehensive Productive Thinking intervention with golfers, enhance emotional control and improve performance (Kirschenbaum, Owens, & O'Connor, 1998). Overall, REBT provides a practical strategy to help athletes understand why they think ineffectively, and to move them toward more Productive Thinking.

Summary: Productive Thinking as the Second P

During the night after the terrorist attacks of September 11, 2001, New York city mayor Rudy Giuliani chose to read about how former British Prime Minister Winston Churchill helped the people of England rally in the face of the Nazi terror bombings of London. Giuliani was searching for the inspiration and insight he needed to help the people of New York think in the most Productive way possible about the surreal shock and horrendous loss of life that resulted from the attacks. Mayor Giuliani understood the importance of instilling confidence and hope in the face of fear and despair, so he used his leadership position to encourage Productive Thinking at a critical time in U.S. history.

Successful people not only think on purpose, they think productively on purpose. They "frame" their failures by thinking "What can I learn from this?" and "How can this help me?" Ask your athletes to become more Productive in their thinking. Help them learn what it means to respond with Productive Thinking as opposed to reacting with Reactive Thinking. Challenge them to choose to think well, because thinking well is a choice and is completely under their control. I've always loved Eleanor Roosevelt's point that "no one can make you feel inferior without your permission." Actually, no one can make you feel anything without your permission! What athletes think about and how they choose to respond to what happens to them in sport largely determines how successful they will be and how enjoyable the sport experience will be for them. Urge them to make the right choice!

Possibility Thinking

The third P in P³ Thinking stands for Possibility Thinking (see Figure 10.1). Possibility joins Purposeful and Productive to complete the P³ formula. Possibility Thinking is what it sounds like—focusing on the possibilities, seeing what you want to and hope will happen, and opening your mind to see beyond the status quo. On May 6, 1954, Roger Bannister ran the first sub-four minute mile in history. Once Bannister broke this time barrier, several other runners quickly followed with sub-four minutes miles as well. The mental, or thinking, barrier that Bannister broke with his historic run was far more important than his breaking of the actual physical record, because it established the possibility in the minds of other runners that a sub-four minute mile was attainable. Possibility Thinking is based on the idea that athletes cannot attain what they cannot see themselves doing.

The opposite of Possibility Thinking is Restrictive Thinking (see Figure 10.1), in which thinking is confined, limiting, and restrained. Here are a few Restrictive Thinking classics from American history (Maxwell, 2003, pp. 165-166):

> *"It is an idle dream to imagine that automobiles will take the place of railways in the long-distance movement of passengers."* American Road Congress, 1913
>
> *"There is no likelihood man can ever tap the power of the atom."* **Robert Millikan,** Nobel Prize winner in physics, 1920
>
> *"There is no reason for any individual to have a computer in their home."* **Ken Olsen,** president of Digital Equipment Corporation, 1977

Obviously, we all enjoy the benefits of automobiles, nuclear power, and computers despite previous Restrictive Thinking about their usefulness. The intent is not to disparage the individuals who made these statements; we all engage in Restrictive Thinking because we all live each day within the current thinking practices of our society. It's hard to look beyond what "is" to see what "can be." Extraordinary people in history who engaged in Possibility Thinking were ridiculed and even killed for the audacity of their thinking. A short list of these people might include Jesus of Nazareth, Martin Luther King, Jr., Lucy B. Anthony, and Patrick Henry. Who are some famous athletes that you consider Possibility thinkers? My list would include Lance Armstrong, Dick Fosbury, Annika Sorenstam, Michael Jordan, and Bonny Warner.

Photo by Cpl. Joe Lindsay, courtesy of USMC

Possibility Thinking completes the P³ Thinking formula, because it adds the important aspect of "what can be" to Purposeful and Productive Thinking. Athletes may think purposefully and productively, but fail to open their mind to the possibilities of their own performance and potential. So without the third P of Possibility Thinking, P³ Thinking is incomplete.

Quotable Quote

"Be realistic: Plan for a miracle."
Bhagwan Shree Rajneesh

Why Possibility Thinking is Important

If you don't believe that Possibility Thinking is important, I urge you to read Martin Seligman's (1998) acclaimed book *Learned Optimism*. Optimism, characterized by believing that defeat is a temporary setback, leads people to try harder, work through obstacles, and look for solutions. On the other hand, pessimists see permanency in bad events, and thus fail to exert effort to effectively manage their lives. Here's what Seligman's (1998, p. 113) research has found:

- Pessimism promotes depression.
- Pessimism produces inertia rather than effort in the face of setbacks.
- Pessimism feels bad (e.g., worried, blue, down, anxious).
- Pessimism is self-fulfilling, because pessimists don't persist when faced with challenges. and therefore fail more frequently.
- Pessimism is related to poor physical health (makes the immune system more passive).

And if these research findings don't get your attention, consider the role of optimism (Possibility Thinking) in sport. By studying the thinking styles of twelve National League baseball teams in 1985-86, Seligman (1998) found that optimistic teams performed better than pessimistic teams. The same result was found for National Basketball Association teams and college swimmers. Seligman (1998) concludes his findings by stating that thinking style (optimism vs. pessimism) predicts how sport teams will do above and beyond their actual talent, and that success is predicted by optimism in the same way that failure is predicted by pessimism.

Another common finding in research examining the psychological characteristics of elite, successful athletes is that they tend to be more preoccupied with their sports in a positive way (Williams & Krane, 2001). That is, these athletes tend to daydream, visualize, and dream about their sport and their performance in very positive ways. This seems to be an indicator of Possibility Thinking, or visualizing what can be in terms of their abilities as athletes. As mentioned at the beginning of this chapter, U.S. Olympic champions were found to be high in optimism and hope, both of which reflect Possibility Thinking in terms of expecting good things to happen and feeling a sense that it will happen (Gould et al., 2002). Research on goal setting has repeatedly shown that difficult goals (think of them as "possibility goals") lead to better performance than easy or moderate goals (Gould, 2001). A great example of a possibility goal is Pia Nilsson's "Vision 54." Nilsson, the Swedish national golf team coach, preaches what she terms "Vision 54," or the belief that an extraordinary round of 18 birdies is possible for her golfers. Although this vision may be seen as idealistic, Annika Sorenstam explains that it enhanced her thinking to enable her to shoot a 59, an extraordinary golf score only attained by two other golfers in competition in history (Sirak, 2003).

A common suggestion in the sport psychology literature is for athletes to set realistic goals (Gould, 2001). However, I never use the word "realistic" with athletes, because I've found it to be amotivational, limiting, and boring. I think goals work when they are audacious and exciting, built upon possibilities. I understand what the research is telling us, which is that athletes should focus on difficult goals, but not so difficult that they are viewed as impossible. If there is no hope of attaining the goal (e.g., playing on the LPGA tour), then the goal is ineffective in driving behavior. However, if athletes have developed their goal maps and are practicing Purposeful and Productive Thinking, then the setting of possibility goals and the motivation of Possibility Thinking will be very effective for them. As a sport psychology consultant, I find limiting goals more of a problem than possibility goals.

Clipboard

Possibility Thinker Bonny Warner

At the age of 14, Bonny Warner wrote down her lifetime goals as part of a school assignment. Her goals were to go to a top college, become an Olympian, work for ABC-TV, obtain her pilot's license, and build a log cabin (Warner, 1999). To give you the bottom line, she attained all her goals. How did she do it? Possibility Thinking. Here are her thoughts on what enabled her to accomplish every single goal:

> "We should expand the list and not limit ourselves to what we know we can do. Mine was a rather 'uninhibited' list, considering the circumstances. As a family, we had no money for such 'dreams' and I was not exactly Olympic caliber in any particular sport. The dream seemed impossible, but is the first step possible? When I accomplished the first step, how much easier the second appeared" (p. 86).

She went to Stanford University on a field hockey scholarship, but then decided to try the luge after watching the Olympic Games on television. She worked in a deli shop to buy a sled, and then flew to Germany on her own to train with the best in the world. The Germans didn't know that she had never done this before, and started her at the top of the hill. Lugers run 80 miles per hour down an ice track with 35-foot banked turns. Warner crashed 52 times in a row learning to ride a sled down a sheet of ice, with her body beaten to a pulp. Here is her description:

> "I was a mess, but bit by bit I learned, finally making it to the finish line on my 53rd try. In luge, if you never crash, then you'll always be afraid of crashing and, as a result, drive the sled too cautiously in competition. In life, too, if we don't fail on occasion, then we're too cautiously choosing our path. Enter the lottery of life now! Don't worry about taking baby steps and don't be afraid of tripping. We really are capable of much more than we think" (p. 90).

Warner competed in the 1984, 1988, and 1992 Olympic Games, earned a degree in broadcast journalism from Stanford, spent years as a commentator/reporter for ABC-TV, and now is a pilot for United Airlines, serving as captain of a Boeing 727 jetliner. Oh, yeah, and she began work on her log cabin in 1999, which if you want to bet, is probably finished by now.

Strategies to Enhance Possibility Thinking

Possibility Thinking, like Purposeful and Productive Thinking, must become habit. It takes reflection and practice, but it is a mental skill that can be developed.

Commit to a possibility attitude. The very first step to enhance Possibility Thinking is to stop focusing on impossibilities, and look for possibilities (Maxwell, 2003). This is a seemingly minor attitude shift, but it is a critical first step. An **attitude** is simply *a way of thinking and feeling that is sustained over time.* So when we say an athlete has a "bad attitude," what we really mean is that he or she is an ineffective thinker. My observation is that athletes with bad attitudes are R³ thinkers who let the events of each day dictate how they think and feel. Instead of telling an athlete that she has a "bad attitude," it may be helpful to engage in conversation with her to help her reflect on the logic of her thinking. Approaching attitude issues as thinking issues gives the coach some concrete ways to help athletes work on the their P³ Thinking skills, as opposed to trying to figure out how they should "change their attitudes."

Use affirmations. One way to practice Possibility Thinking to create a possibility attitude is through the use of affirmations. **Affirmations** are *personal phrases that you repeat over and over to influence your subconscious mind to accept as true.* Affirmations are phrased in the present tense to project to yourself that you are what you intend to be. Affirmation statements should be simple, active, emotive, positive, and stated in the present tense. Examples are "I feel strong and powerful," "I respond with confidence," and "I choose to think well."

One of the most famous affirmations in sport history was Muhammad Ali's repeated use of the phase "I am the greatest!" Of course, he went on to make this statement true. As mentioned in Chapter 7, U.S. speed skater Dan Jansen overcame great adversity and finally won his coveted Olympic gold medal by repeating the affirmation "I love the 1000 meters." Initially, of course, he didn't love this race, but he created an attitude that he needed to feel confident and prepared for the 1000 meter race. He wrote this affirmation on paper and taped it to his bathroom mirror so he would see it and process it repeatedly. Ironically, he won his Olympic gold in the 1000 meters, not his preferred sprint distance of 500 meters.

Affirmations work as a form of Possibility Thinking because over time they create an attitude. By being Purposeful, Productive, and focusing on Possibility in developing affirmations, athletes can create the attitudes that they want. Affirmations are a great tool to practice P³ thinking, and they represent the possibilities of what athletes truly want to be.

Put yourself in a Possibility environment. Possibility Thinking becomes more automatic when you're in an environment conducive to thinking well. Seek out and spend time with people who are Possibility Thinkers, because good thinking, like bad thinking, is contagious. Avoid spending time around or listening to "experts" who are motivated to maintain the status quo because they don't want to stretch their thinking or inconvenience themselves by having to learn more and think differently. Find inspiration and reinforcement for your Possibility Thinking by reading biographies and written accounts of extraordinary people, including master coaches. Learn to enjoy the feeling of discomfort that comes from seeing possibilities and attempting to act on them, instead of maintaining comfortable, yet limiting ways of being. As a coach, instill a Possibility Thinking climate in your athletic program, and talk with athletes about interpersonal guidelines for how they can encourage each other and pursue team goals with a Possibility attitude.

Strategies to Teach P³ Thinking to Athletes

In this final section of the chapter, specific strategies for how to teach P³ Thinking to athletes are provided. The three P's of Purposeful, Productive, and Possibility Thinking are integrated within these strategies, with the overall intent to help athletes become better thinkers.

1. Model P³ Thinking to your athletes at all times.

The Inner Edge is only achieved through consistent, habitual P³ Thinking. You cannot ask your athletes to be mentally skilled if you are not a mentally skilled coach. Mental skill requires good thinking, so the first step for coaches is to model P³ Thinking at all times for your athletes. Being purposeful in practicing effective communication with your athletes (as discussed in Chapter 4) is one way to model effective thinking for them. As discussed in Chapter 5 on leadership, the "stories" that your athletes hear from you each day demonstrate how you think and see the world, and influence how they choose to think about the world.

Avoid being a Reactive or Restrictive Thinking coach. This does not mean that you cannot display emotion, as emotion is often an inspiration or motivation for your athletes. But if you overdo the emotion, it loses its power and you lose credibility with your athletes. Let your athletes see your anger, joy, pride, and sadness when appropriate, but P³ Thinking coaches do not constantly allow their emotions to affect their thinking and the ways in which they communicate their thinking to their athletes. Overall, your thinking and your ability to effectively communicate your thinking to athletes sets the first and most important tone for the development of their P³ Thinking skills.

2. Establish and nurture a P³ Thinking culture in your program.

Coaches usually have guidelines or rules for certain athlete behaviors, such as promptness, effort, and dress codes. I suggest that you also establish guidelines within your team for effective thinking. This might involve a team discussion about P³ Thinking, and then gaining a commitment from athletes to move toward P³ and away from R³ in their self-talk and their communication with others. In Chapter 6, several guidelines were suggested for effective team-building and conflict resolution, and these could be implemented within your team as part of your P³ culture. Goal maps for individuals and the team as a whole might include mental goals as well as physical ones, such as a goal to think and talk Productively during training and competition. You could also suggest a specific focus thought for each training session, such as Purposeful Thinking about exuding confidence or playing with intensity.

3. Normalize the tendency for athletes to experience Reactive and Restrictive thoughts.

This recommendation may sound contradictory to the previous strategy of setting expectations for your athletes to engage in P³ thinking. However, an important part of Productive Thinking is understanding and accepting that you will have negative thoughts, especially at critical times! Coaches should help athletes realize that occasional Reactive or Restrictive Thinking is normal and typical for even the greatest athletes in the world. This normalizing of R³ thoughts helps athletes accept them as inevitable and gives them the confidence to quickly refocus their thinking on P³ thoughts.

4. Ask athletes to complete the P³ Thinking Worksheet so they can specifically identity the P³ thoughts that help them and the R³ thoughts that hurt them.

Athletes should carefully reflect on how they talk to themselves and think in different situations. They need to identify thoughts that prepare them to perform well, increase their confidence and focus, and help them cope with problems. Also, they need to identify the destructive, Reactive, Restrictive, and self-defeating thoughts that typically lead to poor performance. It's also helpful to identify the exact situations or things that cause athletes to engage in R³ Thinking. The self-reflection and self-analysis required to do this is difficult for some athletes, because their thinking is ingrained and seemingly invisible to them. However, encourage your athletes to "be detectives" to sort out their own thinking strengths, weaknesses, and preferences.

The P³ Thinking Worksheet for Athletes is provided in Appendix 10A. This worksheet provides a brief overview of P³ and R³ Thinking for athletes, and then provides some self-reflection exercises that athletes can work through to (a) recognize their R³ thoughts, (b) identify the situations that trigger self-defeating thinking, and (c) develop P³ replacement thoughts for these problem situations. The worksheet is designed so that coaches can use it directly with athletes. Keep in mind that athletes might prefer not to share their "thinking homework" with you because you are their coach. It might work better if you explain the worksheet and the basic premises behind P³ Thinking, and then let them work through the exercises individually or with a teammate.

Table 10.3 How to be an R³ (Random, Reactive, Restrictive) Thinker

1. Demand to be 100% competent in everything you do—demand perfection. Put yourself down if you don't achieve this every time.

2. Remind yourself that you can't stand discomfort or inconvenience because life should be easy and fair, at least for you. Upset yourself every time life isn't easy or fair.

3. Tell yourself that it is awful when coaches or teammates don't act toward you exactly like you want them to at that moment. Pout about this to get their attention and waste their time dealing with you.

4. Never take a risk or chance to better yourself or reach your potential.

5. Demand the approval of just about everyone in your life—and even a few who are not.

6. Don't put any significant amount of effort into working on your problems and limitations.

7. Remind yourself that it is never your fault and thus certainly not your responsibility to do anything about it (when anything happens that is not good).

8. Find a terrific reason for justifying why you are the way you are and refuse to give it up.

9. The second you make a performance error or mistake, remind yourself that you can't do this.

10. Believe that failure is the worst thing that can happen to you and that you can't stand it or accept it when it does.

5. Through conversation (and other methods), challenge athletes to counter their own irrational, illogical, R³ Thinking.

To help athletes identify their irrational, R³ beliefs, look for (Ellis, 1996)

- dogmatic demands (musts, shoulds, never, always, absolutes),
- awfulizing (it's awful, terrible, horrible),
- low frustration tolerance (I can't stand it), and
- self or other labeling (I'm / he / she is lazy, worthless, mean).

A humorous way to get the point across to your athletes about the importance of P³ Thinking and the need to be tolerant, understanding, and accepting of others is to give them a list titled "How to be an R³ Thinker" (adapted from Ellis & MacLaren, 1998, and shown in Table 10.3). By reading the list of irrational, R³ thoughts, athletes can internalize the need for P³ Thinking without having to overtly admit to their own irrational thoughts. Besides being funny, the material in Table 10.3 makes a powerful point about how athletes in your program need to think!

6. Emphasize the need for "triage" in your athletes' thinking during competition.

Triage is a medical term used to describe the sorting and allocation of treatments to patients (especially battle and disaster victims) according to a system of priorities to maximize the number of survivors. Triage is about priorities and the best use of resources. Triage is an important part of P³ Thinking because it prioritizes thinking based on where attentional resources are most needed and best used based on the demands of competition. If you disagree with a teammate's decisions or positioning on the soccer field, you don't have time to get into an argument with him. Your attention during competition must be focused on task-relevant performance thoughts, as opposed to disagreements with teammates. Teach your athletes to use triage in their thinking by prioritizing a performance focus. Other issues can be dealt with later and should be put aside so that athletes' thoughts are focused on performing as well as possible.

Parking is a term that refers to *putting extraneous thoughts aside ("park them") so they don't interfere with focused thinking and performance.* You can also ask athletes to "file it," or to place their extraneous thoughts in a filing cabinet, which they can attend to later after competition. Following triage procedures, athletes must file all thoughts that are not directly related to immediate, task-specific performance demands. There are many ways to set irrelevant thoughts aside or simply get rid of them (e.g., "flush them," "throw them in the garbage," "pack them in a suitcase"). Rhea Taylor, high school basketball coach in California, brushes his shoulder with his hand while making eye contact with a player who has just made a mistake on the floor (Farrey, 2004). This parking trigger reminds his players to "brush off" the mistake and move on. Help your athletes develop specific parking triggers that work well in your sport.

Clipboard

"Putting" R³ Thoughts Where They Belong

Milt Campbell won the gold medal in the decathlon at the 1956 Olympic Games. Here is his unique practice of getting rid of his R³ thoughts (Campbell, 1999, pp. 97-98):

> *"The next challenge for the decathlete is the shot put. In this event, we throw a sixteen-pound lead ball as far away from us as possible. Off the playing field, that ball represents all the negative weight we carry around with us every day. If we're going to achieve our goal, we've got to see that ball as a round container into which we've stuffed every depressing, negative thought we've ever had. Take all those comments from others ('You'll never be able to do that! You're deluding yourself. Get real!') and push them into the ball. Now, mentally toss that ball far, far away. The winner is the person who puts the shot the farthest, who can most completely rid himself or herself of the negative elements that spell defeat."*

Another useful triage strategy to stop R³ thoughts and quickly move to P³ Thinking is to use a mental trigger to "change the channel" on R³ thoughts. Athletes can focus on "changing the channel" as with a television remote control, brush the dirt off the pitching rubber to "wipe away" any negative thoughts (Ravizza & Hanson, 1995), rip the vel-

cro on their golf glove to signify a change in thinking, or slap the floor in basketball to purge R³ thoughts. Suggest a triage trigger for your athletes, making it very specific and meaningful for your sport. Remind athletes prior to competition and training about the importance of using triage in their thinking.

7. Ask athletes to commit to at least one affirmation to create an important P³ thought.

It usually takes athletes some time to identify an affirmation that has personal meaning for them. Because affirmations have been part of slapstick comedy routines on shows like *Saturday Night Live* and *Caddyshack*, athletes often feel silly repeating them. Ask them to do it anyway, and to take it seriously, because affirmations really do work. Explain to them *how* they work, and give them some examples of athletes who have used them. Provide some example affirmations, such as "I choose to think well no matter what," "I accept critical feedback gladly to get better," "My legs feel strong and quick," and "I handle whatever comes up." It's best if affirmations are personalized for individual athletes, but sometimes team affirmations can be very powerful. These often end up on the backs of team t-shirts, which is fine.

> ## Quotable Quote
> *"I've learned to slap down any errant thoughts that intrude on my mind. Kick 'em off the premises and replace them with thoughts only related to the shot at hand."*
> **Patty Sheehan**, LPGA professional and Hall of Fame member *(Freeman, 1998)*

You can have fun with athletes by prescribing different ways to practice their affirmations. One example is putting a small colored adhesive dot on the face of their wristwatches, with the instructions to breathe deeply and repeat their affirmations each time they look at their watches. Athletes can also repeatedly write their affirmations onto goal mapping cards (see Chapter 8). Affirmations can be written on lockers, tacked on bulletin boards, taped to bathroom or car mirrors, and even taped on the ceiling above athletes' beds! I repeat a specific affirmation related to managing my time whenever the phone rings in my office, and it really works to keep me calm and focused. Athletes can engage in Purposeful Thinking about their

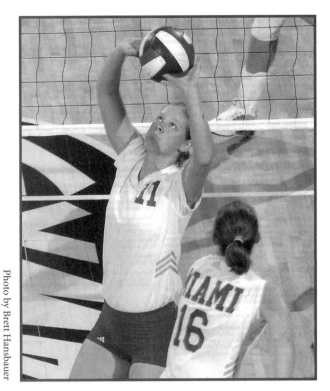

Photo by Brett Hansbauer

affirmations during stretching or warm-ups prior to training and competition.

Practicing P³ Thinking works well in conjunction with other mental training tools. For example, repeating affirmations with controlled breathing in a quiet place (such as prior to going to sleep) is a powerful way to relax your mind to be receptive to P³ thoughts. Athletes should engage in imagery when repeating their affirmations, because this provides a visual along with the verbal stimuli to help the affirmations "sink in" to create powerful beliefs. Athletes can easily create affirmations from their goal maps, which involves taking a goal stated in the future tense ("I will") and making into an affirmation in the present tense ("I am" or "I do"). Affirmations are one of the best ways to actually practice P³ Thinking, so help your athletes to understand and accept the power of this strategy to think better.

Wrapping Up

Thinking well is fairly easy for most athletes in normal circumstances. Effective thinking becomes much more difficult when important goals are at stake, when there is pressure to perform, when athletes don't perform well and make mistakes, and when unforeseen obstacles arise. Like physical training, athletes need mental training in P³ Thinking to develop the supernormal skills needed to cope with these pressures.

All athletes can learn to think better—it is a learnable skill. Because most athletes have never considered monitoring and managing their thoughts, they actually can do quite well when first attempting to practice their thinking skills. The first step is to get athletes to accept that thinking is a choice. The second step is to get athletes to become aware of *how* they think, of their specific R³ thoughts, and what triggers these thoughts. The next step, changing R³ Thinking into P³ Thinking, is where it gets tough. However, this is a good time to remind athletes of just how hard they had to work to gain proficiency in their physical skills and to become physically fit. Remind them to be patient and to persist in their mental training, because it takes just as much work to gain proficiency in their thinking skills as it did for their physical skill development! Encourage them when they get discouraged and struggle in making their new P³ thoughts habitual and automatic. It takes time and work, so challenge them to use P³ Thinking when they struggle with their P³ Thinking! Thinking well builds the Inner Edge for athletes, and will serve them well as a life skill long after their sport careers are over.

Summary Points for Chapter 10

1. Research supports that successful athletes think differently from less successful athletes.
2. P³ Thinking is a mental training tool designed to help athletes think better by being more Purposeful, Productive, and Possibility-oriented in their thinking.
3. R³ Thinking, or engaging in Random, Reactive, and Restrictive Thinking, is the opposite of P³ Thinking and should be avoided.
4. Athletes don't think "on purpose" because they believe thoughts occur involuntarily, they're not sure what to think about, and they allow events in the physical and social environment to dictate how they think and feel.
5. Self-talk, as a form of Purposeful Thinking, has been shown to enhance athletes' performance, motivation, and confidence.
6. Purposeful efforts to not think about something can cause athletes to fixate on unwanted thoughts, unless they allow the thought to

"pass through" and replace it with a Purposeful, Productive thought.

7. Productive Thinking involves choosing to respond, as opposed to reacting with emotion.

8. Thoughts are Productive when they are focused on the present, personally controllable, task-related, and personally relevant.

9. Coaches can use the premises of Rational Emotive Behavior Therapy, or REBT, to challenge dysfunctional philosophies or beliefs held by athletes.

10. REBT is used as a method of countering, which is Productive reasoning to refute the underlying irrational assumptions that lead to Reactive thinking.

11. Possibility Thinking is based on the idea that athletes cannot attain what they cannot see themselves doing.

12. Affirmations are a P³ Thinking practice technique in which self-statements are repeated to create a Possibility attitude and a desired self-fulfilling prophecy.

13. Athletes should "triage" their thinking in competition, to prioritize attentional resources toward task-specific performance concerns.

Glossary

affirmations: personal phrases that you repeat over and over to influence your subconscious mind to accept as true

attitude: a way of thinking and feeling that is sustained over time

countering: using productive reasoning to refute the underlying irrational assumptions that lead to negative thinking

hope: a thinking process characterized by a sense of personal agency and goal-directedness

ironic processes: the tendency for athletes to think in ways that are opposite to the way that they intend to think

optimism: a general expectancy that good things will happen

parking: putting extraneous thoughts aside ("park them") so they don't interfere with focused thinking and performance

self-talk: a verbal dialogue in which athletes interpret their feelings and perceptions, evaluate

themselves, and give themselves instructions or reinforcement

Study Questions

1. What are some of the "thinking characteristics" of successful, elite athletes?

2. Contrast P³ Thinking with R³ Thinking. What do each of these terms mean and how are they different or opposite? Explain why each P is necessary for the P³ formula to work.

3. Explain the three reasons why athletes don't think "on purpose."

4. Define self-talk as a type of Purposeful Thinking, and cite some research supporting its effectiveness as a mental training tool.

5. Use the theory of ironic processes of mental control to explain how and why Purposeful Thinking might hurt athletes' performance. What is the key to the theory that ensures that Purposeful Thinking is facilitative to athletes, and what can coaches do to help athletes do this?

6. What are the four characteristics of Productive Thoughts? Can you identify any other characteristics that might make thoughts productive for athletes?

7. Explain the ABC model that is the basis for Rational Emotive Behavior Therapy. Why is this therapy technique a good thing to use with athletes? How does it work to counter athletes' Reactive Thinking?

8. Explain how affirmations can be used as a Possibility Thinking mental practice technique.

9. Explain the concept of "triage" as an important part of P³ Thinking. Provide several examples of specific strategies athletes in different sports can use to effectively triage their thinking in competition.

Reflective Learning Activities

1. Assess Your Beliefs (adapted from Davis, Eshelman, & McKay, 2000)

Respond to each item in the Beliefs Inventory below. Be honest and respond to each item as you *really* feel, not how you think you *should* feel.

	strongly agree	agree	disagree	strongly disagree
1. It is important to me that others approve of me.	4	3	2	1
2. I hate to fail at anything.	4	3	2	1
3. Frustrating situations tend to upset me.	4	3	2	1
4. I avoid things I cannot do well.	4	3	2	1
5. I want everyone to like me.	4	3	2	1
6. I often get upset about situations I don't like.	4	3	2	1
7. It is highly important for me to be successful in everything I do.	4	3	2	1
8. I usually accept things the way they are, even if I don't like them.	4	3	2	1
9. Although I like approval, it's not a real need for me.	4	3	2	1
10. It bothers me when others are better than I am at something.	4	3	2	1
11. If things annoy me, I just ignore them.	4	3	2	1
12. I often worry about how much people approve of me and accept me.	4	3	2	1
13. It upsets me to make mistakes.	4	3	2	1
14. I am fairly easygoing about life.	4	3	2	1
15. It is annoying, but not upsetting, to be criticized.	4	3	2	1

Scoring:

Add up numbers corresponding to the items listed below for each irrational belief. Items with an R listed means that you reverse score that item (1=4, 2=3, 3=2, 4=1).

I must have approval from others.
(Items 1, 5, 9R, 12, 15R)   Score: _____

I must be unfailingly competent and almost perfect in all I do.
(Items 2, 4, 7, 10, 13)   Score: _____

It's horrible when things are not the way I would like them to be.
(Items 3, 6, 8R, 11R, 14R)   Score: _____

If your score was: 5 - 10   Your thinking is very Productive!

                                  11 - 14   Fair thinker—work to get better.

                                  15 - 20   Your thinking is Reactive and irrational—practice REBT!

Consider your scores and where you scored high on a particular irrational belief. Discuss with a partner why you feel you scored highly on this belief. Attempt to dispute the belief with the help of your partner.

(10 minutes to complete inventory and score it; 10 minutes with a partner to discuss findings.)

2. P³ Thinking Homework Sheet

a.   Individually complete the exercises listed in Appendix 10A of the chapter. This works best as an overnight assignment so participants can give the questions some thought.

b.   Participants then work with a partner to go over their "homework" and get feedback and additional insight from their partner.

c.   After working in pairs, the entire group should discuss (a) what was learned about yourself, (b) what was hard about the assignment, and (c) how can you help athletes make this a meaningful exercise for them.

3. P³ Thinking for Specific Sports

a.   Divide into groups of three by sport. The task of each group is to develop a P³ Thinking plan for its specific sport.

b.   The plan should include the following:

    1.   Suggestions/ideas for Purposeful Thinking (how and when athletes can do this)

    2.   Identification of situations (Activating Events) that trigger Reactive Thinking

    3.   P³ Thinking alternatives and strategies for these situations

    4.   Triage triggers that athletes can use in this sport

    5.   Some example affirmations and how they can be used in this sport by athletes

(Groups should have 20-30 minutes to work, and then present their thinking plans to the other groups)

Chapter

Eleven

Physical Relaxation

Chapter Preview

In this chapter, you'll learn:

- why athletes perform best in a state of relaxed intensity
- how and when physical relaxation might be useful for athletes
- how athletes can use the Power Breathing Response and Quick Power Breath
- four different ways athletes can physically relax.

"When things are going bad, I take a lot of deep breaths and a lot of practice swings, trying to get back a good feel for my swing." **Julie Inkster**, LPGA golf professional and Hall of Fame member

The idea of relaxing seems counterproductive to most athletes who are more concerned with intensity, power, drive, and feeling energized or "psyched up." However, there is a big difference between physical *intensity* that serves as a positive energy fuel for athletes and physical *tension* that results from stress and hurts athletes' performance. A common observation when watching elite athletes perform is that they look fluid, graceful, and effortless in their movements. These athletes appear this way because they have mastered the important skill of performing with relaxed intensity. That is, they have learned to optimize their physical and mental energy to create a positive competitive intensity, but they have also learned to control their muscles to work fluidly with just the right amounts of tension and relaxation for optimal performance.

Fluid performance in all sports requires a certain amount of bodily relaxation so that various muscle groups work in harmony to create a smooth and loose level of movement. Think back to when you were very anxious and tense and attempted to perform a sport skill. If you're like me, you may remember how the physical tension in your muscles made a well-learned skill very difficult to complete successfully. So, even though athletes need to be intense, powerful, driven, and energized, if they can't physically relax enough for fluid and smooth motor control of their muscles, their performance will suffer. In fact, the emphasis on getting "psyched up" may hurt them more than help them!

Athletes respond to the stress of competition in two ways: mentally (called cognitive anxiety) and physically (called somatic anxiety). Of course, mental and physical anxiety are related, such as when worry about performing well causes athletes' muscles to tense. The mental training tools of goal mapping, imagery, and P³ Thinking are all good strategies for athletes to use to reduce mental anxiety. Reducing mental anxiety using these methods will help to reduce some of the physical anxiety experienced by athletes. However, to consistently perform with relaxed intensity, athletes should become proficient in some basic physical relaxation techniques. Physical relaxation focuses on reducing somatic anxiety, or physical symptoms that interfere with smooth, fluid performance.

Physical relaxation, as a mental training tool, is about *willfully controlling bodily functions such as muscular tension, breathing, and heart rate to induce a more relaxed physical state of being*. Research shows that humans can mentally control their autonomic (automatic) body processes to enhance their health and performance (Williams & Harris, 2001). For example, physical relaxation techniques have been included in mental training programs that enhanced athlete performance in basketball shooting (Pates, Cummings, & Maynard, 2002) and distance running (Bull, 1989). In this chapter, some basic physical relaxation techniques that can be taught to athletes are presented. The intent is to provide you the coach with some easily taught, practical strategies to help your athletes physically relax under different conditions.

How Athletes Can Use Physical Relaxation

Why and when would athletes in your sport want to be relaxed? This is a question that you should address to specifically tailor relaxation strategies for your athletes. Here are some suggestions for how athletes can use physical relaxation techniques (adapted from Orlick, 2000 and Williams & Harris, 2001):

1. To create a momentary relaxation response. Athletes can use a brief relaxation strategy or cue to reduce tension and nerves at critical times in competition. This might be prior to throwing a pitch, hitting a golf ball, serving a tennis ball, or diving off the blocks in swimming. It is typical for a momentary relaxation response (usually a deep breath) to be included in pre-performance routines. This takes some learning and practice, but it is an invaluable part of an athlete's mental training tool kit.

2. To create and maintain the feeling of relaxed intensity between periods of competition and inactivity (such as during time-outs; between shifts, innings, heats, or periods; at half-time; or on the bench waiting to go in). Physical relaxation strategies should be combined with P³ Thinking during these

Photo by Master Sgt. Lono Kollars, courtesy of US Army

times of inactivity to optimize mental focus and physical energy needed to perform well.

3. To be relaxed and conserve energy during the final hours leading up to an important competition. Athletes need to optimize their physical and mental energy at the exact time of competition; worrying about an upcoming event can create physical tension that drains athletes' energy levels before competition even starts. Many times athletes appear "flat" during competition, which is typically the result of burning their needed energy and competitive focus prior to the competitive event. Physical relaxation can keep athletes calm and loose, allowing them to conserve energy for competition.

4. To rest and recover while traveling from one competition to another. For athletes in tournaments or who are traveling to another competition site, some practical physical relaxation strategies may help release any tension in their bodies and allow them the full rest and physical recovery that they need to prepare for the next competition. This is particularly true for athletes who have lost in competition or failed to perform to their expectations; physical relaxation along with some other mental training tools can release the tension and pressure they may be feeling from their previous poor performance.

5. To relax enough to engage in restful sleep the night before an important competition. Many athletes have trouble sleeping the night before important competitions, and physical relaxation strategies are sometimes help them relax their bodies to the point where sleep can occur.

6. To learn to relax during physical exertion. The idea of relaxing during extreme physical exertion sounds weird, but as discussed previously, peak performances usually occur in sport when athletes feel loose and relaxed while extending themselves toward full exertion (Orlick, 2000). This is especially helpful for athletes who carry tension in their bodies as the result of heavy training. Coaches can help athletes by asking them to think about how their body needs to feel to perform optimally. Every athlete has a desired or optimal amount of physical and mental energy that tends to help them perform well. It takes self-reflection, self-monitoring, and practice to identify one's optimal body state and to learn to control it.

Methods of Physical Relaxation

Four popular methods of physical relaxation for athletes are presented in this section: (a) imagery, (b) self-talk, (c) Power Breathing, and (d) conscious muscle control. There are many ways to practice physical relaxation, but these four methods are the most typical and seem to be the most practical for athletes. Because imagery and self-talk were reviewed in earlier chapters, they are only mentioned briefly here in relation to their use for physical relaxation.

Imagery

Imagery is probably the easiest way for athletes to physically relax. By consciously visualizing a relaxing image, athletes allow their bodies to unwind and relax. A sample imagery script for relaxation was provided in Chapter 9, and athletes should attempt to identify a specific, personalized image that induces relaxation for them (e.g., favorite place, warm beach, room at home). A golfer with whom I consulted used the image of playing golf by herself when she was in competition. She loved playing golf alone because she focused on the beauty of the course and being outdoors. This image helped her to relax, release tension, and maintain a calm focus when competing with others on the course.

Athletes can also use imagery as a way to induce conscious relaxation in their muscles. Athletes can imagine the blood flowing into their muscles to increase their warmth and elasticity, or imagine making their arms and legs into "cooked spaghetti" or "uncoiled elastic bands." They may imagine the muscles in their necks becoming more elastic and loose as they slowly rotate their heads to release tension. They may imagine drinking a warm liquid and feeling it seep through their bodies, relaxing their faces, necks, shoulders, backs, arms, trunks, legs, feet, and toes. As you learned in Chapter 9, imagined events stimulate our minds and bodies much like real events, so imagery is very useful to program feelings of physical relaxation.

Self-Talk

Self-talk was discussed in Chapter 10 as part of P³ Thinking. Self-talk, as a verbal dialogue that athletes have with themselves, is an easy and quick way to induce physical relaxation. The basic idea is that athletes talk themselves into calming down. Trigger relaxation words and phrases such as "slow down," "breathe and relax," "calm," "ready," and "I'm loose and energized" program the brain to relax the body. Like imagery, self-talk involves programming the mind to control the body to induce a physical relaxation response.

Self-talk cues are also useful in training and competition to remind athletes to relax or stay loose while performing. This is critical in sports such as cross-country running and skiing, swimming, sprinting, and distance running, where a certain amount of relaxation is needed for proper technique. Athletes in these sports must identify where and when tension creeps in to rob them of their fluidity and looseness when performing. After setting the world record in the 100 meters at a blazing 10.48 seconds at the 1988 U.S. Olympic Trials, Florence Griffith-Joyner commented: "The 10.60 [in my previous heat] made me realize if I continued to concentrate on what I'm doing and stay relaxed, my times would continue to drop" (Orlick, 2000, p. 126).

Orlick (2000) suggests that athletes plan verbal reminders to relax yet remain highly focused and intense. These should be very specific to the skill being performed; examples might include "loose and powerful," "reach, pull, relax," or "power, relax." In swimming, each stroke requires power and then relaxation. Swimmers are taught to have "floppy wrists" during the recovery, or relaxation, phase of their crawl strokes. Consider how self-talk was used by a kayaker to induce relaxation in the middle of extreme exertion in the following example:

> "Almost every three seconds or so toward the end I'd have to say 'relax,' and I'd let my shoulders and my head relax, and I'd think about putting on the power, and then I'd feel the tension creeping up again so I'd think about relaxing again, then

> "power, relax." I knew that in order to have that power I had to be relaxed. You can be powerful but tense, and the boat won't go." **Sue Holloway,** Canadian Olympic silver medalist in kayaking (as cited in Orlick, 2000, p. 126)

Using self-talk to induce physical relaxation takes time and practice. Athletes must practice using this relaxation strategy during their training, and during their imagery practice. Through repetitive physical and mental practice, athletes can learn to bring on a relaxation response by using key words during competition.

Power Breathing

A third method to help athletes physically relax is controlled breathing. Athletes' performance, and their overall health, is very much affected by how they breathe. When athletes become anxious, their breathing becomes more rapid and shallow. Shallow breathing reduces the level of carbon dioxide in athletes' bloodstreams, which causes blood vessels throughout their bodies to constrict. This, in turn, reduces oxygen to the brain, creating feelings of tension and shakiness. Improper breathing contributes to anxiety, panic attacks, depression, muscle tension, and fatigue. Breathing is a key component in most Asian philosophies of relaxation, many of which believe that effective breathing can enhance how people feel and think. Controlled breathing is an important aspect of performance in static sports such as archery and shooting, and it is taught in military training to enhance the performance of soldiers and pilots in combat situations. Explain to your athletes that breathing is not some far-out meditation technique, but a key mental training tool to help them master the mental game.

Table 11.1 Differences in Shallow, Ideal, and Relaxation-Focused Breathing (adapted from Wilson, 1995)

Breathing Type	Breaths per Minute	Volume of Air Inhaled per Breath (cc)	Stale Air Exhaled (cc)
Shallow	24	250	2400
Ideal	12	500	4200
Relaxation-Focused	6	1000	5100

Controlled breathing is an effective relaxation technique because, most of the time, we use only a fraction of our lung capacity. When we engage in slower and deeper breathing than normal, we take fewer breaths per minute, inhale a greater volume of fresh air, and exhale a greater volume of stale air. Normally, when we exhale, some air remains in our lungs and airways. This stale air is obviously not as useful to our bodies as fresh air, so it is desirable to exhale as much stale air as possible to enhance respiratory function.

Compare the differences in breathing between shallow, ideal, and relaxation-focused breathing shown in Table 11.1 (adapted from Wilson, 1995). Shallow breathers only use one-third of their lung capacity, take more breaths per minute, inhale less fresh air, and exhale less stale air than ideal breathers. The ideal for everyday breathing is approximately 12 breaths per minute, with this slower breathing rate increasing the volume of fresh air inhaled and stale air exhaled per breath. Individuals who consciously control their breathing to induce relaxation breathe approximately 6 times per minute, inhale twice the amount of fresh air, and exhale a larger amount of stale air as compared to normal everyday breathing. Overall, the deeper and slower we breathe, the more oxygen we provide to our bloodstreams, the more stale air we expel from our bodies, and the more relaxed we feel.

When athletes are anxious and their breathing increases, they breathe from the chest. Chest breathing is shallow and rapid, creating tension in their bodies. Abdominal breathing means that they are using their diaphragms, contracting this thin sheet of muscle downward when inhaling to let the lungs expand, and then pushing the diaphragm up against the lungs with the abdominal muscles to push the air out of the lungs when exhaling. Introduce the concept of "power breathing" to your athletes to emphasize how they should breathe to enhance their physical performance and overall sense of relaxation (Wilson, 1995).

Power Breathing is *the conscious slowing and deepening of breaths using the diaphragm and abdominal muscles to reduce muscle tension and somatic anxiety.* Power Breathing is an essential mental training tool to help athletes calm their bodies and focus effectively. Lead your athletes through the fol-

lowing exercises to enhance their Power Breathing ability:

1. *Breathing Awareness* (Davis et al., 2000)

   a. Lie on your back with knees bent and feet flat on the floor. Place one hand on your abdomen and the other hand on your chest.

   b. Breathe normally for a minute and notice how you are breathing. Which hand rises the most as you inhale—the one on your chest or the one on your abdomen?

   c. If your abdomen moves the most, you are on your way to Power Breathing or breathing from your abdomen or diaphragm. If your chest moves the most, your breathing is shallow and needs to be deepened.

2. *Standing Abdominal Breathing* (Wilson, 1995)

   a. The purpose of this exercise is to get the feel for how your diaphragm works when you are Power Breathing. In a standing position, place your hands on your sides, with your thumbs pointing backwards and positioned in the hollow above each hip. Your fingers extend forward, resting on your abdomen and stretching just below your navel.

   b. Take a breath and feel your abdomen swell beneath your fingers and thumbs. Make sure that your shoulders do not rise and your chest does not puff out.

   c. Now exhale slowly and evenly until you feel your abdomen fall under your fingers. It helps to make one or two full exhalations that push the air from the bottom of your lungs. This creates a vacuum that will pull in a deep Power Breathing breath on your next inhalation.

3. *Supine Abdominal Breathing* (Davis et al., 2000)

   a. Lie on your back with your legs straight and slightly apart, toes pointed comfortably outward, arms at your side and not touching your body, palms up, and eyes closed.

   b. Breathe through your nose. Focus on your breathing and place your hand on the spot that seems to rise and fall the most as you inhale and exhale.

c. Now, gently place both hands on your abdomen and follow your breathing. Focus on how your abdomen rises with each inhalation and falls with each exhalation.

d. To enhance your Power Breathing, press your hand down on your abdomen as you exhale and let your abdomen push your hand back up as your inhale deeply. Do this a few times to "feel" the breathing technique and then just allow your hands to ride softly on your abdomen.

4. *Power Breathing Response* (adapted from Wilson, 1995)

This technique can be practiced in quiet situations and then used in competitive conditions to relax tension and refocus. Here are the steps:

a. Blow out one noisy "whoosh" exhalation through your mouth, puffing out your cheeks as you do so. This is your Power Breathing trigger, which begins your Power Breathing Response. The key is to blow as much air out of your lungs as possible, to prepare for a deep inhalation to flood fresh air into your lungs.

b. Take in a deep breath through your nose. Do this without exertion—neither raising your shoulders nor puffing out your chest. Make it a power inhalation from your abdomen.

Imagine tension from your body being pulled into your lungs as with a vacuum.

c. Slowly breathe out through your nose and mouth, hearing the air as it is exhaled. Imagine the tension leaving your body as you exhale. With each exhalation, let any tension in your body go (say to yourself "*let it go*"). (A variation on this is to think about inhaling *fresh, positive energy* and exhaling *fatigue.*)

d. Continue to inhale through your nose and exhale through your mouth, labeling each breath in ways such as "pull it in" and then "let it go."

Athletes must practice the Power Breathing Response in quiet controlled conditions if they expect it to work in the heat of competition. It helps if they practice their breathing daily, even if for 2-3 minutes, so that they can quickly trigger the Power

Photo by Brett Hansbauer

Breathing Response that they need in competition. When practicing the technique, athletes should imagine themselves in tense situations and see themselves using their Power Breathing Response to create a sense of calm, relaxed intensity, and focus. The Power Breathing Response can also be used by athletes after competition to relax their bodies, let go of tension, and refocus on the next event.

Athletes can also choose a personal cue word to repeat to themselves each time they exhale in the Power Breathing Response. I suggested "let it go" as a good cue to release tension and anxiety, but athletes should personalize their cues and use them each day when practicing Power Breathing. Other example cues might include "relax," "focus," "release," "ready," or "poised." Many athletes like to say *re* on inhalation and *lax* on exhalation because it's easy to remember and provides a slow cadence for their breathing. Daily practice using personal cues can help athletes create a cue-controlled relaxation response that they can quickly use in competitive conditions.

5. Quick Power Breath

The Quick Power Breath can be used as part of a pre-performance routine, such as prior to delivering a pitch, serving a volleyball, shooting a free throw, or kicking a field goal. It can also be used during a break in the action or prior to entering competition from the bench. It involves a simple, deep breath to clear the body of tension and induce a feeling of relaxed intensity:

a. Inhale through your nose slowly and fill your lungs as completely as possible. (Make sure this is a deep breath, with no shoulder or chest movement—feel it in your abdomen.) Drink in the fresh air, flood your body with energy for fluid performance!

b. Exhale through your nose and mouth—feeling relaxed, loose, and ready (energized).

Explain it to athletes as a "Power" Breath because it is used to relax them yet prepare them with energy, focus, and the power to perform loosely.

Conscious Muscle Control

The fourth way that athletes can practice physical relaxation is through conscious control of their muscles. One of the biggest problems that athletes face is that they are often unaware of tension they carry in their muscles. Progressive Relaxation was developed as a conscious muscle control technique in which individuals could learn to recognize and release tension in specific muscle groups to achieve physical relaxation (Jacobson, 1930).

There are many variations on the technique of progressive relaxation, but for your practical use as a coach, three examples of conscious muscle control exercises are provided in this section. These include the Tense-Relax method, Release-Only method, and the Quick Scan and Release technique.

Tense-Release method. The Tense-Release method of physical relaxation requires athletes to progressively tense and then relax the major muscle groups in their bodies. The tensing of muscles allows athletes to experience what extreme muscular tension feels like, and the sudden release of tension allows them to experience the relaxation of that muscle group. Athletes progressively tense and then relax each muscle group, concentrating on how the different sensations of tension and relaxation feel in their muscles. By practicing this Tense-Release method, athletes can learn to recognize unwanted muscular tension when it occurs and release the tension and relax the muscle to facilitate smooth and fluid performance.

I suggest that athletes begin practicing the Tense-Release method using seven muscle groups (right arm, left arm, face, neck, trunk, right leg, left leg) and then once proficiency is gained, move to five muscle groups (arms, face, neck, trunk, legs). Athletes complete two cycles of tension and relaxation

Table 11.2 Timing of Tension and Relaxation Cycles in Progressive Muscle Relaxation

| Cycle 1: | tension | 5-7 seconds | relaxation | 25 seconds |
| Cycle 2: | tension | 5-7 seconds | relaxation | 50 seconds |

Table 11.3 Instructions for Athletes to Tense Each Muscle Group

Right Arm	Bend arm slightly at elbow, make tight fist, press down and in with biceps
Left Arm	Same as right arm
Face	Raise eyebrows, squint eyes, bite down hard, scrunch nose, pull corners of mouth back (make an ugly face!)
Neck	Pull chin down to touch chest while at the same time resisting
Trunk	Pull shoulders back and together; make stomach hard (prepare to be hit in the stomach!)
Right Leg	Lift leg slightly, curl toes down, tense muscles hard
Left Leg	Same as right leg

for each muscle group with the timing of cycles shown in Table 11.2.

Before you begin the actual exercise with athletes, go over the seven muscle groups that will be relaxed and have athletes practice tensing each one. The instructions for you to give to athletes to tense each muscle group are listed in Table 11.3.

Lead them in practicing holding the tension in each muscle group for 5-7 seconds. Use a stopwatch or sweep hand to keep track of time—it really helps. Cue them on each muscle group by saying: "Okay, now I want you to tense the muscles in your right leg by (read how they will do it). When I say 'tense,' hold the tension until I say 'relax.' Ready, TENSE . . . hold it, hold it . . . RELAX. Once the tensing of each muscle group has been practiced, ask if there are any questions. Remind athletes that if they get a muscle cramp (common in the legs and feet), simply skip the tension phase and focus only on relaxing that muscle group. Explain that they will go through two cycles for each muscle group, and to have a passive attitude where they simply follow your verbal directions and focus their attention on their muscles.

Following is a script to help you get started in leading this exercise:

> "Sit or lie in a comfortable position. Close your eyes and take a long, slow, deep breath through your nose, inhaling as much air as possible. Then exhale slowly and completely, feeling the tension leave your body as you exhale. Continue to inhale and exhale slowly and deeply, letting the day's tensions and problems drain out of you with each exhalation. As you are breathing deeply and rhythmically, focus on my voice and follow my instructions. Try not to move any more than necessary to stay comfortable.
>
> We'll start the exercise by tensing the muscles in your right leg. To do this (explain again how to do this). Okay, ready . . . TENSE . . . hold it, hold it . . . RELAX. Concentrate on the feeling of relaxation now in your right leg and contrast that feeling to the previous feeling of tension."

Then, repeat the cycle, this time allowing 50 seconds for the relaxation phase. It's okay to be silent, but preface the silence by cueing athletes to focus on the feelings of relaxation during this time. Periodically, you can also remind athletes to continue breathing slowly, deeply, and in good rhythm to facilitate their relaxation. Once you've completed the tension-relaxation cycles for all muscles groups, cue the athletes to scan their bodies for any additional tension and to let it go. Then cue them to focus on the relaxed state of their muscles and, each time they exhale, to repeat the word "relax." Give them about 2 minutes to relax fully, and then conclude the exercise by saying, "Now that you've enjoyed your deep relaxation state, it's time to return to your day. Begin to move your arms and legs, and when you are ready, open your eyes to feel the alertness flowing back into your body."

Release-Only method. Once athletes have experienced the tension-relaxation difference, they can progress to the Release-Only method. In this method, they progressively work through each muscle group as in the Tense-Release method, but the tension part of the exercise is deleted. Instead, athletes focus on each muscle group and consciously attempt to release any tension they feel in those muscles.

As with the previous exercise, explain the seven (or five) muscle groups that athletes will be focusing on. You of course don't need to explain how to tense each muscle group, but explain that when cued, they should focus the attention on the feelings in that part of their body and attempt to release any tension that they feel. You can cue athletes to release the tension by using various descriptors, such as the ones listed in Table 11.4. Also, athletes only relax each muscle group once, as compared to the two tense-release cycles in the Tense-Release method.

Introduce the exercise the same way as in the Tense-Release method (e.g., get in a comfortable position, slow and deepen breathing, don't move unnecessarily). Then say "We'll now begin the exercise. Focus your attention on the muscles in your [right arm]. Notice any tension that you feel there, and then simply let that tension go. [Let the tension flow down your arm and out your fingertips so your fingers feel like cooked spaghetti.] Tell yourself 'let it go.' Focus now on the feelings of relaxation in your arm and how the muscles feel loose and relaxed." Continue through all the muscle groups, and at the end ask athletes to scan their body for any signs of tension, and to let it go. Finish up the exercise the same way you did in the Tense-Release method.

I have found that athletes often prefer the Release-Only method, but I insist that they practice the Tense-Release method at least three times prior to moving to Release-Only. This is so they have some practice in distinguishing between tension and re-

Table 11.4 Images for Specific Muscle Groups (Release-Only method of conscious muscle relaxation)

Right Arm	Let the tension flow down your arm and out your fingertips so your fingers feel like cooked spaghetti
Left Arm	Same as right arm
Face	Drop your jaw, feel your forehead sag, let your mouth go limp
Neck	Feel the rubber bands running through your neck loosen and go limp
Shoulders and Back	Feel your shoulders drop and your back sink in to the floor
Right Leg	Feel the back of your leg melt into the floor; make your toes feel like cooked spaghetti
Left Leg	Same as right leg

laxation, and are more in tune to identifying what tension feels like in their various muscle groups. At the very least, insist that your athletes try the Tense-Release method at least once, so they can experience the shift from extreme tension to relaxation in their muscles.

Quick Scan and Release technique. The Quick Scan and Release technique is useful as a momentary relaxation strategy during competition. Athletes simply scan their bodies for any tension, and then consciously release tension found in any muscle groups. I find this works best when athletes Quick Scan and Release muscles which are crucial to their performance. For example, I teach golfers to continuously scan the muscles in their neck and back for tension. It is difficult to perform a fluid golf swing when carrying tension in these areas. It works well to add a couple of specific stretches to the Quick Scan and Release technique so that athletes can scan their muscles, stretch them out, and then release the tension (e.g., rolling the head in a slow circle to scan neck muscles for tension). The Quick Scan and Release technique will not work if athletes haven't practiced the Tense-Release method to understand the differences in how their muscles feel when they are tense versus relaxed.

Tips for Coaches

It is typical for coaches to lack confidence in leading athletes in physical relaxation training. In this section, some tips are provided to help you con-sider how you might use this mental training tool with your athletes.

1. Identify commercial products or local experts to lead your athletes in physical relaxation training. It is important for coaches to understand the basics of physical relaxation and how athletes' performance is influenced by tension and somatic anxiety. However, you can rely on other experts for the actual training of your athletes. First, many audiocassettes and videotapes/DVDs are available commercially that include progressive muscle relaxation, breathing exercises, and imagery for relaxation[1]. Second, coaches should check around their communities for sport psychology or stress management professionals who would be willing to lead some physical relaxation sessions with your team. However, there are no secrets or special qualifications needed to lead athletes through the exercises provided in this chapter. You more than anyone understand the relaxation needs of your athletes, so you have the best expertise to customize physical relaxation strategies specifically for your athletes. Be confident and try it—it's really easy once you get started.

2. Practice the physical relaxation exercises yourself. Don't ask your athletes to engage in any mental training techniques that you haven't tried yourself! Practice relaxing yourself through imagery, and then work through the breathing and conscious muscle control exercises listed in the chapter. Decide which ones work for you and might work best with your athletes. You will gain a lot of confidence once

you can do these exercises yourself. Plus, coaches need to relax as much as their athletes, right?

3. Integrate some simple relaxation responses into athletes' physical training. A simple relaxation response should be a part of every athlete's pre-performance routine. Probably the easiest one to use is the Power Breath. You could incorporate Power Breathing or the Quick Scan and Release technique of muscle relaxation as part of a team's post-training cool-down and stretch. Of course, probably the most important role of the coach is in teaching athletes how to cue themselves for appropriate relaxation during their performance. Think of specific verbal cues to use in your teaching to emphasize the need for relaxed, fluid performance.

4. Don't tell athletes to "relax." As I was leaving the huddle as a college basketball player prior to shooting a critical free throw, my coach said, "Just relax, Robin." My immediate thought was, "Gee, am I *not* relaxed?" My coach meant well, but in telling me to relax, she made me think that I wasn't relaxed and that I wasn't ready to shoot. Coaches should help athletes in the development of mental strategies and pre-performance routines, and then let them use these during competition without prompting or telling them to relax. Athletes know they need to relax and focus, so instead of stating the obvious, tell them something useful!

5. Help athletes learn to recognize rushing, which leads to tension and poor performance. Often, athletes who are anxious begin to hurry and rush their performance. Rushing interferes with the smooth coordination needed for optimal performance. Watch for this in your athletes, and then work with them in training so they learn to identify their tendencies to rush when anxious and learn to slow down. With golfers, a technique I call the Slowdown works to help them become more physically and mentally calm. The Slowdown is simply a conscious slowing of walking, talking, thinking, and all movements such as pulling clubs from the bag, lining up shots, and going through the pre-shot routine. The focus during the Slowdown is on calm, efficient use of energy and the feeling of relaxed intensity or relaxed power.

6. Make sure athletes understand that physical relaxation training won't totally eliminate anxiety and tension. Just like athletes will always have negative thoughts, athletes will always experience tension. It is unrealistic to think otherwise. However, just as P³ Thinking helps athletes manage negative thoughts that are bound to occur, physical relaxation helps athletes manage the inevitable physical tension and somatic anxiety that accompanies competition. Athletes can perform successfully when they are anxious, but they must learn and automate strategies to effectively manage anxious thoughts and feelings when they occur. This is when a Power Breath or Quick Scan and Release can be helpful.

7. Remember that there is no right way to relax, or one method that works for everyone. Beyond the physical relaxation strategies presented in this chapter, athletes should consider strategies that work best to keep them relaxed and loose prior to competition. This may involve listening to music, watching a movie for distraction, being alone, being with others, or being outdoors. Within the team concept, coaches should consider providing ways for athletes to mentally and physically prepare for competition in preferable ways. For example, some athletes may like to be a part of a boisterous locker room prior to competition, while others would like access to a quiet space for their mental and physical preparation. There is no right way to relax, and athletes must experiment to find personal relaxation strategies that work for them.

Wrapping Up

As the opposing football team called timeout to "ice" the kicker, his position coach said to him, "Now's the time to use your pre-kick relaxation and focus routine." The player looked at the coach and said incredulously, "Not *now*, coach. *This* is important!" Many athletes go through the motions of mental training, but fail to trust it enough to use it during competition. Athletes must understand that if they practice a few of the techniques described in this chapter, it will pay off for them in managing their physical tension during competition. If you have athletes who simply go through the motions of mental training, tell them to stop wasting your time and theirs.

Like all other mental training methods, keep physical relaxation training simple for your athletes. Start by making sure they can all master deep abdominal breathing and then give them some examples of how they can use the Power Breath in competitive situations. If they like imagery, they can easily master physical relaxation through imagery. And third, teach them some self-talk strategies so that they can trigger the needed relaxed intensity into their performance during the heat of competition.

Physical relaxation is the fourth and final mental training tool in a coach's mental training tool box. As

you will see in the next part of the book, these four mental training tools are typically used together in building mental skills. If athletes develop solid goal mapping plans, they will have identified focus goals that help them engage in Productive Thinking during competition, which in turn induces physical relaxation. Athletes can practice Power Breathing while they are using imagery to mentally focus prior to performance. Imagery can be used to practice the Power Breathing Response in situations where athletes feel they are "losing it." As you will see in Part 3, the big three mental skills of attentional focus, energy management, and self-confidence all require athletes to effectively manage their mental and physical energy. Remind athletes how important physical relaxation and the other mental training tools are to gaining and maintaining the Inner Edge.

Summary Points for Chapter 11

1. Elite athletes can engage in fluid, loose performance movements because they have mastered the important skill of relaxed intensity.

2. Physical relaxation refers to willfully controlling bodily functions such as muscular tension, breathing, and heart rate to induce a more relaxed physical state of being.

3. Athletes can use physical relaxation to create a momentary relaxation response, create the feeling of relaxed intensity in periods of inactivity in competition, conserve energy prior to competition, rest and recover from strenuous competition, prepare the body for sleep, and to relax during the physical exertion of competitive performance.

4. Imagery and self-talk are mind-body techniques that can program the brain to induce a relaxation response in the body.

5. Improper breathing contributes to tension, anxiety, panic attacks, depression, and fatigue.

6. Power Breathing is the conscious slowing and deepening of breaths using the diaphragm and abdominal muscles to reduce muscle tension and somatic anxiety.

7. The Quick Power Breath is a useful relaxation technique to use in pre-performance routines or during a break in competition.

8. Progressive Muscle Relaxation was developed by Jacobson in 1930 as a conscious muscle con-

trol technique in which individuals can learn to recognize and release tension in specific muscle groups to achieve physical relaxation.

9. The Tense-Release method of conscious muscle control requires athletes to progressively tense and then relax the major muscle groups of the body.

10. The Release-Only method works well when athletes are given an image that induces physical relaxation in each muscle group.

11. The Quick Scan and Release technique can be used to relax crucial muscles related to motor movements specific to various sports.

12. Commercial audiovisual products are available that are easily used to lead athletes in physical relaxation training.

13. Rushing is a behavioral tendency of some athletes to speed up their behavior and performance when anxious, which interferes with the smooth muscle coordination needed for optimal performance.

14. The objective of physical relaxation is to help athletes effectively manage somatic anxiety and muscular tension, as opposed to eliminating it.

Glossary

physical relaxation: willfully controlling bodily functions such as muscular tension, breathing, and heart rate to induce a more relaxed physical state of being

Power Breathing: the conscious slowing and deepening of breaths using the diaphragm and abdominal muscles to reduce muscle tension and somatic anxiety

Reflective Learning Activities

1. Sport-Specific Chill Pills

Divide participants into groups of 3 by sport. Each group plans a set of physical relaxation strategies to be used by athletes in their specific sport. These plans should identify which relaxation methods will be used at what times—this must be very specific to the needs of athletes in this particular sport in both training and competition. (20 minutes in groups—additional time if presented to the entire group)

2. Personal Power Breathing

Each participant must identify at least three situations (at work, home, or in sport) in which they could use the Power Breathing response. Once these situations are identified (write them down), participants must practice the appropriate physical relaxation (breathing) response for these situations using imagery at least five times. After working on this Personal Power Breathing intervention, meet with the entire group and discuss each participant's experience in applying Power Breathing to their own stressors. (Assignment over a two-day period)

3. Progressive Partners

Participants pair up and lead each other through the Tension-Release and Release-Only methods of progressive muscle relaxation somewhere outside of class. Afterwards, the entire group meets to discuss the experience. What was difficult about leading the exercises? Which worked better and why? What did you learn and how can you improve in leading the exercises next time?

Note

[1]Use any Internet search engine and type in "physical relaxation for sport" to find many commercially-developed physical relaxation audio-visual products that you can use with your athletes. A favorite site of mine is www.performance-media.com which is for *Performance Media: Products for Maximizing Performance*. They offer a relaxation training CD with instructions for progressive relaxation and breathing.

Part Three

Mental Skills for Athletes: The Big Three

What is the "right mental stuff" for athletes? What are the key mental skills that athletes need to succeed? You could name many characteristics, but in this book, we'll examine the three big mental skills that I believe are crucial for athletes to master to gain the Inner Edge. These are

- to focus their attention where and when needed, no matter what else is going on,
- to manage their competitive energy for optimal mental and physical readiness, and
- to be confident in their abilities as athletes.

You learned about the four basic mental training tools in Part 2. The focus of Part 3 is to use the techniques in your mental training tool box to enhance the "big three" mental skills in your athletes. That is, ath-

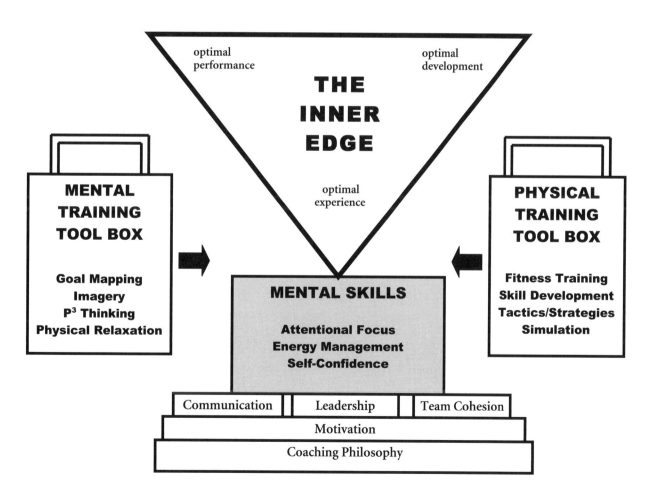

Figure 12.1 Where mental skills fit into the "big picture" of the Inner Edge

letes must learn to focus despite all distractions, manage intense competitive pressure and nervousness, and remain confident despite performance struggles. A tall order!

To refresh your memory of the "big picture," these mental skills are shown in the shaded portion of Figure 12.1. The mental skills rest on the building blocks from Part 1 of the book, and they are enhanced by using tools from both the mental training and physical training tool boxes.

Although some athletes are more mentally tough than others, all athletes can improve their mental skills (just as they can improve their physical skills). It takes time, practice, competitive experience, effective coaching, and the systematic use of mental training techniques described in this book. In reading Part 3, you will gain insight into using mental and physical training techniques to help your athletes be more focused, confident, and properly energized to perform. And remember to apply the lessons learned in this part of the book to yourself. Focused, energized, confident athletes typically have focused, energized, confident coaches—modeling these qualities rubs off on your athletes. So read on to increase your mental skills and those of your athletes!

Chapter Twelve

Attentional Focus

Photo by Brett Hansbauer

Chapter Preview

In this chapter, you'll learn:

- why "paying" attention is costly, as compared to performing on "autopilot"
- the difference in choking and panicking, and what athletes should do when each occurs
- that athletes must master different types of attention to be successful
- how to help your athletes develop routines and focus plans to use in competition

"When life seems to be coming at us head-on, with both barrels blazing, when our schedule can't handle even one more thing, when we feel we've got more plates spinning in the air than a circus performer, don't panic. Focus on one thing at a time, give each task your undivided attention, and you'll be surprised at what you can accomplish. You can do more than you ever dreamed possible." **Greg Barton** *(1999, p. 122)*, who earned two Olympic gold medals on the same day in kayaking, demonstrating uncommon physical capacity and mental focus

"There's always chaos at big meets. Whoever handles the chaos wins." **Marion Jones**, 2000 Olympic Games gold medalist in three track and field events

W hen Jackie Robinson became the first African-American to play major league baseball with the Brooklyn Dodgers in 1947, he was subjected to intense verbal abuse from fans, opposing players, and even his some of his own teammates. When traveling with the Dodgers, Robinson was often refused service in hotels and restaurants. Those heaping the abuse on Robinson hoped that they could bait him to lose control of his emotions and distract him from the mental focus needed to succeed in baseball. Of course, Robinson outlasted those who attempted to destroy his self-control and focus, and he channeled his frustration and anger into a fiery intensity on the field that won the respect of his teammates and opponents. He became an All-Star, World Series champion, and one of the most admired athletes of the 20th century. His personal victory over prejudice was perhaps due more to his ability to maintain focus than it was to his outstanding physical ability in baseball.

Annika Sorenstam was the first woman in 58 years to complete on the PGA tour (since Babe Zaharias in 1945), and her appearance at the PGA Colonial tournament in May 2003 created a flurry of media and public attention that was unprecedented in professional golf. Several male golfers publicly stated that they hoped that Sorenstam failed in her attempt to compete successfully with the men of the PGA Tour. Sorenstam talked prior to the tournament about the difficulty of focusing based on the intense pressure of the international spotlight of media attention: "That's going to be the toughest thing. Golf is a mental sport. I'm not worried about my golf game, but I am worried if I can keep my mind straight and focus on what I have to do. This is something that I've never experienced before" (Sorenstam Stronger, 2003, p. A10).

As I watched Sorenstam on television just prior to her teeing off, there was a brief moment in which I saw fear apparent on her face. Immediately, she stood more erect, smiled, and quickly regained her "game-face" focus. After hitting her first drive down the middle of the fairway, Sorenstam pretended to swoon as if saying, "Wow, I'm glad that's over." She went on to par the first hole and play amazingly well in light of the pressure that she described as the most she had ever felt in competitive golf. Annika Sorenstram demonstrated to herself, and the world, that she could maintain the mental focus needed to succeed despite overwhelming pressure.

To achieve the Inner Edge, athletes must develop their ability to focus attention, especially under pressure. All mental training culminates in the instant an athlete must focus on performance execution. It is simply the most important mental skill. Jackie Robinson was able to maintain his focus on hitting, running, playing defense, throwing—on playing the game of baseball—despite a storm of controversy around him. Robinson chose to focus his attention and efforts on being the best he could be in baseball, and this allowed him to excel and defeat the racist, bigoted attitudes of the time. Annika Sorenstam also displayed the supernormal ability to focus on her performance, as opposed to the media distractions, in her appearance in a PGA tournament event. As you will learn in this chapter, how and where athletes focus their attention makes the difference between choking and peak performance in sport.

If coaches want to help their athletes focus more effectively, they need to understand three key characteristics of attention (Abernathy, 2001; Posner & Boies, 1971). We all know what attention is—it's what we focus on or what we choose to think about at a particular moment. However, we're limited in what we can focus on, which is the first characteristic of attention. Also, our readiness and ability to focus is influenced by our emotional states, which is the second important characteristic of attention. And third, attention involves selectivity, meaning that we all have the ability to engage in selective attention or to choose how to focus in different situations.

Thus, focusing in sport involves attentional capacity, readiness, and selectivity. The first three sections of the chapter discuss these three aspects of attention. Then, in the remainder of the chapter, practical strategies are presented to help you understand how to help athletes focus better in competition. Athletes tend to think that distractions and obstacles hurt their performance, but what actually hurts their performance is how they choose to focus when distractions and obstacles occur. Attentional focusing is a key to gaining the Inner Edge, and athletes must accept responsibility for maintaining a strong, connected focus when they are performing. And they can do it—it just takes some practice! Hopefully, the information in this chapter can enable you as a coach to help your athletes do the mental and physical training needed to become focused, mentally tough competitors.

Attentional Capacity in Athletes

It is very difficult, even impossible, for athletes to focus on more than one thing at a time. In fact, athletes' performance is typically disrupted when they fail to focus their attention on one thing (e.g., dropping a pass in football while thinking about an oncoming tackler). Thus, the first important aspect of attention is that athletes are limited in the amount of information that they can process at one time. That is, they have a limited capacity of attention during performance.

So how do athletes pay attention to all the things they need to focus on when performing their sport? Actually, the key is whether they "pay" attention or have learned to perform the skill automatically without conscious effort. "Paying" attention means athletes pay out part of their limited attentional capacity to think about something (e.g., how to serve a volleyball). "Paying" attention is expensive because it "costs" a great deal in terms of eating up crucial amounts of an athlete's limited attentional capacity. However, through practice, athletes automate their skills, meaning that they are able to perform them without consciously focusing on how to perform. A skilled volleyball player can easily serve a volleyball without "paying" attention to *how* to serve.

"Paying" attention has been termed controlled processing, while the lack of focusing attention on how to do a task is termed automatic processing (Schneider, Dumais, & Shiffrin, 1984). **Controlled processing** is *mental processing that involves conscious attention and awareness of what you are doing when you perform a sport skill.* Controlled processing is used by athletes when they learn a skill, and it is slow, sequential, effortful, and involves self-consciousness about what they are doing. When individuals learn the golf swing, they engage in controlled processing so they can think about how to grip the club, address the ball, and then perform the take-away, backswing, and downswing. This laundry list of sequential things to think about is overwhelming, and anyone who has ever learned the golf swing will tell you that it's very difficult to attend to all these things at this conscious, controlled processing stage (as it is with any sport skill).

Automatic processing is *mental processing without conscious attention.* It is rapid, effortless, integrative, and not part of an athlete's awareness. Athletes engage in automatic processing all the time in their performance of well-learned skills. A point guard can automatically process how to dribble and bring the ball up the floor against defensive pressure, while focusing her attention on the play being run and where she will make the first pass to initiate the offense. A popular example of automatic processing is that most of us can walk and chew gum at the same time, without having to think about how to do these things! All sports require a combination of automatic and controlled processing, because athletes should perform the physical skills of their sport in a reflexive, automatic manner, yet be able to make decisions, use strategy, and consciously focus on dealing with unexpected situations or new information.

The goal for all athletes is the automatic execution of well-learned and highly practiced sport skills.

Automatic processing (or "autopilot") is oftentimes the key to peak performance because athletes are not consciously processing what they're doing, and thus are not open and vulnerable to distractions, self-consciousness, and anxiety. Elite athletes certainly do not focus their attention on what they're doing when they perform at their best. However, all athletes must begin their sports and endure the early learning phases of controlled processing, and with practice, they will "build their machines" and develop the ability to perform on "autopilot" in all types of stressful situations.

Attentional Readiness in Athletes

The second characteristic of attention is that the emotional state of athletes (particularly their level of anxiety), or their degree of readiness, has an enormous influence. Think about how the pressure of competition affects your athletes' abilities to focus on the task as well as your coaching instructions. I remember several athletes that I coached whose abilities to focus and process strategy information were severely hampered by their extreme anxiety during pressurized competitions. Research shows that stress and anxiety can (a) narrow athletes' attention too much so they miss important performance cues and (b) cause athletes to focus on internal processes as opposed to focusing on key external performance cues.

Attentional Narrowing as the Result of Anxiety

As shown in Figure 12.2, the ability of athletes to process cues in the competitive environment is directly affected by their degree of arousal (level of mental and physical readiness) or anxiety (Easterbrook, 1959). At low levels of arousal, athletes are very accurate in identifying peripheral cues and, in fact, even focus on too many things, including cues that are irrelevant and unrelated to performance. This occurs when athletes are not energized enough to perform, and their focus of attention is too broad to "zero in" on what they should be thinking about. Coaches commonly admonish athletes to "get focused" when they observe athletes who don't seem ready to perform. From an attentional standpoint, athletes' lack of readiness means that they waste their attention on irrelevant cues and focus too broadly on too many things.

At high levels of arousal, such as when athletes become anxious, the attentional focus of athletes becomes too narrow, and they fail to process task-relevant cues that are needed to perform successfully (see Figure 12.2). Such is the case of a quarterback who becomes anxious and focuses only on his primary receiver, with his attentional field narrowed to the point where he cannot scan the field to find his secondary receivers or additional options on the play. As a former coach, I remember this "glassy-eyed" look in my athletes when they were very anxious and unable to focus effectively on my instructions as well as what was occurring on the floor during a basketball game. Research has supported that athletes' identification of peripheral cues becomes slower and less accurate at high levels of anxiety (Janelle, Singer, & Williams, 1999; Landers, Wang, & Courtet, 1985; Williams & Elliott, 1999).

As shown in Figure 12.2, moderate levels of arousal lead to optimal attentional focus for athletes. A moderate level of arousal means athletes are appropriately physically and mentally energized for performance, which enables them to focus effectively on task-relevant cues and not allow themselves to focus on irrelevant cues. This is important based on our knowledge that athletes have a limited capacity of attention. Because of this limit, it is critical for athletes to optimize their focus by choosing to think about the important aspects of performance, as opposed to irrelevant or unimportant thoughts that eat up their limited amount of attention.

Self-focused Attention as the Result of Anxiety

Anxiety and stress can also affect attention by making athletes more self-focused. This self-focus may be on perceived inadequacies as they worry about performing well, which interferes with the need to focus externally on the demands of the task (e.g., worrying whether you can hit a pitcher's fastball as opposed to focusing on the ball coming out of her hand).

Self-focused attention as the result of anxiety also causes athletes to attempt to consciously control their performance. As discussed previously, peak performance occurs when athletes engage in automatic processing, where performance is effortless because it doesn't require conscious attention. Thus, self-focused attention disrupts the automaticity that athletes need to perform their best, because they try to consciously monitor and control the performance process. It's almost like the anxiety makes

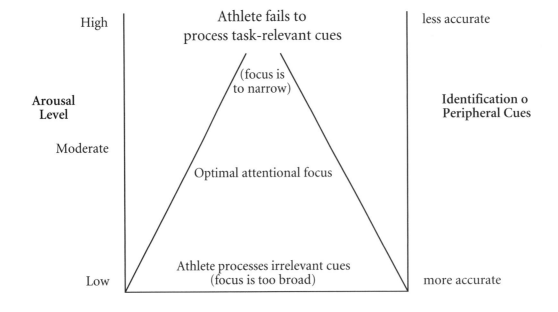

Figure 12.2 Relationship between attention and arousal/anxiety (Easterbrook, 1959)

them regress to an earlier learning stage, where they had to "think" about their performance. Self-focused attention represents an elite athlete's worst nightmare, because they fail to "get out of their own way" enough (attentionally speaking) to let their automatic, well-grooved performance response happen automatically. Research has demonstrated this with field hockey players, who increased their self-focus and attempts to consciously control their performance when anxious (Liao & Masters, 2002).

When anxiety increases too much, athletes become more aware of the situation and the consequences of poor performance, which may cause them to worry and/or attempt to over-control their performance. This is even typical with elite athletes, and the key is for athletes to plan and practice strategies that they can use to focus effectively in stressful situations. Or, athletes can use mental strategies to optimize their arousal levels, because as arousal/anxiety levels become more optimal, athletes are much more likely to focus effectively.

Photo by Robin Vealey

Panicking and Choking in Sport: Why They Occur

We've established that anxiety affects athletes' attention in two ways: by narrowing their attention and creating a self-focus that leads to controlled processing. Actually, these two attentional explanations for how anxiety hurts performance also explain two of the most intriguing phenomena in sport: panicking and choking. People assume that athletes panic and choke as the result of intense competitive pressure, but understanding exactly how and why these dreaded things occur requires attentional explanations. Panicking and choking are different, and in fact, opposite, when explained in terms of attentional focus.

Panicking. Panic is defined in most dictionaries as a sudden, unreasoning, hysterical fear. The key word in these definitions is "unreasoning." **Panic** represents *an extreme emotional state that creates an attentional focus so narrow that individuals are unable to process information (or reason) to help themselves.* In Figure 12.2, panic is represented at the point which the two lines (the breadth of athletes' attention) meet. At this point, a person's attentional focus is zero, and they rely on gut reactions and instinct, as opposed to thinking. Panic is the opposite of reason or any type of information processing, and the often self-defeating behavior that occurs as a result of panic is a simple human reflex. Thus, panic occurs when people stop thinking (Gladwell, 2000).

A typical example of panic is that of scuba divers who lose their air supply while diving deep in the ocean (Gladwell, 2000). Despite their training, novice divers may still attempt to speed to the water's surface when they realize they have no air, which of course results in the deadly bends or decompression sickness. When asked to explain their seemingly illogical behavior, the divers describe an instinctual survivor reflex, which overrides all logical thinking and training. Another example of panic is the plane crash that took the lives of John F. Kennedy Jr., his wife, and his sister-in-law in 1999 (Gladwell, 2000). Air traffic controllers monitoring the flight path of Kennedy's plane observed several curious maneuvers just prior to the crash. These maneuvers indicated to them that Kennedy was desperately trying to find the lights of his destination (Martha's Vineyard, an island off the coast of Massachusetts) while flying over the dark ocean with no lights to guide him or to provide a visual horizon to keep his wings level. Several experienced pilots and air traffic controllers believe that Kennedy's attention was fixated on a desperate search for lights to guide his plane, and that this narrow focus brought on by panic overrode the training that had provided him with the expertise to read the instruments within the plane to keep it steady and avoid crashing.

When people panic, they fall back on their instincts and forget training and reason in their attempt to survive. Panic is only life-threatening in extreme sports, although a complete shutdown of reasoning could certainly be life-threatening in auto racing, downhill skiing, various forms of ski jumping, and other high-risk sports. I have observed athletes panic in sport, such as in pressure situations where athletes are unable to follow a certain strategy (e.g., press-breaker offense in basketball) because their attention is so narrow that they are unable to even process a well-learned response from training.

Choking. **Choking** is a term well known to athletes and sport aficionados, and one of the most dreaded occurrences in sport. It is a *sudden or rapid deterioration of performance below the typical and expected level ability for an athlete performing in a pressure situation.* Why do athletes choke and how is this different from panic? Let's see if you can identify the attentional key to choking by reading the two examples described in the following Clipboard titled "Even Champions Choke!"

Clipboard

Even Champions Choke!

Two of the most famous episodes of choking in the history of sport were committed by Jana Novotna in tennis and Greg Norman in golf. These athletes were outstanding, world-class champions in their respective sports, and they should not be disparaged or ridiculed based on the examples used here.

At the 1993 Wimbledon final, Jana Novotna had a 4-1 lead in the final and deciding set of her match with Steffi Graf. She was serving at 40-30, meaning that she was one point from winning the game and going up 5-1 in this final, decisive set of the most prized championship in tennis. Of course, the All-England Club was packed with spectators, the Duke and Duchess of Kent were watching from the Royal Box, and millions from around the world watched on television. All of a sudden, unbelievably, Novotna's performance faltered. Serving at 40-30, she hit her first serve into the net. Seemingly, something tripped in Novotna's brain, because she then hit a weak, awkward second serve into the net for a double fault. It went downhill from there, followed by a badly missed forehand volley and weak overhead shot. Graf won the game, and instead of leading 5-1, Novotna's lead was 4-2 with Graf serving. Novotna continued to deteriorate, both in her tennis performance and in her body language. She played cautiously, tentatively, and seemed to be in a negative performance spiral with no hope of regaining her poise and ability to execute winning shots. Graf came on to win the match, and everyone who watched will always remember Novotna crying on the shoulder of the Dutchess of Kent, who attempted to console her through her embarrassment and disappointment during the awards ceremony.

Greg Norman seemed to hold an insurmountable lead after the first three rounds of the 1996 Masters Golf tournament. At the time, Norman was arguably considered the best player in the world, playing for the most prestigious championship in golf. He began the final round on Sunday paired with Nick Faldo, over whom he had a six-stroke lead. Everything was fine until the 9th hole, when Norman made a bad error that seemed to unnerve him and touch off something inside of him that had, until then, been dormant. He followed the 9th hole with three straight bogeys, missing fairways, missing putts, and looking like a deer caught in a car's headlights. His swing, which before was fluid and graceful, became mechanical, contrived, and totally out of synch. It was painful to watch one of the best athletes in the world completely choke, as hole after hole he was unable to hit the ball with any amount of precision. Norman gave the tournament away to Faldo, who after they had putted out on the 18th hole, put his arms around Norman and whispered, "I feel horrible about what happened. I'm so sorry" (Gladwell, 2000, pp. 1-5).

Can you identify the attentional explanation for choking suggested in the Clipboard examples of Jana Novotna and Greg Norman? The answer lies in the fact that choking is the opposite of panic (attentionally speaking), so if panic occurs when athletes fail to think, choking occurs when athletes think too much. Choking results from self-focused attention brought on by anxiety, which induces athletes to revert to controlled processing (thinking about how they are performing as they do it) as opposed to automatic processing, in which they just let their performance flow unconsciously (Baumeister, 1984; Gladwell, 2000). Both Novotna and Norman began thinking about their shots when they became anxious. This thinking changed their performance from an effortless, fluid, smooth "just do it" mode to a painfully deliberate, slow, cautious mode. If panic is about reverting to instinct, choking is the loss of instinct (Gladwell, 2000). Athletes choke because they "pay"

attention to how they're performing, and boy, do they ever pay for it in their performance.

So how can coaches use this information? It seems important to understand that anxiety can influence attention in two distinctly different ways. Coaches should carefully observe athletes when they are anxious to identify how their anxiety influences their performance. As we'll discuss in the next chapter, anxiety is a normal response to competition and indicates a level of readiness to perform. Some athletes manage their anxiety effectively, and thus are able to maintain their attentional focus under pressure. However, some become very narrow in focus and tend to panic. When athletes begin to panic, they must manage their arousal levels to calm themselves and regain focused attention. They must learn to recognize that they are too energized and attempt to slow down and verbally remind themselves of what they have to do and that they are trained to do this.

Attempting to intervene when athletes are choking is harder than when they panic, because it's much harder to turn off the controlled processing that occurs with choking. That is, it's easier for athletes to gain conscious control of their thoughts, as compared to attempting to *consciously* make themselves *release conscious control* of their performance. However, there are strategies that athletes can use to refocus when they begin to choke, and even strategies they should follow when they are in the midst of choking. These are presented later in the chapter. At this point, you as the coach should simply understand the difference in panic and choke situations, es-

pecially how anxiety influences athletes' attention to create each of these problematic psychological states.

Attentional Selectivity in Athletes

The third defining characteristic of attention is that it involves selectivity, meaning that athletes have the ability to choose what they focus on. Selectivity in attention is critical for athletic performance when you consider the enormous amount of stimuli that bombards athletes from a variety of sources during competition, including external (e.g., crowd noise, officials, weather, opponents) and internal (e.g., worry, fatigue) distractions. **Selective attention** is *the process in which certain information is selected for detailed processing while other information is screened out or ignored* (Abernathy, 2001). The ability to complete a successful penalty kick in soccer, make solid contact with an oncoming curve ball in baseball, and hit the center of the target in archery requires attention focused only on the most relevant sources of information.

Selective Attention as Part of Expert Performance

Selective attentional ability is crucial for successful sport performance. Research clearly indicates that expert athletes differ from beginning athletes in their selective attentional ability.

Selective processing of cues from the sport environment. Expert athletes in ball sports are superior to novice athletes in their abilities to predict in advance the speed and direction of oncoming ball flight by focusing on the body positions and movements of their opponents (Park, 2003; Starkes, Helsen, & Jack, 2001). More selective processing of cues in sport frees up additional attentional capacity and allows athletes the advantage of anticipating such things as ball flight, rebound trajectory, movement of opponents, and type and placement of the attack shot in volleyball. Although some outstanding athletes are known for their exceptional eyesight, most differences between skilled and unskilled performance is in athletes' ability to process information that is specific to their sport.

Expert athletes in basketball, field hockey, volleyball, soccer, karate, and figure skating were found to be superior to novice athletes in their sports in their ability to recognize, recall, and retain information about structured game situations (Park, 2003;

Starkes et al., 2001). This means that expert athletes are superior in their selective attentional ability to recognize formations and patterns of play, which advantages them in anticipating certain actions in competition. Coaches often speak of the need for anticipation, and this comes from athletes' ability to selectively attend to relevant features of their particular sports.

Expert athletes also use more efficient visual scanning patterns during competition. For example, expert kick boxers focus on their opponents' heads, while using their peripheral vision to attend to their opponents' hands and feet to anticipate certain attacks (Ripoll, Kerlirzin, Stein, & Reine, 1995). Similarly, expert soccer players focus on the player in possession of the ball, and scan the periphery to pick up movements of other players to attempt to anticipate the direction of a pass (Williams & Davids, 1998). Novice athletes use less effective attentional strategies, often focusing on the wrong things at the wrong times (Singer, 2002). Consider the following quote by a former NFL running back, describing his attentional focus when running with the ball: "Even though I'm not thinking, I'm aware of everything. I may run sixty yards without a thought, but when I get to the end zone I can tell you where everybody was and who blocked who. And not just the guys near me, but all over the field" (Zimmerman, 1979, p. 40).

Self-regulation of pre-performance attentional states. Expert performers in sport also show more selective control of their pre-performance states, which serves to enhance their performance. This research is conducted using psychophysiological measures such as electroencephalogram (EEG), which assesses brain activity and heart rate to measure degree of body activation. EEG measures can determine the amount of stimulation in certain parts of the brain that relate to attention. Expert shooters show greater relaxation in the left hemispheres of their brains (analytical part of brain) prior to shooting as compared to novice shooters, which indicates that the experts significantly decreased their controlled processing and engaged their automatic processing ability prior to performance (Janelle, Hillman, Apparies, et al., 2000). Interestingly, as novice archery athletes improved their performance, their EEG patterns began to resemble the brain patterns of elite archers (Landers, Han, Salazar, et al., 1994). These changes in brain patterns indicated an increase in automatic processing and a quieting of the left hemisphere, suggesting a decrease in controlled processing. Research also shows that elite shooters, archers, and golfers decelerate their heart rates just prior to trigger pull, arrow release, or putting, indicating more efficient attentional control (Boutcher, 2002). Overall, elite athletes have refined their selective attentional ability, which then becomes part of the automatic processing they engage in during their performance.

Types of Attention Needed by Athletes

Athletes know they need to focus. They hear this a lot from coaches, but what should they focus on? If the key to effective sport performance is selective attention, we need to provide athletes with some specific guidelines as to where they should focus their attention. Obviously, every sport requires specific types of attention at specific times. However, there are some unique types, or dimensions, of attention that are important in all sports.

Two dimensions of attention. Attention in sport may be thought of as having two dimensions (Nideffer & Sagal, 2001). As shown in Figure 12.3, attention varies by both width and direction. Athletes' *width* of attention can range from very broad to very narrow (the horizontal axis in Figure 12.3). Think of attentional width as a spotlight, which can vary from a narrow, pinpoint, laser-like point of light to a broad, all-encompassing field of illumination. Like the spotlight, athletes can open their attentional field up to focus broadly or they can narrow it to focus specifically on one thing. Returning serve in tennis requires a narrow focus of attention, while a field hockey goalie needs to focus broadly to attend to all the players on the field and the flow of play.

Athletes' *direction* of attention can be focused either internally or externally (the vertical axis in Figure 12.3). Athletes focus internally to monitor their bodies, gather their energy, or to visualize how to shoot a free throw. They focus externally to visually lock on to a target, opponent, or incoming projectile. I use popular labels describing the dimensions of attention to help athletes remember them. Any type of broad attention is "big picture," and narrow attention means to "zoom in". Focusing externally is cued by being "out there," while focusing internally means being "in here" (it helps to point to your head to indicate where "in here" actually is).

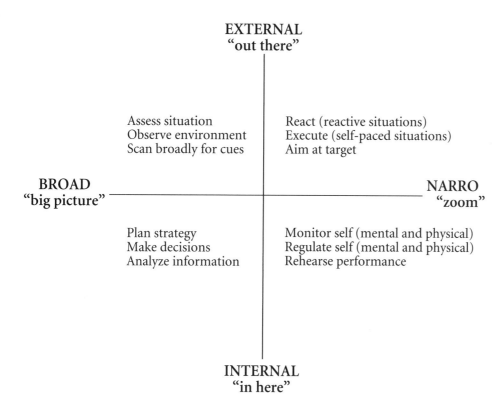

EXTERNAL
"out there"

Assess situation
Observe environment
Scan broadly for cues

React (reactive situations)
Execute (self-paced situations)
Aim at target

BROAD
"big picture"

NARRO
"zoom"

Plan strategy
Make decisions
Analyze information

Monitor self (mental and physical)
Regulate self (mental and physical)
Rehearse performance

INTERNAL
"in here"

Figure 12.3 Types of attention needed in sport

Four types of attentional focus needed in sport. As shown in Figure 12.3, the two dimensions of attention create four separate quadrants, which represent the types of attentional focus required in sport: broad-external, narrow-external, broad-internal, and narrow internal. A broad-external focus enables athletes to assess, observe, and scan the environment and situation around them ("big picture out there"). A narrow-external focus allows athletes to zoom in as with a camera zoom lens, to execute a specific performance skill, react to specific performance stimuli, and/or aim at a target ("zoom out there"). A broad-internal focus enables athletes to plan strategy and analyze information ("big picture in here"). And finally, a narrow-internal focus allows athletes to monitor and regulate their mental and physical functioning as well as to mentally rehearse their performance ("zoom in here").

Attentional demands of different sports. Different sport situations require different types of attention, and athletes should understand how to focus differently based on the demands of the situation. One big attentional difference in sports is that the type of focus needed is dependent upon whether the sport is reactive or self-paced. In reactive sports such as basketball, soccer, softball, and hockey, athletes perform in relation to and in response to their opponents. Much of their performance involves reacting to actions by their opponents, and attentional demands are variable, fast-paced, and unpredictable. In self-paced sports such as gymnastics, shooting, archery, and the field events in track and field, the performance (and attentional) demands are more stable and predictable. These sports typically involve aiming at targets, or executing specific motor skills in relation to fixed equipment such as the high jump bar, the pole vault, or the balance beam.

Personal Plug-In

Before reading further, identify the different types of attention needed in your sport. Think of the many situations that make up your sport and describe the type of focus needed by athletes in each one. Does your sport have a primary type of attention? Also, where do athletes tend to get distracted or stuck, or where and when do they fail to make the necessary shifts to the appropriate types of attention needed in certain situations?

Most sports require athletes to shift from one focus to another. Golfers use a *broad-external* focus to assess terrain, distance, and wind speed/direction, and then move to a *broad-internal* focus to analyze the information and make a decision about club selection and type of shot. They then engage in a pre-shot routine to get themselves physically and mentally ready to execute the shot, and they rehearse the shot in their mind prior to hitting it (*narrow-internal* focus). Finally, they zoom in on the ball using a *narrow-external* focus, and they execute the shot. Athletes can think of this attentional progression as "get the big picture," "zoom in here," "zoom out there." "POW"—then they hit the ball with an automatic focus or feel for the shot.

A similar focus sequence would be followed by a baseball hitter and tennis player receiving serve, with the only difference coming at the final narrow-external focus phase, where the hitter and tennis receiver "zoom out there" to react to the pitched or served ball.

Cross-country skiers constantly shift back and forth between a narrow-internal focus to concentrate on their technique and self-regulation to a narrow-external focus on the trail that they're skiing. A hockey goalie spends a lot of time scanning the ice and patterns of play using a broad-external focus. He must know exactly when to zoom in to react and execute when a shot is made on goal. Narrow-internal attention is used by distance runners to monitor how their bodies are feeling, and to keep their mental focus and technique in form during their races. A narrow-internal focus is also used by weight-lifters and in the throwing events in track and field. The concentration for these athletes is internal, as they focus inwardly on pulling together or fusing their energy to manipulate objects in a single explosive strength movement. A broad-internal focus is used by athletes in many sports to make decisions and use strategy.

Summary of types of attention. Attention is optimal when athletes focus on the right things at the right times. Athletes should carefully analyze their sports and, with help from coaches, be sure that they understand how they should focus at different times in competition. Athletes must also identify where and when their focus breaks down, which typically occurs when they become distracted and fail to maintain the right attentional focus for effective performance in their sports. Keep in mind that with practice and the development of automatic processing, athletes automatically shift their focus using different types of attention much faster than they can consciously process. Once skills are mastered and athletes learn to manage their attention effectively, they don't consciously think about moving from narrow-internal to narrow-external and so forth. However, it's important that you as the coach understand these different types of attention, so you can recognize focus problems when they occur in your athletes and know what types of attention athletes need at certain times.

Differences in Attentional Skills

We've established that different attentional demands are required in various sport situations. As a coach, you've probably noticed that some of your athletes are better at certain attentional demands than others. Certain athletes are better at zooming in to focus narrowly, while others are better at external scanning to anticipate the actions of teammates and opponents. Some athletes are skilled in attentional flexibility so that they are able to shift their focus effectively to meet the different demands in their sports. Thus, some athletes are more attentionally suited for their sports than others (Nideffer & Sagal, 2001). Of course, you can train a point guard in basketball to scan more effectively to "see the floor" and

Photo courtesy of Miami University IT Communications

control a team's offense, but there are certain athletes whose attentional skills just fit what is needed in certain situations in sport.

There are paper-and-pencil tests developed by sport psyschologists that assess athletes' attentional skills. A popular one is the Test of Attentional and Interpersonal Style (Nideffer & Sagal, 2001), which measures an athlete's

- ability to engage in a broad-external focus,
- ability to engage in a broad-internal focus,
- ability to narrow their focus to avoid distractions,
- tendency to become overloaded with external distractions,
- tendency to beome overloaded with internal distractions, and
- inability to shift attention from one focus to another.

The TAIS generalizes to all sports and is not sport-specific in assessing athletes' responses. Research has shown that sport-specific versions of the TAIS are better in predicting athletes' behavior than the generalized TAIS. A tennis-specific version of the TAIS predicted match play results and showed that advanced players had more attentional skill than intermediate and beginning players (Van Schoyck & Grasha, 1981). A baseball/softball specific version of the TAIS showed that batting performance was positively related to attentional ability (Albrecht & Feltz, 1987). Finally, a basketball-specific version of the TAIS demonstrated that athletes' attention was related to various performance scores, including field-goal percentage, free throw percentage, assists, steals, and personal files (Bergandi, Shryock, & Titus, 1990).

Should coaches use tests such as these to assess the attentional skills of their athletes? Probably not. As a coach, you are in a unique position to observe your athletes in many practices and competitions. Through these observations, you can pinpoint the attentional strengths and weaknesses of your athletes without having to use paper-and-pencil tests. However, if interested, you could give your athletes an attentional questionnaire to make them more aware of their attentional strengths and weaknesses (or find a local sport psychology expert to do this for you). The intent of this exercise should be to educate your athletes about the types of focus they need and

to make them more self-reflective about their attentional skills. A test should not be used to make decisions about which athletes are better than others, who should play or not, and/or who should stay on the team and who should be cut. An alternative to the tests used in sport psychology research such as the TAIS is a simple rating scale that you could give your athletes to assess their attentional abilities. An example of this practical way of getting your athletes to self-assess their focus abilities is presented later in the chapter.

Associative and Dissociative Attention

What do athletes in long distance events think about during the long hours of training and competition? For example, what do marathoners think about during a 26-mile race? Or how about the Iron Man competitions and other ultra-endurance events that last for many hours? How in the world can anyone focus for *that long*? What *should* endurance athletes focus on to enhance their performance?

Interviews with marathon runners found that these athletes selected two main forms of attention: association and dissociation (Morgan & Pollock, 1977). **Associative attention** is when athletes *focus internally to monitor and self-regulate their physical, mental, and technical performance*. Associative attention also involves *focusing on the task of racing itself, such as monitoring progress and race strategy*. **Dissociative attention** involves *distraction or focusing attention away from the activity itself*. In dissociation, athletes can day-dream about many things (e.g., building a house, planning a vacation) or simply focus on the beauty of the external environment.

Overall, research suggests that performance in endurance events (running, swimming, rowing) is enhanced when athletes use associative strategies (Connolly & Janelle, 2003; Couture, Jerome, & Tihanyi, 1999; Scott, Scott, Bedic, & Dowd, 1999; Tammen, 1996). Associative attention is a useful strategy for both elite and novice athletes, and it makes sense that athletes' performance is enhanced by focusing on their body sensations and competitive decisions. Obviously, athletes engage in some dissociation, particularly in training and in different parts of competition to relax their minds. However, as the intensity increases in competition, athletes become more associative. Research has shown that as runners become more experienced, they learn to control their thoughts and use more specific and sophisticated associative strategies (Schomer, 1986). Thus, overall, it is helpful for endurance athletes to learn how to associate their attention to monitor their performance in ways that are most appropriate for them. Dissociation seems to be a good way to break up the monotony of long training sessions and can even be used for positive imagery and other mental training exercises.

Attentional Selectivity Problems

Athletes' performance is controlled by what cues they select to process from the environment and their own minds. Although the attentional skill of athletes varies, in normal circumstances most athletes can direct their attention effectively. In the heat of competition as the pressure builds, the skill of attentional selectivity becomes more difficult for athletes (Abernathy, 2001; Nideffer & Sagal, 2001). Three main problems in attentional selectivity are commonly observed in athletes: (a) selecting the wrong focus of attention, (b) becoming distracted, or allowing one's focus to drift, and (c) becoming stuck in one focus and unable to shift attention when needed.

Selecting the wrong attentional focus. Athletes fail to focus effectively if they are unaware of the specific focus needed for a particular performance. This is typical when learning sport skills. At early stages of skill development, athletes have not yet learned how to focus or what to focus on, and they also are expending large amounts of attention on performing the skill itself (controlled processing). Beginning racquetball players run all over the court chasing the ball, because they focus on the flight of the ball as opposed to the angles of rebound from the walls. Experienced racquetball players focus on the type of shot hit by opponents and move to the area of the court where the ball will finally come off the wall. In the words of Wayne Gretzky, "I skate to where the puck is going, not where it is now."

We all have experienced the "eureka!" effect of being taught a specific way to focus that enables us to leap forward in our skill development. I vividly remember finally "getting" the volleyball spike down when a coach made me focus on keeping the ball in front of my hitting shoulder. From then on, I had it—but I needed that one focus cue to master the skill. Coaches must teach not only the physical or motor progression of a skill to athletes, but also the

attentional focus progression to move from novice to elite skill levels. In addition, even elite athletes at times have developed bad habits or simply do not select the most appropriate cues to focus on. Training sessions should be specific to ensure that athletes know exactly how to focus their attention during the performance of different skills.

Becoming distracted. Becoming distracted, or letting one's attention drift to unwanted sources, is probably the biggest focus problem for athletes. Allowing distractions to break the focused connection needed to perform well is a primary cause of poor performance. Research has shown this to be a particular problem at big events, such as championship tournaments and the Olympic Games (Greenleaf et al., 2001). Research has also shown that the most successful athletes at these big competitions not only have focus plans, but also have developed distraction control plans that they practiced ahead of time and use religiously at the competition site (Orlick & Partington, 1988). Physical training sessions should be used to practice in the face of different distractions to train athletes to maintain a connected focus no matter what.

Clipboard

Amazing Comebacks and Last-Second Heroics

When teams make amazing comebacks or execute last-second plays to win, it is usually because they have diligently practiced these plays as part of their normal training. We know that athletes' attention narrows with increases in stress, so it's important to train athletes for last-second plays to make them well-learned and automatic. The following story, told by starting center Mitch Kupchak, describes how North Carolina's men's basketball team came back from incredible odds to beat Duke in one of the greatest comebacks in sport history. Kupchak gives due credit to Coach Dean Smith of North Carolina and how he prepared them to execute under pressure.

> "At home against Duke in 1974, we were down eight points with 17 seconds left. There was no three-point shot, so we had to score four times to tie it. His [Coach Smith's] calm throughout was amazing. The way he walked us through those 17 seconds, it was as if he said, 'Don't think about this. Just do as I say and we'll win.' There he was in the huddle, looking up at us with a kind of smile, saying, 'Bobby [Jones], make these two free throws, then we'll go into this defense, steal the inbounds pass, score and call time-out.' He didn't let us think about being down eight. He gave us step one—just do that. So Bobby made both free throws. We stole the pass. We scored. We called time-out. It all happened so fast. I remember the last play in particular. We had the ball under their basket and had to go the length of the floor. Coach calmly told us to run the 5-3-5 . . . We'd run the play in practice so often that we wondered when we'd really need it . . . The plan was to get Walter [Davis] the ball, have him take one dribble, and shoot. He did, and banked in a 35-footer. We won in overtime. The key to it all was that we were prepared—and that we believed. I'll tell you, we believed a lot more afterward, too" (Wolff, 1997, p. 40).

Getting stuck in a focus and not shifting when needed. The third attentional selectivity problem is when athletes get stuck in one type of attentional focus and can't make the needed shift to change it. The previous problem of distraction occurs when athletes shift attention without wanting to, while getting stuck occurs when athletes can't make an attentional shift when they need to. Athletes get stuck in a broad-external focus ("big picture out there") when they become overwhelmed with irrelevant information from their environment. They get caught up in worrying about everything and fail to zoom back in on themselves or their performance. This is exhausting when it happens! Another problem for athletes is overanalysis, which means they get stuck in a broad-internal focus and can't release their attention to narrow in and engage in automatic processing of their skills. Getting stuck in a narrow-internal focus occurs when athletes worry, have

self-doubts, and focus attention on whether they have the ability to succeed. And finally, some athletes get so focused in a narrow-external perspective that they fail to shift to another focus when needed. I worked with a football tight end who caught every pass thrown his way, but who was unable to do anything but fall down once he caught the pass. He had trained himself to focus so narrowly on catching the ball that he only thought about this. We developed a focus progression for him that included the cue words of "catch - balance - daylight." He used imagery to practice focusing on catching the ball, immediately balancing himself, and scanning for "daylight" or an opening into which to run.

Concentration as a double-edged attentional sword. The attentional problem of getting "stuck" brings up the issue of concentration vs. attention. Coaches use the popular term "concentration" as another name for focus. **Concentration** is *the ability to sustain a non-distractible attentional focus on a specific task.* We buy concentrated liquids because they are stronger and not diluted by other things. Similarly, concentrated attention is strong and not diluted by other thoughts. However, concentration is only one aspect of attention. Athletes can diligently concentrate, or focus their attention on one thing, and not make the necessary attentional shifts that are required for success in their sport. I once wrecked a car because I was concentrating so intently on reading street signs that I failed to yield the right-of-way to an oncoming car. Similarly, all of us have driven our cars on autopilot while concentrating on some deep thought, only to look up and realize we don't remember driving for the last few minutes. We should all realize that driving a car requires many attentional shifts!

Getting "stuck" in one focus of attention and not shifting when needed is an example of how concentration can sometimes be bad. Concentration is an important part of attention, because it is the ability to deeply focus and lock in attention despite distractions. However, too much concentration can hurt athletes if they can't be flexible and shift to other focus demands when they arise in sport. I've heard athletes describe this by saying, "Gee, I didn't pick that up because I was concentrating so hard on [something else]." The take-home point is that attention involves selecting the right cues, concentrating on them, and then being flexible and skilled enough to shift attention when needed.

Strategies to Enhance Athletes' Attentional Focus

Attention in sport has been discussed in terms of athlete's attentional capacities, their attentional readiness as related to arousal and anxiety, and their abilities to select and maintain the needed attentional focus for success in their sports. The remainder of the chapter is designed to provide you, the coach, with some practical ideas about how to enhance the attentional focus abilities of your athletes.

1. Athletes should build a strong physical machine and wire a trustworthy autopilot switch.

One of your main jobs as coach is to increase your athletes' abilities to engage in automatic processing. This is why you lead your athletes in repetitive practice so they can make their skills as automatic as possible. There is simply no substitute for the thousands of repetitions that athletes must make to automate their skills. And importantly, these repetitions should be fundamentally sound as the old adage that "practice makes perfect" only rings true if the practice is perfect as well. Attention to details and a focus on consistent execution of fundamental skills are essential in automating performance that will withstand the pressures and distractions of competition.

I like to tell athletes that they must "build their machine" by practicing over and over again to make their skills automatic. I also like to tell them that they are responsible for installing the wiring for their autopilot switches. They all want to use their autopilot switches and just let their performance flow, but they can't trust the switch under pressure unless they've worked hard to wire the machine so that the autopilot can work flawlessly. They need a trustworthy autopilot system to serve them well in stressful, pressurized performance situations. Encourage them to "build their machine" and "wire themselves" to be strong and efficient enough to withstand any pressures. If athletes take shortcuts in physical training, no amount of mental training can make up for their failure to build a strong machine for their performance.

2. Overload athletes with processing demands in training.

Similar to the premise that overload in weight training makes athletes stronger, attentional overload is a useful way to optimize athletes' attentional capacities and enhance their performance. Practice drills should be designed to require dual and even triple processing demands, such as adding a sixth player on defense in basketball, asking quarterbacks to make multiple reads of changing defenses, and drilling outfielders on responding correctly to different game situations as they are fielding grounders and fly balls.

Coaches should also overload athletes' attention by simulating distracters that are common in their

sports. Example distracters include crowd noise, loud music, rough play, trash talking by opponents, mistakes by officials, and environmental conditions such as rainy or cold weather. Football teams practice "wet ball" drills and high jumpers should practice in rainy conditions. In team sports, injuries to key players should be simulated, so that teams learn to incorporate reserve athletes in critical situations without losing focus. Create unexpected situations all the time in training your athletes (Orlick 2000). Provide them more or less warm-up time, change the order of practice, move practice to a different venue, and practice overcoming as many obstacles as you can think of to train your athletes to focus despite any expected occurrences.

Clipboard

Training a Tiger

Tiger Woods' father employed many attentional distractions while teaching his son selective focus in golf. Earl Woods, the father, would do things like drop his golf bag in the middle of Tiger's backswing, roll a ball across his putting line just prior to Tiger's putt, remind him not to snap hook his drive into the nearby houses, rip the Velcro on his golf glove in the middle of Tiger's backswing, jingle the change in his pockets before his bunker shots, and kick his own ball out of the rough when Tiger was looking. If Tiger had a wedge shot, his father would stand 15 feet in front of him and say, "I'm a tree," and Tiger would obligingly hit over him to the green. Earl Woods had one goal driving his seemingly bizarre training methods: "I wanted to make sure he'd never run into anybody who was tougher mentally than he was" (Reilly, 1995, p. 65).

3. Athletes should practice focusing in training sessions.

Talk to your athletes about the importance of focused training, because this leads to focused performance in competition. I find many athletes go through the motions in training, just "getting their reps in" without practicing the focus needed to succeed in competition. When these athletes hit typical obstacles in competition, they can't maintain their

Photo by Dale Sparks, All-Pro Photography

needed focus because they haven't practiced focusing through distractions. Coaches should set up certain drills by specifying the focus needed for that drill. A volleyball transition drill might require a quick, reactive focus, various training runs in track and field could emphasize a relaxed focus to increase speed, and difficult, intense drills can be run at the end of practice to train the ability to focus through fatigue. Athletes are very vulnerable to losing their focus when fatigued, and you should challenge them to develop their focus skills to remain connected even though they feel depleted at the end of competition.

Athletes should experiment with different focus cues that help them to maintain attention when performing different skills in practice. They can use cue words as simple focus reminders when practicing swimming or track starts, training in long distance events, and even when receiving criticism from their coaches and teammates. Focusing results from productive thinking, so coaches should emphasize and athletes should practice P³ Thinking during training sessions. Athletes should use self-talk cues (simple words) to trigger automatic execution of their skills and purposefully plan and practice how they will think and focus in pressure situations. Remind your athletes that thinking (and focus) is most productive when athletes stay in the present (focus on the "now"), occupy their minds with key performance thoughts, and keep their focus on things they control. Remind athletes to triage their thinking (discussed in Chapter 10) to prioritize their attentional resources to focus on the key things that will help them perform well.

Athletes must take (and be given) responsibility to focus. If they rely totally on coaches to verbally remind them to focus and how to think, they will never develop the personal attentional skills needed to succeed in competition. Educate your athletes about the types of focus you expect during training, timeouts, competition, and team meetings. Challenge them to catch themselves when distracted and to refocus immediately on their performance. Related to this, coaches should allot some practice time each day where athletes engage in a flow of performance without any prompting, directing, or teaching from coaches. Explain the purpose of this practice time to your athletes and challenge them to maintain their focus without constant reminders from you as the coach.

4. Teach athletes how and when to selectively attend when performing in their sports.

As discussed previously, athletes need to know how and what to selectively attend to in their sports. Master teachers and coaches do just this, by carefully instructing athletes what to look for and how to pay attention at different times. For example, in volleyball, blockers are taught to follow the ball until it leaves the setter's hands and then shift their attention to the oncoming hitter to set the block in the correct place. Here are some other examples: What should a basketball player focus on when playing defense? What should a field hockey goalie focus on and when should she shift her attention? What should a swimmer think about when doing the butterfly stroke? Where should a strong safety in football focus his attention during the snap count?

Obviously, coaches should start simple with young athletes who must initially focus their attention on learning the fundamental skills in their sports. As their skill increases and they move from controlled to automatic processing, athletes can progress in their attentional training to learn anticipatory cues, which they can pick up from opponents' movements and specific patterns of play.

5. Athletes need to focus on the right goals at the right times.

In training and competition, athletes should use personalized goal maps that include focus goals (see Chapter 8) to keep their attention on relevant aspects of performance. In particular, athletes should remember that the outcome, or milestone, goals that they set are to motivate them in training and provide high standards for them to pursue. However, these outcome goals should not be the main focus of attention for athletes. Athletes tend to lose focus and become anxious when they place too much emphasis and attention on achieving important outcomes. Athletes must engage in Productive Thinking so that they focus on performance and process goals in pursuit of their longer-term outcome goals. Focusing on the wrong goals, especially uncontrollable outcome goals, creates anxiety and attentional distractions for athletes and should be avoided.

Related to goals, athletes should constantly revisit their passion, or sense of purpose, in playing their sport. This sense of purpose was discussed in Chapter 8 as an important part of goal mapping.

Athletes lose their focus when they lose sight of why they are playing. Most athletes participate in their sport because they love it, and when they lose sight of their enjoyment of playing, they often lose their focus. Focusing on the quality of the experience is part of the Eastern philosophy of Zen, which is a focus method that emphasizes that you should be one with your activity. Zen is about being wholly there, totally present, and automatically connected with the activity that you're doing. Athletes can develop simple cue words to remind them of their passion, such as *fun*, *enjoy*, or *pure skill*. Refocusing on one's reason for participation is a good way to gain the perspective needed to calm your mind and perform effortlessly without "trying too hard." Imagery can be used to recreate the focus and feelings that athletes had in their sport in their earlier years of participation (Orlick, 2000). This mental return to a simpler, easier time when focusing was automatic reminds athletes of the ease and joy with which they can perform, similar to when they were younger.

Quotable Quote

"I've learned not to focus on the outcome of any event. Although you dream about it, and I dreamed about the gold medal for many years, I think the best thing for me is that I've learned to concentrate on what I need to concentrate on. I needed to concentrate on having a good warm-up, on being very smooth, very quick, looking for speed in the course. I went to the start and I wasn't concentrating on the final result, I was concentrating on what I needed to do to ski my very best. It just became natural for me. I went through the same motions I go through every race. It just happened naturally." **Kerrin Gartner,** Canadian downhill skier and Olympic gold medalist *(cited in Orlick, 2000, p. 31)*

---

6. Athletes must effectively manage their competitive anxiety or arousal levels.

Because attention is related to arousal, athletes can optimize their attentional focus by optimizing their levels of arousal or anxiety. Athletes should practice and have ready for competition some quick and basic physical relaxation strategies to calm their bodies, which in turn helps to calm their minds. As they learn to identify anxiety in their bodies, they can use the Power Breathing technique or simply take a Power Breath to manage their physical tension. They can use imagery to visualize smooth and perfect execution and then turn their body over to autopilot. A more extensive discussion of energy management for athletes is presented in Chapter 13. However, coaches should remember that athletes tend to focus better when they are at their optimal energy levels for performance.

7. Help athletes become more aware of their attentional skills and how they can improve.

Coaches can raise athletes' focus awareness by leading them through a self-assessment exercise. The Attentional Focusing Questionnaire for Athletes is provided in Appendix 12A. Make a copy of the questionnaire and the "Assess Your Focus Skills" worksheet provided in Appendix 12A for each of your athletes. In a team setting, ask them to complete the questionnaire, which they should do in about 10 minutes. Be sure to tell them that this is an exercise for them to assess themselves and learn more about focusing. You as the coach will not see their answers or use the information to decide which athletes are better than others. Stress that this is an educational exercise for athletes to learn about themselves, not an evaluative one for coaches to gather and use information about athletes.

Once athletes have completed the questionnaires, take them through the scoring procedures in the first two steps listed on the "Assess Your Focus Skills" worksheet. Then, you can either lead them through the rest of the worksheet as a group, or ask them to work individually through the worksheet themselves. If they do it by themselves, I recommend that you take time at the beginning to describe each of the five focus types and make sure they understand them. It works well to have a group discussion at the end about how these focus types work in your sport. This is a good time for you as the coach to provide tips to athletes about when these focus types are important and to suggest some sport-specific strategies to help athletes focus effectively in each area. Conclude the exercise by emphasizing that (a) mentally tough athletes are those that focus no matter what, and (b) focus skills can be learned and improved. Overall, make the exercise and discussion informative, interesting, non-threatening, and even fun for your athletes.

8. Athletes should develop, practice, and consistently use pre-performance routines.

A useful focus strategy for athletes to use just prior to performing is the **pre-performance routine**. This is a *preplanned, systematic sequence of thoughts and behaviors that an athlete engages in prior to performing a specific skill*. Some routines are quite simple (e.g., a deep breath) while others have more steps. Some routines have become famous, such as the pre-free throw routine of Steve Alford when he was playing for the Indiana Hoosiers in the1980s. Alford was one of the best collegiate free-throw shooters in the nation, and his routine of touching his socks, wiping his hands on his shorts, taking the ball from the referee, and then bouncing it three times prior to shooting was legendary. Indiana fans began chanting "socks, shorts, bounce, bounce, bounce" as Alford ran through his routine, until Coach Bob Knight asked them to stop. Interesting that the Indiana fans could have distracted Alford during his routine, which was designed to keep him focused from distractions!

Most pre-performance routines are used in self-paced activities like the basketball free throw, and other examples include volleyball and tennis service, penalty kick in soccer, diving, bowling, football and rugby kicking, golf, field events in track, and all shooting sports. Routines seem to work best when there is a lapse in competitive action, which means that athletes need to fill this lapse with Productive Thinking or routines that help them think and feel optimally. However, in reactive sports there are also lapses in which athletes could benefit from a brief routine, such as the time between pitches for softball/baseball fielders and the time between plays for football players. Coaches should consider the nature of their sports to decide if and when routines might be useful for athletes.

Clipboard

Routines for Swingers

Read over the following examples of preshot routines used by professional golfers (Ready, Set, 2004) and note the simplicity and personal nature of each routine:

• *"I begin by taking a practice swing next to the ball, along the line of the shot. Then I move three steps back and look at the target while holding the club in my right hand and squeezing the thumb, index finger, and middle finger of my left hand together. (It sounds strange, but I do it for concentration.) Then I pick a spot on my line in front of the ball and set up to that."* **Catrin Nilsmark**

• *"The most important thing about a preshot routine is to do the exact same thing every time. I take one practice swing behind the ball, look at my target, take one little waggle and then go. My focus is generally on the target or on a specific feel in my swing. It won't be a swing thought but a feel thought."* **Heather Daly-Donofrio**

Nilsmark uses an interesting focus cue (squeezing her fingers together) to lock in her preshot focus. Daly-Donofrio's use of a "feel thought" indicates that she creates a kinesthetic image or body feeling as part of her routine prior to swinging. As shown by the routines of these "swingers," the key is to find what works best for each athlete!

Why and how routines aid athletes' attention and performance. The most successful athletes use pre-performance routines, and athletes with the most consistent routines have been shown to perform the best (Cohn, Rotella, & Lloyd, 1990; Thomas & Over, 1994; Wrisberg & Pein, 1992). Research has shown that elite archers, shooters, and golf putters demonstrate effective attentional control as assessed by changes in their brain activity and heart rate during pre-performance routines, indicating that their well-learned routines help focus their attention and enhance their performance more so than beginning athletes with less sophisticated routines (Boutcher, 2002).

When you ask athletes about how their routines help them, you get many answers. Athletes usually say that their routines make them feel confident and more in control. Part of this control is attentional control, with the idea being that the routines cause athletes to focus on how they want to feel and what they want to think about, as opposed to being vulnerable to distractions and pressure. Other athletes describe their routes as a priming mechanism, to get their brain and muscles primed to execute a perfect motor performance skill. This is why many routines involve a practice swing/stroke/move, or the mental rehearsal of the upcoming skill. This priming idea also applies to athletes using routines to prime themselves to perform on autopilot. The routine serves as the autopilot switch by taking the athlete through well rehearsed, familiar behavior patterns that lead right into automatic execution. Overall, the purpose of pre-performance routines is to enable athletes to think and feel the way they want just prior to performance, whether that is feeling confident, relaxed, intense, energized, focused, or ready. Each athlete should personally develop his or her own routines for relevance and practicality. However, some team-oriented routines can be taught to athletes, as illustrated in the following example.

Example team routine. A simple, yet effective routine was developed for the University of Nebraska football team to keep players focused on one play at a time (Ravizza & Osborne, 1991). The routine, taught to the team by a sport psychologist along with the help of the coaches, was termed the 3 R's, which stood for the three steps of "ready, respond, and refocus." When the quarterback or defensive signal call was ready to call the play in the huddle, he gave the verbal cue of "ready." This was the cue for players to look at the signal caller's face and be in the present moment. The "ready" cue also triggered players to put any distractions or mental thoughts

© iStockphoto.com

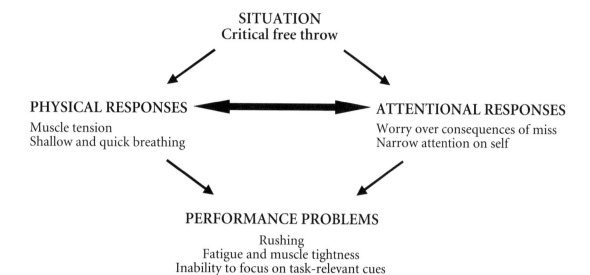

Figure 12.4 How physical tension and attentional distraction hurt performance

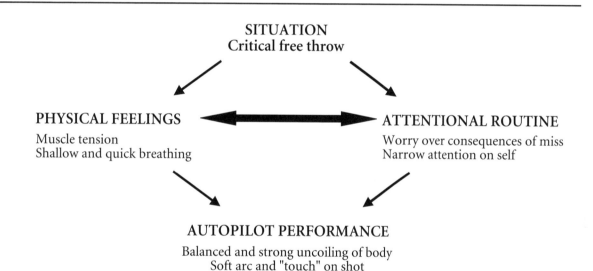

Figure 12.5 Centering for effective focus and performance

from the previous play out of their heads. Players were individually responsible for mentally rehearsing their performance for the upcoming play after it was called. (You could add a fourth R and ask athletes to "ready, rehearse, respond, and refocus.") Players were taught to shift to a pure reactive mode during the snap count and to focus on responding automatically when the ball was snapped. After each play, players were encouraged to take a moment to evaluate and make any mental adjustments needed based on the play, and then refocus to the present to get ready for the next play. Overall, the team routine

was successful because it was developed and incorporated into the physical training regimen of the Nebraska team.

Centering. A specific type of pre-performance routine that works well with athletes is centering. **Centering** is a *pre-performance routine that creates a physical readiness to perform and a desired attentional focus* (Nideffer & Sagal, 2001). Look at the centering examples in Figures 12.4 and 12.5 (modified from Nideffer & Sagal, 2001). Figure 12.4 shows how physical tension and shallow breathing interact with a loss of focus to create performance problems in the basketball free throw. In Figure 12.5, the athlete follows a planned routine of centering in which he creates a desired physical feeling and focuses on a set sequence of attention. He feels balanced, loose, and strong in his legs, and takes a Power Breath to relax his body. He dribbles three times to establish rhythm, and then coils his legs, feeling their strength. His focus just prior to shooting is "soft" over the front of the rim. This leads into the automatic execution of a softly arcing shot controlled by a strong uncoiling of his legs. Notice that in the first example, one of the performance problems was rushing. Routines help athletes remain consistent and deliberate in their thoughts and behavior to avoid rushing when performing under pressure.

A helpful exercise is to use blank centering templates (see Appendix 12B) and ask athletes to create centering responses for situations in which they would like to enhance their focus. On the left side of the centering worksheet shown in Appendix 12B, athletes identify a situation in which they would like to focus more effectively. Being self-reflective (and very honest), athletes should identify any physical and attentional problems that interfere with their performance. It helps if they specify exactly how these things affect their performance. Then, athletes move to the right side of the page and consider how they prefer to feel and focus in this situation. This should be kept very simple, and athletes should be encouraged to try different things until they get their routines just right.

Guidelines for developing routines. There are no rules or scripts for effective pre-performance routines. The main objective is that the thoughts and behaviors in athletes' routines should create the feelings that lead them to the automatic execution of their performance. (My four-year old son insists that he kicks the soccer ball better when he yells "Geronimo!" as he strikes the ball. Whatever works!)

I suggest that athletes develop their routines by considering four things:

(1) Create the physical and mental feelings that you want. Many pre-performance routines include a deep breath, because it's the most practical way to relax and reenergize our bodies to prepare to perform. Often, a key phrase can set the tone for your body and mind, such as feeling "strong and smooth" in your golf swing. Typical physical feelings include feeling loose, energized, coiled like a spring, strong,

and explosive. Mental cues might include feeling calm and focused, intense, confident, and relaxed.

(2) Develop a rhythm for yourself. Your routine should give you the feeling of rhythm that you want, which leads to smooth and effortless performance execution. Many athletes rush under pressure without realizing it. Think about the thoughts and behaviors that provide you with the best performance rhythm. Example behaviors that develop rhythm include pre-shot bouncing of the ball in tennis, volleyball, and basketball, and practice swings in golf, baseball, and softball. Rhythm can also be established be a sequence of thoughts, such as cueing a gymnastic floor routine or particular dive (e.g., push, coil, extend, and reach).

(3) Rehearse your performance. Most pre-performance routines contain a rehearsal component, meaning that athletes either mentally (imagery) or physically (simulate a volleyball serve) rehearse their upcoming performance. Rehearsal is often part of establishing a rhythm, but not always. "Seeing" and "feeling" yourself perform perfectly is typically a good thing to include in pre-performance routines.

(4) Develop your "lock-in cue." Just prior to execution, athletes should have one focus cue that locks in the focus they need for optimal performance. In golf, this is called a swing thought. The previous centering routine for a basketball free throw used the lock-in cue of "soft" over the front of the rim. Archers may just visually lock into the center of the target, without having to use a verbal cue to focus them on this. This lock-in cue should not interfere with the actual execution, but rather set the stage for automatic execution to occur. The lock-in cue seems to tell the brain "just do it" so that automatic, and hopefully perfect, performance follows. At the point of actual performance execution, elite athletes will tell you that they think about nothing at all. Think of the pre-performance routine as a mental plan that leads you to think about nothing at all! Ironic, isn't it?

As with all mental skills, athletes should start simple with pre-performance routines. A deep breath and focus cue are a good start, and athletes can modify their routines as they become more proficient. Pre-performance routines only serve to enhance attention and performance if they are practiced repetitively to become second nature. That is, routines will only trigger automatic performance if the routines become automatic themselves! Coaches should require athletes to practice their routines in physical training sessions, under varying conditions of pressure and distraction.

Clipboard

Training a Softball Routine

The following routine is for softball outfielders, and it is appropriate for beginning levels. It includes defining the attentional demands of the task, the specific routine, and exercises to train athletes in the skill and the routine.

A. Define the central task (to catch the ball [in the air or on the ground]).

B. Define peripheral tasks (call others off, listen to be called off, be aware of position of runners and where to throw, listen to infield on where to throw)

C. Routine to be followed:

  1. Before each pitch:

    a. Assess batter's potential or tendencies

    b. Repeat out loud where to throw (for ball hit in air and on ground)

    c. Touch glove to ground (trigger to narrow attention and focus on batter)

  2. If ball is not hit or fouled off: repeat steps 1b and 1c

  3. If ball is hit:

    a. Central visual narrowing on ball—pick up speed, spin, trajectory

    b. Peripheral auditory widening—listen for teammates voices

D. Training Exercises

  1. Work on catching fly balls - concentrate on sound of bat and first jump - call "mine."

  2. Hit fly ball between two players - call one to catch - make them call "mine."

  3. Fielder catches fly ball or grounder and responds to voices to throw to different positions

  4. Simulated game situations - athletes practice routine before each pitch.

9. Athletes should develop, practice, and consistently use focus plans.

Another attentional strategy for athletes is the development and use of focus plans. A **focus plan** is *a plan of how to think, feel, and act during various parts of competition to create an optimal mental focus for a particular performance* (Orlick, 1986a). Research has shown that focus plans lead to successful performance in sport (Mallet & Hanrahan, 1997; Orlick & Partington, 1988). Athletes develop and use focus plans because they do not allow their attention in competition to be left up to chance. Similar to the premise behind P³ Thinking, focus plans enable athletes to think and act "on purpose" in the pursuit of their goals. Tell your athletes that focus plans allow you to "make a nice day" as opposed to hoping that you'll "have a nice day." World-class athletes leave very little to chance in terms of their physical preparation, and they do the same with their mental preparation. They have well-defined and well-practiced focus plans that they use consistently to maximize their mental and physical energy for their performance (Greenleaf et al., 2001; Orlick & Partington, 1988).

Example focus plans. Focus plans range from very simple to extremely detailed. Some plans are sequential across time, such as planning one's focus during the first, middle, and end of a race. For example, 100 meter sprinters ran faster when they focused on race cues related to technical needs during the first ("push" during the acceleration phase), middle ("heel" for maximum velocity phase), and end ("claw" for speed endurance phase) of the 100 meters (Mallet & Hanrahan, 1997). Another example focus plan comes from a successful Olympian in pairs kayak:

> *"My focus was very concentrated throughout the race. We have a start plan, and in it I concentrate only on the first few strokes. I've found that if I concentrate beyond that, those first strokes won't be strong enough. Then I concentrate on the next little bit of the race. Then we come to the 250, and I say, 'Poof,' and we put in an extra burst to get the boat up and moving . . . Then it's getting to the end, and we have to really push . . . Almost every 3 seconds or so towards the end I'd have to say, 'Relax,' and I'd let my shoulders and my head relax, and I'd think about putting on the power, and then I'd feel the tension creeping up again so*

> I'd think about relaxing again, then power, relax . . . I look ahead down the lane. The last 100 meters are marked with red buoys and I knew how many buoys ahead of that to start our finish, because we had practiced for the course. When it was time for the very last part of the finish, we just go all-out power, forgetting style and everything else. Crossing the line, the thing I remember was just letting the emotion go, and being able to say, 'That's it, it's over!' I just knew that we'd gone our very hardest" (Orlick & Partington, 1988, p. 116).

Other focus plans are repetitive across structured types of competition such as a baseball player's focus while batting, while in the field, and while in the dugout between innings. Similarly, a volleyball player may plan a focus for playing the front row, playing back row defense, and for serving. A terrific example of this type of focus plan is Jack Nicklaus' (1993) "peak and valley" attentional regimen for his competitive golf rounds:

> "I was blessed with the ability to focus intensely on whatever I'm doing through most distractions. Nevertheless, I still can't concentrate on nothing but golf shots for the time it takes to play 18 holes. Even if I could, I suspect the drain of mental energy would make me pretty fuzzy-headed long before the last putt went down. In consequence, I've developed a regimen that allows me to move from peaks of concentration into valleys of relaxation and back again as necessary.
>
> My focus begins to sharpen as I walk onto the tee, then steadily intensifies as I complete the process of analysis and evaluation that produces a clear-cut strategy for every shot I play. It then peaks as I set up to hit the ball and execute the swing, when ideally my mind-picture of what I'm trying to do is both totally exclusionary and totally positive. Unless the tee shot finds serious trouble, when I might immediately start processing possible recoveries, I descend into a valley as I leave the tee, either through casual conversation with a fellow competitor or by letting my mind dwell on whatever happens into it.
>
> The next build-up of concentration begins as I reach the marker from which I'll pace the distance to my ball and start figuring yardages. My focus then gradually tightens as my caddie and I complete the math and I again finalize a clear-cut playing strategy, until it again peaks at address and during the swing. As I walk toward the green I return to the valley, although rarely quite as deeply as after the tee shot. Then I gradually begin to

emerge again at whatever point I can begin to assess my next shot, be it a putt, chip, pitch, sand shot, or whatever. The third peak occurs during the setup and swing, after which my focus remains fixed and sharp until the ball is finally in the hole. I try to adhere to this pattern whether I'm playing at my best or worst, but obviously have to work harder at it when things aren't going well. If there's a delay in play for whatever reason, I try not to let it irritate me by using the time to relax both mentally and physically" (pp. 47-48).

Focus plans can also be simple in terms of representing a focus philosophy. A focus plan or philosophy for baseball pitchers is based on the idea that pitchers don't have to make great pitches all the time to get batters out (Ravizza & Hanson, 1995). Pitchers should focus on being professional glove hitters and recognize that hitting the catcher's mitt is the only thing a pitcher can control. A suggested focus is to throw to the catcher, not to the batter. Pitchers must keep in mind that getting a hit in baseball is difficult, but it becomes much easier when the pitcher walks batters and gets behind in the count. Ravizza and Hanson suggest a focus plan for pitchers based on making good pitches—not great ones—which allows pitchers to be focused on the catcher's mitt and feel confident about their ability to do what is within their control. This is a simple focus concept, but one that can have drastic performance results for athletes.

Developing focus plans. Coaches can help athletes determine how to divide their events into meaningful segments for a focus plan. The next step is for athletes to decide how they want to feel, focus, and function during the different segments of their events. For each segment, athletes should identify what their their focus of attention should be and then design personally relevant cues to direct attention appropriately in that situation.

Orlick (1986a) suggests that athletes develop both pre-competition and actual competition plans. Athletes' pre-competition focus has three main objectives:

- to strengthen feelings of being prepared to solidify confidence
- to keep attention focused away from distractions and self-defeating thoughts
- to create an optimal pre-performance state

When athletes awake on competition day, they begin their focus plan of feeling confident, eager to compete, and prepared to do well. They must put themselves in a good mood anticipatory of performing well. I'm always amazed at athletes who wake up the day of a big competition only to "find themselves" in a bad mood. A major premise behind focus plans is that athletes must *choose* to think well and focus effectively. This happens automatically only once in a blue moon, so tell your athletes to avoid sitting around waiting for their blue moons to appear! As athletes move into their pre-competition routines of stretching and warming up, they should be engaged in a mental warm-up as well by concentrating on relevant things identified in their focus plans.

An example focus planning sheet for the jumping events in track and field is provided in Appendix 12C. Athletes in these events must plan their focus based on the nature of their event, in which they engage in a series of jumps, with rest and waiting time between each one. The focus plan allows them to identify an early competition day focus, a pre-jump physical and mental warm-up focus, a pre-performance routine for their jumps, and a post-jump routine. The planning sheet also incorporates refocusing responses, which is discussed more fully in the next section. This part of any focus plan involves anticipating how athletes will respond and focus when obstacles and problems arise. Coaches can modify the planning sheet in Appendix 12C to fit the demands and timetable of other sports.

10. Athletes should understand how to manage themselves when they lose focus, choke, and panic.

The final attentional strategy athletes must learn is the hardest one. Despite their best intentions and hard training, athletes will face situations in competition where they must steer their focus away from distractions of all kinds. In addition, and even though they don't like to think about it, athletes must prepare to manage themselves effectively in situations where they choke or panic.

Refocusing. Of all the things that set champion athletes apart from ordinary athletes, the ability to manage their focus and deal with distractions and setbacks is the most distinguishing factor (Orlick & Partington, 1988). To be mentally skilled, and especially mentally tough, athletes must learn to refocus. Thus, along with pre-competition and competition focus plans, athletes must have refocusing plans that outline how they would prefer to respond in distracting situations.

One of the best examples of refocusing occurred during the women's all-around gymnastics final at the 2000 Olympic Games (Grandjean, Taylor, & Weiner, 2002). The vault was inadvertently set 5 cm too low for half of the women competing in this event. As you might expect, the height difference negatively affected the gymnasts' performance, even though they didn't realize the problem was in the equipment. Five of the first 18 vaulters fell, including one athlete who had to leave the arena in a wheelchair. Most of the others stumbled and scored significantly lower then they had in the qualifying round. The error was found and corrected for the remaining gymnasts in the competition. The question of interest is how did those gymnasts who vaulted on faulty equipment, at the Olympic Games no less, respond to this huge distraction that hurt their performance? The answer is they responded like champions. Statistical analyses showed that the vaulting mishap had no significant effect on their subsequent performances on other pieces of equipment, and had no effect on the final standings in the all-around competition. In a situation that would shake up most competitors, these world-class gymnasts were able to refocus and regain the narrow attentional concentration needed for their subsequent performance.

It's nonsensical that athletes tend to get upset when things don't go perfectly. How many times do things go perfectly? Maybe once or twice in a lifetime, if you're lucky! So challenge your athletes to expect things to go wrong, to expect performance screw-ups, to expect bad weather, bad calls, bad opponents, and bad news. For example, expect conditions to be different when playing on the road, and expect conditions to be a lot different in championship events (Orlick, 2000). Expect teammates (and sometimes coaches) to act differently at stressful times, and don't get caught up in their behavior.

> ## Quotable Quote
>
> *"The mark of a champion isn't how you play when everything is going right, it's how you play when you're struggling."* **Jay Haas**, professional golfer *(cited in Feinstein, 1999, p. 149)*

Distractions only distract athletes if they let them. Remind athletes of the importance of triage in their thinking, so they prioritize their attention and their energy towards performance.

Athletes can do several things to refocus. They should remain present-oriented and refuse to focus on the past. They should use their focus, or process, goals. They should work their newly developed focus plan and adhere to their pre-performance routines.

Table 12.1 Sport Situations That May Require Refocusing
(adapted from Orlick, 1986b)

1. Pre-event hassle

2. Non-ideal conditions

3. Delay in competition

4. Overwhelmed with distractions the day of competition (family, friends, exams, deadlines)

5. Poor performance at beginning of competition

6. Big mistake (error)

7. Criticism from coach or teammate

8. Mind wandering and distracted

9. Fear opponent and doubt own ability

10. Feeling focused and ready, but not performing as well as usual

Table 12.2 Losing Focus, Choking, and Panicking: What They Are and What to Do

	Lose Focus	Choke	Panic
What Is It?	Thinks wrong thing at wrong time	Thinks too much	Doesn't think
Why Does It Happen?	Attention distracted by irrelevant things	Attention becomes self-focused and athlete attempts to control performance	Attention narrows so much that athlete can't reason
Objective When It Happens	Refocus by managing thoughts and attention	Return to autopilot	Gain control of attention; rational thinking
Strategies To Use	"Park" or "file" it Get in "the now" Visualize process goals Grind - work to focus	Perspective shift to purpose/passion What the hell - let it go Imagery and autopilot triggers Small performance increments	Do the Slow Down Power Breath(s) Big picture focus - RET Centering strategy

They should engage in P³ Thinking, and "park" or "file" any thoughts that interfere or don't help them perform better. They can use centering techniques or imagery to change to the focus they desire. But all of these strategies should be planned beforehand and practiced in training sessions. Athletes can use the Refocusing Worksheet for Athletes (Orlick, 1986b) provided in Appendix 12D to help them identify situations or distractions that cause them to lose their focus. They can identify the mentally skilled response they would prefer and designate a cue word or focus trigger to bring on the desired response in that situation. Another useful exercise that gets athletes thinking about how to refocus is to ask them to work through a list of potential distractions/obstacles by noting how they can best respond and refocus in these situations. Some general situations are shown in Table 12.1 (adapted from Orlick, 1986b), but coaches should develop a list of situations specific to their sports that typically require refocusing.

Managing choking and panic situations. As discussed previously in the chapter, choking and panicking may be attentionally explained as thinking too much and not thinking respectively. Choking occurs when the pressure of achieving an important outcome causes athletes to start "pressing," or attempting to control their performance. This controlled processing interferes with the smooth, effortless autopilot type of performance that athletes hope to attain. Panic occurs when athletes are so anxious or overwhelmed that their attention narrows to the point where they stop thinking. Their ability to reason to calm themselves down and think more effectively is severely hampered.

The different attentional problems of losing focus, choking, and panicking are summarized in Table 12.2. The goal for athletes who choke is to return to autopilot. Actually, once they're in the middle of choking, this may be too much to ask. I tell athletes to try to release and relax their bodies and mind a little at a time. Thus, when athletes begin to choke, they can't just magically return to automatic processing (autopilot), but they can recognize the need to "let go" and use some focus cues to trigger the feelings that stimulate automatic, relaxed performance. It helps to attempt to gain perspective ("Isn't this crazy that you're so uptight you just can't play?" or "This is a diving competition, not brain surgery. You're a skilled diver—let it happen"). Athletes

should strive for small performance increments and not force things by trying to make the save-all, unbelievable plays. From this point, athletes can slowly gain confidence and trust in their autopilot, and let it take over more and more. They should do a lot of Power Breathing and think focus thoughts such as "smooth" to focus their brains on the automatic execution of their skills.

When athletes begin to panic, they must first learn to recognize what's happening. Athletes tend to panic when they feel overwhelmed by information or demands, so a good strategy is to slow down thinking and acting, and deliberately do one thing at a time. Centering strategies work well for panic, because they calm the body and focus the mind on some concrete thoughts. Rational thinking is critical to warding off panic, so athletes susceptible to panicking should reflect on the logic underlying how they think. To overcome panic, athletes must be reasonable and focus on the "big picture" of what's happening, which is the opposite of managing choking, where athletes need to zoom in to their autopilot modes.

Clipboard

Thinking Straight to Avoid Panic

Peter Vidmar, U.S. Olympic gold medalist in gymnastics, describes his experience with panic and how he dealt with it by thinking productively when the feeling came over him at the Olympic Trials:

"I was petrified . . . because I missed my first two routines. I was starting to panic thinking I might not make the Olympic team, even though I was still in third place. All of a sudden, I just calmed down and started thinking straight. Just as I started thinking, things started to click for me. It turned out to be the best routine of my life up to that point. I don't have that type of panic anymore; it was really scary then. As the years went on, though, I got rid of that element of panic because I triggered myself somehow into saying, 'Okay, something is wrong now. What can I do about it?' as opposed to saying, 'Something's wrong. I can't believe it's happening!' (Ravizza, 1993, p. 96)

Think like A PRO! To remind athletes of productive responses for losing focus, choking, or panicking, use the acronym A PRO. That is, athletes should follow these sequential steps to think like a pro:

A   ACCEPT the situation. Manage the feeling, even though it doesn't feel good. Don't try to make it go away, deny it's happening, try harder not to think about it, or press. The first step is to say, "I knew this could happen. I'm prepared." Face it head-on and deal with it.

P   Maintain a confident POSTURE. Exude physical poise and confidence by keeping your head and shoulders up and your eyes focused on something relevant. I tell athletes to "fake it 'til you make it," meaning that even if you don't feel confident and focused, you act like you are. Our mind often takes cues from our bodies, so maintaining your physical presence helps get your focus back on track.

R   RELAX yourself physically. Take a Power Breath or take a moment and stretch. If appropriate in your sport, consciously slow down your speech, walk, and thoughts. Become more deliberate and relaxed in your thoughts and actions.

O   OCCUPY your mind using your focus plan, refocusing strategy, or centering technique. "File" or "park" any thoughts that don't help you at the moment—get 'em out of there! Think in terms of "one task, one focus" or "what do I need to do right now?" and focus on that one thing and do it. A big part of P^3 Thinking is preplanned Purposeful Thinking, and it really helps to have planned some focusing strategies for these moments. Otherwise, it is hard to move the destructive thoughts out and make room for the P^3 thoughts.

Wrapping Up

I'll say it one more time. The ability to focus, especially under pressure, is the most important mental skill for athletes. In the next two chapters, you'll learn about the mental skills of energy management and self-confidence. These are important skills that indirectly help athletes manage their attention. By optimizing their arousal or energy levels, athletes tend to focus more effectively. And clearly, confidence is a huge help mentally in providing athletes with personal beliefs about their competence, allowing them to focus without worries and distractions.

However, as important as energy management and confidence are to athletes, they are not as critical as the ability to maintain a focused connection with performance. There are times in competition when athletes are anxious and fearful, and they still can and must focus despite their fears. There are times in competition where athletes lack confidence, and they still can and must focus, despite worries and concerns about their abilities. Other mental skills make it easier to focus, but athletes can maintain a strong focus without these supporting (and comforting) skills. The key point is that attentional focusing takes work to make it bulletproof for competition. When athletes get into the "zone" and enjoy the automatic, effortless focus that guides their performance, that's great. However, they must also take personal responsibility to train and prepare themselves for those days (the majority of days) in which they will struggle to maintain optimal focus for performance. Challenge your athletes to work on enhancing their focus ability. They'll find that learning how to "pay" attention in the right ways buys them the ultimate mental skill needed to gain the Inner Edge.

Summary Points for Chapter 12

1.   The most critical skill for the Inner Edge is to focus attention, especially under pressure.

2.   Focusing in sport involves attentional capacity, readiness, and selectivity.

3.   Expert performance in sport occurs when athletes engage in automatic processing without conscious attention to the execution of skills.

4.   Stress and anxiety can narrow athletes' attention too much so they miss important performance cues and also cause athletes to focus on internal processes as opposed to focusing on key external performance cues.

5.   Panic occurs when athletes' attentional focus is so narrow that they fail to reason and process relevant information.

6.   Choking, as a sudden or rapid deterioration of performance in pressure situations results from self-focused attention, which induces athletes to revert to controlled processing.

7.   Selective attention is the process in which certain information is selected for detailed pro-

cessing, while other information is screened out or ignored.

8. Expert athletes differ from beginning athletes in their selective attentional ability.

9. Attention has both width and direction dimensions, which creates four types of attentional focus needed by athletes in sport.

10. Different sport situations require different types of attention, and athletes should understand how to focus differently based on the demands of the situation.

11. Associative attentional strategies are more conducive to endurance performance in sport than dissociative attentional strategies.

12. Common attentional problems in sport include selecting the wrong attentional focus, becoming distracted, and getting stuck in a particular focus by concentrating too much.

13. Athletes need to engage in repetitive physical training to automate their skills and build an autopilot that can withstand pressures and distractions.

14. Coaches should overload athletes with processing demands in training sessions to enhance their attentional capacity and selectivity.

15. Goal mapping, P³ Thinking, imagery, and physical relaxation all enhance athletes' focus in competition.

16. Athletes can develop pre-performance routines and focus plans to enhance their attentional focus during competition.

17. Mental skill and toughness require athletes to master the difficult skill of refocusing in the face of distractions, obstacles, and setbacks.

18. To combat choking, athletes must use strategies to engage automatic processing, while dealing with panic situations requires more conscious reasoning and rational thinking.

Glossary

associative attention: an internal focus to monitor and self-regulate physical, mental, and technical performance, as well as competitive strategy

automatic processing: mental processing without conscious attention, which is rapid, effortless, integrative, and separate from an athlete's awareness

choking: a sudden or rapid deterioration of performance below the typical and expected level of ability for an athlete performing in a pressure situation

concentration: the ability to sustain a non-distractible attentional focus on a specific task

controlled processing: mental processing that involves conscious attention and awareness of what you are doing when you perform a sport skill

dissociative attention: focusing attention away from the competitive activity or how one feels when performing

focus plan: a plan of how to think, feel, and act during various parts of competition to create an optimal mental focus for a particular performance

panic: extreme emotional state that creates an attentional focus so narrow that individuals are unable to process information (or reason) to help themselves

pre-performance routine: a preplanned, systematic sequence of thoughts and behaviors that an athlete engages in prior to performing a specific skill

selective attention: process in which certain information is selected for detailed processing while other information is screened out or ignored

Study Questions

1. Explain the difference in "paying attention" vs. performing on autopilot. When should each attentional approach be used by athletes?

2. Explain the relationship between arousal and attention. What two attentional problems occur at high levels of anxiety? How does choking and panicking relate to these attentional problems?

3. How do experts and novices differ in their selective attention ability?

4. Explain the four types of attentional focus, and provide examples of situations in which athletes need to use each type of focus.

5. What are the three main attentional selectivity problems faced by athletes? How can concentration be a problem?

6. Explain the concept of centering and give an example of effective centering.

7. Identify at least eight other strategies that can be used to enhance athletes' attention in sport.

Reflective Learning Activities

1. The Paradox of "Control"

Discuss the paradoxical problem in attempting to let go of conscious control to combat choking (and "pressing" which leads into choking). Is it realistic to employ conscious strategies to avoid choking or is it an inevitable occurrence that just has to happen? What do you recommend as the best strategy to deal with choking in sport?
(Discuss in groups of 3 for 10 minutes; then share thoughts within large group discussion)

2. Creating a Plan

Create a specific focus plan for athletes in your sport. Your plan should include pre-competition focus, competition focus, and refocusing strategies for unique situations in your sport.
(Complete individually)

3. Assess your Attention

Complete the Attentional Focusing Questionnaire in Appendix 12A and then work through the "Assess Your Focus Skills" worksheet. Consider your attentional strengths and weaknesses. Talk as a group about how this exercise would work best with athletes.

4. Front and Center

Create a simple and practical centering response you could teach to an athlete in your sport. (Complete individually and share in small groups of 4)

Chapter Thirteen

Managing Energy

Chapter Preview

In this chapter, you'll learn:

- that all forms of competitive energy can be positive as well as negative for athletes
- that the optimal energy zone involves a unique recipe of feeling states for each athlete
- how to help athletes reframe negative energy
- how to help athletes develop and use an Optimal Energy Profile

> "But for all the frustrations, the beatings, and the booings I endured, I'd still be in football if I could be guaranteed a certain feeling just three times a game. It's when you get into a zone or groove . . . in which everything appears to be moving in slow motion . . . On those occasions, the 3 1/2 seconds between the snap from center and the time you release the ball seem like a month. It's the most exhilarating feeling you could ever imagine: very pure, simple . . . It doesn't happen every game, but when it does it's so satisfying. But it's frustrating too, because sometimes you find yourself waiting for it to happen, and it doesn't." **Pat Haden**, former NFL quarterback
>
> "When I first experienced pre-competition jitters, Coach Brown said, 'Learn to love the feeling.' Ever since, I adjust by telling myself, 'I love this feeling, I love to be nervous, I embrace the uncertainty.' Yes, I had sweaty palms, the shaking, the incessant yawning, but I told myself it was a good sign. It was a sign I cared about my involvement and the results.'" **Justin Huish**, 1996 U.S. Olympic gold medalist in archery (Huish, 1999, p. 247)

Energy management is the second of the "big three" mental skills presented in this part of the book, and enhancing athletes' skills in this area is very important. Why? Have you ever had your performance disrupted because you were tense, nervous, or "tried too hard"? Have you ever let your anger or frustration hinder your performance? On the other hand, can you remember performing "in the zone," where time seemed to stand still and you experienced an almost spiritual feeling of focus, sense of control, and total immersion in your sport? Similarly, can you recall the intoxicating joy of winning a championship with teammates in an intense competition with a rival? All these examples—the gut-wrenching anxiety and pressure of competition, the debilitating effects of anger spinning out of control, the exhilaration of peak experiences in sport, and the pure joy of winning a championship—are examples of the ways in which athletes experience and use energy in sport. Managed effectively, athletes' competitive energy can help them perform at the highest levels possible for them. Unmanaged, athletes' competitive energy can block them from ever fulfilling their potential and even discourage them from continuing their participation in sport.

We play sport because we love it, because it is part of our identity, and because we value the goals inherent in competition. We experience deep satisfaction and the profound joy of pursuing and achieving goals as part of a team. However, these reasons that we play make us vulnerable to negative emotions and thoughts, because we want to do well. Because sport competition involves the public pursuit of highly valued, personal goals and intense public comparison with others, it can create crushing pressure and intense anxiety. Consider the combination of negative and positive energy experienced by Cristie Kerr, professional golfer, as she talks about playing in the Solheim Cup for the United States against the European team: "You live to make the team. You can feel the tension building in your stomach. Last year, the veterans warned us rookies that we'd feel like puking on the first tee. But you don't want the week to end. The high is inexplicable" ("Eyeing the Solheim," 2003, p. 25).

The two quotes at the beginning of the chapter represent the two main objectives of energy management as a mental skill for athletes. First, athletes should understand how to mentally prepare to put themselves in a position to get into flow, or the optimal energy zone where athletes perform their best. The quote by former NFL quarterback Pat Haden aptly describes the wonder of this optimal energy zone, but it also illustrates how frustrating it is waiting for flow to happen. Through mental training, athletes can learn and use strategies to put themselves in a position to make flow happen, instead of waiting around for it to happen by chance.

The second objective of energy management is for athletes to effectively manage their competitive energy when they're *not* in the zone. To do this, athletes must practice and master mental strategies to cope with the unpleasant feelings that interfere with their performance. It's normal and understandable

that athletes get nervous, that they worry, and that they occasionally choke. However, they can develop their skills to manage their thoughts, feelings, bodies, and behaviors to harness the human energy that is a major part of sport competition. Justin Huish reminds athletes that they should learn to love the precompetition jitters because even though these jitters don't feel great at the time, they simply mean that athletes are ready and primed to perform their best. However, as we'll learn, athletes interpret these feelings in many ways, and sometimes their lack of productive, focused thinking allows these negative feelings of energy to really hurt their performance. As a coach, you need to understand the nature of competitive energy and, in particular, how to help athletes optimize their positive energy and manage/cope with the negative energy that is a normal part of sport competition.

Competitive Energy as a Natural Resource

The energy that athletes have inside them is a natural resource. Athletes must learn how to manage, conserve, interpret, and release their energy in the most effective ways to enhance their performance and wellbeing. Consider the ways that athletes attempt to manage their physiological energy. They engage in precise aerobic, anaerobic, and weight training methods, they taper their physical training to optimize their cardiovascular and muscular energy for competition, and they follow a specific diet and eat a pre-competition meal at a precise time to maximize the fuel available to their muscles for the upcoming competitive event. All of these activities are designed to build, manage, conserve, and release athletes' physiological energy in the most optimal manner for performance.

But what about athletes' mental energy? What training methods and precompetitive activities do athletes engage in to optimize their mental energy for competition? Some athletes have psych-up routines or focus plans, but the vast majority leave the optimization of mental energy for competition up to chance. Luckily, athletes' minds and bodies become conditioned to the demands of competition, and they automatically "rev up" for competition. However, sometimes these systems "rev up" too much or too less, and athletes fail to perform well because their energy is not optimized at the time of competition. Also, athletes interpret the feelings of energy differently, and for some the energy is negative, threatening, and even draining.

Athletes can learn to become more aware of their mental energy needs for competition, and can learn to manage their energy to optimize their performance. Like physiological energy, athletes must plan ways to consciously manage their mental energy so that at the point of competition, they are at their optimal energy peak for outstanding performance. As their coach, you would never allow them to approach their physical training in a haphazard way, so why not ask them to make the same commitment to enhancing their mental training for energy management? Read on to learn how!

There are a lot of terms for energy in the sport psychology literature, such as arousal, anxiety, stress, activation, mood, and emotion. These terms differ in subtle ways, but basically they are all concerned with human energy. **Energy** refers to *physical and mental readiness, or a capacity for vigorous action.* **Competitive energy**, therefore, is *an athlete's physical and mental readiness for competition.* Obviously, we are most interested in competitive energy, and how athletes can manage their physical and mental readiness to perform their best. The scientific term "arousal" is synonymous with energy as defined in this chapter. **Arousal** is *a state of bodily energy or physical and mental readiness.* Activation is another term used to describe energy states of athletes, and for the purposes of this book we'll just consider it synonymous with arousal and energy.

Whatever term is used, the state of readiness occurs as the body mobilizes its energy resources in response to specific demands, incentives, and threats. Thus, athletes' competitive energy or arousal results from the ways in which athletes' minds and bodies respond to competition. The mental skill of energy management requires athletes to consciously prepare to mobilize their energy resources in the most effective way to enhance their performance. As you'll learn in this chapter, the ways in which athletes use and manage their competitive energy vary widely based on individual preferences and personalities, as well as the mental and physical demands of different types of sports.

Different Feeling States Experienced by Athletes

We've established that competitive energy, also known as arousal, is an athlete's state of physical and mental readiness. Think of this energy as the RPMs of a car engine, which vary from a slow idle to a highly revved state (Martens, 1974). Thus, an athlete's energy state may be of low or high intensity, depending on the how much the athlete revs his or her engine. However, unlike a car engine, where the RPMs represent just intensity, the energy of human machines like athletes varies in intensity *and* direction. By that, I mean athletes experience their competitive energy as different types of feeling states—some which are pleasant and some which are unpleasant.

Feeling States Result from Intensity and Direction of Competitive Energy

The different feeling states experienced by athletes are shown in Figure 13.1. Athletes' feeling states can be of high or low intensity, and can be more or less pleasant (Hanin, 1997, 2000c; Watson, Clark, & Tellegen, 1985). High intensity pleasant feeling states include feeling vigorous, enthusiastic, and competitive. High intensity unpleasant feeling states include feeling anxious, tense, fearful, or angry. Low intensity pleasant feelings include calm and relaxed, in contrast to low intensity unpleasant feelings such as sadness, tiredness, and lethargy. Athletes experience many different feeling states based on the intensity and pleasantness/unpleasantness of their competitive energy in response to the demands of competition. Mentally skilled athletes learn the specific feeling states that help them to perform better (even the unpleasant ones!), and they use various combinations of these states to achieve their desired levels of competitive readiness (we'll discuss this more fully later in the chapter).

The types of feeling states shown in Figure 13.1 have been studied in various ways in sport psychology. Athletes' mood states as well as their emotions have been studied extensively in relation to performance, overtraining, and injury occurrence (e.g., Hanin, 2000a). In particular, the field of sport psychology has focused more on the study of high intensity unpleasant feeling states (e.g., anxiety, fear of failure, tension) much more than the other types of feelings. This is somewhat understandable given the

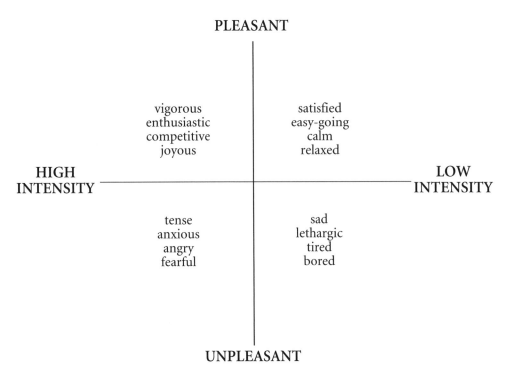

Figure 13.1 Types of energy states based on intensity and direction

common anxiety and stress brought on by the demands of competition. However, I believe it is helpful to talk to athletes about managing their overall energy and multiple feelings states, as opposed to focusing only on the one aspect of energy that involves managing stress or reducing anxiety (high intensity unpleasant feeling state).

Anxiety is *a high intensity unpleasant feeling state that typically results from a demand or threat.* We all have experienced anxiety over the threat of physical harm, such as a physical attack from an-

other person, falling from a high and narrow cliff, or riding in a car with a reckless driver. However, the anxiety most studied in sport psychology is based on the threat of failure and/or evaluation, such as when athletes compete in front of spectators and the media. The threat inherent in these situations is to the athlete's sense of self or self-esteem, which occurs when important and self-defining goals are threatened. Much of the research in the sport psychology literature on competitive energy and feeling states has focused on anxiety, but keep in mind that

	MENTAL	PHYSICAL	MENTAL	PHYSICAL
HIGH INTENSITY	worried concerned angry nervous	tense jittery tight	focused confident excited	explosive energized vigorous
LOW INTENSITY	tired lethargic confused sad	fatigued depleted tired exhausted	calm relaxed sleepy tranquil	loose fluid relaxed
	UNPLEASANT		PLEASANT	

Figure 13.2 Mental and physical energy states based on intensity and direction

this is only one type of feeling state that athletes must manage.

Athletes Experience Feeling States Mentally and Physically

Competitive energy affects athletes both mentally and physically. So along with high/low intensity and pleasant/unpleasantness, competitive feeling states are experienced by athletes as thoughts (mental) and as bodily sensations (physical). Think about how anger works mentally and physically. When an athlete becomes angry, he typically is thinking things like "It's not fair!", "I'll get even," or, at extremes, "I'm going to knock this guy's lights out!" Anger causes several bodily responses, such as increased blood flow to the extremities, tension and shaking, and feeling hot in the face or all over. When an athlete is tired or exhausted, he may experience mental exhaustion from attentional overload as well as the physical fatigue and lethargy associated with spent muscles and/or overall body tiredness. Example mental and physical feeling states categorized by intensity and direction are shown in Figure 13.2.

The different mental and physical components of anxiety have been a major focus of study in sport psychology. Multidimensional anxiety theory distinguishes between cognitive (mental) and somatic (physical) anxiety (Martens, Vealey, & Burton, 1990). When athletes experience **cognitive anxiety**, they *worry about how they will perform and whether they have the skills to be successful.* When athletes experience **somatic anxiety**, their *bodies feel tense and jittery, their heart rate, breathing, and sweating increase, and they feel "butterflies" in their stomachs.* To help athletes effectively manage their feelings of anxiety, it is important to understand exactly how they are experiencing this unpleasant feeling state. Later in the chapter, I'll provide some suggestions to help athletes differentiate between types of anxiety and how to manage these feelings more effectively.

All Forms of Competitive Energy are Potentially Positive and Negative

The competitive energy athletes have stored in their bodies is like nuclear power. If used efficiently and carefully, it can produce exceptional performance. However, if athletes misuse their energy, it

© Eyewire Images

Quotable Quote

"It's natural to be nervous. I use the energy and tell myself it means I'm psyched and ready to play." **Kelli Kuehne**, LPGA golfer

can be disastrous. Positive and negative refer to the effects of energy on athletes' performance and wellbeing. This should not be confused with the dimension of pleasant and unpleasant presented in Figure 13.1. A feeling state can feel unpleasant to an athlete (e.g., anxious or angry), but may have a positive effect on performance for that athlete. Likewise, a feeling can be pleasant (e.g., calm), but have a negative influence on performance. For example, I don't know many defensive linemen in football who would say that feeling calm helps their performance! Research with college athletes from a variety of sports found that athletes rated anger and fear as positive influences on their performance, and relaxed and calm as negatively related to performance (Mellalieu, Hanton, & Jones, 2003). The basic point is that all forms of competitive energy, or feeling states, have the potential to affect athletes' performance and wellbeing in both positive and negative ways.

Purposes of Feeling States

All of the feelings that we experience as humans serve a purpose, or at least did so as part of our evolution (Goleman, 1995). When we are worried or fearful, we prepare ourselves for the challenge. When we are angry, we prepare our bodies to fight. Even sadness functions to help us grieve, which aided primitive humans by keeping them close to home when they were most vulnerable due to their grief (Goleman, 1995). Athletes should understand that all of their feelings, or energy sources, have purposes. Worry is useful to rehearse how an athlete will respond to a challenge—it focuses the mind on a problem so that a solution can be found. Thus, anxiety can have a positive influence on athletes' preparation for competition. Similarly, feeling tired cues an athlete to accurately read her body and seek needed rest and recovery. Obviously, anxiety that distracts attention and fatigue that saps energy at the moment of competition are problematic, but these unpleasant feeling states serve athletes in other useful ways. The key is for athletes to understand their unique pattern of feeling states and prescribe how they want to feel when preparing for competition, as well as what feeling states optimize their energy and focus at the point of competition.

Clipboard

Using, Not Losing, Your Temper

Bob Rotella (1992), sport psychology consultant for many professional golfers, states that the goal of energy management is not to control your temper. Rather, it is to use your emotions to be as successful as you can be. Coaches talk a lot about athletes keeping their composure, but Rotella argues that composure doesn't mean that athletes should perform without emotion. Composure is about staying focused on the task at hand, and he argues that sometimes emotions can help athletes do that. In fact, Rotella cautions against suppressing emotions, which can bottle up energy and interfere with the external focus athletes need to have in competition.

Athletes should express emotion to empty themselves of distraction, not to create more. Athletes can and should be expressive, such as by showing a moment of anger or frustration, but the key is to then leave that emotion behind and move on with relevant performance thoughts and feelings. Rotella uses pro golfer Ben Crenshaw as a good example of how to make emotion work for you. Crenshaw has always been a top putter, yet he often shows irritation and anger after missing a putt. How is this helpful? Rotella says that Crenshaw's emotional self-talk reinforces to himself that he's a great putter, as his emotional outbursts are often along the lines of "How did that not go in?" Thus, Crenshaw's showing of emotion reinforces his confidence and belief in his putting ability.

Rotella suggests that athletes experiment with finding the right emotional "temperature" for themselves during competition. Athletes can then become more aware of when and how to get mad at themselves to kick in the right level of energy, as well as when and how to ease back on the intensity of energy to relax and just play. Help your athletes understand how emotion can work for them as well as against them, and encourage them to figure out the special mix and intensity of emotions that helps them to perform their best.

Why Stress is Important for Athletes

Stress is typically assumed to be a form of negative energy for athletes, but stress actually serves the important purpose of stimulating growth. **Stress** may be simply defined as *a demand placed on an athlete*. We stress athletes all the time through weight training and exhaustive physical repetitions of their sport skills. By stressing them in these ways, their bodies and skills adapt and are improved. However, too much physical stress in the form of overtraining causes athletes' bodies to break down. By following a careful progression, coaches incrementally build the physical stress tolerance of athletes so they can withstand the higher levels of stress that occur during competition.

The same idea works for mental stress. To manage the pressure and mental demands of competition, athletes must learn to cope by using mental training tools to enhance their mental skills. If athletes have the skills to cope effectively with the stress, then it is not negative. Thus, stress is a stimulus for growth and development, and in the right amounts it is a very positive influence on our lives. Athletes love competition because they understand that the stress of competition challenges them to perform optimally.

Competitive stress is also useful in small, progressive doses because it can serve as an "inoculation" to help athletes cope with increasing levels of stress

Quotable Quote

"I hope I never get over the jitters. If you don't have them, you should be doing something else." **Kelly Robbins**, LPGA golfer

(Martens, 1978). An inoculation given to prevent disease actually involves giving people a mild form of the disease so that their bodies develop antibodies to become immune to harsher forms of the disease. Through training and a gradual introduction to competition, athletes are subjected to progressive levels of stress, and they adapt so they are able to cope effectively with higher and higher levels of stress. This, I believe, is a strong argument in favor of youth sport programs that are structured to allow children to develop competitive coping skills. All of us need coping skills for life—called life skills—to manage our energy effectively in evaluative achievement situations.

Jim Loehr, mental training consultant for many professional athletes, emphasizes that effective energy management involves the oscillation (or rhythmic movement) between energy expenditure (stress) and energy renewal (recovery) (Loehr & Schwartz, 2001). Loehr states that stress itself is not a problem and emphasizes that stress is necessary to bring out our ultimate energies to perform in ways that we may not realize without the prodding of stress. The problem occurs when athletes do not engage in adequate recovery. Chronic stress without adequate recovery burns out athletes' energy reserves and causes their performance as well as their bodies to break down.

Thus, energy management is not the avoidance of stress. Effective energy management requires athletes to be subjected to progressive levels of stress, with intermittent recovery periods so that their bodies and minds can adapt and rest. Their training should include physical practice as well as mental training and practice (e.g., imagery, relaxation, P³ Thinking, focus plans). Athletes need progressive levels of stress, intermittent recovery periods, *and* mental training to inoculate them in preparation to withstand the bigger stress of sport competition.

Flow: The Optimal Energy Zone

When athletes' natural resources of energy are at their optimal state, the experience of flow occurs. As defined in Chapter 1, flow is an optimal mental state characterized by total absorption in the task (Csikszentmihalyi, 1990), typically referred to by athletes as "the zone." Think of it as the optimal energy zone. Flow is a mental state filled with pleasant feelings or energy, including enjoyment, fun, and joy, and it is the one area of positive energy that has been studied

extensively in sport psychology (e.g., Jackson, 1992, 2000; Jackson et al., 2001). Although flow and peak performance are not exactly the same thing, in sport athletes who experience flow typically enjoy peak performance as well. Thus, helping athletes identify their special recipes of feeling states that lead to their optimal energy zones will certainly enhance their performance (Gould & Udry, 1994).

Flow as a Balance Between Challenge and Skills

Flow occurs when athletes experience a balance between their skills and the challenges that they perceive in the situation (see Figure 13.3). As shown in Figure 13.3, athletes' skills and challenges must be at a high enough level to be interesting, or else the result will be apathy. Low levels of skill and a lack of challenge are not enough to stimulate flow, even if they are in balance (dotted line area in Figure 13.3) Thus, flow occurs when the skill-challenge balance is at a higher than average performance level. We've all experienced the exhilarating feeling of testing our skills against a challenging opponent. It seems that this challenge sharpens our focus and brings out positive feeling states that lead us into the zone.

When the competitive challenge far outweighs athletes' skills, they experience anxiety. Conversely, when athletes' skills far outweigh the challenges they face, they experience boredom. Coaches should find ways to optimally challenge athletes in training and competition, to set the stage for the flow of optimal energy that occurs when skills and challenges are in balance. A combination of milestone, challenge, and focus goals (see Chapter 8) would be helpful to get athletes excited about achieving an important outcome, yet focused on intermediate performance (challenge) goals and the process by which they can achieve these goals (focus goals and goal achievement strategies).

Why Flow Leads to Peak Performance

Flow is an optimal energy experience that leads to peak performance in sport. When athletes are in flow, they enjoy a bullet-proof cocoon of focused, pleasant energy. Through interviews with athletes, researchers have identified several characteristics that define this positive energy state. First, flow involves complete *absorption in the task*, often described as the *merging of action and awareness*. That is, athletes are aware of what they're doing, but

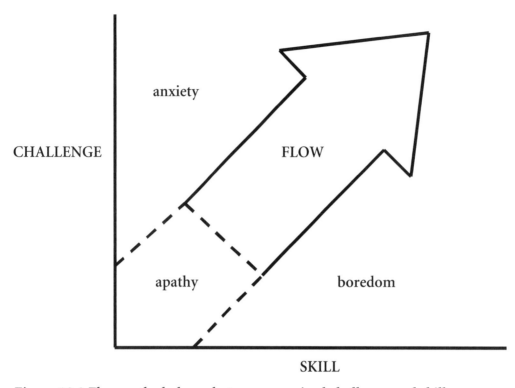

anxiety

CHALLENGE

FLOW

apathy

boredom

SKILL

Figure 13.3 Flow as the balance between perceived challenge and skills

they're not aware of their awareness. They are locked into autopilot, and their performance feels and looks effortless. This absorption allows them to engage in total concentration or *exceptional focus* (second characteristic), because their focus of attention is so optimal that worries and self-doubts have no room to creep into their consciousness.

A third characteristic of flow is a *sense of control*, as if athletes are controlling not only their performance, but also their anticipation and reading of their teammates' and opponents' actions. Fourth, athletes in flow *lose their self-consciousness*, which protects them from the problems of controlled processing and self-focused attention. Because of their total absorption in the task, they have no attentional capacity for worries, self-doubts, or analysis of performance. Fifth, athletes in flow experience *clarity in their purpose or goals*, and *unambiguous and instantly useful feedback*. Athletes automatically know what to do, where to focus, and instinctually incorporate ongoing performance feedback into their continuing performance. Sixth, athletes and others that experience flow (artists, surgeons, writers) often feel a *transformation of time*, typically when they are oblivious to its passing. I remember the warm summer evenings of my childhood when I would become so totally absorbed in games with my friends that I would completely lose track of time and miss dinner (and be in trouble!).

And finally, flow is *autotelic*, defined in Chapter 1 as engaging in an activity for intrinsic reasons. Even though flow is usually accompanied by out-

Photo courtesy of USAF

standing performance outcomes, the irony is that when in flow, athletes are not thinking about performance outcomes at all. In fact, the most striking feature of flow is that the focus is on the joy of the experience, and many athletes have admitted that winning was the last thing on their mind when in this positive energy state. This is a key point to consider, as it's very hard to get across to athletes that the best way to win is to avoid thinking about winning! Mental training helps athletes release their focus on outcomes by using personal goal maps to create focus goals, practicing purposeful and productive thinking to keep their minds in the present, and creating focus plans that occupy their thoughts with relevant, task-oriented cues and images.

Can Athletes Train for Flow?

Although some athletes believe that flow is controllable (Jackson, 2000), I don't buy it. Controllability is an illusion; you cannot totally control your energy or feeling state. A better idea is to suggest to athletes that they can manage their thoughts, feelings, and behaviors to *put themselves in a position for flow to occur*. How should athletes do that? Quality physical training and preparation for specific competition is the first step. Quality mental training follows so that athletes identify personalized mental focus plans that help them lock into the non-distractible task focus that they need. Following pre-competitive and pre-performance routines helps

athletes ease into a familiar focus and positive feeling states that can lead to flow. Athletes have also stated that optimal environmental conditions and positive team interactions facilitate their abilities to get into flow (Jackson, 2000). All the mental training tools presented in this book are designed to help athletes prepare for flow, or peak performance, to occur. By focusing on appropriate goals, creatively using imagery to program perfect mental responses in competition, being able to release tension and relax their muscles, and engaging in P³ Thinking, athletes can prime themselves for flow to occur. Self-confidence has also been identified as an important precursor to achieving flow in competition (Jackson, 2000).

As a coach, you should remember that flow occurs when higher than average skills are balanced in relation to competitive challenges. Coaches should attempt to structure challenging situations in training and allow athletes to perform for a period of time in these situations without interruption or feedback. Although providing feedback and evaluation is a responsibility of coaches, constant feedback and evaluation is disruptive to athletes' performance flow. Although difficult, coaches should set aside training time for scrimmage or performance trials where no overt coaching occurs. Athletes can be cued to energize and focus appropriately during these training sessions to attempt to reach their optimal energy states.

Explain to your athletes that evaluation prevents and disrupts flow. Perfectionistic athletes often have trouble refocusing after analyzing their skills, but they should be urged to do this occasionally so that their performance can simply flow. Team members should also be aware that analysis, evaluation, and consciously thinking about how one is performing all serve to disrupt flow. I can remember a flow experience as a college basketball player that was rudely interrupted at halftime when one of my teammates said, "Robin, you're having a career game—20 points at halftime!" I started the second half aware that I was having a great game, while in the first half I was just playing without consciously thinking about it. Needless to say, the bubble burst and I returned to reality in the second half! Baseball players are well aware of this phenomenon and stay away from any pitcher who is working on a no-hitter during a game. Athletes should understand that trash-talking and even casual comments made by opponents are often intended to disrupt their positive energy and flow states. As discussed in Chapter 12, athletes should have a quick refocusing cue that they use to center themselves after distractions such as these.

How Competitive Energy Influences Athletes' Performance

You've learned that flow, or the optimal energy zone, leads to peak performance in athletes. However, there are a lot of other aspects of competitive energy that influence athletes' performance, which you should know about.

Intensity of Competitive Energy (Arousal) and Performance

We can establish a few general points about how the *intensity* of competitive energy, or arousal, affects athletes' performance.

1. As athletes' levels of arousal increase, they are more likely to exhibit their dominant responses (see Figure 13.4). Dominant responses refer to performance behaviors that are most typical for individual athletes. For a skilled athlete, her dominant response is correct performance because her skills are well learned and ingrained. For a young athlete in the

early stages of skill learning, her dominant response is incorrect performance. She makes a lot of mistakes because she is learning how to do the skill. So think about how having an audience present to watch each of these athletes perform would affect them. The presence of the audience should increase each athlete's arousal level, which according to our prediction should increase each athlete's emission of dominant responses. So which athlete's performance should be enhanced by the audience? Which athlete's performance should be hampered by the audience?

Right! For the skilled athlete, the presence of spectators increases her arousal, which increases the emission of her dominant response, which is correct. Thus, increases in competitive energy or arousal *enhance* the performance of this athlete—she performs better with higher levels of arousal. Similarly, for the beginning athlete, the presence of spectators increases her arousal, which increases the emission of her dominant response. However, her dominant performance response is incorrect—she makes more mistakes than correct performances because she is learning the skill. Thus, increases in competitive energy or arousal hurt the performance of the beginning athletes—she performs better in the learning stages with lower levels of arousal.

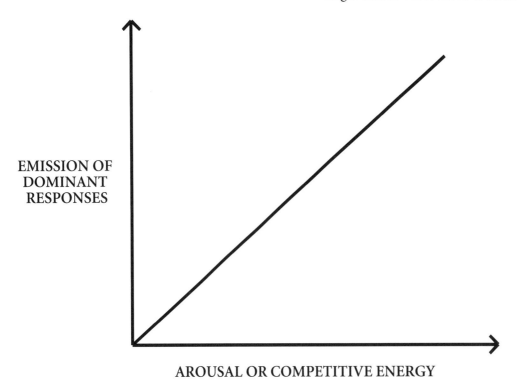

EMISSION OF DOMINANT RESPONSES

AROUSAL OR COMPETITIVE ENERGY

Figure 13.4 Arousal increases athletes' emission of dominant responses

This relationship between arousal and the emission of dominant performance responses comes from drive theory (Spence & Spence, 1966). This is an older and overly simplistic theory that is not part of mainstream sport psychology research today. Do you think it's too simplistic? Study the graph in Figure 13.4, and think about college athletes. Will their performance continue to get better as arousal gets higher and higher?

Basically, we can agree that increase in arousal helps athletes with well learned skills—it energizes them, sharpens their focus, and gets their bodies and minds ready to perform. However, the theory becomes questionable once that diagonal line in Figure 13.4 moves out toward the end of the graph. It seems obvious that athletes can get so highly energized or aroused that their performance is hurt by these high energy levels. This is particularly true in sport situations that require fine motor control (archery), accuracy (free throw shooting, field goal kicking), and a lot of complex decision-making (soccer and hockey goalies, football quarterbacks). Higher levels of arousal would be more helpful for sport situations that require a lot of speed (running) and strength (weight lifting, line play in football), but even then extremely high arousal levels would probably interfere with quality decision-making that is required even in large muscle activities (Landers & Arent, 2001).

If the theory is outdated, then why talk about it? I think there are some useful practical points about arousal and performance that coaches should understand from drive theory. First, remember that arousal increases the emission of athletes' dominant responses. Obviously, you would want to control the teaching and learning environment to ensure that athletes learn skills and new strategies in a climate void of pressure (e.g., no spectators, no competition, no fear of making mistakes while learning). As their learning increases, you can slowly begin to create higher arousal levels to stimulate them to perform better. Once athletes have learned skills, then coaches should create many different energizing situations in training (e.g., competitive drills, spectators, scrimmages with incentives) to bring out their best performances.

Another practical point from drive theory is to be aware that as athletes feel more pressure and their arousal increases, they will tend to engage in familiar (dominant) behaviors. A basketball player may rely on a favorite offensive move (e.g., pull up and shoot versus run the team offense or drive to the basket) or a quarterback will revert to a favored play (e.g., running out of the pocket). Coaches should be aware of athletes' tendencies to revert to dominant performance responses and bring this to their attention so that it doesn't detract from their performance. As discussed in Chapter 12, panic occurs at the highest levels of arousal and incites protective, instinctual behaviors. These represent the most dominant response we all have—to survive. However, instinctual responses are not always good or helpful, so athletes must learn to manage the intensity of their competitive energy levels and learn effective refocusing strategies (discussed in Chapter 12) to manage their performance and behavioral responses at high levels of arousal.

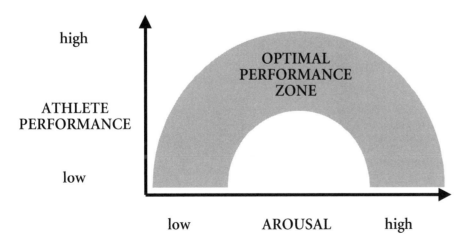

Figure 13.5 Inverted-u model of arousal or competitive energy

2. Generally, athletes perform better at moderate levels of arousal. Based on the weakness of drive theory just discussed, a better way to draw the relationship between arousal and athletes' performance is shown in Figure 13.5. Basically, arousal and performance are related in a curvilinear fashion, as shown by the inverted-u shape in Figure 13.5. This means that athletes perform better as their arousal increases, up to some optimal point, which is shown in Figure 13.5 as the optimal performance zone. However, when arousal increases past an optimal point, athletes' performance decreases. They've moved past their zone and are now over-aroused. Thus, the inverted-u model indicates that athletes perform best when they achieve an optimal (or balanced) energy or arousal state. Research has supported the inverted-u model, although of course the curve isn't as smooth and continuous in real life as shown in Figure 13.5.

Clipboard

Arousal and Little League Performance: Research Test of the Inverted-U Model

In an interesting field study, two researchers observed the performances of 11- and 12-year-old baseball players across a season (Lowe & McGrath, 1971). They evaluated each player's hitting performance based on how well they contacted the ball. The better the ball was contacted by the batter, the better the performance rating. This controlled for lucky bloop hits or the multitude of errors made by youth baseball players in the field, and focused just on how well each player hit the ball (regardless of whether it was scored as a base hit, out, or error). The researchers also recorded the players' heart rates and rated how fidgety their behavior was as they waited on deck to bat. These measures of heart rate and behavioral fidgetiness were used to assess the players' arousal levels.

The researchers also recorded the importance of each game and each situation in which players' batted. Game importance was rated the highest when the two teams at the top of the league standings played each other late in the season. Situation importance was rated the highest when it was the final inning, the score was tied, and the bases were loaded.

The researchers used this method to categorize games and situations as low, medium, and high in importance. Thus, each time a player batted, the researchers recorded an arousal score, game importance score, situation importance score, and player performance rating.

The results of the study are shown in Figure 13.6, and lo and behold, they look like an inverted-u! That is, players performed better in games and situations of medium importance, and performed less well when game and situational importance was low or high. The arousal evaluations of players supported the findings, as players' arousal levels corresponded to how important the games and situations were in which they batted. Highest arousal levels were shown for the high importance games/situations, and the lowest arousal levels were shown for the low importance games/situations. Overall, these field study results of Little League baseball supported the inverted-u model of arousal and performance in sport.

3. The optimal intensity of athletes' arousal differs according to situational demands of specific sports. Do you think that the optimal arousal point or zone is the same for all sport situations? Of course not. It's just common sense that different sports and the different situations within them require different levels of arousal to facilitate performance. A football linebacker can be at a much higher arousal level and perform well as compared to a archer, whose optimal arousal level for performance is somewhat lower in comparison (see Figure 13.7). Optimal arousal levels differ even within the same sport for athletes. Basketball players must perform at high intensity levels, hustling up and down the court, and then abruptly stand at the free throw line, where they must decrease their arousal intensity to coolly shoot free throws. If you observe basketball, most players have learned to take a deep breath and engage in pre-performance routines to calm themselves and focus effectively. Athletes must consider the various performance demands in their sports, and learn brief strategies to energize appropriately ("psych up" or "psych down") for the different demands.

4. The optimal intensity of arousal depends on unique factors associated with individual athletes.

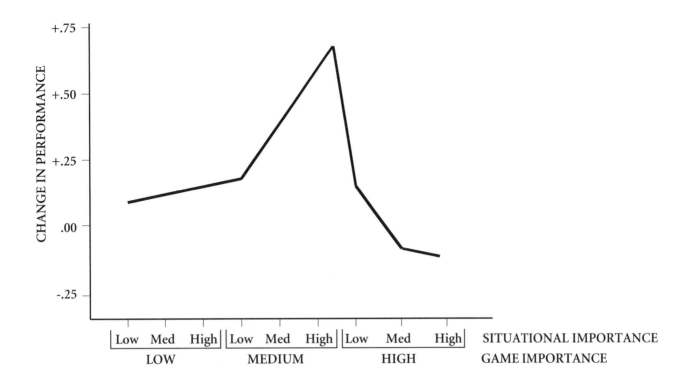

Figure 13.6 Batting performance of Little Leaguers as the result of game and situational importance

Not all athletes have the same optimal arousal level—not even athletes playing the same position in the same sport! Some prefer and perform better at really high RPM levels of energy, while others prefer and perform better at lower intensities of arousal. In fact, the Little League study of arousal presented in the previous Clipboard showed an overall group effect supporting the inverted-u model (see Figure 13.6). However, when the researchers looked at each individual player's scores, they found that the players' optimal arousal levels differed (Lowe & McGrath, 1971). Some players performed better at low levels of arousal, others at high levels, and still others at moderate levels. So even though the group results supported the inverted-u model, individual players had very unique optimal arousal zones or patterns.

Individual factors that may affect preferred arousal levels include personality characteristics, coping ability and style, and skill level. A famous study illustrating how arousal differs based on skill level assessed arousal intensity (as measured by heart rate) of both beginning and experienced parachutists before, during, and after a jump (Fenz & Epstein, 1967). As shown in Figure 13.8, there were differences in arousal intensity between parachutists based

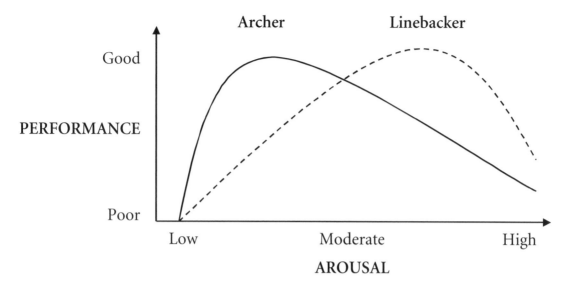

Figure 13.7 Optimal arousal levels for specific sports

on experience. Can you explain the different patterns of arousal, why they occurred, and how they might affect performance? Consider how the experienced parachutists managed their competitive energy to perform well on the jump, as opposed to the beginning parachutists who seemed unable to manage their energy effectively.

Many times athletes fail to understand the individualized nature of optimal arousal, and they copy the behaviors or strategies that their teammates use to get energized for performance. Obviously, that doesn't always work well. Educate athletes about the need to find their optimal intensity zones. They can recreate feelings and thoughts associated with good performances as well as bad performances to experiment with strategies that work for them.

5. As athletes' arousal levels increase, their attention narrows. The first four points in this section discussed how arousal intensity influences athletes' performance. But we haven't talked about *why* or *how* arousal affects athletes' performance. One of the most important ways that arousal affects athletes' performance is by narrowing their attention. In Chapter 12, you learned about the cue utilization model (Easterbrook, 1959), which portrays attention as a beam of light that goes from broad to very narrow (see Figure 12.2). The model is repeated in this chapter to emphasize how the intensity of competitive energy can influence athletes' abilities to focus effectively.

The cue utilization model indicates that there is an optimal zone of arousal that facilitates athletes'

attention and competitive focus. This means that all athletes have an arousal zone, not too low and not too high, in which their focus is best for their performance. At low levels of arousal, athletes' attention is too broad, and their focus is on too many irrelevant things. They're not "zoomed in" to the sharp competitive focus they need to perform well. At really high levels of arousal, athletes' attention is too narrow, and they are so "juiced" that they have tunnel vision and fail to pick up important peripheral cues that are needed for effective performance. You see this occur when basketball players mistakenly pass the ball to opponents in pressure situations, fail to read changing defenses, or are unable to scan and find an open teammate under full court defensive pressure.

With regard to their expectations for athletes' performance in pressure situations, coaches should be aware of this relationship between arousal and atten-

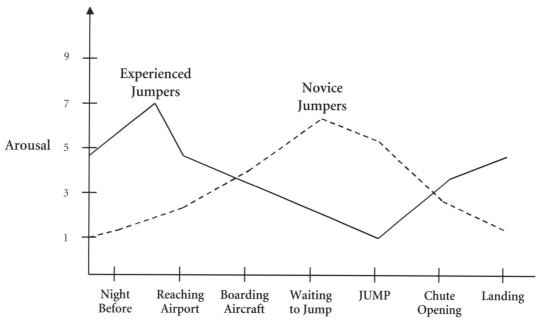

Figure 13.8 Arousal levels of beginning and experienced parachutists (adapted from Martens, 1987)

tion. As a college basketball coach, I made a big mistake in the pressurized closing seconds of a tight game. My mistake was that I provided too much information and too many options for my players. They were highly energized due to the pressure, and their attention was narrowed because of this. By not keeping it simple, I set my players up for failure, and they were unable to execute effectively under the pressure. I learned from this, and later in the season, when faced with a high pressure situation, I gave them very clear and simple instructions. They executed the play effectively by each concentrating on one key thing, and we actually won the game. I've never forgotten the real life lesson I learned about athletes' attentional narrowing in pressure situations. When coaching athletes in pressure situations where their arousal levels are high, KISS and KICK ("Keep It Simple and Systematic" and "Keep It Crystal Klear")!

Pleasant and Unpleasant Feeling States Related to Performance

Thus far, we've only focused on the *intensity* of athletes' competitive energy in relation to their overall arousal levels. We've established that athletes need to understand what RPM levels of competitive energy work best to energize them for optimal performance. However, competitive energy is made up of feeling states that differ not only in intensity, but also direction (pleasant or unpleasant). Thus, the purpose of this section is to examine how the *direction* of arousal or competitive energy influences athletes' performances.

Typical feeling states preferred by athletes to enhance performance. Yuri Hanin, a Russian sport psychologist now working with Olympic athletes in Finland, has pioneered the study of pleasant and unpleasant feeling states related to sport performance. He has found that athletes use a wide variety of individually relevant words to describe the pleasant and unpleasant feeling states that both help and hurt their performance (Hanin, 2000b). Table 13.1 lists the top eight pleasant feeling states that athletes from a variety of sports identified as positive and negative influences on their performance. Pleasant feeling states that were identified as predominantly positive in their effects on performance are listed on the left side of Table 13.1. Pleasant feeling states that were identified as predominantly negative in their effects on performance are listed on the right side of Table 13.1. Then, for each set of pleasant feeling states, the percentage of athletes who viewed them as positive and negative are listed.

The pleasant feeling states identified as positively influencing performance (left side of Table 13.1) seem to represent high energy (*energetic, charged, motivated*), confidence (*certain, confident*), and feelings of strong will (*purposeful, willing, resolute*). The pleasant feeling states identified as negatively influencing performance (right side of Table 13.1) seem to represent low energy (*easygoing, tran-*

Table 13.1 Top Eight PLEASANT Feeling States Identified by Athletes as Positive and Negative for Performance (Hanin, 2000)

Predominantly POSITIVE Influence on Athletes' Performance			Predominantly NEGATIVE Influence on Athletes' Performance		
Pleasant Feeling States	% viewed as +	% viewed as -	Pleasant Feeling States	% viewed as -	% viewed as +
Energetic	40	6	Easygoing	30	7
Charged	40	4	Excited	23	19
Motivated	38	0	Tranquil	18	3
Certain	30	14	Relaxed	17	10
Confident	29	2	Animated	17	1
Purposeful	29	0	Overjoyed	15	1
Willing	23	2	Fearless	15	9
Resolute	22	0	Satisfied	15	4

quil, relaxed), a lack of seriousness (*excited, animated, overjoyed*), and overconfidence (*fearless, satisfied*). Even though the majority of athletes found specific feeling states to be either positive or negative, the percentages show that individual athletes differ from the majority in their interpretations of certain feeling states. For example, 30% of the athletes identified *certain* as a pleasant feeling state that helped their performance, although 14% identified *certain* as a pleasant feeling state that hurt their performance. Also, 17% of the athletes identified *relaxed* as a pleasant feeling state that hurt their performance, yet 10% of the athletes viewed *relaxed* as having a positive influence on their performance.

The unpleasant feeling states identified by the athletes as positively influencing performance (left side of Table 13.2) all seem to represent high energy (*tense, vehement, intense, nervous, furious, irritated*), which appears to be channeled toward overcoming an opponent or achieving difficult goals (*dissatisfied, attacking, provoked, angry*). Unpleasant feeling states identified as negatively influencing performance

(right side of Table 13.2) represent lack of energy (*tired, sluggish,, exhausted*), lack of motivation or will (*unwilling, lazy*), lack of confidence or fear (*uncertain, distressed, afraid*), and inappropriate moods for competition (*depressed, sorrowful*). As with the previous list, notice that most unpleasant feeling states are experienced as positive and negative, depending on the perspective of individual athletes.

These findings provide us with a general picture of the types of competitive energy, or feeling states, that most athletes view as helpful and hurtful to their performance. However, athletes' preferences for different feeling states are influenced by their individual personalities and also the specific nature of the sports in which they compete (Hanin, 2000b).

Individual approaches to optimizing feeling states to enhance performance. Because of the personalized nature of optimal feeling states for athletes, athletes must understand which types of competitive energy work best for them, and then create and maintain their special recipes of feeling states that lead to their optimal energy zones. Optimal en-

Table 13.2 Top Ten UNPLEASANT Feeling States Identified by Athletes as Positive and Negative for Performance (Hanin, 2000)

Predominantly POSITIVE Influence on Athletes' Performance			Predominantly NEGATIVE Influence on Athletes' Performance		
Unpleasant Feeling States	% viewed as +	% viewed as -	Unpleasant Feeling States	% viewed as -	% viewed as +
Tense	49	10	Tired	44	3
Dissatisfied	49	6	Unwilling	40	1
Attacking	35	0	Uncertain	37	5
Vehement	25	0	Sluggish	29	1
Intense	22	3	Depressed	27	0
Nervous	20	10	Lazy	23	1
Irritated	20	4	Distressed	20	6
Provoked	13	4	Sorrowful	17	0
Angry	12	4	Afraid	16	4
Furious	11	2	Exhausted	15	0

ergy zones have been shown to be important predictors of individual athlete's performance (Hanin, 1997, 2000b, 2000c).

Athletes can create personalized optimal energy zones by identifying:

(a) pleasant feeling states that help their performance (P+),

(b) pleasant feeling states that hurt their performance (P-),

(c) unpleasant feeling states that hurt their performance (U-),

(d) unpleasant feeling states that help their performance (U+), and

(e) their preferred intensity of each feeling state on a scale from 0 to 10.

Thus, athletes have to know *how* they want to feel and *how much* they want to feel each of these ways, and then work to create the most optimal levels of feeling states they can for competition.

To most completely assess the effects of competitive energy on performance, athletes must understand both the positive and negative effects of various feeling states (Hanin, 1997, 2000c). Different combinations of feeling states interact to influence athletes' performance in specific ways, so they must experiment to find their personal recipe of optimal feeling states that works best for them. By only focusing on positive feelings, or even negative feelings, they miss the key interactive nature of multiple competitive feeling states. This idea of finding the best recipe of "mixed emotions" works in sport, as athletes often tell me they want to feel *relaxed* yet *intense*, or *anxious* yet *confident*, or *angry* yet *focused*.

An example of an individually created optimal energy zone for an ice hockey player is shown in Fig-

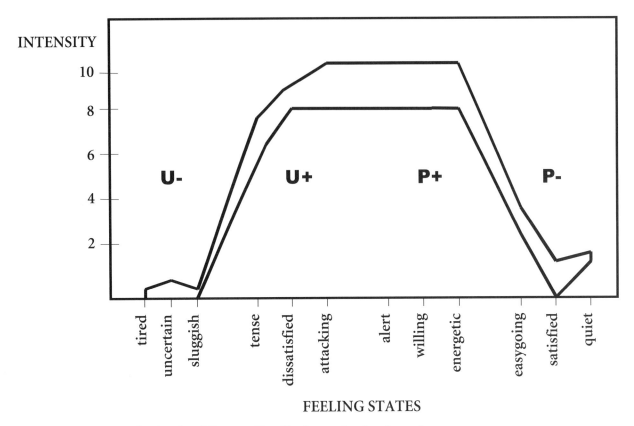

Figure 13.9 Example Optimal Energy Profile for an ice hockey player

ure 13.9 (modified from Hanin, 2000b). The player selected the feeling states that energize him in the most positive ways for optimal performance (P+ and U+), as well as the feeling states that affect his energy and performance in the most negative ways (U- and P-). Then, he identified his preferred intensity levels for each of his feeling states on a scale from 0 to 10. The optimal energy zone for this athlete includes high intensities of P+ and U+, and low intensities of U- and P- feeling states.

Research shows that when athletes stay within their prescribed zones, they perform better. Think of the graph in Figure 13.9 as the new and improved inverted-u model! Athletes can chart their preferred intensities of helpful (positive) feeling states in the middle, and then chart their preferred intensities of hurtful (negative) feeling states on each side of their graphs. This creates their optimal energy zones. The preferred higher intensities of positive energy in the middle and the lower intensities of negative energy on the sides create an inverted-u, which increases the probability of good performance. If an athlete's inverted-u flattens out, he or she is more likely to ex-

perience average performance. If an athlete's energy profile flips to a u-shape (lower in the middle than the sides), then they are likely to experience poor performance and even choking (Hanin, 2000c).

Later in the chapter, I'll provide some specific directions for how you can lead athletes in an exercise to chart their personalized optimal energy zones. The key take-home point for now is that each athlete has a unique individual recipe of feeling states that make up his or her optimal energy zone and leads to peak performance.

Clipboard

Different Strokes for Different Folks

Athletes are very idiosyncratic about managing their energy for competition. Andy Roddick, 2003 U.S. Open tennis champion, embraces the "anti-'stay in your room and focus'" strategy. He describes his optimal energy approach to competition as "Chill out, play video games . . . and save all that intensity and energy for when you go on the court" (Wertheim, 2003, p. 76).

Jeff Blatnick, U.S. Olympic wrestler, had a routine he performed with his father just prior to every match. His father would look at him and say, "Get mad, son!" Blatnick would reply, "If you get mad, you get stupid!" Obviously, anger was not a preferred feeling state for Blatnick during competition. His quote emphasizes that for him, the emotion of anger clouded his ability to make effective decisions and focus optimally on his wrestling (Blatnick, 1999, p. 51).

Former PGA golf great Sam Snead wanted to be in a zone where he felt "cool-mad." He described this as staying intense but on an even keel—just a little bit above his everyday energy level. On the other hand, Hale Irwin, another former PGA champion golfer, describes how he focuses on controlled intensity, as opposed to coolness: "I try to make the pressure and tension work for me. I want the adrenaline to be flowing. I think sometimes we try so hard to be cool, calm, and collected that we forget what we're doing. There's nothing wrong with being charged up if it's controlled."

Which approach would work best for you? The answer is none! We all have to understand ourselves well enough to develop our own approach to energy management in competition. Even though the athletes described here are great champions, it simply doesn't work to try to copy their mental styles of energy management. Let your athletes know that they have to establish an individualized optimal energy plan that works best for them!

Anxiety and Performance

As defined previously, anxiety is a high intensity unpleasant feeling state that typically results from a demand or threat. The influence of anxiety on athletic performance has been studied more by sport psychologists than any other feeling states.

Optimal zones of anxiety. Anxiety has been specifically studied using the concept of optimal zones for performance enhancement. Research supports that athletes perform better when they are in their optimal anxiety zones, which are individual preferences for certain levels of cognitive and somatic anxiety (Hanin, 2000b). For example, a mental training program helped adolescent tennis players perform better by teaching them how to manage their anxiety based on the unique intensities and types of anxiety experienced by each athlete (Annesi, 1998).

Types of anxiety related to performance. Athletes' performance is affected differently depending on whether they experience more cognitive or somatic anxiety. For example, a study with high school softball players found that athletes experiencing higher cognitive anxiety had more mental errors in competition than athletes who experienced lower cognitive anxiety (Bird & Horn, 1990). This means that mental training should focus on helping athletes manage the specific types of anxiety that interfere most with their performance. As an example, a cognitive-oriented self-talk mental training intervention was designed for semiprofessional soccer players who experienced high levels of cognitive anxiety (Maynard, Warwick-Evans, & Smith, 1995). The mental training program was successful in decreasing the athletes' cognitive anxiety and enhancing their decision-making, which is an important part of performance negatively affected by cognitive anxiety.

Somatic anxiety creates physical tension and bodily nervousness, and is typically related to athletes' performance in an inverted-u manner (moderate levels are best, with low and high levels negatively related to performance). Athletes who experience specific symptoms of somatic anxiety (e.g., tension in the shoulders of golfers, jitteriness in hands of shooters and archers) should practice physical relaxation techniques such as Power Breathing and conscious muscle control to help reduce the negative effects of somatic anxiety.

Interestingly, it is the *combination* of cognitive anxiety and physiological arousal that seems most likely to affect athletes' performance (Hardy, 1996). This interactive effect is described as the "catastrophe" model, and the effects on performance are as ominous as they sound! Catastrophes may be thought of as choking, or sudden and complete decrements of performance for athletes. Catastrophes tend to occur when athletes are in a high state of cognitive anxiety and their physiological arousal increases to a breaking point where . . . boom—their performance drops off drastically and the catastrophe occurs!

What can coaches learn from this catastrophe model? First, cognitive anxiety isn't by itself a bad thing. Some athletes accept and even welcome the worry and mental strain of cognitive anxiety as a readying or focusing mechanism. These athletes seem to manage their other energy states (e.g., self-confidence, control of their physiological arousal) to create a positive overall energy zone for themselves that includes cognitive anxiety. The key is that, when their cognitive anxiety is high, athletes must be able to control their physical arousal to prevent the interactive catastrophe effect (Hardy, 1996).

Another important implication for coaches is that once athletes choke, or experience a catastrophic overdose of anxiety and subsequent performance blackout, they can't refocus or rebound by simply easing back on their RPMs, or intensity of energy. If you can envision the inverted-u model, this means that athletes can't move back up the inverted-u once they've gone past their optimal zone. Rather, they need to de-energize by stepping off the u (so to speak), and climb back on at the lower side and start over. It's almost like they need to restart their engines once the catastrophe stalls them. They can't slow their engines back down to moderate cruising speed without restarting and revving them back up.

Interpretation of anxiety as positive or negative. Even though anxiety is an unpleasant feeling state, certain athletes perceive it as performance-enhancing (Hanin, 2000c). Athletes who are elite, who perform better, who are more competitive, and who are more confident all perceive anxiety as more facilitative to their performance as compared to non-elite, lower performing, less competitive, and less confident athletes (Jones & Hanton, 1996). Recent research indicates that it's not the anxiety per se that facilitates athletes' performance. Rather, mentally skilled athletes use anxiety as a cue to engage in coping and focus strategies to gain control over and confidence in their mental and physical skills to perform (Hanton & Connaughton, 2002).

This emphasizes how important mental skills are for athletes! If they perceive they have the ability to cope with the anxiety they experience and still achieve their goals, then anxiety may be a very positive cue for them to lock in to their mental focus strategies and reach their optimal energy zones (Jones & Hanton, 1996). Explain to your athletes how they can use anxiety as a performance enhancer

to trigger them to focus and energize in response to competitive demands. Anxiety, as a type of unpleasant competitive energy, doesn't always *feel* good, but it can be a very useful natural resource for athletes to harness as a performance enhancer.

How anxiety influences performance. As just discussed, anxiety is sometimes a helpful form of competitive energy that serves to get athletes focused and ready to perform. However, high levels of anxiety that are not managed effectively can create worries and self-preoccupation that draw athletes' attention away from relevant task-related processing that is needed for optimal performance (Eysenck & Calvo, 1992). Research has shown that athletes that experience anxiety as negative and debilitative spend more time processing negative cues in the competitive environment (Eubank, Collins, & Smith, 2000). That is, these athletes focus their attention on the threatening aspects of competitive (what can go wrong, how I might screw up) as opposed to the challenging and exciting aspects of competition.

Obviously, athletes whose performance is disrupted by anxiety would greatly benefit from creating and practicing optimal energy focus plans. However, it seems simplistic to only examine anxiety as one feeling state in athletes' optimal energy zones, because it is the interactive effects of different combinations of feeling states that are most likely to affect performance (Hanin, 2000b, 2000c; Hardy, Jones, &

Photo by Brett Hansbauer

Gould, 1996). Thus, I encourage athletes to develop their personalized optimal energy zones using all types of feeling states. If anxiety is an important U-feeling state that interferes with their performance, then we can work to manage their energy to decrease or refocus the anxious feelings. One way to do this is by emphasizing the P+ and U+ feeling states to create a positive, helpful sense of competitive energy. Overall, athletes should view anxiety as a normal and expected source of competitive energy and mentally train to manage this unpleasant feeling state to make it work *for* them instead of *against* them.

How to Optimize Competitive Energy in Athletes

You've learned a lot about competitive energy and the ways in which it influences athletes' performance. Now it's time to think about how you as the coach can help athletes manage their energy and spend time in their optimal energy zones in pursuit of flow and peak performance.

P^3 Thinking and Feeling in Response to Competitive Pressure

You might want to go back and reread Chapter 10! How athletes think and respond to what happens to them determines how they feel. Successful energy management by athletes requires P^3 (Purposeful, Productive, Possibility) Thinking. R^3 (Random, Reactive, Restrictive) Thinkers allow their thoughts and feelings to be controlled by what happens to them. Thus, R^3 Thinkers don't manage their energy, they just experience whatever forms and levels of energy happen to occur to them. And based on Murphy's Law, negative energy states are going to rear their ugly heads at the absolute worst time for athletes, such as in championship competitions.

P^3 Thinking leads to P^3 Feelings! Athletes must engage in Purposeful, Productive, and Possibility Thinking, which then creates Purposeful, Productive, and Possibility Feelings. Athletes ultimately choose how to think and feel about competition, and these thoughts and feelings determine how well they will perform.

How pressure leads athletes into R^3 Thinking and Feeling traps. Athletes' thoughts and feelings are influenced by many things in the competitive situation, including crowd size, importance of the com-

petition, presence of college or professional scouts, television exposure, number of family members present, and personal goals and expectations. The unpleasant feeling state of **pressure** occurs *when attractive and highly valued incentives create an urgent and compelling force on the athlete to succeed.* Athletes feel pressure when highly valued personal goals are threatened, such as not living up to expectations (their own and others), not performing to potential, and appearing untalented, among other things (Lewthwaite, 1990; Wilson & Eklund, 1998).

Clipboard

Game 7 Pressure

Luis Gonzales stepped into the batter's box with the bases loaded, bottom of the ninth, and the score tied 2-2 during Game 7 of the 2001 World Series. Gonzales describes how the pressure affected his thinking: "I felt the weight of the city, of my teammates, of my family—the weight, in a way, of all baseball. I mean, the weight of that situation in a Game 7 . . . If you let it, it can crush you. It's like nothing you feel at any other time . . . You have to concentrate, but there're so many things going through your mind. What adjustments should I make? Then those thoughts, what you *should* be thinking about, are pushed out by things you *shouldn't* be thinking about. Where in the city will I hide if I strike out? I can feel my friends and my teammates pulling for me. What if I let them down? This isn't Game 1 or Game 2 where you still have time. This is Game 7!"

Gonzales went on to hit a single into short left field, which scored the winning run and won the Series for the Diamondbacks. And like all great competitors, he looked back at the situation and relished the pressure: "When I think back on it now, what I wish is that my family, my friends, and all our fans could experience what I experienced in that short time. I wish I could bottle that Game 7 feeling. Because there's nothing like it" (McCallum, 2004, pp. 58, 65).

The pressure of competition, especially championship competition like Game 7 of the World Series, can be devastating. But as described by Gonzales, it's also why we play and what we truly relish about sport. When athletes feel pressure, they should remind themselves that this is what it's about—it's why they play. Tell your athletes to drink in the pressure and to relish it as a true competitor.

Seventy-one percent of U.S. National Champion figure skaters experienced *more* stress and anxiety after winning their titles than they did before winning them (Gould, Jackson, & Finch, 1993). The "top dog" pressures experienced by these athletes were expectations to skate flawlessly, never have a bad day, be better than their previous championship year, and live up to the daily expectations of being a national champion. This could be quite a burden! In addition, unexpected stressors that come up in competition have been shown to elicit more R^3 Thinking and Feeling than expected stressors, and athletes have admitted that they tend to hold back or fail to respond appropriately when faced with unexpected stressors (Dugdale, Eklund, & Gordon, 2002).

Thus, it's easy to see how pressures inherent in sport competition trap athletes into R^3 Thinking and

Feeling. Ah, but there's the rub! It *is* a trap. Athletes fall into the trap because they believe that pressure (or any other competitive distraction) hurts their performance. But it isn't the pressure that hurts their performance—it's their *responses to* the pressure. As shown in Figure 13.10, how athletes respond to pressure depends on how they think and feel about it, and how they act in response to the pressure. Some athletes thrive on pressure and welcome it, even though it doesn't feel pleasant at the time. Others wilt under pressure as the unpleasant feelings are interpreted as negative and become overwhelming. Athletes must learn to respond to pressure with P^3 thoughts and feelings, as opposed to reacting with R^3 thoughts and feelings. Reacting means that the athlete allows the pressure to dictate how they think and feel. Responding means that athletes have planned and mentally practiced effective thoughts and feeling states to manage the negative energy that can interfere with their performance.

Enhancing P^3 Thinking and Feeling to handle pressure. So what can coaches do to help athletes think and feel better when facing pressure situations?

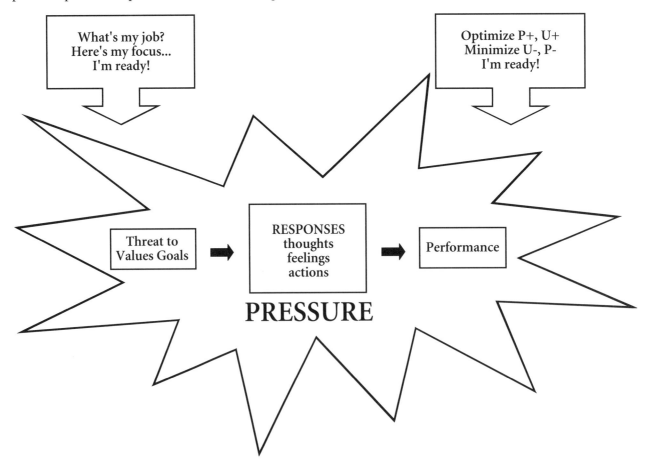

Figure 13.10 P^3 Thinking and Feeling in response to pressure

Because pressure involves threat to valued goals, the first place to start is by building athletes' skills in goal mapping (review Chapter 8). If athletes focus on SMAART goals and know which goals to focus on at what times, this is an important first step to managing pressure. If athletes learn to "climb the performance tree" as shown in Chapter 8, then they will have performance and process goals they can focus on during competition. Consider how the performance and focus goals of Annika Sorenstam help her to focus and energize optimally before she hits a golf shot in pressure situations: "I commit to a shot 100 percent and I don't worry about the result. What the ball does after it leaves my clubface is beyond my control, so I accept the outcome" (Freeman, 1998, p. 76).

Using their goal maps as a base, athletes should develop focus plans and pre-performance routines (see Chapter 12) that are used to mentally train the responses that they want to occur in pressure situations. As shown in Figure 13.10, P³ Thinking as part of a focus plan means that athletes respond to pressure by assessing what must be done ("What's my job?"), and then planning and practicing the focus that is needed to do this. Also shown in Figure 13.10 is athletes' P³ Feeling responses, where athletes respond to pressure by optimizing the feeling states that help their performance (P+, U+) and minimizing the feeling states that hurt their performance (U-, P-).

Acceptance is an important step for athletes in dealing with pressure, and I advocate athletes practicing acceptance in two ways. First, they must resolve to themselves prior to competition that they will accept themselves and their performance no matter what happens. This is difficult and takes maturity, emotional intelligence, and perspective. But self-acceptance is a powerful antidote to keeping worry in perspective (Orlick, 1986). It doesn't mean athletes won't feel pressure and worry, but it lessens the severity of the worry and negative influence of pressure. Coaches can help athletes by countering their irrational thoughts that they *have to* win or perform well (review Chapter 10 on REBT).

The second key to acceptance is that athletes should accept the pressure that goes along with competition. I remind them often that that is why they play! I've found that some athletes love the pressure, while others don't. For those that don't, I simply ask that they work on acknowledging it, accepting that it's part of what they feel, and meet it

head on by working with it, not against it. If athletes don't enjoy the pressure, then they should at least make friends with it. By focusing on the feeling states that occur when they experience competitive pressure, athletes can learn to use pressure as a positive energy source. Brian Goodell (1999), Olympic swimming champion, explains that athletes can dismiss fear and worry, but only if they face it head on. He explains that fear is often unjustifiable, if you just take the time to think through it rationally:

> *"Confronting the fear, like turning on the light in a haunted house, forces the fear to justify itself and often it can't"* (p. 177).

Sean McCann (2003), sport psychologist at the U.S. Olympic Training Center in Colorado Springs, suggests that asking athletes the right questions helps them ingrain the key thoughts and feelings they want to have in response to competitive pressure. He explains that the best questions you can ask athletes are ones that direct their focus to what they want to do, not what they want to avoid. Here are the four key questions that McCann advocates asking athletes who are nervous before big events (p. 13):

(1) What is your job? (Sample answer, "wrestle well tomorrow.")
(2) How do you do that? (Sample answer, "Attack the first minute, then go harder.")
(3) Can you do that? (Sample answer, "Yes! I'm in amazing shape.")
(4) Will you do that? (Sample answer, "Yes!")

McCann notes that questions such as these allow coaches to see how athletes are thinking and feeling. However, more importantly, these questions allow athletes to find their own solutions instead of agreeing with their coaches' solutions. Athletes are more likely to believe and internalize effective responses when they come from within.

Of course, this works only if your athletes have practiced P³ Thinking and focus planning for competition. So make sure that before you ask these questions, you've mentally prepared your athletes for competitive pressures. For example, 8 to 9 year-old-children in youth sport often believe that pregame nervousness and worry means they're less skilled than other kids (Weiss, Ebbeck, & Horn,

1997). Obviously, young athletes are susceptible to interpreting unpleasant feeling states as negative and abnormal. One of the first things that youth sport coaches should do is help young athletes understand the normal and even helpful nature of competitive energy. An old adage in sport psychology that works with kids is to tell them that the "butterflies" they're feeling are normal, and these butterflies mean that their bodies are ready to go! Tell them that the trick is to get their butterflies flying in the right formation (Orlick, 1986)! This gets across the point that we all experience the unpleasant sensations of nervousness, but if we use that energy in the right way then it can help us.

Coaches should become familiar with their athletes so they can recognize signs of under-arousal as well as over-arousal when they are out of their zones. McCann (2003) says that coaches need to know the difference between "good quiet" and "bad quiet" before competition. "Good quiet" is when athletes are focusing on performance and getting mentally and physically energized. "Bad quiet" is when they are trying to look as if they're focused and ready, but when in reality they are out of their zones and probably worrying about uncontrollable things. Learn to read your athletes, and be prepared to "touch base" with them to reassure them that they're ready or to ask the key questions about what their job is and how they are going to do it. A simple comment or dialogue with them can help athletes make the mental reversals they need to manage their energy more effectively.

Clipboard

How Do You Make a Diamond? Pressure and Heat!

Here's a great analogy to use with your athletes about the positive effects of pressure:

Diamonds are the most precious stones on Earth, and are very valuable based on their unique physical and chemical properties. Yet diamonds are almost pure carbon, the same element that makes up graphite, which is a common substance with properties very different from diamonds. How can two materials (diamonds and graphite) with basically the same chemical composition be so different? Why is it that diamonds are so rare, when carbon occurs so commonly in other forms and compounds?

The answer is PRESSURE and HEAT! Diamonds form about 100 miles below the earth's surface, in the molten rock of the earth's mantle. The carbon that turns into diamonds must be subjected to an exact amount of heat and pressure to transform it into a diamond. In order for a diamond to be created, carbon must be placed under 435,113 pounds per square inch of pressure at a temperature of at least 752 degrees Fahrenheit. If the pressure and heat are any less than this, then graphite is created.

What's the lesson here? Without the right amount of pressure, we fail to become extraordinary. Welcome the pressure! Take the heat! Use it to make yourself into a diamond, or an athlete who shines in becoming the best you can be. Pressure and heat don't always feel good, but make friends with these feelings instead of fighting or avoiding them. Use the pressure to move from being a common lump of graphite (average athlete) to a sparkling diamond, or an athlete with championship physical and mental skills. Remember—welcome the pressure, take the heat—and be a diamond!

Emotional preparation. Cal Botterill, successful sport psychologist for many Canadian and National Hockey League teams, emphasizes that athletes must engage in "emotional preparation" the same way they engage in physical preparation (Botterill, & Patrick, 2003). In particular, athletes need to prepare for feeling states that get triggered when things don't go right. So athletes should prepare for how they will think and feel in every situation that might occur in competition or training (e.g., bus breaks down, a teammate goes off on me, I start playing great, I start playing lousy, a key teammate gets injured, the officials are terrible, play is really rough, my opponent is trash-talking me, we're late/early for warm-ups).

Botterill and Patrick (2003) also suggest that athletes mentally prepare to respond to specific emotions that arise during competition. As an example, athletes should prepare to respond effectively to surprise, both negative and positive. How many times have you heard the adage, "I don't want any surprises" when people are preparing for an event? Well, none of us may like them, but surprises are part of life and particularly a part of competition. Athletes and teams should prepare for their opponent's best and most annoying performances, and rehearse effective responses for these situations. Athletes and teams should also prepare for their own surprisingly effective starts, and not be vulnerable to the pleasant feeling states of joy and excitement, which could interfere with their performance. Other surprises that athletes should be ready for include officiating, weather, delays, and last minute changes. Overall, athletes should prepare for a range of emotions including anger, embarrassment, and low energy emotions such as sadness or depression. Athletes should consider what emotions they are most susceptible to as well as which emotions tend to interfere the most with their performance. They can then prepare effective responses to these emotions when they occur in competition.

Emotional preparation includes planning effective responses (P³ thoughts and feelings) for situations that the athlete identifies as potentially disruptive. This planning could include identifying typical negative thoughts and feelings that arise in these specific situations, and then developing a counterplan that includes productive self-talk, focusing cues, and/or imagery triggers for how he or she wishes to respond. Athletes should attempt to trigger the negative feelings that may come up, and then rehearse a quality physical, mental, and emotional response for each feeling (Botterill & Patrick, 2003). This should be planned and practiced well ahead of competition (weeks and months), so that athletes feel totally prepared as competition time nears. Then, the day before or of competition, athletes can mentally rehearse their focus plan for competition, including their planned and practiced P³ Thinking and Feeling responses to typical stressors and resulting emotions.

In addition, athletes need to prepare their thinking and feeling responses for situations that they haven't even considered! This sounds weird because they can't prepare specifically for something they aren't aware of, but they can prepare to respond with P³ Thoughts and Feelings no matter what happens! "No matter what happens" should be your athletes' mantra! Remind them over and over that they can choose whether to manage their thoughts and feelings or to let them be managed by what happens to them. The mentally tough choice is the first one—no matter what.

Coaches should challenge athletes to take personal responsibility for their emotional readiness for competition. Often, feeling states that are experienced by individual athletes spill over into the team. Actually, in team sports it is possible and desired to create collective feeling states such as "readiness," "attacking," or "energized." It only takes one athlete to disrupt the feeling state that the team is trying to create (Botterill & Patrick, 2003). Thus, athletes must take responsibility to create their own optimal energy zones, but also to contribute positively to the collective optimal energy feelings needed by the team.

Summary. In summary, optimizing competitive energy in athletes requires P³ Thinking and Feeling. It requires self-acceptance and the acceptance of competitive pressure as a potential ally. As shown in Figure 13.10, athletes must take personal "response-ability" to focus on what they have to do, how they'll do it, and how they'll think and feel while doing it. Athletes should identify helpful P+ and U+ feeling states that they will optimize and disruptive U- and P- feeling states that they will minimize. Mental rehearsal of these feeling states and all possible emotional responses to potential (and unforeseen) competitive stressors should culminate in a feeling of "I'm ready!" And it will!

Managing Negative Energy

In attempting to manage negative feeling states, athletes have two options. First, they can use mental training tools to decrease the intensity of their negative feelings. This means athletes attempt to decrease their internal RPMs, or the speed at which their internal engines are working. For example, a distance runner could train herself using Power Breathing, conscious muscle control, and imagery to relax the bodily tension she experienced prior to competition. A high jumper could use imagery and self-talk within a focus plan to decrease the intensity of cognitive anxiety prior to each jump. These methods have been shown to work with athletes in decreasing energy intensity (e.g., Hardy et al., 1996; Williams & Harris, 2001).

Reframing negative energy into positive. The second way that athletes can manage negative energy is to reframe negative feeling states into positive feeling states. Reframing is a type of coping where athletes change their perspective to view things more productively. We've already talked about accepting pressure and going with it, as opposed to resisting the unpleasant feelings that are part of pressure. This is an example of reframing to optimize competitive energy. A mental training program targeted for swimmers who experienced anxiety as a negative and disruptive feeling state successfully modified the swimmers' perceptions of anxiety so that it became a positive feeling state useful for their performance (Hanton & Jones, 1999). The mental training intervention included preliminary goal mapping and imagery rehearsal, which allowed them to experience the energy of anxiety as helpful and natural. Swimmers were also taught individualized pre-race routines that incorporated productive self-talk and imagery rehearsal of optimal performance.

Mental reversals. Athletes interpret their feeling states as positive or negative depending on their "motivational moods." This idea comes from reversal theory (Apter, 1982; Kerr, 1997), which contends that athletes' interpretations of feeling states depends on their motivational mood at that point in time. The motivational moods that seem to be most relevant for energy management in athletes are whether the athlete feels playful or goal-oriented.

As shown in the double-arrow lines on the graph in Figure 13.11, an athlete in a playful mood prefers high levels of arousal, interprets this arousal as exciting, and thus seeks out situations of high energy intensity (e.g., competition, risk activities, social activities with friends). Athletes in playful moods interpret low intensities of arousal as boring, and would prefer not to be in this feeling state. The reverse is true for an athlete in a goal-oriented mood. This athlete prefers a low level of arousal, interprets this arousal as relaxation, and avoids high intensities of arousal, which are interpreted as anxiety.

To manage energy effectively, athletes should learn to induce mental reversals in their motivational moods. These reversals are shown as the block arrows in Figure 13.11. When an athlete feels anxious, he can reframe this unpleasant high intensity energy state into excitement by reversing his motivational mood from goal-oriented to playful. This may sound dubious to you—why would you want an athlete to become playful in the middle of competition, where goal achievement is the main focus? The answer lies in the characteristics that we know are associated with flow or peak performance. Feeling playful or lost in one's task without conscious processing of goals or outcomes leads to flow, optimal energy

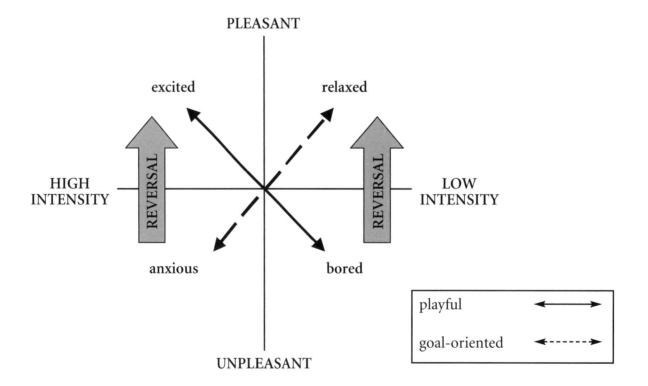

Figure 13.11 Reversing negative energy to positive by altering motivational moods

zones, and peak performance. Research with elite athletes has shown that playful motivational moods are related to better performance (Males, Kerr, & Gerkovich, 1998; Perkins, Wilson, & Kerr, 2001).

Changing motivational mood to feel more playful and less anxious is a common mental training strategy to get athletes to gain perspective and focus on their love of the feelings associated with sport. Many elite golfers hum a familiar and pleasant song during their rounds to keep their motivational mood from becoming so goal-oriented that anxiety becomes a problem. Athletes also use self-talk cues such as "enjoy" and imagery rehearsals that focus on the feelings of enjoyment and the thrill of performing. Athletes should plan a cue that they can use in competition to induce a mental reversal from anxiety to excitement or joy. This cue can be anything that focuses them away from outcome pressure and toward enjoyment and passion. The other mental reversal shown by the block arrow in Figure 13.11 is moving from unpleasant to pleasant low intensity feelings. The graph shows a reversal from bored to relaxed, but athletes can also use this to attempt to move from tired to relaxed. This is important for recovery and rest from training and competition.

Athletes should understand that they will experience many mental reversals during the course of a competitive event. They should become aware of the factors in competition that cause their motivational shifts and subsequent changes in feeling states. Typically, performance problems and frustration lead athletes to become more goal-oriented and full of negativity. However, some athletes lose their focus and optimal energy zone because they are not goal-oriented enough, and should learn to monitor themselves to stay on task, focused, and dialed in to their preferred feeling states.

Managing pleasant energy that hurts performance. We've talked a lot about pressure and strategies that athletes can use to manage the unpleasant feeling states associated with pressure. However, high intensities of pleasant feeling states, such as being really psyched up, can interfere with performance as well. Read the following quote by Peter Vidmar, U.S. Olympic gold medalist in gymnastics, who describes how high intensity pleasant feeling states negatively affected his performance, and how he and his coach managed this energy:

"[He] always would make me try to think about practice as though it were competition. And then when I got to competition, he would reverse it and try to get me to imagine it as a workout instead of a real meet. In that way, my emotions would balance out. I mean, for the competition, you get so keyed up that all of a sudden you're stronger than you normally are for your regular workout. You have a lot more power, but because of the extra power it doesn't mean you have a lot more control. If you're training every day by doing just routines over and over again without really thinking about them . . . you haven't done anything to get yourself ready mentally. So you walk into a meet and you're all pumped up—you're really strong but mentally you haven't gotten yourself in the frame of mind to know how to control that adrenalin. So what we do is try to feel our adrenalin when we're doing our routine. Especially when it got close to the Olympics, we did that. Every routine was critical; every routine had to be perfect" (Ravizza, 1993, p. 94).

Vidmar's example emphasizes the need for optimal intensity of energy, regardless of whether it is pleasant or unpleasant. This seems particularly important in sports where precision is necessary and could be negatively influenced by pleasant feelings, which can tip the balance of energy so that athletes have more power than usual. But learning how to manage the intensity of your RPMs is difficult, especially with the excitement generated by competitive sport. Think about the energy generated in an athlete as he runs into Ohio Stadium in front of 100,000 people, or as she goes to the starting line for the 100-meter race at the Olympic Games. It takes practice to identify and habituate the strategies that work for each athlete in optimizing his or her energy states for competition.

Creating Optimal Energy Profiles for Athletes

If you're sold on the idea that athletes need to identify their optimal energy zones to improve performance, you're probably wondering how to help them do this. Good question! An exercise titled "Optimal Energy Profile" is provided in Appendix 13A to teach athletes how to identify and monitor their feeling states or competitive energy needed for competition. Read through the entire exercise so you understand what is involved. As a first step, I recommend that you assess and monitor your OEP as a coach. I've done this with coaches and they feel it is very helpful in preparing to manage their emotions and energy for competition.

Before you begin the exercise with athletes, make extra blank copies of Parts B and C. These are worksheets that athletes should use repeatedly to assess their feeling states after competition to chart whether they are performing in their Optimal Energy Zone. You can lead this exercise in a group setting, or you can explain it to athletes in a group, and then let them complete it on their own time. Athletes need time to engage in self-reflection for this exercise to work, so it's a good idea to give them time and space to complete it on their own. Emphasize the need to identify the specific types of feelings that really help and hurt their performance. Each athlete's Optimal Energy Profile should be uniquely personalized. Encourage them to complete the worksheets after several competitions, so they can begin to understand what things may have interfered with their performance.

Athletes should try to adhere to the same mental/behavioral preparation strategies and routines before every competition. These routines should help them achieve their desired feeling states that put them in the position for peak performance. Along with mentally preparing to get into their zones, athletes should also pay attention to things during competition that take them out of their zones. If they continually fall out of zone on a certain feeling state that is important to them, they should carefully assess why this occurs and develop a refocusing strategy (Chapter 12) to get them back into their zone. Athletes should think of their OEP as their energy thermometer, and by taking their temperature after each competition, they can become more in tune with their optimal energy needs and preferences.

Energy Management for Coaches

The entire chapter has focused on helping athletes manage their energy. However, it's clear that coaches can also benefit a great deal from energy management strategies.

Energy management for coaches is critical for two reasons. First, your athletes look to you as the primary model for how to manage competitive pressure and the excitement of competition. Displaying just the right amount of emotion can inspire your athletes, displaying too much emotion can push them out of their zones, and displaying too little emotion makes your athletes wonder if you care. Although each athlete must develop their own optimal energy states and should not copy what you do as coach, your personal example of knowing yourself and managing your energy states provides a powerful model for them to follow. The second reason why you must manage your competitive energy is to ensure that you remain effective. Nothing interferes with effective decision-making more than emotion. This doesn't mean that emotion is bad—it's not—but it means that you need to understand your personal emotional tendencies under pressure so that you can remain effective as the coach.

Consider the following examples of how ineffective energy management can hamper your coaching ability (McCann, 2003). Nervousness is contagious and your staff and athletes will catch it from you because they look to you as the leader. Just the right amount of worry means that you prepare your team well and look after important details; endless worry exhausts you and your staff, and makes your athletes question their preparedness. Nervousness can lead to over-coaching and talking too much, which can make your communication ineffective and expose your nervousness. Nervousness can also make you go quiet and stop coaching, which of course is just as ineffective and just as noticeable by your athletes. It is helpful if you have a trusted assistant coach or someone close to your program that can give you honest feedback about your behavioral tendencies under pressure (McCann, 2003). This feedback is helpful in developing strategies to manage your own energy and coaching behaviors in pressure situations.

Photo by Julie C. Elliott, courtesy of © stock.xchang iv

Other feeling states can hurt your performance much like anxiety. For example, unmanaged anger can lead to embarrassing behaviors and even expulsion from competition. A common strategy for coaches susceptible to anger is to ask an assistant to step in with a rational voice when anger is building. However, like athletes, coaches must take personal responsibility for managing their own feeling states, so coaches that experience anger that hampers their performance should develop a brief strategy to manage this anger. This should be something simple, such as a quick relaxation response (Power Breath with shoulder shrug) followed by a self-talk trigger to focus away from the anger ("coach the game"). If the anger is directed at an official, it would be appropriate to express and release the anger, and then refocus on coaching the game.

Coaches, like athletes, should also plan their desired responses to surprise. For coaches, this could include situations like tactical surprises from opponents, an athlete or the team performing better or worse than expected, an injury to a key player, or timing devices failing or officials doing something unexpected. The coach's response to surprising events sets the tone for the team. I've often noticed that when coaches continue to whine and complain when basketball games get overly physical and the officiating is questioned, their players do the same thing. This means that the players lose their performance focus and worry about the officiating as opposed to managing their feelings and just playing. Like athletes, coaches should mentally prepare and practice for effective responses to all situations that can occur in their sports, including different emotions that arise.

Interviews with 21 expert Canadian coaches in field hockey, ice hockey, volleyball, and basketball, identified by their National Sport Organizations as being the most knowledgeable and respected in the country, indicated that most all these coaches used mental rehearsal as part of their game-day routine (Bloom, Durand-Bush, & Salmela, 1997). More than 90% of the coaches interviewed took time during the day to review in their minds typical scenarios that may arise in the upcoming competitions, including how they would respond to key matchups, late game substitutions, and poor officiating. One basketball coach stated,

> *"My biggest problem is emotional control during games, so I have to mentally rehearse all the situations and decide in advance how I am going to react. When I see who is officiating . . . I visualize those people making the usual screwups that they make and how I am going to react. I have to do that or I would be out of control" (p. 133). An ice hockey coach explains, " . . . I would think about who I was going to use against whom. Also, if somebody got hurt, who would I replace him with? I tried to visualize what might happen, different scenarios; if this line is not going well, who would I move into that position? So I would rehearse . . ." (p. 133).*

Coaches should pay attention to their behavioral and emotional tendencies under stress or pressure, and develop mental plans for how they want to think and act in these situations. Develop your own Optimal Energy Profile as a coach and assess yourself after several competitions to become more aware of the feeling states you need to manage to do your job well. Remember the powerful modeling effect that you have on your athletes, and let optimal energy management in your program start with you!

Wrapping Up

The important life skill of emotional intelligence begins with self-awareness, which involves understanding our internal states, preferences, resources, and limitations. Daniel Goleman (1998), originator of the emotional intelligence concept, states that without this awareness, we can be sidetracked by emotions that run amok. He goes on to explain that this takes some effort, because in the rush of everyday life, our minds are preoccupied with constant thoughts and plans. He likens our internal feeling states to a subterranean energy force that is always with us, but typically not in our consciousness. In his words, "our feelings are always with us, but we are too seldom with them" (p. 56).

The point of this chapter is to encourage athletes (and coaches) to pay attention to the feelings that help them perform better as well as those that distract them or hurt their performance. By more effectively managing their competitive energy, athletes do two key things. First, they put themselves "on deck" for flow. Athletes can't force flow or peak performance to happen, but they can put themselves in a position to increase the probability that it will occur.

Second, the ability to effectively manage energy is an important coping skill for the many competitive situations in which athletes aren't in flow or when peak performance just isn't happening.

Athletes should shoot for the new inverted-u or "Peak" each time they perform, based on their Optimal Energy Profiles. Similar to the idea of Purposeful Thinking advocated in Chapter 10, athletes should also engage in Purposeful Feeling, or the systematic, preplanning, focused effort on creating the feeling states that they need to perform their best. Effective energy management means that athletes respond productively to manage how they think and feel, no matter what happens to them in competition. This takes a great deal of mental practice to prepare for the competitive demands and emotions that they must regulate within themselves. Encourage them to tap into their most important human resource—their energy. Advise them—use it effectively or it will use you!

Summary Points for Chapter 13

1. The goals of energy management are to (a) mentally prepare to achieve an optimal energy zone, and (b) effectively manage competitive energy when not in the zone.

2. Athletes are typically very systematic about optimizing their physiological energy, but tend to allow their mental energy to occur naturally without attempting to optimize it for performance.

3. Energy, synonymous to the term arousal, is a state of physical and mental readiness.

4. Athletes experience their energy as different types of feeling states, which can be high or low intensity, unpleasant or pleasant, and experienced mentally as thoughts or physically as bodily sensations.

5. Anxiety is a high intensity unpleasant feeling state that typically results from a demand or threat.

6. Cognitive anxiety is worry, while somatic anxiety is physical symptoms such as muscle tension, increased heart rate and breathing, and jitteriness.

7. All forms of competitive energy, or different feeling states, are potentially positive and negative in relation to athletes' performance.

8. All of the feelings that we experience as humans serve a purpose and developed as part of the evolution of our species.

9. Stress is a demand placed on an athlete, which helps athletes by stimulating growth and inoculating them to cope with higher levels of stress.

10. Flow may be thought of as the optimal energy zone, and it occurs when athletes experience a balance between their skills and the challenges that they perceive in a situation.

11. Flow is characterized by a complete absorption in the task, sense of control, loss of self-consciousness, clarity in purpose, unambiguous feedback, and intrinsic motivation.

12. Constant feedback and evaluation are disrupting to an athlete's flow.

13. As athletes' levels of arousal increase, they are more likely to exhibit their dominant responses.

14. Generally, athletes perform better at moderate levels of arousal, shown in graphic form as the inverted-u.

15. The optimal intensity of athletes' arousal differs according to situational demands and individual preferences.

16. As athletes' levels of arousal increase, their attention narrows.

17. Athletes use a wide variety of individually relevant words to describe the pleasant and unpleasant feeling states that both help and hurt their performance.

18. Athletes can create personalized optimal energy zones by identifying the types and intensities of pleasant and unpleasant feeling states that help and hurt their performance.

19. The new and improved inverted-u model is created when athletes optimize their positive feeling states and decrease their negative feeling states within their optimal energy profiles.

20. Athletes perform better in their optimal anxiety zones, which are preferences for certain levels of cognitive and somatic anxiety.

21. When athletes are in a high state of cognitive anxiety and their physiological arousal increases too much, they suffer catastrophic performance decrements (choking).

22. Athletes who are elite, who perform better, who are more competitive, and who are more confident all perceive anxiety as more facilita-

tive to their performance as compared to non-elite, lower performing, less competitive, and less confident athletes.

23. High levels of anxiety that are not managed effectively can create worries and self-preoccupation that draw athletes' attention away from task-related processing that is needed for optimal performance.

24. Pressure is an unpleasant feeling state that occurs when attractive and highly valued incentives create an urgent and compelling force on the athlete to succeed.

25. Pressure itself does not hurt athletes' performance, rather athletes' *responses* to pressure influence how well they perform.

26. Coaches can help athletes cope with pressure by teaching them effective goal mapping, self-acceptance of performance, acceptance of pressure as part of competition, and P³ Thinking and Feeling responses.

27. Athletes must mentally prepare to respond effectively to any situations and/or emotions that may arise during competition.

28. To manage negative energy states, athletes can decrease their intensity or reframe them into positive feeling states.

29. Reversal theory contends that athletes' interpretations of feeling states depend on their motivational mood at that point in time.

30. Athletes can develop their Optimal Energy Profiles to become more aware of their optimal energy zones.

31. Coaches must manage their energy to be role models for their athletes and make effective decisions.

Glossary

anxiety: a high intensity unpleasant energy state that typically results from a demand or threat

arousal: a state of bodily energy or physical and mental readiness

cognitive anxiety: worry and/or unpleasant self-focused thoughts about one's abilities in relation to competitive demands

competitive energy: an athlete's physical and mental readiness for competition

energy: physical and mental readiness, or a capacity for vigorous action

pressure: an unpleasant feeling state experienced by athletes when attractive and highly valued incentives create an urgent and compelling force on them to succeed

somatic anxiety: athletes' perceptions of their physical responses to competitive stress, typically involving body tension, feeling jittery, and increased heart rate, breathing rate, and sweating

stress: a demand placed on an athlete

Study Questions

1. What is competitive energy and why should athletes think of it as a natural resource? Explain its many forms based on intensity, direction, and possible effects on performance.

2. Explain why stress is important for athletes, and how a lack of stress would keep them from performing their best. When does stress become a problem? Provide several examples of this in your sport.

3. Define flow and list 5-6 characteristics of the flow experience.

4. Identify and explain five key predictions about how the intensity of arousal influences athletes' performance.

5. Explain why unpleasant feeling states can be helpful to performance. What are some examples of unpleasant feeling states that may be helpful to athletes? In particular, explain how anxiety can be helpful as well as disruptive to athletes' performance.

6. What is pressure? What are some specific mental strategies that athletes and coaches can use to help manage the pressure associated with competition?

7. Specifically describe the two ways that athletes can manage negative energy. In particular, explain how mental reversals can be used to reframe negative energy.

8. Explain why energy management is important for coaches.

Reflective Learning Activities

1. Finding Your Zone

a. Develop your own Optimal Energy Profile by completing the exercise in Appendix 13A. Pick a specific activity, such as a sport you play regularly or your competitive performance as a coach. Assess your OEP over at least three competitions and attempt to regulate your energy to optimize your feeling states and stay within your zone. (Assign for a 4-5 week period)

b. In small groups, discuss your OEP and what you learned about yourself. Were you able to stay in your zones? Did it help your performance? (Groups of 3 for 15 minutes)

2. Flowing in Your Sport

Divide into small groups by sport type and discuss the following:

a. How does flow work in your sport?

b. What are some specific things athletes can do in your sport to facilitate getting into flow?

c. What are typical things that disrupt flow in your sport?

d. Identify some training strategies that coaches can use to facilitate flow in their athletes in this sport.

(15 minutes in groups and then 15 minute overall discussion of ideas)

3. Surprise, Surprise, Surprise!

A key to energy management is to prepare effective responses to all types of situations and emotions that can arise during competition. That is, coaches and athletes must prepare for surprises. Identify key situations, emotions, and/or surprises that may occur in your sport, and develop an energy management strategy for each situation.
(Work in groups of 3 from similar sports for 18 minutes)

4. Why Not Just Think Positive?

In developing their Optimal Energy Profiles, athletes are asked to identify feelings that hurt as well as help their performance. Why is it necessary to think about and plan for negative feeling states? Why shouldn't athletes just focus on the positive feelings they want to have and prepare themselves to have these feelings? (Group discussion for 10 minutes)

Fourteen

Self-Confidence

Chapter Preview

In this chapter, you'll learn:
*   what confidence is and what it is not
*   how and why self-confidence acts as the "mental modifier" for athletes
*   which sources of confidence are best for athletes
*   how to help athletes build their confidence through Perspiration, Regulation, and Inspiration

Pete Rose was being interviewed in spring training the year that he was about to break Ty Cobb's all-time hit record in major league baseball. A reporter asked him, "Pete, you only need 78 hits to break the record. How many at-bats do you think you'll need to get the 78 hits?" Without hesitation, Rose very matter-of-factly said, "78." The reporter retorted, "Ah, come on Pete, you don't really expect to get 78 hits in 78 at-bats, do you?" Rose replied, "Every time I step to the plate, I expect to get a hit. If I don't expect to get a hit, I have no right to step in the batter's box in the first place. If I go up hoping to get a hit, then I probably don't have a prayer. It is a positive expectation that has gotten me all of the hits in the first place."

Pete Rose became the all-time hits leader in baseball because of his physical ability to hit a baseball and his confidence in his ability to do so. He completed his baseball career with 4,256 hits, a record that seems unbreakable. Only players who have stellar seasons in their prime achieve 200 hits per season, and breaking Rose's record would require a player to achieve 200 hits for 21 seasons! Pete Rose, a beloved figure in Cincinnati where he played most of his career, was disliked by many opponents and opposing fans because of his outrageous confidence. However, it is no accident that baseball's all-times hits leader was one of the most confident athletes to ever play the game.

In this chapter, self-confidence, as the third key mental skill for athletes, is discussed. The word "confidence" is used a lot by athletes and coaches, and there are many misconceptions about confidence in sport, so we'll start by distinguishing between what confidence *is* and what it is *not*. Then we'll talk about confidence as the "mental modifier" for athletes, and present evidence to support this concept. Next, we'll get into the key sources of confidence for athletes and teams. Finally, we'll wrap things up by considering several strategies that coaches can use to enhance confidence in their athletes.

What Confidence IS and What It Is NOT

To get started, take a moment to complete the following Confidence Quiz, which contains five true-or-false statements about the nature of self-confidence in athletes. You'll learn the answers to the Confidence Quiz as you read through the chapter.

1. You can never be too confident.   True   or   False

2. Confident athletes get nervous and experience anxiety prior to competition.   True   or   False

3. Athletes must win to be confident.   True   or   False

4. Performance mistakes destroy confidence.   True   or   False

5. World-class athletes have unshakable confidence.   True   or   False

Understanding Confidence

According to most dictionaries, confidence is about believing in your abilities or feeling certain about your ability to do something. **Self-confidence** in athletes may be defined as the *beliefs or degree of certainty athletes possess about their ability to be successful in their sports* (Vealey, 2001). Confidence is based on beliefs. Skill is not enough—athletes have to *believe* in their skills to use them most effectively. For confidence, the key belief is an athlete's perception of his or her ability in relation to what is demanded in the situation[1] (Bandura, 1997). Can I make this penalty kick? Can I complete a double axel? Can I make a free throw despite a loud and hostile crowd? Can I recognize the defense and make the right read as the quarterback? Another key to understanding confidence is that it is based on athletes' perceptions of success. Confidence focuses on beliefs about being "successful." As you will see in this chapter, an important key to self-confidence for athletes is to personally define success as opposed to letting others define success (usually in unproductive ways) for them.

Coaches often use the term "overconfident" when describing a team or athlete who performed poorly, seemingly because they failed to adequately prepare or give full effort needed to succeed. **Overconfidence** is a *false confidence in which athletes' abilities do not match their beliefs in their abilities* (Bandura, 1997; Martens, 1987). False confidence, or overconfidence, often leads to neglect in preparation and a lack of effort and intensity in performance. However, overconfidence does not mean that an athlete has *too much* confidence. Athletes can never have too much confidence. True athletic self-confidence involves a strong belief that one has the abilities to succeed in a situation, with the realistic understanding of the effort, preparation, and persistence it will take to succeed in that situation. Mike Eruzione, captain of the 1980 U.S. Men's Ice Hockey Team who won the Olympic gold medal, stated, "Confidence does not negate the need to work; rather, it often highlights it" (Eruzione, 1999, p. 258).

So overconfidence isn't too much confidence. It's not even real confidence. It is a false sense of confidence in which an athlete overestimates his or her abilities and subsequently fails to prepare adequately. True confidence can never be too strong, because it has to do with how much a person believes in his or her abilities, with the full knowledge of the preparation and effort needed to maximize these abilities. Research supports that confidence provides the motivational fuel to prepare well and work hard to showcase one's talents.

Myths About Confidence

Because confidence is such a popular term, there are many myths or misconceptions about it. These myths include (a) bragging demonstrates confidence, (b) athletes must win to be confident, (c) mistakes destroy confidence, and (d) successful athletes have unshakable confidence.

Bragging. The first myth is that those athletes who talk the loudest and brag the most have the most confidence. Brash athletes who boast about their abilities may be confident, but their showmanship often betrays an undercurrent of uncertainty and a fear of failure. What athletes publicly say may be far different from what they really feel inside. Self-confidence is based on what athletes really feel about their abilities, not what they say with false bravado. Truly confident athletes present themselves with self-assurance, have presence or charisma, and even inspire those around them. At times, extreme self-confidence often looks like arrogance when athletes lack social and communication skills. However, this behavioral self-assurance is congruent with their internal beliefs or confidence and is not the same as bragging to pretend to be confident. Pretending to be confident by bragging indicates that athletes lack self-awareness, an important part of emotional intelligence, and this is an obstacle for these athletes to develop true confidence (Goleman, 1998).

Coaches may want to talk individually to those athletes who brag and act brashly, to understand these athletes better and help them develop a strong and consistent confidence in their abilities. Often, young athletes engage in brash "trash-talking" because they believe the myth that acting boldly means you are confident. Explain to them that truly confident athletes do not have to shout at the world about their abilities, but simply believe and trust in themselves and their abilities. Use examples of extremely confident athletes who carried themselves with humility and class, such as Pete Sampras, Annika Sorenstam, Bonnie Blair, Joe Dumars, and Peyton Manning.

Must win. The second myth about self-confidence in sport is that you must win to be confident.

Photo by Brett Hansbauer

A variation of this is the myth that confident athletes must believe they will win. Neither is true. The reason these myths are untrue is because no matter what coaches, athletes, parents, or the news media say, winning is an uncontrollable outcome, and confidence should never be based on something that is beyond athletes' personal control.

Nothing breeds confidence like success, but the trick is to define success as more than winning. Confidence is an athlete's belief in his or her ability to succeed. To build and maintain resilient confidence, athletes cannot narrowly define success as winning. Winning is important and is the unstated goal in any competition, but sport provides many opportunities for success beyond winning. Examples include achieving personal bests, mastering a new skill, or performing at one's highest level. Athletes must learn to be rational and mature in defining personal success. Personalized goal maps provide success steps for athletes on their way to important milestones, which often include winning. Athletes must be confident to win, and thus they must gain confidence on their way to winning by defining their success in personal ways to put themselves in the best position to win. In addition, athletes must acknowledge defeat and use competition as a means of gauging their progress as an athlete. I've often heard athletes talk about the confidence they've gained from losing, because they learned important lessons from these losses and they faced their fear of losing, which then freed them up to perform more confidently after the loss. As you can see, athletes who engage in productive (P³) thinking are able to frame both winning and losing in ways to build their confidence.

True confidence comes from knowing that you've performed well and that you've successfully demonstrated competence and skill. There is always negative emotion associated with losing a sport contest—no one likes to lose and everyone likes to win—but each athlete's sense of confidence is affected by how he or she performs, irrespective of winning. As professional golfer Greg Norman stated after a particularly painful loss, "I'm a winner. I just didn't win today."

Mistakes destroy confidence. The third myth about self-confidence is that mistakes destroy confidence. Research clearly refutes this myth, as confident athletes typically make more mistakes because they're not afraid to make them. Confidence allows athletes to push the envelope in improving their weaknesses. Athletes who lack confidence often spend time practicing well-learned skills, because they want to avoid making the inevitable mistakes that come from learning new skills. Athletes must learn to build their confidence despite repeated mistakes or failures by selectively attending to whatever small improvements or positive experiences are gained.

A mark of extraordinary individuals is their ability to maintain confidence and perseverance in the face of repeated failures. Thomas Edison tried and failed more than 1,000 times in the process of inventing the light bulb. Gertrude Stein continued to submit poems to editors for 20 years before one was finally accepted for publication. Vincent Van Gogh sold only one painting during his life. Consider the fate of this man: he failed as a businessman, suffered the death of two young sons, was defeated twice as a Congressional candidate and twice more as a Senate candidate, and was defeated as a Vice-President candidate. This was Abraham Lincoln, considered one of the most successful Presidents in American history. Confidence creates the resiliency needed to weather obstacles and setbacks that are part of any achievement endeavor. A highly successful Soviet volleyball coach explained how he selected mentally tough players: "I don't choose the players who handle success most easily; I choose the players who respond best after failure" (Kiraly, 1999, p. 208).

Mistakes are a normal part of pursuing excellence in any field. It's not the mistakes that hold athletes back from reaching their potential; it's their fear of making mistakes. Help your athletes understand that mistakes are part of the learning and performing process. Betsy King, LPGA golfer and Hall of Fame, member states, "The first time I won a tournament, the thing that surprised me the most was how many mistakes you could make and still win" (Freeman, 1998, p. 28). Also, help athletes distinguish between mistakes that occur in competition because it's impossible to be perfect every time as opposed to mis-

takes that occur because they lose their focus or choke. Many times athletes lose confidence when they make a critical error in competition because they accept the popular assumption that they "choked" or that they were not mentally tough. Mistakes and performance errors occur in sport competition, despite athletes' mental toughness, confidence, and diligent preparation. The mark of a confident athlete is to accept these mistakes for what they are, and to keep them from becoming a bigger deal than just a simple mistake. Figure skater Tara Lipinski explains her confident response to a critical fall in competition: "I felt like I was going for it, and it just kind of went wrong. The mistake I made is not a big deal. I'm glad it's not from doubt—it was just a mistake" (Rosen, 1998, p. 18). Following this competition, Lipinski went on to win the gold medal at the 1998 Olympic Games in Nagano.

Quotable Quote

"Every strike brings me closer to my next home run." **Babe Ruth**

Overall, confidence allows athletes to think productively and to frame their errors in ways that enhance confidence. Remind athletes that what happens to them isn't nearly as important as how they respond to what happens to them. Help your athletes to respond to mistakes and performance errors as temporary setbacks from which they can extract important lessons, learn what they need from the experience, and then discard the negative images of the mistakes.

Successful athletes have unshakable confidence. The final myth about self-confidence is that successful athletes have unshakable confidence. Consider the following quotes from successful, world-class athletes:

- *"It crossed my mind a few times that day that I didn't really belong up there with some of those guys."* Elite decathlete, talking about overcoming his lack of confidence at the international level (Dale, 2000)
- *"The thing about confidence I don't think people understand, is it's a day-to-day issue. It takes constant nurturing. It's not something you go in and turn on the light switch and say, 'I'm confident,' and it stays on until the light bulb*

As Mia Hamm notes, confidence is not something that is achieved and then remains strong for the rest of an athlete's career. Hamm admittedly lacks confidence at times due to her perfectionistic standards and actually asked the coach to let a teammate take her place in the lineup for a critical penalty kick in the 1999 World Cup shootout against China (Smith, 2003). Her coach prevailed upon her to take the kick, and the rest is history: she made the kick and the American team went on to win the World Cup. But Hamm's example indicates that no athlete is immune from lapses in confidence. Athletes' confidence is always based on their perceived abilities in relation to their specific reference groups. Thus, world-class athletes assess their abilities in relation to world-class competition, which means they are as vulnerable to lapses in confidence as recreational athletes. One reason talented athletes sometimes lack or lose self-confidence is their tendency to cling to, or revert back to, a less talented self-image (Orlick, 1986a). Orlick explains that coaches can help athletes recognize and accept that their images of their less talented selves are no longer valid.

Quotable Quote

"The greater the artist the greater the doubt; perfect confidence is granted to the less-talented as a consolation prize." **Robert Hughes**

Another factor that influences the confidence of successful athletes is the expectations that get loaded onto them based on their previous successes. Athletes in this situation really need well-practiced mental training plans to help them manage these often unrealistic and irrational expectations. Sean McCann (1998), sport psychologist at the U.S. Olympic Training Center in Colorado Springs, explains that high expectations can become a distraction, source of pressure, and reason to be defensive for many athletes. This negative mindset distracts athletes from the focused and confident mindset they need to perform their best. Mia Hamm had to carry the label as best female soccer player in the world and Nike icon (a building at Nike headquarters is named after her) onto the field for that famous penalty kick. Try performing in front of millions with those expectations on your back!

McCann (1998) suggests that coaches should listen to their athletes to hear whether the expectations are creating worry ("I have a great chance to win, but I'm afraid of screwing it up.") or giving them confidence ("I feel I can perform well, if I do a few key things and keep focused."). He suggests that coaches talk to athletes directly about this, because unloading their negative thoughts and feelings of pressure is the first step in keeping it in perspective. Remind athletes of their preparation and training, and help them develop a simple performance focus plan that they should follow deliberately. Obviously, Mia Hamm had the mental skill to focus and successfully execute her penalty kick despite her initial lack of confidence. Finally, coaches can emphasize that the athlete's job is to perform well, period, and that any other expected outcomes are unrealistic and uncontrollable.

Personal Plug-In

For your sport, identify when and how different types of confidence are important for athletes. Also, identify ways that you can specifically train these different types of confidence.

What Do Athletes Need to Be Confident About?

We've established that confidence is about believing in one's abilities to be successful. To understand confidence fully, we should consider all the things that athletes should be confident about. Too often, we as coaches think about confidence as an athlete's belief in executing physical skills (e.g., hitting a jump shot). However, a basketball player has to be confident about her ability to make the shot, make the shot in traffic, make the shot under pressure, read the defense to get open to take the shot, and remain focused and confident even though she missed her last four shots.

Based on the nature of sport and competition, athletes need to be confident about their abilities in three basic areas (Vealey & Knight, 2002). First, athletes need to be confident that they can *physically execute the skills* needed to perform successfully. Divers must believe they can execute the intricate body movements needed to successfully perform each of their dives. Triathletes must believe they have the muscular and cardiovascular endurance to perform successfully. Second, athletes need to be confident in their *mental skills to maintain focus and make effective decisions* needed to succeed in their sports. Quarterbacks must believe they can effectively read opposing defenses and make the right decisions in running their offense. Endurance athletes must develop confidence that they can maintain the focus needed to push their limits in physically taxing events. Third, athletes need to be confident in their *resilience*, or their ability to regain focus after errors, bounce back from performing poorly, and overcome setbacks and obstacles to be successful.

Quotable Quote

"I stayed calm. I told myself to forget all those other expectations. The most important thing to remember was my expectation for myself, which was to skate my best. Period." **Michelle Kwan**, Olympic medalist in figure skating

---

In a study of confidence in collegiate swimmers, confidence in resilience and mental focus skills were the strongest predictors of performance in a critical, pressurized meet (Vealey & Knight, 2002). Of course the swimmers needed to have confidence in their swimming ability, but this confidence was overshadowed by the need to remain focused and resilient in an important, highly emotional meet with a major rival. Obviously, all three types of confidence are important for athletes, but it may be that certain types are more important at specific times during the competitive season. Coaches should consider this and work to enhance athletes' beliefs in not just their abilities to perform, but their abilities to mentally focus and perform well despite obstacles, distractions, and setbacks. Athletes can complete the Sport-Confidence Inventory provided in Appendix 14A to assess their confidence in these three critical areas for competition. Scoring instructions are provided, along with some brief tips for ways that athletes can strengthen their confidence in each area.

Confidence as the "Mental Modifier"

Confidence may be thought of as the Mental Modifier for athletes, because confidence modifies how athletes perceive and respond to everything that happens to them in sport (see Figure 14.1). The left side of the continuum shown in Figure 14.1 represents peak performance, flow, and/or being in "the zone." As athletes move from right to left across the continuum, their mental skills and mental approach to competition are enhanced. In the best cases, they are focused and consistent in their performance. On days when athletes struggle to focus and lack consistency in their performance, they still can "grind" and focus on performing the best they can that day. Confident athletes do this—they believe in their ability enough to hang in there and not give up. The true mental test for athletes is how well they can perform on those days when they aren't "on" or able to perform effortlessly with full focus and consistency. Confidence helps athletes pass this big mental test because it provides them with a strong belief in their ability, even their ability to perform well when it doesn't come easy to them.

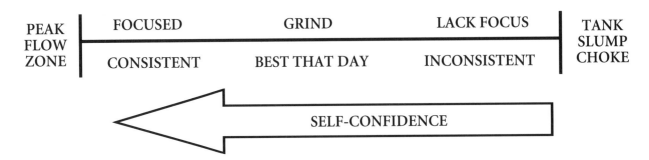

Figure 14.1 Confidence as the Mental Modifier

On those days when performance doesn't go smoothly and athletes struggle to focus and perform on autopilot, it is their confidence that keeps them from sliding to the right side of the continuum. This end of the continuum represents tanking, slumping, and choking. Athletes "tank" when they lack the mental toughness to work hard to focus and maintain effort in their performance on the days when it doesn't come easy to them. They give in to their own lack of expectations. If athletes lack confidence, they are also susceptible to allowing their poor performance to turn into a prolonged slump. And of course, confidence also keeps athletes focused to help them avoid choking.

The basic premise in Figure 14.1 is that confidence, as the Mental Modifier, directly influences athletes' movement across the performance continuum. In particular, confidence helps athletes from sliding all the way to the right side of the continuum when they have off days or less than desirable performances. Research supports that confident athletes perform better than less confident athletes in a variety of sports (e.g., Feltz & Lirgg, 2001; George, 1994; Treasure, Monson, & Lox, 1996; Vealey, 2001). Athlete confidence was identified by coaches and athletes as one of the strongest reasons for athlete success at the 2000 Olympic Games (Gould et al., 2002). Overall, the evidence is overwhelming that confidence is a critical mental modifier in influencing the performance of athletes in sport.

But how does confidence modify athletes' performance? In this section, I'll explain how confidence enhances athletes' performance through (a) challenging goal choices, increased effort, and greater persistence, (b) cognitive efficiency, or better thinking, and (c) emotional adaptiveness (Maddux & Lewis, 1995).

Goals, Effort, and Persistence

Confident athletes tend to work harder than less confident athletes. Specifically, confident athletes set more challenging goals, exert more intense effort in training, and persist longer despite obstacles and setbacks when compared to athletes who lack confidence. Athletes with confidence set their sights high, and those that lack confidence settle for less challenging goals. As we know, clear and challenging goals lead to greater achievement (Locke & Latham, 1990). Because athletes with low confidence lack the conviction that they can meet tough challenges, they

don't have the self-assurance to plunge ahead as do confident athletes. Pete Sampras (1997) has stated that confidence allows athletes to demonstrate persistent effort at "crunch time" in matches, which he feels is important to let opponents know that you're not going to give in at all or tank the match due to mental or physical fatigue.

Bandura (1997) explains how goals act as incentives to differentially influence the motivation of athletes, which ultimately dictates their level of confidence. When athletes fall short of their goals, they are dissatisfied. For confident athletes, this dissatisfaction turns into incentive, and they will increase their effort and persistence to reach their goals. For athletes who lack confidence, this dissatisfaction turns into disincentive and they will give up. Think about why this happens. How does it relate to the definition of confidence? Again, it emphasizes the importance of believing in your abilities, because these beliefs create a positive response after failure ("I can do this."). For athletes who lack confidence and whose beliefs about their abilities are shaky, these beliefs create a negative response after failure ("See—I knew I couldn't do this.") Self-confidence is the ultimate self-fulfilling prophecy, because athletes allow their beliefs to affect how hard they work and how they respond to failure, and ultimately their achievement (or lack of) conforms to their beliefs, completing the self-fulfilling prophecy.

The influence of self-confidence on athletes' effort and persistence had been demonstrated in several research studies. In a study of baseball players, more confident athletes reported that they put more effort into their hitting than less confident athletes (George, 1994). In this study, the players were asked to report how much effort they put into their hitting in that day's game on a scale from 0 to 100% effort. Other research studies have experimentally manipulated athletes' levels of self-confidence to see how they will respond in terms of effort and persistence. Two studies of weight lifting demonstrate how this works (Fitzsimmons, Landers, Thomas, & van der Mars, 1991; Wells, Collins, & Hale, 1993). First, the lifters established their one-repetition maximum (1-RM, or the most weight each could lift at one time) in the bench press. In the next session, they lifted a weight they were told was equal to their 1-RM, but the weight was actually 10 pounds lighter than their 1-RM. This deception or manipulation was designed to enhance their self-confidence in their weightlifting ability, which it did. At the next session, those participants whose self-confidence had been increased via the deception executed a significantly heavier bench-press 1-RM. Because no strength training was done between sessions, these findings indicated that the change in performance was due to confidence. Those lifters that did not have their confidence manipulated did not significantly increase their performance. Thus, increases in self-confidence related to increases in strength performance. (See the Clipboard below for another example of this research.)

Clipboard

Research Example: Effects of Confidence on Muscular Endurance

A study by Weinberg, Gould, and Jackson (1979) examined the influence of self-confidence, or expectations, on the performance of a muscular endurance task. Research participants were brought into a room and asked to sit on a table and extend their leg for as long as they could (to test the muscular endurance of the thigh muscles). The participants competed on the task with another person, and this person was a confederate, which means that he or she was part of the experiment, although the participants didn't know this at the time. The researchers manipulated the participants' levels of confidence just prior to the activity. To create high levels of confidence, the researchers told the participants that their competitor was coming off a leg injury (thus participants felt they could do better than this person). To create low levels of confidence, the researchers told the participants that their competitor was an elite sprinter with outstanding leg strength (thus participants felt they could not perform as well as this person). The confederate secretly placed a deflated sponge ball under his/her leg just prior to the activity, which gave him/her a distinct advantage in the competition. So actually, the confederate was just a normal individual, although participants had been led to believe otherwise to manipulate their confidence.

Participants in the high self-confidence situation extended their legs longer than participants in the low self-confidence situation. In addition, after failure, the more confident participants showed increased persistence while the low confidence participants showed decreased persistence. Overall, the results showed that self-confidence enabled the participants to exert more effort and persistence in their performance. Amazing, isn't it, what our beliefs allow us to do!

Cognitive Efficiency

Along with enhancing goal striving, effort, and persistence, self-confidence in athletes also serves as the mental modifier by enhancing athletes' cognitive efficiency (Maddux & Lewis, 1995). To be cognitively efficient means that athletes use their mental, or cognitive, resources more productively. Or more to the point, confident athletes think better than less confident athletes.

Confident athletes have the mental skill to ignore distractions and manage their thinking, thus confidence enhances P³ Thinking. Confidence gives athletes the freedom to focus their attention on the task as opposed to worrying about their inadequacies and possible performance failures. For example, research with basketball players showed that more confident players were better able to narrow their attention effectively and were less likely to experience attentional overload and reduced attention (Roberts & Vealey, 1992). Confident athletes are more decisive and better able to focus on the present and leave performance errors in the past. Confident athletes make more productive attributions for their performance outcomes by attributing success to their ability, effort, and preparation, while less confident athletes tend to attribute success to uncontrollable factors (Vealey, 1986).

Quotable Quote

"On race day at the Olympics, it was very flat light, very foggy, which is not pleasant in downhill. The first positive thing I did was say to myself, 'You're good in flat light; you're one of the best skiers in flat light. This is your opportunity right now—go for it!' I really am one of the better skiers in flat light. Although I don't like it more than anyone else, I can still be aggressive and I can still ski like I want to ski." **Kerrin Gartner**, Olympic downhill champion *(cited in Orlick, 2000, p. 28)*

Confident athletes used more problem-focused coping strategies, as opposed to emotion-focused strategies (Grove & Heard, 1997). This again demonstrates an efficient and skillful use of cognitive resources, as coping should be problem-focused to address important task issues, as opposed to coping by responding with emotion, which does not directly address the problem and a solution. And finally, confident athletes engage in more mastery imagery and have better imagery ability than less confident athletes (Moritz, Martin, Hall, & Vadocz, 1996). Overall, self-confidence helps athletes' cognitive efficiency, and enables them to think better about competition and respond with productive thoughts no matter what happens.

Emotional Adaptiveness

The third way in which confidence acts as the mental modifier with athletes is by enhancing their emotional adaptiveness (Maddux & Lewis, 1995). Athletes who have strong beliefs about their abilities are able to manage the emotions associated with competition much more efficiently than athletes who lack confidence. This is not to say that confident athletes don't experience anxiety and stress—they do, but they don't allow this anxiety to overwhelm them and interfere with their performance. Confidence allows athletes to effectively manage and cope with this anxiety, and it frees up their minds to focus their attention on the sport situation and what they

Table 14.1 Sources of Confidence for Athletes

1. Achievement	prior success; winning; demonstrating ability compared to others; mastering skills; improving skills; achieving goals
2. Preparation	physical training; developing well-practiced strategies to execute; mental preparation and training; knowing you're prepared for the situation
3. Self-Regulation	developing and using skills and strategies to maintain focus and manage emotions, thoughts, and behaviors that lead to optimal performance
4. Models	seeing others, such as teammates, friends, and other athletes, perform successfully; watching videotape of self; using imagery to view oneself performing perfectly
5. Feedback/ Encouragement	receiving useful feedback, as well as support and encouragement, from coaches and others (teammates, parents, friends)
6. Coach's Leadership	believing that your coach is skilled in decision-making and leadership in terms of running the team and program
7. Environmental Comfort	feeling comfortable in a competitive environment
8. Physical Self-Presentation	feeling that you look good in terms of your physical self (e.g., body, uniform, appearance)
9. Situational Favorableness	feeling that the breaks or momentum of the situation are in your favor

want to do, as opposed to worrying about their abilities and possible failures.

As discussed in the previous chapter on energy management, stress responses occur when athletes perceive that the task demands overwhelm their response capabilities. Athletes who believe they can't successfully meet the demands of competition perceive more threat, thus experience more negative emotions. Confidence mentally modifies this process, allowing athletes to create a strong coping mechanism and making them better able to cope with competitive anxiety (George, 1994; Treasure et al., 1996). Overall, self-confidence helps athletes experience adaptive emotional responses to competition, while a lack of confidence is related to debilitating anxiety, depression, and dissatisfaction.

Sources of Confidence for Athletes

So now you know what confidence is, what it isn't, and how it acts as the Mental Modifier to affect athletes' effort, persistence, goal choices, thinking ability, and their ability to manage their emotions effectively. Hopefully, you agree that confidence is important for athletes! Because it's so important, coaches should be aware of where athletes get their confidence to perform successfully. What are the important sources for athletes' confidence in sport? Actually, there are several sources that athletes use to gain confidence, and these vary according to age, gender, and individual athlete preference. Nine sources for athletes' confidence are summarized in Table 14.1. I'll overview these sources of confidence in this section, so you as the coach can become more aware of the various ways that athletes develop and enhance their confidence.

Achievement

Without question, the most important source of athletes' confidence is their past performance or achievement (Bandura, 1997; Feltz & Lirgg, 2001). Most all of us are confident in our abilities if we have succeeded in the past in a particular area. If a soccer goalie has performed well all season and made many different types of saves for her team, she typically will be confident going into the post-season tournament because she knows she has succeeded and thus can succeed in the future. Research supports previous performance as the best predictor of athletes'

confidence in baseball (George, 1994) and swimming (Theodorakis, 1995). Achieving success is the most direct evidence of athletes' capabilities—it's tangible proof that they can do it because they've done it before. Obviously, past failures can weaken confidence for the same reason—we question our ability because we have yet to be successful.

However, remember that achievement takes many forms. For example, research shows that athletes use both *mastery* (improving their skills or mastering new skills) as well as *demonstration of ability* (showing off skills to others, demonstrating more ability than an opponent, or winning) as important sources of confidence (Vealey, Hayashi, Garner-Holman, & Giacobbi, 1998). That is, achievement can be subjectively defined for athletes as more than just winning or beating an opponent. As discussed in Chapter 8, effective goal maps include performance goals that are controllable so that success is within the athletes' control. Interestingly, male athletes tend to use demonstration of ability as a more important source for their confidence as compared to female athletes (Vealey et al., 1998). Coaches should understand that males are typically socialized to demonstrate ability in sport skills, and that they tend to base

their confidence on successful comparisons with others (e.g., winning). All athletes, particularly male athletes, should be encouraged to define success and achievement in controllable ways (e.g., mastery) to help keep their confidence stable and resilient through the ups and downs of competition.

Preparation

The second source of confidence for athletes is preparation. Abraham Lincoln once said that if he had had seven hours to cut down a tree, he would spend six hours sharpening his axe. Athletes should use this analogy to sharpen their axes for competition, which means spending time in preparation to perform optimally. Coaches readily agree with this, as they have rated physical conditioning as their top strategy in developing confidence in athletes (Gould, Hodge, Peterson, & Giannini, 1989). Athletes have also rated physical and mental preparation as one of their top sources of confidence (Vealey et al., 1998), and successful world-class athletes have particularly emphasized the importance of *quality* training for their confidence and performance success (Orlick & Partington, 1988). Lance Armstrong, six-time winner of the grueling Tour de France, explains his confidence based on his preparation: "My job is to suffer. I make the suffering in training hard so that the races are not full of suffering" (Saporito, 2003).

Self-Regulation

The third source of confidence is self-regulation, which involves developing and using skills and strategies to maintain focus and manage one's thoughts, emotions, and behaviors that lead to optimal performance. Self-regulation as a source of confidence is closely related to preparation, because athletes must mentally prepare and practice their self-regulation strategies for them to work in competition. However, using these strategies during competition often serves as an important source of confidence. A common example is the use of routines to create a familiar and comfortable plan for how to act and think as the time to compete nears. Athletes indicate that these routines help them feel a sense of control and confidence in relation to the upcoming competition. Research and a great deal of experiential evidence from successful athletes indicate that pre-competition routines, rituals, and focus plans are critical predictors of how well athletes perform, especially in championship or pressure situations (Gould et al., 2002, Greenleaf et al., 2001; Orlick & Partington, 1988).

Models

A fourth source of confidence for athletes is watching successful models. Commonly, a teacher or coach will demonstrate a skill to athletes while at the same time presenting information about how to perform the skill. This combination of verbal instruction and visual modeling gives athletes confidence to successfully complete the skill themselves. Coaches are important models for athletes not only in skill execution, but also for modeling confident behavior, decision-making, and strategy development. Coaches who are more confident in their coaching abilities have been shown to have more successful teams and more satisfied athletes than less confident coaches (Feltz, Chase, Moritz, & Sullivan, 1999).

Teammates also serve as confidence-building models for athletes by demonstrating their ability to perform at crucial times. In the 1990 World Series, Eric Davis of the Cincinnati Reds hit a home run off of the Oakland Athletics' fire-balling ace pitcher Dave Stewart in the first inning of Game 1. The Reds, huge underdogs to the powerful A's team, went on to sweep the Series in four games. Several of the Reds' players commented how Davis's home run at the beginning of the first game inspired them with confidence that they could win the Series and sent a message to the A's that the Reds were not intimidated.

An important source of confidence that is used more and more by athletes is self-modeling. This usually involves watching videotapes of one's own performance, although imagery could also be used to visualize one's performance to serve as a model. Athletes who are in slumps and/or who are struggling with confidence often view videotapes of their previous performances when they were in a groove to serve as a model to improve their performance and "get their stroke" back. A common confidence-builder is the development of personal highlight videotapes for athletes, where their best performances are captured on tape along with energizing music, often selected specially by the athlete. Watching personal highlight videotapes has been shown to enhance self-confidence in college basketball players (Templin & Vernacchia, 1995) and professional ice hockey players (Halliwell, 1990).

Feedback/Encouragement

We've all built confidence when our parents or coaches gave us encouragement and made us believe in ourselves in various achievement situations. I believe in myself because my parents showed me how much they believed in me, which helped me to believe in myself and my abilities. The encouragement and feedback we receive from significant others in our lives is an important source of confidence. As discussed in Chapter 4, coaches can be a positive source of confidence for athletes if they provide contingent praise and feedback. Research has supported that children who played for coaches who gave frequent praise, technical instruction, and error-contingent encouragement significantly increased their self-esteem over the course of the season (Smoll, Smith, Barnett, & Everett, 1993). Similarly, coach feedback in terms of praise and information was positively related to self-confidence in adolescent athletes (Allen & Howe, 1998). When U.S. Olympic athletes were asked to list the best coaching actions to enhance athletes' performance, providing support and confidence was ranked second (Gould et al., 1999).

Interestingly, sources of confidence change as athletes age (Horn, Glenn, & Wentzell, 1993; Horn & Weiss, 1991). Research shows that children age 9 years and under use adult feedback from parents, teachers, and coaches as the most important source for their confidence. However, in late childhood from age 10-13 years, children tend to focus on how they compare to their peers as their most important source of confidence. Then, as children move through adolescence during the ages of 14-17, they gradually shift to using self-referenced standards such as improvement, mastery, and the achievement of personal goals as their most important source of confidence. Coaches working with young athletes should keep these developmental trends in mind to understand what sources of confidence are most salient to athletes at different age levels.

Other Sources

Several other sources of confidence for athletes are shown in Table 14.1 (Vealey et al., 1998). *Coach's leadership* is a source of confidence derived from believing in your coach's decision-making and leadership skills. There are many examples throughout this book of the ways in which outstanding coaches such as John Wooden, Mike Krzyzewski, Doc Counsilman, Pat Summitt, Pia Nilsson, and Dean Smith have inspired confidence in their athletes through their outstanding leadership. As with all mental skills, confidence begins with you the coach. You must exude confidence and earn the confidence of your athletes by being a skilled leader for your program.

Environmental comfort is a source of confidence that comes from feeling comfortable in a competitive environment, such as a particular gymnasium or pool. The "home advantage," or finding that home teams in sport competition win over 50% of the games played under a balanced home-and-away schedule (Courneya & Carron, 1992), is often anecdotally cited as a source of confidence for athletes. *Physical self-presentation* is defined as athletes' perceptions of their physical selves, or body image. Athletes are often very concerned with the appearance and evaluation of their bodies (Martin & Mack, 1996), thus their perceptions of their bodies often serve as a source of confidence. That is, feeling like they "look good" or in strength sports that they "look big" in terms of muscle mass and definition creates a sense of confidence for them. Research with individual sport athletes found that physical self-presentation was a more important source of confidence for females as compared to males (Vealey et al., 1998). *Situational favorableness* involves gaining confidence by feeling that the breaks of a situation are in one's favor. Athletes get the feeling that "things are going my way," which enhances their confidence. One example of this is the popular notion of "momentum" in sport, which typically creates a surge of confidence.

Are Some Sources of Confidence Better Than Others?

Although we've identified nine sources of confidence available to athletes in sport, some sources are better than others. All these sources are available to athletes and can be used, but some are more controllable, more enduring, and lead to stronger and more resilient self-confidence. Higher levels of confidence are related to focusing on sources or strategies that athletes personally control, such as mastery of physical skills and preparation (Vealey et al., 1998). Confidence is more stable and resilient when athletes directly control the sources upon which their confidence is built. If athletes base their confidence on environmental comfort, they will continue to lack confidence in unfamiliar or uncomfortable competitive settings. If athletes base their confidence on feedback/encouragement, they will lack the internally controlled confidence they need to pursue excellence when social support is not readily available. All sources of confidence are useful at times for athletes, but focusing on mastery and improvement, achieving personal performance goals, exhaustive training and preparation, and personal self-regulation serve as the best sources for strong and stable confidence.

Research has also supported that some sources have greater effects on athletes' confidence. The most effective way to build athletes' confidence is to provide them with opportunities to succeed (Bandura, 1997). Athletes must succeed and believe that their success is directly related to their ability and hard work, not because you made it easy for them. Thus, athletes have to achieve success in optimally challenging situations. Research has also shown that encouragement/feedback is a weak source of confidence by itself, but when this feedback follows successful performance, the combination of performance success and verbal feedback enhances confidence even more than just performance success alone (Wise & Trunnell, 2001). The verbal messages of encouragement that athletes receive after success seem to reinforce the new beliefs they have formed about their ability based on their success.

Overall, then, keep these sources in mind when attempting to build your athletes' confidence. To gain confidence, they have to be able to do it (e.g., make the shot, swim fast, execute a dive). Help them define "doing it" based on their own performance standards using a personalized goal map. Encourage them to engage in careful preparation and self-regulation to enhance their ability to do it and do it well. If athletes are injured or can't do it, they should watch others doing it. Injured athletes can observe practices and teammates running through plays and formations. If it is an individual activity, injured athletes should watch themselves on tape or engage in imagery to enhance their mental blueprints and build their mental skills in preparation for their return to competition. When athletes are successful, coaches should verbally reinforce the specific abilities that the athletes just demonstrated to provide a follow-up source of confidence after performance success. Coaches should model strong and resilient confidence through P^3 Thinking, effective communication and leadership behaviors, and self-regulation of their own emotions. Coaches should train athletes to create environmental comfort in all competitive situations, to think productively in any situation, and to accept their physical selves as part of who they are. Use all the sources to help your athletes maintain the resilient confidence needed for success in sport, and understand which sources are most important and how to use the sources in combination to build athletes' confidence.

Self-Confidence in Teams

So far in the chapter, we've focused on self-confidence in individual athletes. However, as a coach, I'm sure you know that your team has its own collective level of confidence as well. **Team confidence** is *the shared beliefs of team members in the ability of the team to perform successfully* (Bandura, 1997). Coaching for the Inner Edge requires you as the coach to not only help individual athletes develop confidence, but to lay the foundation for strong team confidence in your program. Individual athletes may be very confident about their individual abilities to perform successfully, but at the same time they may have little to no confidence in the team's ability to succeed. Team confidence is particularly important for highly interactive teams (e.g., volleyball, hockey, basketball, soccer) as opposed to coaching teams such as track and field, swimming, or golf (Bandura, 1997).

Research has supported the importance of team confidence. Team confidence has been shown to be a better predictor of team success than the aggregate of individual levels of confidence for all team members in both ice hockey (Feltz & Lirgg, 1998) and volleyball (Spink, 1990). Also, team confidence increased after team success and decreased after team losses, while individual confidence is not influenced by team outcomes. Teams high in team confidence are typically more cohesive in terms of athletes' feelings of involvement with the team's productivity (Spink, 1990). Finally, athletes' beliefs that there is strong leadership within the team has been shown to be related to overall team confidence, particularly for teams that were unsuccessful the previous season (Watson & Chemers, 1998). This finding suggests that the confidence of teams coming off losing seasons can really be enhanced if strong leaders emerge within the team to help build confidence. Thus, exceptional leadership, from athletes as well as coaches, is an important source of team confidence.

Overall, team confidence is likely to influence how hard athletes on the team work, and how much they persist when they hit obstacles and setbacks. Like individual self-confidence, team confidence can serve as a self-fulfilling prophecy. Teams mired in losing streaks often lack the confidence needed to come from behind, and instead give in by saying "here we go again" when faced with the prospect of losing. Explain to your teams that self-confidence serves as the mental modifier for the team as a whole, as well as for individual athletes. Building cohesiveness and an effective group norm for productivity (discussed in Chapter 6) should help in creating a team culture that includes team confidence. However, as with individual confidence, the most important source of team confidence is team success in performance. Coaches must find ways for teams to succeed, including winning, but also including performance statistics and mastery goals that enable team members to see progress on their way to winning.

Strategies to Enhance Confidence in Athletes

A good way to think about how to build confidence in athletes is to take the nine sources of confidence just discussed and organize them into three broad categories. Coaches can help athletes build their confidence through perspiration, regulation, and inspiration (see Figure 14.2). It sounds silly, but it's true! Quality training that leads to achievement (perspiration), mental training and practice (regulation), and a social environment that provides contingent feedback and encouragement, strong models, and outstanding leadership (inspiration) are the three main ways to enhance confidence in your athletes.

Perspiration

Earn confidence through quality physical training. Athletes have to *earn* the right to be confident through persistent deliberate practice and training (or "perspiration"). There are no shortcuts or quick fixes when it comes to confidence. Athletes are unable to "relax and trust" by switching to autopilot when performing unless they have done the exhaustive physical work that allows their bodies to engage in automatic execution. Systematic physical preparation allows athletes to trust themselves in executing their skills during the pressure of competition. No mental training strategy can ever take the place of the physical skill and conditioning needed to perform well in sport. World record holder and Olympic champion sprinter Michael Johnson has stated, "My confidence is in knowing that I have trained harder than anyone I am going to run against."

Coaches should develop strategies to enhance the quality and impact of physical training on athletes' confidence and performance levels. Examples of practice management to enhance confidence include simulation of pressure situations and creating unexpected situations to train adaptability. Persistent deliberate practice is what sets great athletes apart from others—encourage your athletes to always be prepared to respond with confidence knowing that they've paid the price in their workouts. Athletes should think of their training as money in the bank that they can withdraw when they need it

Figure 14.2 Three ways to build confidence in athletes

during competition (an analogy used by an elite decathlete, cited in Dale, 2000, p. 34): "Leading up to it I was training, busting my butt and everything was positive. I went to the meet knowing what I could do. It's kind of like . . . having a lot of money in the bank—you just keep putting money in, keep training, keep training, everything is building up and looking good . . . and then when it's time to withdraw, you have all that money."

Teach athletes to focus on performing at their best level FOR THAT DAY. Perspiration is particularly needed by athletes on those days when things don't go easy for them. Based on the research presented in this chapter, you should understand that confidence affects our effort and persistence, without us even realizing it. Explain this to your athletes. Get them to understand how important it is for them to work hard to focus and "grind" out their best performances on those days when they aren't "in the zone" or when they are not feeling automatically confident. Challenge them to focus on performing at their best levels *for that day.* This is the ultimate mental test for athletes, and it is what sets great athletes apart from good ones. Great athletes don't wait until they feel like performing great; they attempt to perform great all the time even when they don't feel like it.

Coaches should first get a commitment from their athletes to work on this aspect of the mental game, and then help them train to do this by working their focus (and refocusing) plans (see Chapter 12) on days when things aren't coming easily to them. Experienced athletes are most proud of when they perform well (maybe not terrifically, but well) on those days in which they struggle to focus and hang in there, as opposed to those days when they perform terrifically on autopilot. An important part of athletes' confidence is their beliefs in their abilities to perform well on these "off" days. Help them develop this confidence by successfully focusing and refocusing in training sessions on days when they struggle with their physical skills.

Help athletes personalize goal maps to define success appropriately. As you know, the strongest source of confidence for athletes is success. The biggest reason athletes lose and lack confidence is that they allow others to define success for them. Each athlete must develop a personalized goal map that identifies very specific and individualized milestone, challenge, and focus goals for him or her (see Chapter 8 on building goal maps). Athletes who buy into their personal goal maps gain control over their own success, which is an important key to building confidence. You as the coach must reinforce progress and achievement for each individual athlete based on their personal goals. If you expect athletes to habitually use personal goal maps, you must reward them based on these maps (as opposed to what the community or media glorifies). Stable confidence is based on the pursuit and achievement of SMAART goals (specific, measurable, aggressive yet achievable, relevant, and time-bound—review Chapter 8 for more details on SMAART goals). Particularly in relation to self-confidence, athletes need help in identifying and pursuing aggressive yet achievable goals. All athletes should be encouraged to push their limits and extend their performance and skills, but not at ridiculously unrealistic levels and definitely not in comparison or competition with others. Help athletes keep confidence manageable by focusing on personalized SMAART goals and individual success.

Regulation

Perspiration is the first step in building confidence, so that athletes *earn* the right to be confident. Athletes then move from *earning to learning,* as they learn to regulate their thoughts, feelings, and behaviors in ways that enhance their confidence and their performance. Thus, the second key to building confidence in athletes is helping them to become skilled at self-regulation.

Practice and use mental training tools and skills. Athletes learn to self-regulate by using the mental training tools and skills outlined in this book. You as the coach can help them by introducing them to these tools and skills, and by systematically developing ways for athletes to use these tools and skills in training and competition. As just discussed, athletes should develop and focus on personalized goal maps to define and mark their successes (Chapter 8). They can use imagery to enhance confidence in two ways

(Chapter 9). First, they can visualize themselves successfully performing specific skills to provide perfect mental models for their performance. Second, they can use imagery to create a productive task focus of "what they will do" in the upcoming competition, and/or by creating positive emotion to energize their confidence and performance just prior to competing.

Athletes must build Purposeful, Productive, and Possibility Thinking (P³) into their focus plans for competition to effectively manage typical doubts and negative thoughts that pop up under pressure (Chapter 10). They should learn and practice an easy-to-use physical relaxation response, such as Power Breathing, to manage their physical anxiety and let their bodies communicate a sense of confidence and readiness to their brains (Chapter 11). They should develop some well-practiced pre-performance routines and/or focus/refocusing plans to manage their attention (Chapter 12).

Specific tips to regulate confidence. Here are some reminders from previous chapters that are important in regulating confidence in athletes. First, athletes should mentally prepare with focus and refocusing plans not only for optimal performance, but also for total disaster. This is helpful because when athletes begin to experience feelings of panic or choking, feeling prepared (in terms of knowing these conditions could occur and having planned responses) helps them to maintain perspective and manage the feelings. Athletes can start by jotting down some responses to this question: what do you do or say to yourself that leaves you feeling confident in your performance? Instead of worrying by focusing on reasons why you might perform poorly, look for reasons why you can perform well (Orlick, 1986a). When feelings of doubt creep in during performance, remind yourself that you've performed well in less than ideal conditions, and that you can do it now.

Second, athletes should always exude a physical or behavioral level of confidence no matter what. That is, athletes must learn to control their behavior, body actions, facial expressions, and posture so that they always convey a sense of confidence and personal control. As I like to say to athletes, "fake it until you make it": act confident no matter what is happening to you. This physical poise and behavioral confidence should be an important part of your team culture or program "code." An affirmation that serves as a useful reminder for acting with confidence is "I respond with confidence." Athletes

should mentally prepare themselves for typical performance errors, criticism, bad calls from officials, and even their own self-doubts by practicing the affirmation "I respond with confidence" along with a Power Breath or while they are doing Power Breathing. Their goal is to create a strong attitude that they always respond with confidence, as opposed to reacting with emotion. Responding with outer poise or confidence makes it easier to respond with inner confidence, or to believe in yourself.

Clipboard

Quick Mental Prep Routine for Pre-Competition Confidence

1. Visualize where you will perform
2. Create the physical and mental energy you want (your body, your feelings, your thoughts).
3. Focus on the demands of competition and your role.
4. Visualize meeting these demands by performing successfully.
5. Visualize handling problems: practicing grinding/regaining focus, responding with confidence.
6. Affirm "I respond with confidence"

Third, I suggest that athletes use a strategy for dealing with doubts that is the opposite of the strategy espoused in Chapter 13 for dealing with fears. As discussed in Chapter 13, athletes should confront their fears by dealing with them head-on to reframe them as manageable and even silly. However, the doubts that creep in to weaken our confidence should not be given the privilege of athletes' attention, as they are simply pesky irrelevant thoughts. Brian Goodell, Olympic champion swimmer, sums up what I believe is the difference in responding to fear as opposed to doubts:

"Fear is the worry that something bad will happen, while doubt is the concern that something good might not . . . The treatment for fear is to confront it, and the treatment for doubt is to ignore its suggestions . . . Doubts are like uninvited guests. Don't entertain them" (Goodell, 1999, pp. 176-181).

Remind athletes that doubts are Random, Reactive Thoughts. They should expect that they will occur and be prepared with a Purposeful and Productive Thinking (or focusing) alternative when doubts arise. Athletes should channel their focus into performance and use the doubts as cues or reminders to shift to their P³ Thinking channel. Confidence in athletes is the result of particular thinking habits that have been consistently practiced to be automatic and natural. That is, it is the result of Perspiration to set the physical foundation for confident thoughts, and then Regulation to create the habit of P³ Thinking and the ability to focus attention where it counts.

Quotable Quote

"You cannot succeed without believing in yourself, and that belief is completely under your control—nobody else can generate it for you." **Karch Kiraly**, 3-time Olympic gold medalist in volleyball *(Kiraly, 1999, p. 205)*

Inspiration

Athletes control their Perspiration and Regulation through quality physical and mental training to build the strong and resilient levels of self-confidence needed to succeed in sport. Less controllable are those sources of confidence that represent this third category of confidence-building strategies, or Inspiration. Coaches should realize that Perspiration and Regulation are the two key ways to help athletes enhance their confidence, and that Inspiration acts as a supporting source of confidence for athletes. Confidence-supporting strategies that fall into the Inspira-

tion category include social support, coaches' leadership, athlete leadership within the team, and effective modeling within the team. The main idea is that confidence can be inspired in athletes through their social associations with significant people in their lives (particularly within their team and overall program).

Social support. With regard to social support, coaches should remember that all athletes, like all people, need unconditional acceptance as human beings. This means that you as a coach should distinguish between feedback related to athletes' performance and communication related to their self-worth as human beings. If coaches mix messages and make athletes feel that they are less worthy in their coach's eyes when they perform poorly, they may continue to struggle with confidence. It's much easier to be confident when you know that the people around you accept you unconditionally for who you are.

Another important aspect of social support that all coaches should remember is to remain confident in athletes who are struggling with their performance. Developing resilient confidence requires athletes to experience overcoming setbacks through persistent effort and training (Bandura, 1997). This experience of bouncing back gives athletes a stronger sense of confidence and helps them to persevere in the face of future adversity. It helps athletes' confidence to have coaches who stick it out with them through tough times, with supportive patience and encouragement to keep working.

The third thing that coaches can do to enhance athletes' confidence through social support is to create a program climate where P³ Thinking is the norm. Create a team that thinks well, that has a strong and committed group norm for productivity, that is mentally tough, and that has internalized a commitment and passion for excellence in your sport. This social environment in your program creates a "confidence climate" where athletes can "perspirate" and "regulate" on their way to becoming skilled, confident performers.

Leadership and modeling. Your leadership as a coach influences athletes' confidence in several ways. Coaches should model confident decision-making, manage their emotions appropriately, and exude a behavioral or physical presence of confidence at all times. You set the tone for how your athletes think and feel, and confidence is contagious. So let your athletes catch it from you! Coaches also build confi-

dence in their teams by designing systems of play that take advantage of the unique strengths of particular teams. Athletes must believe in the "system" being used by the team, and have confidence that they can perform well within the system.

Confidence in teams is also enhanced by having strong athlete leaders within the team. It is difficult to "manufacture" leaders on teams where seemingly no natural leaders are apparent. However, coaches should prescribe leader behaviors that are needed by the team to individuals most likely to serve as team leaders. Specifically explain what it means to be a leader, what the team needs in terms of leadership, and ask these athletes to discuss with you their thoughts about serving in leadership roles.

Finally, confidence is enhanced by observing effective models. Again, this starts with you the coach as the most important model for your athletes. Important models in your program also include senior or experienced team members who "set the tone" for how athletes conduct themselves in the program. The group norm that is set for behavior, effort, performance, and confidence is a crucial social influence on athlete confidence within the team. Encourage your experienced athletes to socialize with incoming athletes in ways that enhance their confidence in becoming a successful, organized, committed, supportive team member.

Wrapping Up

The overall goal for athletes is not a quick fix of confidence here and there to keep them going. Rather, strong and resilient confidence is needed by athletes to weather the inevitable setbacks and performance failures. Deeply rooted, resilient confidence is based on a strong physical training foundation, an individualized definition of success, self-regulatory skills to manage thoughts and emotions during competition, and a team culture that models and expects confidence and commitment from its athletes.

Educate your athletes about the true nature of self-confidence. They should understand that it is not about trash-talking, does not mean they will not make mistakes, and is not necessarily tied to winning. Explain how confidence works as the Mental Modifier, to modify how they think about and respond to everything that happens to them during competition. Challenge them to

- perform the best they can with the ability they bring to competition each day,
- respond with confidence after making mistakes, getting criticized, or performing poorly,
- maintain strong effort and persistence on days that they struggle with performance and confidence, and
- believe in their ability to bounce back and be resilient performers.

Summary Points for Chapter 14

1. Confidence is about believing in your abilities or feeling certain about your ability to do something successfully.

2. Overconfidence is a false confidence in which athletes' abilities to not match their beliefs in their abilities.

3. Typical myths about confidence in sport are bragging demonstrates confidence, athletes must win to be confident, mistakes destroy confidence, and successful athletes have unshakable confidence.

4. Types of confidence important to athletes include confidence in physical skill execution, mental skills needed to maintain focus and make effective decisions, and resilience to overcome obstacles and setbacks.

5. Confidence may be thought of as the "mental modifier" because it modifies how well or poorly athletes respond to their performance abilities on a day-to-day basis.

6. Research supports that confident athletes perform better than less confident athletes in a variety of sports.

7. Confidence enhances performance by influencing athletes' goal choices, effort, persistence, cognitive efficiency, and emotional adaptiveness.

8. Important sources of confidence for athletes include achievement, preparation, self-regulation, models, feedback/encouragement, coach's leadership, environmental comfort, physical self-presentation, and situational favorableness.

9. The strongest source of athletes' confidence is their prior performance, or achievement success.

10. Sources of confidence change as children age from middle childhood to late adolescence.

11. Stronger levels of confidence in athletes are related to focusing on sources or strategies that athletes personally control, such as mastery of physical skills and preparation.

12. Team confidence is the shared beliefs of team members in the ability of the team to perform successfully.

13. Team confidence is predictive of overall team success and team cohesion.

14. Confidence-building strategies may be thought of as falling within the broad domains of Perspiration, Regulation, and Inspiration.

Glossary

overconfidence: a false confidence in which athletes' abilities do not match their beliefs in their abilities

self-confidence: belief or degree of certainty athletes possess about their ability to be successful in their sport

team confidence: the shared beliefs of team members in the ability of the team to perform successfully

Study Questions

1. What is the difference between self-confidence and overconfidence?

2. Why do people think that you must win to be confident? Why is this partly true, but overall a myth about confidence?

3. Explain the three types of confidence, and give specific examples of each type for your particular sport.

4. Discuss why confidence is the "mental modifier" using specific examples.

5. Explain the research that shows that confidence influences athletes' effort and persistence.

6. Provide specific examples of how confidence affects athletes' cognitive efficiency and emotional adaptiveness.

7. Identify and explain the nine sources of confidence presented in the chapter. Then, describe how coaches can put each source into practice with athletes to enhance their confidence.

8. What are the best sources of confidence for athletes? How can you use these sources when athletes are struggling through a performance slump or losing streak?

9. How is team confidence different from individual confidence?

10. How can coaches build confidence in athletes through Perspiration, Regulation, and Inspiration?

Reflective Learning Activities

1. Confidence: What and When?

a. Individually complete the Sport-Confidence Inventory provided in Appendix 14A.

b. In groups of three, discuss what types of confidence you feel are most important in your sport. Does the importance of these types change across the season or during competition? How can coaches train each of these types of confidence? (12 minutes)

2. Confidence Through Committee

As discussed in the chapter, confidence can be nurtured in athletes through "Inspiration," or the social support, leadership, and modeling within a team or program. In groups of four (same sport), identify as many specific examples as you can for confidence-building ideas within teams. Be creative and be specific! (10 minutes)

3. Confidence Quiz

In groups of four, discuss the five items in the Confidence Quiz from the beginning of the chapter. Come to a consensus about the correct answer for each question. In particular, make sure that you understand why each question is true or false. (10 minutes)

Part
Four

Putting It All Together

This final part of the book is designed to help you to put it all together. You have a lot of information about the Inner Edge such as imagery, goal mapping, relaxation, energy management, confidence, and attentional focusing. However, it's hard to know how to put things together into useful mental training plans or to know when to use what. The purpose of this part of the book is to provide you with some suggestions and strategies for how to use the material in integrative ways in your program (see Figure 15.1).

Think about all the topics that you've read about in Chapters 1-14 as being on a restaurant menu. In Chapter 15, I'll provide some suggestions for how to select from the menu in using sport psychology with your athletes. Some practical tips and implementation ideas for applying mental training are suggested, and example mental plans for specific situations are provided. In Chapter 16, I'll provide some "special recipes," or ideas for how to deal with common challenges faced by coaches, such as slumps, inconsistency, perfec-

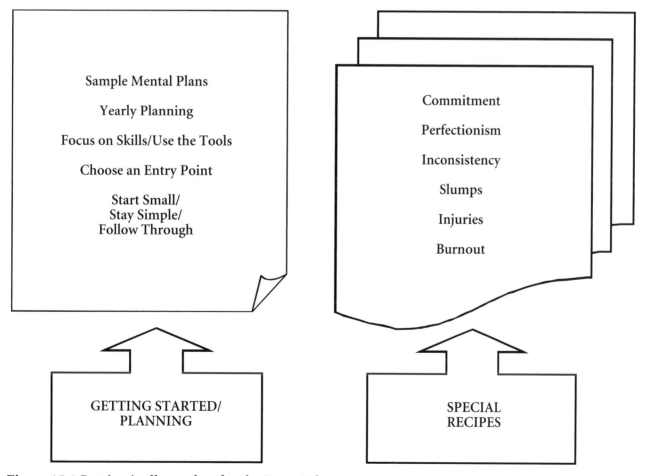

Sample Mental Plans

Yearly Planning

Focus on Skills/Use the Tools

Choose an Entry Point

Start Small/
Stay Simple/
Follow Through

Commitment

Perfectionism

Inconsistency

Slumps

Injuries

Burnout

GETTING STARTED/
PLANNING

SPECIAL
RECIPES

Figure 15.1 Putting it all together for the Inner Edge

tionism, lack of commitment in athletes, helping athletes return from injury, and dealing with burnout (both athlete *and* coach burnout!).

Overall, the intent of Part 4 is to raise your confidence in helping your athletes gain the Inner Edge by providing examples of how things fit together in practical and useful ways. I hope you find it useful!

Fifteen

Implementing Mental Training: Selecting from the Menu

Chapter Preview

In this chapter, you'll learn:
- how to implement mental training in your program
- about entry points for mental training
- how to periodize mental training along with your seasonal physical training program
- to start small, stay simple, and follow through

> "*If you want your ship to come in, you must first build a dock.*" **Benjamin Franklin**
>
> "*If opportunity doesn't knock, build a door.*" **Milton Berle**

W hew! You just read 14 chapters and probably have more information about the Inner Edge than you can process! That's okay. The purpose of this chapter is to help you view all the topics from the previous chapters as a restaurant menu. I'll give you some examples of how you can pick and choose a few topics a la carte to introduce to your athletes, and I'll also provide some full course dinners, which are examples of how you could integrate many of the topics from the book into comprehensive programs for your athletes. Use this chapter as your guide for how to get started in helping your athletes and team gain the Inner Edge.

Commit to the Inner Edge

Although they lived a couple of hundred years apart and had very different careers (18th century inventor/statesman vs. 20th century comedian), Benjamin Franklin and Milton Berle, as reflected in the quotes at the beginning of the chapter, share the same thought processes. Building a door or building a dock are symbolic examples of doing what is necessary to make things happen for yourself. Success in sport through optimal performance, development, and experiences requires building a door or a dock—doing the proactive, purposeful things that lead to success, as opposed to leaving the Inner Edge up to chance and hoping that athletes are mentally prepared for competition. If you want your athletes to be more focused, teach them some simple mental preparation strategies and how to center themselves in competition. If you want your athletes to perform well under pressure, help them understand their optimal energy zones as well as their irrational beliefs that create negative energy.

In short, I hope that at this point in the book you are ready to commit to the Inner Edge. Many coaches tell me that they don't have the time to spend on mental training, but I think this is either a cop-out or an instance of underestimating all that is involved in coaching to get the Inner Edge. Whether or not they call it mental training, the best coaches at all levels of sport coach the Inner Edge and coach it well. You can't read a book written by a successful coach and not come away with a feel for how he or she coached the Inner Edge. You can do as much or as little as you feel comfortable with in coaching the Inner Edge, but the key comes in incorporating the ideas presented in this book in some way in training your athletes. If you don't want to ever utter the words "mental training" or "sport psychology" with your athletes, that's fine. You can still do it—almost without them realizing it!

Put First Things First

Effectively coaching the Inner Edge means working from the front of this book to the back. I don't mean that you have to do everything presented in all the chapters, but I mean that first things come first. Nothing is more basic or foundational to the mental skills of your athletes than the philosophy you establish for your team and program. All of the outstanding coaches quoted in these pages (e.g., John Wooden, Mike Krzyzewski, Pia Nilsson, Doc Counsilman) base their approach to the Inner Edge on well thought out philosophies that they implement as teaching strategies, expectations for athletes, and styles of communication and feedback.

So I would start by focusing on Chapters 2-6, and write out some of the following:

(a) key points in my coaching philosophy or ideas about leadership
(b) ways my philosophy is communicated to and practiced by athletes in the program

(c) my vision and action plan for the overall program and this team in particular
(d) my expectations for interpersonal communication within the team
(e) my ideas to build a sense of "team" and commitment to the program (team building)

These are the essential parts of the Inner Edge. Doing these things well takes a lot of time and thought. A clearly articulated philosophy and vision for your program, attention to leadership and communication effectiveness, and a commitment to building team cohesion and performance effectiveness are the most fundamental parts of coaching the Inner Edge. Before you progress to more specific mental training strategies, ensure that these critical foundations are in place. If this is all you focus on in developing the Inner Edge for your program, that's fine. Athletes' mental skills are enhanced when these fundamental aspects of the Inner Edge are clearly established by coaches. However, once you are confident that the basic foundations have been established, I encourage you to begin to structure your program to incorporate more specific mental training strategies for your athletes.

Start Small - Stay Simple - Follow Through

The mantra for mental training is "start small - stay simple - follow through." Say this to yourself several times to make sure you remember it. The most common mistake in implementing mental training with athletes is overloading them with information or asking them to do too much. Just like physical training, athletes need time to digest and assimilate information about mental skills. *So start small!* Any type of mental training should be focused on making things easier and better for athletes, not to complicate their lives or confuse them. Athletes will use what they retain, and they'll retain what they understand and what is practical and easy to use. *So stay simple!* The second most common mistake in teaching mental skills to athletes is to get them started with some new ideas and strategies, and then forget about it as the season progresses. Not only is this ineffective and a waste of time, but it also gives athletes the message that mental training is really not that important. *So follow through!* The actual mental skills you focus on and the strategies you use with athletes are not that important—what *is* important is that you start small, stay simple, and follow through.

For example, you could choose to work with athletes on developing and using pre-performance routines (Chapter 12). First, you could have a brief team discussion about routines and provide some examples. Ask your athletes to think about and develop a brief routine for one specific skill (e.g., volleyball serve, prior to each dive, prior to high jump). After they've had time to do this and talk with you about it if needed, explain how they should use mental rehearsal to practice the routine each day (Chapter 9). Periodically, ask athletes about their routines (how they're working), and prompt athletes to use their pre-performance routines during physical training sessions. Focusing on one mental strategy and following through across the season is much more effective than confusing athletes by giving them too many things to think about.

So start small, stay simple, and follow through. Don't make a big deal about how the team is going to "try some new mental training." It works better to incorporate mental training ideas from the menu within the seasonal, weekly, and daily routines of your athletes, without identifying them as something separate or special. Overall, athletes should understand that they must be physically and mentally prepared for competition, and that training sessions will focus on developing both these areas.

Choose an Entry Point

Entry points are activities that serve as starting places for mental training with athletes. They're something to get the ball rolling, and to use as a point of departure to get athletes engaged in mental training. Choose one activity to use as an entry point, and then follow through by working from your entry point. Here are some suggested entry points, or starting places for mental training.

Goal Mapping as an Entry Point

Developing team and/or individual goal maps is often a good entry point (explained in Chapter 8). This activity requires athletes to figure out their sense of purpose, and to identify milestone, challenge, and focus goals. You could continue the activity across several meetings, as follows:

First team meeting. Discuss why goals work; what makes goals SMAART; goal map concept; key to using goal maps effectively is knowing *what* goal to focus on *when*; discussion on team sense of purpose or feeling that feeds this team's goals; brainstorming possible milestone goals for team.

Second team meeting. Develop a preliminary team goal map; get some consensus on a collective sense of purpose; establish milestone goals; identify challenge goals the team needs to achieve to make milestone goals reachable; brainstorm focus goals, or key mental focus triggers needed to achieve challenge goals.

Following through. Along with team goal maps, individual athletes can develop their own goal maps. As the season progresses, team and individual goal achievement strategies can be developed to focus on ways to achieve goals. Using goal mapping as an entry point easily leads to developing focus plans for competition based on specific goals. Work on the goal map weekly throughout the season—don't just identify goals, write them down, and forget about them. Encourage athletes to consult their goal maps weekly by checking their progress, revising their goals, and planning strategies to achieve their goals. Their focus in training sessions and competition should logically progress from their goal maps.

Identifying Critical Success Factors as an Entry Point

Another good entry point in coaching the Inner Edge is the Critical Success Factors activity found in Chapter 6. This activity should be done in the off-season or early preseason for college teams and in the early preseason for high school teams.

First team meeting. Develop a worksheet like the example shown in Appendix 15A, and provide one copy to each athlete. Explain that Critical Success Factors (CSFs) are things that the team has to do well to be successful, and emphasize that every team has different CSFs. Ask your athletes: What does *this team* have to do well to succeed, achieve its goals, and fulfill its potential? Start with brainstorming, where everything that is identified is written down on a chalkboard or whiteboard in front of the team. Once all possible CSFs are identified, athletes then rank them in order of importance to the team's success.

Second team meeting. Prepare for the second team meeting by taking the top five CSFs identified by the team, typing them into the worksheet (Appendix 15A), and making new copies for the athletes. Then in the meeting, ask athletes (a) if they agree with the key CSFs, (b) to rate the attention given to each CSF on the team, and (c) to identify strategies to strengthen each CSF.

Following through. Typically, athletes identify both physical and mental CSFs in this activity, and you can encourage them to do so. Their recommendations to strengthen CSFs can include such things as physical training drills, more coaching attention given to certain areas, and specific strategies for individual athletes to practice. This activity easily leads into goal mapping by focusing on goals based on the CSFs identified by the team. You can also print up the team's CSFs in big type and place them in a prominent place in the locker room. You can focus on the team's CSFs throughout the season and ask athletes periodically, "Are we strengthening our . . . (CSF)?" Throughout the season, you can pick and choose from the mental training menu to use various strategies to enhance different CSFs.

I often use the CSF activity in the off-season and then put together a "Mental Skills Checklist" for athletes based on the CSFs identified for the team. For a college volleyball team, we did the CSF activity in the spring, and then the coach gave them a Mental Skills Checklist along with their physical training program for the summer (see Appendix 15B for an example checklist). The idea is to get athletes to focus on physical and mental training prior to and during the season that directly addresses the CSFs that they have identified as crucial for their performance in the upcoming season.

Self-Evaluation Activities as Entry Points

Self-evaluation activities where athletes have to reflect on their typical and/or desired mental responses in competition are often good entry points for mental training. These work well with individual athletes, whereas the previous two examples focused more on team entry points. For example, you could use the P³ Thinking Worksheet for Athletes provided in Appendix 10A to get athletes reflecting on how they want to think and feel in competition. This entry point could serve as the basis for promoting P³ Thinking in your program, and following through by building P³ Thinking into pre-performance routines, competition focus plans, and/or Optimal Energy Profiles.

Another good entry point self-evaluation activity is the Attentional Focusing Questionnaire and Assess Your Focus Skills Worksheet found in Appendix 12A. Instructions for leading this exercise are in Chapter 12. This entry point can lead athletes into developing focus plans, pre-performance routines, and/or refocusing strategies as the season progresses.

Focus on the Skills - Use the Tools

Along with choosing an effective entry point for mental training with your team, it is also helpful to choose one mental skill to focus on and build your program around. The "big three" mental skills presented in Part 3 are attentional focusing, energy management, and self-confidence. A good strategy is to focus on one of these as the theme for your team's mental training, and then use the menu of other training skills and tools to build this skill.

The mental training tools presented in Part 2 (goal mapping, imagery, P^3 Thinking, and physical relaxation) can be used by athletes to build mental skills. It's more effective to use the tools in a systematic way rather than randomly, by themselves. For example, instead of randomly practicing imagery, athletes should use imagery in specific ways to build confidence, enhance attentional focus, or manage competitive energy. Similarly, athletes should use P^3 Thinking, goal mapping, and physical relaxation as tools to build key mental skills. It is less useful to teach athletes how to physically relax if they do not know how and when to use relaxation. Part of their training should include a plan for how relaxation can help them manage negative physical energy prior to competition or to use Power Breaths as part of their pre-performance routines to enhance attention. The indiscriminant use of mental training tools without being part of an overall mental training focus is not useful and often a waste of time.

Which skill should you choose to focus on? There's no right answer, and it isn't a hugely critical decision because all mental skills boil down to the ability to think and feel optimally during competition. You should focus on a mental skill that you are most interested in and that best fits your program. As you'll see in the following examples, all mental training skills and tools dovetail and work in combination, so you'll probably end up addressing all three skills before you're finished. Three outlines are presented representing a mental training progression for each of the "big three" mental skills. These are just examples, and can be modified in many ways. Use them as a framework, and personalize a plan that works best for you and your athletes.

Focus on Confidence

A. Confidence as the Mental Modifier
   1. Discuss what confidence is and what it is not
   2. Examples in your sport of how confidence keeps athletes from sliding to the right (Figure 14.1)
   3. Example quotes or descriptions of athletes in your sport who display confidence
   4. Team discussion about what helps them feel confident (what teammates and coaches can do that enhances confidence)
B. Goal Mapping
   1. Effective and appropriate goals serve as basis for confidence
   2. Goal maps (key is what goals to think about when)
   3. Sense of purpose (tree trunk of the goal map) serves as "confidence cushion" by giving athletes perspective they need under pressure
   4. Emphasize use of focus goals during competition
C. P^3 Thinking
   1. Confidence and success come from thinking well (P^3 vs. R^3 Thinking)
   2. Set expectations for P^3 Thinking in all aspects of program (get leaders to buy in)
   3. Athletes complete P^3 Thinking Worksheet (Appendix 10A) for self-reflection/evaluation
D. Planning a Confident Focus
   1. Take results from P^3 Thinking Worksheet and develop competition focus plan (Appendix 12C)
   2. Take results from P^3 Thinking Worksheet and develop refocusing plans (Appendix 12D)
   3. Plan a simple and personalized pre-performance routine
E. Rehearsing My Confident Focus and Responses
   1. Use imagery daily to mentally rehearse focus and refocusing plans

2. Mentally prepare and practice via imagery for unexpected occurrences in competition

3. Mentally rehearse losing confidence and working to stay focused despite change in confidence

F. Key Coach Behaviors to Focus on Confidence

1. Drill athletes repeatedly in pressure situations

2. Focus on athletes' strengths, push them to work on weaknesses

3. Catch athletes doing things right and reinforce this

4. Catch athletes making mistakes, yet trying to strengthen a weakness, and reinforce this

5. Demonstrate confident decision-making, P³ Thinking, and confidence in your athletes, especially in pressure situations

Focus on Managing Energy

A. Competitive Energy Key Concepts

1. A natural resource, with all forms being potentially useful

2. Stress as positive energy—focus on this and welcome/use the pressure

3. Examples of famous athletes using effective energy management strategies

4. Team discussion of ways to use energy effectively in this sport

B. Customizing Optimal Energy Profiles

1. Explain that individuals use and prefer energy very differently (everyone has optimal zones for different types of energy)

2. Athletes complete Optimal Energy Profile (Appendix 13A)

   a. Give out blank copies of Parts B and C of the OEP

   b. Athletes complete Parts A, B, and C

   c. Athletes refer to Part D as a guide to practice

3. Athletes monitor their OEPs by completing Parts B and C for each competition

4. Athletes revise their OEPs to create more functional zones for themselves

5. Coaches should monitor progress and remind athletes to energize appropriately in training and in preparation for competition

C. Goal Mapping

1. Effective and appropriate goals serve as basis for energy management

2. Developing personal goal maps (key is what goals to think about, when to create appropriate energy for that situation)

3. Sense of purpose (tree trunk) gives athletes perspective they need to manage energy under pressure

4. Develop focus goals related to optimal energy feeling states desired in competition

D. Focus Plan to Create and Maintain Personal OEP

1. Develop competition focus plan to create OEP for competition (Appendix 12C)

2. Develop refocusing plans (Appendix 12D) for when you get out of zone

3. Plan a simple and personalized pre-performance routine for feelings of optimal energy

4. Use imagery to mentally rehearse focusing and refocusing strategies every day

5. Create a simple physical relaxation response for when you're out of zone

E. Key Coach Behaviors to Focus on Managing Energy

1. Develop your own OEP to manage energy appropriately (avoid eruptions and giving off nervous cues)

2. Physically and mentally prepare athletes for unexpected occurrences in competition

3. Avoid getting athletes too emotionally high for competition; rather, remind them to focus on their optimal zones

4. Require athletes to manage energy appropriately in training (e.g., simulation of pressure, getting optimally energized even for practice)

5. Reinforce athletes when they manage energy effectively

Focus on Focus

A. Goal Mapping

1. Effective and appropriate goals serve as basis for focus needed in competition

2. Developing personal goal maps (key is what goals to think about to create appropriate focus for that situation)

3. Sense of purpose (tree trunk) gives athletes a controllable feeling state to focus on as opposed to uncontrollable outcome (milestone) goals that detract from optimal focus

4. Develop focus goals to create task focus for key competitive situations

B. P³ Thinking

1. Focusing requires athletes to think well (P³ vs. R³ Thinking)

2. Set expectations for P³ Thinking in all aspects of program (get leaders to buy in)

3. Athletes complete P³ Thinking Worksheet (Appendix 10A) for self-reflection/evaluation

C. Developing Focus Plans for Competition

1. Develop competition focus plan (Appendix 12C)

2. Develop refocusing plans (Appendix 12D)

3. Plan a simple and personalized pre-performance routine to lock in focus

4. Use imagery to mentally rehearse focusing and refocusing strategies every day

E. Key Coach Behaviors to Enhance Athletes' Focus

1. Use distraction strategies in training sessions

2. Teach athletes what to focus on in different competitive situations

3. Work with team to define needed team focus for different competitions

4. Reinforce athletes for demonstrating mental focus skills in different situations

5. Set strong expectations for optimal focus during training, expect athletes to come into training with this focus, and to maintain a strong focus no matter what happens in training

Yearly Plans for Optimal Physical and Mental Training

Once you develop some experience in implementing mental training, you can design yearly plans for optimizing both physical and mental training for your athletes. This is called periodization, which simply refers to longitudinal training plans. Periodization in physical training is common in elite sport, where coaches and athletes plan a training regimen across a calendar year and into the competitive season to optimize their competitive energy and focus for a certain time (usually a championship competition).

An example yearly plan for coaching the Inner Edge is shown in Table 15.1. Coaches should progressively plan across the off-season, preseason, and competitive season. Periodization of mental training follows the same logic as the periodization of physical training, including broad to narrow, fundamental to specialized, and stable foundation to specific focus. The example program in Table 15.1 shows a progression for a coach who wants to emphasize the mental skill of attentional focus. This coach uses the off-season to clarify his philosophy, vision, expectations, and ideas about how to communicate these things to his athletes. He also connects with his team leaders to nurture their leadership abilities and commitment, and to discuss critical success factors and possible goal maps for the team with them.

The preseason is the best time to get athletes focused on mental training, and it should be integrated with preseason physical training. The coach communicates his vision and expectations to athletes, focuses on building team cohesion, and uses P³ Thinking and Performing as his key expectation for athletes. A P³ Thinking activity is used as the entry point, and it leads athletes into the development of focus and refocusing plans for competition. Goal mapping and imagery are also used as critical mental training tools to help athletes plan for and practice effective focusing for competition. The coach creates unique training situations to challenge athletes to remain focused and refocus from distractions.

Mental training during the competitive season becomes very specific in relation to each particular competition. Athletes should mentally practice specific focus goals, focus strategies, and refocusing strategies that could possibly be needed for each competition. Mental rehearsal for each competition should be used to practice P³ Thinking and Performing based on the questions "What will it be like?" and "How will I respond?"

Sample Mental Plans

In this section, three case studies are presented with examples of mental plans that these athletes could use. These examples attempt to demonstrate how coaches can think of the mental training ideas presented in the book as a menu, from which they can select different tools or skills to use in various situations.

Case Study 1: Redding High School Redhawks

It is the off-season and you are preparing for the upcoming preseason training for your high school softball team. Your team is relatively young, with

Example Yearly Progression for Mental Training

Off-Season

✓ Clarify philosophy in key points that define program/focus/expectations

✓ Clarify vision for program in short vision/mission statement

✓ Develop preliminary goal map for team to clarify critical success factors for this team

✓ Prescribe off-season physical conditioning program for athletes

✓ Prescribe off-season mental training activities for athletes

✓ Meet with team leaders to develop communication, understanding, and expectations

Preseason

✓ Communicate philosophy/vision/expectations to athletes (P³ Thinking and Performing)

✓ Team building activities, discussions, and expectations (P³ Thinking within team)

✓ Entry point activity ("P³ Thinking" worksheet)

✓ Introduce mental skill that will be main focus of mental training (focus)

✓ Progressively lead athletes through mental preparation activities

- SMAART goals lead to effective focus
- Goal mapping activity (team and individuals)
- Design weekly physical and mental goal maps for athletes
- Direct athletes to develop competition focus plans (start simple!)
- Direct athletes to use imagery to practice focus plans
- Direct athletes to develop refocusing strategies (Refocusing worksheet)
- Direct athletes to use imagery to practice refocusing

✓ Physical training to create pressure, demand focus and refocusing

Season

✓ Mental and physical preparation for specific competitions

✓ Challenge and focus goals for specific competitions

✓ Direct athletes to mentally rehearse strategies for upcoming competition

✓ Direct athletes to mentally rehearse focus plans for upcoming competition

✓ Direct athletes to mentally rehearse refocusing strategies for upcoming competition

Table 15.1 Example Yearly Progression for Mental Training

your key players being juniors and even a few sophomores. Last year's team graduated four seniors that were fairly good athletes and who served as leaders for the team. However, their leadership was too "nice" in that they focused too much on everyone getting along and feeling good about each other. This year's team will have more physical talent, but you feel they need a "mental makeover." They lacked mental toughness in holding leads in late innings, fighting back when behind, and putting opponents away. They did not create the inner team competitiveness, confidence, and focus you feel they must have to become champions. How will you institute this "mental makeover" for the team?

Mental Training Intervention Plan for the Red-hawks:

A.   Mental training theme: Build the Diamond!

1. Story about how diamonds are created through intensive pressure and heat (see Clipboard in Chapter 13)
2. Take the heat, use the pressure—build the diamond!
3. Use pressure as a natural source of energy: expect it, accept it, like it, harness it, use it!

B. Build the Diamond! mental training picture (see Figure 15.2)
  1. Create locker room bulletin board with diamond
  2. Create handout for each player (colorful for locker)
  3. Explain three steps in building the Redhawk diamond

  Commit to being PERFORMANCE PARTNERS
  Choose to FOCUS
  Be tough and RESPOND

  4. Players must get to first, second, and third base to achieve these three steps
  5. Goal for the team is a Grand Slam (achieving all three steps)
  6. Each athlete has to hit a grand slam every day (training and practice) for the team to build the diamond
  7. Emphasize personal responsibility every day for these three things

C. Becoming PERFORMANCE PARTNERS (lead meeting to present and discuss this)
  1. Performance partners means teammates never let each other be less than they can be
  2. Performance partners insist on effort, focus, performance

3. Emphasis is on support and challenge in process of becoming champions
4. Different than "everyone getting along" or feeling good about each other
5. Expect more from your teammates every day; expect more from yourself
6. Conflict is not bad—performance partners accept conflict and get better
7. Questions for discussion:
  How can you be performance partners for each other?
  What should you expect from each other and yourselves?
  Will you accept conflict and use it?
  What are ways we'll resolve conflict yet stay performance partners?
8. Follow through with "performance partners" theme throughout season
  a. Explain your goal map with your performance partner (team activity)
  b. Selected team building activities (e.g., Critical Success Factors to build the diamond)

D. Choosing to FOCUS
  1. Repetitive, detail-oriented physical preparation to build automatic responses in your athletes
  2. Pre-performance routines for all players for batting
  3. Pre-performance routines for pitchers
  4. Focus plans that include P^3 Thinking and productive behaviors for:
    a. pre-competition and warm-up

BUILD THE DIAMOND!

Plan/Use Your FOCUS

Be Tough: RESPOND

Be A PERFORMANCE PARTNER

GRAND SLAM!

Figure 15.2 Building the Diamond: A team intervention

b. between innings in dugout

c. while playing defense in the field

5. Teach focus cues for offense and defense (what to look for, what to think about)

6. Prompt athletes to practice focus plans/pre-performance routines during training

7. Lead a group session on using imagery to practice focus plans and strategies

8. Prompt athletes to work their focus plans in warm-ups and during game

E. Being tough and RESPOND

1. Lead group session of refocusing strategies

2. Key skill related to taking heat and using pressure—to build the diamond!

3. Steps for athletes to plan and practice:

a. Identify key situations or occurrences when you lose focus or confidence

b. Develop a simple mental strategy to use in this situation—think like A PRO to build the diamond!

c. Take them through the A PRO steps—give them specific steps (Chapter 12)

d. Teach the concept of "parking" or "triage" (Chapter 10)

e. Mentally prepare for all types of possible situations and emotions (Chapter 13)

F. Key Coach Behaviors

1. Model and expect P3 Thinking to build the diamond

2. Emphasize focus and responding in training; constant simulation of pressure situations with an emphasis on focus and respond

3. Help athletes know when to use milestone, challenge, and focus goals

4. Emphasize the build the diamond theme, and three key sub-themes (performance partners, focus, respond) throughout physical training sessions and in preparation for competition

Case Study 2: Brooke

Brooke is a senior in high school, and an outstanding cross-country and distance runner in track and field. She was All-State her junior year, and has received a lot of media attention and interest from college recruiters going into her senior year. As the competitive cross-country season began, Brooke uncharacteristically began to struggle with her performance. She had some minor nagging injuries, but it seems to you that Brooke lacks confidence to perform. When you talk with Brooke, she says that running isn't fun anymore and that she's tired of the pressure and expectations. She says her parents are driving her crazy, but then in tears admits she hates to let them down. She says she's sorry she's letting you and the team down, but she doesn't know what's wrong and why running isn't natural and easy for her anymore.

Mental Training/Intervention Plan for Brooke:

1. Refocusing Brooke on why she runs

a. Goal mapping exercise (only identify sense of purpose and focus goals)

b. Focus is on passion/why she runs and focus goals

c. Point is to forget milestone and performance goals and just run for right reason

d. Only goal: recreate feeling and feel it each time she runs (forget other goals for now)

2. P^3 Thinking

a. REBT dialogue with Brooke

b. Lead her into reflecting about how others are controlling her running, instead of her

c. Could work through P3 Thinking Worksheet (Appendix 10A)

3. Recreate optimal energy and focus

a. Begin with "How would you like to feel when you run" or "How do you feel when you run well?"

b. Brooke develops Optimal Energy Profile for herself (Appendix 13A)

c. Uses imagery to create OEP and recreate previous OEPs that led to good performance

4. Culminate previous work into a competition focus plan (Chapter 12)

a. Objective is to help Brooke gain control over competitive thoughts/feelings/goals

b. Plan can include OEP thoughts/feelings and energy that flows from her passion for running

c. Teach her to park or triage "pressure points" such as parents, outcome goals, expectations (Chapter 10)

5. Key Coach Behaviors:
    a. Demonstrate support for and acceptance of Brooke as a person—unrelated to her performance
    b. Demonstrate support for her unique goal map (emphasis on passion—not performance or outcomes)
    c. REBT dialogue to help her think productively and rationally (Chapter 10)

Case Study 3: Scott

Scott has just finished his sophomore season on the college basketball team that you coach. He is the best athlete on the team with outstanding physical abilities, and he plays extremely well in practice. However, during his first two years on the team, he was unable to achieve the same performance level in games that he did in practice. He becomes very anxious prior to games, which seems to hurt his performance. Scott has told you he doesn't know why he gets so uptight before games, but he does. He is now heading into the off-season, and you and your staff are prescribing off-season physical and mental training programs for your athletes. What would you prescribe for Scott?

Mental Training/Intervention Plan for Scott:

A. Develop goal map
    1. Work to identify key sense of purpose or perspective for playing (why he plays)
    2. Develop meaningful focus goals and practice these during physical training sessions
B. P³ Thinking Worksheet for Athletes (Chapter 10)
    1. Emphasize thinking "on purpose" and responding (not reacting) to competition
    2. Teach parking and identify key thoughts Scott must park
C. Use information learned from P³ worksheet to create Optimal Energy Profile
    1. Scott monitors self across training sessions attempting to get into his zones

2. Imagery practice every day to internalize OEP and productive responses to competition
D. Develop pre-competition/competition focus plan
    1. Includes focus goals, P3 thoughts, response-oriented images, and optimal energy key words
    2. Practice focus plan using imagery and in physical training sessions
    3. Identify specific distractions/pressures and develop refocusing strategies for each
E. Key Coach Behaviors
    1. Simulation of competitive pressure to practice focus strategies
    2. Demonstrate support for and acceptance of Scott irrespective of his performance
    3. Maintain high expectancies for his performance in competition
    4. Provide him specific focus cues to lock in on during different performance situations

Wrapping Up

Start small, stay simple, follow through. Remember this mantra of mental training. Decide on a key mental skill to serve as your theme (focus or confidence or managing energy), and then slowly and progressively build mental training into your overall physical training regimen. Although you can think about a yearly mental training plan, it's fine just to plan some simple mental training exercises for the preseason and season. Also, remember that first things are first. The most important part of coaching the mental game is developing your philosophy, your vision for your program, and your leadership, communication, and team building skills. The ways in which you structure your program, communicate your vision and philosophy to your athletes, and model productive thinking, feeling, and acting are the most essential parts of coaching for the Inner Edge.

Use the ideas presented in this book to develop mental training outlines and worksheets for your athletes. Whenever I have a mental training discussion with athletes, I always provide pencils and brief outlines/worksheets to ensure that they are actively engaged in the activity. Get your athletes personally involved in any activity so they can evaluate themselves and plan their own mental strategies. One of the best things you can do is to use examples and quotes about the importance and use of mental skills from famous athletes. This convinces your athletes to "buy into" mental training, and also provides interesting examples of the many ways that mental training can be used.

Start small, stay simple, and follow through. You'll find that once you get started, your ability to integrate mental training with your athletes' physical training becomes second nature. You'll also develop your own unique ways of teaching mental skills to your athletes, and then maybe I can learn from you in writing the second edition of this book! Good luck!

Summary Points for Chapter 15

1. Working on the Inner Edge begins with the development of a clear philosophy and vision, attention to leadership and communication effectiveness, and ideas to build team cohesion and commitment.

2. The mantra for mental training is "start small – stay simple – follow through."

3. Two common mistakes in mental training are (a) to overload athletes with too much information, and (b) to fail to continue mental training strategies as the season progresses.

4. Entry points are activities that serve as starting places for mental training with athletes.

5. Example entry points include goal mapping, identifying critical success factors, and self-evaluation activities.

6. A good strategy for coaches to use in mental training is to focus on one skill as a theme (e.g., confidence), and then use various mental training tools to work on that skill.

7. The indiscriminate use of mental training tools without being part of an overall mental training plan is not useful and often a waste of time.

8. Coaches can plan a longitudinal approach to mental training across the off-season, preseason, and competitive season, similar to the periodization of physical training for athletes.

Study Questions

1. What should coaches first focus on when making a commitment to the Inner Edge? Why is this important?

2. What are common mistakes typically made in implementing mental training with athletes? How can coaches avoid making these mistakes?

3. Why is an entry point helpful in getting athletes engaged in mental training? Besides the examples provided in the chapter, identify some activities you think would be useful as entry point activities for mental training with athletes. Why do you think these would be effective?

4. Explain how the random or indiscriminate use of mental training tools could be problematic for athletes.

5. Outline a yearly plan for mental training in your particular sport. Discuss how the mental training would be integrated within the physical training.

Reflective Learning Activities

1. Pick Your Skill

What mental skill would you build your mental training program around and why? Outline a progression of steps or phases you would follow in developing this mental skill in your athletes. Be specific in integrating mental and physical training in your sport. (Individual assignment)

2. Let's Be Real

Break into small groups (3-4 persons) by type and level of sport you are coaching or interested in coaching. Discuss implementation ideas for mental training for this sport (e.g., high school soccer). Identify the unique challenges in implementing mental training in this situation, such as what might work, what wouldn't, and why. Be realistic yet open-minded in deciding what mental training strategies may or may not work in this situation.

3. It's Your Show

Pick one mental skill or tool and develop a brief mental training presentation/activity for athletes of a certain age in a specific sport (e.g., middle school tennis team). Develop a one page handout or outline that you would use in teaching this mental strategy to the athletes. Remember to keep it simple and make it entertaining. (Individual assignment or in pairs)

Common Challenges Faced by Coaches: Special Recipes

Chapter Preview

In this chapter, you'll learn:
- how to implement mental training in your program
- about entry points for mental training
- how to periodize mental training along with your seasonal physical training program
- to start small, stay simple, and follow through

"You find talent, not by looking for it, but by working for it." **Nancy Lopez** *(cited in Freeman, 1998)*

"The people who get on in this world are the people who get up and look for the circumstances they want, and, if they can't find them, make them." **George Bernard Shaw**

This is the special recipe chapter. Use it as a reference guide when you need to respond to a specific issue or problem that wasn't covered in a regular chapter of the book. I've identified several issues regarding athletes that might call for special recipes. These special recipes involve you as the coach putting all your new knowledge about the Inner Edge to use in helping athletes through these issues. Two very specific issues that you're bound to confront include burnout (both for you and your athletes) and mental training for injured athletes. Examples of other issues that require some special recipes include slumps, inconsistency, perfectionism, and commitment. Of course I can't foresee all the special recipes you'll need in your program. However, you'll quickly learn how to cook up your own recipes for problems that arise by trying out the different mental training strategies presented in the book.

Burnout

"I don't know, Coach. I just feel burned out." How many times have you heard this statement from athletes? But what is burnout? Is it the same thing as stress? Is it real? Or is it a lack of mental toughness? How can you as the coach help your athletes avoid burnout, and what can you do to help athletes who are experiencing burnout?

Burnout is real, and it has several distinguishing characteristics. First, it involves feelings of exhaustion, including *mental, emotional, and physical exhaustion*. It's easy to see how the physical demands of training coupled with the mental and emotional demands of competition interact to create burnout in athletes. Second, this exhaustion leads to *negative moods and feelings* (depression, despair) and a *negative change in athletes' responses to others,* such as cynicism, feeling alienated from teammates, and a lack of empathy for others. Third, athletes experiencing burnout *feel a lack of accomplishment*, which decreases their performance level and feelings of self-esteem. Fourth, athletes experiencing burnout become *disillusioned with their sport involvement,* as shown in the following quote by a junior elite tennis player experiencing burnout, "I just never wanted to practice anymore and . . . it just wasn't there for me . . . I felt like I don't want to do this anymore and it is just wasting my life. I didn't want to be there so I didn't

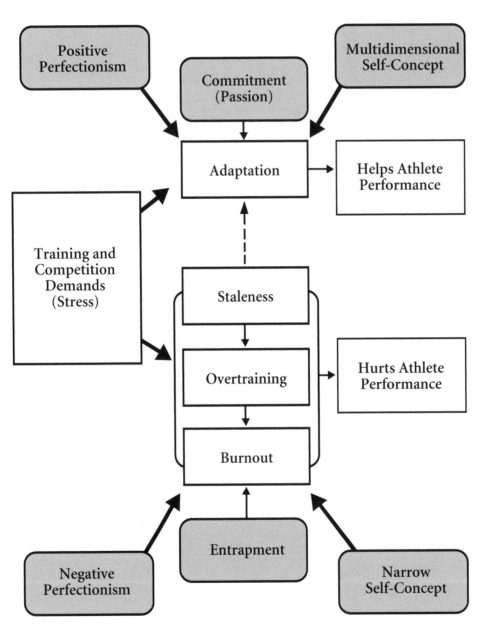

Figure 16.1 Positive and negative adaptation to competitive demands

feel like trying" (Gould, Tuffey, Udry, & Loehr, 1996, p. 345).

Why Do Athletes Burn Out?

There's not one answer to the question why athletes burn out in sport. Burnout is a complex condition that occurs when key personality characteristics of athletes interact with the social and environmental stressors found in competitive sport. Let's work through Figure 16.1 to understand how and why burnout occurs in athletes.

Training and competitive demands. Starting at the left side of Figure 16.1, everything begins with the demands of training and competition. This is also known as stress, which was defined in Chapter 13 as a demand placed on an athlete. Remember that stress is not necessarily bad for athletes, and in fact is an important stimulus for growth. As shown by the upper arrow leading from the stress box in Figure 16.1, when athletes adapt to the stress of training and competition, their performance is enhanced. It is through adaptation to stress that athletes incorporate the benefits of training into their performance through increased skill, strength, endurance, and mental skills such as focus, confidence, and energy management.

However, as shown by the lower arrow leading from the stress box in Figure 16.1, sometimes athletes are not able to adapt to the training and competitive stress imposed upon them. This can happen for many reasons, such as inadequate rest and recovery, conflict, multiple life demands, mental pressure, and fatigue (Silva, 1990). Burnout doesn't happen immediately in this case, because burnout is the result of a long-term or chronic lack of adaptation to stress. That is, burnout develops over time as athletes are unable to adapt to and cope with various demands placed upon them.

Staleness. As shown in Figure 16.1, athletes first experience **staleness** when they fail to adapt to stress. Just like bread that gets stale, athletes' energy can get stale, and they *lose their vigor and performance effectiveness.* Athletes feel stale when they are either *bored with or worn down by the tedious and familiar nature of the repetitive training that is necessary for athletic excellence.* Staleness is very common in sport training, because training for high level performance requires tedious, repetitive, focused work. I tell athletes all the time that if it were easy, everyone would

be a great athlete! Staleness is a temporary state that athletes often experience after a long day or week of practice. In fact, staleness by itself can even lead to adaptation (see the dotted line in Figure 16.1), because athletes often hit performance plateaus (no improvement) when they feel stale and must train through these plateaus to persist and get better (Silva, 1990).

Overtraining. However, if athletes cannot adapt by using recovery time or rest, and their staleness continues, they can move down the negative path toward overtraining. **Overtraining** is *when athletes train beyond a level that is ideal for maximum benefits to their performance.* This is not a desired overload or demand placed on athletes to help them adapt, which ultimately enhances their performance. This is a *negative* condition brought on by *repeated* failures of athlete's bodies and minds to adapt to competitive and training demands over a period of time, which hurts their performance.

Burnout as the end result. As shown in Figure 16.1, the negative spiral of non-adaptation to stress leads from staleness to overtraining to burnout. That's why burnout just doesn't happen overnight—it takes time to develop as the unmet demands and the lack of adaptation to them create the physical and mental feelings of exhaustion, negative feelings and moods, and amotivation and disillusionment that define burnout in athletes. Often, athletes who are burned out quit their sports, and there are many examples of young superstars in sports like tennis, women's gymnastics, and golf who have burned out. However, many athletes stay in their sports while experiencing burnout, and their performance as well as overall health is hurt by the negative physical and mental symptoms of burnout.

Why Are Some Athletes More Susceptible to Burnout Than Others?

Even though stress gets the ball rolling in terms of burnout, it is not the sole reason why athletes experience this negative condition. Research shows that some athletes are more susceptible to burnout than others. As shown at the bottom of Figure 16.1, three characteristics of athletes make them susceptible to burnout.

Feeling trapped. First, athletes who feel trapped in their sport participation experience more burnout than athletes who participate because they are committed and love their sports (Raedeke, 1997). Athletes experience this "entrapment" when they feel they *have to* continue in their sports, because of family pressure, their own expectations, college scholarships, and even the prospect of college scholarships. The opposite of entrapment is shown at the top of Figure 16.1 as commitment or passion for one's sport. Passionate commitment, or love of one's sport, helps athletes endure the grueling training and mental demands placed on them.

Negative perfectionism. A second characteristic of athletes that leads to burnout is negative perfectionism. Perfectionism is a funny thing. It has its positive qualities, such as high personal standards of success and effective organizational skills. However, perfectionism can be negative when it makes one overly concerned with mistakes and unrealistic expectations for flawless performance, which can lead to anxiety and self-focused attention. This negative type of perfectionism has been found in athletes who are burned out (Gould, Udry, Tuffey, & Loehr, 1996).

Narrow self-concept. A third characteristic of athletes who tend to experience burnout is a narrow self-concept. Adolescent athletes identified as burned out have been shown to have very narrow and constrained life pursuits, all at the expense of their sport participation (Coakley, 1992). Thus, their self-concept and personal identity is completely wrapped up in being an athlete. It seems obvious that the demands, pressure, and stress on an athlete would be far greater and much more conducive to burnout if the athlete's sole identity is based on their sport success. The perspective and mental rejuvenation gained through participation in activities other than sport provides athletes some relief from the oppressive nature of sport training and expectations for performance. Athletes who narrowly specialize and have no other "eggs in their basket" put themselves at risk for undue pressure and burnout (Gould, Tuffey, Udry, & Loehr, 1997).

Helping Athletes Avoid and Deal With Burnout

We've probably all experienced burnout at some point in our lives, so to think that you as the coach can and should prevent burnout in your athletes is unrealistic. A better objective is for you as the coach to be aware of how burnout occurs and then strive to help athletes who are prime candidates for burnout manage their lives and approach their sport

© Media Focus International, LLC

in productive ways to avoid the burnout trap. Here are some suggestions:

1. Use challenge and variety in training to combat staleness. Even though repetition is needed for skill development, coaches should find challenging and innovative ways to train athletes that vary enough to enhance motivation and avoid staleness. Interval training is useful to balance easy and hard drills within practice, as well as easy and hard training days each week. Explain to athletes the importance of rest and recovery and provide them adequate time for this. Above all, make their sport participation meaningful and exciting. This doesn't mean that every practice drill has to be fun, because excellence in sport requires diligent and intense training. But athletes are less likely to get stale when they are part of an exciting and meaningful quest to achieve team goals.

2. Don't confuse overload with over overtraining. One of the most difficult decisions for coaches is how hard to push athletes. Unfortunately, there's no formula for what is optimal and what is too much. We all know that overload, as a basic training principle, is necessary for performance enhancement. Athletes have to be overloaded in practice to get better, stronger, more focused, and more skillful. But at some point overload turns into overtraining, at which point the benefits of training cease and athletes actually lose performance effectiveness. As the rewards for sport success have become more glamorous and sport training has become more sophisticated, there's a strong tendency to think that more is better in terms of training. The injury rates in athletes have skyrocketed as we place more and more demands on athletes, and they respond with overuse injuries such as stress fractures and tendonitis. Burnout represents the mental overuse injury that results from long-term overtraining.

Coaches should focus on the *quality* of training to help athletes stay physically healthy and mentally focused. Of course athletes must be pushed, but the intensity of training should be periodic with appropriate recovery time between intensive training sessions. Ask your athletes to give you their absolute physical and mental best for a period of quality, focused practice. Reward them for their focus and effort by keeping training sessions within reasonable limits. If athletes realize that practices will be kept to a certain time limit if they focus and work hard, they tend to accept this responsibility and give optimal effort during an abbreviated practice as opposed to going through the motions in the drudgery of a three-hour training session.

Clipboard

Coach K's Burnout Intervention

Coach Mike Krzyzewski (2000) provides a great example of how he worked with a burned out athlete to find a good solution for him. After Duke won the men's national collegiate basketball championship in 1991, star player Christian Laettner told Coach Krzyzewski that he was worn out and wanted to rest instead of participating in the prestigious Pan American Games that summer. Krzyzewski told Laettner that he understood how he felt and that he needed rest, but asked him to think about why the Pan Am Games were important to him. He made Laettner realize that, by playing on this team with exceptional talent, he would get better as a player, earn the respect and be a key leader for his teammates next season, and put himself in a great position to make the 1992 Olympic Team (the original "Dream Team" of basketball superstars). However, instead of just talking Laettner into playing, Krzyzewski suggested that he not touch a basketball for six weeks, relax and have fun as a college student, and then start working out a couple of weeks ahead of the Pan Am practices. He also proposed that Laettner could then take another month off after the Pan Am Games to rest and forego the team preseason program based on his summer training. Laettner agreed because the compromise allowed him the rest and rejuvenation he needed, yet also allowed him to enhance his skills to come back as a strong leader for the 1992 Duke team. By helping Laettner plan how to get the recovery time he needed yet still participate in international play, Krzyzewski helped him enter the 1992 season with strong energy and focus, as opposed to staleness and burnout. It must have worked—Duke, led by Christian Laettner, won another national championship in 1992!

---

3. Deemphasize intense specialization in one sport at the exclusion of all other activities. A trend in high school athletics is to push athletes to specialize their abilities in one particular sport. Proponents of this strategy say that it gives athletes the best chance for quality skill development and the opportunity for college scholarships, but it's also true that coaches demand specialization to advantage their programs, not the athletes. Participating in multiple sports and other activities gives athletes the variety, freshness, and stimulation to stay focused and "into" what they're doing, which combats staleness, overtraining, and burnout.

If you coach athletes who have chosen to specialize in one sport, at least encourage them to participate in other activities along with their sport participation. The key is for athletes to have a multi-faceted identity or self-concept with several areas of interest or expertise. One thing I ask athletes to do when they meet with me is to draw their "personal pies." They draw a circle, and then slice up the circle into pieces that represent who they are or what is important to them. For example, an individual might draw a pie with pieces that represent herself as a tennis player, good student in school, family member, drama club member, and friend having quality social time with her peers. The size of each pie piece represents how important that part of the person's identity is to them. If athletes' identities as athletes take up most all of their personal pies, they could be candidates for burnout. Help athletes develop a multi-faceted "personal pie" which gives them many areas to excel in and focus on, as well as a variety of life activities needed to provide perspective and balance.

4. Intervene with athletes whose personalities and/or life situations predispose them to burnout. We all want committed athletes, but remember that if that commitment is based on negative perfectionism, then these athletes will experience self-induced stress related to concern over mistakes and unrealistic performance expectations. Athletes high in burnout often feel pressure to perform perfectly and focus on inappropriate goals that lead them to overtrain. Demonstrate your acceptance of their mistakes when they make them in practice and competition, to get them focused on striving to perform well as opposed to avoiding performing poorly. Help them design personalized goal maps to identify individualized performance and focus goals (Chapter 8). Bombard these athletes with P³ Thinking (Chapter 10), and help them develop simple focus plans for thinking rationally and productively about competition (Chapter 12). Help them develop Optimal Energy Profiles so they can learn to create positive feelings and manage negative feelings related to

competition (Chapter 13). They can use imagery to mentally rehearse their focus plans and feelings of optimal energy in preparing for competition.

Another helpful intervention for overtrained or burned out athletes is to help them create Optimal Energy Profiles for competition *and* for post-competition. The idea is to help athletes optimize their energy to compete, and also their energy to recover. It's almost like developing a focus or feeling recovery plan for how to think about their previous performance, extract the lessons from mistakes, feel proud of accomplishments, and then focus on feeling calm and restful to rejuvenate their energy levels. Athletes can use the forms in Parts B and C of Appendix 13A to create their OEPs for post-competition. An example post-competition OEP is shown in Figure 16.2. This athlete attempts to manage her thoughts and feelings to enhance *relaxation, calmness, acceptance,* and *reflection,* while at the same time decreasing feelings of *tension, guilt, anger,* and feeling *revved up* for competition. Athletes need to understand that opti-

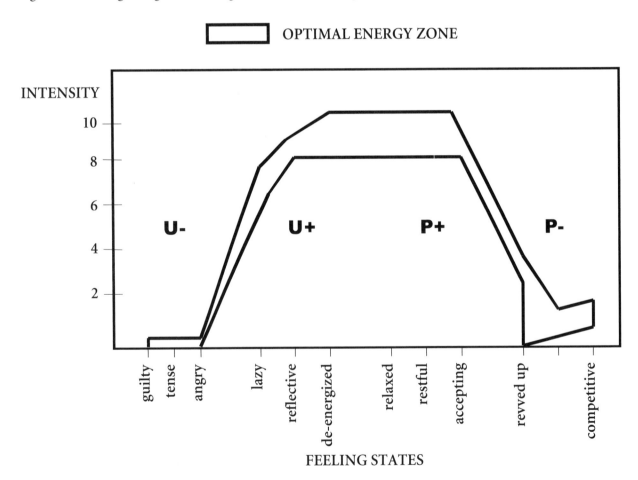

Figure 16.2 Post-competition Optimal Energy Profile

mal recovery is just as important as optimal performance, and that optimal recovery *leads to* optimal performance.

In addition to perfectionism, athletes who lack passion—or love of playing—are candidates for burnout, because they are playing for the wrong reasons and feel entrapped by their sport participation. Talk with these athletes using the REBT-type of questions and dialogue presented in Chapter 10 to get at the following: How do you feel about playing? What would make you enjoy playing more? What can we do to make playing fun for you again? Entrapped athletes feel that they "have to" stay in sport and perform well. Use REBT to dispute the "have to" and help them figure out if they "want to" and how they can change their lives to "want to" more.

Another good exercise for these athletes is creating their personal goal maps as presented in Chapter 8. As you may remember, the first step in goal mapping is for the athletes to identify their sense of purpose for why they are playing. Help athletes figure out a way to label the "trunk of the tree" in their goal maps, to remind them of how they want to feel when they play and why they are playing. This is more important than their goals, because it is the reason that they have goals. Without the sense of purpose or passion, the goals are meaningless. Athletes that tend to burn out have many positive qualities that lend themselves to excellence in sport and life, such as dedication, intensity, and a narrow task or performance focus. However, if they don't have the perspective needed to keep their pursuit of sport excellence rational and balanced, they are prone to burnout.

Coaches and Burnout

It's ironic that we've spent all this time talking about athletes. You as the coach are more susceptible to burnout than your athletes! This is because burnout occurs most frequently in the "helping" professions, such as nursing, social work, counseling, and yes, coaching. In a study of collegiate tennis coaches, over half experienced moderate to high levels of burnout in the form of emotional exhaustion (Kelley, Eklund, & Ritter-Taylor, 1999). Not a good thing!

Coaches become burned out for many of the same reasons that athletes become burned out. Swim coaches who felt trapped in their coaching positions for whatever reasons were high in burnout, while those coaches who were positively committed and highly attracted to coaching were lower in burnout (Raedeke, Granzyk, & Warren, 2000). However, like athletes, coaches that are committed because of their love of coaching are less predisposed to the stress that causes burnout (Kelley et al., 1999). Coaches high in burnout also have identified an overload of demands and a lack of control over their programs as contributing to their stress and burnout (Vealey, Udry, Zimmerman, & Soliday, 1992).

As a coach, the expression "being spread too thin" is probably one you are familiar with when it comes to honoring all the commitments you make. Mike Krzyzewski (2000) describes how he took on more and more after winning his first national championship until his body and mental state broke down. He had to step down from coaching during a competitive season to heal from the extreme burnout and physical deterioration that he experienced. He talked about how he learned to set boundaries and to accept that he couldn't be all things to all people. Your first responsibility as coach is to ensure that you're trained and ready, just like you expect your athletes to be. Work hard and take on the stress of being the best you can be, but remember the need for oscillation between stress and recovery discussed in Chapter 13. If you don't manage your time effectively for your own health and wellbeing, you will not be effective as the coach of your program.

Research has shown that burnout leads to negative coaching behaviors, and athletes are susceptible to burnout from these negative behaviors from coaches high in burnout themselves (Vealey, Armstrong, Comar, & Greenleaf, 1998). Develop your own goal map, with goals related to coaching success but also personal health and wellbeing. Develop strategies for relaxation and activities away from coaching that reenergize you and give you perspective. Take it from a recovering workaholic, you can be deeply committed and work hard at your job, but at the same time still make sure that you have the recovery time needed to create your own personal optimal energy levels. Coaches can enhance their lives by excelling in both the gold and green zones (Orlick, 1998). The gold zone is your life as a coach, and the green zone is the rest of your life. The key to achievement and wellbeing is to perform well in both zones and to prioritize both zones equally. If you only focus on your gold zone, you'll burn out. If you only focus on your green zone, you won't achieve your career goals. Find ways to live fully in both zones and be totally focused on gold and green when you are in those zones. By giving your full attention to both work and recovery, you'll achieve more—and live better as well!

Wrapping Up Burnout

Burnout is not a sign of weakness or a simple response to stress. It occurs over time as athletes and coaches are unable to adapt to the demands placed on them. The reasons for this lack of adaptation are many, and can involve self-induced pressure, expectations from others, escalating training demands on athletes, and the narrow specialization of training in one sport to the exclusion of other activities. Watch for the early signs of staleness and overtraining in your athletes, and assess your own energy levels and mental state to keep yourself committed in a positive, passionate way, as opposed to feeling the pressure of *having to* do things. Observe and listen to your athletes, and structure their training for optimal stress and optimal recovery. Provide them with some simple mental strategies such as goal mapping, energy management, or focus plans to help them keep the right perspective about their sport experiences.

Coaching for the Inner Edge with Injured Athletes

The second special recipe for coaching the Inner Edge involves helping injured athletes use mental strategies and skills to enhance their recovery and return to competition. When athletes get injured, the focus is on their physical recovery. But research has shown that athletes' mental recovery from injury is just as crucial, if not more crucial, in helping them get back to competitive form. Thus, your understanding of the relationship between mental skills and injury, your responses to your athletes' injuries and rehabilitation efforts, and your help in providing mental training strategies during injury rehabilitation are important responsibilities for coaching the Inner Edge.

Mental Skill Reduces Athletes' Vulnerability to Injury

We've spent a lot of time in this book talking about how mental training enhances athletes' performance, development, and experiences. Would you believe that mental skill also reduces athletes' vulnerability to injury? It's true. Athletes who experience more life stress and cope less effectively with these stressors are injured more frequently than athletes with lower stress and better coping skills (Williams, Rotella, & Scherzer, 2001). Conversely, athletes who are more focused and relaxed tend to be less injured than athletes with less productive mental states (Williams, Hogan, & Andersen, 1993). Pretty amazing!

We tend to think of injuries as random or instances of bad luck, or that they are caused by taking extreme risks. Although both of these points are somewhat true, the link between mental skills and injury indicates that injuries can be somewhat predicted by athletes' mental skills in competition (Williams et al., 2001). First of all, muscular tension increases an athlete's risk of injury, whereas a relaxed body is less susceptible to injury. Second, stress and anxiety narrow athletes' attentional focus, which reduces their ability to respond to peripheral dangers. Third, attentional distractions also lessen the task focus athletes need to be aware of things happening around them in the competitive environment.

When athletes engage in mental training, their injury risk decreases. For example, injuries were reduced by 52% for swimmers and 33% for football players during a season in which they practiced relaxation and imagery (Davis, 1991). Elite gymnasts who mentally trained in energy management skills were significantly less injured than gymnasts who did not mentally train (Kerr & Goss, 1996). Overall, mental skills help athletes adapt effectively to competitive stress and make them less vulnerable to injury.

Mental Training With Injured Athletes

Once athletes become injured, a productive mental approach by everyone is critical. Athletes' confidence and belief in their ability to recover is greatly influenced by the interactions they have with trainers and coaches. Coaches should respond to athletes as people ("How are you feeling about this?") as opposed to responding only to their injuries ("How's the knee?). Empathy is very important, particularly in the early stages of injury, to focus on the athletes' feelings and thoughts as opposed to focusing on how the injury will be "fixed." Because injured athletes often feel isolated and lose their sense of connection with the team, keep them as integrated within team activities

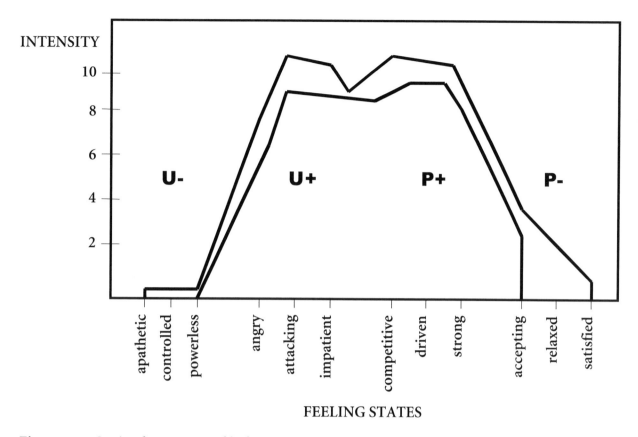

Figure 16.3 Optimal Energy Profile for injured athlete undergoing rehabilitation

as possible. If practical, injured athletes should attend training sessions, and instead of standing around on the perimeter, they should be involved in timing, providing feedback, and learning new strategies and tactics as they are taught by the coaches. In particular, injured athletes should use this time of physical inactivity to mentally rehearse as much as possible. They should imagine themselves performing the drills and plays in practice, and vividly feel and see their perfect performance responses.

Athlete responses to injuries. Athletes experience many forms of negative energy and thoughts when coping with severe injuries (e.g., Gould, Udry, Bridges, & Beck, 1997b; Tracey, 2003). These include questioning ("Will I make it back?"), feeling loss ("I'll miss my last tournament."), having difficulty watching others perform ("I should be there."), fear of losing their spot on the team, frustration, and anger. Two of the biggest mental obstacles are a sense of isolation from the team and the fear of re-injury. Interestingly, the mental stress experienced by in-

jured athletes is typically more difficult to cope with than the physical rehabilitation process itself (Gould et al., 1997b).

However, research has shown that athletes use unpleasant feeling states to enhance their recovery process (U+), much like they use unpleasant feeling states to create their optimal energy zones for competition. Feeling states like anger, impatience, and frustration seem to be related to athletes' urgency to return to their sports after injury, and can be used as positive energy during the long and difficult rehabilitation process (Wiese-Bjornstal, Smith, Shaffer, & Morrey, 1998). For example, as shown in Figure 16.3, an Optimal Energy Profile for an athlete undergoing rehabilitation from knee surgery includes high levels of unpleasant positive feelings (U + = *angry, attacking, impatient*) and low levels of pleasant negative feelings (P- = *accepting, relaxed, satisfied*). Athletes should develop their personal OEPs to describe the exact feeling states that they want to create to optimize their rehabilitation performance.

And they should think of it as performance. This is now their performance arena, and they should throw themselves into it using all of their physical and mental capacities just like they do in their sport performance. Every mental training tool and strategy presented in this book can and should be adapted and used by athletes undergoing injury rehabilitation. This is their game now, and the Inner Edge is just as important rehabbing on the sideline as it is performing between the lines!

Elite athletes have reported that despite the agonizing experience of injury and rehabilitation, they clearly gained important skills or perspectives that benefited them as athletes (Tracey, 2003; Udry, Gould, Bridges, & Beck, 1997). They described achieving personal growth and clarifying priorities, becoming mentally tougher and more resilient to obstacles, and even enhancing their physical skill development by learning to perform better and smarter. These feelings are captured in the following quotes by skiers that experienced major season-ending injuries:

> *"With my injury, I would say that I learned a whole new work ethic. My pain tolerance got much higher, and so my tolerance for training got a lot higher. So, I guess the injury helped shift my training up a notch"* (Udry et al., 1997, p. 230).
>
> *"The grass is always greener on the other side . . . When there is something that you can't have and that you want so badly, you start to work for it . . . When you are totally healthy and things are going great, you just can't work that hard. You have to really need and want something badly"* (Udry et al., 1997, p. 243).
>
> *"I don't think I would have been successful without the adversity and without those injuries because I needed that time to train mentally; it taught me a lot. It taught me that I have to take time out of my busy schedule to train mentally. I have to spend some time alone to prepare for what I'm going to do. It taught me how to climb through adversity, how to win, and to know how to win again"* (Orlick, 1998).

These quotes represent much more than reframing negative experiences. They truly are mentally productive responses to huge setbacks. I have always believed that people who have overcome adversity in their lives are advantaged with stronger internal "stuff" than those who have not yet weathered personal adversity. Coaches should "talk this talk" with

athletes and challenge them to respond with determination, focus, and the belief that something will be gained by persevering through their injuries. A key affirmation for this is "Adjust and find meaning" (Udry et al., 1997). It may sound existential, but that's what mentally skilled and emotionally tough individuals do in this life—they adjust and find meaning. A major characteristic of P³ Thinking is to always respond, as opposed to reacting with negative emotions or disruptive thoughts. Encourage athletes to respond to their injuries with determination, focus, a learning approach, and a sense of accomplishment and resilience that can serve them well when they return to competition.

Mental strategies for injured athletes. Research clearly supports the effectiveness of mental training in enhancing athletes' recovery from injuries (Cupal, 1998). Specifically, mental training has been shown to improve mood, optimize effort, enhance recovery time, and reduce pain, stress, and anxiety. One thing that mental training does for injured athletes is to give them something to do, which helps them become an ac-

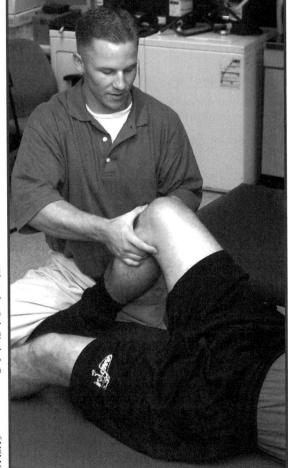

Photo by Cpl. Cindy L. Pray, courtesy of USMC

Table 16.1 Refocusing Worksheet for Injured Athletes

Situation or Distraction	Preferred Response	Focus or cue word (to bring on preferred response)
physical pain in rehab exercises	Use it (to get stronger!) Welcome it—it's good pain. Trust my trainer.	Pain is gain! Love it!
watching teammates and feeling that I'm losing ground/getting replaced	Can rebuild a stronger machine. Use this time—get mentally tough. I'll be stronger and more resilient. Focused mental training/ planning.	Coming back stronger! New attitude!
fear of re-injury pops up in workouts and hurts my performance	Feel the fear—it's normal. Face the fear—stare it down - response = strength and confidence.	Trust it! Beat it!

tive and empowered participant in the recovery process. Challenge athletes to focus their competitive energies and drive into performing well in this new game—the game of pushing their bodies to recover and gain new strength and perspective. Athletes experience more successful recoveries when they actively engage in mental training strategies such as energy management, focus plans, and imagery as compared to relying on others for social support through the process (Gould, Udry, Bridges, & Beck, 1997a).

Coaches or athletic trainers can assist athletes in developing rehabilitation goal maps, beginning with defining a sense of purpose for their recovery and including key milestone, challenge, and focus goals. Imagery can be used in many ways. Athletes should attend team training sessions, if possible and practical, and mentally rehearse all aspects of training that their teammates are doing. Injured athletes should use this recovery time to hone their Inner Edge, and a good way to do that is to engage in daily imagery practice. This may include mentally rehearsing skill repetitions, effective decision-making in competitive situations, and practicing focus plans, pre-performance routines, and refocusing responses to dis-

tractions. It may be helpful to develop refocusing responses for obstacles that occur during rehabilitation. As shown in Table 16.1, athletes can identify key situations in rehab that interfere with their desired focus, develop the responses they want to have in these situations, and create personalized focus cues to affirm a mentally tough attitude. Breathing exercises and conscious muscle control practice can be useful in managing pain and training athletes' bodies to relax and energize appropriately. Often, the abilities that athletes gain in managing bodily tension during rehabilitation can be applied to optimizing their bodily feelings during competition. The physical inactivity that frustrates athletes during injury rehabilitation should be seen as a key opportunity for mental training.

The final hurdle in injury rehabilitation is athletes' reentry into competition, and it is typical that their physical readiness is ahead of their mental readiness at this stage. Normalize the feelings that athletes express at this reentry stage, which often include doubt, fear of re-injury, anxiety, and a lower level of confidence than they are used to feeling. It is useful to create goal maps for reentry and to focus on reentry as a process, not one point in time. Athletes returning from serious injuries have reported that it took them up to six weeks after their first attempts at reentry to focus fully on their performance, have confidence in their injured body parts, and not be distracted by thoughts and fears of re-injury (Evans, Hardy, & Fleming, 2000). Make sure that they (and you) understand that reentry to competition after injury is a gradual process, in which their physical and mental energies, focus, confidence, and ultimately performance are warming up to get back to full speed. Athletes must focus on appropriate goals during this stage and avoid unrealistic expectations. The recovery process is not yet complete, and they should understand this and complete their recovery by gradually moving to optimal competitive form. They will get there!

Slumps

An issue that sends a lot of athletes to mental training consultants for help is the experience of performance slumps. A **slump** is *a decline in performance that athletes experience over a period of time that is atypical for them*. If a career .300 hitter in softball goes 3 for 30 in a period of games, she's in a slump. When athletes slump, questions abound: Is it physical or mental? Should she work harder or ease off? Should I talk to her about it or leave her alone? In the remainder of the section, several suggestions are provided to help athletes work through slumps.

1. Normalize slumps as inevitable, natural, and unavoidable. If you're an athlete, you're going to experience flow and peak performance, but you're also going to experience choking and slumps. That's why mental skill is so important: it makes athletes resistant to the highs and lows of sport participation. So let your athletes know that slumps are normal, but that they are temporary setbacks and will not last forever. The key is to accept them and respond appropriately.

2. Slumps are created by a variety of factors. A common response to slumps is to immediately and fervently search for the reason why the slump is occurring. Sometimes this is easy, such as when athletes adopt new equipment such a new golf driver, new skis, or a new bow in archery. Typically in these cases, athletes accept the "slump" as a normal performance regression due to the unfamiliar new equipment.

Sometimes a drop in performance results from a key technique error, such as "coming over the top" in the golf swing or pulling back instead of following through when shooting in basketball. Once athletes become aware of the error and correct it, their performance improves. Other factors influencing slumps include life stressors, such as family concerns and academic pressure. Often, athletes experience performance decrements when they have minor injuries, which keeps them from performing at their best and also can precipitate bad habits or problematic technique changes as the result of the injury.

3. Athletes' mental responses to their performance are the most important factor in dealing with slumps. Although many factors can contribute to slumps, athletes must understand that the most important thing for them is to respond productively when slumps or even off days occur. Bad days can become the foundation of slumps if they are mentally mishandled. For example, athletes can "will" themselves into a slump by exaggerating the poorness of their performance or failing to accept an off day as an off day (Taylor, 1988). Review Figure 14.1 in Chapter 14, which shows that confidence, as the mental modifier, allows athletes to accept off days and think productively as opposed to overreacting, second-guessing, worrying, and talking themselves into performance slumps. Confidence enables athletes to keep bad performances in perspective, accept them as unfortunate but "one of those things," and move forward both mentally and physically.

In the 1995 NBA playoffs, Nick Anderson of the Orlando Magic missed several critical free throws down the stretch of a key game. Anderson was shaken by these misses and allowed them to affect his confidence. He experienced a shooting slump during the next season and admitted that his slump was induced by his loss of confidence and inability to accept his critical free throw misses and move on. Conversely, Diana Taurasi, women's basketball player at the University of Connecticut, went 1 for 15 in field goal shooting as a freshman in the 2001 Final Four. However, she accepted it, even made fun of the absurdity of it, and immediately put her thoughts in forward motion to leave the bad performance behind (Deford, 2003). That is, she saw it as the anomaly that it was, accepted it as "not like me," and moved on. She then went on to win three national championships and twice became national player of the year. Like

Diana Taurasi, athletes should think of their bad performances as "not like me," yet learn from the experiences, remain mentally tough, and look forward to performing again. When I have a bad round in golf, all I want to do is to immediately play again, so I can "type over" that bad round in my head and get it out of there! Athletes should think of their next performance as a way of "whiting out," or "typing over" their previous bad performances.

Slumps occur when athletes have unproductive mental reactions to bad days. Athletes must learn to think well, not only when they get into slumps, but to make themselves as resistant as possible to slumps. Thus, P³ Thinking is a critical mental strategy for athletes. They must think productively after poor performances, and they must think productively when mired in slumps.

4. Don't use the S-word. A good strategy to use is to stop thinking about slumps as slumps (Bennett & Pravitz, 1987). Don't use the S-word. When athletes start focusing on the dreaded word "slump," and continuously think things like "What's wrong with me?", "Why I am in this slump?", or "I've lost my shot," they are affirming all these things to their subconscious. Their minds then fixate on the negative thoughts and images, which of course prolongs the slump or makes it worse.

Don't allow your athletes to use the S-word. Their performance might be a little off, they are grinding to perform well, or they are experiencing a temporary lapse, but it's natural, normal, to be expected, and they will come around. Don't give a slump life by naming it, or by fixating on it. A great example of this was Tiger Woods' performance during the 2003 professional golf season. As the number one golfer in the

world and winner of several major championships, Woods did not win a major in 2003 and the media started writing about his "slump." Woods repeatedly scoffed at the idea that he was in any kind of slump and refused to acknowledge and thus believe that he was. Ironically, Woods finished the 2003 season with the lowest scoring average in the world, was second in money earnings, and was named Player of the Year. So much for his so-called "slump"!

5. Athletes should use focus plans and focus goals to wire and engage their autopilot. Like choking, athletes in slumps tend to revert to controlled processing, because they're trying so hard to perform well they can't let go of conscious control (discussed in Chapter 12). Just like choking, the goal in overcoming slumps is to get back to smooth and easy autopilot and let performance happen freely. Athletes should create and work focus plans and mentally practice refocusing responses to distractions. As part of their goal maps, they should use their focus goals to lock into their autopilot performance mode and resist thinking about performance outcomes.

Coaches often question whether athletes experiencing slumps should step back and take time out to relax or whether they should train through the slump. I usually advocate a combination where the athlete focuses on a mental "time out" but continues with the physical repetitions of training. Mentally, the idea is to take the pressure off of thinking about performance (e.g., what's wrong, what's right), and just focus "inside" the performance itself. They should continue physical training, with the intent of engaging in numerous, quality, smooth, no-pressure repetitions of their performance. In other words, just play! *Let* it happen and quit trying to *make* it happen.

Continuing to engage in quality physical training and remaining mentally focused and productive during a performance slump is a difficult thing to ask athletes to do. Ask them anyway. I remind athletes of former U.S. swimmer Nancy Hogshead, who describes how she went two and half years without improving a single time in her events. Yet she kept getting in the water every day and went on to win four Olympic medals, including three golds in 1984 (Hogshead, 1999). Remind athletes that what happens to them is not as important as how they *respond* to what happens to them. Their responses to slumps will reflect a great deal about their ultimate commitment to being the best they

can be. As their coach, support them, but don't allow them to buy into the S-word and get caught up in the negativity surrounding it. Encourage and help them to respond like champions, because only by responding like one can they become one!

Inconsistency

If there were a surefire recipe for consistency in athletic performance, it would be served in every restaurant around the world! Inconsistency in athletes' performance is frustrating for both athletes and coaches. Who are the most consistent athletes you can think of? My thoughts turn to Chris Evert and Bonnie Blair. Chris Evert, multiple Grand Slam tennis champion, was known as the Ice Maiden for her consistent, make-no-mistakes approach to competitive tennis. As a baseliner, she was renowned for her machine-like accuracy and stamina, which would wear down opponents, even those that were more athletically gifted.

Bonnie Blair was known for her ultra-consistent pre-competition routines, which remained the same no matter what the event. Her coach Nick Thometz credits her work habits and lifestyle as reasons why she was best in the world in women's speed skating from 1988 to 1995 and won five Olympic gold medals (Rushin, 1994). As if to emphasize her consistency, she achieved a lifelong goal by breaking the 39-second barrier and skating a 38.99 at a 500-meter invitational meet in Calgary exactly one month *after* her gold medal performance at the Lillehammer Olympic Games. Fifty people saw her achieve this incredible milestone, which is a credit to Blair's mental skill of performing consistently at a high level no matter what the stakes.

Importance of Emphasizing Consistency

Consistency in performance is a mental and behavioral skill that is underemphasized in the glitzy world of 21st century sport. Competitive highlights shown on television glorify the flamboyant, not the consistent. However, coaches in all sports know that consistent performance throughout and across competitive events is the key to success. Sell this to your athletes. Baseball highlights show the home runs, but defense, pitching, and consistent offensive production win championships. Basketball highlights show the dunks and spectacular plays, but

solid team defense and consistent offensive effectiveness (e.g., repeatedly hitting those boring 15-foot jump shots and free throws!) win championships. Tennis highlights show the booming aces and between the legs winners, but consistency in holding serve and grinding out precision ground strokes wins championships. Before athletes become consistent, they must understand what consistency is and the type of consistency in performance that is most important in their sport.

What Consistency Means

Consistent performance requires consistent thoughts, focus, feelings, and behavior. It requires consistent mental and physical preparation. It requires systematically following focus plans (Chapter 12). It requires systematically using refocusing strategies to manage situations that lead to inconsistency (Orlick, 1986). It requires a consistent self-image, where athletes know who they are and play to their strengths. Inconsistency occurs when athletes deviate from their game plans and try to be what they are not. And finally, consistent performance requires consistent preparation. Many times athletes complain about being inconsistent, yet they have not practiced at a high level of performance consistency, and thus their performance is not inconsistent at all. If fact, it is consistent with how they practice! If a golfer is not a good putter, and fails to consistently practice putting, then he can't say he's inconsistent when he doesn't putt well during competition.

Athletes should first establish what is consistent for them. Consistency should be defined as a *range* of effective performance for each athlete. It also involves a range of effort, feelings, confidence, thoughts, and focus. Athletes can control their consistency through effort and energy management, if nothing else. For example, basketball players may shoot inconsistently during a game, but they can be consistent in their defense and hustle. Golfers can putt inconsistently during a round, but they can mentally grind to work their focus, hit fairways, and play as consistently as possible with whatever game they have that day.

Responding to Inconsistencies

Although it sounds paradoxical, athletes must learn to respond consistently to their inconsistencies. A champion tennis player who double faults at a crucial moment must respond productively by seeing this performance gaffe as an anomaly, or as inconsistent with who they are and how they typically perform. The player should then accept the error (this doesn't mean they like it but accept that it happened), refocus to the current task, and move on mentally and behaviorally. When things happen that are unexpected or inconsistent with what athletes are used to, they must respond productively. This requires mental skill and mental preparation for unexpected occurrences (Chapter 13).

Help athletes sort out what things interfere with their consistency. A softball player told me that her hitting would become inconsistent when she focused on hitting for power, such as attempting to hit home runs when teammates were in scoring position. When she focused on driving the ball, her swing was smoother, more on plane, and she hit better. Thus, we developed a focus plan and pre-performance routine for her to channel her thoughts, images, and feelings into driving the ball. As discussed in Chapter 13, high intensities of competitive energy can interfere with performance, even if they feel pleasant (e.g., excitement). Athletes should carefully

© iStockphoto.com

monitor their Optimal Energy Profiles, because consistency in energy and feeling states across competition leads to consistency in performance.

"Playing to the Level"

A common type of inconsistency with athletes is "playing to the level of the competition" (Bennett & Pravitz, 1987). This refers to athletes or teams who lack consistency in performance because they perform just well enough to win. When athletes or teams compete against weaker opponents, their performance drops and is inconsistent with their performance against stronger opponents. "Playing to the level of competition" means that athletes are allowing the situation to manage them, as opposed to them managing the situation. The actual competition, in terms of winning and losing, doesn't demand consistency. Rather, athletes have to demand it from themselves. They must realize that "playing to the level" will catch up with them when they lose an important competition that they should have won because they failed to be mentally and behaviorally consistent.

Orlick (1986) provides an example of an alpine skier who "played to the level" because she performed better on more difficult and challenging courses, while performing poorly in less challenging situations. By observing her performances, competitive energy, and mental focus across competitions, she realized that her inconsistency was based on her lower than optimal energy states for courses that were less challenging. She made the classic mistake of relying on the external competitive challenge to get her energized and focused, as opposed to taking personal responsibility to get herself energized and focused, no matter what the situation. To her credit, she identified a key mental focus strategy by stating, "Maybe I have to work harder when it's easier" (p. 93). Athletes have to work harder to create the competitive energy states that are optimal for them when they don't naturally occur as the result of competitive excitement and challenge. They have to create optimal energy zones and a sharp mental focus for themselves, no matter what opponent they are facing.

Overall, consistent performance is achieved by being consistent in physical and mental preparation. Encourage athletes to work their goal maps to push their personal performance envelopes in every competition. The greatest compliment that can be given to athletes is that they never "take a day off," which is a testament to their consistency of effort, focus, and performance. Help athletes understand that with every peak of emotion, there usually is a corresponding valley. Help them smooth out their energy and focus levels to avoid the highs and inevitable lows of competition, and instead train to maintain a consistent mental and physical approach to competition, as well as consistent and productive responses to things that occur in competition. It might sound boring, but boring is consistent, and consistency rocks!

Perfectionism

Most coaches want athletes in their programs to be perfectionists. Well, sort of. That is, they want athletes who *have high personal standards of achievement and behave with intense effort and drive to reach these high personal standards*. The problem with **perfectionism** is that it's a double-edged sword.

Positive and Negative Perfectionism

Research shows that there are two types of perfectionism: negative and positive (Blatt, 1995; Hamachek, 1978). Positive perfectionism means that athletes set high personal standards of achievement, are driven to succeed, are highly motivated to do their best, and get pleasure from the efforts of pursuing goals. In addition, positive perfectionists take their performance setbacks in stride and accept that they cannot and do not always perform perfectly.

Negative perfectionism means that athletes set high personal standards of achievement, but they focus on avoiding failure, leave themselves little freedom to make mistakes, are overly critical in evaluating their performance, and rarely feel good about their performance even when they give their best effort. For these reasons, negative perfectionists are prone to feelings of inadequacy and performance problems. High-level achievement in sport requires risk-taking and worry-free performance, and the achievement of negative perfectionists is stunted because they focus on avoiding mistakes, as opposed to making things happen. Negative perfectionism leads to competitive anxiety, burnout, social physique anxiety (worrying about negative evaluations of one's body), and even disordered eating habits in athletes (Frost & Henderson, 1991; Gould et al., 1996; Haase, Prapavessis, & Owens, 2002).

Identifying Negative Perfectionist Athletes

Negative perfectionist athletes are easy to spot (McCann, 1998). They often give up early after they make a mistake. I once consulted with a golfer who would quit and start his round over if he had a bad hole. Of course, it was hard to train his mental refocusing skills when he simply quit and started over! Negative perfectionists also may avoid pressure situations. They would like to be the hero, but the prospect of being the goat prevents them from trying. Obviously, negative perfectionists also struggle with anxiety and negative energy states that prevent them from achieving their optimal energy zones for competition. Athletes high in negative perfectionism also may be identified by their self-talk. They typically engage in a lot of reactive thinking ("I have to play perfectly"), and coaches should counter athletes' unrealistic and irrational thinking by using REBT-type questions such as "How does thinking you have to play perfectly help you?"

Coaching Negative Perfectionistic Athletes

Coaches must help negative perfectionistic athletes to refocus in more productive ways. McCann (1998) suggests that coaches can help athletes define mistakes in ways that motivate them to focus on success, as opposed to avoiding failure. For example, basketball players can learn that passing up an open shot is a bigger mistake than missing the shot. When athletes assert themselves in pressure situations, coaches should reinforce their behaviors. When developing focus plans for negative perfectionistic athletes, the focus of attention should be on the specific behaviors the athletes will engage in, *not* the behaviors they want to avoid (McCann, 1998). Overall, these athletes need to understand that trying to play their best, and accepting what their best is each day, is far better than trying to be perfect. As most coaches know, trying to play perfectly is often the worse thing an athlete can do (McCann, 1998)!

Clipboard

Perfectionist Mia Hamm

Mia Hamm, leading scorer in elite women's soccer, achieved greatness and battled personal demons because of her perfectionism. Just prior to the 1999

World Cup, Hamm, the most prolific scorer in soccer history, failed to score during eight consecutive matches for the U.S. team. Twice during that time, the United States lost to its main rival, China. Hamm's coach, Tony DiCicco, observed that Hamm's behavior on the field changed. She seemed reluctant to challenge defenders and seemed hesitant with the ball. DiCicco stated, "Mia, because she is so hypercritical, has always had to deal at times with less confidence than she wants. She puts so much demand on herself. It's why she's the greatest scorer in history. But those high standards are hard to reach on a consistent basis. If she doesn't feel she can reach those demands, she feels inadequate. It wears on her. I respect how she got through the year. It was a tremendous mental battle for her."

Hamm admits that she's a perfectionist and describes how it turned against her in 1999: "I want to do things as perfectly as I can. Obviously, it's not going to happen, but it's a good source of motivation. Sometimes it can work against me . . . I wasn't enjoying what I was doing . . . I was worried about what people outside my support system were saying. I needed to go out and play for the reason I always played, because I loved what I do. I lost sight of that . . . I wasn't having any fun out there. I was critiquing every little thing I did. Tony was great. He told me we had a lot of time, it wasn't the end of the world. [He said,] 'Quit putting so much pressure on yourself. We'll take it one step at a time.'" Hamm played brilliantly in the 1999 and the 2003 World Cup tournaments. But she's a great example of a world-class athlete who fights to keep the negative aspects of her perfectionism from overriding the positive, which drove her to be the exceptional athlete that she is (Hamm & Heifetz, 2000, p. 125).

Commitment

The last special recipe issue is probably the toughest one. How can we help athletes enhance their commitment to being the best they can be in their sport? How can we get athletes to commit to the team, and the goals and mission of the team? Probably the most important question is this: Is it possible to enhance athletes' commitment or is it something that they just "have?" Like all mental skills, some athletes are and will always be more committed than others. However, I believe we can help athletes enhance their commitment by making it more behavioral, more describable, and less abstract. Commitment has to be more than a word written on the locker room wall—it has to be defined for athletes in specific terms so they understand what commitment actually looks like.

What is Commitment?

Commitment and motivation are closely related, so rereading Chapter 3 on motivation may be helpful. But while motivation can be thought of as the force of water running through a garden hose, commitment is the purposeful, efficient, and persistent use of the water in very focused and productive ways. Or you can think of motivation as a ball of energy inside athletes' bodies, which fuels their commitment in the form of a focused, precise, white-hot laser beam that is applied to achieve specific goals. Athletes can be motivated, yet lack commitment if they cannot apply the energy of motivation in laser-like ways to train with intensity and persistence.

Commitment also involves will, or a strong and fixed purpose. This sense of purpose binds athletes to their sport in almost mystical ways. Pete Sampras' display of emotion at his retirement ceremony at the 2003 U.S. Open demonstrated his deep commitment to and love for the game of tennis, which had defined his life up to that moment. Athletes base their commitment on their love of the game, their personal investment in their sport, the opportunities they've gained, and their clear sense that they play because they want to, not just because of obligation (Scanlan, Russell, Beals, & Scanlan, 2003). Athletes describe their commitment as meaning that no priorities are more attractive, and this is often the distinguishing feature between those athletes who are truly committed and those who just "talk the talk."

Without question, the most distinguishing characteristic of world-class, successful athletes is their commitment (Orlick, 2000; Orlick & Partington, 1988; Scanlan, Russell, Wilson, & Scanlan, 2003). Best stated by a member of the highly elite and world famous All Black rugby team of New Zealand, "[Commitment] is probably about 85 to 90% of my success . . . probably the start and the finish of sport at an elite level is commitment" (Scanlan et al., 2003, p. 375).

Quotable Quote

"There are only two options . . . you're either in or you're out; there's no such thing as in between." **Karch Kiraly**, Olympic volleyball champion on commitment *(Kiraly, 1999)*

But we can't force athletes to commit—only they can do that. So what can we do?

Building Commitment in Athletes

First of all, athletes have to see what commitment is when they look at their coaches. Whatever you want their commitment to be, you must be that. This might include your commitment to your program, to your athletes, to your family, and to your health. Second, coaches have to define commitment for athletes so they understand what commitment looks like. What does commitment look like in this team? What behaviors do we engage in that demonstrates our commitment? These could include intensity and focus in training, no matter what else is happening in athletes' lives. It could include P³ Thinking at all times during training and competition. It could include taking personal responsibility for being on time, working hard when the coach isn't watching, and beginning the season with a strong and conditioned body. It could include specific expectations for interpersonal communication with each other (see Chapter 4). A team I consulted with made the commitment to forego desserts (or any type of sweets) during their entire competitive season. I asked about this, because for many of the athletes the extra calories presented no problem to maintaining weight for competition. They informed me that it was a team commitment, and something that they did to demonstrate their commitment to each other, especially those athletes who were working to maintain optimal competitive weights.

Clipboard

Commitment as Defined by NHL Coaches and Scouts

Following are some of the behavioral examples of the type of commitment that coaches and scouts in the National Hockey League feel are prerequisites

for excellence in professional ice hockey (excerpts from Orlick, 2000, p. 45):

- Does constant work on the ice; is in on the action, always after the puck, the check, or the goal; gives a little extra when it is important.
- Never gives up (for example, takes a check, gets back into the play quickly, tries and tries again).
- Plans, evaluates, and corrects with line mates on the bench; encourages others.
- Takes tips, asks questions, listens, admits errors and corrects them without excuses; shows that he wants to learn.
- Pursues activities both in and out of season to maintain conditioning and improve skills (fitness training, power skating).
- Learns how to come back and play well after a setback, mistake, missed chance, call against him or team, or bad penalty.
- Learns to control temper (for example, does not needlessly retaliate after a hit or setback). Learns to respond to referee, coach, teammates, and fans in a mature way, especially in big games.
- Learns to stay cool and confident under pressure (for example, is not moody and not a worrier).

A good exercise for a team is to write out their covenant, or their specific definition of commitment for their team for that season (see example in Chapter 6). In this team covenant, athletes specifically describe key behavioral examples of commitment that they believe in and pledge to follow. Another way to do this is to talk of commitment as a mission, and ask athletes to define their mission each day by focusing on one or two key things for that training session (Ravizza & Hanson, 1995). A variation on this is to ask athletes to define the key mission for the team for each training session, and then ask athletes to grade themselves on how well they fulfilled their stated mission during that session. Another useful exercise at the beginning of the season is to ask the team to visualize the end of the season banquet where the coach describes the team's season (Ravizza & Hanson, 1995). Ask athletes to identify what they would like to hear said about their team. Challenge them to commit to that, and ask how they will exactly practice this commitment. Ask each athlete to identify what he or she would like to hear said about him or her. Then tell them, "Okay, commit to that!"

After identifying behaviors that define their commitment, teams could also put these behavioral descriptions into a checklist format. An example behavioral checklist is shown in Appendix 16A (adapted from Martin & Toogood, 1997), titled the "Act Like Champions Checklist." As seen in the checklist, athletes identify behaviors that define their commitment to being champions. The checklist is then used at two or three practices each week to ensure that they follow through on their commitment every day in training. The trick is to get athletes to buy into using the checklist as a self-evaluative exercise to enhance their commitment. Coaches shouldn't use the checklist to berate athletes or "check up on them." When I use it with teams, each athlete posts her checklist in her locker and quietly monitors herself over a period of time. The intent of the checklist is to make athletes reflective and responsible for their own behavior, and to learn to practice their commitment daily. It's a reminder of what they want to be, and how they want to act.

A final example is an off-season or early preseason exercise that asks athletes to evaluate their commitment. It begins by defining commitment in a certain way, asking athletes to evaluate themselves and then identify strategies to strengthen their commitment both physically and mentally. This commitment evaluation would be a nice lead-in to the development of personal goal maps for the season. The use of goal maps, including goal achievement strategies, is one of the best ways that athletes can define and chart their commitment (see Chapter 8).

Don't ever let athletes off the hook when they tell you that they're committed. Immediately ask them what they've done, what they are doing today, and what they will do to "walk" their commitment. You can't ever force commitment, but you can help athletes understand what it looks like and prescribe ways for them to develop and deepen their commitment. You've then done your part—the rest is up to them!

Wrapping Up

Coaches need a lot of special recipes for mental training. The ones offered in this chapter are for the typical situations that come up in any sport team. Helping athletes return from injury, deal with slumps, burnout, and negative perfectionism, and become more consistent and more committed requires a lot of coaching skill and knowledge. I hope some of the ideas presented in this chapter help you in dealing with these special issues. However, remember that many of the ideas presented in this chapter (and book) come from outstanding coaches. You are in the best position to take the basic ideas from the information in this book and apply them in your own innovative ways. Develop your own recipes for the Inner Edge! Good luck!

Summary Points for Chapter 16

1. Burnout is characterized by mental and physical exhaustion, negative feelings, negative change in responses to others, perceived lack of accomplishment, and disillusionment or amotivation.

2. Staleness and overtraining are progressive phases of non-adaptation to stress, which often leads to burnout.

3. Personality characteristics that make athletes and coaches susceptible to burnout are feeling trapped in sport participation, negative perfectionism, and a narrow self-concept.

4. The increasing emphasis on specialized and heavy training creates an environment conducive to burnout.

5. Athletes who are less mentally skilled and cope less effectively with stress are injured more frequently than athletes with better mental and coping skills.

6. Athletes respond to injuries with a range of feeling, including positive perspectives of priorities, mental toughness, and resilience to future obstacles.

7. Mental training enhances athletes' recovery from injury by improving mood, optimizing effort, enhancing recovery time, and reducing pain and anxiety.

8. Athletes can use the same mental training tools and skills learned for performance enhancement in their rehabilitation from injury.

9. Slumps, which are declines in performance over a period of time, are inevitable and normal.

10. The key mental factor in overcoming slumps is to respond effectively to poor performance or a prolonged slump.

11. Athletes can improve their performance consistency by enhancing the consistency of their mental approach to competition.

12. Positive perfectionism involves high standards of performance, yet the acceptance of performance mistakes.

13. Negative perfectionism also involves high standards of performance, but a focus on avoiding failure and an overconcern about making mistakes.

14. Coaches must help negative perfectionist athletes refocus in more productive ways, such as by redefining mistakes and becoming more assertive in pressure situations.

15. Coaches and athletes identify highly skilled athletes as higher in leadership ability.

16. Although coaches can attempt to enhance leadership ability by specifying critical leader behaviors for the team, they should not force leadership roles of a certain type on athletes who are uncomfortable in those roles.

17. Athletes can be motivated, yet lack commitment if they cannot apply the energy of motivation to train with intensity and persistence.

18. Coaches must find ways to specifically and behaviorally define what commitment is within a particular team or program.

Glossary

burnout: the result of chronic non-adaptation to training and competitive demands, characterized by physical, mental, and emotional exhaustion, negative feelings and responses to others, a perceived lack of accomplishment, and disillusionment with sport participation

overtraining: when athletes train beyond a level that is ideal for maximum benefits to their performance

perfectionism: having high personal standards of achievement and behaving with intense effort and drive to reach these high personal standards

slump: a decline in performance that athletes experience over a period of time that is atypical for them

staleness: typically a short-term condition in which athletes lose vigor and performance effectiveness because they are bored with or worn down by the tedious and familiar nature of the repetitive training that is necessary for athletic excellence

Study Questions

1. Explain why burnout is a long-term response to athletes' inability to adapt to stress or competitive demands.

2. Why are some athletes more susceptible to burnout than others?

3. What can coaches do to help athletes avoid burnout, and what can they do to help athletes who are experiencing burnout?

4. What are some possible explanations for why mental skill reduces athletes' vulnerability to injuries?

5. Give some specific examples of how mental training tools and skills can be used to help athletes who are recovering from injuries.

6. What are three key things coaches can do to help athletes avoid and/or manage performance slumps?

7. Why are athletes inconsistent in performance, and what are some mental strategies to enhance athletes' consistency?

8. Distinguish between good and bad perfectionism. What are some ways that a coach can respond to negatively perfectionistic athletes to help them?

9. Is it possible to develop leadership in athletes, and if so, how can coaches do this?

10. Identify several strategies for building commitment in athletes.

Reflective Learning Activities

1. The Psychodoping of Athletes

In an article on burnout in adolescent athletes, Jay Coakley (1992) suggested that mentally training athletes was a form of "psychodoping" that is largely ineffective because burnout is based on the problematic structure of sport. His point seemed to be that sport psychology is providing athletes a "band-aid" that is largely ineffective due to the huge injurious nature of organized sport, and that the only way to combat burnout is to change the structure of sport.

Do you agree with Coakley? Why or why not? If you do agree, what then should be done to solve the burnout problem? If you don't agree, what can coaches and sport psychologists do to take into account the structural problems in sport that lead to athletes' burnout? (Discuss in groups of 3-15 minutes)

2. Coaching the Inner Edge with Injuries

a. Describe a specific injury to an athlete in a specific sport (e.g., knee, shoulder, back, broken bone). The injury is season-ending, and occurs at the beginning of the season.

b. Develop a comprehensive mental training program for this athlete during their recovery and up to the point of reentry into competition. Be specific in describing how the athlete will use various mental training tools and skills. (Complete individually or in pairs)

3. Create Your Own Recipe

Choose a specific issue faced by coaches that was not covered in the chapter. Develop guidelines and/or a plan for how coaches can use the mental training ideas from this book to effectively address this issue. (Groups of 3-20 minutes)

4. Nature or Nurture?

The case was made in the chapter that commitment can be taught to athletes. Do you agree with this? In small groups, discuss the innate vs. learned nature of commitment. In particular, try to identify what aspects can be learned (if any) and what aspects are more innate (if any).

Postscript

Postscript

Here are some parting words about coaching for the Inner Edge. These tips come from small college, Division I college, and Olympic coaches (Burns, 2001; "Critical coaching," 2003; Krzyzewski, 2000; Wooden, 1997), who say it much better than I could. I agree these are wise words, and a good postscript for the book. Good luck, and good coaching!

1. Remind your athletes before each competition to enjoy the experience.
2. Be an example. Act like a champion, with class, passion, and professionalism.
3. No matter how much pressure you feel, don't stop caring about people.
4. Be reliable and dependable, even if you are tired and overworked.
5. Be a good psychologist; listen to what your athletes need.
6. Show self-discipline, in all areas.
7. If you don't know, say so.
8. Do planning, then plan again, then modify the plan.
9. De-escalate crisis.
10. Teach your athletes the wonderful freedom that comes from learning to lose with grace and dignity and without excuse.
11. Have a detailed plan—then sell it.
12. Laugh! Keep your sense of humor. Your athletes need it.
13. Have the courage to say no when the answer is no.
14. Show some passion on occasion. They have to know you care.
15. Convey to your players the intrinsic honor that comes from training and playing hard.
16. Keep in mind that the joy of winning fades immediately and precipitously.
17. Don't posture—a confident person need not convince anybody of anything.
18. Convey to your athletes your love of the game.
19. Be consistent in behavior, communication, and preparation.
20. Always finish positive with athletes when giving corrections.
21. At the end of every season, thank your team for their effort.
22. Be confident, act confident.
23. Listen to your athletes when you're too tired to listen.
24. Focus on the controllable.
25. Plan for the unexpected.
26. Set your standards early and don't compromise them.
27. Believe in your athletes.
28. The single most intimidating element of competition, aside from raw talent, is a team working and playing hard for the entire game.
29. Find a kind way to tell your athletes the blunt truth.
30. Speak succinctly. Don't lose track of the value of being uncomplicated.
31. Where there is a will, there is not always a way—but sometimes there is.
32. Don't second guess yourself—make the best decision you can and move on.
33. Make game day your best day.
34. It is unnecessary to raise your voice to be heard if your athletes believe you have something important to say.
35. Winning is overrated, and the singular quest for it leads to unhappiness.
36. Confrontation simply means meeting the truth head-on.
37. Embrace the heck out of personal responsibility.
38. It's the perfection of the smallest details that make big things happen.

39. Understand that the harder you work, the more luck you will have.

40. Fairness is giving athletes the treatment they earn and deserve.

41. Too may rules get in the way . . . people set rules to keep from making decisions.

42. Teach your athletes that peace of mind is a result of giving all that they have.

43. Greet each athlete personally at the beginning of training each day.

44. Believe in yourself!

45. Deal with a little negative thing immediately—before it becomes a big negative thing.

46. Balance praise and criticism—too much of either can be harmful.

47. A leader has to show the face his team needs to see.

48. Don't allow one or two athletes to ruin things for the rest of the team.

49. When things go wrong for you and your team, assume responsibility.

50. Every season is a journey. Live it with exuberance and excitement. Live it right.

Resource Guide for Coaches

Coaching Books Related to the Inner Edge

DiCicco, T., & Hacker, C. (2002). *Catch them being good.* New York: Penguin.

Dorfman, H. A. (2003). *Coaching the mental game.* Lanham, MD: Taylor Trade.

Dorrance, A., & Averbuch, G. (2002). *The vision of a champion.* Ann Arbor, MI: Huron River Press. (soccer)

Gregg, L. (1999). *The champion within.* Burlington, NC: JTC Sports. (soccer)

Janssen, J., & Dale, G. (2002). *The seven secrets of successful coaches.* Cary, NC: Winning the Mental Game.

Leith, L. M. (2003). *The psychology of coaching team sports.* Toronto: Sport Books.

Lynch, J. (2001). *Creative coaching.* Champaign, IL: Human Kinetics.

Coaching Philosophy and Leadership

Biro, B. D. (1997). *Beyond success: The 15 secrets to effective leadership and life based on legendary coach John Wooden's pyramid of success.* New York: Perigee.

Goleman, D., Boyatzis, R., & McKee, A. (2002). *Primal leadership.* Boston: Harvard Business School.

Krzyzewski, M. (2000). *Leading with the heart.* New York: Warner.

Maxwell, J. C. (1998). *The 21 irrefutable laws of leadership: Follow them and people will follow you.* Nashville: Thomas Nelson.

Murphy, S. (1999). *The cheers and the tears: A healthy alternative to the dark side of youth sports today.* San Francisco: Jossey-Bass.

Summitt, P. (1998). *Raise the roof.* New York: Broadway.

Thompson, J. (2003). *The double-goal coach.* New York: HarperCollins.

Wooden, J. (1997). *Wooden: A lifetime of observations and reflections on and off the court.* Lincolnwood, IL: Contemporary.

Team Building

Heermann, B. (1997). *Building team spirit.* New York: McGraw-Hill.

Janssen, J. (2002). *Championship team building.* Cary, NC: Winning the Mental Game.

Rohnke, K., & Butler, S. (1995). *Quicksilver: Adventure games, initiative problems, trust activities and a guide to effective leadership.* Dubuque, IA: Kendall/Hunt.

Athletes' Views on the Inner Edge

Naber, J. (1999). *Awaken the Olympian within.* Torrance, CA: Griffin.

Books for Athletes on the Inner Edge

Orlick T. (2000). *In pursuit of excellence* (3rd ed.). Champaign, IL: Human Kinetics.

Porter, K. (2003). *The mental athlete.* Champaign, IL: Human Kinetics.

Sport-Specific Books on the Inner Edge

Beswick, B. (2001). *Focused for soccer.* Champaign, IL: Human Kinetics.

Miller, S. L. (2003). *Hockey tough.* Champaign, IL: Human Kinetics. (ice hockey)

Ravizza, K., & Hanson, T. (1995). *Heads-up baseball: Playing the game one pitch at a time.* Lincolnwood, IL: Masters Press.

Sport Psychology Textbooks

Gill, D. L. (2000). *Psychological dynamics of sport and exercise* (2nd ed.). Champaign, IL: Human Kinetics.

Lidor, R., & Henschen, K. P. (2003). *The psychology of team sports.* Morgantown, WV: Fitness Information Technology.

Weinberg, R. S., & Gould, D. (2003). *Foundations of sport and exercise psychology* (3rd ed.). Champaign, IL: Human Kinetics.

Williams, J. M. (Ed.). (2001). *Applied sport psychology: Personal growth to peak performance* (4th ed.). Mountain View, CA: Mayfield.

Managing Energy

Davis, M., Eshelman, E., & McKay, M. (2000). *The relaxation & stress workbook* (5th ed.). Oakland: New Harbinger.

Hanin, Y. L. (Ed.). (2000). *Emotions in sport.* Champaign, IL: Human Kinetics.

Jackson, S. A., & Csikszentmihalyi, M. (1999). *Flow in sports.* Champaign, IL: Human Kinetics.

McKay, M., & Rogers, P. (2000). *The anger control workbook.* Oakland: New Harbinger.

P³ Thinking

Ellis, A., & Harper, R. A. (1997). *A guide to rational living.* Hollywood, CA: Wilshire.

Maxwell, J. C. (2003). *Thinking for a change.* New York: Warner.

Seligman, M. E. P. (1998). *Learned optimism.* New York: Free Press.

Seligman, M. E. P. (2002). *Authentic happiness.* New York: Free Press.

Academic Books on Coaching

Jones, R., Armour, K., & Potrac, Paul. (2004). *Sports coaching cultures.* London: Routledge.

Lyle, J. (2002). *Sports coaching concepts.* New York: Routledge.

Websites for Coaching and Sport Psychology Resources

www.aaasponline.org (Association for the Advancement of Applied Sport Psychology website, a professional organization of sport psychology researchers and consultants)

www.jeffjanssen,com (books, videotapes, audiotapes related to the Inner Edge)

www.mindtools.com (Inner Edge resources)

www.peaksports.com (Inner Edge resources developed by Dr. Patrick Cohn)

www.positivecoach.org (site of Positive Coaching Alliance)

References

Abernathy, B. (2001). Attention. In R.N. Singer, H.A. Hausenblas, & C.M. Janelle (Eds.), *Handbook of sport psychology* (2nd ed., pp. 53-85). New York: Wiley.

Albrecht, R. R., & Feltz, D. L. (1987). Generality and specificity of attention related to competitive anxiety and sport performance. *Journal of Sport Psychology, 9,* 231-248.

Allen, J. B., & Howe, B. L. (1998). Player ability, coach feedback, and female adolescent athletes' perceived competence and satisfaction. *Journal of Sport & Exercise Psychology, 20,* 280-299.

Amorose, A. J., & Horn, T. S. (2000). Intrinsic motivation: Relationships with collegiate athletes' gender, scholarship status, and perceptions of their coaches' behavior. *Journal of Sport and Exercise Psychology, 22,* 63-84.

Andersen, M. B. (2001). When to refer athletes for counseling or psychotherapy. In J.M. Williams (Ed.), *Applied sport psychology: Personal growth to peak performance* (pp. 401-415). Mountain View, CA: Mayfield.

Anderson, M. P. (1959). What is communication? *The Journal of Communication, 9,* 5.

Annesi, J. J. (1998). Applications of the individual zones of optimal functioning model for the multimodal treatment of precompetitive anxiety. *The Sport Psychologist, 12,* 300-316.

Apter, M. J. (1982). *The experience of motivation: The theory of psychological reversals.* London: Academic Press.

Armstrong, L. (2001). *It's not about the bike.* New York: Berkley.

Atkinson, J. W. (1974). The mainstream of achievement-oriented activity. In J.W. Atkinson & J. O. Raynor (Eds.), *Motivation and achievement* (pp. 13-41). New York: Halstead.

Bakker, F. C., Boschker, M. S. J., & Chung, T. (1996). Changes in muscular activity while imagining weight lifting using stimulus or response propositions. *Journal of Sport & Exercise Psychology, 18,* 313-324.

Bandura, A. (1997). *Self-efficacy: The exercise of control.* New York: Freeman.

Barnett, N. P., Smoll, F. L., & Smith, R. E. (1992). Effects of enhancing coach-athlete relationships on youth sport attrition. *The Sport Psychologist, 6,* 111-127.

Baumeister, R. F. (1984). Choking under pressure: Self-consciousness and paradoxical effects of incentives on skillful performance. *Journal of Personality and Social Psychology, 16,* 361-383.

Becker, B. (1998, March). The price of greatness. *Tennis,* pp. 50-55.

Beilock, S. L., Afremow, J. A., Rabe, A. L., & Carr, T. H. (2001). "Don't miss!" The debilitating effects of suppressive imagery on golf putting performance. *Journal of Sport & Exercise Psychology, 23,* 200-221.

Bendaly, L. (1996). *Games team play: Dynamic activities for tapping work team potential.* New York: McGraw-Hill.

Bennett, J. G., & Pravitz, J. E. (1987). *The profile of a winner: Advanced mental training for athletes.* Ithaca, NY: Sport Science International.

Bergandi, T. A., Shryock, M. G., & Titus, T. G. (1990). The Basketball Concentration Survey: Preliminary instrument development and validation. *The Sport Psychologist, 4,* 119-129.

Best Tip. (2004, February). *Golf Digest,* p. 14.

Bird, L. (1989). *Drive: The story of my life.* New York: Bantam.

Bird, A. M., & Horn, M. A. (1990). Cognitive anxiety and mental errors in sport. *Journal of Sport & Exercise Psychology, 12,* 217-222.

Biro, B. D. (1997). *Beyond success.* New York: Perigee.

Blank, W. (1995). *The 9 natural laws of leadership.* New York: Amacon.

Blatt, S. J. (1995). The destructiveness of perfectionism: Implications for the treatment of depression. *American Psychologist, 50,* 1003-1020.

Blatnick, J. (1999). Escape, counter, and attack. In J. Naber (Ed.), *Awaken the Olympian within* (pp. 44-53). Torrance, CA: Griffin.

Bloom, B. S. (1985). *Developing talent in young people.* New York: Ballantine.

Bloom, G. A., Durand-Bush, N., & Salmela, J. H. (1997). Pre- and postcompetition routines of expert coaches of team sports. *The Sport Psychologist, 11,* 127-141.

Botterill, C., & Patrick, T. (2003). Understanding and managing emotions in team sports. In R. Lidor & K. P. Henschen (Eds.), *The psychology of team sports* (pp. 115-130). Morgantown, WV: Fitness Information Technology.

Boutcher, S. H. (2002). Attentional processes and sport performance. In T.S. Horn (Ed.), *Advances in sport psychology* (2nd ed., pp. 441-457). Champaign, IL: Human Kinetics.

Bull, S. J. (1989). The role of the sport psychology consultant: A case study of ultra distance running. *The Sport Psychologist, 3,* 254-264.

Bump, L. A. (1989). *American Coaching Effectiveness Program master series sport psychology study guide.* Champaign, IL: Human Kinetics.

Burnett, J. (1997, September/October). The lady is a champ. *Golf for Women,* pp. 20-22.

Burns, R. (2001, June 4). Top 25 (or so) truths for college coaches. *The NCAA News,* p. 4.

Burton, D. (1989). Winning isn't everything: Examining the impact of performance goals on collegiate swimmers' cognitions and performance. *The Sport Psychologist, 3,* 105-132.

999). How to win your personal decathlon. In J.
 , *Awaken the Olympian within* (pp. 95-104).
 : Griffin.

 ...an, M. M., Wheeler, J. & Stevens, D. (2002).
 ...performance in sport: A meta analysis. *Jour-*
 Exercise Psychology, 24, 168-188.

 ..., ... (1993). Leadership. In R. N. Singer, M. Murphey,
& L. K. Tennant (Eds.), *Handbook of research on sport psy-*
chology (pp. 647-671). New York: Macmillan.

Cleary, T. J., & Zimmerman, B. J. (2001). Self-regulation differences during athletic practice by experts, non-experts, and
novices. *Journal of Applied Sport Psychology, 13,* 185-206.

Coakley, J. (1992). Burnout among adolescent athletes: A personal failure or social problem. *Sociology of Sport Journal, 9,*
271-285.

Cohn, P. J. (1991). An exploratory study on peak performance in
golf. *The Sport Psychologist, 5,* 1-14.

Cohn, P. J., Rotella, R. J., & Lloyd, J. W. (1990). Effects of a cognitive-behavioral intervention on the preshot routine and
performance in golf. *The Sport Psychologist, 4,* 33-47.

Compton, K. C. (1998, April). Doin' it for yourself: Why your
source of   motivation means the difference between
fun and fear. *Women's Sports and Fitness,* pp. 60-62.

Connolly, C. T., & Janelle, C. M. (2003). Attentional strategies in
rowing: Performance, perceived exertion, and gender considerations. *The Sport Psychologist, 15,* 195-212.

Courneya, K. S., & Carron, A. V. (1992). The home advantage in
sport competitions: A literature review. *Journal of Sport and
Exercise Psychology, 14,* 13-27.

Couture, R. T., Jerome, W., & Tihanyi, J. (1999). Can associative
and dissociative strategies affect the swimming performance of recreational swimmers? *The Sport Psychologist,
13,* 334-343.

Covey, S. R. (1989). *The seven habits of highly effective people.*
New York: Simon & Schuster.

Critical coaching behaviors that an Olympic coach must do to
perform well at the games. (2003, Spring). *Olympic Coach,*
p. 12.

Csikszentmihalyi, M. (1990). *Flow: The psychology of optimal experience.* New York: Harper & Row.

Cumming, J., & Hall, C. (2002). Athletes' use of imagery in the
off-season. *The Sport Psychologist, 16,* 160-172.

Cupal, D. D. (1998). Psychological interventions in sport injury
prevention and rehabilitation. *Journal of Applied Sport Psychology, 10,* 103-123.

Curry, L. A., & Snyder, C. R. (2000). Hope takes the field: Mind
matters in athletic performance. In C. R. Snyder (Ed.),
Handbook of hope: Theory, measures and applications (pp.
243-259). San Diego: Academic Press.

Daggett, T. (1999). How bad do you want it? In J. Naber (Ed.),
Awaken the Olympian within (pp. 143-150). Torrance, CA:
Griffin.

Dale, G. A. (2000). Distractions and coping strategies of elite de-
cathletes during their most memorable performances. *The
Sport Psychologist, 14,* 17-41.

Davis, J. O. (1991). Sports injuries and stress management: An
opportunity for research. *The Sport Psychologist, 5,* 175-
182.

Davis, M., Eshelman, E. R., & McKay, M. (2000). *The relaxation
& stress reduction workbook* (5th ed.). Oakland, CA: New
Harbinger.

Deci, E. L., & Ryan, R. M. (1985). *Intrinsic motivation and self-
determination in human behavior.* New York: Plenum.

Deford, F. (1999, May 10). The ring leader. *Sports Illustrated,* pp.
96-114.

Deford, F. (2003, November 24). Geno Auriemma + Diana
Taurasi = Love, Italian style. *Sports Illustrated,* pp. 124-133.

Diaz, J. (1999b). A year beyond his years. *Sports Illustrated, 91*
(November 15), pp. 46-49.

Diaz, J. (1999a). Peace be with him. *Sports Illustrated, 90* (June
28), p. G56.

Dicicco, T., Hacker, C., & Salzberg, C. (2002). *Catch them being
good.* New York: Penguin.

Dieffenbach, K., Gould, D., & Moffett, A. (2002). The coach's
role in developing champions *Olympic Coach, 12,* 2-4.

Dorfman, H. A., & Kuehl, K. (1995). *The mental game of baseball*
(2nd ed.). South Bend, IN: Diamond.

Dorrance, A., & Averbuch, G. (2002). *The vision of a champion.*
Ann Arbor, MI: Huron River Press.

Dugdale, J. R., & Eklund, R. C. (2002). Do *not* pay any attention
to the umpires: Thought suppression and task-relevant focusing strategies. *Journal of Sport & Exercise Psychology, 24,*
306-319.

Dugdale, J. R., Eklund, R. C., & Grodon, S. (2002). Expected and
unexpected stressors in major international competition:
Appraisal, coping, and performance. *The Sport Psychologist,
16,* 20-33.

Durand-Bush, N., & Salmela, J. H. (2002). The development and
maintenance of expert athletic performance: Perceptions
of world and Olympic champions. *Journal of Applied Sport
Psychology, 14,* 154-171.

Durand-Bush, N., Salmela, J. H., & Green-Demers, I. (2001).
The Ottawa mental skills assessment tool (OMSAT-3*).
The Sport Psychologist, 15, 1-19.

Easterbrook, J. A. (1959). The effect of emotion on cue utilization
and the organization of behavior. *Psychological Review, 66,*
183-201.

Elko, P. K., & Ostrow, A. C. (1991). Effects of a rational-emotive
education program on heightened anxiety levels of female
collegiate gymnasts. *The Sport Psychologist, 5,* 235-255.

Ellis, A. (1996). *Better, deeper, and more enduring brief therapy:
The rational emotive behavior therapy approach.* Bristol, PA:
Brunner/Mazel.

Ellis, A., & MacLaren, C. (1998). *Rational emotive behavior therapy: A therapist's guide.* Atascadero, CA: Impact.

Ericsson, K. A. (2003). Development of elite performance and
deliberate practice: An update from the perspective of the
expert performance approach. In J. S. Starkes & K. A. Ericsson (Eds.), *Expert performance in sports* (pp. 49-83).
Champaign, IL: Human Kinetics.

Eruzione, M. (1999). It wasn't a miracle on ice. In J. Naber (Ed.),
Awaken the Olympian within (pp. 252-263). Torrance, CA:
Griffin.

Eubank, M, Collins, D., & Smith, N. (2000). The influence of
anxiety direction on processing bias. *Journal of Sport & Exercise Psychology, 22,* 292-306.

Evans, L., Hardy, L., & Fleming, S. (2000). Intervention strategies
with injured athletes: An action research study. *The Sport
Psychologist, 14,* 188-206.

Eysenck, M. W., & Calvo, M. G. (1992). Anxiety and performance: The processing efficiency theory. *Cognitive and
Emotion, 6,* 409-434.

Farrey, T. (2004, March 20). The power to motivate positively. *ESPN Outside the Lines.* Retrieved from http://espn.go.com/ nba/s/2003/0313/1523176.html

Feinstein, J. (1986). *A season on the brink: A year with Bobby Knight and the Indiana Hoosiers.* New York: Simon & Schuster.

Feinstein, J. (1999). *The majors.* Boston: Little, Brown.

Feldman, D. A. (1999). *The handboo k of emotionally intelligent leadership.* Fall Church, VA: Leadership Performance Solutions.

Feltz, D. L., Chase, M. A., Moritz, S. E., & Sullivan, P. J. (1999). Development of the multidimensional coaching efficacy scale. *Journal of Educational Psychology, 91,* 765-776.

Feltz, D. L., & Lirgg, C. D. (1998). Perceived team and player efficacy in hockey. *Journal of Applied Psychology, 83,* 557-564.

Feltz, D. L., & Lirgg, C. D. (2001). Self-efficacy beliefs of athletes, teams, and coaches. In R.N. Singer, H. A. Hausenblas, & C. M. Janelle (Eds.), *Handbook of sport psychology* (2nd ed.; pp. 340-361). New York: Wiley.

Fenz, W. D., & Epstein, S. (1967). Gradients of physiological arousal of experienced and novice parachutists as a function of an approaching jump. *Psychosomatic Medicine, 29,* 33-51.

Fitzsimmons, P. A., Landers, D. M., Thomas, J. R., & van der Mars, H. (1991). Does self-efficacy predict performance in experienced weightlifters? *Research Quarterly for Exercise and Sport, 62,* 424-431.

Fosbury, D. (1999). Maybe you're right and everyone else is wrong. In J. Naber (Ed.), *Awaken the Olympian within* (pp. 62-73). Torrance, CA: Griffin.

Flynn, G. (Ed.). (1973). *Vince Lombardi on football.* New York: New York Graphics Society.

Freeman, C. (1998). *The wisdom of women's golf.* Nashville, TN: Walnut Grove Press.

Garfield, C. A., & Bennett, H. Z. (1984). *Peak performance: Mental training techniques of the world's greatest athletes.* Los Angeles: Tarcher.

George, T. R. (1994). Self-confidence and baseball performance: A causal examination of self-efficacy theory. *Journal of Sport & Exercise Psychology, 16,* 381-399.

Gibbons, T.,& Forster, T. (2002). A landmark study: The path to excellence. *Olympic Coach, 12,* 6-7.

Gilbert, W. D., & Trudel, P., & Haughian, L. (1999). Interactive decision making factors considered by coaches of youth ice hockey during games. *Journal of Teaching in Physical Education, 18,* 290-311.

Gill, D. L. (2000). *Psychological dynamics of sport and exercise* (2nd ed.). Champaign, IL: Human Kinetics.

Gladwell, M. (2000). The art of failure: Why some people choke and others panic. *The New Yorker* (August 21), 1-10.

Glenn, S. D., & Horn, T. S. (1993). Psychological and personal predicators of leadership behavior in female soccer athletes. *Journal of Applied Sport Psychology, 5,* 17-34.

Goleman, D. (1995). *Emotional intelligence.* New York: Bantam.

Goleman, D. (1998). *Working with emotional intelligence.* New York: Bantam.

Goodell, B. (1999). Fear and doubt: The evil twins. In J. Naber (Ed.), *Awaken the Olympian within* (pp. 174-182). Torrance, CA: Griffin.

Gordon, D. (2001). The dominator. *Newsweek, 137* (June 18), 42-47.

Gould, D. (2001). Goal setting for peak performance. In J. M. Williams (Ed.), *Applied sport psychology: Personal growth to peak performance* (4th ed., pp. 190-205). Mountain View, CA: Mayfield.

Gould, D., Dieffenbach, K., & Moffett, A. (2002). Psychological characteristics and their development in Olympic champions. *Journal of Applied Sport Psychology, 14,* 172-204.

Gould, D., Eklund, R. C., & Jackson, S. A. (1992a). 1988 U.S. Olympic wrestling excellence: I. Mental preparation, precompetitive cognition and affect. *The Sport Psychologist, 6,* 358-362.

Gould, D., Eklund, R. C., & Jackson, S. A. (1992b). 1988 U.S. Olympic wrestling excellence: II. Thoughts and affect occurring during competition. *The Sport Psychologist, 6,* 383-402.

Gould, D., Eklund, R.C., & Jackson, S.A. (1993). Coping strategies used by U.S. Olympic wrestlers. *Research Quarterly for Exercise and Sport, 64,* 83-93.

Gould, D., Finch, L. M., & Jackson, S. A. (1993). Coping strategies used by national champion figure skaters. *Research Quarterly for Exercise and Sport, 64,* 453-468.

Gould, D., Greenleaf, C., Guinan, D., & Chung, Y. (2002). A survey of U.S. Olympic coaches: Variables perceived to have influenced athlete performances and coach effectiveness. *The Sport Psychologist, 16,* 229-250.

Gould, D., Greenleaf, C., Lauer, & Chung, Y. (1999, Summer). Lessons from Nagano. *Olympic Coach,* pp. 2-5.

Gould, D., Guinan, D., Greenleaf, C., Medbery, & Peterson, K. (1999). Factors affecting Olympic performance: Perceptions of athletes and coaches from more and less successful teams. *The Sport Psychologist, 13,* 371-394.

Gould, D., Hodge, K., Peterson, K., & Giannini, J. (1989). An exploratory examination of strategies used by elite coaches to enhance self-efficacy in athletes. *Journal of Sport & Exercise Psychology, 11,* 128-140.

Gould, D., Jackson, S. A., & Finch, L. M. (1993). Life at the top: The experiences of U.S. national champion figure skaters. *The Sport Psychologist, 7,* 354-374.

Gould, D., Tuffey, S., Udry, E., & Loehr, J. (1996). Burnout in competitive junior tennis players: II. Qualitative analysis. *The Sport Psychologist, 10,* 341-366.

Gould, D., Tuffey, S., Udry, E., & Loehr, J. (1997). Burnout in competitive junior tennis players: III. Individual differences in the burnout experience. *The Sport Psychologist, 11,* 257-276.

Gould, D., & Udry, E. (1994). Psychological skills for enhancing performance: Arousal regulation strategies. *Medicine and Science in Sports and Exercise, 26,* 478-485.

Gould, D., Udry, E., Bridges, D., & Beck, L. (1997a). Coping with season-ending injuries. *The Sport Psychologist, 11,* 379-399.

Gould, D., Udry, E., Bridges, D., & Beck, L. (1997b). Stress sources encountered when rehabilitating from season-ending ski injuries. *The Sport Psychologist, 11,* 361-378.

Gould, D., Udry, E., Tuffey, S., & Loehr, J. (1996). Burnout in competitive junior tennis players: I. A quantitative psychological assessment. *The Sport Psychologist, 10,* 322-340.

Grandjean, B. D., Taylor, P. A., & Weiner, J. (2002). Confidence, concentration, and competitive performance of elite athletes: A natural experiment in Olympic gymnastics. *Journal of Sport & Exercise Psychology, 24,* 320-327.

Greenleaf, C., Gould, D., & Dieffenbach, K. (2001). Factors influencing Olympic performance: Interviews with Atlanta and Nagano U.S. Olympians. *Journal of Applied Sport Psychology, 13,* 154-184.

Gregg, L. (1999). *The champion within.* Burlington, NC: JTC Sports.

Greenspan, M. J., & Feltz, D. L. (1989). Psychological interventions with athletes in competitive situations: A review. *The Sport Psychologist, 3,* 219-236.

Grove, J. R., & Heard, N. P. (1997). Optimism and sport confidence as correlates of slump-related coping among athletes. *The Sport Psychologist, 11,* 400-410.

Guilar, J. D. (2001). *The interpersonal communication skills workshop.* New York: Amacom.

Haase, A. M., Praavessis, H., & Owens, R. G. (2002). Perfectionism, social physique anxiety and disordered eating: A comparison of male and female elite athletes. *Psychology of Sport and Exercise, 3,* 209-222.

Hackfort, D., & Schwenkmezger, P. (1993). Anxiety. In R. N. Singer, M. Murphy & L. K. Tennant (Eds.), *Handbook of research on sport psychology* (pp. 328-364). New York: Macmillan.

Hall, E. G., & Erffmeyer, E. S. (1983). The effect of visuo-motor behavior rehearsal with videotaped modeling on free throw accuracy of intercollegiate female basketball players. *Journal of Sport Psychology, 5,* 343-346.

Halliwell, K. (1990). Providing sport psychology consulting services in professional hockey. *The Sport Psychologist, 4,* 369-377.

Hamachek, D. E. (1978). Psychodynamics of normal and neurotic perfectionism. *Psychology, 15,* 27-33.

Hamm, M., & Heifetz, A. (2000). *Go for the goal: A champion's guide to winning in soccer and life.* New York: Quill.

Hanin, Y. L. (1997). Emotions and athletic performance: Individual zones of optimal functioning model. *European Yearbook of Sport Psychology, 1,* 29-72.

Hanin, Y. L. (Ed.). (2000a). *Emotions in sport.* Champaign, IL: Human Kinetics.

Hanin, Y. L. (2000b). Individual zones of optimal functioning (IZOF) model. In Y. L. Hanin (Ed.). *Emotions in sport* (pp. 65-89). Champaign, IL: Human Kinetics.

Hanin, Y. L. (2000c). Successful and poor performance and emotions. In Y. L. Hanin (Ed.) *Emotions in sport* (pp. 157-187). Champaign, IL: Human Kinetics.

Hanton, S., & Connaughton, D. (2002). Perceived control of anxiety and its relationship to self-confidence and performance. *Research Quarterly for Exercise and Sport, 73,* 87-97.

Hanton, S., & Jones, G. (1999). The effects of a multimodal intervention program on performers: II. Training the butterflies to fly in formation. *The Sport Psychologist, 13,* 22-41.

Hardy, L. (1996). Testing the predictions of the cusp catastrophe model of anxiety and performance. *The Sport Psychologist, 10,* 140-156.

Hardy, L., & Callow, N. (1999). Efficacy of external and internal visual imagery perspectives for the enhancement of performance on tasks in which form is important. *Journal of Sport & Exercise Psychology, 21,* 95-112.

Hardy, J., Gammage, K., & Hall, C. (2001). A descriptive study of athlete self-talk. *The Sport Psychologist, 15,* 306-318.

Hardy, L., Jones, G., & Gould, D. (1996). *Understanding psychological preparation for sport: Theory and practice of elite performers.* Chichester: Wiley.

Hargrove, R. (1995). *Masterful coaching.* San Francisco: Jossey-Bass.

Hecker, J. E., & Kaczor, L. M. (1988). Application of imagery theory to sport psychology: Some preliminary findings. *Journal of Sport & Exercise Psychology, 10,* 363-373.

Heermann, B. (1997). *Building team spirit.* New York: McGraw-Hill.

Hogshead, N. (1999). Success is a learned skill. In J. Naber (Ed.), *Awaken the Olympian within* (pp. 132-140). Torrance, CA: Griffin.

Hollander, D. B., & Acevedo, E. O. (2000). Successful English Channel swimming: The peak experience. *The Sport Psychologist, 14,* 1-16.

Holmes, P. S., & Collins, D. J. (2001). The PETTLEP approach to motor imagery: A functional equivalence model for sport psychologists. *Journal of Applied Sport Psychology, 13,* 60-83.

Horn, T. S. (2002). Coaching effectiveness in the sport domain. In T. S. Horn (Ed.), *Advances in sport psychology* (2nd ed., pp. 309-354). Champaign, IL: Human Kinetics.

Horn, T. S., Glenn, S. D., & Wentzell, A. B. (1993). Sources of information underlying personal ability judgments in high school athletes. *Pediatric Exercise Science, 5,* 263-274.

Horn, T. S., & Harris, A. (1996). Perceived competence in young athletes: Research findings and recommendations for coaches and parents. In F. L. Smoll & R. E. Smith (Eds.), *Children and youth in sport: A biopsychosocial perspective* (pp. 309-329).

Horn, T. S., Lox, C. L., & Labrador, F. (2001). The self-fulfilling prophecy theory: When coaches' expectations become reality. In J. M. Williams (Ed.), *Applied sport psychology: Personal growth to peak performance* (pp. 63-81). Mountain View, CA: Mayfield.

Horn, T., & Weiss, M. R. (1991). A developmental analysis of children's self-ability judgments in the physical domain. *Pediatric Exercise Science, 3,* 310-326.

Huish, J. (1999). It's time for a change. In J. Naber (Ed.), *Awaken the Olympian within* (pp. 242-250). Torrance, CA: Griffin.

Isaac, A. R. (1992). Mental practice - does it work in the field? *The Sport Psychologist, 6,* 192-198.

Isaacson, M. (1990, February 4). The final bows: Doc and the shoe say so long. *Chicago Tribune,* pp. 3-1, 3-10.

Jackson, S. (1992). Athletes in flow: A qualitative investigation of flow states in elite figure skaters. *Journal of Applied Sport Psychology, 4,* 161-180.

Jackson, S. A. (2000). Joy, fun, and flow state in sport. In Y. L. Hanin (Ed.), *Emotions in sport* (pp. 135-155). Champaign, IL: Human Kinetics.

Jackson, S. A., Mayocchi, L., & Dover, J. (1998). Life after winning gold: II. Coping with change as an Olympic gold medallist. *The Sport Psychologist, 12,* 137-155.

Jackson, S. A., Thomas, P. R., Marsh, H. W., & Smethurst, C. J. (2001). Relationships between flow, self-concept, psychological skills, and performance. *Journal of Applied Sport Psychology, 13,* 129-153.

Janelle, C. M. (1999). Ironic mental processes in sport: Implications for sport psychologists. *The Sport Psychologist, 13,* 201-220.

Janelle, C. M., Hillman, C. H., Apparies, R. J., Murray, N. P., Meili, L., Fallon, E. A., & Hatfield, B. D. (2000). Expertise differences in cortical activation and gaze behavior during rifle shooting. *Journal of Sport & Exercise Psychology, 22,* 167-182.

Janelle, C. M., Singer, R. N., & Williams, A. M. (1999). External distraction and attentional narrowing: Visual search evidence. *Journal of Sport & Exercise Psychology, 21*, 70-91.

Janis, I. L. (1972). *Victims of groupthink*. Boston: Houghton Mifflin.

Jansen, D. (1994, July 15-17). Winning big. *USA Weekend*, pp. 4-7.

Jansen, D. (1999). There's more to life than skating around in a circle. In J. Naber (Ed.), *Awaken the Olympian within* (pp. 3-14). Torrance, CA: Griffin.

Janssen, J. (2002). *Championship team building*. Cary, NC: Winning the Mental Game.

Janssen, J. (2004). *The team captain's leadership manual*. Cary, NC: Winning the Mental Game.

Jones, G., & Hanton, S. (1996). Interpretation of competitive anxiety symptoms and goal attainment expectancies. *Journal of Sport & Exercise Psychology, 18*, 144-157.

Jones, R., Armour, K., & Potrac, P. (2004). *Sports coaching cultures*. London: Routledge.

Kane, T. D., Baltes, T. R., & Moss, M. C. (2001). Causes and consequences of free-set goals: An investigation of athletic self-regulation. *Journal of Sport and Exercise Psychology, 23*, 55-75.

Kelley, B. C., Eklund, R. C., & Ritter-Taylor, M. (1999). Stress and burnout among collegiate tennis coaches. *Journal of Sport & Exercise Psychology, 21*, 113-130.

Kelley, H. H., & Thibaut, J. W. (1969). Group problem solving. In G. Lindzey & Arconson (Eds.), *The handbook of social psychology* (2nd ed., Vol. 4, pp. 1-101). Reading, MA: Addison-Wesley.

Kendall, G., Hrycaiko, D., Martin, G. L., & Kendall, T. (1990). The effects of an imagery rehearsal, relaxation, and self-talk package on basketball game performance. *Journal of Sport & Exercise Psychology, 12*, 157-166.

Kerr, G., & Goss, J. (1996). The effects of a stress management program on injuries and stress levels. *Journal of Applied Sport Psychology, 8*, 109-117.

Kerr, J. H. (1997). *Motivation and emotion in sport: Reversal theory*. East Sussex, UK: Psychology Press.

Kingston, K. M., & Hardy, L. (1997). Effects of different types of goals on processes that support performance. *The Sport Psychologist, 11*, 277-293.

Kiraly, K. (1999). Making winners out of nobodies. In J. Naber (Ed.), *Awaken the Olympian within* (pp. 202-210). Torrance, CA: Griffin.

Kirschenbaum, D. S., Owens, D., & O'Connor, E. A. (1998). Smart golf: Preliminary evaluation of a simple, yet comprehensive, approach to improving and scoring the mental game. *The Sport Psychologist, 12*, 271-282.

Klawans, H. L. (1996). *Why Michael couldn't hit*. New York: Freeman.

Kobasa, S. (1979). Stress life events, personality, and health: An inquiry into hardiness. *Journal of Personality and Social Psychology, 37*, 1-11.

Kotter, J. P. (1996). *Leading change*. Boston: Harvard Business School Press.

Kramer, J. (1968). *Instant replay*. Evanston, IL: Holtzman Press.

Krzyzewski, M. (2000). *Leading with the heart*. New York: Warner.

Lambert, S. M., Moore, D. W., & Dixon, R. S. (1999). Gymnasts in training: The differential effects of self- and coach-set goals as a function of locus of control. *Journal of Applied Sport Psychology, 11*, 72-82.

Landers, D. M., & Arent, S. M. (2001). Arousal-performance relationships. In J. M. Williams (Ed.), *Applied sport psychology: Personal growth to peak performance* (pp. 206-228). Mountain Grove, CA: Mayfield.

Landers, D. M., Han, M. Salazar, W., Petruzzello, S. J., Kubitz, K. A., & Gannon, T. L. (1994). Effects of learning on electroencephalographic and elecrocardiographic patterns in novice archers. *International Journal of Sport Psychology, 25*, 313-330.

Landers, D. M., Wang, M. Z., & Courtet, P. (1985). Peripheral narrowing among experienced and inexperienced rifle shooters under low and high stress conditions. *Research Quarterly for Exercise and Sport, 56*, 122-130.

Lang, P. J. (1979). A bio-informational theory of emotional imagery. *Psychophysiology, 16*, 495-512.

Latane, B., Williams, K. D., & Harkins, S. G. (1979). Many hands make light the work: The causes and consequences of social loafing. *Journal of Personality and Social Psychology, 37*, 823-832.

Layden, T. (2004, March 29). The upset. *Sports Illustrated*, pp. 70-80.

Lazarus, A. (1984). *In the mind's eye: The power of imagery for personal enrichment*. New York: Guilford.

Lee, M. J., Whitehead, J., & Balchin, N. (2000). The measurement of values in youth sport: Development of the youth sport values questionnaire. *Journal of Sport and Exercise Psychology, 22*, 307-326.

Lewthwaite, R. (1990). Threat perception in competitive trait anxiety: The endangerment of important goals. *Journal of Sport & Exercise Psychology, 12*, 280-300.

Liao, C., & Masters, R. S. W. (2002). Self-focused attention and performance failure under psychological stress. *Journal of Sport & Exercise Psychology, 24*, 289-305.

Lieber, J. (1999). USA won't kick habit of believing. *USA Today*, July 6, pp. 1c-2c.

Locke, E. A., & Latham, G. P. (1990). *A theory of goal setting and task performance*. Englewood Cliffs, NJ: Prentice-Hall.

Loehr, J. E. (1984, March). How to overcome stress and play at your peak all the time. *Tennis*, pp. 66-76.

Loehr, J., & Schwartz, T. (2001, January). The making of a corporate athlete. *Harvard Business Review*, pp. 120-128.

Lowe, R., & McGrath, J. E. (1971). *Stress, arousal and performance: Some findings calling for a new theory* (Report No. AF1161-67). Washington, D. C.: Air Force Office of Strategic Research.

Lyle, J. (2002). *Sports coaching concepts*. New York: Routledge.

Lynn, A. B. (2002). *The emotional intelligence activity book*. New York: Amacom.

Maddux, J. E., & Lewis, J. (1995). Self-efficacy and adjustment: Basic principles and issues. In J. E. Maddux (Ed.), *Self-efficacy, adaptation, and adjustment* (pp. 37-68). New York: Plenum.

Males, J. R., Kerr, J. H., & Gerkovich, M. M. (1998). Metamotivational states during slalom competition: A qualitative analysis using reversal theory. *Journal of Applied Sport Psychology, 10*, 185-200.

Mallett, C. J., & Hanrahan, S. J. (1997). Race modeling: An effective cognitive strategy for the 100m sprinter? *The Sport Psychologist, 11*, 72-85.

Marks, D. F. (1983). Mental imagery and consciousness: A theoretical review. In A. A. Sheikh (Ed.), *Imagery: Current theory, research and application* (pp. 96-130). New York: Wiley.

Martens, R. (1974). Arousal and motor performance. In J. H. Wilmore (Ed.), *Exercise and sport science reviews*. New York: Academic Press.

Martens, R. (1978). *Joy and sadness in children's sports*. Champaign, IL: Human Kinetics.

Martens, R. (1987). *Coaches guide to sport psychology*. Champaign, IL: Human Kinetics.

Martens, R. (1990). *Successful coaching*. Champaign, IL: Human Kinetics.

Martens, R., Vealey, R. S., & Burton, D. (1990). *Competitive anxiety in sport*. Champaign, IL: Human Kinetics.

Martin, G. L., & Toogood, A. (1997). Cognitive and behavioral components of a seasonal psychological skills training program for competitive figure skaters. *Cognitive and Behavioral Practice, 4*, 383-404.

Martin, K. A., Moritz, S. E., & Hall, C. R. (1999). Imagery use in sport: A literature review and applied model. *The Sport Psychologist, 3*, 245-268.

Massimo, J. (1973). *A psychologist's approach to sport*. Presentation to New England Gymnastic Clinic, Newton, MA.

Maxwell, J. C. (1998). *The 21 irrefutable laws of leadership: Follow them and people will follow you*. Nashville: Nelson.

Maynard, I. W., Warwick-Evans, L., & Smith, M. J. (1995). The effects of a cognitive intervention strategy on competitive state anxiety and performance in semiprofessional soccer players. *Journal of Sport & Exercise Psychology, 17*, 428-446.

McCallister, S. G., Blinde, E. M., & Weiss, W. M. (2000). Teaching values and implementing philosophies: Dilemmas of the youth sport coach. *The Physical Educator, 57*, 35-45.

McCallum, J. (2004, May 24). It's that time again. *Sports Illustrated*, pp. 54-65.

McCann, S. (1998, Spring). High expectations: Blessing or curse. *Olympic Coach*, p. 9.

McCann, S. (1998, Summer). The perfect performance vs. trying to be perfect. *Olympic Coach*, p. 9.

McCann, S. (2003, Fall). So you want to be a great "big event coach"? *Olympic Coach*, pp. 11-13.

McKay, M., Davis, M., & Fanning, P. (1983). *Messages: The communication book*. Oakland: New Harbinger.

McPherson, S. L. (2000). Expert-novice differences in planning strategies during collegiate singles tennis competition. *Journal of Sport & Exercise Psychology, 22*, 39-62.

Mears, P., & Voehl, F. (1994). *Team building: A structured learning approach*. Delray Beach, FL: St. Lucie Press.

Meeker, L. (1994). *Experiential activities for high performance teamwork*. Amherst, MA: HRD Press.

Mellalieu, S. D., Hanton, S., & Jones, G. (2003). Emotional labeling and competitive anxiety in preparation and competition. *The Sport Psychologist, 17*, 157-174.

Miller, A., & Donohue, B. (2003). The development and controlled evaluation of athletic mental preparation strategies in high school distance runners. *Journal of Applied Sport Psychology, 15*, 321-334.

Miller, S. C., Bredemeier, B. J. L., & Shields, D. L. L. (1997). Sociomoral education through physical education with at-risk children. *Quest, 49*, 114-129.

Moore, K. (1996). The man. *Sports Illustrated, 85* (August 12), pp. 26-32.

Morgan, W. P., & Pollock, M. L. (1977). Psychological characterization of the elite distance runner. *Annals of the New York Academy of Sciences, 301*, 382-403.

Moritz, S. E., Martin, K. A., Hall, C. R., & Vadocz, E. (1996). What are confident athletes imaging?: An examination of image content. *The Sport Psychologist, 10*, 171-179.

Murphy, A. (2001). Magnifique! *Sports Illustrated, 95* (August 6), pp. 34-39.

Naber, J. (1999). No deposit, no return. In J. Naber (Ed.). *Awaken the Olympian within* (pp. 55-64). Torrance, CA: Griffin.

Nack, W., & Munson, L. (2000). Out of control. *Sports Illustrated, 93* (July 24), pp. 86-95.

Nakamura, R. M. (1996). *The power of positive coaching*. Boston: Jones and Bartlett.

Newburg, D., Kimiecik, J., Durand-Bush, N., & Doell, K. (2002). The role of resonance in performance excellence and life engagement. *Journal of Applied Sport Psychology, 14*, 249-267.

Nicklaus, J. (1974). *Golf my way*. New York: Simon & Schuster.

Nideffer, R., & Sagal, (2001). Concentration and attention control training. In J. M. Williams (Ed.), *Applied sport psychology: Personal growth to peak performance* (4th ed., pp. 312-332). Mountain View, CA: Mayfield.

Orlick, T. (1986a). *Psyching for sport*. Champaign, IL: Human Kinetics.

Orlick, T. (1986b). *Coaches training manual to psyching for sport*. Champaign, IL: Human Kinetics.

Orlick, T. (1990). *In pursuit of excellence* (2nd ed.). Champaign, IL: Human Kinetics.

Orlick, T. (1998). *Embracing your potential*. Champaign, IL: Human Kinetics.

Orlick, T. (2000). *In pursuit of excellence* (3rd ed.). Champaign, IL: Human Kinetics.

Orlick, T., & Partington, J. (1988). Mental links to excellence. *The Sport Psychologist, 2*, 105-130.

Park, S. (2003). Anticipation and acquiring processes of visual cues on a spiker's attack patterns and directions as a function of expertise in volleyball players. *International Journal of Applied Sport Sciences, 15*, 51-63.

Pates, J., Cummings, A., & Maynard, I. (2002). The effects of hypnosis on flow states and three-point shooting performance in basketball players. *The Sport Psychologist, 16*, 34-47.

Patrick, T. D., & Hrycaiko, D. W. (1998). Effects of a mental training package on an endurance performance. *The Sport Psychologist, 12*, 283-299.

Pelletier, L. G., Fortier, M. S., Vallerand, R. J., Tuson, K. M., Briere, N. M., & Blais, M. R. (1995). Toward a new measure of intrinsic motivation, extrinsic motivation, and amotivation in sports: The sport motivation scale (SMS). *Journal of Sport and Exercise Psychology, 17*, 35-53.

Pelletier, L. G., & Vallerand, R. J. (1996). Supervisors' beliefs and subordinates' intrinsic motivation: A behavioral confirmation analysis. *Journal of Personality and Social Psychology, 71*, 331-340.

Perkos, S., Theodorakis, Y., & Chroni, S. (2002). Enhancing performance and skill acquisition in novice basketball players with instructional self-talk. *The Sport Psychologist, 16*, 368-383.

Perman, S. (2002). The agony (not to mention the public humiliation, financial disappointment and long-term psychological trauma) of defeat. *Sports Illustrated for Women, 4* (February), pp. 78-83.

Posner, M. I., & Bois, S. J. (1971). Components of attention. *Psychological Review, 78*, 391-408.

Perkins, D., Wilson, G. V., & Kerr, J. H. (2001). The effects of elevated arousal and mood on maximal strength performance in athletes. *Journal of Applied Sport Psychology, 13*, 239-259.

Perry, M. (2002). Five questions with Carlos Boozer. *Cincinnati Enquirer* (January 12), p. D4.

Raedeke, T. D. (1997). Is athlete burnout more than just stress? A sport commitment perspective. *Journal of Sport & Exercise Psychology, 19*, 396-417.

Raedeke, T. D., Granzyk, T. L., & Warren, A. (2000). Why coaches experience burnout: A commitment perspective. *Journal of Sport & Exercise Psychology, 22*, 85-105.

Ravizza, K. (1977). Peak experiences in sport. *Journal of Humanistic Psychology, 17*, 35-40.

Ravizza, K. (1993). An interview with Peter Vidmar, member of the 1994 U.S. Olympic gymnastics team. *Contemporary Thought in Performance Enhancement, 2*, 93-100.

Ravizza, K., & Hanson, T. (1995). *Heads-up baseball: Playing the game one pitch at a time.* Chicago: Masters Press.

Ravizza, K., & Osborne, T. (1991). Nebraska's 3 R's: One-play-at-a-time preperformance routine for collegiate football. *The Sport Psychologist, 5*, 256-265.

Ready, Set, Go. (2004, May/June). *Golf for Women*, p. 118.

Reilly, R. (1995). Goodness gracious, he's a great ball of fire. *Sports Illustrated, 83* (March 27), pp. 62-72.

Riley, P. (1993). *The winner within: A life plan for team players.* New York: Putnam's Sons.

Ripoll, H., Kerlirzin, Y., Stein, J. F., & Reine, B. (1995). Analysis of information processing, decision making, and visual strategies in complex problem solving sport situations. *Human Movement Science, 14*, 325-349.

Roberts, W., & Vealey, R. S. (1992, October). *Attention in sport: Measurement issues, psychological concomitants, and the prediction of performance.* Paper presented at the Association for the Advancement of Applied Sport Psychology Conference, Colorado Springs.

Rodgers, W., Hall, C., & Buckolz, E. (1991). The effect of an imagery training program on imagery ability, imagery use, and figure skating performance. *Journal of Applied Sport Psychology, 3*, 109-125.

Rohnke, K., & Butler, S. (1995). *Quicksilver: Adventure games, initiative problems, trust activities and a guide to effective leadership.* Dubuque, IA: Kendall/Hunt.

Rosen, K. (1998, January/February). Who's the Olympic favorite? *Olympian*, pp. 16-18.

Rosenfeld, L. B., & Richman, J. M. (1997). Developing effective social support: Team building and the social support process. *Journal of Applied Sport Psychology, 9*, 133-153.

Rotella, R. J. (1992, September)). How to use - not lose - your temper. *Golf Digest*, pp. 78-80.

Rotella, R. J. (1995). *Golf is not a game of perfect.* New York: Simon & Schuster.

Rushall, B. S., Hall, M., Roux, L., Sasseville, J., & Rushall, A. S. (1988). Effects of three types of thought content instructions in skiing performance. *The Sport Psychologist, 2*, 283-297.

Rushall, B. S., & Shewchuk, M. (1989). Effects of thought content instructions on swimming performance. *The Journal of Sports Medicine and Physical Fitness, 29*, 326-334.

Rushin, S. (1994, December 19). Out of the shadows. *Sports Illustrated*, pp. 72-80.

Russell, B., & Branch, T. (1979). *Second wind: The memoirs of an opinionated man.* New York: Random House.

Ryan, E. D. (1980). Attribution, intrinsic motivation, and athletics: A replication and extension. In C. H. Nadeau, W. R. Halliwell, K. M. Newell, & G. C. Roberts (Eds.), *Psychology of motor behavior and sport - 1979* (pp. 19-26). Champaign, IL: Human Kinetics.

Sackett, R. S. (1934). The influences of symbolic rehearsal upon the retention of a maze habit. *Journal of General Psychology, 13*, 113-128.

Sampras, P. (1997, November). You can come through at crunch time. *Tennis*, pp. 36-38.

Saporito, B. (2003, September 29). Ten questions for Lance Armstrong. *Time*, p. 8.

Scanlan, T. K., Russell, D. G., Beals, K. P., & Scanlan, L. A. (2003). Project on elite athlete commitment (PEAK): II. A direct test and expansion of the sport commitment model with elite amateur sportsmen. *Journal of Sport & Exercise Psychology, 25*, 377-401.

Scanlan, T. K., Russell, D. G., Wilson, N. C., & Scanlan, L. A. (2003). Project on elite athlete commitment (PEAK): I. Introduction and methodology. *Journal of Sport & Exercise Psychology, 25*, 360-376.

Scheier, M. F., & Carver, C. S. (1992). Effects of optimism on psychological well-being: Theoretical overview and empirical support. *Cognitive Therapy and Research, 16*, 201-228.

Schomer, H. H. (1986). Mental strategies and perceptions of effort of marathon runners. *International Journal of Sport Psychology, 17*, 41-59.

Schneider, W., Dumais, S. T., & Shiffrin, R. M. (1984). Automatic and control processing and attention. In R. Parasuraman & R. Davies (Eds.), *Varieties of attention* (pp. 1-27). Orlando, FL: Academic Press.

Scott, L. M., Scott, D., Bedic, S. P., & Dowd, J. (1999). Need title. *The Sport Psychologist, 13*, 57-68.

Seligman, M. E. P. (1998). *Learned optimism.* New York: Free Press.

Sexton, J. (1998, March 6-8). "I don't mind being tough." *USA Weekend*, p. 20.

Short, S. E., Bruggeman, J. M., Engel, S. G., Marback, T. L., Wang, L. J., Willadsen, A., & Short, M. W. (2002). The effect of imagery function and imagery direction on self-efficacy and performance on a golf-putting task. *The Sport Psychologist, 16*, 48-67.

Silva, J. M. (1990). An analysis of the training stress syndrome in competitive athletics. *Journal of Applied Sport Psychology, 2*, 5-20.

Simons, J. (2000). Doing imagery in the field. In M. Andersen (Ed.), *Doing sport psychology* (pp. 77-92). Champaign, IL: Human Kinetics.

Singer, R. N. (2002). Preperformance state, routines, and automaticity: What does it take to realize expertise in self-paced events? *Journal of Sport & Exercise Psychology, 24*, 359-375.

Sirak, R. (2003). Passion to be perfect. *Golf for Women* (March/April), pp. 116-123.

Smith, D. K. (1999). *Make success measurable! A mindbook-workbook for setting goals and taking action.* New York: Wiley.

Smith, D. M. (1997). *The practical executive and leadership*. Lincolnwood, IL: NTC Business Books.

Smith, G. (2003, September 22). The secret life of Mia Hamm. *Sports Illustrated*, pp. 58-73.

Smith, R. E., & Christensen, D. S. (1995). Psychological skills as predictors of performance and survival in professional baseball. *Journal of Sport and Exercise Psychology, 17*, 399-415.

Smith, R. E., Schutz, R. W., Smoll, F. L., & Ptacek, J. T. (1995). Development and validation of a multidimensional measure of sport-specific psychological skills: The athletic coping skills inventory-28. *Journal of Sport and Exercise Psychology, 17*, 379-398.

Smith, R. E., & Smoll, F. L. (1990). Self-esteem and children's reactions to youth sport coaching behaviors: A field study of self-enhancement processes. *Developmental Psychology, 26*, 987-993.

Smith, R. E., Smoll, F. L., & Curtis, B. (1979). Coach effectiveness training: A cognitive behavioral approach to enhancing relationship skills in youth sport coaches. *Journal of Sport Psychology, 1*, 59-75.

Smoll, F. L., Smith, R. E., Barnett, N. P., & Everett, J. J. (1993). Enhancement of children's self-esteem through social support training for youth sport coaches. *Journal of Applied Psychology, 78*, 602-610.

Sorenstram stronger, relaxed, and prepared to play her best. (2003, May 22). *Cincinnati Enquirer*, pp. A1, A10.

Spence, J. T., & Spence, K. W. (1966). The motivational components of manifest anxiety: Drive and drive stimuli. In C. D. Spielberger (Ed.), *Anxiety and behavior*. New York: Academic Press.

Spink, K. S. (1990). Group cohesion and collective efficacy of volleyball teams. *Journal of Sport & Exercise Psychology, 12*, 301-311.

Starke, J. L., & Ericsson, K. A. (Eds.) (2003). *Expert performance in sports*. Champaign, IL: Human Kinetics.

Starkes, J. L., Helsen, W., & Jack, R. (2001). Expert performance in sport and dance. In R. N. Singer, H. A. Hausenblas, & C. M. Janelle (Eds.), *Handbook of sport psychology* (2nd ed.; pp. 174-201). New York: Wiley.

Summitt's spoof motivates team. (2004, April 2). *Cincinnati Enquirer*, p. C10.

Swift, E. M. (1992). All that glitters. *Sports Illustrated, 77* (December 14), pp. 70-80.

Tammen, V. V. (1996). Elite middle and long distance runners' associative/dissociative coping. *Journal of Applied Sport Psychology, 8*, 1-8.

Taylor, J. (1988). Slumpbusting: A systematic analysis of slumps in sport. *The Sport Psychologist, 2*, 39-48.

Taylor, P. (1995). Resurrection. *Sports Illustrated, 82* (March 27), pp.18-22.

Templin, D. P., & Vernacchia, R. A. (1995). The effect of highlight music videotapes upon game performance of intercollegiate basketball players. *The Sport Psychologist, 9*, 41-50.

Tharp, R. G., & Gallimore, R. (1976, January). Basketball's John Wooden: What a coach can teach a teacher. *Psychology Today*, pp. 75-78.

Theeboom, M., De Knop, P., & Weiss, M. R. (1995). Motivational climate, psychological responses, and motor skill development in children's sport: A field-based intervention study. *Journal of Sport and Exercise Psychology, 17*, 294-311.

Thelwell, R. C., & Greenlees, I. A. (2001). The effects of a mental skills training package on gymnasium triathlon performance. *The Sport Psychologist, 15*, 127-141.

Thomas, P. R., & Over, R. (1994). Psychological and psychomotor skills associated with performance in golf. *The Sport Psychologist, 8*, 73-86.

Thompson, J. (2003). *The double-goal coach*. New York: HarperCollins.

Thomsen, I. (2000). Heavenly ascent. *Sports Illustrated, 93* (July 24), pp. 40-48.

Tour tips. (2003, March/April). How to stop the bleeding. *Golf for Women*, p. 86.

Tracey, J. (2003). The emotional response to the injury and rehabilitation process. *Journal of Applied Sport Psychology, 15*, 279-293.

Treasure, D. C., Monson, J., & Lox, C. L. (1996). Relationships between self-efficacy, wrestling performance, and affect prior to competition. *The Sport Psychologist, 10*, 73-83.

Tuckman, B. W. (1965). Developmental sequence in small groups. *Psychological Bulletin, 63*, 384-399.

Udry, E., Gould, D., Bridges, D., & Beck, L. (1997). Down but not out: Athlete responses to season-ending injuries. *Journal of Sport & Exercise Psychology, 19*, 229-248.

Vallerand, R. J., & Fortier, M. S. (1998). In J. L. Duda (Ed.), *Advances in sport and exercise psychology measurement* (pp. 81-101). Morgantown, WV: Fitness Information Technology.

Van Schoyck, S. R., & Grasha, A. F. (1981). Attentional style variations and athletic ability: The advantages of a sport-specific test. *Journal of Sport Psychology, 3*, 149-165.

Vealey, R. S. (1986). Conceptualization of sport-confidence and competitive orientation: Preliminary investigation and instrument development. *Journal of Sport Psychology, 8*, 221-246.

Vealey, R. S. (1994). Current status and prominent issues in sport psychology interventions. *Medicine and Science in Sports and Exercise, 26*, 495-418.

Vealey, R. S., Armstrong, L., Comar, W., & Greenleaf, C. A. (1998). Influence of perceived coaching behaviors on burnout and competitive anxiety in female college athletes. *Journal of Applied Sport Psychology, 10*, 297-318.

Vealey, R. S., & Greenleaf, C. A. (2001). Seeing is believing: Understanding and using imagery in sport. In J. M. Williams (Ed.), *Applied sport psychology: Personal growth to peak performance* (4th ed., pp. 247-283). Mountain View, CA: Mayfield.

Vealey, R. S., & Knight, B. J. (2002, October). Conceptualization and measurement of multidimensional sport-confidence. Paper presented at the Association for the Advancement of Applied Sport Psychology Conference, Tucson.

Vealey, R. S., Udry, E. M., Zimmerman, V., & Soliday, J. (1992). Intrapersonal and situational predictors of coaching burnout. *Journal of Sport & Exercise Psychology, 14*, 40-58.

Viesturs, E. (2000). Each mountain a collection. In B. McDonald & J. Amatt (Eds.), *Voices from the summit* (pp. 72-77). Washington, D. C.: Adventure Press.

Wahl, G., & Wertheim, L. J. (2003, December 22). A rite gone terribly wrong. *Sports Illustrated*, pp. 68-77.

Walton, D. (1989). *Are you communicating*? New York: McGraw-Hill.

Walton, G. (1992). *Beyond winning: The timeless wisdom of great philosopher coaches*. Champaign, IL: Human Kinetics.

Wanlin, C. M., Hrycaiko, D. W., Martin, G. L., & Mahon, M. (1997). The effects of a goal-setting package on the performance of speed skaters. *Journal of Applied Sport Psychology, 9*, 212-228.

Warner, B. (1999). It might as well be me! In J. Naber (Ed.), *Awaken the Olympian within* (pp. 85-94). Torrance, CA: Griffin.

Watson, C. B., & Chemers, M. M. (1998). *The rise of shared perceptions: A multilevel analysis of collective efficacy.* Paper presented at the Organizational Behavior Division for the Academy of Management Meeting, San Diego, CA.

Watson, D., Clark, L. A., & Tellegen, A. (1985). Towards a consensual structure of mood. *Psychological Bulletin, 98*, 219-235.

Wegner, D. M. (1994). Ironic processes of mental control. *Psychological Review, 101*, 34-52.

Wegner, D. M., Ansfield, M., & Pilloff, D. (1998). The putt and the pendulum: Ironic effects of the mental control of action. *Psychological Science, 9*, 196-199.

Weinberg, R., Gould, D., & Jackson, A. (1979). Expectations and performance: An empirical test of Bandura's self-efficacy theory. *Journal of Sport Psychology, 1*, 320-331.

Weiner, B. (1986). *An attribution theory of motivation and emotion.* New York: Springer-Verlag.

Weiss, M. R., Ebbeck, V., & Horn, T. S. (1997). Children's self-perceptions and sources of physical competence information: A cluster analysis. *Journal of Sport & Exercise Psychology, 19*, 52-70.

Weiss, M. R., & Petlichkoff, L. M. (1989). Children's motivation for participation in and withdrawal from sport: Identifying the missing links. *Pediatric Exercise Science, 1*, 195-211.

Wells, C. M., Collins, D., & Hale, B. D. (1993). The self-efficacy-performance link in maximum strength performance. *Journal of Sport Sciences, 11*, 167-175.

Wertheim, L. J. (2003, November 10). Andy Roddick is just like you. *Sports Illustrated*, pp. 72-76.

White, A., & Hardy, L. (1998). An in-depth analysis of the uses of imagery by high-level slalom canoeists and artistic gymnasts. *The Sport Psychologist, 12*, 387-403.

Wiese-Bjornstal, D. M., Smith, A. M., Shaffer, S. M., & Morrey, M. A. (1998). An integrated model of response to sport injury: Psychological and sociological dynamics. *Journal of Applied Sport Psychology, 10*, 46-69.

Wilcox, S., & Trudel, P. (1998). Constructing the coaching principles and beliefs of a youth ice hockey coach. *Avante, 4*, 39-66.

Williams, A. M., & Davids, K. (1998). Visual search strategy, selective attention, and expertise in soccer. *Research Quarterly for Exercise and Sport, 69*, 111-128.

Williams, A. M., & Elliott, D. (1999). Anxiety, expertise, and visual search strategy in karate. *Journal of Sport & Exercise Psychology, 21*, 362-375.

Williams, J. M., & Harris, D. V. (2001). Relaxation and energizing techniques for regulation of arousal. In J. M. Williams (Ed.), *Applied sport psychology: Personal growth to peak performance* (4th ed., pp. 229-246). Mountain View, CA: Mayfield.

Williams, J. M., Hogan, T. D., & Andersen, M. B. (1993). Positive states of mind and athletic injury risk. *Psychosomatic Medicine, 55*, 468-472.

Williams, J. M., & Krane, V. (2001). Psychological characteristics of peak performance. In J. M. Williams (Ed.), *Applied sport psychology: Personal growth to peak performance* (4th ed., pp. 162-178). Mountain View, CA: Mayfield.

Williams, J. M., Rotella, R. J., & Scherzer, C. B. (2001). Injury risk and rehabilitation: Psychological considerations. In J. M. Williams (Ed.), *Applied sport psychology: Personal growth to peak performance* (4th ed., pp. 456-479). Mountain View, CA: Mayfield.

Williams, J. M., & Widmeyer, W. N. (1991). The cohesion-performance outcome relationship in a coacting sport. *Journal of Sport and Exercise Psychology, 13*, 364-371.

Wilson, P. (1995). *Instant calm.* New York: Penguin.

Wilson, P., & Eklund, R. C. (1998). The relationship between competitive anxiety and self-presentational concerns. *Journal of Sport & Exercise Psychology, 20*, 81-97.

Wise, J. B., & Trunnell, E. P. (2001). The influence of sources of self-efficacy upon efficacy strength. *Journal of Sport & Exercise Psychology, 23*, 268-280.

Wolff, A. (1996a, August 12). Power grab. *Sports Illustrated*, pp. 58-61.

Wolff, A. (1996b, July 22). Roadshow. *Sports Illustrated*, pp. 94-97.

Wolff, A. (1997, December 22). Fanfare for an uncommon man. *Sports Illustrated*, pp. 32-48.

Wooden, J. (1988). *They call me coach.* Chicago: Contemporary Books.

Wooden, J. (1997). *Wooden.* Chicago: Contemporary.

Wright, R. J. (1997). *Beyond time management: Business with purpose.* Boston: Butterworth.

Wrisberg, C. A., & Anshel, M. H. (1997). The use of positively-worded performance reminders to reduce warm-up decrement in the field hockey penalty shot. *Journal of Applied Sport Psychology, 9*, 229-240.

Wrisberg, C. A., & Pein, R. L. (1992). The preshot interval and free throw shooting accuracy: An exploratory investigation. *The Sport Psychologist, 6*, 14-23.

Yukelson, D. (1997). Principles of effective team building interventions in sport: A direct services approach at Penn State University. *Journal of Applied Sport Psychology, 9*, 73-96.

Zielinski, D. (1998, February). Bringing out the actor within: How to find your authentic stage presence. *Presentations*, pp. 41-52.

Zimmerman, P. (1979, November 26). All dressed up: Nowhere to go. *Sports Illustrated, 51*, 38-40.

Appendices

Appendices List

Personal Shield Exercise (instructions)

Draw something that represents a peak performance you recently achieved

Draw something about yourself that few people know

Sketch how you like to spend your spare time

Draw something at which you are the BEST

Write or draw something that epitomizes your personal motto

Appendix 4B

Personal Shield Exercise (blank)

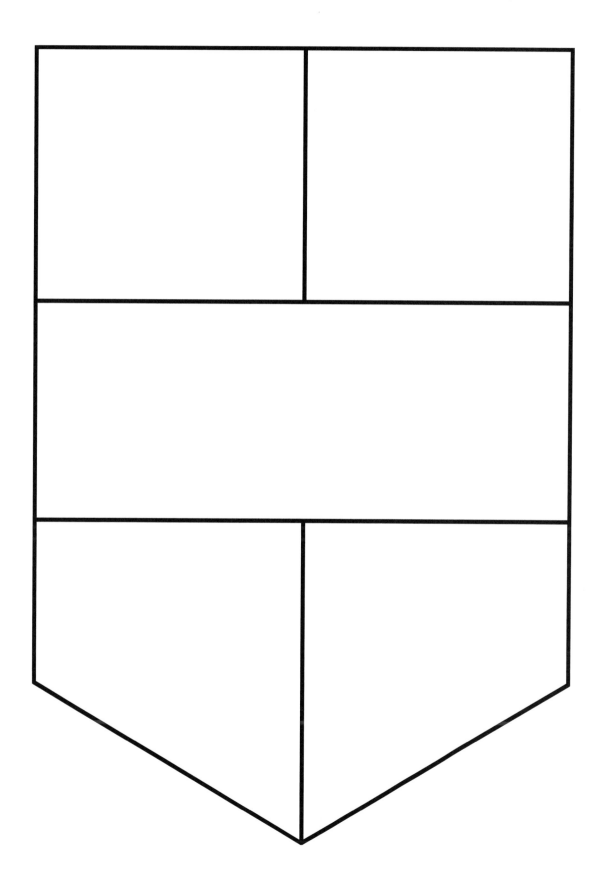

Appendix 10A

P³ Thinking Worksheet for Athletes

Introduction

1. To be a mentally tough athlete, you have to **think well**. Thinking well means that you follow the P³ formula: **Purposeful + Productive + Possibility** Thinking.

2. When you lose focus or choke, it's from **poor thinking**. Self-defeating thoughts in sport come from the R³ formula: **Random + Reactive + Restrictive** Thinking.

3. Look at the differences in how athletes think using the P³ and R³ Thinking formulas in the following example situations.

Example A: My field hockey team arrived at the competition site 45 minutes late due to transportation problems, and we have less time than usual to warm up.

P³ Thinking	R³ Thinking
Purposeful	*Random*
Warm up quickly and deliberately, but don't rush—prepare to play well.	I feel rushed and unfocused.
+	+
Productive	*Reactive*
Focus on readiness of body, skillful stick handling, and confidence—I'm ready!	This is not fair!
+	+
Possibility	*Restrictive*
We might play better with a shorter warm-up period!	I can't get ready to play that quickly.

Example B: A swimmer is put in a preliminary heat with the defending state champion, with only two swimmers advancing to the finals.

P³ Thinking	R³ Thinking
Purposeful	*Random*
I love the challenge—it's why I compete.	I can't beat her.
+	+
Productive	*Reactive*
Quick start, feel strong, solid technique, swim my race.	How did I draw this heat? I *have* to make the final.
+	+
Possibility	*Restrictive*
I'm primed—time for the training payoff.	Don't take chances—get second and qualify.

4. Here's some tips to help you become a better (and P³) thinker:

   a. **Think "on purpose."** Your thoughts are changeable and controllable. Decide what to think about or how you want to think in tough situations.

   b. Decide right now that you are going to **manage your thoughts to manage your life**. Athletes who lack mental toughness let their lives and what happens to them control how they think. Control your thoughts or they will control you!

c. In situations where you struggle, think negatively, or choke, **plan some brief trigger words** or thoughts and practice these ahead of time. Your thoughts are Productive in competition when they are focused on the present, personally controllable, task-oriented, and personally meaningful.

d. When you have self-defeating or R³ thoughts, that's okay. Mentally tough athletes have R³ thoughts occasionally—they just refuse to focus on them and let them "pass through" their heads. Immediately replace an R³ thought with a P³ thought. **It's okay for R³ thoughts to occur—just don't give them the privilege of your attention!**

e. **Focus on what you want to happen and/or what you hope for.** See this vividly. If you picture what you DON'T want to happen or what you fear, quickly replace this image with an image of your best possible performance or response in this situation.

f. **Choose to RESPOND (cool thoughts); don't REACT with emotion** (hot thoughts). Remember that what happens to you is not nearly as important as how you RESPOND to what happens to you. Thinking is a choice!

g. **Mentally practice your P³ thinking** by going through how you want to think in different situations. Visualize yourself to think well by responding and using the P³ formula.

Exercises

1. Think carefully and reflectively about **thoughts and feelings that you associate with GOOD performances.** What thoughts and feelings prepare and enable you to perform well while also remaining focused and confident in competition?

Personal thoughts and feelings that enable me to perform well and remain focused and confident:

_____

_____

_____

_____

2. Now, think carefully and reflectively about **thoughts and feelings that you associate with POOR performances.** What thoughts and feelings do you have when you are performing poorly or feeling less confident and focused in competition?

Personal thoughts and feelings typically occurring prior to and during my POOR performances:

_____

_____

_____

_____

3. Identify any **situations or things** that happen to you in sport that **trigger you to have self-defeating thoughts or feelings** (e.g., criticism from coach, mistakes, officials, teammates). Be **very specific** in describing the exact thing that triggers you to think Reactively or feel badly:

Situations or things that trigger me to think or feel badly:

Specific thing that happens to me:	*What I think (self-defeating R^3 thoughts):*	*How it makes me feel or how it hurts my performance:*
a.		
b.		
c.		
d.		
e.		

4. In the previous exercise, you identified self-defeating R³ thoughts that hurt your performance in certain situations. Your task now is to **plan the P³ thoughts that you will use to immediately replace the R³ thoughts when they occur in each situation.**

Tip: your replacement thoughts must be believable—don't just go through the motions. Write down what you actually believe and that has meaning for you in that situation.

Situations or things that trigger me to think or feel badly:

Specific thing that happens to me:	*How I can think better (replacement P³ thought):*	*How this will enhance my feelings and performance:*
a.		
b.		
c.		
d.		
e.		

5. Spend a few minutes each day visualizing the situations you've identified, and **mentally practice thinking well in these situations by using your P³ replacement thoughts.**

6. When your old self-defeating thoughts come back at times in competition, remind yourself that you knew they could, but **immediately choose to think about your planned replacement thoughts.** Keep it simple—make your thoughts short and easy to remember—and focused on what you have to do at that moment in competition. Give yourself a **perfect mental picture** of your performance as you repeat your P³ thoughts. Good luck!

Appendix 12A

Attentional Focusing Questionnaire for Athletes

Respond to each item by circling the number that represents **how much you feel this way in competition**. There are no right or wrong answers. Be honest, so you can learn how you can improve your focus.

		always	frequently	sometimes	rarely	never
1.	I don't think about my performance in competition—I just do it.	4	3	2	1	0
2.	I get distracted in competition by things that shouldn't matter.	4	3	2	1	0
3.	I am good at looking at a competitive situation and assessing what is going on.	4	3	2	1	0
4.	I can quickly refocus my attention when it is interrupted.	4	3	2	1	0
5.	I can "zoom in" my focus when I need to.	4	3	2	1	0
6.	I perform on autopilot by trusting and letting my performance flow freely.	4	3	2	1	0
7.	I maintain my focus even when I fall behind or perform poorly.	4	3	2	1	0
8.	It is hard for me to take everything in and analyze it quickly.	4	3	2	1	0
9.	I quickly regain my performance focus after an error or setback.	4	3	2	1	0
10.	It's hard to for me to focus on my task when there is a lot going on around me.	4	3	2	1	0
11.	I over-think my performance and try to control it too much.	4	3	2	1	0
12.	I handle bad calls or situations that go against me by staying in focus.	4	3	2	1	0
13.	I am good at analyzing opponents' strengths and weaknesses.	4	3	2	1	0
14.	After I receive criticism from my coach, I quickly regain my competitive focus.	4	3	2	1	0
15.	It is easy for me to focus on one thing at a time when I compete.	4	3	2	1	0
16.	I get lost in my performance and forget problems and distractions.	4	3	2	1	0
17.	Things like officiating, opponents, and crowd noise bother me.	4	3	2	1	0
18.	I can quickly process things as they happen in competition.	4	3	2	1	0
19.	When something upsets me in competition, I put it aside and quickly regain my focus.	4	3	2	1	0
20.	It is easy for me to narrow my thoughts and focus on one key thing.	4	3	2	1	0

Assess Your Focus Skills

1. The Attentional Focusing Questionnaire for Athletes assesses **five types of focus needed by athletes to perform successfully**. Compute your focus scores by adding up your individual scores for each subscale that represents a certain type of focus. An "R" after the item number means that you **reverse score** that item (4=0, 3=1, 1=3, 0=4). Each of your scores should range between 0 and 16.

Autopilot (sum items 1, 6, 11R, 16)   Score: _____

Focusing Through Distractions (sum items 2R, 7, 12, 17R)   Score: _____

Big Picture (sum items 3, 8R, 13, 18)   Score: _____

Refocusing (sum items 4, 9, 14, 19)   Score: _____

Zoom (sum items 5, 10R, 15, 20)   Score: _____

2. What do your scores mean? Here's a quick way to interpret them. If you scored:

    13 - 16   Outstanding competitive focus in this area—a focus machine!
    9 - 12   Good focus ability, just need some fine-tuning.
    5 - 8   Average focus skills, so you can really improve with practice!
    0 - 4   You have some work to do!

3. **Which focus skills are you good at, and which skills do you need to work on?** All athletes have attentional strengths and weaknesses. Your focus abilities are like your muscles—they respond to training! So the intent of this exercise is to help you understand what you're good at focusing on and what you need to work on to enhance your ability to focus and perform well.

    Each focus area is described below, and **tips to enhance each type of focus** are provided. Read through each description and think about how you can improve your focus ability in that area. Jot down a couple of things you can do in each area to help yourself be a more mentally focused athlete.

Autopilot: Your best performances occur when you "let them happen" and perform automatically. We lose this focus when we "try too hard" or attempt to control or steer our performance.

When I need to use Autopilot:

_____

_____

_____

To get this focus:
Train hard and do many reps to "build your machine" to perform automatically; visualize performance and then let it flow effortlessly; use verbal cues to trigger the automatic movements you want to feel; think about the joy of performing and forget about the outcome or winning; practice "letting go" in training; just play.

How I can improve My Autopilot:

_____

_____

_____

Focusing Through Distractions: Your most important mental goal as an athlete is to maintain a focused connection to your performance, no matter what! Distractions don't hurt your performance, you let them hurt your performance by giving them your attention! Don't let distractions take your focus. Expect the unexpected. Expect to be inconvenienced, criticized, cheated, made uncomfortable, surprised, angry, and to not perform well at times. These distractions are inevitable in sport, but only you decide whether or not to give them your attention.

When I need to Focus Through Distractions:

_____

_____

_____

To get this focus: Simulate distractions in your training; mentally practice handling distractions and staying focused; tell yourself to "stay in the present" and only focus on what is happening right now and what you have to do; triage your thinking in competition to only focus on the performance at hand; "file" your distracting thoughts away and deal with them later.

How I can improve my ability to Focus through Distractions:

_____

_____

_____

Big Picture: Ability to analyze what's happening in competition; to make decisions and use strategy; analyzing opponent's strengths and weaknesses; recognizing what needs to be done to succeed in competition.

When I need to focus on the Big Picture:

_____

_____

_____

To get this focus: Remind yourself to intermittently "read" what's going on; talk to your coach to get tips for doing this in competition; become a student of your sport; scan, read, and recognize while on the bench.

How I can improve My Big Picture focus:

_____

_____

_____

Refocusing: How well and quickly you can shift your focus back to where it should be after being distracted; ability to shift focus when needed to talk to coach or teammate and then get right back into flow; ability to quickly "change the channel" and put your mind back where it needs to be to perform.

When I need to Refocus:

_____

_____

_____

To refocus: Identify situations that distract you and come up with a refocusing cue to help you "change the channel" back to performance; accept distractions and performance errors—let them go and lock back in to your focus; "file" distractions and use your refocus cue; stay in the present, be in "the now."

How I can improve my Refocusing:

_____

_____

_____

Zoom Focus: How well you can "zoom in" to think about one key thing while performing; a laser-like narrow focus in which all surrounding distractions become irrelevant; focusing on one thing at a time.

When I need to Zoom:

_____

_____

_____

To get this focus: Develop a pre-performance routine to help you zoom in; practice nondistractible zooming in training; repeat a key word or phrase to help you lock on to the exact performance you want to have; visualize yourself in a narrow beam of light—make yourself a laser.

How I can improve my Zoom?

_____

_____

_____

Appendix 12B

Centering Yourself to Focus Under Pressure

PROBLEM SITUATION   FOCUS SITUATION

_____   _____

_____   _____

PHYSICAL PROBLEMS	FOCUS PROBLEMS	PHYSICAL FEELINGS	FOCUS ROUTINE
_____	_____	_____	_____
_____	_____	_____	_____
_____	_____	_____	_____
_____	_____	_____	_____

↓   ↓

PERFORMANCE PROBLEMS   FOCUSED PERFORMANCE OUTCOMES

_____   _____

_____   _____

_____   _____

Appendix 12C

Focus Planning Sheet

Focus Feelings and Thoughts Early in Competition Day	Pre-Jump Physical and Mental Warmup Routine and Focus	Pre-Jump Routine (performance)	Post-Jump Routine	Refocusing Responses

Appendix 12D

Refocusing Worksheet for Athletes

Situation or Distraction	Preferred Response	Focus or Cue Word (to bring on preferred response)

Appendix 13A

Optimal Energy Profile

The purpose of this exercise is for you to **identify the feelings** that help you **perform your best** as well as the feelings that **hurt your performance**. All athletes have their own personal Optimal Energy Zone, and your goal in this exercise is to begin to identify your zone where you perform your best.

All types of energy, or feelings, are useful to help athletes perform well. You will be asked to identify:

- **pleasant** feelings that **help** your performance (P+)
- **unpleasant** feelings that **help** your performance (U+)
- **unpleasant** feelings that **hurt** your performance (U-)
- **pleasant** feelings that **hurt** your performance (P-)

It's easy to understand how pleasant feelings help you to perform better and unpleasant feelings hurt your performance. However, sport competition requires athletes to push themselves beyond their typical comfort zones to excel. Because of this, unpleasant feelings are often helpful to get athletes focused and ready to perform well, even though they don't always feel good! So it's important that you carefully think about unpleasant feelings that don't feel good, but that help you perform better.

As you work through the exercise, it's very important that you think about exact feelings in your own personal words. The example words are just examples—there are no right or wrong answers.

Before you start the exercise, make extra photocopies of Part B and Part C. You'll use these more than once, so you'll need blank copies.

Part A: Identifying Feelings

Recall some of your **BEST and WORST PERFORMANCES**. Visualize in your mind the feelings you had just prior to and during these events. These feelings may include **your mental state** (e.g., ready, calm) as well as **how your body felt** (e.g., quick, tense).

1. **What PLEASANT feelings really HELP your performance?** Write **at least 3** and no more than 6 words that describe:

My mental state (e.g., confident, ready, charged, intense, calm) and/or **how my body felt** (e.g., quick, strong, smooth, light, wired, energized, relaxed, fast, loose):

_____

_____

_____

2. **What UNPLEASANT feelings really HELP your performance?** Write **at least 3** and no more than 6 words that describe:

My mental state (e.g., worried, angry, fearful, intense, nervous) and/or **how my body felt** (e.g., tight, jittery, tense, tired, wired):

_____

_____

_____

3.   **What UNPLEASANT feelings really HURT your performance?** Write **at least 3** and no more than 6 words that describe:

My mental state (e.g., worried, angry, fearful, intense, nervous, depressed) and/or **how my body felt** (e.g., tight, jittery, tense, tired, wired, relaxed):

_____

_____

_____

4.   **What PLEASANT feelings really HURT your performance?** Write **at least 3** and no more than 6 words that describe:

My mental state (e.g., calm, happy, satisfied, certain, determined) and/or **how my body felt** (e.g., quick, strong, smooth, light, wired, energized, relaxed, fast, loose)

_____

_____

_____

Part B: Identifying Preferred Intensity of Feelings

1.   Look back over the feelings that you've identified in Part A. **In each group** of feelings, **select 2-3 that affect your performance the most.** Circle these in Part A.

2.   **Write the feelings you've selected in the spaces provided below.** P+ is for pleasant feelings that help performance; U+ is for unpleasant feelings that help performance; U- is for unpleasant feelings that hurt performance; P- is for pleasant feelings that hurt performance. You should have at least 2 feelings for each category listed below, and no more than 3 for each one.

3.   After writing in your feelings for each category, **circle the number** next to it that represents **HOW MUCH you want to feel** that way. If you circle 10, you want to feel "the most you can feel that way"; 8-9 is "a lot"; 6-7 is "pretty much"; 5 is "average"; 3-4 is "some"; 1-2 is "hardly any"; and 0 is "not feeling that way at all."

	not at all	hardly any		some			pretty much		a lot	most I can feel
	0	1	2	3	4	5	6	7	8	9	10

P+ Feelings:

0	1	2	3	4	5	6	7	8	9	10
0	1	2	3	4	5	6	7	8	9	10
0	1	2	3	4	5	6	7	8	9	10

U+ Feelings:

0	1	2	3	4	5	6	7	8	9	10
0	1	2	3	4	5	6	7	8	9	10
0	1	2	3	4	5	6	7	8	9	10

U- Feelings:

0	1	2	3	4	5	6	7	8	9	10
0	1	2	3	4	5	6	7	8	9	10
0	1	2	3	4	5	6	7	8	9	10

P- Feelings:

0	1	2	3	4	5	6	7	8	9	10
0	1	2	3	4	5	6	7	8	9	10
0	1	2	3	4	5	6	7	8	9	10

Part C: Developing Your Optimal Energy Profile (OEP)

1.   **Write in the names of your feeling states at the bottom of the graph in the appropriate categories** (see next page for an example).

2.   Then, **plot your scores** by making a circle on the graph to show your **preferred intensity for each feeling** (see circles on example graph).

3.   Then, **draw your Optimal Energy Zone**, which goes from one point below and one point above each circle. As shown on the example graph, the U- feeling of "tight" is preferred by the athlete to be a 1 in intensity level. So her zone for this feeling is 0 to 2. Plot the upper and lower points of your zone, and then connect the lines to create your overall OEP. Color it your favorite color—it's your zone!

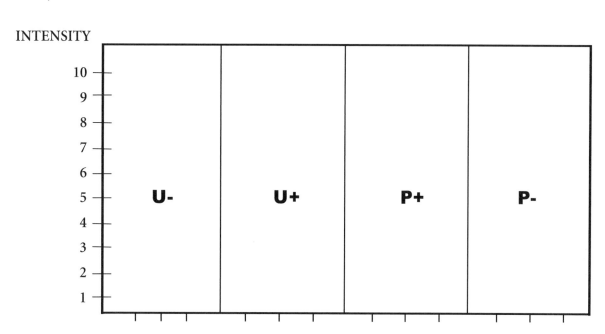

INTENSITY

FEELING STATES

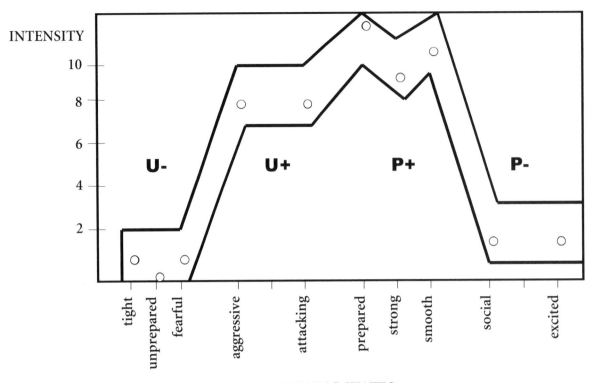

INTENSITY

10

8

6

4

2

U-   **U+**   **P+**   **P-**

tight unprepared fearful aggressive attacking prepared strong smooth social excited

FEELING STATES
Example Optimal Energy Profile for Elite Golfer

Part D: Using Your Optimal Energy Profile (OEP)

Congratulations! You've just figured out your Optimal Energy Zone and created an Optimal Energy Profile for yourself. Now, how do you use it? Here are some steps to follow:

1. **Mentally prepare to put yourself in your zone prior to and during your performance.** Using the elite golfer's example OEP, she wants to feel as prepared and smooth as possible. She also wants to feel strong, aggressive, and attacking. She wants to avoid feeling tight, unprepared, and fearful, and also doesn't want to feel social or excited as these tend to distract her from playing her best.

    a. **Mentally rehearse the feeling states that you want** to have during competition. Feel these feelings in your **mental practice,** and also attempt to feel these feelings during **physical training.**

    b. **Develop a plan for your physical and mental warm-up to put yourself in the mood you want and to bring out your positive feelings.** For example, the golfer would avoid being social, keep her excitement contained, and focus on smooth swing and feeling strong and prepared in her warm-up. She would hit shots focusing on being aggressive with those clubs and attacking the pins. If her body starts to feel tight, she takes Power Breaths and shrugs the tightness from her shoulders. If she thinks of fear or feeling unprepared, she catches these negative thoughts and replaces them with thoughts of being ready for every shot and welcoming the fear because it gives her aggressive energy to play her best. Her pre-shot routine involves thinking "smoooooth" during her practice swing and then committing fully to a strong and aggressive (yet smooth) swing.

2. **Keep blank copies of Parts B and C of this exercise, and complete them after each competition.** That is, you'll assess the intensity of your feeling states, and then plot them to look at your OEP for each competition. **Your objective is to stay within your zone,** because this is where you should perform your best. As you learn more about your competitive energy and feelings, you can **revise your key feeling states and even change your OEP.** Your main objective is to find the OEP that works best

for you in enhancing your performance, and then mentally and physically prepare to get into your zone during competition.

3.   Your performances should be good when your OEP looks like a **Peak** (higher in the middle and low on the sides). If your OEP looks like a **Valley** (lower in the middle and high on the sides), that means you're totally out of zone for that competition and your performance should be bad. If your zone is a **Plateau** (straight across the middle), you're experiencing the same levels of positive and negative feelings and your performance should be average. If your zone is a **Flatline** (straight across the bottom), check your pulse—you're not feeling anything and probably need CPR to perform at all!

Appendix 14A

Sport-Confidence Inventory
Sport-Confidence Inventory

Athletes need many different abilities to succeed (e.g., physical skills, mental focus, optimal fitness). In this survey, you are asked to assess many of **your abilities as an athlete.**

Read the example item listed below, and then decide **how certain you are** that you can **successfully** do what is described in that item.
For this survey, consider "**success**" to be whatever you define as successful for you (your **personal definition of success**).

Respond to each item based on how you feel *right now* **about your abilities in relation to the upcoming competitive season.**

Use the continuum shown below to guide your self-assessment. What number would you circle for the example item?

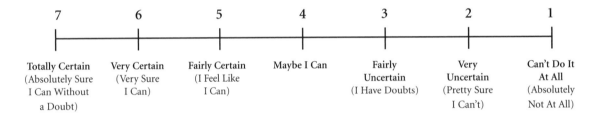

7	6	5	4	3	2	1
Totally Certain (Absolutely Sure I Can Without a Doubt)	Very Certain (Very Sure I Can)	Fairly Certain (I Feel Like I Can)	Maybe I Can	Fairly Uncertain (I Have Doubts)	Very Uncertain (Pretty Sure I Can't)	Can't Do It At All (Absolutely Not At All)

EXAMPLE ITEM:

How certain are you that ... you can perform successfully under pressure?

       7   6   5   4   3   2   1

Be honest in your assessment.

    If you think **MAYBE you can do this**, you would circle 4.
    If you're **pretty sure you CAN'T do this**, you would circle 2.
    If you're **very sure you CAN do this**, you would circle 6.
    Only if you're **ABSOLUTELY sure without any doubts** would you circle 7.

Keep in mind that 7 and 1 represent **absolute levels** in which you are totally certain that you can do this or absolutely sure that you cannot.

On the following page, read each item and **circle the number** that represents HOW CERTAIN YOU FEEL that you can do what is described in that item.

Your answers will be kept strictly confidential. Please answer as **you really feel**, being totally honest (as opposed to answering as you would LIKE to feel or think that you are SUPPOSED to feel). All athletes are different in their abilities, and **there are no right or wrong responses.**

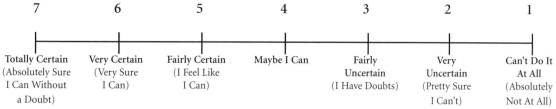

7	6	5	4	3	2	1
Totally Certain (Absolutely Sure I Can Without a Doubt)	Very Certain (Very Sure I Can)	Fairly Certain (I Feel Like I Can)	Maybe I Can	Fairly Uncertain (I Have Doubts)	Very Uncertain (Pretty Sure I Can't)	Can't Do It At All (Absolutely Not At All)

HOW CERTAIN ARE YOU THAT ...   (CIRCLE ONLY **ONE** NUMBER FOR EACH ITEM)

7   **totally certain** (ABSOLUTELY sure I CAN without a doubt)
6   **very certain** (VERY SURE I CAN)
5   **fairly certain** (I feel like I CAN)
4   **MAYBE I** can
3   **fairly uncertain** (I have DOUBTS)
2   **very uncertain** (PRETTY SURE I CAN'T)
1   **can't do it at all** (ABSOLUTELY NOT AT ALL)

1.   you can **execute the physical skills** necessary to succeed?

       7   6   5   4   3   2   1

2.   you can keep **mentally focused** throughout the competitive event?

       7   6   5   4   3   2   1

3.   you can **bounce back** from performing poorly to successfully execute your skills?

       7   6   5   4   3   2   1

4.   your **physical training** has **prepared** you enough to succeed?

       7   6   5   4   3   2   1

5.   you can successfully **make critical decisions** during competition?

       7   6   5   4   3   2   1

6.   you can **regain your mental focus** after a performance **error**?

       7   6   5   4   3   2   1

7.   your **physical fitness level** will allow you to compete successfully?

       7   6   5   4   3   2   1

8.   you can effectively **use strategy** needed to succeed?

       7   6   5   4   3   2   1

9.   you can **overcome doubt** after a poor performance?

       7   6   5   4   3   2   1

7	6	5	4	3	2	1
Totally Certain (Absolutely Sure I Can Without a Doubt)	Very Certain (Very Sure I Can)	Fairly Certain (I Feel Like I Can)	Maybe I Can	Fairly Uncertain (I Have Doubts)	Very Uncertain (Pretty Sure I Can't)	Can't Do It At All (Absolutely Not At All)

HOW CERTAIN ARE YOU THAT ...   (CIRCLE ONLY **ONE** NUMBER FOR EACH ITEM)

7   **totally certain** (ABSOLUTELY sure I CAN without a doubt)
6   **very certain** (VERY SURE I CAN)
5   **fairly certain** (I feel like I CAN)
4   **MAYBE I can**
3   **fairly uncertain** (I have DOUBTS)
2   **very uncertain** (PRETTY SURE I CAN'T)
1   **can't do it at all** (ABSOLUTELY NOT AT ALL)

10.   you can successfully **perform the physical skills** required in your sport?

          7   6   5   4   3   2   1

11.   you can **maintain the mental focus** needed to perform successfully?

          7   6   5   4   3   2   1

12.   you can **overcome problems and setbacks** to perform successfully?

          7   6   5   4   3   2   1

13.   you have the **physical preparation** that is needed to compete successfully?

          7   6   5   4   3   2   1

14.   you can successfully **manage your nervousness** so that it doesn't hurt your performance?

          7   6   5   4   3   2   1

Scoring Instructions

1.   Sum items 1, 4, 7, 10, and 13, and divide this sum by 5. This is your *SC-Physical Skills and Training* score.

                                             _____

2.   Sum items 2, 5, 8, and 11, and divide this sum by 4. This is your *SC-Cognitive Efficiency* score.

                                             _____

3.   Sum items 3, 6, 9, 12, and 14, and divide this sum by 5. This is your *SC-Resilience* score.

                                             _____

SC-Physical Skills and Training: confidence in your ability to execute the physical skills necessary to perform successfully

SC-Cognitive Efficiency: confidence that you can mentally focus, maintain concentration, and make effective decisions to perform successfully

SC-Resilience: confidence that you can regain your focus after performance errors, bounce back from performing poorly, and overcome doubts, problems, and setbacks to perform successfully

Analyzing and Enhancing Your Confidence

1.   What area(s) of confidence are you strongest in? Weakest in? Can you explain why you have these strengths and weaknesses? Understanding why you are confident and what your confidence is based on is the first step in developing a strong and resilient confidence needed for performance success.

2.   Here are some tips for building confidence in each area. These are just tips—only you can take responsibility and do the work to build your own confidence. Good luck!

Confidence in your Physical Skills/Training: Earn the right to be confident through intense physical practice. If you don't do the reps, you won't be able to relax and trust your performance when it counts in competition. Identify your strengths and focus on those, but take time to identify and work on your weaknesses. Develop and constantly monitor a personal goal map, which is your individualized prescription for success. Shortcuts in training rob you of confidence when you need it. Plan your path—do the work—reap the results!

Confidence in your Cognitive Efficiency: Work with your coach to create a focus plan for competition and/or a pre-performance routine for yourself. Monitor yourself to understand the thoughts and feelings you have prior to and during good performances, and mentally practice a routine where you consciously make yourself think and feel these ways in preparation for competition.

Confidence in your Resilience: Have you ever rebounded from errors, slumps, and poor performances? Of course you have! Reaffirm to yourself that you have the mental toughness to work through obstacles and bounce back from setbacks and poor performances. On those competition days when you are struggling, make it a priority to perform the best you can those days with no loss of effort. Work to maintain your focus, even when it's hard. Practice focusing in training sessions on days when things don't come easily, and you can develop your ability to remain resilient in your effort, focus, and performance no matter what happens during competition. Also, develop a refocusing plan by identifying situations or distractions in which you lose your focus. Plan a mental strategy for how you will refocus in these situations, and practice your refocusing strategies both mentally and in training sessions. Remember—good thinking is a choice. Distractions don't cause you to lose focus, rather you choose to allow your focus to be distracted. Choose to think well, and train hard to think well in the pressure of competition. Grow a thick skin—and be a resilient, mentally tough athlete!

Appendix 15A

Critical Success Factors Activity

Identifying Critical Success Factors

Critical Success Factors (CSFs) are **areas to which a team must give full attention and achieve success** if it is to reach its goals and fulfill its potential.

Critical Success Factor (CSF)	Attention presently given to this CSF (Rate on 1 to 10 scale where 1=low and	Recommendations for strengthening this CSF 10=high)

Appendix 15B

Mental Skills Checklist

Miami Volleyball 2003

Mental Preparation for a Championship Season

I. Critical Success Factors identified by you for the 2003 season:

A. Demanding excellence in preparation and performance
B. Resilient confidence
C. Effective mental preparation—for practices and matches, for individuals and team
D. Solid serve receive performance—communication and execution
E. Solid and seamless transition from defense to attack

The top three ranked CSFs that this team chose last spring focus on mental toughness, confidence, and mental preparation. **What have you done, what are you doing, and what can you do now heading into the season to achieve these important goals?**

II. Mental Skills Checklist

Read through the following checklist of characteristics and behaviors that define what it means to be a mentally skilled athlete. Ask yourself "**What components am I missing?**" and work heading into the preseason to become a more complete and mentally tough player.

❑ **Highly motivated and welcomes challenge.** Only YOU are responsible for your preparation and training. Let the tradition of this program and the determination of this team motivate you to train and prepare this summer, and to come into the preseason in top physical AND mental shape.

❑ **Takes personal responsibility every day for self AND team.** Recognize the importance and influence of your behavior and actions on your teammates, coaches, and team as a whole.

❑ **Strong self-concept.** See yourself as a great player who has something important to contribute to this team. If you're part of Miami Volleyball, then the program thinks you're a great player and you should always think the same. ALWAYS.

❑ **Supports and contributes to team cohesion at all times.** This team has prided itself on becoming a team that battles together, in practice and during matches. How do you (and how will you) contribute to a strong team cohesion? Can you control your moods, your temper, your frustrations, your gripes, to always support the team and your teammates? Can you cope with criticism that is fair or even unfair?

❑ **Resilient confidence across all situations.** EVERYONE is confident when they are playing well and things are going great. Only mentally tough athletes maintain confidence across time NO MATTER WHAT. Resilience is "the ability to recover from or adjust to misfortune or change." How resilient is your confidence? Identify things that deflate your confidence, and then develop strategies to make it more resilient. Mentally practice confident responses to mistakes, misfortunes, injuries, illness, and the changing of your role on the team. RESPOND with confidence—don't react with emotion.

❑ **Instantly changes negatives into productive ways of thinking.** *This is the key to championship teams.* The U.S. Women's Soccer team has an "in" list (things they choose to focus on) and an "out" list (things they refuse to focus on or think about). Identify your negative thinking, work out a productive way to think about this, and move the negatives to your "out" list. Remember—there always is a way.

❑ **Resilient focus across all situations.** Can be trusted to stay disciplined and focused NO MAT-TER WHAT is happening around you. This summer and preseason, plan the mental approach that is best for you that you will use every match and throughout the entire match. Develop strategies to focus on specific elements of the game—the controllables—that will make a posi-tive contribution, and learn to ignore the distractions that negatively affect your game. This takes incredible amounts of practice and patience. Make mental toughness a habit—develop an unflappable mental cocoon for yourself.

❑ **Constantly self-references and adapts—a learning player.** Do you take ownership or and responsibility for your pluses and minuses as a player? Do you take ownership of or and responsibility for your progress as a volleyball player? What are you striving for? What are your goals for self-improvement this season?

❑ **Courageous performer** who WANTS the serve, pass, or set to make things happen for the team when it counts the most. This type of courage comes from confidence that is   EARNED through deliberate focused practice with no shortcuts. Train hard so you can trust yourself and WANT to make the big play for the team.

❑ **Never loses the pure enjoyment and fun of playing volleyball.** Love of the game is the key to your commitment. How much do you love the game? Do you play and practice with passion to play at your highest level?

III. Tips to Build and Strengthen your Mental Skills

How many components of mentally skilled athletes could you check off? Consider the following questions: "What am I doing right now?"; "How can I become a more complete player?"; and "How will I propel myself forward into the preseason in top physical and mental condition?" Consider the tips in this section to help you build your mental skill.

A. **Develop your goal map.** Attached is blank goal map. It looks like a tree with the trunk on the left and branches that become denser as you move to the right. The trunk asks you to identify your **sense of purpose**, or the feeling you like to have when you are playing. This purpose should remind you of why you like to play, such as enjoying the feeling of pure skill, or enjoy-ing the thrill of competition, or striving for self-challenge to be the best you can be.

As you start to fill in your goal map, consider important goals for you this season. **Milestone goals** are usually outcome oriented, such as being All-Mac, winning the league, or winning a starting position. **Challenge goals** are the performance-oriented goals that help you reach your milestones, such as serving and hitting percentages, or maintaining mental skills during com-petition. Finally, **focus goals** are specific things that you think about during competition that enhance your performance execution. You might develop some focus goals for serving, for mental toughness when things aren't going well, and for other physical performance or mental skill areas.

Play with your goal map some to identify areas to work on and towards in the preseason. Your map can change a lot, so do it in pencil or make several copies.

B. **EARN, LEARN, and then BURN with self-confidence.** EARN the right to be confident this sea-son by taking no shortcuts in your physical and mental training. Evaluate your skills and then behaviorally commit to getting better. Do the extra rep, spend the additional 15 minutes, work on a weak spot despite feeling foolish, attend to the exact details, do what most others wouldn't to earn confidence. LEARN how to self-regulate to enhance the resilience of your confidence. Develop strategies to respond with confidence. Create an "in" and "out" list of how you will think as a player. BURN with a passion for your sport, for being a competitor, for loving the challenge. Having this "burn" for what you do really builds resilience in confidence because what you do is real and an essential part of who you are.

C. **Critically reflect on your communication strengths and weaknesses.** If you all want to demand excellence in each other, you must communicate well. Identify ways that you can communicate more effectively to take personal responsibility for team cohesion and team performance. Be honest about this with yourself!

D. **Make productive thinking a habit.** Building from your "in" and "out" list, identify situations that cause you to start thinking negatively. Consider how to manage these thoughts and reframe them in productive ways. World-class athletes always do this! You are what you dwell on, so work to dwell on the most positive aspects of any situations. Once you start doing this, you'll be amazed at how it can become a habit!

Some keys: keep your thoughts in the present, focus on your focus goals during competition, have a mental plan for how to respond effectively.

E. **Control distractions** by making a checklist of everything that might push you off track from accomplishing your goal. Ask yourself what it is that you can control and focus on in the present in that situation. Plan your focus, practice your focus plan in practice and through visualization, and then work your plan in competition.

F. **Be accountable and self-responsible.** There is no "I" in team, but there is a "me." You MUST take total responsibility for the way you train, the way you interact with coaches and teammates, the way you respond to pressure, criticism, adversity, and the ways that you contribute to the team's cohesion. Volleyball is a sport in which athletes are MOST dependent upon each other. Do the extra work when no one's watching, sacrifice for the team without anyone knowing, take responsibility even when it's not your fault. If you all do this, your team will grow in unbelievable ways. **What you do as an individual always affects the team as a whole—be responsible for everything about your team.**

*Commit right now to a successful season.** You have talked the talk in identifying your Critical Success Factors, and now you must walk the walk to make these happen for yourself and this team.

No matter what happens in terms of wins and losses, you can take personal responsibility to make the season a championship season. Champions:

> play a certain way,
> act a certain way,
> respond a certain way,
> win a certain way,
> lose a certain way,
> work together a certain way,
> take criticism a certain way
> face and resolve problems a certain way, and
> prepare a certain way.

> **PREPARE to be champions this season.** It's up to you.

Appendix 16A

ALC "Act Like Champions" Checklist

Dates:																	
1. I deliberately put myself in a productive mood and focus at the start of practice.																	
2. I set an A/A physical goal for practice.																	
3. I set an A/A mental goal for practice.																	
4. I overtly supported my teammates in practice.																	
5. I participated in every drill with 100% effort.																	
6. I participated in every drill with 100% focus.																	
7. I responded and refocused when I got distracted, received critical feedback, or performed poorly.																	
8. I improved a critical skill in practice today.																	
9. I overtly challenged my teammates today to get better.																	
10. Before leaving practice, I told the coach one thing I think the team did well or that I liked about practice.																	

Index

consequences
logical, 40
natural, 40
consistency, 348
control, 93–96
controlled processing, 241, 265
Coop, Richard, 19
Counsilman, James "Doc," 77, 322
countering, 213, 222
Couples, Fred, 178
Covey, Stephen, 49, 56
Crenshaw, Ben, 272
critical success factors (CSFs), 123–124
    as an entry point, 323–324
Csikszentmihalyi, M., 7

D

Daggett, Tim, 212
Dakich, Dan, 49
Daly–Donofrio, Heather, 256
Davis, Eric, 309
Day, Colleen, 170–171
decision-making styles
autocratic, 93
democratic, 93, 94–96
permissive, 93
defensiveness, 58, 66, 70
defensiveness threshold, 117
Dekker, Erik, 24
Dewey, John, 32
Dhammapada, 201
DiCicco, Tony, 39, 59, 63, 99, 113, 195, 351
Dietrich, Marlene, 75
Disney, Walt, 85
distractions, 250–251
dominant responses, 276–277
Dorrance, Anson, 15, 37, 113, 133
"double-goal" model, 15
double messages, 65
doubts, 314–315
drive theory, 277
Dryden, Ken, 187

E

Edison, Thomas, 14, 24, 302
Edwards, Teresa, 106, 108
Eisenhower, Dwight D., 75, 82
electroencephalogram (EEG), 246
Ellis, A., 212
emotional adaptiveness, 307–308
emotional bank account (EBA), 56–57
deposits in, 56–57
emotional competence, 55–56
Emotional Intelligence (Goleman), 92
emotional temperature, 64
emotions, 153, 184, 218
    expression of, 272
empathy, 56, 72, 92–93, 100
empowerment, 81, 100
encouragement, 307, 310
energy, 269, 297

competitive energy, 269–273, 297
    energy as a natural resource, 268–269
energy management, 9, 192, 267–268, 296
    for coaches, 294–295
    mental training progression for, 325–327
Energy Room, 192
environmental comfort, 310, 316
Epictetus, 212
Eruzione, Mike, 300
evaluation, 275–276
Evert, Chris, 189, 347
extrinsic reinforcers. *See* reinforcement

F

failure-oriented athletes, 33–34, 45
feedback, 61–65, 192, 275, 307, 309–310
contingent feedback, 65
receiving feedback, 62, 74
feeling states, 269–272, 340
    collective feeling states, 291
    purposes of, 272
    and recovery from injury, 343
    related to performance, 281–285
filtering, 58
flow, 7, 11, 30, 158, 205, 273, 293
    athletic training for, 275–276
as autotelic, 7, 11, 275
as a balance between challenge and skills, 273–274
why it leads to peak performance, 274–275
See also being in the zone
Flutie, Doug, 53
focus plan, 259–260, 265, 289, 309, 313, 347
Ford, Bob, 184
Ford, Henry, 24
Fosbury, Dick, 86, 203
Foster, Will A., 150
Foudy, Julie, 113
Franklin, Ben, 108, 157, 252, 321

G

Gandhi, 57, 88
"GAP thinking," 85–86
Gardner, Howard, 92, 207
Gartner, Kerrin, 254, 306
getting stuck, 251
Gilbert, Brad, 145
Giuliani, Rudy, 214
Goal Achievement Strategies (GAS), 164
goal board, 168
goal evaluation card, 168
goal mapping, 6, 9, 31, 87, 149–150, 173, 253, 254, 265, 289, 308, 311, 313, 341
    definition of a goal, 149, 173
    as an entry point, 323
    importance of, 150–153

SMAART goal mapping, 155–157, 173, 313
    steps of, 157–171
    tips for coaches, 171–173
goals, 173
    challenge goals, 162, 173
    and effort, 305
    focus goals, 162, 173
    long-term goals, 155
    milestone goals, 162, 173
    outcome goals, 153, 173
    performance goals, 153, 174
    and persistence, 305
    process goals, 153, 174
    short-term goals, 155
Goethe, 75
Goleman, Daniel, 55–56, 92, 295
Golf Is Not a Game of Perfect (Rotella), 178
Gonzales, Luis, 287
Goodell, Brian, 289, 314
Gould, D., 142, 171, 306
Gretzsky, Wayne, 24–25, 39, 177, 250
Griffey, Ken, Jr., 141
Griffith, Coleman, 27
Griffith-Joyner, Florence, 228
"grinding," 145
groupthink, 110, 126

H

Haas, Jay, 261
Hacker, Colleen, 15, 39, 185
Haden, Pat, 267
Hamm, Mia, 37, 59, 113, 166, 202, 302–303, 350–351
Hanin, Yuri, 281
hardiness, 35, 45
Hargrove, R., 61
Harper, Ron, 173
Harvey, Mary, 63
hazing, 110
Henrich, Christy, 16, 18
Hickcox, Charles, 77
hidden agendas. *See* meta-messages
Hill, Grant, 84
Hoeppner, Terry, 51
Hogshead, Nancy, 159–160, 347
Holloway, Susan, 228
home advantage, 4, 26, 310
hook and challenge, 38–39
hope, 202, 222
Huggins, Bob, 39
Hughes, Robert, 303
Huish, Justin, 267
hyperconformity, 21, 22, 110, 126

I

Iacocca, Lee, 14
Ideal Self-Image (ISI), 192
identifying, 58
imagery, 8, 131–132, 139–140, 178, 198, 313

can imagery hurt athletic performance? 187–188
definition of, 178, 198
does imagery work? 181–185
example exercises, 196–197
how to use imagery, 188–194
and injured athletes, 344–345
internal and external imagery, 181, 198
making imagery more effective, 194–196
as a mental training tool, 180–181
    as a polysensory experience, 179–180
    as recreating and creating, 178–179
    symbolic images, 189
    team imagery, 188
inconsistency, 348–350
information, 97
injury
    mental training with injured athletes, 342–345
    overuse injuries, 338–339
recovery from, 194
reducing vulnerability to, 342
Inkster, Julie, 225
Inner Edge, 8–9, 11
and a balanced triad, 8, 15–16
"big picture" of, 8–10
building blocks of, 8
commitment to, 321–322
definition of, 11
mental skills and implementation tips, 10
and the mental training tool box, 9–10
inspiration, 312, 315–316
intensity, 225
ironic processes, 206, 222
irrational beliefs, 211
Irwin, Hale, 285
Ito, Midori, 17
It's Not About the Bike (Armstrong), 137–138

J

Jackson, S., 306
Jacobson, 52–53, 235
James, William, 177
Janelle, C. M., 207
Jansen, Dan, 18, 143, 154, 217
Johnson, Jimmy, 63
Johnson, Michael, 3–4, 312
Jones, Marion, 239
Jordan, Michael, 23, 34, 145
Joyner-Kersee, Jackie, 23

K

Kelley, H. H., 94
Kelly, Angela, 119
Kendall, G., 183
Kennedy, John F., 34, 85
Kennedy, John F., Jr., 243

Kerr, Cristie, 268
Kerrigan, Nancy, 179
KICK, 281
kinesthetic sense, 179, 197, 198
King, Betsy, 302
King, Roch, 118
Kiraly, Karch, 315, 351
KISS, 171, 281
Knight, Bob, 77, 255
Knoblauch, Dee, 89–90, 96
Kramer, Jerry, 29
Krzyzewski, Mike, 50, 79, 84, 116, 339, 341
Kuehne, Kelli, 271
Kupchak, Mitch, 250–251
Kwan, Michelle, 304

L

Laettner, Christian, 116, 339
Latham, 151
leadership, 8, 76, 100, 315
definition of, 76, 100
nurturing it in athletes, 98–99
three-ring circus model of, 83–85
See also leadership myths; transactional leadership; transformative leadership
leadership myths
Born Leader, 81
Formula Leader, 82–83
Rah-Rah Leader, 81–82
Leading with the Heart (Krzyzewski), 15
Learned Optimism (Seligman), 215
learning
double-loop, 78–79, 100
single-loop, 78–79, 100
triple-loop (transformative), 78–79, 100
LeMond, Greg, 133
Leslie, Lisa, 106, 119
life skills, 273
Lilly, Kristine, 185
Lincoln, Abraham, 24, 157, 302, 309
Lipinski, Tara, 302
Lobo, Rebecca, 106, 115
Locke, 151
Loehr, Jim, 143, 273
Lombardi, Vince, 16, 29
Lopez, Nancy, 241, 335
losing focus, 260–262
Love, Davis, III, 275

M

Macinness, Helen, 36
Making The Big Time Where You Are (Westering), 19
Marcus Aurelius, 209
Martens, R., 33, 65
Masterful Coaching (Hargrove), 61
mastery, 308
Maxwell, J. C., 89, 95
McCann, Sean, 289–290, 294, 303, 350
McClain, Katrina, 106

McGee, Carla, 106
McPherson, S. L., 202
mental frames, 78
mental practice, 182
mental skills, 139–140, 147
Mental Skills Checklist, 324, 397–399
mental training, 134, 147
    does it work? 142–143
    entry points, 323
    how coaches should approach it, 143–144
    how it is misunderstood,137–139
    sample training plans, 328–332
    "start small – stay simple – follow through," 322–323, 332
    what it is, 139–142
    why it is neglected, 135–136
    yearly plans for,327
mental training tools, 139, 147, 205, 226, 313
    See goal mapping; imagery; P^3 Thinking; relaxation
meta–messages, 65
Mickelson, Phil, 191
Miller, Shannon, 155
Millikan, Robert, 215
mind reading, 57–58
"Mission Possible," 44
mission statement, 121, 159
mistake ritual, 63
mistakes, 301–302
Mize, Larry, 208–209
modeling/models, 64, 87–88, 307, 309, 315
Montana, Joe, 24
Morales, Pablo, 186–187
motivation, 8, 24–25, 36–37, 45, 150, 152, 351
and athletes' needs, 29–30
and the balanced triad, 44–45
and choice, 24
definition of, 24–25
development and enhancement of, 38–44
and effort, 24
extrinsic motivation (EM), 37, 45
intrinsic motivation (IM), 36–37, 45
keeping motivation fine–tuned, 37–38
and persistence, 24–25
positive cycle of, 32
strategies for enhancing, 31–32, 34–35
test of motivation I.Q., 25
See also motivation myths; self–determination
motivation myths
exploding these myths, 28–29
jug-and-mug myth, 25–27, 65
natural talent myth, 27–28
you-have-it-or-you-don't myth, 27
motivational moods, 292–293
motivational packages, 26
Mullins, Aimee, 25

About the Author

Robin S. Vealey, Ph.D.

Dr. Robin S. Vealey is a Professor in the Department of Physical Education, Health, and Sport Studies at Miami University in Ohio. She completed a B.A. at Marshall University and a M.S. at Indiana University with a specialization in Coaching Science. After completing the Master's degree, Dr. Vealey taught and coached at Linfield College in Oregon where her basketball and volleyball teams received national recognition and she was a finalist for the small college Basketball Coach of the Year. Her experiences as an intercollegiate athlete and coach led her to complete a Ph.D. in sport psychology in 1984 at the University of Illinois.

Dr. Vealey teaches courses in sport psychology and coaching effectiveness at Miami, where she has received numerous teaching awards. She co-authored the book *Competitive Anxiety in Sport*, and has published multiple articles and book chapters related to sport psychology and coaching effectiveness. She has also made over 200 scholarly and applied presentations to regional, national, and international audiences. She has been honored as a research fellow by three national organizations and received the Distinguished Scholar Award from the Australian Psychological Society.

Dr. Vealey is a former President of the Association for the Advancement of Applied Sport Psychology (AAASP), and former Editor of *The Sport Psychologist*. She is a Certified Consultant of AAASP and is listed in the United States Olympic Committee Sport Psychology Registry. Dr. Vealey has worked as a sport psychology consultant for the U.S. Nordic Ski Team, U.S. Field Hockey, elite golfers, and is involved in mental training with athletes and teams at Miami University and the surrounding community. She has extensive experience in coaching education, serving as a National Instructor for the coaching certification course within the American Sport Education Program. A former collegiate basketball player, she now enjoys the mental challenge of golf.